CANADA'S GLOBAL VILLAGERS

Ruth Compton Brouwer

CANADA'S GLOBAL VILLAGERS

CUSO in Development, 1961-86

UBCPress · Vancouver · Toronto

21 20 19 18 17 16 15 14 13   5 4 3 2 1

Printed in Canada on FSC-certified ancient-forest-free paper (100% post-consumer recycled) that is processed chlorine- and acid-free.

Library and Archives Canada Cataloguing in Publication

Brouwer, Ruth Compton, author
    Canada's global villagers : CUSO in development, 1961-86 / Ruth Compton Brouwer.

Includes bibliographical references and index.
Issued in print and electronic formats.
ISBN 978-0-7748-2603-7 (bound). – ISBN 978-0-7748-2604-4 (pbk.).
ISBN 978-0-7748-2605-1 (pdf). – ISBN 978-0-7748-2606-8 (epub).

    1. CUSO – History. 2. CUSO – Biography. 3. Economic assistance, Canadian – History –
20th century. 4. Technical assistance, Canadian – History – 20th century. I. Title.

HC60.B78 2013   338.91'7101724   C2013-903842-6
                                                                      C2013-903843-4

Canadä

UBC Press gratefully acknowledges the financial support for our publishing program of the Government of Canada (through the Canada Book Fund), the Canada Council for the Arts, and the British Columbia Arts Council.

This book has been published with the help of a grant from the Canadian Federation for the Humanities and Social Sciences, through the Awards to Scholarly Publications Program, using funds provided by the Social Sciences and Humanities Research Council of Canada.

UBC Press
The University of British Columbia
2029 West Mall
Vancouver, BC V6T 1Z2
www.ubcpress.ca

To my remarkable sisters – Libbie, Isabel, Sophie, Hope, and Anne

"Our age will be remembered because it is the first generation since the dawn of history to believe it is practical to make the benefits of civilization available to the whole human race."

– Arnold J. Toynbee, as quoted by
Prime Minister Pearson in a message
of support for CUSO, 1966

Contents

Illustrations

Preface

It has now been many decades since international development assistance has been regarded as an unequivocally "good thing." To the extent that critics of development have referred to the presence of nongovernmental organizations (NGOs) in the development process, even the sternest of them has usually found initiatives to commend. As for the NGOs themselves, though, far from being complacent, many were already engaging in self-reflection in the 1970s. Nonetheless, the publication of book-length critiques of the roles and relevance of NGOs by practitioners and former practitioners is largely a twenty-first-century phenomenon. Whether calling for the transformation of NGOs or their effective dissolution and whether writing from an international or a national perspective, these authors share an emphasis on how much has changed since the hopeful days of amateurs in the first Development Decade. Among those reflecting from a Canadian perspective, none, so far as I know, has harkened back to the existence of "a pre-Harper paradise lost," as a recent polemic suggests.[1] Indeed, they are far from romanticizing the good old days. Yet some of them, writing with strong institutional memories, *do* recall what was in many respects a better time for northern NGOs, a time, especially before the mid-1980s, when the governments that helped fund them remained comparatively supportive and non-prescriptive even in the face of politically inconvenient NGO activism; a time before the corporatization of NGOs, on the one hand, and the rise of volunteer tourism, on the other; a time when many NGOs were a good match with existing needs in the Global South and so successful at what they did that they contributed to their own obsolescence.[2] Canadian University Service Overseas (CUSO), the NGO I write about in this book, was part of that better time.

Canada's Global Villagers is intended as a contribution to historical scholarship rather than a commemorative work. As such, it engages in the kind of critical analysis of sources expected in the history profession. My sources, however, go beyond documents: they include more than one hundred living men and women, former CUSO volunteers and staff. In the course of conducting my research, I have developed a deep admiration for them, formed personal friendships, and felt more than a touch of envy for youthful pasts more adventurous than my own. These CUSO alumni are listed in an appendix and acknowledged along with many others whom I thank at the end of the book.

Abbreviations

AGM	annual general meeting
ANC	African National Congress
AUCC	Association of Universities and Colleges of Canada
CCC	Canadian Council of Churches
CCIC	Canadian Council for International Cooperation
CESO	Canadian Executive Service Overseas
C-FAR	Citizens for Foreign Aid Reform
CIDA	Canadian International Development Agency
COV	Canadian Overseas Volunteers
CUSO	Canadian University Service Overseas
CVCS	Canadian Voluntary Commonwealth Service
CYC	Company of Young Canadians
EAO	External Aid Office
ECSA	East, Central and Southern Africa
FSO	field staff officer
GAD	gender and development
IDRC	International Development Research Centre
IRM	inter-regional meeting
MSF	Médicins Sans Frontières
NFCUS	National Federation of Canadian University Students
NGO	nongovernmental organization
OECD	Organization for Economic Co-operation and Development
RV	returned volunteer
SCI	Service Civil International
SCM	Student Christian Movement
SUCO	Service Universitaire Canadien Outre-mer
SUPA	Student Union for Peace Action
TESL	teaching English as a second language
UNDP	United Nations Development Program

UNESCO	United Nations Educational, Scientific and Cultural Organization
UNICEF	United Nations Children's Fund
USC	Unitarian Service Committee
USAID	United States Agency for International Development
VSO	Voluntary Service Overseas
WAD	women and development
WID	women in development
WUS	World University Service
WUSC	World University Service of Canada

CANADA'S GLOBAL VILLAGERS

Introduction

Global Villagers. It was a catchy label for CUSO volunteers, especially in the age of McLuhan. *Maclean's* magazine used it in an appreciative article about the volunteers in 1969, at the height of the Nigerian civil war.[1] In the beginning, though, a different label had routinely been used: Canada's Peace Corps. Back in 1961, it had seemed the readiest phrase for CUSO and the media to use to capture the nation's attention and convey a sense of the new organization's youthful makeup and overseas focus. But the label was misleading in several respects, not least because CUSO was a nongovernmental organization (NGO) rather than a creation of the state. And with the growth of a new and more radical Canadian nationalism in the last half of the 1960s, many members of the CUSO community came to detest the phrase, so much so that in 1967, at CUSO's sixth annual meeting, a resolution was passed calling for an end to the use of the words *Canada's Peace Corps* in all campus advertising.[2] "To Serve and Learn," "Development Is Our Business," and other slogans would likewise come and go as CUSO itself developed and sought to redefine itself. This book takes CUSO beyond labels and slogans. Drawing on the personal reflections of CUSO alumni as well as on archival and private collections, it introduces readers to an organization that engaged thousands of young Canadians in the practice and politics of development in and beyond the two so-called Development Decades.

Portrayed as poster kids for idealism in the early years and as irresponsible radicals by some on the right at the end of the 1970s, the volunteers were like the decades themselves, a mix of contending tendencies.

Founded in 1961 as Canadian University Service Overseas, CUSO was the first Canadian NGO to undertake development work from a secular stance and in a context of rapid decolonization. By 1965, it was said to be "the fifth largest peace corps programme in the world"; twenty years later it claimed some nine thousand returned volunteers.[3] When I first thought of writing a book about CUSO, I was motivated by two related factors, one personal, the other professional. A high school classmate – studious, actively involved in church work, and likely, it seemed, to follow her Uncle Roy into missionary service in the United Church of Canada – unexpectedly joined CUSO in 1966 and went off to teach in Kenya. Over the years I lost touch with my friend, who died in 1999, but vague memories of her CUSO involvement recurred and had increased resonance as I researched a book about three Canadian professional women and their mission-based work in the interwar era. I was struck by the ways in which the institutional and social service work of mainstream Protestant missions in that period anticipated the kinds of development work that new NGOs undertook in the 1960s. By the end of the sixties, the overseas activities of such churches had themselves effectively become "NGOized."[4] Why, then, did my friend and thousands of other young Canadians, often church-raised like her, instead choose a secular vehicle for acting on the idealism, the adventurism, and the varied other motives that took them into development work? Was it a minor transition or a sea change? And what did they actually do as secular volunteers? Inevitably, as my research on CUSO proceeded, other questions came to the fore, and this book took on a life of its own. Before saying more about its content, I use the next few paragraphs to remind readers of salient terms and events related to the broad international and national context within which CUSO came into existence.

As practices and entities, both *development* and *NGO* have long histories. But the terms acquired much of their present meaning and became common coinage in the post–Second World War era through agencies of the United Nations.[5] The proposal to assist "underdeveloped areas" as "a cooperative enterprise ... through the United Nations and its specialized agencies whenever practicable," famously made by President Truman as Point Four in his inaugural address in 1949, effectively "*inaugurated the 'development age*,'" writes historian

Gilbert Rist.[6] In the context of the Cold War, addressing underdevelopment through economic assistance and the application of modernization theory acquired increasing urgency and indeed came to be seen as crucial to the interests of the United States and other Western nations.[7] The term *Third World*, introduced in 1952 by French anticolonialist Albert Sauvy to refer to underdeveloped regions that were part of neither the Communist nor Western blocs but rather places where their rivalries would be played out, quickly entered the development lexicon. Present-day Western writers employ the term sparingly and with unease, but as Vijay Prashad points out, it was quickly appropriated by Frantz Fanon and by non-aligned leaders like Nehru, who saw its utility for uniting former colonies around a common project to resist the legacy and continuation of imperialism.[8]

The first United Nations Development Decade, proclaimed in 1961, set the stage for ambitious new commitments and expectations for multilateral and bilateral assistance to the developing world.[9] It was also in this decade that, metaphorically speaking, a thousand NGOs bloomed. In introducing their study of NGOs in contemporary Britain, James McKay and Matthew Hilton caution against what they call "the 1960s fetish" and observe that in the international development sector, such agencies as Oxfam and Christian Aid were already in existence.[10] Had they extended their study beyond Britain, McKay and Hilton could have added other, earlier internationally minded NGOs, such as World University Service (WUS), whose roots go back to 1920s Geneva and the European Student Relief wing of the World Student Christian Federation; and Service Civil International (SCI), whose pacifist founder, Pierre Ceresole, went in 1934 to earthquake-ravaged Bihar, India, with a few Swiss and English companions and his trademark strategy of work camps, thereby perhaps making SCI the first secular agency to send volunteers from the West to the South.[11] The 1950s saw the emergence of more organizations with a focus on the non-West, sometimes, as with World Vision, out of strong roots in evangelism. For Canadians able to recall this decade, the most memorable organization was the Unitarian Service Committee (USC). Founded by Lotta Hitschmanova in 1945 to assist postwar Europeans in need, USC began providing aid to Korea after the civil war there.[12] In 1957, World University Service of Canada (WUSC) was incorporated as a Canadian NGO. WUSC became the vehicle through which numerous soon-to-be-prominent Canadians, including Pierre Elliott Trudeau, participated in international seminars in countries such as India and

Ghana.[13] Many more Canadians, the author among them, would get a more accessible taste of WUSC's attempts to broaden their international horizons as its annual Treasure Van brought developing-world crafts to university campuses in the 1960s. A year after WUSC was established, Operation Crossroads Africa began encouraging young Canadians to develop empathy and international understanding through a few months of hands-on work on diverse projects alongside their contemporaries in new African countries. Taken up by the United Church of Canada at the suggestion of an African-American minister who had established the organization in the United States, Crossroads would later sever its church connection and expand its focus beyond Africa, but as Crossroads International, it lives on as a vehicle for sending volunteers abroad on short-term assignments.[14] Finally, across the world in Australia, and particularly noteworthy as a 1950s initiative that had an important influence on CUSO, was the Volunteer Graduate Scheme, launched, it was said, out of an urge to atone for white Australia's past racist relationships with its non-white neighbours.[15]

These examples notwithstanding, the 1960s was a decisive decade for the expansion, transplanting, and creation of development-focused NGOs. The Mennonite Central Committee, the Canadian Catholic Organization for Development and Peace, and Oxfam Canada became important Canadian NGOs, and, of particular relevance for this study, organizations to send young volunteers from industrialized to developing countries multiplied internationally.[16] UN Secretary-General U Thant's much quoted observation, "I look forward to the time when the average youngster – and parent or employer – will consider that one or two years of volunteer work for the cause of development either in a faraway country or in a depressed area of his own community, is a normal part of one's education," reflected and resonated with the times.[17] As the author of *New Trends in Service by Youth* noted, the growth of such programs all over the world during the 1960s was "nothing short of spectacular."[18] In England, Voluntary Service Overseas (VSO), founded in 1958 by Alec Dickson, became an independent NGO in March 1961 following the "palace revolution" that sidelined Dickson. In the same month, by executive order, President Kennedy established the Peace Corps, vastly bigger, more ambitious, and influential than any of its nongovernmental "Peace Corps cousins."[19] Though early CUSO volunteers and supporters rightly pointed out that CUSO's organizational antecedents predated the Peace Corps, it was not until June 1961 that the Canadian cousin officially came into existence.

Canadians think of their nation as having a tradition of generosity in terms of development assistance. The emergence of NGOs in the 1960s and the optimistic mood of the period may have contributed to this perception.[20] Until recently, historians have not devoted much attention to separating myth from reality in regard to Canada's role in development assistance, or even to charting its course, largely leaving the task to political scientists, journalists, aid practitioners, and consultants.[21] The beginning of Canada's official contribution to development assistance is usually dated to 1950 and the launch of the Colombo Plan. In 1966, political scientist Keith Spicer, one of CUSO's founders, published an early critical analysis of Canada's contribution to the Colombo Plan, highlighting what he argued were flawed assumptions in federal aid policy overall. Three years later, journalist Clyde Sanger published *Half a Loaf: Canada's Semi-Role in Developing Countries* following his tour of a dozen countries where Canada had involvement and largely confirmed Spicer's analysis. Canada's official aid was frequently neither bold nor generous, nor was it well conceived, Sanger argued, commenting more approvingly on what he had seen of assistance provided by churches and NGOs.[22] Canadian official development assistance policies received attention in 1976 in some of the essays in *Canada and the Third World,* and they were subjected to close-grained critical analysis in several works written or edited by Cranford Pratt, for whom a key analytical theme was the triumph of pragmatism over "humane internationalism" in such policies.[23] But it was not until 1998 with *Aid and Ebb Tide* that another political scientist, David Morrison, provided a full-fledged study of the Canadian International Development Agency (CIDA), the major vehicle for orchestrating Canada's official aid. And it was only in 2010 that historians Bruce Muirhead and Ronald Harpelle introduced readers to CIDA's innovative and little-known offspring, the International Development Research Centre (IDRC).[24]

CUSO's work overseas and its influence within Canada have received passing attention in some of these studies. CUSO, though, did not wait for the attention of outsiders: its returned volunteers (RVs) and staff began early on to document their own history. In 1968, CUSO's first full-time executive director, Bill McWhinney, framed a varied collection of volunteer narratives with a lengthy introduction to CUSO's origins. In 1985, Ian Smillie, also an RV and former executive director, published a much different insider history before going on to a long career as an author and consultant on international development issues.[25] Beginning in the mid-1960s, several RVs wrote graduate theses on aspects of CUSO.[26] Other former volunteers who went on to careers linked to international development have provided broader analyses of the NGO phenomenon in Canada, largely with a view to improving NGOs' self-understanding and performance.[27] Meanwhile, especially as early CUSO volunteers have reached the stage of retirement, several have published collections of their youthful letters home.[28]

What has not yet appeared despite the passing of more than half a century since Canadians began to participate in the age of development is an academic history of CUSO or of any other development-focused NGO. This lacuna is not peculiarly Canadian: as Akira Iriye has observed, when historians study international relations, they typically do so from a state-centred perspective.[29] I hope that my book will be the beginning of a succession of alternative and complementary perspectives. Studies of the origins and evolution of secular NGOs such as CUSO and Oxfam Canada and of faith-based organizations such as KAIROS and its antecedents can enhance our understanding of the evolution of Canada's global consciousness beyond the missionary era and complement analyses of the role played by Canada in international development through bilateral and multilateral agencies. In choosing to make CUSO the specific focus of my study I was motivated by several factors in addition to those mentioned earlier. CUSO was the first NGO to receive government assistance for development work and during this period received larger amounts than any other NGO. Indeed, it was pressure from the CUSO community and its supporters that resulted in a significant shift in external aid policy: the establishment within CIDA in 1968 of a specific division to assist NGOs on an ongoing basis. In taking this step, CIDA became something of a role model internationally among official aid agencies. Moreover, like the missionaries before them, CUSO's thousands of volunteers became the human face of Canada in many parts of the developing world, a presence for some years in more than forty countries. Beginning with the civil war in Nigeria in the late 1960s, CUSO volunteers and staff also became, along with activist churches, Oxfam Canada, and other groups, a major lobbying constituency in trying to influence Canadian foreign and aid policies. By the end of the 1970s, CUSO's forays into development education and its controversial support for anticolonial and anti-apartheid activism in southern Africa had made it a target of right-wing criticism and as such a source of vulnerability and potential embarrassment for CIDA and for the federal government more generally. As these and other aspects of the organization's reach and activism are recovered, it is less likely that CUSO will remain absent in histories of Canada's role in the Global South.

This book deals only with CUSO's first quarter century. CUSO still exists as a volunteer-sponsoring organization, by now claiming some fifteen thousand alumni. But since its 2008 merger with VSO, its British counterpart, it has operated under two different names: first CUSO-VSO and now Cuso International. Especially with these name changes, it is unquestionably less familiar to Canadians than NGOs such as Oxfam and Médicins Sans Frontières (MSF), whose involvement with emergency aid and relief work periodically brings them into the limelight. In choosing to focus on the years 1961-86, and especially on the two Development Decades, I am dealing with the period when CUSO was in its heyday, its volunteers still overwhelmingly *young* Canadians, often straight out of university. Demographic and other changes accelerating in the early- to mid-1980s as the organization placed fewer volunteers, typically older, professionally trained, and experienced, resulted in what insiders called "a new CUSO." As its records become available, it will merit its own history.

Chapter 1 of *Canada's Global Villagers* analyzes CUSO's competing founding narratives and provides a profile of the 1960s volunteers. Most members of the first cohort went to India, where placements ended after just a decade. To the extent that India lingers in CUSO's institutional memory, its work there is associated with its pioneering phase, with naive expectations and hair-shirt idealism. The early India volunteers subscribed to a philosophy of service that gave pride of place to the promotion of international goodwill and understanding through simple grassroots living. But as I argue in Chapter 2, without abandoning that philosophy, the volunteers quickly moved beyond an inevitable early naïveté and actively sought niches for useful work. Their maturity and commitment helped overcome early reservations about CUSO in official Ottawa, while the eclectic nature and challenges of their postings provided important early lessons in development and drew them into such new areas as family planning and the green revolution. Meanwhile, as government funding became available to CUSO from the mid-1960s, the organization lost its early bootstraps character. What had been a tiny secretariat at its Ottawa headquarters became an emerging bureaucracy invested in the "business" of development. This period also saw the emergence internationally of scathing critiques of development[30] and the return of politicized volunteers. These changes set the stage for the intense debates and substantial upheaval within CUSO in the 1970s that are the subject of Chapter 3. Nigeria, which became, early on, the biggest placement country for CUSO, was also in several respects its most daunting field, as Chapter 4 shows. The everyday challenges of living and working in Africa's most populous country quickly emerged, followed by a civil war that sharply divided the CUSO community on the ground and in Canada. In the 1970s, programming in Nigeria came under further criticism within the organization, especially from politicized volunteers and staff who declared that the ongoing concern with providing teachers to that country was not *real* development. In Chapter 5, the focus of the book again turns homeward to consider the question of the long-term impact of the volunteer experience on Canadian society and on the volunteers themselves. Numerous CUSO alumni remained involved in development through official agencies and NGOs or did analogous work on domestic issues such as those confronting First Nations peoples. Many more RVs, shaped irrevocably by their overseas experience, undertook to tutor their fellow Canadians about the needs – and the cultural richness – of the developing world, whether in their workplaces or in the communities to which they returned. It became something of a refrain to say that CUSO's greatest contribution to development was made within Canada. As for the early slogan "To Serve and Learn," CUSO volunteers interviewed for this book were nearly unanimous in turning it around to declare that they had learned far more than they had served. In the Conclusion to *Canada's Global Villagers*, I return briefly to this point and to the metaphor of "gnat against elephant" used by an early RV to put the immensity of the overseas challenge and the volunteers' realism about their own contribution into perspective.

There are several aspects of CUSO's first quarter century that receive scant coverage in this book, among them its fractious relationship with SUCO, its francophone sibling. There is also limited coverage of CUSO's overseas work outside India and Nigeria, although interviews with volunteers who served in other placement regions have yielded valuable insights and fruitful comparisons. Moreover, CUSO's connections with eastern and southern Africa receive a good deal of attention, particularly in Chapter 3, as the site of inspiration and engagement for many volunteers and staff who became political activists in the 1970s. Throughout the book, I make abundant use of personal anecdotes as a way of considering how individual lives intersect with large-scale movements, particularly, in this case, with the secular and reformist impulses animating contemporary Canada and with the international movements for development and decolonization that drew the volunteers abroad. Their recollections tell us much about how they remember themselves as individuals responding to these larger forces. Collectively, they convey a vivid sense of young Canadians discovering worlds very different from their home communities and in the process engaging in voyages of self-discovery and personal growth.

During the decades considered here, CUSO as an organization was itself in development. Through close attention to how it responded to specific issues, it may be possible to contribute insights into some of the "big questions" that have also challenged other NGOs: What are the trade-offs when an NGO accepts substantial state funding? How does its interpretation of its mission change in response to on-the-ground issues and new development paradigms (development as a "business," for instance, and "women in development")? Should NGOs begin or continue to work in countries notable for corrupt regimes and deplorable human rights practices? Should they intervene in the internal politics of a country if they believe intervention is the best way to advance aid and development, or simply concentrate on sending qualified workers?[31] Should they try to stay on in a country that starts to withdraw its welcome mat if they believe that they can still function to meet community needs? How do they avoid self-destructing in the face of ideological challenges such as those that arose when internationally influential figures like Ivan Illich began decrying the export of Western-style institutions, especially formal education, the very kind of work in which volunteers were most heavily involved? One question that CUSO seems to have spent relatively little time considering was that of concentration versus dispersion. Why did it spread itself across so many countries, especially since the dispersion approach has so frequently been criticized in regard to official aid? Finally, given the fact that NGOs like CUSO *did* carry on despite increasingly sharp critiques of development work and their own intense soul-searching and internal debates, how did they redefine themselves in order to justify an ongoing role?

A significant number of volunteers, and particularly volunteers-turned-staff, *did* engage with the big questions. But during their two-year assignments, volunteers mainly had to deal with the everyday realities of their placements. For a few, there would be a significant boredom factor, and as they themselves acknowledged, they could not always triumph over adverse circumstances to make a success of their assignment. Furthermore, there were undeniably some who went into CUSO ill-equipped motivationally, academically, or psychologically to cope with the realities of their placements. Still, when one early supporter referred to the first cohort of volunteers as "fine young Canadians" in introducing them to community groups whose financial support he courted, he was identifying an unmistakable strand of commitment and idealism, however quaint his phrase may sound now and however much it amused and embarrassed the young men and women he was describing, who were very much conscious of complexity in their own motives. The strand of idealism arguably remained among their successors even when they restyled it *pragmatic* idealism and perhaps especially when they became advocates of more politicized approaches to development.

Collectively, the volunteers who participated in these Development Decades returned home enriched by their overseas experience and anxious to make Canada a less parochial and more generous country. Collectively, too, they embody the interconnectedness of our country's overseas and domestic narratives. The first of these narratives is paramount for this book, but I hope that my account also contributes to a broader understanding of salient themes in this period of Canadian history. Organizationally, CUSO was shaped by, and in some cases influenced, new university and state initiatives and new ideas about civil society. At an individual level, the young volunteers personified the complexities and ironies of an increasingly secular Canada and new, more capacious ways of thinking about race and sexuality and gender roles. CUSO gave them an open road and a chance to grow. Transnationalists,[32] idealists, and engaged citizens, they pushed Canada to live up to its own best self-image. It has been a pleasure to follow them on their journeys.

1

"Fine Young Canadians"
Visionaries and Volunteers in CUSO's First Decade

> Bliss was it in that dawn to be alive, but to be young was very heaven.
> – William Wordsworth, *The Prelude*[1]

In May 1966, journalist Tom Alderman's "What's Bugging the Committed Kids?," a feature story on Canadian youth groups, was published in a weekend magazine: "Like, what's with this SUPA? And Crossroads Africa? And Summer of Service '67, Operation Beaver, CYC, TEQ, CUSO and UGEQ, and CMJQ, and CIASP, and something called KAIROS? Seems you can put any combination of letters in the alphabet together and come up with another new youth organization."[2] Like Alderman's mock-jovial writing style, most of these groups have long since disappeared, though SUPA (Student Union for Peace Action) and the CYC (Company of Young Canadians) are still familiar to students of this period in Canadian history, thanks to scholarly studies and nostalgic reminiscences.[3] CUSO was established several years earlier than SUPA and the CYC. It involved far larger numbers of students, and it has survived the vicissitudes of a turbulent half century. Yet it remains largely invisible in chronicles of youth movements in Canada's 1960s. Its absence is ironic but not surprising: CUSO began with students who were born a little too early to have the cachet of baby boomers, its New Left moment happened mainly in the seventies, and its youthful activism had an international focus.

Emerging more or less simultaneously on several Canadian campuses in 1960 and 1961, the "committed kids" who came together as CUSO had idealistic visions of helping out in newly decolonized countries and thereby promoting international understanding. To the older group of visionaries who set in motion the meetings that resulted in the official founding of CUSO, they seemed altogether admirable in their intentions but too amateurish to be left to their own devices. This chapter begins with these two competing strands in the CUSO founding narrative and describes early organizational and fundraising efforts before focusing on the volunteers themselves. The last part of the chapter deals with some of the changes facilitated by federal funding from the mid-1960s and foreshadows the politicization that marked CUSO's 1970s.

Success Has Many Fathers: CUSO's Origins

Officially established at McGill University on 6 June 1961, CUSO was to serve as a "national co-ordinating agency to develop and promote schemes to send young Canadians to serve abroad."[4] The founding meeting was held in conjunction with the annual meeting of the National Conference of Canadian Universities and Colleges (later absorbed into the Association of Universities and Colleges of Canada). University of Toronto President Claude Bissell was named CUSO's first honorary president, and Father G.-H. Lévesque, vice-chairman of the Canada Council, became honorary vice-president. A previously drafted constitution was adopted at the meeting, and Rt. Rev. H.J. Somers, president of St. Francis Xavier University, was chosen as chairman of CUSO's first Executive Committee. Donald B. Wilson, associate secretary of the Student Christian Movement (SCM), became the first secretary-treasurer. Lewis Perinbam, associate secretary of the Canadian National Commission for UNESCO (United Nations Educational, Scientific and Cultural Organization), became CUSO's acting executive secretary.[5]

The initiative for bringing the proposal to the university presidents' conference had come from Dr. Francis Leddy, the internationally minded dean of Arts and Sciences at the University of Saskatchewan and president of the Canadian National Commission for UNESCO. Leddy, in turn, had been approached by Perinbam, who remained an important figure for CUSO long after he ceased to have direct involvement. Born in the British colony of Malaya, where his Tamil father was a prominent physician in the state medical service, and educated from boyhood in Scotland, Lewis Perinbam had come to Canada in 1953 to work for World University Service (WUS). Struck by the parochialism of Canadian students and familiar with an Australian scheme that was putting student volunteers into Indonesia, he had approached the federal government in 1959 with a proposal that it help Canadian university graduates provide volunteer service in developing countries and, through such service, gain international experience and understanding. Perinbam had a personal reason to value the promotion of international understanding. His father had been brutally executed by occupying Japanese troops during the Second World War, and after spending time in Japan for a WUS seminar in 1955, Lewis pondered how it was that "such peaceful gentle kind people" could have been persuaded to commit such atrocities.[6] Though Ottawa had been unresponsive to Perinbam's 1959 proposal, he made another overture in March 1961, now working through his UNESCO office and advising the External Aid Office (EAO) of a forthcoming "consultative" meeting to be held later that month. The March consultation effectively laid the groundwork for what became the founding meeting at McGill.[7] Following that June meeting, Perinbam, as noted, became CUSO's interim executive secretary, with his UNESCO office in Ottawa serving temporarily as CUSO headquarters. In July, after meeting with the director of Voluntary Service Overseas (VSO) in London and obtaining assistance from officials in England and France, he left for South and Southeast Asia to investigate opportunities for Canadian volunteers.[8]

In his history of CUSO, Ian Smillie begins his account of founding figures with Perinbam. Yet it was initiatives undertaken by Keith Spicer, a University of Toronto graduate student studying Canada's role in the Colombo Plan, that led to the placing overseas of the first group of Canadian student volunteers.[9] In his 2004 memoir, Spicer recalled that at the Canadian Institute on Public Affairs Couchiching Conference in August 1959 he had "stumbled on a book that seized me and wouldn't let go," Donald K. Faris's *To Plow with Hope*, published the previous year. Faris, a United Church of Canada China missionary-turned-UN-aid-worker, had surveyed the problems of the developing world from what he called "a human-economic standpoint." While he welcomed evidence of growth and coordination in existing government and volunteer aid programs, the thrust of his message was that the West must do much more and that what developing peoples needed was assistance in improving their existing ways of life, rather than wholesale transformations based on Western models. Using storytelling devices, he suggested such strategies as promoting functional literacy, family planning, and – his own specialty – locally feasible methods for improving agriculture and nutrition. In a few pages near the end of his book, Faris suggested that educated young Westerners could play an important part in providing such assistance. Through their skills and idealism they could contribute not just technical services but "lasting values such as friendship, goodwill, and understanding."[10] It was this brief call to youth that had captured Spicer's attention.

Armed with chutzpah and some preparatory notes, Spicer went directly to Prime Minister John Diefenbaker, who readily offered moral and diplomatic support for Spicer's idea of establishing an organization to send university graduates for a period of service in developing Commonwealth countries. In January 1960, Spicer travelled to South and Southeast Asia for his political science doctoral research, at the same time securing meetings with various Canadian and Asian officials with a view to obtaining information and establishing contacts for placing Canadian volunteers. About a year later, he again met personally with Diefenbaker and submitted what was now a more fully developed "Scheme for Commonwealth Graduate Volunteers." The explicit reference to Commonwealth in the title reflected Spicer's assumption that the Royal Commonwealth Society would support his scheme financially and that such a reference would appeal to Diefenbaker. When no money was forthcoming from either source, the scheme was revised and renamed and incorporated as Canadian Overseas Volunteers (COV). Like Perinbam, Spicer cited the Australian student volunteer scheme as the most feasible model to follow for organizing Canadian students.[11] Among the "grey-haired guys" whom Spicer later remembered as assisting in critiquing his unfolding plans were Professors Paul Fox, Nathan Keyfitz, and James Eayrs, the latter his thesis supervisor, and John W. Holmes, former diplomat and now head of the Canadian Institute of International Affairs (CIIA). More crucial than any of these men, however, was Toronto lawyer and Conservative MP Fred Stinson, a classic Red Tory whom Spicer had met at the Couchiching Conference and who became president and chief fundraiser of the incorporated COV. The two men sought volunteer sponsorships from newspapers, businesses, churches, and service organizations. By the time of the June 1961 meeting at McGill that officially established CUSO, Spicer and a few fellow students, strongly supported by Stinson and a handful of other mentors, had selected fifteen Canadian Overseas Volunteers, put them through a series of preparatory lectures, and had them ready for an August departure for Asia.[12]

Meanwhile, possibilities for sending Canadian students to developing countries were being discussed in other Canadian academic settings.[13] There were several nascent groups in Quebec, including Volontaires Canadiens Outre-Mer at Laval University, which, though closely linked with COV, was not so far along in its planning. At the University of British Columbia (UBC), the President's Committee on Student Service Overseas came into existence early in 1961, thanks largely to initiatives taken by two undergraduates who were, if anything, even more idealistic than Spicer. One of them, Mike Clague, had met Spicer at a conference. Following his return to UBC, Clague and his friend Brian Marson wrote to Spicer to obtain information about his evolving plans. They also prepared a letter to President Norman "Larry" MacKenzie outlining their ideas and took it directly to his home. MacKenzie was away at the time, but his wife promised to put their letter on his pillow so that he would be sure to see it on his return![14] Back in Toronto, Guy Arnold, a young Englishman teaching at nearby Pickering College, was the key figure behind Canadian Voluntary Commonwealth Service (CVCS). Arnold initially envisioned brief cross-cultural encounters in work camps within Canada as well as overseas service for high-school and university-aged students in Commonwealth countries, beginning with summer placements in the Caribbean.[15] Spokesmen for these groups were invited by Leddy to the June 1961 meeting with twenty-one university presidents or their alternates, as were representatives of such organizations as Catholic Action, the SCM, and WUSC. Altogether, representatives of twenty-two organizations in addition to the UNESCO and university officials themselves were in attendance.[16]

Representatives of church mission boards were not invited. The SCM's Donald Wilson was probably correct in thinking that a concerted effort was being made to prevent the new organization from having any appearance of denominational ties or falling under the churches' control. Having been present as an observer at the March consultative meeting organized under the umbrella of the Canadian National Committee for UNESCO, Wilson reported that there had been "a general air of not wishing to accept anything from the churches, apart from money, and the rather obvious feeling on the part of some members present there that the whole movement must be kept clear of any religious implications." While such a feeling was understandable, he wrote, there was, ironically, "a general flavor of the spirit which I imagine pervaded early SVM [Student Volunteer Movement for Foreign Missions] days when the world was to be helped, and renewed by the youthful vigour of a North American generation," and scant knowledge of the ways that mainstream missions had changed since the Victorian era.[17] For their part, officials in the Department of Overseas Missions of the Canadian Council of Churches (CCC) – an ecumenical umbrella group of mainly liberal churches – were very much conscious that the various plans being discussed for student involvement in development had important implications for their own work and that of the indigenous churches. Thus, in the spring of 1961, they contacted spokesmen for Protestant mission organizations in Britain as well as leading Asian and African churchmen in order to ascertain their views on the nascent student volunteer schemes.[18] Despite the cautious tone in a number of the responses they received, several member denominations in the CCC, most notably the United Church of Canada and the Presbyterian Church in Canada, became early and enthusiastic supporters of COV and CUSO.[19] Even the selection of Francis Leddy, an ardent, outspoken, and high-profile Catholic layman, as CUSO's first chairman, was evidently not a deterrent.[20]

Meanwhile, for Spicer and Stinson, the university officials and faculty members who participated in the March and June meetings that established CUSO were johnny-come-latelies to the idea of Canadian university students in overseas service. Months earlier, Spicer had become suspicious of and frustrated by some faculty members on the newly forming UBC President's Committee on Overseas Student Service. He had written back helpfully when Marson and Clague had contacted him about his evolving overseas volunteer scheme and had urged them to move quickly to get university support so that UBC students could participate in a joint effort with COV and Laval to send volunteers in 1961. However, some UBC faculty members, following up on the contacts with Spicer made by Marson and Clague, had first sought ideas and documents from Spicer and then cast doubts on COV's ability to carry on as a student-run organization. Anthropology professor Cyril Belshaw, who chaired the President's Committee and who would serve as a vice-chairman on CUSO's first slate of officers, was particularly patronizing to Spicer, who in turn suspected Belshaw of making perfidious use of COV correspondence in an attempt to undermine his plans.[21] Stinson was even more frustrated than Spicer by what he saw as efforts to highjack or derail the original COV plan. Both men wanted to maintain the small-scale, student-run structure with which COV had begun.[22] Likewise, following the March consultative meeting, Don Wilson had expressed concern about the loss of student initiative in the proposed CUSO plan and about the likely centralization and bureaucracy, especially if this were to lead to the perception in developing countries that the new Canadian organization was to be an agency of government like the Peace Corps.[23]

Yet the logic of one national organization to channel regional enthusiasms for overseas student volunteer service into one central structure with a permanent institutional home ultimately prevailed. Even University of Toronto President Claude Bissell, while praising the COV plan as "sensible and intelligently conceived" several months earlier, had gone on to declare that the times called for such efforts to be "mobilized on a larger plane."[24] The group lined up by Spicer and Stinson at the University of Toronto did go to Asia under COV auspices, as noted, leaving in August 1961, followed by a second group in July 1962. But for Spicer, who had a doctoral thesis to finish, active involvement largely ended with the departure of the first COV contingent. A period of overlap in the existence of COV and CUSO followed, lasting for more than a year. It was marked by some cooperative activities but also by lingering COV resistance to the CUSO approach.[25] Spicer's August 1961 invitation to Donald Faris to return to Canada from his UNICEF post in India and take up the secretaryship of both organizations reflected these dual tendencies. In what seems to have been one of his last letters on behalf of COV, Spicer acknowledged that he had no formal authority to speak for CUSO, but he went on to assure Faris that some CUSO executive members would favour his appointment. Faris, he believed, could bring to CUSO "the student enthusiasm, local initiative and guidance" that had made COV a success, use CUSO as a vehicle to promote national unity and international understanding, and, at the same time, head off ill-advised attempts to centralize volunteer work. The following spring, Stinson likewise proposed that Faris consider the position of CUSO executive secretary, since a permanent appointment to that position was soon to be made.[26] But a quite different proposal, emanating from the COVs in India, changed the future of both organizations and ultimately brought them together.

In a long and tactful letter to Stinson, the COVs, writing as a group from the site where they had gathered for a reunion in February 1962, urged that one of their own, Bill McWhinney, who had joined them from his bank placement in Ceylon (Sri Lanka), be brought back to Toronto to take over the administration of COV. In making this suggestion, they stressed that they were not expressing a lack of confidence in Stinson or in Ozzie Schmidt, Spicer's successor as the main student organizer for COV. But given other demands on their time (Stinson was facing an election campaign; Schmidt was doing graduate work) and the increasing burden of administering COV, it would be desirable to have

Lewis Perinbam, interim executive secretary of CUSO, 1961-62 *(left)*, and Bill McWhinney, his successor, who served until 1966 *(right)*. Both men later worked at CIDA. Perinbam was vice-president for special programs from 1974 until his retirement in 1991. McWhinney came to CIDA as senior vice-president in 1981 and was acting president in 1982-83. Photo of Perinbam, ca. 1983, courtesy of Ian Smillie; of McWhinney, 1961, courtesy of Stephen Woollcombe.

a full-time administrator in Toronto with field experience. Their proposal, they added, was endorsed by Faris. Before the month was out, Stinson acted on the COVs' suggestion and asked McWhinney to return.[27]

McWhinney worked in Toronto with COV until August. Then, abandoning embryonic plans to study at Oxford, he accepted an invitation to become CUSO's Ottawa-based executive secretary, replacing Lewis Perinbam.[28] Big Bill – it was a fond nickname for the towering McWhinney – was an ideal choice as a bridge figure: endowed with the *gravitas* and business training to impress university administrators, government officials, and potential donors, but linked by his youth and shared overseas experience to his fellow volunteers. With one of their own at the helm of the national organization, the COV support team in Toronto gradually resigned themselves to a new role as CUSO's local campus committee. Reflecting the transition, they made the initial selection of Toronto-area volunteer candidates for South Asia for 1963, leaving the final decisions about appointments and arrangements to the CUSO national office.[29]

As for Spicer, reflecting on his passionate engagement with student inter-nationalism almost half a century and several careers later, he had a bittersweet perspective on what had happened: COV had been absorbed. It was "the end of student control: heartbreaking at the time, but probably an inevitable and solidifying outcome." Even as he had turned back to his overdue doctoral thesis in the spring and summer of 1961, Spicer's feistiness had lessened and he had become resigned to letting others carry on with his scheme.[30] At UBC, a report that fall for the Alma Mater Society acknowledged that COV had provided the "inspiration and vitality" that had led to the establishment of UBC's President's Committee on Student Service Overseas. But as faculty chairman of the committee, Belshaw made no such acknowledgment, instead maintaining that UBC delegates at the June meeting had been "instrumental in securing the formation of Canadian University Service Overseas."[31] Others elsewhere, and Leddy most egregiously, would later put themselves at the centre of the founding narrative. Leddy and several other officials interviewed by Ian Smillie as part of the research for his history of CUSO showed a tendency to dismiss the student initiatives as amateurish and unimportant. They appeared unaware of, or unwilling to acknowledge, the extent to which the student groups and COV in particular had engaged in concrete planning and inter-campus networking.[32] These officials' claims to founder status notwithstanding, the fact remains that it was a young graduate student ("abrasive, difficult" but "tremendously talented"[33]) with a handful of supporters who conceived and launched the pilot project that sent the first cohort of Canadian student volunteers into overseas development work.

The Canadian initiatives to send educated young adults to developing nations for a period of volunteer service were part of a rapidly growing international phenomenon in the early 1960s. The declaration of the United Nations Development Decade and to an even greater extent publicity surrounding J.F. Kennedy's plan for a Peace Corps gave the phenomenon momentum. Introduced in unscripted remarks to an enthusiastic university student audience during the presidential campaign in the fall of 1960 and established by an executive order in March 1961, the Peace Corps was immeasurably influential in creating popular support for other national youth groups.[34] The fifteen COVs who departed for Asia the following August were proud that their organizational initiatives predated the Peace Corps – proud, too, that they were serving independent of government and without the comforts and constraints of their more richly endowed US counterparts, a vastly larger organization conceived as an arm of US foreign policy and perceived as a tool in the Cold War.[35] Given the COV's pioneering status and its dogged and innovative fundraising efforts, Stinson found it frustrating that national media initially seemed more attuned to the nascent Peace Corps than to the inspirational Canadian story. At the same time, in early publicity pieces by COV and CUSO, as well as in pieces written about them, it was common practice to speak of these organizations as the Canadian version of the Peace Corps. Nor was this usage confined to Canada. For a time, the term was used as a generic label for *any* national volunteer youth group engaged in development work.[36] As for the volunteers who served in the Canadian and US organizations, they had a great deal in common. Once overseas, many Canadian volunteers enjoyed the largesse and socializing available at get-togethers with their Peace Corps cousins on holidays or at work camps or in-country orientations. In some regions, they were posted to the same area, where friendships and occasionally marriages resulted. The obverse was a certain *schadenfreude* within CUSO when the Peace Corps experienced unpopularity in a country where it was serving. In short, the combination of rivalry and connectedness in the Canadian volunteers' attitudes toward their far more numerous and better-known US counterparts reflected larger and long-existing patterns in Canadian-American relations.

Getting Started as CUSO: The Shoestring Era

In the conclusion to the report on his Asian tour in the summer of 1961, Lewis Perinbam assured his readers that Canada held an enviable and respected position in the world. It was "in a sense 'a city set on a hill whose actions cannot be hid,'" and thus had an important role to play in aiding the developing world. Furthermore, graduates of Canadian universities had the necessary skills, humility, and goodwill to render valuable international service and in so doing could bring credit to their country. Nonetheless, in the portions of the report dealing in more detail with the Asian response to his visit and to proposed CUSO placements, Perinbam made it clear that newly independent nations like India were by no means unreservedly enthusiastic about receiving young North American volunteers, no matter how well intentioned they might be:

> There was a strong feeling that young Canadian graduates were, in a sense, coming to "civilize" and that this was why many of them wanted to work in villages rather than in the towns and cities where the life might be more sophisticated ... I was asked how Americans and Canadians would react and respond if Asian countries offered to send their unemployed young graduates to work in business, industrial,

"Fine Young Canadians"

and governmental concerns in North America and 'to help' people in our part of the world.[37]

Mindful of the skepticism he had encountered in parts of Asia but undeterred by it, Perinbam set about establishing local committees to publicize and recruit for CUSO, all of them on university campuses. Acting in his capacity as CUSO's secretary-treasurer, Donald Wilson of the SCM did a recruitment tour of western Canadian universities. Likewise, Walter McLean, newly licensed as a Presbyterian minister but not yet ordained, visited Canadian campuses in his role as president of the National Federation of Canadian University Students (NFCUS) in 1961-62, using each stop to promote the idea of international service through CUSO.[38] Some forty committees were established during the academic year, though in reality, the "committee" was often just one person, a faculty member acting as the CUSO representative on a volunteer basis.[39]

This was not, of course, the case where campus committees predated CUSO, as at the University of Toronto and UBC, where they remained vibrant. Committees like these played a major role not only in recruiting but also in interviewing and screening applicants. Beginning early in 1962, the SCM's newly appointed secretary at McGill University, an ordained American with developing-world experience, served for several years as executive secretary of the campus CUSO committee.[40] McGill was one of several campuses where the SCM played a key role in local CUSO committee work in the early years. Elsewhere, WUSC was sometimes designated to act for CUSO on campuses where no local committee was yet formed, or CUSO and Operation Crossroads Africa shared a common representative.[41]

Early guidelines from CUSO's Ottawa office sought to establish national procedures and systematic two-way communication with campus committees.[42] Much of what was being recommended was a continuation of practices that COV, and to a lesser extent the UBC President's Committee, had employed – for instance, enlisting the expertise of faculty, community members, or visitors with developing-world experience in the work of the committees. There were as yet no specific national criteria to guide those interviewing and making recommendations about would-be volunteers. In the absence of such criteria, campus selection committees in this early period took an ad hoc approach to this task.[43] Prior to the interview, they were meant to have access to the applicant's transcript and letters of reference as well as his or her completed information

CUSO founding figures and several early volunteers, recipients of twenty-fifth anniversary awards, pose with Governor General Jeanne Sauvé, 6 June 1986. *Front row, from left:* Les Johnson (India), Geoff Andrew, Marcel Cloutier, Madame Sauvé, Keith Spicer, J. King Gordon, Chris Bryant (Grenada). *Centre:* Anne Jones Hume (India). *Back row, from left:* Guy Arnold, Francis Leddy, Bill McWhinney, Lewis Perinbam, Fred Stinson. *CUSO Forum,* September 1986. Courtesy of Cuso International.

form. The latter sought data on such matters as extracurricular reading, church affiliation, and emotional health as well as education, motivation, work experience, and language skills. Based on the interviews and the materials available to them, campus committees ranked applicants' files and forwarded them with comments to Ottawa for final decisions by the National Selection Committee.[44]

As at the campus level, persons with relevant knowledge or experience were asked to serve on the National Selection Committee. Dr. Davidson Dunton, president of Carleton University, chaired the inaugural committee, which also included Rev. J.M. Quirion, dean of Social Sciences from the University of Ottawa; SCM staffperson Katharine Hockin; NFCUS president and soon-to-be missionary Walter McLean; and representatives from the National Research Council, the Canadian Universities Foundation, and the External Aid Office.[45] Working with the National Committee, CUSO's small staff had to come to terms

"Fine Young Canadians"

with applications from students whose academic records were sometimes less than stellar, and in these circumstances the argument that a positive attitude in a volunteer was more important than academic excellence was probably persuasive.[46] In this start-up period, CUSO had a smaller pool of applicants from which to draw than its Peace Corps counterpart, proportionately as well as absolutely, and thus could not afford to be as discriminating in making its selections.[47]

Once volunteers had been selected, CUSO staff turned to the challenge of matching individuals with requests from host countries for specific types of services and skills. In theory, like COV before it, CUSO's policy was that its volunteers would go only where they were requested by indigenous agencies or governments. (In practice, a great deal of effort would go into finding placements, as later chapters will show.) Likewise, volunteers' salaries were to come from their host employer and be comparable to salaries paid to indigenous workers with the same level of training and responsibility.[48] One important change from COV practice was in regard to the length of volunteers' service. Having been advised by various individuals and groups that a one-year appointment was too short to be practical and worthwhile, CUSO, like most of its international counterparts, opted for a two-year contract for its volunteers.[49]

In the autumn of 1962, Perinbam's term as interim executive secretary of CUSO came to an end, as did CUSO's interim organizational relationship with the Canadian National Commission for UNESCO. Perinbam had given CUSO as much time and attention as could be managed while still holding his UNESCO position. But he had been handicapped by the fact that the first chair of the executive committee had provided lacklustre leadership; by problems in retaining successful applicants (many withdrew when overseas postings could not be rapidly confirmed); and by CUSO's lack of money.[50] The new arrangements instituted that autumn put CUSO on a better footing. Not only did the organization now have a full-time executive secretary in the person of the bridge-building Bill McWhinney; the newly established International Programmes Division of the Canadian Universities Foundation (CUF), with UBC professor Geoffrey Andrew in charge, assumed executive and administrative responsibility for CUSO. CUF also provided for office space and related expenses.[51] It did not, however, cover the costs of such matters as orientation or volunteers' travel and supplies. Much remained to be done to ensure CUSO's viability.

Acknowledging that CUSO's activities in its first year had "fall[en] short of professional standards," Andrew, who was also on CUSO's executive committee, took the lead in fundraising initiatives, aggressively seeking financial support from big business as well as from the kinds of organizations that COV had courted.[52] J.M. Macdonnell, a former Diefenbaker cabinet minister with a strong interest in the developing world, agreed to head up a national fundraising campaign for CUSO. The first such campaign, conducted in 1963, yielded the sum of $137,000. In-kind assistance also began, and three provinces provided small grants.[53]

It was all helpful and encouraging. But it was not enough if CUSO was to respond to increasing opportunities for placing volunteers. A second national fundraising campaign secured only 45 percent of its objective.[54] The most obvious place to turn for significant financial help as requests for volunteers and applicant numbers increased was the federal government. The initial outlook was not promising. Diefenbaker's early moral support for Keith Spicer's idea notwithstanding, his government remained unwilling to provide money to volunteer aid organizations. As Diefenbaker's external affairs minister, Howard Green took the position that Canada's Colombo Plan funds could not be allocated to any nongovernmental agency.[55] EAO head Herb Moran was equally resistant to appeals from Perinbam. Perhaps fearing pressure in a public setting, Moran declined even to send an EAO representative to CUSO's first annual meeting, held in Hamilton in June 1962.[56] Meanwhile, in their correspondence with COV a year earlier, Canadian diplomatic representatives in South Asia had conveyed their understanding that they had no mandate from Ottawa to provide any help beyond that of "a consular character" to would-be student volunteers. Canada's high commissioner to India, Chester Ronning, had written Spicer to that effect. As Canada's high commissioner in Ceylon, James George likewise observed that since the Canadian government had no involvement in Spicer's scheme beyond "sympathetic good wishes, my role must be pretty informal too." George ended his letter by asking COV for copies of all relevant correspondence while "not involving us more directly than you can help."[57]

With the election of the Liberals under Prime Minister Lester Pearson in 1963, there were prompt and substantial increases in official foreign aid – an acknowledgment of, and attempt to improve on, Canada's weak record in comparison with other developed nations.[58] The new aid climate benefited CUSO directly. Early in 1964, the minister of external affairs, Paul Martin Sr., announced that CUSO volunteers would be flown to their destinations on RCAF transport. The following year, Pearson's government announced a $500,000 special grant to CUSO.[59] It was a remarkable change. But CUSO's new access to

"JONES TO SAIGON ... BROWN TO CYPRUS ... GAGNON TO CHICAGO STADIUM ... "

Although *The Toronto Telegram* was an enthusiastic supporter of the early CUSO, cartoonist Al Beaton couldn't resist poking fun at "Canada's Peace Corps" when the federal government announced a half-million-dollar grant from External Aid funds in April 1965. Courtesy of Sun Media Corporation.

federal assistance was more than simply a matter of the election of a government with a more expansive view of how to support development. Continuing its earlier pattern of polite lobbying, CUSO and its supporters had systematically prodded Liberal leaders to adopt that more expansive view. Like Perinbam before him, McWhinney was invariably diplomatic, even deferential, in dealing with government representatives at all levels and grateful for *any* type of support for CUSO's goals, at the same time demonstrating a careful, businesslike approach to his job such as would inspire confidence in the young organization.[60] In December 1963, together with Leddy, Andrew, and Monsignor J. Garneau, CUF's associate director, McWhinney met with Pearson and Martin and presented a brief asking the federal government to match grants to CUSO from the private sector.[61] In February 1965, McWhinney prepared another presentation to the government, making the case for the kinds of benefits that could accrue to Canada from an enlarged CUSO presence overseas while at the same time demonstrating that such a presence could not be achieved on the basis of privately raised funds. In the wake of the government's commitment to the provision of RCAF transport and later the half-million dollars, McWhinney expressed his appreciation of all concerned, not forgetting the aircrews.[62]

Now, too, warm endorsements of the volunteers' work were being received from Chester Ronning and others attached to the Canadian High Commission in India. Acknowledging that his office had initially had misgivings about the COV/CUSO initiative, Ronning wrote early in 1964 to say that the volunteers had proven to be a dedicated and self-reliant group of young Canadians; they were creating a favourable impression for Canada and merited some government support.[63] Meanwhile, once the national media had become aware that Canada had its own "peace corps," its coverage had been laudatory. Several newspapers urged the government to support what the *Toronto Star* labelled "young Canadian idealism at work."[64] Beginning with the COVs, departing or returning volunteers were invited as speakers to churches, women's groups, service clubs, and local branches of UN associations. Clearly, numerous Canadians now shared the view that Stinson had repeatedly expressed in speeches on behalf of COV: the volunteers were "fine young Canadians."[65] From the world of Canadian transnational businesses, Thomas Bata showed up at the 1963 orientation to assure the volunteers that they could go into any Bata shoe store in the world if they needed help. (His company's deplorable employment practices in its factories in apartheid South Africa would only later be widely exposed.)[66] In the House of Commons, Thomas Berger of the NDP and Red Tory Gordon Fairweather used private members' bills to request help for CUSO. Fairweather's notice of motion in June 1963 was enthusiastically supported by MPs from the three major parties.[67]

The two-year delay in actually implementing financial aid to CUSO was not simply a matter of a foot-dragging bureaucracy. As Pearson's external affairs minister, Paul Martin reportedly had some misgivings. It was not a matter of his doubting the value of youthful volunteerism. He had lent moral and advisory support to COV, and in 1964 his own daughter went to Senegal with Crossroads Africa.[68] Rather, his concern as minister, it was said, was that if funds were granted to CUSO, other development-minded groups, including churches and missionaries, would be led to seek similar treatment.[69] Still, having agreed to allowing CUSO volunteers to travel on RCAF transport, Martin seemed open to the idea of further aid to the organization so long as it could be given without impairing CUSO's independent status and making it effectively an agency of government. Thus, writing in 1964 to Leddy as the chairman of CUSO's Executive Committee (and soon to be a prominent member of Martin's riding as the incoming president of the University of Windsor), Martin declared, "we ought to be considering a greatly expanded voluntary service overseas and I hope that you will join with me sometime next fall in reviewing this whole situation with a view to considering how we can develop a programme for 1965."[70] Timely pressure from Leddy and from Duncan Edmonds, Martin's executive assistant and an important early advocate for CUSO, was undoubtedly valuable in overcoming Martin's initial reluctance.[71] Moreover, with the prime minister, diplomats, MPs, and the public all onside to help CUSO, it would have been difficult to remain aloof and declare that it could not be done.[72]

Yet the spring 1965 announcement of federal funding for CUSO did not bring unalloyed relief to CUSO, for it came just after the Liberal government's speech from the throne presented a plan for the creation of an entirely new organization, the Company of Young Canadians (CYC). Initially, the CYC's mandate appeared to include overseas as well as domestic development work. Did this mean that CUSO was going to become a direct agency of government as part of CYC rather than an independent NGO aided by some federal financing? Many members of the inner CUSO community worried that this was in the offing. They thus welcomed Prime Minister Pearson's assurance early in 1966 that CUSO would continue to be "the principal Canadian agency devoted to providing opportunities for young Canadians to serve as volunteers on long-term contracts in developing countries" and that the federal government would "continue to add its own substantial financial support to the very necessary contributions received from the public at large."[73]

Still, the creation of the CYC had inflicted at least short-term harm on CUSO. The resulting confusion in the public mind did some damage to the 1965 fundraising campaign. Ironically, the CYC also cost CUSO its stellar executive secretary.[74] McWhinney, named to *Maclean's* magazine's list of outstanding Canadians of 1965 and featured on the cover of its first issue in 1966, had been asked by Pearson to become the CYC's interim director. Pearson policy adviser Tom Kent told *Maclean's* that CUSO had been the inspiration for the founding of the CYC (a view echoed by many participants in parliamentary debates on the bill to establish the CYC). The *Maclean's* article went on to declare that McWhinney epitomized all that was best in the new mood of youthful activism in Canada.[75] As it turned out, McWhinney's interval with the CYC would be brief and frustrating. He had no enthusiasm for grappling with the fuzzy ideas about community development or the New Left rhetoric that quickly came to the fore in the organization, while for their part CYC radicals found him hopelessly "square."[76] Though McWhinney did not return to CUSO, his ties with the organization remained emotionally strong and strategically valuable.

As for CUSO itself, after a brief interim period under the direction of acting executive secretary Terry Glavin, it, too, moved on, hiring as Glavin's replacement Hugh Christie, a senior bureaucrat from the EAO. In 1966, at his first executive committee meeting, Christie observed that CUSO had entered a new phase and that "the setting of new policies would be required."[77] A period of rapid expansion followed: "In the four years following McWhinney's departure, the number of volunteers tripled, from 341 working in twenty-nine countries to 1,110 in forty-two countries; the staff complement grew almost twice as fast."[78]

Volunteers: Background and Preparation

Available personal data on volunteers from English Canada reveal some broad general patterns among those serving during this decade.[79] They typically came from middle-class or skilled working-class backgrounds and were born in Canada, the children of urban and suburban families of Anglo-Saxon or Anglo-Celtic background. Although most volunteers with French ancestry came from Quebec and went overseas with SUCO, some francophones did serve with CUSO. The decade's volunteers also included one or more men or women from Dutch, Egyptian, First Nations, German, Japanese, Russian, and South African national backgrounds. Religiously, Jewish, Lutheran, Mormon, Muslim, and Sikh traditions were represented. Mainly, though, volunteers were from mainstream Protestant or Catholic backgrounds, some of them still from large farm families, just as they had been in the missionary era when such families had produced vocations in abundance. Although few Canadian families were classified as without any religious identity even in the 1970s,[80] some volunteers reported non-observant backgrounds. Several respondents came from well-to-do families, and in the early 1960s, volunteers from private-school backgrounds were probably over-represented. Yet the volunteer who emerges as *most* typical from all the data available for 1960s English Canada is a young man or woman of English, Irish, or Scottish ethnicity from a comfortable urban Ontario home and from a mainstream Protestant, often United Church of Canada, background.[81]

Volunteer Marie Smallface, from the Blackfoot Nation, Cardston, Alberta, was eager to encourage other "Indians" to join CUSO. "When I return home," she wrote, "I intend to use my African experience to help bring Canada out of its racial dark ages." *CUSO/ SUCO Bulletin,* December 1968. Courtesy Cuso International and Marie Smallface Marule.

This social profile is consistent with what is known about immigration and university attendance patterns in Canada in this decade. Immigrants continued to come mainly from Europe, Britain, and the United States. And even in Ontario, the province that attracted the largest number of immigrants and that had the largest number of universities, it was late in the twentieth century before a significant number of students from southern and eastern Europe and from so-called visible minority backgrounds were in a position to attend university.[82]

Given the campus recruitment setting, it should come as no surprise to learn how young the 1960s volunteers were. Still, this aspect is striking. Drawing on data up to September 1967 for his introductory chapter in *Man Deserves Man,* McWhinney gave the volunteers' average age as "in the neighbourhood of twenty-four to twenty-five," with some as young as nineteen or twenty and others as old as seventy-nine.[83] McWhinney's average was somewhat misleading, pulled up by a few elderly volunteers such as a retired pediatrician who went to Nigeria and a retired engineer who served in Uganda, and by a recent increase in the enrolment of nurses. McWhinney seemed anxious to de-emphasize volunteers' youthfulness. Certainly, the two COV cohorts had been younger than his average. Biographical data on nineteen COVs slated for South and Southeast Asia in the second cohort showed that eight of them were just twenty-one; five were twenty-two. The oldest was a twenty-eight-year-old nurse. And data in CUSO's annual report for the recruitment year 1965-66 showed that 359 of the 571 applicants were under the age of twenty-four.[84] At an early date, CUSO began rethinking its focus on new university graduates as the norm for its volunteers and sought to attract more mature applicants with work experience. But no substantial change could be expected while universities and colleges remained the main sites for recruitment. Dropping *university* from the organization's name, a possibility discussed briefly in 1964, proved unworkable. In any case, so long as promoting international understanding stood with being technically useful as one of CUSO's two principal objectives, an argument could be made for sending young and unencumbered volunteers.[85]

With their new university degrees,[86] most of these young volunteers were in possession of what was still a rare commodity in Canadian society. Even in the mid-1960s, only about one in ten eighteen-year-old Canadians was enrolled in university, a number that would rise to one in six by the early 1970s.[87] Some of the volunteers had honours degrees, and a few had postgraduate degrees in arts or science. Overall, however, as in the Peace Corps, the most common qualification was a general bachelor of arts degree. In volunteer parlance they were known as BAGs.[88] In 1965-66, out of the total of 571 applicants, there were 254 new arts graduates and fifty-five applicants with newly acquired science degrees. It seems likely that most of the forty-five people who applied with secondary-school teaching experience also had BA degrees.[89]

After university graduates, the next largest category of applicants in 1965-66 was nurses. Only two of the sixty-five applying that year had degrees, a reflection of the fact that the three-year nursing diploma was still overwhelmingly the norm in Canada.[90] Still, nurses with degrees perhaps came to be overrepresented in CUSO's ranks.[91] The increasing number of nurse applicants in the last half of the 1960s reflected a response to CUSO's advertising outreach to this group, which, in turn, reflected a growing interest in some host countries – India and Colombia most notably – in obtaining their services, particularly for teaching and mentoring roles.[92] Unlike university graduates who became secondary-school teachers overseas, the nurses often had several years of work experience by the time they volunteered; sometimes in challenging non-urban settings. Having worked, they were also somewhat older than other volunteers in their cohort.[93]

The growth in the number of volunteers who were nurses after mid-decade added to an already-strong female presence in volunteer ranks. Seven of the fifteen volunteers in the first COV cohort were women, among them two nurses and a francophone doctor from Quebec. In the second cohort, the majority were women. Writing about CUSO applicants in May 1963, Bill McWhinney expressed concern that more women than men had again applied.[94] When allowance is made for the fact that in 1961 only about 26 percent of Canadian university graduates with first degrees were women, and that even in 1971 the figure was still just 38 percent,[95] it becomes clear that women were, proportionately, over-represented in applicant and volunteer numbers.[96] Overall, male volunteers may have outnumbered females in both the 1960s and the 1970s, albeit only slightly.[97] Unlike their Peace Corps counterparts, young Canadian men did not have the chilling prospect of a letter from the draft board and a tour in Vietnam as an incentive to join CUSO.[98]

Whether male or female, with the exception of the nurses, few 1960s volunteers had experienced the work world other than in summer jobs. Still, some of them had more usable pasts than others so far as work was concerned. A period of a few months as a clerk in a store or even as a camp counsellor could do little to prepare one for a developing world assignment, especially if the placement was in a remote area or in an ill-defined job. What *was* an advantage in such a setting for a number of male volunteers who went to India and who were given challenging agricultural assignments was their farm background. They were certainly in very different rural environments from the ones in which they had grown up, thrust into leadership roles and responsible for tasks whose specific requirements were far outside their range of experience. Still, the things they had done – and done without – growing up on the family farm were, in their way, perhaps as helpful as their professional agricultural training.[99] The work experience that some male volunteers had gained through Frontier College also stood them in good stead. Its roots going back to the Reading Camp Association established by a Presbyterian minister in 1899, Frontier College enabled university students to work as labourer-teachers alongside immigrants and other labourers in remote settings, assisting them to acquire literacy and other life skills.[100] Though Dave Godfrey's day job with CUSO in Ghana was teaching literature in an elite high school under an Oxford-educated headmaster who valued his Stanford MA, Godfrey had his Frontier College experience to draw upon when he started a night-school class for working men in a nearby town. Likewise, in India, John R. Wood, having spent summers with Frontier College in northern Manitoba and Newfoundland, was perhaps more inclined than would otherwise have been the case to go beyond the confines of a middle-class school and, in his free time, undertake work with village farmers and the children of Dalits. At a minimum, summers with Frontier College had given young men like Godfrey and Wood, Tom Schatzky, Steve Woollcombe, and Jim Morrison, a taste of an unfamiliar and challenging milieu and a chance to exercise initiative, even if it was on Canadian soil. For Morrison, after two summers with Frontier College, going overseas with CUSO seemed "a natural progression." Ross Kidd spent three summers with Frontier College, responsible in his final year for supervising forty labourer-teachers. For Kidd, whose father was recognized internationally for his leadership in adult education, Frontier College was excellent preparation for the job awaiting him in Zambia: selecting, training, and supervising teachers in adult-education methods at the College of Applied Arts and Commerce in Lusaka.[101]

Among volunteers slated to be teachers, a lack of relevant work experience and professional preparation was, nonetheless, the norm. And yet, as in the Peace Corps, teaching assignments were, by a large measure, the single most frequent type of placement for volunteers. Despite CUSO's stated desire to diversify and attract candidates with a broader range of vocational skills, the number of teachers would increase significantly in the course of the decade, especially as newly independent African nations sought teachers from the West. Meanwhile, in 1962, of forty teachers recommended for Nigeria by local screening committees, the vast majority lacked any teaching experience.[102] It was in an effort to deal with these gaps in volunteers' backgrounds as well as to prepare them culturally that CUSO in 1962 began providing orientation sessions.[103] Held in July at Macdonald College in Montreal for thirty Africa-bound volunteers, the first CUSO orientation was headed by Professor Wayne Hall, the acting director of the College's Institute of Education. Along with several of those assisting him, Hall had some experience of working in Africa. The most senior Africanist was British anthropologist Margaret Read, formerly with the University of London's Department of Education in Tropical Areas. Donald Wilson and Katharine Hockin from the national SCM played active roles.[104] Both, like

Read, had links with the international missionary community. Remarkably, neither the Macdonald College sessions nor the orientation held at the University of Ottawa a year later involved actual practice teaching. Yet for a time, instructors with mission links continued to be involved. However surprising this may seem in view of CUSO's efforts to eschew mission connections during its founding, it reflected the reality that missions were the only Canadian organizations with extensive experience in preparing personnel for such overseas service. As CUSO's new executive secretary, Bill McWhinney had promptly sought help with orientation from the CCC. In 1963, Father Romeo Guilbeault. of the University of Ottawa, newly returned from years of educational administration and university work in Basutoland (Lesotho), assisted with orientation. Although "Father G." would remain a fixture on the CUSO/Ottawa scene into the late 1970s, occupying leadership roles in recruitment and selection as well as orientation, his contribution in 1963 illustrated the makeshift character of early orientation sessions: one volunteer recalled that he gave classes in an African language that had no relevance for any of their postings.[105] External Aid Office personnel with overseas teaching experience shared instructional duties for the following year's orientation, one component of which was held at the University of Toronto. Yet feedback remained unenthusiastic. Indeed, it highlighted the need for more useful and stimulating sessions than CUSO had so far been providing. The practice teaching element, while "a commendable innovation," did not involve real students and thus was "too artificial to be of much value."[106] As the number of placement countries and volunteers grew, especially from 1965, the need for better planned, more diversified orientation programs became increasingly obvious. In that year, a total of 365 volunteers experienced more intensive and specialized sessions on five campuses from Nova Scotia to British Columbia, and for the first time some volunteers practice-taught in front of a live class.[107]

By 1967 and 1968, when orientation for the large contingent of West Africa volunteers was contracted to Althouse College of Education at the University of Western Ontario, the measures taken to prepare the volunteers had become more thorough, more geared to the professional needs of would-be teachers, and far more culturally diverse. In 1968, the month-long orientation for 140 West Africa volunteers – all but twenty-four of whom were to work in education – provided a substantial practice-teaching component using local high school students as subjects. The staff of fifty-five included thirteen Africans and seventeen RVs. Don Simpson, the young Althouse professor who directed the orientations in both years, was upbeat about what had been accomplished. Yet feedback from volunteers following the 1968 orientation included a variety of complaints: it made too many demands on their time (area studies, critical analysis of Canadian society, language and sensitivity training, and health tips as well as teacher training); it sought to force them into a mould; and its un-stated but built-in function of deselecting those considered unsuited for overseas service was emotionally disturbing.[108] These and other volunteer concerns about orientation will be examined later in this chapter. What is clear, however, is that after mid-decade, the orientations were attempting to prepare the largely in-experienced and professionally untrained volunteer educators more thoroughly and creatively than had been possible earlier in the decade.

Volunteers: Expectations and Motivation

When Joan Barrett of Port Credit, Ontario, was told that she was being posted to Sarawak, she had never heard of the place. Nor had Catherine Duffy and her PEI farm family when her term there began in 1965.[109] A former British colony on the island of Borneo, and part of Malaysia from 1963, Sarawak was admit-tedly a particularly distant and exotic place for Canadians. But even a Common-wealth country like India that had historically loomed larger in Canadians' consciousness seems to have been understood largely in terms of generaliza-tions about poverty and suffering, generalizations unattuned to regional and class differences and to the country's sensitivity about receiving outside aid. Even a comparatively knowledgeable and well-travelled academic like UBC's Cyril Belshaw anticipated in 1961 that India would be prepared to absorb "any number of students."[110] A *Toronto Star* reporter who was eager to help COV in 1962 by doing a story on its work in South Asia admitted to confusion about the spelling and location of the place he was writing about. Even several years later, the *Star*'s well-intentioned coverage of a York University orientation for Africa-bound volunteers could do no better than feature horror stories about what they might encounter as they left Toronto "for high adventure and lonely labor in some of the hottest, dampest, poorest and most frustrating countries on earth."[111] As David Morrison has observed, prior to the Colombo Plan era few Canadians "had even indirect connections with what were seen to be distant and exotic lands."[112] In the early 1960s, even the names of former colonies were changing at dizzying speed, particularly in sub-Saharan Africa, much of which had been coloured imperial red on school maps in the volunteers' childhoods.

Given their understandable lack of much advance knowledge about the history, geography, and government of the countries where CUSO had work, and the fact that decisions about their future posting were frequently made or changed shortly before, or even after, their departure,[113] it was not surprising to learn that volunteers had few advance expectations about their posting. By the time they completed the area-studies component of their orientation program, and especially if they had followed through on suggested readings, they were certainly better informed than they had been a few weeks earlier. But it was scant preparation for the enormous changes awaiting them. Almost invariably there was at least a brief period of culture shock, even if the volunteer's posting turned out to be in a city or town where other expatriates were working rather than the stereotypical mud hut outpost featured in some of the early literature.

At the same time, the volunteers had an attitude of openness to new experiences and a good deal of hopefulness about what they were about to undertake. Optimism about what could be done to help the Global South was characteristic of the early years of the first Development Decade among volunteers and government-funded experts alike. Behind the concept of a Development Decade was the assumption, associated most closely with the work of US economist Walt Rostow, that the challenges facing the "Third World" – typically countries newly emerged or about to emerge from colonialism – were challenges that could be met with assistance from the West through short-term provision of expert personnel, modernizing values and techniques, and financial and material aid. These outside interventions, it was assumed, would be necessary only until developing countries could carry on with their own modernization, the benefits of which would in time trickle down even to the poorest.[114] The intended role for young Western volunteers in this process was frequently referred to as filling a gap: by providing junior- or middle-level skills and services until such time as an adequate number of indigenous professionals became available. In introducing his book *The Alms Bazaar,* Ian Smillie illustrated the hopeful mood by referring to the first episode in his own development career: a teaching job with CUSO in Sierra Leone in 1967-69. An independent country from 1961, Sierra Leone still seemed in 1967 permeated by "a feeling of optimism: of growth, energy and a promising future." The young Smillie saw himself as contributing, like numerous other NGO workers in the developing world, "to what most of us thought was the business of 'putting ourselves out of business.'"[115]

Interviewed almost forty years after he first set foot in Africa, Smillie readily acknowledged the strain of idealism that played a part in his decision to apply to CUSO. But he went on to add that for himself and probably most CUSO applicants, wanting to do something useful was frequently mixed in with elements of escapism and a desire for adventure. He had planned to study law after completing his McGill University BA (crusading lawyer Ralph Nader was his hero). But then, during his last year, he had been part of an audience of two for a promotional film shown by an enthusiastic RV. The film captivated him, he recalled, for although it was obviously staged, it had wonderful scenery and great appeal. Having passed the subsequent CUSO interview, Smillie was asked about accepting a placement in India. Negative media images of the country made him unenthusiastic. What, then, about a posting in Nigeria or Sierra Leone? Since, on the one hand, he had heard of political trouble brewing in Nigeria (the civil war was about to begin), and, on the other, he had liked Sierra Leone's stamps during his boyhood stamp-collecting days, he had opted for Sierra Leone. At age twenty-two he was off to West Africa and an assignment teaching English, French, and history in a United Evangelical Brethren secondary school that by then had neither white brethren nor evangelical expectations of its staff.[116]

The particular combination of background circumstances and preferences that launched Smillie's long career in development work was unique. But his retrospective perspective on his own and other CUSO volunteers' youthful motivation meshes reasonably well with what Bill McWhinney had to say on this subject in 1968 in his introduction to *Man Deserves Man*. Identifying guilt as one factor – "in those who are struck by the extent of the material prosperity which is their birthright" – McWhinney went on to identify a smorgasbord of motives:

> Although volunteers continue to react against the label of idealism, an element of this is also involved, but of the pragmatic rather than the naive variety ... possibly combined with a religiously motivated altruism, a desire to serve, as Cardinal Léger has expressed it, with deeds as well as words ... Yet one need not deny the element of self-interest ... There is no doubt that a romantic attachment to overseas countries exists, plus a strong desire for travel and self-testing and self-exploring adventure. But, deeper than these, there has been a realization of the tremendous educational value which can be derived from living and working in another culture. Volunteer

service is thus seen as a complement to formal education, from both the professional and personal point of view.[117]

Writing from the perspective of one who had served as CUSO's first full-time executive secretary and as a member of the first contingent of COVs, McWhinney was probably in as good a position as anyone to comment on the question of motivation in the first half of the 1960s. *Man Deserves Man* was clearly meant to inform would-be applicants and facilitate recruitment, so one might expect an emphasis on pragmatic idealism as well as elements located along a spectrum of self-interest. But what is perhaps most noteworthy is the fact that a book published in 1968 with a young, university-educated audience in mind would still quote in its introduction Christian internationalists like Cardinal Léger, Albert Schweitzer, and Donald Faris, all of whom unhesitatingly invoked idealism in their calls for service to the world's neediest countries. McWhinney cited Faris's optimistic perspective: "Our youth possess a tremendous potential of energy, idealism and enthusiasm, just waiting to be tapped. The one reagent needed is the challenge that life's fullest expression is found in serving others." Even the foreword to *Man Deserves Man,* written by India's recently retired philosopher-president, Dr. Sarvepalli Radhakrishnan, invoked idealism as the explanation for the desire of educated and privileged young Westerners to help those "suffering from ignorance, disease and poverty." "The only answer," Radhakrishnan wrote, for the problems of a world riven by inequalities and threatened by dangerous new weapons of destruction, was to "make idealism effective. Religion is love in action."[118]

What about those other motivational elements that McWhinney identified under the category of self-interest and the two in particular that Smillie highlighted: adventure and escapism? In response to questions about motivation, many RVs who served in the 1960s unhesitatingly acknowledged the former and sometimes the latter as well. One woman, looking back from a long career in development, wrote, "above all ... I wanted to travel and see the world – get away from upper middle class Toronto."[119] One of the few RVs who requested anonymity spoke of joining CUSO as, for him, the modern equivalent of running away to sea. Some volunteers had an interest in a particular country and saw CUSO as a way to get there. Unlike Smillie, a number of them were attracted rather than repelled by what they had heard or read about India. One RV recalled the impression made on him in childhood by a bubble-gum card that had featured Mahatma Gandhi.[120] Others spoke of a more diffuse interest in "getting to know what was beyond [the] white western world."[121]

A wide variety of factors could come together to turn a vague interest into a firm decision to volunteer. University of Toronto graduate Sally Bambridge remembered stimulating contacts with international students hosted by her aunt, a university staff member. Then, in her last term of study, Bambridge covered a presentation on COV for *The Varsity* and thought what she heard sounded sufficiently interesting and worthwhile to herself become part of the cohort.[122] Other volunteers who had had a brief taste of the developing world through organizations like Crossroads Africa and WUSC determined that they wanted more. Family constellations of volunteers were nowhere more evident than among the nephews of the CIIA's John W. Holmes; four of them joined CUSO.[123] Many other volunteers also followed siblings or classmates or community members who had served with CUSO. As for the element of escapism, it could reflect a variety of quite personal situations in addition to those mentioned, including dissatisfaction with a job or reluctance to settle into a permanent career or a marriage. Unresolved issues about their sexual identity, which in turn contributed to tensions with dating partners and family, were recognized retrospectively by two volunteers as among the factors that contributed to their decision to join CUSO.[124] At a more prosaic level, the desire to escape from a small-town environment had been with some young adults well before they had ever heard of CUSO; usually, of course, they had had a mundane destination in mind.

Two very different volunteers for whom a CUSO posting was a calculated and strategic time out from a career path were Adel Nafrawi, a middle-aged Egyptian-born doctor, and Shirley Caldwell Tilghman, a future president of Princeton University. Dr. Nafrawi had come to work in Canada in 1964 after an exchange arrangement in the US had expired and out of reluctance to return to Nasser's Egypt. After reading about CUSO in the *Globe and Mail,* Nafrawi had volunteered and been accepted in 1969 for what proved to be a satisfying and memorable year in Nigeria.[125] A year earlier, after graduating in chemistry from Queen's University, Shirley Caldwell had gone to Sierra Leone to teach chemistry, math, and English. Interviewed by Canadian media in 2011 about her career at Princeton and as a world-renowned molecular biologist and a director of Google, Shirley Caldwell Tilghman spoke about her decision to undertake what proved to be two wonderful and "relaxing" years in Sierra Leone. The

CUSO placement was her time out before climbing on what she knew would be the rigorous treadmill of a graduate program in chemistry research. Although her parents objected to her two-year hiatus in Sierra Leone, Tilghman looked back on the interval as a richly rewarding break from intellectual pressures: "two years available to myself."[126]

Still, veteran aid advocates like Faris were not misguided in perceiving idealism in the era's youth. Even RVs like Tilghman who put self-interest in the foreground in recalling their own motivation acknowledged that an element of idealism had also played a part in their decision to join CUSO. Furthermore, a good many RVs recognized that their motivation might have owed something to the religious tradition in which they had been raised. Several volunteers recalled missionary ancestors. Others had siblings who were missionary nuns.[127] A significant number of volunteers from various parts of Canada and from both Catholic and Protestant backgrounds indicated that, as children or young teenagers, they themselves had fleetingly thought about ministry or missionary service.[128] Such volunteers may not have had any familial role models, but they had grown up at a time when stories about the work of Dr. Albert Schweitzer in French Equatorial Africa (Gabon) and Dr. Tom Dooley in Southeast Asia were internationally known and still deeply inspirational. Dooley, who died of cancer in 1961 at age thirty-four and whose work President Kennedy praised later that year when he established the Peace Corps, was especially inspirational for young Catholics, but his influence cut across religious lines.[129] Closer to home there were clergy who, far from providing a "comfortable pew," touched young consciences with stirring sermons on the needs of the wider world. Nor did all these young people outgrow a sense of calling: two volunteers who went to India with CUSO midway through the 1960s spoke of first seeking opportunities for missionary service. One of the two, a nurse whose Baptist denomination had mission work in India, was unable to acquire the necessary visa to follow in that tradition. The other, who had a farm background and graduate training in agriculture, applied to CUSO only after learning that he would be unable to obtain a mission appointment that made use of his background.[130] An early volunteer in Sarawak who later trained as a United Church minister and served in Brazil regarded joining CUSO both as a chance for a break before undertaking divinity studies and as "congruent with" his Christian goals.[131] As Cobbs Hoffman has noted with regard to the Peace Corps, something akin to a missionary impulse could resonate even with non-Christian volunteers. A CUSO volunteer from the early years whose original plan after graduation had been travel in India saw a good fit between the social and religious values of her left-leaning Jewish family and her later decision to marry and go with her husband to Ghana under CUSO auspices.[132]

Yet even if one focuses on the few for whom a mission board appointment was the preferred route for serving in a developing country, there is no reason to believe that had they received such an appointment, evangelism would have been a priority, especially since, during the 1960s, the mainstream churches were themselves becoming increasingly "NGOized."[133] Meanwhile, what emerges with vividness from personal information provided by 1960s volunteers is a pattern of religious declension: a church upbringing from which the volunteer had deliberately broken or was gradually falling away by the time he or she joined CUSO. How does one reconcile the strong evidence of this pattern with Bill McWhinney's firm assertion in 1963 that "the great majority of our person-nel are practicing Christians"? Quite simply, the statement needs to be under-stood in context. McWhinney was writing to address a concern raised by the educational secretary of the Christian Council of Nigeria about the lack of fit between secular CUSO volunteers and the requests of some missions for vol-unteers who would conform to their faith observances. In practice, CUSO field staff quickly learned to avoid making placements in mission institutions that made explicit religious demands on their volunteers, but since missions were so often the sites of placements in many African countries, McWhinney clearly wanted to be reassuring at this early stage about volunteers' backgrounds.[134]

As well as declension in religious observances in the volunteers' personal lives, there was unease, sometimes profound unease, with any semblance of a link between what the volunteers were undertaking and what they understood as traditional missionary activity. This was certainly the case with one of three volunteers who were children of clergy in the second COV cohort.[135] What was happening, it appears, was not so much a wholesale rejection of core values taught in a faith-based upbringing as a break from traditional creeds and ob-servances and from once-inviolate moral/social norms. It was a break that was reflective of the decade's increasing secularization.[136] Historian Doug Owram's observation about campus activists in this period also seems relevant for CUSO volunteers: "One of the persistent themes of the sixties," Owram writes, "is the link between student activism and a religious sense of duty ... the first stop on the road to campus activism was often in organizations like the Student Christian Movement. The belief in service, duty, and commitment brought them there, and the same beliefs often led them onward to new stops and new organizations."[137] Meanwhile, for the typical CUSO volunteer, whether he or she had begun from a faith position, it seems clear that there was seldom a single motivational factor. Rather, a conjunction of chance and circumstance meshed with the volunteer's personal background and predisposition – and with the spirit of the times – to make joining CUSO an attractive step. Keith Bezanson (Nigeria, 1963), looking back on what turned out to be a call to a lifelong career in development, summed up the elements as follows: "It was Canada's Pearsonian age of internationalism; Kennedy was in the White House and had launched the Peace Corps and the Alliance for Progress; a newly independent country seemed to be born every week. I was part of that age and its ethos. Volunteering was just the natural thing to do."[138]

Recent scholarly writing on post–Second World War humanitarianism – both the phenomenon generally and development and volunteerism in particular – posits the existence of an ongoing element of colonial-style paternalism in motivation and discourse, albeit generally shorn of the crude and infantilizing language of the earlier era.[139] What is striking from the interviews with RVs conducted for this book and from the paper trails left from their early period of youthful engagement is how eager most CUSO volunteers were to strike out on a new path in regard to race relations and ways of living and working in the non-Western world.[140]

CUSO from the Mid-1960s: Growth, Growing Pains, New Agendas

Writing as chairman of CUSO's National Executive Board in 1966, Professor J. King Gordon explained that while CUSO was now the fourth-largest international peace corps program in the world, it was still not in a position to meet the numerous requests it received for qualified volunteers.[141] Fortunately, the provision of government money to CUSO that had begun in 1965 continued. As head of the EAO from 1966, and then from 1968 of CIDA, Maurice Strong was a firm believer in the value of CUSO and other NGOs to Canada's international aid program. From 1968, government funding for NGOs was disbursed through CIDA's Special Programs Division, whose first head was Lewis Perinbam. CUSO was (and remained) by far the largest NGO recipient of money from the division.[142] By 1970-71 the CIDA grant totaled $4,250,000. Private-sector assistance from corporations and from Miles for Millions walks, service organizations, and individual donors all remained vital for CUSO's continuing

James Amissah *(left)*, first secretary Ghana High Commission, joins a CUSO team in a Miles for Millions walk. RV Helen Forsey (Ecuador) is to his right. CUSO's director of fundraising anticipated that his organization's share of funds from the 1969 campaign might be in excess of a quarter-million dollars. *CUSO/SUCO Bulletin,* Summer 1969. Courtesy of Cuso International.

identity as an NGO, but such assistance provided less than a quarter million dollars in total in that year. Universities associated with AUCC and AUCC's facilities in Ottawa also continued to provide valuable services and space at no cost, and host country employers typically paid volunteers' salaries.[143] Still, it was clear that CUSO's capacity for growth hinged on the maintenance of government support. And grow CUSO did, sending more than seven hundred volunteers in 1970, a record-high number. Meanwhile, government funding had also made possible rapid staff growth in the Ottawa office and the establishment of specialized departments.[144] More time and attention and in some cases professional expertise could now be brought to bear on such matters as fundraising, recruitment, selection, and orientation, with the first two of these functions facilitated by increased media coverage and public service announcements.[145]

Draft recruitment materials prepared for CUSO by a professional advertising firm for its 1967-68 recruitment campaign illustrated the new approach. The advertisements were designed to appeal to prospective applicants' self-interest or to reflect the countercultural spirit of the times, with old-fashioned idealism a less prominent part of the message ("Why two years with CUSO may put you five years ahead in your field"; "So you're not a hippie. Here's how to register another kind of protest"). There was also some targeting by occupational category, as shown in an advertisement prepared for use in *Canadian Nurse*: "We won't take just any nurse: only those committed nurses willing to work for a low salary under demanding conditions in any of 45 developing countries around the world." A spokesman for the advertising firm that designed these materials recommended more CUSO staff and more targeting of specific groups to deal with an increase in enquiries and to attract "*quality* as well as numbers." And while CUSO should continue to use public service announcements, the adman advised, it should also undertake the production of full-fledged commercial materials in both languages for use in a television campaign for the following year.[146] Another manifestation of the new approach was the commissioning of films showing volunteers at work. In what proved to be the first stage in a lifelong career in development communication, Neill McKee was hired to do this on his way home from his own posting in Malaysia.[147] Clearly, it was all a long way from the bootstraps days at U of T and UBC, when recruitment had been the task of a handful of students using posters on campus notice boards and stories in the campus press to facilitate word-of-mouth approaches to would-be volunteers – a long way, too, from Perinbam's forty-odd CUSO campus recruitment committees that had often been committees of one.

As shown above, McWhinney's introduction to *Man Deserves Man* had given a good deal of attention to idealism and enthusiasm as aspects of a volunteer's motivation even though the book was published in 1968, when those motives were becoming suspect. But *Man Deserves Man* was by no means all of a piece in tone and content. As in the professional advertising copy cited above, some of the articles written for *Man Deserves Man* by RVs sounded coolly pragmatic. Thus, the chapter on adaptation by Mary Lou and Jon Church, twenty-eight-year-olds who had already served in India and Ghana, put the emphasis on professional preparedness: "CUSO interviewing teams cannot select the most enthusiastic individual if he does not have a particular skill required in one of the newly independent countries. These countries want teachers, engineers, nurses and a thousand and one other types of skilled people, but they send few requests to CUSO for idealists or social activists." India RV John R. Wood's chapter on orientation was equally emphatic about CUSO's new concern with professional competence and the limitations of a simple BA.

Wood's main focus, however, was on the ways that orientation had improved since the early days. Now, he claimed, there was more, and more specialized, professional preparation: "midwifery and family planning for nurses, and wet-rice cultivation for agriculturalists" as well as better teacher training for the vast majority destined for classrooms. There was also significantly more time and technology invested in language training. As for the area-studies component, it was now more engaging, more fun, thanks to such innovations as having visiting foreign students teach Nigerian highlife (contemporary club music) or Jamaican ska (precursor to reggae) and the simultaneous scaling back of "dull windy lectures by ancient missionaries or pedantic orientalists."[148]

Did the growth in CUSO's budget and staff and more specialized approaches to such tasks as recruitment and orientation make CUSO more effective at these tasks? On the matter of orientation, comments provided by RVs some forty years after their own experience suggest mixed assessments. Robin Jeffrey, who went on to become a prominent historian of modern India, recalled his 1967 orientation at York University as a "wonderful experience – learned Devanagari script, a knowledge which I have benefitted from for 43 years." A doctor who in 1968 was about to be sent to northern Nigeria likewise recalled his orientation at the University of Western Ontario as exciting and helpful. The area-studies aspect and some basic Hausa vocabulary proved to be useful preparation. He also valued the efforts to alert young volunteers like himself to development problems in their own Canadian backyard (black activist Rocky Jones and a spokesman on Aboriginal issues were featured speakers that year). Similarly, Gini Dickie recalled the orientation at Western a year later as excellent: she now had at least some preparation for her forthcoming secondary-school teaching assignment, she had enjoyed learning to dance to highlife music, and she had some assurance that she would fit into her new cultural milieu.[149]

Some RVs, however, recalled their orientation in less positive terms. This was particularly true of the sensitivity-training aspect. Several recalled it as insensitive: amateurish, personally invasive, even potentially harmful. One woman whose orientation for India in 1966 was otherwise remembered as "a time of learning, adventure and fun" had very negative recollections of the "T groups." Another who went through orientation for Nigeria several years later and who looked back some thirty years thereafter from her perspective as a trained and experienced psychotherapist felt even more strongly than she had done at the time that "it was inappropriate, if not completely unethical, for an orientation program to have included the expectation of disclosure and exploration of

Orientation group, Montreal, 1966. The volunteers were preparing for postings in Kenya, Tanzania, Uganda, and Zambia. Donald Savage of Loyola's History Department *(front row, right)* led their training. Courtesy of David Beer.

personal issues on the part of volunteers about to depart for their postings."[150] In the article on orientation just mentioned, John Wood sought to emphasize the positive intent behind sensitivity training, but he was not alone among orientation leaders in acknowledging that this aspect was controversial, sometimes resented by and traumatizing for volunteers.[151] Wood's article also overstated the extent and rigour of volunteers' preparation for such specialized fields as family planning. As for the ticklish matter of "deselecting" those volunteers who appeared during orientation to be unsuitable for an overseas assignment, CUSO's claim that it did less of this than the Peace Corps, thanks to the screening done earlier by its local committees, seems to have been valid. Still, deselecting was not always done with finesse or discrimination, or even determination. One young male volunteer simply refused to be deselected for West Africa by orientation leaders. He may well have appeared arrogant and stubborn at the time in his disregard for rules and expectations, but the same independence of spirit served him well in Biafra in the immediate aftermath of the Nigerian civil war.[152]

Overall, CUSO files on various aspects of orientation around the end of the decade reveal a good many concerns about the process among those in charge and an absence of consensus on how to make it more effective. While some who had participated as leaders or facilitators wanted more of the orientation to take place in the host country, or to involve more RVs, or more foreign nationals living in Canada, others recommended more advanced study of the host country so that volunteers would arrive with a sound knowledge base. Writing from New Delhi in 1969, Nancy Garrett was concerned that some RVs, drawing on the worst of their own experiences, told "'war' stories" to the new recruits and thus unintentionally fostered racism. British VSOs, with less orientation than their CUSO and Peace Corps counterparts, actually adjusted to India more easily, she believed.[153] As for the use of resident foreign nationals in orientation programs, the unidentified author of a detailed orientation report saw limitations as well as benefits in their participation: usually they were university students, not necessarily up to date on events in their own country, sometimes "defensive when problems are discussed," or participating only for "some easy money for the holidays and a good bash." Cultural sensitivity was vital, he agreed, but fostering and testing for this quality at an orientation held just prior to departure was wrong-headed. Instead, applicants should be required to attend a course on cultural sensitivity before even being accepted by the local committee, and part of the process should involve contact with a Canadian subculture different from their own.[154]

These late-1960s comments on orientation programs were an apt reflection of an organization remarkably open to self-criticism and anxious to be culturally sensitive in a period of social turbulence. Clearly, efforts were being made to deal more explicitly with issues of "race" than had been the case earlier in the decade. The challenges that CUSO faced in this respect and the way that its good intentions could backfire were dramatically illustrated at the closing banquet in Montreal for the 1969 East Africa orientation. Like other orientations of the period but perhaps to a greater degree, the East Africa program had included speakers "strongly critical of neo-colonialism, neo-imperialism, 'do-gooderism' and aid in general." Such speakers, Ian Smillie writes, and especially some of the Black Power activists who had been invited to participate, "spread doubt and guilt among the middle-class Canadians as though they were sprinkling herbicide on a weed bed." The resulting tensions resulted in a physical brawl that ended the banquet "in unhappy disarray." This incident, which CUSO was naturally anxious to keep from the media, followed the much bigger and widely publicized race-based eruption of tensions that had taken place at Sir George Williams University earlier in the year.[155]

The sheer size of orientation programs such as the one for the large East Africa contingent in 1969 (there were 275 CUSO workers in five East African countries two years later)[156] added to the challenge of making them effective and relatively tension-free experiences. Moreover, the fact that they brought together volunteers from all across the country precluded the degree of camaraderie and cohesiveness and the strong sense of personal responsibility for their shared new venture that had been such defining characteristics of the two COV cohorts. In assessing gains and losses in orientation over the decade, it is worth reflecting briefly on the efforts to prepare those early cohorts. Drawn mainly from the University of Toronto and destined mainly for assignments in India, the 1961 COVs had been able to attend preparatory lectures and gather for publicity and fundraising activities during the winter term, while those in 1962 had come together in evening and weekend sessions spread over several summer months. Though she was initially an outsider to the 1962 group, one woman, a twenty-five-year-old British-Columbia-born nurse from a working-class Sikh family, remembered the sessions appreciatively for the sense of inclusiveness and cohesiveness they fostered.[157] In those early days in a still very uncosmopolitan city and campus, the two COV orientations had relied heavily for expertise on lecturers with university faculty and mission connections. As for the reading lists, they certainly offered less theory and breadth than the lengthier lists recommended for CUSO volunteers at the end of the decade, when recent critiques of North American society were included along with books by (for instance) Frantz Fanon, André Gunder Frank, and Albert Memmi.[158] Nonetheless, works used with the COVs such as books by Nehru,

Barbara Ward, and Faris and the best-selling novel *The Ugly American,* added for 1962, may in practice have been more widely read, especially if they were provided directly to the volunteers. (Stinson evidently purchased 150 copies of Faris's book for distribution.)[159] Working intensely with these small groups, the COV organizers could promote a level of personal engagement that was simply less attainable in later years. There were, then, some losses as well as significant gains as the later orientations became larger and more ambitious. Meanwhile, on a lighter note, the "fun" quotient probably increased after mid-decade as more casual attitudes to dating and partying became part of the orientation experience.[160]

If CUSO's diverse approaches to orientation from the mid-1960s were challenged as well as challenging, how did CUSO fare in this later period in regard to recruitment? This aspect will be considered first in terms of CUSO's concern to recruit more volunteers with a broad range of skills and experience and then in regard to the question of whether a shift was taking place in the ethos of volunteers. In terms of reaching out beyond the campus, CUSO, as noted, was most effective in regard to attracting nurses. This was more than a matter of numbers. Volunteers with a nursing background brought a high level of commitment as well as experience and maturity to their CUSO placements, and following their assignments a significant number remained engaged in some form of development work or pursued advanced studies. The organization made fewer gains, however, in attracting other types of volunteers who could bring maturity and new skills to overseas service. Following the launch of the first national advertising campaign in 1966, the *CUSO/SUCO Bulletin* reported a tripling of letters of enquiry, among them many from older and technically skilled enquirers. And yet National Selection Committee data indicate that as of September 1971, the single biggest group of applicants was still quite young – between twenty-one and twenty-three years of age – and that the median age overall was 23.6.[161] Moreover, as Gérard Aubry, the chairman of CUSO's board of directors, acknowledged in his 1971 report, developing countries' requests for teachers *with experience* and for "all types of technical personnel – from motor mechanics to electronics technologists were still largely unmet," and the reason seemed clear: "CUSO has been, and is, geared to recruiting on campus, where the organization had its beginnings."[162]

While CUSO's recruitment activities were still centred on Canadian campuses, these were places that had undergone significant change in the course of the decade. By the mid-1960s, existing universities were expanding and new ones were being created to meet the surge of baby boomers who were starting to arrive. "In the five years between 1963 and 1968," Owram writes, "Canadian university enrolment increased as much as it had in the previous fifty!" Among the new students, only a small percentage came from racial and ethnic minority backgrounds, but they had far more diverse socio-economic backgrounds than previous generations of undergraduates. And they were being taught by faculty who were younger and less privileged than their predecessors. Like their professors, the students were part of a social milieu awash in new and sometimes contradictory values and discourses.[163]

Did this rapidly changing demographic and social context and CUSO's ability to sponsor more personnel result in the sending of volunteers with a different level of commitment from that of their predecessors? Certainly, there were those who thought they perceived some change – and those who thought so included both CUSO's friends and its critics. *Globe and Mail* journalist Clyde Sanger, a member of CUSO's board of directors in 1969, was both friend and critic. Sanger began a *Globe* article that year by citing a question posed in UBC's alumnus magazine: "Has success spoiled CUSO?" His answer was no ... and perhaps. On the plus side, unlike the Peace Corps, CUSO had never been asked to leave a country, and in several developing countries, it was the main Canadian presence. Moreover, as a group, its RVs were better informed about the problems of developing countries than other groups of Canadians. And far from being "retired volunteers," they were activists. But therein lay a complication: if the campaign of "public education and political action" within Canada for which some RVs were calling was interpreted as a criticism of Canadian foreign policy – and it was – it could jeopardize federal funding. As for the question of whether the current crop of volunteers was made of the right stuff, a question being asked by some of the old-time "hair-shirt volunteers," Sanger, who had recently returned from a tour of countries where Canadians were doing development work, *did* voice some concerns. "The critics have a point when they complain too many today seem more interested in accoutrements for their Hondas [motorbikes] than in the job ahead of them. Also, with 140 CUSO people in Nigeria, and 200 spread between Zambia and Tanzania, there's a temptation to cluster in Canadian colonies." As Sanger put it in the book that followed his tour, CUSO was "at the Crossroads."[164]

One RV, reflecting some forty years later on his own experience and that of others in the early "hair-shirt" cohorts and comparing their motivation with that of those who came after, pondered the early CUSO motto "To Serve and

Learn" and the question of what had changed. He thought that RVs like himself who had participated in recruitment after their return had perhaps unwittingly contributed to a weakening in the volunteer ethos:

> In an attempt to deflect the "praise" about the service aspect of our time overseas, I think we emphasized the learning aspect, and all of a sudden people were signing up to go "get an experience" or because it would look good on a resume. We, of the first generation, were a bit bewildered by the motivation of some who went after us. Maybe they were [just] more honest than we were. I know that I wanted an adventure, but felt that I had to justify it by service.[165]

In the same way that the efforts of early volunteers to deflect praise for their "sacrifices" may have had an unintended effect on later volunteers' motivation, attempts to damp down expectations about what individual volunteers could expect to accomplish in the developing world during their brief period of involvement may also have had unintended outcomes. To be sure, the need to establish realistic expectations had been expressed by members of the pioneering cohort from their first months in the field, as Chapter 2 will show, but warnings on this subject had usually been confined to exchanges among the volunteers themselves and with their home-base colleagues in Toronto. As the decade wound down, it was a message intended for would-be volunteers. The authors of a statement originating with the CUSO Regional Conference in Bangkok in 1969, for instance, called for volunteers' expectations to be set "at a realistically modest level" so that they would be aware that their efforts would be "at best, peripheral."[166]

By the early 1970s, some national staff responsible for recruitment and selection were concerned that volunteers frequently did not know much about development problems in their own country (a non-issue a decade earlier), and that they knew less about the developing world than had previously been the case. In regard to the latter, a letter from the Ottawa office to local selection committees stated, "We remain *very* concerned about the general level of awareness and preparedness of people applying to CUSO to work overseas. People applying nowadays are simply not as well informed about CUSO, about development, and about overseas conditions as previously."[167]

What is one to make of these concerns about declension? Taken together, they appear to indicate that CUSO's ability to draw from a larger recruitment pool and put larger numbers of volunteers in more countries was contributing to the sending of young men and women less imbued with an ethic of service and less well informed about the developing world than had been the case in earlier years. Sanger attributed some of the organization's difficulties with more recent volunteers to the terms of its funding relationship with CIDA. With 90 percent of its working funds coming from CIDA and with the amount based on a formula directly related to the number of volunteers being appointed, "more than a few are now being sent abroad who should never have gone." Sanger especially deplored the "sloppiness" in appointments to nearby Jamaica, "whose government has been casual in its way of accepting virtually anyone offered," and at CUSO headquarters, for "not filtering applicants more carefully." The result, he wrote, was that in 1968-69 almost half the volunteers sent to Jamaica returned before the year was over.[168]

CUSO at the Crossroads

Perceptions of declension in the volunteering ethos in CUSO in the late sixties and early seventies occurred simultaneously with the emergence of a significant group of politicized RVs, as Sanger noted. This group of RVs and RVs-turned-staff was arguably as engaged as the earliest volunteers and, in their way, as idealistic, however much they rejected what they called naive idealism and argued for a more sophisticated understanding of barriers to development. Indeed, some of them, drawn from the early cohorts, had themselves once epitomized that kind of idealism. Now, reflecting a larger international pattern among development NGOs, they sought to use CUSO's new resources to further an agenda that included critical thinking about development issues and strategies for political activism. The rhetoric and activities of this radicalized subset became a major source of internal division and external criticism, as Chapter 3 will show.

Yet as CUSO ended its first decade, it continued to benefit from a large fund of national goodwill – cultivated by such eminent university-based supporters as King Gordon and expressed tangibly in its numerous local committees and private-sector assistance, at the highest levels of state, and in generous media coverage. The title and content of a 1969 *Reader's Digest* article typified media warmth: CUSO was "Canada's Foreign Aid Extraordinary." Reviews of *Man Deserves Man*, launched from the home of Governor General Roland Michener and his wife and chosen as the nonfiction selection of the *Canadian Reader*, were also kind to a fault. Donald Savage, the academic who reviewed the book for *Canadian Forum,* had directed the orientation for East and Central Africa in 1966 and had thus seen the volunteers up close. His comments on the tone of "high-mindedness" and the "overwhelming impression of Victorian earnestness" that permeated much of *Man Deserves Man* would have been cringe-inducing for many in the organization, since these were the very images they were seeking to dispel. But Savage went on to add that the book's tone should not be a basis for academic condescension, for with its "experience, elan, and flexibility ... CUSO has become that curious thing, a Canadian success story."[169]

2

A Passage to India
Early Lessons in Development

It is not your aptitude; it's your attitude.
– Prime Minister Nehru, 1962[1]

On 15 August 1961, fifteen Canadian Overseas Volunteers (COVs) left Canada for what became CUSO's first overseas placements, travelling by plane to London and then by P&O liner to Bombay (Mumbai), India, where they docked on 4 September. Three of the volunteers continued onward to assignments in Ceylon (Sri Lanka), while another two, CUSO's first married couple, went on to Sarawak. The remaining ten, five men and five women, served in India, effectively making that country CUSO's first major site for development work.[2] Although CUSO terminated its work in India in 1972, the experience there remains significant in the organization's history for several reasons. It was CUSO's largest placement country in Asia during the 1960s. In the early years, programming in India was influenced by a philosophy of volunteer service that gave pride of place to promoting international goodwill and understanding rather than providing vocational expertise. The initiative, adaptability, and commitment shown by the early volunteers contributed substantially to a positive image back home, and in so doing, helped CUSO win public and government support. Especially

Canadian Overseas Volunteers (COV) on the SS *Arcadia* nearing Bombay (Mumbai), September 1961. Courtesy of Stephen Woollcombe.

compared to the much larger programs that would be built up in West Africa, where teaching opportunities dominated from the outset, India provided the volunteers with an eclectic mix of placements. In addition to conventional teaching jobs, assignments included work in Gandhian ashrams, leadership on agricultural initiatives, aid to Tibetan refugees, and opportunities to participate in India's burgeoning family planning programs. This range was a reflection of the development context in 1960s India, but it also reflected the role played by the volunteers and coordinators and their advisers in seeking out contacts with potential employers. The wide array of placement opportunities provided many of the volunteers with a development experience that was richly rewarding at a personal level. They forged lasting ties with the communities in which they served and were led to professional interests that became the basis of future careers. Inevitably, however, there were assignments that proved to be a poor fit with what the volunteers had to offer or that, for a variety of other reasons, simply did not work out. Though such problems were fewer as CUSO gained experience and became more job focused and as more resources could be put into the coordinator's role, they did not disappear. Given these and other challenges, India served CUSO as the site of important early lessons in development.

Two images of the India experience that emerged early on in CUSO mythology were that of the hair-shirt volunteer, malnourished and alone in a mudhut setting, and that of the young naïf. Probably the hair-shirt image *did* have more reality in the experience of the volunteer in India than in any other country. But in this chapter, I want to challenge some aspects of the second mythic image and instead show how quickly these early volunteers moved beyond their initial naïveté about the developing world and about what they themselves could contribute. Although as returned volunteers (RVs), many of them would be uneasy with the ways CUSO was changing after the mid-1960s, that did not mean that they saw their own development experience as a model for emulation by their successors or that they had any illusions about what they and their organization could contribute to the lessening of the frightful social and economic divide between the Northern and Southern worlds. India had a way of inducing a humbling sense of proportion and scale soon after the Westerner's arrival. The cliché about being "a drop in a very big bucket" quickly took on meaning for the earliest volunteers.[3] Chapter 2 explores this early lesson as one of several aspects of the CUSO/India experience.

Why India?

When Lewis Perinbam approached the federal government in 1959 seeking support for a plan to get Canadian students involved in overseas work, it was the newly independent nation of Ghana that he had in mind as the first setting for their placements. For the COV's Keith Spicer, however, as Chapter 1 explains, the focus was on the Commonwealth countries in South and Southeast Asia where his graduate research took him in the first half of 1960. Spicer had used the trip to investigate opportunities for volunteers as well to research his thesis, and in the "Scheme for Canadian Overseas Volunteers" that he prepared in the spring of 1961, he named India and Ceylon as "two potential host countries" that could be counted upon as a result of personal contacts. Meanwhile, following the official creation of CUSO in June 1961, it was to this same region that Lewis Perinbam travelled on his fact-finding survey as CUSO's acting executive secretary. Prior consultation with various Canadian agencies, including the External Aid Office (EAO), had made it clear that CUSO's initial focus should

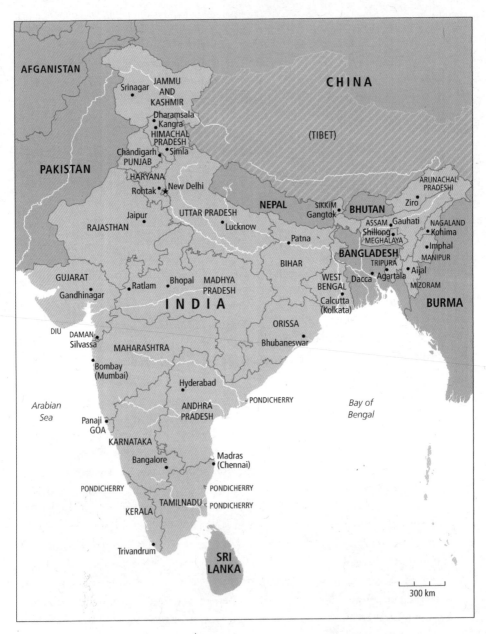

India, ca. 1976

be those Asian countries "with which Canada was associated in the Common-wealth and in the Colombo Plan."[4]

In their respective research trips, both Spicer and Perinbam had spent more time in India than in any other Asian country. It was a reflection of how large that nation loomed in terms of Canada's foreign aid priorities at this period. In the late 1950s and early 1960s, expenditures in India on Canadian capital projects in health, welfare, and education dwarfed similar expenditures else-where in Asia, or in Africa or the Caribbean. They included the Canada-India Reactor, said to be the largest aid project of its kind in the world.[5] In addition to being (along with Pakistan) the first non-white British colony to obtain in-dependence, India was perceived simultaneously as an immense, and immensely needy, country, a Commonwealth "family concern," and a Third-World nation of great importance to Cold War politics. Internationally, India loomed especially large as the leader among new Asian and African nations following the Bandung (Indonesia) Conference in 1955, where Prime Minister Nehru urged a policy of non-alignment with the power blocs of the first and second worlds.[6] For the US, India was a crucial site for directing aid and applying modernization theory, both for humanitarian reasons and in order to undermine the appeal of Com-munism. For the same reasons it would also be one of the "naturals" when it came to deciding where to dispatch Peace Corps volunteers.[7]

Nehru's acceptance of US aid and the aid that flowed from his pragmatic decision to accept British Commonwealth membership was an acknowledg-ment of the reality that substantial outside assistance would be necessary to address India's subsistence and development challenges. The 1961 census showed that India's population had grown in a decade from 361.1 million to 439.2 million people, and while agricultural and industrial output had increased in that period, India could not meet its food needs without accepting outside assistance, par-ticularly wheat from the US, Canada, and Australia. As for literacy rates, they were still only 24 percent overall, and much lower in rural areas, where more than 80 percent of Indians still lived. Still, as Judith Brown observes, Nehru was uneasy about "the distorting cultural influences which went with aid."[8] Such concerns certainly did not end with his death in 1964. Nor were they the pre-serve of national leaders. Quite the contrary: foreign cultural influences were more likely to be a cause of concern for state and local leaders than for the pragmatic and cosmopolitan Nehru.

The tensions resulting from India's unease with dependency had effects that went well beyond its international and bilateral relations with major donor countries. Inevitably, they also affected the experiences of the thousands of young volunteers arriving in 1960s India through such organizations as the Peace Corps, Voluntary Service Overseas (VSO), and CUSO. The volunteers came, initially, equipped with more goodwill than thorough preparation, believing that they were needed and wanting, in the classic volunteer phrase, "to make a difference." But among the many paradoxes that would soon confront them was that of an underdeveloped country with a sizable educated and wealthy class, especially by comparison with places like Papua New Guinea and many countries in Africa. In what sense, then, were they needed? Even if there were many parts of India where the needs were great – especially in the hundreds of thousands of villages, where illiteracy and abysmal health care were norms and where too few of its urban elites felt a call to serve – did the young Westerners have the personal and professional qualifications to adapt and be useful? And what if their initial assignment fell through or was not what they had anticipated? Could they perhaps make a contribution in a different location? Together with their international fellow travellers, the Canadian volunteers had to confront such questions soon after their arrival in India.

The Start-Up Years: Idealistic Aims and Problematic Placements

Two cohorts of volunteers served one-year assignments as COVs before surrendering their separate identity and formally coming under the umbrella of CUSO's organizational structure.[9] How did an organization established and run by young Canadians with no experience of living in a developing country begin the process of "serving and learning" in such a setting? The arrangements described in Spicer's "Scheme" had sounded well advanced and reassuring. But as it turned out, placements in India were still far from having been secured when Spicer returned from his research trip in 1960.[10] That autumn, therefore, he had sought assistance from Donald K. Faris, whose *To Plow with Hope* had been the original source of his inspiration for starting what became COV. Following the end of the Second World War, Faris had at various times worked for UN agencies in China, Korea, and Thailand. When Spicer's letter reached him, he was newly arrived in India to implement UNICEF's Applied Nutrition Programme (ANP).[11] Spicer introduced himself to Faris as "the most fanatical" of "several hundred fervent disciples" at universities across Canada, told him that *To Plow with Hope* would be assigned reading for all COV volunteers, and that he had urged the federal government to buy copies for all of its overseas technical experts. He also invited Faris to be the honorary patron for his volunteer scheme. The main object of Spicer's letter, however, was to ask for Faris's help in contacting Shri Dharampal, the general secretary of AVARD (Association of Voluntary Agencies for Rural Development), whom Spicer had briefly met while in India, in order to obtain his assurance that AVARD would be willing to place the Canadian volunteers whom he proposed to send.[12] Faris replied enthusiastically to Spicer's letter and acted promptly to consolidate this important early placement linkage for COV/CUSO. Although he did canvass other agencies about jobs in the months leading up to the arrival of the first COVs, AVARD would in fact handle all placements for that first year.[13]

A New Delhi–based NGO established in the late 1950s, AVARD was a national consortium of major voluntary agencies designed to serve as a "'common platform and clearing house' for voluntarism."[14] It was a good fit with an important if often overlooked aspect of development planning in independent India. As Benjamin Zachariah has observed, Prime Minister Nehru's development strategies are associated most strongly in historical memory with his national Planning Commission and with a focus on heavy industry and technological change. Yet Nehru's government also acknowledged a need for "decentralized initiatives and rural welfare" in India's development. Embodied from 1952 in Community Development schemes, the initiatives "incorporated Gandhi as a crucial legitimating icon" and included such goals as rural cooperatives, village industries, and new versions of colonial-era "village uplift" schemes.[15] Although it was an NGO rather than an arm of the national Planning Commission, AVARD sought to serve such goals. Many of its links, and thus job opportunities, were with village ashrams inspired by Gandhian economic thought and devoted to community development.[16] But there were also opportunities through AVARD for more specialized placements beyond the village level, such as in rural training institutes or in other development initiatives undertaken by *zilla parishads,* the elected district-level bodies that were becoming more common in India.[17] As will be seen below, concerns about some of the placements found for COV through AVARD would emerge within months. But Dharampal himself, a committed believer in Gandhian social and economic ideas for village-level development, would remain a valued friend and adviser to COV/CUSO over the next several years.

Meanwhile, Donald Faris's ideas about what young Western volunteers could contribute to the developing world would be the single most important early philosophical influence on COV/CUSO in India. Those ideas, as set out in *To Plow with Hope* and in his correspondence with the volunteers and their supporters, in many ways dovetailed with Dharampal's approach. *To Plow with Hope*, as its title indicated, was concerned with rural development, but it was not primarily a how-to book. Although Faris came from a farm background and had taken courses in agriculture during mission furloughs, his professional background was in ministry. Still, as a missionary in northern China in the interwar era, he had increasingly devoted his energies to the subsistence challenges facing peasants. *To Plow with Hope* came out of a period when he was between UN assignments. He made only modest claims for the book, calling it a kind of primer. Yet the information it provided about official and voluntary agencies assisting newly decolonizing countries, the mix of realism and optimism about possibilities for modest improvements in peasant life, and perhaps especially the humane spirit in which it was written seemed to fit the mood of the times. Many who were older and more worldly wise than Spicer and his band of would-be volunteers, including CUSO's Lewis Perinbam, spoke of the book as inspirational.[18] It was favourably reviewed in North America and England, where Victor Gollancz sought the rights from its New York publisher and obtained a blurb from Sir Julian Huxley, the first director general of UNESCO.[19] It was also well received in India, where an adviser in the national Ministry of Community Development wrote to Faris to commend its "deep sympathy and understanding." While one former missionary colleague seemed disappointed that Faris had not been more explicit about missionaries' pioneering roles in development-type work, the downplaying of that connection probably helped make the book more acceptable to contemporary audiences, especially young enthusiasts like Spicer and those in the Netherlands who planned to use it in preparing youthful Dutch volunteers for community development work.[20]

The section near the end of *To Plow with Hope* that specifically addressed young Westerners took up only two of the book's more than two hundred pages, but its call for "junior experts" who could "after an intensive period of orientation ... go into any country where they were invited ... to work with indigenous leaders in the world's needy villages" obviously struck a chord. "If, in addition to technical skills, these junior experts were equipped with humility and courage, with sincerity and wisdom, they would be able to transmit not only physical satisfactions to the needy but also lasting values such as friendship, goodwill and understanding."[21] Viewed from the distance of half a century, the term *junior experts* is jarring. It was also an inappropriate term for conveying

Faris's intent. Faris was seeking to differentiate the youth he was addressing from senior technical specialists in governmental and UN agencies ("balding experts") rather than to narrow his call only to those young Westerners with specific types of technical expertise. Indeed, in his correspondence with Spicer and others about COV and CUSO, Faris made clear his conviction that the personal contacts established by volunteers with the individuals and communities where they served – what he called the human element in relationships – and the spirit of internationalism such relationships could foster was more important than any skill or service the young Canadians could provide. (It is worth noting that a similar emphasis was present in Sargent Shriver's approach to the early Peace Corps, albeit more tinged by pragmatic motives of state.)[22] Faris also believed that a small, informal organization like COV rather than a bureaucratic and narrowly job-focused organization would be more effective in cultivating such relationships. Early letters by Spicer and Fred Stinson as well as by many of the volunteers themselves reveal how much they were attracted by this ambassadorial vision for COV/CUSO. Stinson, for instance, writing to Dharampal at the end of 1961 to thank him for his patience with their rookie volunteer operation, commented: "Of one thing I am certain – on returning to Canada the volunteers now in India will be able to do a great deal to promote good relations and friendship between your country and mine."[23]

This was all very well as an ideal. But especially when a volunteer's placement was with a small agency in a village ashram doing community development (a notoriously vague concept at the best of times), where perhaps only the supervisor and one or two others spoke English and where food, housing, and sanitary arrangements were of the most basic type, how was the volunteer to cope on a daily basis, much less communicate with unschooled villagers in any meaningful way, whether to foster good relations or undertake a specific task? Most volunteers seem to have adapted willingly to the physical hardships, but the lack of structure in such placements was initially frustrating even for volunteers who later fared well. (One of Gandhi's most ardent Western devotees, Mira Behn, had gone through something similar decades earlier – she later recalled it as a period of "inner misery and outer aimlessness" – when she was without productive work at his ashram at Sevagram.)[24] For some of the young Canadians, it was simply too much. One promising volunteer, an engineer assigned to work in Sevagram, in fact had a breakdown that required his being returned to Canada.[25] Another, just nineteen years old, mercurial and unwell, left his post without explanation to the considerable consternation of his project supervisor. "It is good to develop Indo-Canadian relationship," the young man's supervisor wrote to Faris, "but it is necessary for them [volunteers] to select lines of work which will help the villagers of India." Doctors, nurses, and even trained high school teachers, he suggested, could function effectively in many Indian settings, but future volunteers coming into a rural-development project such as the one he supervised and expecting to work with peasants should be able to speak or understand Hindi and be physically and mentally adaptable.[26]

Others, including Dharampal and the volunteers themselves, were already conscious of problems with existing arrangements for recruiting, preparing, and placing volunteers. A February 1962 conference at Juhu Beach, Bombay, involving Dharampal, Faris, and all of the volunteers provided the setting for lengthy discussions of philosophy and strategy. Was the volunteers' purpose in India to accomplish a particular technical task, or to promote mutual international understanding, or both? Did they feel sufficiently useful in their assignment to recommend it for another volunteer? Were they filling a position that could and should be filled by an Indian? Should the relationship with AVARD continue, or should they seek to work with other agencies, including government agencies? For his part, Dharampal was already finding the task of coordinating all of the Canadian volunteers' activities and placements burdensome and thus recommended that COV provide its own person for this task. The volunteers turned to Dale Posgate, who, while feeling redundant at Sevagram, was by no means defeated by India. Until he left for home near the end of 1962, Posgate acted informally as coordinator for the group, investigating possible placements for the forthcoming second cohort of volunteers and at the same time providing an evaluation of what his own cohort was achieving. Meanwhile, it was also at this mid-year conference (such gatherings became annual events) that the volunteers suggested that Bill McWhinney return to Canada from his post in Ceylon to handle administration and fundraising for COV on a full-time basis.[27]

From COV to CUSO: Continuity *and* Change

In Toronto with COV for the next several months and then, from September 1962, in Ottawa as CUSO's first full-time executive secretary, McWhinney continued to correspond with Dharampal and Faris and his fellow volunteers in India about future directions for their work. The correspondence made it clear that shifts were taking place. Yet they were matters of emphasis rather than a wholesale break with the philosophy and practices of the first year. Posgate's views as peer-designated coordinator are illustrative, simultaneously hard-headed *and* idealistic about what COV had done and could do. Writing in July 1962 to McWhinney, Posgate maintained that only one of their number, a nurse caring for infants in a Bengali village, had made a difference "in concrete terms," and given India's population problem, even that was a questionable accomplishment. And yet Posgate was certainly not suggesting that COV should quit India. For the most part, he believed, the volunteers were making good contributions in terms of personal relationships and in their openness and adaptability in their particular settings. He cited the example of DH, who had recently written articles for the Toronto *Globe* about his experience in India (teaching English and economics in an ashram in Madras state). The articles themselves, Posgate declared, "are the type of result we should recognize as valuable. It wouldn't have made a damn bit of difference, in terms of development, improvement, betterment, etc etc if ... [DH] had never left Oakville. But his personal accomplishments among the people he worked with and with the villagers that he met is considerable, and one which I think we should be proud of and recognize as a real accomplishment. To ask for more is unrealistic." Like Faris in India and Stinson in Toronto and like virtually all his fellow volunteers, Posgate believed strongly in the value of COV as a learning experience and as a vehicle for promoting mutual knowledge and understanding among individual Indians and Canadians. Indeed, his own six months at Sevagram had epitomized that kind of approach. When his job there, at an institute for training government rural-development employees, had turned out to be wholly undefined, he turned his hand to a variety of other things, including helping to organize a work camp at which volunteers worked with Indians to build a water tower.[28]

In his long and appreciative reply to Posgate, McWhinney made clear the extent to which he shared his views. "In my speeches and discussions here, I have tried to play down any tendencies people may have of feeling that we are going to make a fantastic technical contribution. Rather I have stressed the fact that we are going abroad to serve in very much secondary posts and with a sense of humility." This approach, he believed, and "living as the people ... and working with them and under their guidance" distinguished the COVs from "the Colombo Plan expert" and even from "our American cousins" in the Peace Corps. And yet, McWhinney maintained, the goal of promoting mutual understanding would be better served if the volunteers were doing "a tangible job." Moreover, "the initiative on placement should come from the host authorities

... They would have to feel that we could be useful to them and theirs would be the responsibility for any charges of taking jobs away from indigenous personnel."[29]

The question of who should take the initiative on finding placements would remain a challenge for CUSO. Other assignments found through AVARD in addition to those already mentioned had proven to be a poor fit. Several women volunteers, feeling under used or ill placed in their posts, had opted after several months to travel and seek out worthwhile work elsewhere in India.[30] Following the volunteers' February gathering, some of them had been anxious to supplement Posgate's efforts by keeping an eye out for worthwhile placements for the next cohort. Marilyn Cook, who was part of that next cohort and whose own first placement quickly proved unproductive, became a job-scouting activist. In response to cautions from McWhinney about the volunteer-as-searcher approach, Cook sensibly pointed out that potential employers could not know, unless they were told, that young Canadians were available and eager to serve.[31] By the end of 1962, when COV had surrendered its separate existence and merged into CUSO, something of a compromise approach was being worked out: the volunteers were not to go "ferreting out jobs" to the neglect of their own assignments, but if, through their own placements, they learned of agencies with a potential interest in a volunteer, they were to put such agencies in touch with CUSO/Ottawa. They were also to be supplied with pamphlets from CUSO for use with interested agencies.

A form letter from Ozzie Schmidt at the University of Toronto to the India volunteers explained these and other aspects of the new regime and added, "CUSO has pretty rigid specifications about the usefulness of a volunteer, about the necessity for down-to-earth, concrete work ... upon *request*."[32] Schmidt himself was in general sympathy with the stronger emphasis on usefulness. So also was John R. Wood, the *de facto* leader of the second cohort of volunteers to arrive in India and a nephew of John Holmes. All the volunteers should come prepared to do a "tangible" job, Wood wrote. But they should also want to make an "intangible" contribution by promoting "international understanding." It is "a wornout phrase, I know," he acknowledged, "but if organizations like COV do not help promote mutual appreciation between West and East, then they might as well pack up and go home. I think in the light of world tension and conflict of ideology there should be a desire by liberally-minded university graduates to help, even if in an infinitesimal way, to reduce the danger of these pressures."[33]

A Passage to India

So ... concrete jobs meeting real needs or goodwill assignments? The ambivalence and the two approaches would continue to exist to some extent throughout CUSO's time in India. But even as the jobs emphasis became stronger within CUSO as an organization, there was no predicting or controlling what a particular assignment would yield, especially if placements continued to be made in remote village ashrams, as they sometimes were even in the mid-1960s. Nor could CUSO predict how its volunteers would respond in such settings: villages were accessible only by bullock cart or on foot; mud-hut housing had no amenities; prayers, meals, and ablutions were communal rituals; personal privacy was non-existent. One volunteer, for whom such a placement in the state of Orissa initially appeared (to himself and others) to be wholly unsuitable, found a strong sense of belonging through participation in daily rituals, and a degree of usefulness as he participated in community tasks over and above his teaching assignment.[34] Another, a nurse in a Gujarat ashram serving tribal people who still wore loin cloths and carried bows and arrows, found her post enormously challenging but ultimately worthwhile. Through her medical work, she felt that she had done "at least a little bit of good for a few individuals" even though, overall, there would be "no lasting impact beyond that of reinforcing the importance of the work my fellow ashramites were doing." She had respected the work of the ashram, which "had a reputation for honesty," and its founder and supervisor, and, like her teaching colleague in the Orissa ashram, she still remained in contact with some of her associates decades later. [35] Yet her successor at this ashram, also a nurse, regarded the place as essentially a sham. She and her husband, an agricultural volunteer, were there, they believed, only "as foreign status symbols – proof to skeptical business donors that the institution was worth sponsoring." As for the supervisor, he was "a dominating employer with a smooth tongue and confident charm [that] can go a long way in deception." After pondering how best to respond to their situation, this task-oriented couple left for what proved to be a more satisfying and productive assignment.[36]

They were by no means the only volunteers to believe that they were on show as Westerners to lend an indigenous organization greater credibility for fundraising purposes. But as (or if) volunteers came to believe in "their" organization's long-term goals and legitimacy, they did not necessarily see their deployment for this purpose as corrupt or demeaning, particularly if they could also get on with a "real" job.[37] Indeed, rather than feeling exploited or on show, volunteers could experience a sense of pride in symbolically representing their country in an Indian institution, particularly during an event of national significance. This was the case for Don Millar, who was teaching English in a boys' college in Uttar Pradesh in January 1966 when Nehru's successor, Lal Bahadur Shastri, died suddenly while in office. Asked by the principal to address the student body after his Indian colleagues had spoken, Millar used the occasion of the prime minister's death to express a sense of shared international sorrow and solidarity. Then, with one of his colleagues, he crowded into a third-class train carriage and travelled to Delhi to join the thousands of other Indians witnessing the funeral procession and cremation. For Millar, and presumably for his Indian students and co-workers, sharing this intense national experience was both moving and memorable.[38]

The Importance of Friends on the Ground

The Faris/Dharampal philosophy remained influential even after COV had officially become CUSO. Likewise, during the next few years, the volunteers continued to rely on the practical assistance and advice of Faris and Dharampal and a small number of other Western and Indian advisers as they struggled to learn by trial and error how to function in India. Though AVARD, institutionally, was not used as a source of placements after COV's first year, Dharampal himself, as noted earlier, remained a friend and adviser to the volunteers. He placed even less priority than did Faris on the volunteers' practical skills and technical usefulness and instead emphasized the larger goal of promoting international goodwill. He realized that local organizations that accepted volunteers often did so not because they needed them for a particular task but "partly because of the novelty of the idea of a foreign person coming and living with them." Given that fact, the volunteers, he thought, should perhaps "take their own talents a little less seriously," and "the[ir] outlook has to be a little different." In making these remarks, Dharampal was not belittling the young Canadians. Indeed, he obviously admired them, not least for their ability to handle rugged living conditions. And though he did not want to remain responsible for orchestrating their placements, he was prepared to provide a new Canadian coordinator with modest office space at AVARD, as he had done for Posgate, along with ongoing advice and information about contacts.[39] Thus when Stephen Woollcombe, who had taught near Ahmedabad in the first COV cohort, came to Delhi to serve as volunteer coordinator from April to

November of 1963, he maintained CUSO's ties with Dharampal, as did Bill McWhinney back in Ottawa.[40]

Meanwhile, the role of Don Faris and his wife, Marion, extended to the familial. The couple, already in their sixties when Don took up his UNICEF appointment in India, were said to have rented a large residence in New Delhi specifically so that the volunteers would have a Canadian "home away from home."[41] As volunteer coordinators, both Posgate and Woollcombe spent long periods of time there. Marion Faris's correspondence as well as her later account of this period in her husband's career contains affectionate references to these and other volunteers who stayed at their home. They came at Christmas and on other occasions and particularly when they were ill. Hepatitis, typhoid, amoebic dysentery, and other illnesses were a serious problem for the early India volunteers, whose advance preparations in Canada did not yet include rigorous preventive health measures and whose mode of living in India made them vulnerable to infections.[42] One volunteer, whose situation epitomized some of the most difficult living conditions, lost more than thirty pounds during his teaching year there, a newspaper back home reported. As coordinator, Woollcombe maintained that it was actually a disservice to CUSO if volunteers put themselves at risk by not taking proper precautions ("being careless of their health does not make them more 'volunteer-ish' or 'mud-hutish'"). Yet once placements had been made in settings that involved such features as communal meals and housing in a rat-infested-thatched-roof hut with little or no readily available medical aid, a physically challenging existence was a fact of life rather than a lifestyle.[43] Moreover, when the volunteers travelled within India, opting by necessity and choice for inexpensive, non-Western-style accommodation, they were also vulnerable to illnesses. The Farises arranged for the hospitalization of some volunteers who became dangerously ill. More usually, as well as providing nourishing meals, Marion Faris, a public health nurse by training, dosed her patients/volunteers with vitamins and other remedies of her own devising to restore them to health, sometimes accommodating them for six weeks or more.[44] Not surprisingly, volunteers' letters written at this time and even years later contain moving tributes to *Mamaji* and *Papaji*, and, back in Canada, the Farises received further thanks from grateful parents.[45]

Arthur Kroeger, the Oxford-educated second secretary at the Canadian High Commission, provided backup space for male volunteers who were ill or in need of temporary accommodation in New Delhi. More typically, Kroeger's

Marion and Don Faris, *Mamaji* and *Papaji* to the early volunteers in India, ca. 1959.
Courtesy of the Faris family.

role was that of a kind of business agent for the volunteers, seeing to financial arrangements, communications, customs, and other practical matters at a time when COV/CUSO still lacked the money, the facilities, and the expertise to take care of such matters on its own. It was Kroeger and Faris who handled such sensitive matters as repatriating the young volunteer whose breakdown required his return to Canada in the first year.[46] Because he was so directly involved with volunteers' activities, Kroeger often received copies of CUSO correspondence, and because he was only about a decade older than the volunteers, his relationship with them was that of a close friend as well as a source of diplomatic and practical support until he returned to Canada late in 1963.[47] Even then, back in Ottawa, where he would eventually rise through the civil service to become "the dean of deputy ministers," Kroeger continued to assist CUSO by serving on the National Selection Committee, and Ottawa-based RVs continued to count him as a friend.[48]

The volunteers' relationship with Chester Ronning, the head of the Canadian High Commission, was more formal. Yet Ronning arguably did the India volunteers, and CUSO overall, a vitally important service when, in 1964, he wrote

A Passage to India

to the under-secretary of state for external affairs to express his admiration for the volunteers' self-reliance, dedication, and ability and to commend them as a credit to their organization and to Canada. Interestingly, while Ronning recommended that the federal government provide CUSO with some financial assistance, he did not want to see it become a substantially larger and richer organization like the Peace Corps, or narrowly specialized, like federally appointed technical experts. What CUSO was doing, he conceded, was only "a drop in the bucket." Still, a CUSO that remained small and independent and that continued to work at a grassroots level could make a positive impression while yielding great benefits to the volunteers themselves. An accompanying memo, probably written by Kroeger, affirmed and elaborated on Ronning's message on the basis of more intimate knowledge: the volunteers had responded creatively to the challenges they had met, including the early inappropriate placements; their willingness to endure austere living, isolation, third-class travel, and other hardships had enabled them to get closer to "the people."[49]

Outside of diplomatic circles, another Canadian, Dr. W.D. (David) Hopper, a gifted New Delhi–based agricultural economist with the Ford Foundation, also became a valuable friend to CUSO. By the time the volunteers came to know Hopper, he and his wife had a large house with a staff of servants. During David's student-researcher phase, however, the Hoppers had lived in an Indian village and were thus in a position to understand and appreciate the experiences of volunteers serving in village placements. Like Faris and Kroeger, Dr. Hopper helped volunteers with personal and practical advice, placements, and orientation. Later, as the volunteers prepared to move on, Hopper supplied several with references for graduate studies.[50] The Hopper connection would also pay dividends for the volunteers back in Canada years later when Hopper became the first head of the International Development Research Centre (IDRC).

There were also non-Canadian friends and associates on the ground who helped the volunteers get their bearings. The first three cohorts of volunteers had had some type of orientation in London, England, as well as in Canada by the time they arrived in India. But for many, the experience of being together in New Delhi for an in-country orientation before they went their separate ways was uniquely valuable as a cultural experience as well as for classroom sessions. The Peace Corps, arriving in India at the end of 1961, proved to be generous kin. Despite a tendency by some Canadian volunteers to make disparaging remarks about the Corps' greater affluence and their tendency to cluster, there was a recognition that CUSO and the Peace Corps had a great deal in common

Newly arrived volunteer Judy Ransom meets the president of India, Sarvepalli Radhakrishnan, during orientation, New Delhi, September 1964. Courtesy of Judy Ransom.

and that the latter was often generous about sharing resources, whether for language training at orientations or at gatherings such as one organized by the Peace Corps in Kashmir in 1962 to discuss learning experiences.[51] Nevertheless, it was early contacts with helpful Indian individuals, organizations, and leaders that mattered most as the volunteers sought to adjust and fit in. These went beyond Dharampal and AVARD. Even use of the Juhu Beach guesthouse where the COVs met for their first conference had been provided by a wealthy Indian sympathizer, Woollcombe recalled. Another RV remembered with gratitude orientation lectures from "a wonderful old Indian gentleman about Indian manners and culture" as well as being billeted at the Ladakh Buddha Vihara – "both a culture shock and a great orientation experience."[52] Orientation assistance also came from such agencies as the Institute of Economic Growth. In the meantime, as coordinator, Woollcombe established a variety of informal but supportive Indian contacts as well as more formal links with the national Planning Commission. The 1962 and 1963 cohorts had opportunities to meet with Nehru and with India's philosopher-president, Sarvepalli Radhakrishnan. The fact that Prime Minister Nehru gave the Canadians about a half hour of his time for the 1963 meeting was a source of great satisfaction, though in all likelihood the chief practical outcome of these meetings was wonderful publicity photos for use back in Canada. As president, Radhakrishnan probably had more time to spare for the volunteers, who, in 1962, in response to his request for a Canadian song, gave an Anglo rendition of "Alouette!"[53]

Late in 1963, John R. Wood, who succeeded Woollcombe as volunteer coordinator, rented as office and living space two rooms in a wholly Indian bazaar area in New Delhi. It felt somewhat like the beginning of a new era, Wood wrote to McWhinney, and "marks a new step of CUSO maturity."[54] The move *did* make CUSO somewhat less dependent on Don and Marion Faris and on the Canadian High Commission. Kroeger's return to Canada and the departure of the Farises, first for a brief home leave in 1964 and then permanently in 1966, necessitated such steps toward increasing self-reliance. Yet until federal funding started to have an impact, CUSO/India remained very much a shoestring operation. Neither Wood nor his successor was allowed to budget for a phone, for instance. Office filing cabinets were made from whisky boxes "donated from fellows down at the High Commission," and there was certainly no such thing as a CUSO automobile. In these circumstances, early friends like Kroeger and the Farises were neither forgotten nor taken for granted.[55] Even beyond the shoestring era, supportive relationships with Roland Michener, Geoffrey Pearson, James George, and others in the Canadian High Commission remained an important element in the CUSO/India experience.

Gender Matters

Questions about how to integrate the needs of women into development initiatives and how to facilitate women's leadership within development organizations emerged as substantive and ongoing issues in organizations like CUSO only from the mid-1970s. Yet from CUSO's first year in India, what would later come to be called gender issues arose, reflecting both the composition of CUSO's volunteer population and the volunteers' attempts to understand and respond to India's complex cultural practices regarding appropriate roles and behaviours for men and women. Especially because of the volunteers' desire to live as much as possible as part of "their" Indian communities rather than apart in expatriate enclaves, CUSO's young men and women could not afford to live their lives as if local values and social taboos need not be taken into account; in these circumstances, as they quickly discovered, the absence of privacy was a real and often frustrating fact of life. Yet the challenges went beyond a simple loss of personal privacy, and they were especially significant for female volunteers. The young women experienced, on the one hand, an expansive sense of possibilities and broadened horizons through their roles as volunteers and, on the other, a vivid consciousness of local cultural constraints. The women's warm camaraderie with their male counterparts and their desire to make good in their jobs seem generally to have outweighed their frustrations with indigenous understandings of appropriate gender behaviours and with their organization's concern that they not give offence. Still, the existence in India of more rigid codes of gendered conduct than those with which they had been raised could not be gainsaid.[56]

As Chapter 1 notes, relative to their numbers in university-student populations in the 1960s, women were over-represented in the ranks of CUSO volunteers, and in some years, female volunteers equalled or exceeded their male counterparts in absolute numbers.[57] As noted, too, the high ratio of women volunteers in India became a matter of concern for Bill McWhinney in his first year as CUSO's executive secretary.[58] While he did not elaborate on his reasons for regarding this phenomenon as a problem, he might have been concerned about finding suitable placements for female volunteers, their lesser experience in leadership roles, or their perceived inability to adapt themselves to the patriarchal constraints of Indian society. The latter issue had been drawn to his attention as a problem by Woollcombe, who as volunteer coordinator had prepared a paper on the subject in the spring of 1963 in anticipation of orientation for the incoming cohort of new volunteers. Woollcombe was not suggesting that the young Canadian women were being flirtatious or sexually aggressive, but rather that "such seemingly insignificant matters as smoking, loud spokenness, indiscreet dress, and where and how she takes an outing in the town" could lead to gossip and misunderstandings, and thereby undermine CUSO's credibility and respectability. Also, what came across in India as female "boldness" could give offence to employers.[59] Back in Canada, both McWhinney in Ottawa and Ozzie Schmidt at the University of Toronto undertook to interpret Woollcombe's concerns to the women who were about to become part of the third cohort of India volunteers. Unfortunately, in this context and in the young men's earnest desire to do well by their organization, some of the very qualities that could signal female volunteers' aptitude for leadership roles – "straight forwardness, zeal, and application to work" – were perceived and presented as potential problems.[60] Moreover, especially in the first year or so, in their concern to win acceptance in India, some of the volunteers perhaps rushed to judgment and underestimated adventurous female colleagues' ability to evaluate the parameters of what was acceptable female behaviour in a particular setting and to respond accordingly.[61] One such woman, whose departure from her first placement evoked mild criticism from some volunteers and reportedly offended Dharampal, in fact proved so acceptable in a new placement, where she taught and assisted in a maternity centre, that her employer requested a replacement for her when her year was up.[62]

And yet there were evidently some settings in which a female volunteer's reputation and usefulness could be compromised if she did not conform to local standards. JF, a physiotherapist whose placement was in a rural health institute south of Bombay, had anticipated that her fiancé, a doctor, would be able to come out from Canada to live and work for part of the year in the same community. The proposed arrangement did not involve cohabitation, but there was apprehension that even for the engaged couple to appear together in the community could lead to gossip. Following correspondence with CUSO/Ottawa and consultation with Kroeger, the Farises, and others, and after the fiancé's arrival, it was decided that the couple should marry before leaving New Delhi to return to JF's work site. Thus were the most important personal plans in their young lives altered by CUSO's reading of a particular cultural context and by JF herself in coming to accept that reading.[63]

Perhaps no other personal life-change in the service of CUSO was as dramatic as this one. Furthermore, constraining social pressures on volunteers' conduct seem to have varied a good deal in different institutional settings and between rural and urban areas. BH, an experienced nurse-educator who served in two successive senior positions in a large and venerable Methodist mission hospital, was cautioned about dating a pilot at the nearby air base: "I ... was called into the [Indian male] Medical Superintendent's office and informed this was not proper behaviour for a nice young woman. That was that!!!" BH's personal conduct otherwise conformed fully to the mission's standards. But even in the late 1960s the matter of dating, especially across the "race" divide, was still a taboo for those who ran this historic institution.[64] Another woman, volunteering earlier in the decade, quickly understood that most Indian families did not want their offspring to become romantically involved with Westerners. She herself dated a Western-educated Indian during a brief period in New Delhi, but when he later paid a day visit to the rural school where she taught, her principal and fellow teachers were shocked.[65] Certainly, big cities and secular institutions with modernizing values provided more space for fraternal or romantic relationships within or across the Western/non-Western divide, but because most placements were not in such settings, volunteers realized that they could not simply behave as if they were still back home in Canada.

Indian families typically kept their daughters under their supervision or in the care of surrogate institutions until they entered arranged marriages. Understandably, then, for young Western women to be arriving unsupervised in rural settings thousands of miles away from their families was at least problematic. Those in charge of such placements seem typically to have provided the kind of living and working arrangements that kept the newcomers from gossip or harm. Clearly, however, such arrangements could be excessively restrictive. Nor were restrictions and double standards always directly related to matters of sexuality. KH, whose first placement was in a new, Bata-sponsored dispensary operated by a local district council, had a boss who was determined to remain in control. As for her monthly pay, when it was not forthcoming, she was told by the council head that she should simply ask for what she needed, as a "sister" would do, rather than expect regular payments. KH's situation was probably complicated by the fact that she was of South Asian parentage. Decades later when she reflected on this placement, she concluded that the situation was really no one's fault and that posting a volunteer in the newly established dispensary had probably just been premature. But at the time, her difficulties were viewed by CUSO as ones from which she should be rescued. Accordingly, Kroeger and one of the male volunteers brought her back to Delhi, where, after a period of frustrating idleness, she moved on to a more satisfactory placement and one where she could make at least some use of her native Punjabi.[66]

What about possibilities for female volunteers to play leadership roles within CUSO/India? Here again, contingent circumstances rather than fixed assumptions seem to have determined outcomes. Soon after her arrival in 1962, Marilyn Cook stood out for her initiatives in searching out placements and for her general sense of joie de vivre in her new Indian environment. However, it seems not to have occurred to her male colleagues, or perhaps to Cook herself, that she could have been appointed officially as coordinator[67] even though she functioned unofficially in that role for several months before April 1963, when Steve Woollcombe took over, and even though she continued to work with him for some time thereafter and was generally acknowledged to have done an outstanding job.[68] Among a core group of early COV/CUSO leaders there was a robust male camaraderie as well as a very strong sense of responsibility for their organization's well-being. As some of their correspondence shows, such attitudes and concerns could sometimes slip over into assumptions that would later be viewed as sexist and that led them to look first to new male volunteers for future leaders.[69]

And yet in 1964, Judy Ransom from the 1963 cohort succeeded to the co-ordinator role, thereby becoming for a brief period the only full-time coordinator in any country where CUSO had work.[70] Ransom's appointment did not signal an early wave of feminist influence from Canada or a waning of concerns about appropriate female volunteer behaviour in India. Rather, it seems to have re-flected a realistic appraisal by the volunteers themselves of who among them, male or female, could effectively take on the coordinator's role while causing minimal disruption by leaving a placement prematurely.[71] Ransom had spent the first part of her year in an isolated posting in southern India to which CUSO had been directed by the Unitarian Service Committee's Lotta Hitschmanova. A rural health and community development project established and run by an Englishwoman, an ex-Communist and ardent Gandhian, the project would eventually grow into a multi-faceted hub of social services. But in 1963 it was not a good fit for Ransom's honours degree in modern languages, and it was far from providing the collegial relationships with Indian teachers and teen-aged pupils that she had envisioned in anticipating a teaching appointment. Moreover, even before leaving Canada, Ransom had been recognized for her leadership potential. She was thus open to a job change and, in the prevailing circumstances, an obvious candidate for the coordinator role.[72]

Ransom was coordinator until April 1965. The position brought several challenges. The location of the apartment-cum-office that John Wood had occupied was deemed unsuitable for a single Western woman. She therefore made do with makeshift arrangements until she obtained her own place in the home of a Sikh family. (In one such arrangement, she had found herself in the ironic position of living in the home of the Hoppers – who were on leave – surrounded by seven servants but meanwhile having only enough money for basic food supplies.) Like Wood, she had no phone, and though she owned a typewriter, she could not type. Communications with Ottawa and the volunteers were thus a time-consuming process. Travel to find and assess placements was extensive and still by third class. CUSO/Ottawa was eager to have her identify good solid jobs for some twenty-five incoming volunteers, by now all on two-year assignments. Yet the majority of the new volunteers were the so-called BAGs – BA generalists – the type of volunteers perceived as most likely to take positions that could otherwise go to educated Indians. An additional complicating factor was that most volunteers completing their terms were not recommending that their own position be refilled.[73]

The two coordinators who followed Ransom, Bob Pim and Brian Marson, were men appointed by CUSO/Ottawa to take the India program beyond its grassroots approach. Neither one had India experience, and they were viewed skeptically by some volunteers. But from 1968, when teacher Christina Cassels and nurse Carol McPherson were chosen by their fellow volunteers to be co-directors, until 1972, when the India program closed, women would again be country coordinators. Meanwhile, back in Canada, Ransom was asked by McWhinney to join the Ottawa staff, first as associate secretary and, in her second year, as director of Asian programs. Clearly, then, even before the so-called WID era (women in development), there were some instances in which organizational needs, collegial decision making, and individual abilities ultimately trumped preconceived, gendered notions about who could do what in a development NGO.

Placements from the Mid-Point: Responding to Crises and National Priorities

The waning of the original philosophy informing decisions about placements in India, especially after the mid-1960s, contributed to a lessened emphasis on rural postings and a greater emphasis on obtaining volunteers with professional training and experience. The shift reflected a number of factors on the ground and in Ottawa, about which more will be said below. At their annual reunion in 1964, the India volunteers had determined that flexibility should be "the watchword for programming policy ... CUSO should consider all types of assignments, in both urban and rural settings, from large sophisticated universities and mission schools to rural Gandhian ashrams."[74] There had in fact been flexibility about making assignments almost from the beginning: teaching positions in post-secondary institutions, for instance, physiotherapy appointments in urban mission hospitals, and other assignments that could certainly not be construed as grassroots.[75] Moreover, there had been some ashrams that, though they promoted such Gandhian values as pride in Indian identity, a social service ethic, and international understanding, served elite groups. Despite being part of the pioneer cohort, Stephen Woollcombe had found himself appointed to a school serving this kind of constituency. Shreyas, founded by the wealthy daughter of a cotton-mill magnate, provided a high-level academic education, albeit of a distinctly Indian nature. Teaching in such a place was certainly not what Woollcombe had expected to be doing in a country as poor as India, and in his follow-up assessment of his placement, he did not recommend that another volunteer be placed there. Yet that did not mean that he had felt useless or unhappy at Shreyas. In addition to helping his students improve their English, he had initiated such extracurricular activities as a school newspaper and a debating club. Living on-site and increasingly adapting himself to the culture of Shreyas, he had formed lasting bonds with its founder and staff. A year later, his friend John Wood, also finding himself in an ashram where the clientele seemed too privileged to meet his need to feel useful, went beyond assigned classroom tasks during weekends and holiday periods to do manual labour alongside farmers in a nearby village and to help organize a village night school. Without neglecting their formal assignments or actually relocating, other teacher-volunteers in very different settings also initiated extracurricular activities or sought out work camps during holiday periods, especially if they felt under-utilized. Indeed, this was the kind of thing that CUSO, like the Peace Corps, expected any good volunteer to do.[76]

At the other extreme, the CUSO/India experience around mid-decade comprised some assignments where, however serendipitously, volunteers with the right mix of skills and personality found themselves among vulnerable groups and in truly challenging circumstances, employed to the fullest and able to make substantial, even life-determining contributions. Gordon Banta's and Hans-Henning Mündel's agricultural assignments and the involvement of Lois James and Judy Pullen with Tibetan refugees are vivid examples. A twenty-two-year-old from an Alberta farm family, Banta had arrived in Toronto in the summer of 1963 with a certificate in mechanics and a BSc in agriculture for an orientation that prepared him for work in Ceylon.[77] When the Ceylon job fell through, he was given a choice between a teaching assignment at Benares Hindu University or working in a recently founded leprosy colony in a place in Orissa "that no one could find on a map." By the time he arrived at the colony, the doctor who had founded it had died of a heart attack, and the two volunteers who had been at the site were about to flee. He had in fact come into a situation that John Wood as coordinator described as an "organizational mess," involving officials from multiple agencies. "Gord has done an amazing job of getting 'in' with all local officials," Wood wrote, "and he will become, effectually, the guts of the whole development of Hatibari as far as on-the-spot decisions and carrying-out go."[78] Banta himself, recollecting the experience, was low-key and matter-of-fact. There were few others at Hatibari who were not leprosy patients. Banta quickly recognized that since there was no food supply, his primary objective should be to plant a crop and "get the colony as close to self-sufficiency in food as possible." This was a matter of hard and relentless physical work, for which his farm background and a tough summer job had been helpful preparation, and of learning enough Oriya to communicate with patients and officials. Had he known about the leprosy-colony assignment in advance, he recalled, "I might have made a different and wrong choice," but as things turned out, "I ... ended up running the place." Banta extended his contract to help get the next crop planted, and, years later, like many of his fellow India volunteers, returned to the site of his work. Unlike them, however, he found no welcoming voices: "Everyone I knew was dead."

Arriving in India in 1966 for what would be a three-year stay, Mündel began an assignment in the Nilgiri Hills of Madras state (now Tamil Nadu), where he was appointed as farm manager of a newly established settlement colony for some twenty-five families of Paniyas. The Paniyas were Adivasis who had until recently been bonded servants to small landowners in the region. Employed by the Nilgiri Adivasi Welfare Association (NAWA), Mündel was located more than one hundred miles from NAWA headquarters and entirely responsible for the day-to-day affairs of the new colony. In addition to organizing the Paniyas for land clearing and planting fast-maturing food crops, Mündel undertook to get the community's children into the local school, a step that meant he first had to arrange for them to be washed, clothed, and supplied with breakfast, and he himself had to be declared their official guardian before the school would accept them. Although there were plenty of setbacks during his year in this challenging community, he had a strong sense of responsibility for its welfare and an enduring emotional investment, as a recently published book of his letters home shows.[79]

Lois James and Judy Pullen, arriving in India in the same year as Banta, faced conditions in some respects even more harrowing than his but, like Mündel, they would eventually be able to look back on happier long-term outcomes. Twenty-two-year-old Pullen, the daughter of a well-to-do Oakville, Ontario, family, had a University of Toronto degree in physical education, a year of teacher's training, and a summer's experience in the Caribbean with Canadian Voluntary Commonwealth Service when she went to India. Having learned about a month prior to her departure that she was to work with Tibetan refugees, she borrowed all four books on Tibet from the Oakville Public Library and began preparing for what would be a life-altering experience. Nurse Lois James, from Timmins, Ontario, had worked in the Canadian Arctic and travelled in Europe before joining CUSO at age twenty-four. Different as they were in background and personality, the two women had in common the necessary adaptability, initiative, and commitment to see them through the challenges that lay ahead.

CUSO had learned about possibilities for volunteer work among the Tibetan refugee community from several informants. One of them was writer George Woodcock, who with his wife, Ingeborg, established the Tibetan Refugee Aid Society in Vancouver in 1962 following their travels in India and their meeting with the Dalai Lama.[80] The work assigned to Pullen and James was with child refugees in Kangra. It was about two hours by bus from Dharamsala in northern India, where the Dalai Lama had established his Tibetan government-in-exile following his flight from Lhasa in 1959. Arriving in Kangra in late September 1963, they were initially accommodated by Dr. Florence Haslam, a veteran of three decades' service at the Canadian Anglican mission hospital there. Haslam helped care for the sickest of the child refugees and administered funds for the Tibetan Refugee Aid Society and other agencies. Pullen and James moved into the cramped building that served as accommodation and transit school for the several hundred children with whom they worked until the children could be transferred to a permanent facility. While Judy Pullen taught the children, Lois James nursed the many who were undernourished and in poor health. As Pullen became more drawn into Tibetan culture and language study, she was asked to teach monks as well as children. From May 1964, she was involved full-time at the Tibetan teachers' training college at Dharamsala, the only institution of its kind, established under the sponsorship of the Dalai Lama. She first taught English and then was asked by the Tibetan director of education to establish "a *real* teachers' training programme [such] as we have in the West" in order to help prepare monks to offer instruction in Western subjects as well as their own culture. Together with a Tibetan lama who was a leading educator and textbook writer, Pullen travelled through northern India to select monks and a few nuns for the teacher training course. Having served well beyond her initial one-year CUSO contract, she returned to Canada in 1967. A year later, in Oakville, she married a Western-educated Tibetan, T.C. Tethong, a deputy minister of Tibetan affairs for the government-in-exile and for some years an interpreter for the Dalai Lama. Following their marriage, they returned to India, this time to Mysore state in the south, where Tethong was to head up a second settlement for the hundreds of refugees who were now arriving in India.[81]

Lois James's CUSO experience remained bound up with the child refugees.[82] Dr. Tom Dooley had been one of her heroes, and it was from a foundation established in his name that she obtained, early on, some much needed basic medical supplies. Soliciting help from such organizations, dealing with well-meaning but time-consuming and sometimes judgmental "charitable" visitors, and adapting to Spartan and unsanitary living conditions quickly became routine. The high points for her were her first Christmas at Kangra, when donations from Canadians and local Peace Corps volunteers made it possible to provide 260 children with new underwear and special treats, and her personal meeting with the Dalai Lama; the most physically and emotionally draining experience was dealing with the arrival of a new group of desperately ill child refugees. Ranging in age from four to seventeen years, the 140 children, many of them orphans, had been held for months without shelter at the border inside Nepal until the Indian government was pressured into admitting them. James moved to Dharamsala to help care for the new refugees. At the nadir of this episode, she assisted some older Tibetan boys who had been instructed to make a funeral pyre for a child who had died in her arms en route to Dr. Haslam's hospital. Observing post-mortem movement in the child's body, probably caused by still-active worms, one frantic boy pleaded that the child was still alive and tried to stop the cremation. "It was a grizzly affair which seemed to last forever," Lois wrote, "and by the end I wept from both exhaustion and sorrow." Visited next morning by the Tibetan director of education, she was gently told to pull herself together: "If I collapsed there would be no one to care for the children. The overwhelming kindness of the many Tibetans gave me the strength to continue."[83] Lois James did survive the ordeal, but her health, seriously impaired by earlier, variously diagnosed illnesses, remained precarious. The leisurely return journey to Canada that she had planned to share with fellow volunteer Suki Falkner had to be aborted in Bangkok in 1965. More than three decades later, back in northern India, she would meet the man who as a teenager had shared the cremation trauma with her. Now a deputy minister in the Tibetan government-in-exile, he typified the positive changes that had occurred. Although refugees continued to arrive on a monthly basis, the Tibetan community in

Dharamsala had become self-sufficient. "I saw educated, healthy, well dressed competent Tibetans in charge of everything from the hospital to the computer centre. I also realized the focus had now shifted from saving lives to ensuring the survival of their heritage and culture."[84]

Like Banta and Mündel, Pullen and James had found useful placements in communities in crisis. But to the extent that it could, CUSO sought after the mid-1960s to respond more systematically to India's national development priorities as set out in its five-year plans. In his report for 1965-66, CUSO's acting executive secretary Terry Glavin identified agriculture and family planning as the country's "areas of greatest need."[85] Brian Marson, arriving as coordinator in late 1966 direct from the Ottawa office, was anxious to focus on those priorities. Marson's involvement with CUSO went back five years to his undergraduate role in establishing the University of British Columbia President's Committee on Student Service Overseas. He had joined CUSO's small secretariat in 1964 as associate director of Asian programs and director of fundraising. After his India year, he would return to CUSO's Ottawa office until 1969, when he left to do graduate studies in economics and government at Harvard University.[86] Marson's report from India, written six months into his new role there, made it clear that he aspired to be something of a new broom in his approach to programming, especially by moving away from ad hoc placements to carefully selected assignments. There was no talk, as in the early CUSO/India days, of promoting cultural understanding. Rather, Marson spoke in terms of "a technical assistance programme" in India, one in which the jobs assigned, even in teaching, should have a "multiplier effect," be subjected to more rigorous performance evaluation, and, ideally, be geographically concentrated in northern Hindi-speaking states. In keeping with the new approach, several volunteers were reassigned from their original placements to positions in which they would have "a maximum impact on the development process."[87]

With regard to the two national development priorities identified by Glavin and Marson, the emphasis on agriculture was very much linked to the beginnings of India's green revolution with its aggressive (and ultimately controversial) strategies for increasing agricultural productivity through such means as selective plant breeding for high-yielding varieties of food grains, more intensive cultivation and irrigation, and use of pesticides.[88] Dr. David Hopper, from 1966 the associate director of the Rockefeller Foundation's agricultural program and, as such, an important early contributor to the green revolution, was anxious to direct suitable CUSO volunteers toward this area of service. Hans-Henning Mündel was one such volunteer. Hopper believed that someone with Mündel's professional background – master's degrees in agronomy/plant breeding and international agricultural development – could be more usefully employed in the task of modernizing Indian agriculture than in helping a few families of Paniyas. Despite his emotional investment in his work with the Paniyas, Mündel himself eventually agreed: even his small salary was a drain on the scarce funds available from NAWA for the Paniyas community, and he was not the best fit with its needs. Transferring to the site to which Hopper had originally tried to direct him, Mündel worked for the next two years in an agricultural research institute in Maharashtra state, assigned to start a safflower breeding and development program. As in his previous assignment, he was highly motivated, paying for private lessons in Marathi, for instance, in order to communicate with technical support and field staff. Although it was by no means the end of his involvement with the Paniyas, the plant-breeding assignment was the real beginning of Mündel's professional career.[89]

Several other CUSO volunteers with specialized training were also in on the early stages of the green revolution. Jim Ward, in India from 1964, had endured an unsatisfying first-year placement in an ashram with his wife, Sheila, before moving north to Bharatpur in Rajasthan. Here, too, the Wards initially struggled to find productive work. After consulting with Hopper, Jim Ward was able to move in a new and more satisfying direction. As he became involved in hybrid seed development and other matters related to grain production, his work in Bharatpur took off. At one stage, he even wrote a column on agriculture for the *Hindustan Times*.[90] Meanwhile, George Janzen, born and raised on a Saskatchewan farm, was involved in the production and marketing of hybrid corn, sorghum, and millet seed for a farmers' cooperative in Andhra Pradesh. Although he declined to stay on in a lucrative salaried position to run the cooperative at the end of his volunteer term, Janzen briefly returned to India with CUSO in 1970 to work with Pat Phillips in a coordinator role.[91]

Mündel, Ward, and Janzen were not the only volunteers to serve in India's green revolution, but from CUSO's perspective they were a disappointingly small group. Back in Canada from 1968, Jim Ward worked for three years with CUSO/Ottawa. Despite his and other staff members' repeated attempts to recruit volunteers with appropriate professional qualifications for the opportunities in agricultural development in India (and elsewhere), there was a dearth of such volunteers. And unlike the Peace Corps, CUSO was evidently not inclined to put BA generalists into such positions.[92]

So far as CUSO/India was concerned, family planning appeared to be a development niche where there was, by contrast, a good fit between a national priority in the host country and volunteer supply. The volunteers in this case were mainly nurses. Given the fact that until 1969 birth control was illegal in Canada and that Canadian nurses had typically not been trained in procedures, technologies, and attitudes related to the promotion of contraception, this match on the surface seems problematic and calls for explanation, beginning with the India context.[93]

Though a birth control movement had existed in colonial India, it was the work of small groups of indigenous and Western social reformers. With the rapid growth of India's population in the decade following independence, the situation changed dramatically. Even the initially skeptical Nehru concluded that trying to address development challenges without tackling population pressures was counterproductive. India became the first country in the world to establish a family planning program. The Third Five Year Plan, which became operative in 1961, contained an unprecedented commitment to family planning.[94] When Indira Gandhi became prime minister in January 1966 following Shastri's sudden death, family planning became an even higher priority. Indeed, the day after Gandhi was sworn into office, the Ministry of Health was renamed the Ministry of Health and Family Planning. International pressure on India to get its population growth under control as a condition of receiving food aid, especially from the US, reinforced national planners' own strong interest in this aspect of facilitating development.[95]

Birth control advocates in the colonial era had typically looked to doctors for leadership and expertise or had themselves been indigenous or Western physicians. Given the scale of the task being contemplated in 1960s India and the new technologies available, it was deemed neither possible nor necessary to rely exclusively on doctors for the educational campaigns and some of the procedures envisaged. Rather, many advocates claimed, public health nurses and Lady Health Visitors could lay the attitudinal groundwork and also, where feasible, train auxiliary health workers to perform simple contraceptive procedures, of which the most common in this period was insertion of intrauterine devices (IUDs, commonly called loops). The problem was that when family planning became a major state and NGO initiative in 1960s India, most Indian nurses were still not in a position to take on leadership roles or work independently in this highly sensitive area of practice, given the nature of their backgrounds and training and existing cultural constraints.[96]

CUSO volunteers of both sexes were quick to recognize the importance of family planning as a possible area for involvement. Several members of the 1962 cohort indicated that they had had, or been encouraged to have, some involvement in family-planning activities in their placements even though they had no medical background and such activities had not been part of their assignments.[97] In what seems to have been the first official reference to CUSO involvement, Terry Glavin's annual report for 1965-66 indicated that a number of CUSO nurses in India were doing some family-planning work, one of them on a full-time basis. The full-timer was probably Sheila Ward, by then in Bharatpur. She had originally been hired by local officials to teach midwifery in the district hospital and conduct public health visits in the surrounding villages. The district, according to these officials, was "conservative and backward." Yet as she travelled to villages by bicycle, Ward encountered women who requested in whispered Hindi, "Benji, baccha bund karo" ("Sister, stop us having children").[98] Elsewhere in India there would soon be other CUSO nurses working full time in family planning, for with the arrival of Brian Marson and Wendy Marson, CUSO's engagement with this national priority took off.

The Marsons were unusual within CUSO in having relevant background in this area of work.[99] Soon after their arrival in New Delhi, having learned about a family-planning project operated by the Christian Medical Association of India (CMAI), the Marsons travelled to Ratlam in Madhya Pradesh to meet the man celebrated by the CMAI as the project's founder, United Church of Canada medical missionary Bob McClure. It was through their contact with McClure that they learned about placement possibilities for CUSO nurses within the CMAI's family-planning project. Wendy Marson herself became the first such placement.[100] Working out of New Delhi as the regional director of the project in northwest India, she functioned, she recalled, as a kind of "circuit rider," calling on mission hospitals and seeking the support of staff for family-planning initiatives. She also met with patients and outpatients, and she sometimes accompanied hospital staff members as they went on village-visiting assignments and encouraged them to add family planning to their existing work. Before the Marsons' year in India was out, Wendy had published an article in *Canadian Nurse* on "India's Project number one," outlining for her readers the nature and scope of the CMAI's family-planning project and the opportunities that existed for more nurse volunteers.[101]

CUSO, as noted, had a good track record in recruiting nurses, typically women who were somewhat older than other volunteers and equipped with personal and professional experiences that had broadened their horizons. Recognizing their lack of professional training in contraception work, the family-planning nurses as a group had the maturity and motivation to educate themselves in their new line of work and in the broad cultural context in which it was to be conducted.[102] Although they were typically to be nurse educators rather than hands-on contraceptive workers or purveyors of devices, they needed to be familiar with the types of procedures and aids being made available and the nature of the resistance that existed among potential users, not only because of cultural and economic factors but also as a result of myths and misunderstandings and the existence of physical problems. One of the early rumours they would encounter held that IUDs were in fact worms imported from the West that worked by eating the fetus. Yet physical problems resulting in pain, bleeding, and other difficulties would prove to be anything but rumours, especially if the loops had been inserted incorrectly and without follow-up.

The experience of Vancouver-born Patricia Ann Phillips provides insights into the CUSO nurses' learning curve in this new line of work.[103] Twenty-nine years old when she arrived in India in 1968, Phillips became part of a four-member mobile team working out of the CMAI's project headquarters in Bangalore and travelling to mission hospitals in the states of Mysore and Tamil Nadu. Her Canadian preparation for her assignment had consisted only of a brief visit to a Vancouver birth control clinic. Now she immersed herself in the professional literature that was being made available to workers like herself. Her preparation also involved an orientation program organized for project workers before they set out on their assignments. Her team comprised a professional Indian Christian nurse with a public health background, a Muslim driver and, for a time, a social scientist. Working with mission hospitals of various sizes and degrees of complexity, the team's mandate was to help hospital staffs themselves to develop and promote awareness of India's population problem and a knowledge and acceptance of birth control techniques, both within the hospitals and in the surrounding communities. Over the course of her two-year assignment, Phillips and her Indian nurse-partner spent countless hours deciding how best to teach and train hospital staffs and tracking down effective resources. The challenge was to win over not only senior medical workers but also all hospital staff, including sweepers, since even non-medical personnel could become conduits of information – or misinformation – especially if they shared caste or linguistic ties with patients. Learning on the job was part of the job, as was learning to listen to the non-specialists on staff, since "their questions are the ones that voice the doubts of the majority of India's population."[104]

One of the three regional directors to whom Phillips's team reported at the base in Bangalore was another CUSO nurse, Joyce Relyea. Relyea had previously worked for some months on the CMAI's family-planning project in New Delhi, where one of her tasks had been helping to organize a major conference, initiated and funded by the government of India as outreach to medical and nursing superintendents in mission hospitals. In Bangalore, she and her fellow directors aimed to have eight mobile family-planning teams at work by the end of 1968, each to include a CUSO nurse. Relyea's "A New Concept in Family Planning Education," published that year in the CMAI *Journal*, described the details and aims of the new concept in optimistic terms. Three years later, CUSO nurse-educator Jean Stilwell, working in the state of Orissa, echoed other *Journal* accounts of a gratifying increase in family-planning work among CMAI member hospitals, such that some were now able to hire their own full-time workers from the community for both in-patient and village-outreach work. Stilwell also touched on another hopeful pattern in the organization's family-planning work: a greater focus on such related matters as maternal and child nutrition.[105]

The CMAI as the umbrella organization of mainstream Protestant missions in India had given cautious support to birth control as far back as the 1930s. State officials recognized that mission personnel as part of the voluntary sector had done pioneer work in family planning well before the national government took up the cause. Their contributions remained important, for even in the 1970s, mission-founded medical institutions were still the largest group of non-state actors in the health-care field in India[106] – hence, the national government's willingness to engage with and involve mission medical leaders through conferences and other cooperative activities and by sharing resources (albeit not without numerous bureaucratic hurdles and delays and despite its unease with other aspects of mission work); hence, also, the fact that the CMAI became the single largest employer of the CUSO nurses who became involved in family planning.

In 1967, for the first time, nurses outnumbered teachers among new volunteers assigned to India.[107] Of forty-eight CUSO volunteers overall in India in September 1968, ten were involved in family planning. In addition to the six in CMAI employ, one volunteer was identified as a special assistant to the minister of health and family planning. Several others were employed in the state of Haryana. One of them, probably a reassigned teacher, worked in the demography unit of the state government.[108] Nancy Garrett, filling in for a nurse who had been sent to Calcutta for further training, worked in the Family Planning Training Centre of the state's Medical College Hospital at Rohtak. Art photographer Vicki Henry served in the same college but as an assistant in the design of posters promoting nutrition and family planning. Meanwhile, Sheila Ward, by now on her third assignment in India, was the director of a field survey research project funded by USAID and conducted among rural women in Rohtak district who had been fitted with IUDs. The aim of the survey was to compare the experiences and retention rates of those women whose IUD insertions had been carried out by doctors with those of women whose insertions had been carried out by auxiliary nurse midwives. The latter were cheaper workers for family planning centres to employ and more readily available. But if, as many doctors claimed, they were less adept at doing successful insertions, this information was obviously important to have if the devices were to gain widespread acceptance.[109]

Small as their total numbers were, CUSO's family-planning volunteers were doing varied and valued work in India in the last half of the 1960s. It appeared that in the country's burgeoning family-planning movement CUSO had found a niche where it could effectively place volunteers. So important did family planning seem to be in CUSO's vision of its future in India in 1967 and 1968 that the in-country orientations for new cohorts in those years provided background information on the movement to all new volunteers. As coordinator in New Delhi in 1967, Brian Marson arranged for the newly arrived nurses to meet with officials in several organizations and agencies broadly related to their future work. There were even arrangements for taking tea at the residence of the minister of health and family planning.[110] A March 1969 report on the work of CUSO/India claimed that twenty-three volunteers were involved in health and family-planning activities. As a result of some organizational changes, CUSO's work overall in India was said to have been stabilized in a most encouraging way, and relations between CUSO/India and state and national government officials with whom it had dealings were said to be excellent.[111]

Yet within the next few years it would become clear that all was not well for CUSO in India, and that its relations with the state were far from excellent. No new volunteers were sent in 1971. A year later, at CUSO's Asia Regional Meeting in Bangkok, a report announced plans to "deactivate" CUSO's work in India after August. By way of explanation, the report spoke of difficulties in getting postings confirmed for volunteers, of the high unemployment rate in India among the educated, and of the Indian government's "obvious desire to 'go it alone' in the development field."[112] CUSO was not actually excluded from India, as one scholar has claimed, but along with other Canadian NGOs, including the Unitarian Service Committee and Oxfam, it was experiencing what he referred to as a period of "diminishing Indian cooperation."[113] As Pat Phillips, the last CUSO staff person to work in India, recalled, "The writing was on the wall."[114] The same thing was happening to Britain's VSO and to the Peace Corps. Indeed, Dick Bird's insider account of VSO claims that in 1972 the government of India called for an end to the recruitment of all foreign volunteers, seemingly in response to anti-American feeling resulting from US support for Pakistan in the recent war. The Peace Corps, which for a time in the 1960s had had India as its biggest placement field, was ordered in 1972 by Indira Gandhi's government to reduce its numbers from over 500 volunteers to just 50.[115]

The withdrawal of the welcome mat was undoubtedly awkward. CUSO's India volunteers had, as seen, won praise for their dedication and adaptability, especially in the first half of the 1960s. Even in 1968, when *Man Deserves Man* was published, India still seemed to loom large in CUSO, as the book's foreword by India's scholarly former president signalled.[116] Perhaps understandably, the organization was low-key about its decision to end programming there. But was there also equanimity about the departure? Certainly, from the perspective of an increasingly ambitious development NGO, there were other factors, in addition to the Indian government's waning support, to make a decision to withdraw seem timely. Even at the best of times, India had proven to be a challenging country in which to work, and a costly one. Although CUSO's general practice was to have its volunteers paid by their host employers at local salary levels, in India CUSO sometimes had to supplement volunteers' salaries in order to make their stay viable. Volunteers' health problems, although less

common than in the first few years, did not disappear despite the introduction of gamma globulin shots and other preventive measures. Nor did there cease to be ineffectual placements. Paradoxes abounded. Teaching placements, the easiest to make, were often in institutions that, from a comparative perspective, needed the volunteers least: mission schools, for instance, and other private schools, and even some specialized state schools and ashrams. When teacher-volunteers *were* placed among the truly disadvantaged, as in a Gujarati ashram serving Adivasis, a placement that Les Johnson skilfully critiqued for *Man Deserves Man,* they were often unable to develop sufficient language skill and cultural understanding to make contributions that felt useful. Or they could be wanted by the institution that had hired them and at the same time resented by their Indian co-workers, as Johnson's fellow Manitoban Allan Collier quickly learned in 1968 in his first teaching placement.[117] One woman was so frustrated in her teaching assignment at Chandigarh in the Punjab that she transferred to work with Mother Teresa in Calcutta even though she was Jewish. Even an appointment that seemed to be a good fit between institutional needs and volunteer qualifications could provoke soul searching. Barbara Kerfoot, a professional librarian with graduate training in adult education and part of the last cohort to be sent to India, had a placement with a new NGO called Literacy International. Based in New Delhi, the placement was comfortable in terms of both working and living arrangements. But Kerfoot had hoped to be located "somewhere more rural," and "I guess I hoped that there might have been more hands-on experience in the field of literacy." Looking back, she recalled that "all of us in India grappled with what we were doing – teaching, nursing, etc. India had many trained people, so why should we be doing some of the work we were? Were we taking jobs from them?"[118]

Even in regard to family planning, comparatively a success story for CUSO, there were some concerns. The backlash in India against family planning would not reach crisis levels until 1976-77, when the coercive methods implemented nationally by Indira Gandhi's government under her son Sanjay would contribute to the prime minister's electoral defeat.[119] But even at the beginning of the decade, there were some states such as Orissa, where Jean Stilwell's CMAI team worked, where the movement was deeply unpopular. And articles were already appearing in international media that raised questions about the effectiveness and the ethics of family planning as a tool for development, especially if it was coercive and not part of a larger, multi-pronged strategy that addressed poor families' concerns about their future security. To be sure, the media alarms were sounded primarily about large state-sponsored interventions pushed by the West. Still, articles of this sort were being reproduced in collections of readings for CUSO's own constituency,[120] and inevitably they stimulated questioning. In the spring of 1970, as coordinator for health and medical work, Nancy Garrett was asked by CUSO/Ottawa's medical director, Dr. Ed Ragan, for an assessment of India's family-planning initiatives and the place of the CMAI project within them. "It would ... be interesting to know if the CUSO participants consider the project to be viable and worth supporting in the long term," Ragan wrote. And should CIDA be encouraged to support it? In her reply, Garrett stated that while the CMAI's mobile teams had done commendable work, the project overall was not well administered. And any CIDA aid to family planning should go to state governments with an interest in such work, especially since the CMAI project appeared set to receive a very large grant from USAID.[121]

There were, then, concerns about various aspects of CUSO's programming in India as well as the undeniable reality of government officials' "diminishing ... cooperation." Bureaucratic complexities and delays had been a norm in CUSO's dealings with all levels of government, but now the delays signalled the end of a welcome for volunteers. In any case, as Kerfoot's reflections indicate, the volunteers themselves were mindful of the issue of their real or perceived redundancy. A symbolically significant shift had already taken place within the CMAI family-planning project. Joyce Relyea's position on the central supervisory team at Bangalore had been filled after her return to Canada in 1969 by Sujatha De Magry, the Indian public health nurse who had been Pat Phillips's colleague and friend. Phillips, in India until June 1972, recalls that by the early 1970s there was already a significant Indian middle class. And in terms of family planning, there were more Indian nurses who, like De Magry, were prepared culturally and qualified professionally to take on the kinds of roles that CUSO nurses had briefly occupied, in effect filling a gap that existed in the early days of the CMAI's project. Nancy Garrett, leaving India two years before Phillips, had likewise recognized the reality that India now had a substantial population of educated men and women, many of them not adequately employed. Given that reality, she recalls, she had recommended the termination of CUSO's India program once the cohort serving there had completed its term.[122]

Meanwhile, in contrast to India, in many other developing countries there was a high demand for CUSO volunteers. In Papua New Guinea, where, before leaving CUSO, Brian Marson had acted on the suggestion of diplomat Arthur Menzies and investigated opportunities for Canadian volunteers, there was virtually no educated class.[123] Broadly speaking, the biggest growth area was in former British colonies in Africa, where teacher-volunteers were very much in demand. Given greater ease in placing volunteers in countries like these, it was difficult to justify trying to hang on in India.

And then, next door to India, newly independent Bangladesh was heavily reliant on international aid following its bloody break from Pakistan in 1971. For a time, CUSO believed that Bangladesh was a country where it could make a significant volunteer contribution. Following the completion of her regular two-year term in July 1971, Jean Stilwell worked among refugees from the former East Pakistan in India's Bihar state before returning to Canada and undertaking a cross-country tour to publicize the plight of the millions of refugees. For her part, after briefly working back home in Vancouver, Phillips travelled to Bangladesh in 1973 to investigate opportunities for a CUSO health program in the new country.[124] Jean Pelletier had been sent a year earlier to establish a CUSO presence, especially with a view to placing an initial twenty volunteers. Given his recent experience with a postwar reconstruction project in Biafra, Pelletier, the son of Trudeau cabinet minister Gérard Pelletier, was considered well suited for his new assignment. But Bangladesh lacked the infrastructure and other resources to provide even minimal support for a cadre of volunteers. Nor was it possible to find twenty volunteers who could contribute effectively in a setting with so little in the way of necessary structures and resources. Given these challenges, and the presence of numerous other aid agencies in Bangladesh, CUSO in 1974 opted not to follow its usual volunteer-placement pattern. Instead, under field staff officer Raymond Cournoyer, a former Holy Cross brother and Oxfam worker with years of experience in Bangladesh, CUSO provided support for projects that largely reflected locally defined needs and that strengthened indigenous leadership.[125] When at the end of the 1970s Pat Phillips returned to Bangladesh as CUSO's field staff officer, she had just one Canadian worker to supervise. Now her main responsibility was formulating proposals for social development appropriate to the local context and finding the resources to support such projects.[126] It was indicative of the way CUSO's approach had changed in its work in many countries in the course of the 1970s and of how much had changed overall since 1961, when the first cohort of volunteers had arrived by ship in India.

"More Learn Than Serve": What the Volunteers Took from India

During his meeting with Sargent Shriver in 1961 and responding to Shriver's proposal to place Peace Corps volunteers in India, Nehru is reported to have observed, "I am sure young Americans would learn a great deal in this country and it could be an important experience for them." But, he added, "I hope you and they will not be too disappointed if the Punjab, when they leave, is more or less the same as it was before they came."[127] Perhaps Nehru's comment to the 1962 cohort of Canadian volunteers about attitude being more important than aptitude was meant to convey a similar message. In any event, within a year of the arrival of the first cohort, many of them were already well schooled in realistic expectations. As ad hoc coordinator, Dale Posgate had been candid on the subject. Likewise, Stephen Woollcombe, in his political science master's thesis on CUSO as a case study of an overseas volunteer program, completed in 1965, found that most of the RVs he surveyed believed they had made only a "very limited concrete contribution" to India. Writing that year from Varanasi, where she was about to start her second year of teaching, one volunteer stated, "I don't think any of us in CUSO feel that we are making a great contribution to India, but at least we have broadened our horizons and deepened our understanding tremendously."[128] Contrary to what journalists would later suggest when, covering a more radical CUSO, they depicted the first cohorts as "downy-cheeked students" seeking, missionary-like, to bring enlightenment to the backward, even the earliest of the India volunteers *did* understand very quickly that their efforts were "small potatoes."[129] And they were at pains to pass that message on to their successors. When in 1968, at the first Returned Volunteers' conference, an effort was made to recruit *recently* returned volunteers for political education work within Canada, the message of one document was that "good old India '62 with his box of slides" should willingly retreat to the sidelines along with others from the "bygone era."[130] "Good old India '62" was probably being sidelined not because he was presenting an overblown image of past achievements but rather because he was still hewing to a philosophy of volunteering as small-scale international bridge-building at a time when new and different visions of CUSO were emerging.

While the India volunteers acknowledged that their contributions had been small potatoes, that did not mean that as a group they had experienced a sense of uselessness during their time in the subcontinent. In addition to contributing to "the abstraction known as international understanding,"[131] there had been

A Passage to India

tangible individual satisfactions. Even teacher-volunteers, the most likely to experience a feeling of redundancy, could look back on worthwhile extracurricular and community involvement as well as on whatever they had done for and with individual pupils. A few agricultural volunteers had participated in the making of India's green revolution, regarded, at least briefly, as an unproblematically valuable aspect of development. In a small number of cases, volunteers had played crucial roles in the lives of vulnerable groups, as in Mündel's year among the Paniyas, Banta's work in a leprosy colony, and the involvement of Judy Pullen and Lois James with Tibetan refugees. The majority, serving in less pressing circumstances, would probably have agreed with the retrospective perspective of Sally Bambridge from the first cohort of volunteers. Asked like other interviewees to reflect on the early CUSO motto "To Serve and Learn," Bambridge wrote that it had been "[m]ore learn than serve," but that "I served enough to earn my learning, I think."[132]

In 1998, in an article titled "How Five Idealistic Young People Ventured Forth – And Didn't Save the World," John Stackhouse, the New Delhi-based development issues reporter for the *Globe and Mail,* used first-person accounts from five former volunteers to describe their original assignments and what they had found when they returned to their placements some thirty-five years later. They neither took credit for what had been accomplished nor bemoaned disappointing outcomes or reproached themselves for youthful naïveté. Rather, through vivid, moving accounts, they conveyed a sense of what their India years had meant to them personally.[133] The five were perhaps unusual in being in a position to make this return journey, but they shared a perspective that was common among their fellow volunteers, a perspective conveyed in Sally's apt phrase *more learn than serve.* There were numerous variations in expressing the idea. For teacher Anne Jones, in India at the beginning like Sally as part of the first COV cohort, it was "the most important choice I could have made in terms of global learning." For Phillips, there at the very end, it was "an experience worth gold ... Changed my life!"[134] India was, simultaneously, a hard early lesson in the challenges of development and, for individual volunteers, a cherished and life-altering experience.

3

"Development Is Disturbance"
Change, Politics, and Conflict in CUSO's 1970s

In a talk prepared for the April 1968 Conference on Inter-American Student Projects, Monsignor Ivan Illich reminded his audience of his well-known opposition to the presence of "all North American 'do-gooders' in Latin America." A year later, the Committee of Returned Volunteers of the Peace Corps dismissed the Corps as "a graduate school for imperialism" and recommended its abolition.[1] These two expressions of disillusionment with Western efforts to help the Global South were distinctive only in that they specifically targeted the efforts of youth-based groups and came from people who had themselves been "do-gooders." Otherwise, the admonitions were very much in keeping with broader critiques of neocolonialism and development by other First- and Third-World writers and activists in the late 1960s. Far from downplaying such critiques, CUSO publicized them to its various constituencies. In doing so, it was reflecting the extent to which, in common with other NGOs within and outside Canada, its understanding of development had changed in the course of a decade. Gone was the easy optimism that had marked the beginning of the first Development Decade with its faith that modernization and goodwill could facilitate sustained growth in the developing world and amicable relationships with its peoples. Rather, for organizations such as CUSO, the new default position appeared to be critical self-reflection and guilt, not just about the West's historical sins in the Global South but also about its contemporary failings even when it tried to help – indeed, sometimes especially when it tried to help.[2] Yet denunciations such as Illich's notwithstanding, there was no serious thought of abandoning the cause of development. CUSO entered the 1970s as a large and increasingly ambitious NGO, and while competing visions emerged within the organization about how it should "do" development, giving up altogether on the development project was clearly not an option.

As shown earlier, CUSO's own development had been characterized by expansion from the mid-1960s when federal funding had begun. Growth in numbers of volunteers, field staff, and placement countries was outpaced only by the expansion of staff and bureaucracy at Ottawa headquarters as the organization sought to reinvent itself as a more professional and businesslike NGO. One ironic outcome of the coexistence of a bigger, more bureaucratized, and better-funded CUSO and late-sixties social ferment was that politicized members of the CUSO community had far more opportunities and venues in which to express and act on their concerns than would otherwise have been the case. As had been the pattern from the McWhinney era onward, returned volunteers (RVs) held most of the senior staff positions in CUSO's Ottawa office.[3] The desire of other RVs for input on CUSO decision making was facilitated by changes that assured them a voice on CUSO's board of directors, at annual general meetings (AGMs), on local campus committees, and in other settings. Among activists who wanted CUSO to be a politically engaged, even radical, organization, there tended to be a standard discourse: CUSO should do more than just send volunteers. It should speak out and intervene on "big" issues related to development. It should take a stand on the side of the colonized and oppressed in developing countries by actively supporting liberation movements and analogous struggles. Within Canada, attention should be directed to the complicity of multinational corporations and the state itself in policies and practices that exacerbated Third World poverty and oppression. This contingent of activists was probably never as numerous as those within CUSO who favoured a pragmatic approach to development and who believed that their organization should eschew politics and instead concentrate on sending capable volunteers and initiating worthwhile projects. Yet particularly in CUSO's ECSA region (East, Central, and Southern Africa), and for a time during the mid-to-late 1970s within CUSO's Ottawa office, the "radicals" appeared to be in the ascendant.

Although CUSO's leftward tilt was part of a larger pattern among development NGOs, the politicization within CUSO from the late 1960s had some elements that set it apart. Emerging tensions with SUCO, CUSO's francophone counterpart, and the challenges that arose from the complex relationship between these sibling organizations were the most important of such elements. CUSO's relationship with CIDA and the federal state more broadly also had some distinctive aspects, for along with the tensions and the sense of vulnerability that came with its financial dependency on CIDA, there was also a strong symbiosis and numerous personal links. This chapter begins with a broad overview of the CUSO landscape at home and abroad in the late 1960s and early 1970s before turning to CUSO's political activism and the concerns it engendered within and outside the organization. In 1979, CUSO's *annus horribilis,* the internal conflicts and external concerns created a crisis that briefly threatened the organization's existence, after which, under a new executive director, it was put back on a more even keel. It is worth stressing that the divisions between CUSO's radical and moderate factions were generally over means rather than ends: debates about the best basic strategies for aiding the people of the Global South. Meanwhile, matters related to gender and race did not come to the fore as significant issues of contention within CUSO during the turbulent 1970s. The last part of the chapter considers why this was the case.

Diverse Tendencies and New Directions in an Expanding NGO

The growth and change that had begun when Hugh Christie was seconded from the External Aid Office (EAO) to replace Bill McWhinney as executive secretary accelerated when Frank Bogdasavich was appointed to the position in 1968. An RV like McWhinney, Bogdasavich fostered an organizational culture markedly different from the one over which McWhinney had presided as CUSO's first full-time executive secretary. A lawyer by training, Bogdasavich had served in Tanzania, functioning as national program coordinator while also tutoring in the Faculty of Law at University College, Dar es Salaam. Back in Canada, he joined the CUSO secretariat as director of the East and Central Africa program and while in that role initiated a research department. As executive director (the title adopted in this period to replace executive secretary), he oversaw further growth and change, including an increased number of specialized departments and more use of paid staff or outside professionals to coordinate such tasks as recruitment and fundraising.[4] Whereas in 1965, there had been seven national staff overall, by the end of 1968, there were fifteen anglophone

"Development Is Disturbance"

staff officers and six francophone officers in a now separately managed SUCO, each one with a secretary and/or an assistant.[5]

During Bogdasavich's term at the helm, CUSO also undertook a review of its constitution, and the early slogan "To Serve and Learn" gave way to "Development Is Our Business."[6] The new slogan was more than a cosmetic change. Especially during the early years in India, as Chapter 2 shows, there had been a strong commitment to the bridge-building aspects of the volunteer experience. Volunteers and their supporters believed in promoting international understanding through individual contacts with village cultures and simple, grassroots living. Now, to those who talked in terms of the "business" of international development, of CUSO as a "technical supply" or "manpower resource" agency, and of the need for "realism" and a "functional approach,"[7] the style and aspirations of those early volunteers were bound to seem naive and unfocused. CUSO, the business-minded believed, should concentrate on sending volunteers trained in the specific skills that specific developing countries wanted.

The shift in ethos and emphasis from serving and learning and hair-shirt living to volunteers as "professionals" certainly did not happen without regret on the part of some of those associated with the pioneering cohorts, who warned against what they saw as the transformation of CUSO into a "placement agency" and an excessive concern with professionalism. Still, Bogdasavich was part of a growing segment within CUSO eager to dispense with the idea of the volunteer as someone whose idealism and willingness to endure hardship could compensate for the absence of the specific professional skills being sought by host countries. Indeed, some RVs were now uncomfortable with the very term *volunteer,* though it would remain in use until replaced by cooperant about a decade later.[8] In truth, terms like *hair-shirt volunteers* and *skilled professionals* were contrasting tropes rather than accurate labels for what had been or would be within CUSO. But as indicators of distinct ideological positions, they were regularly deployed in the late 1960s until, by the early 1970s, those most strongly associated with the former position had largely moved on or been silenced.[9] Furthermore, labels like these, and, in the 1970s, "conservative" or "pragmatic" versus "political" or "radical" sometimes reflected and were reinforced by the kinds of personality conflicts that came to the fore as the organization went through a period of rapid growth.[10]

Bogdasavich's address to the 1968 AGM indicated the kinds of changes he considered necessary in overseas policies in order to make CUSO a more businesslike NGO, more responsive to the needs of its client countries. One recommendation was providing volunteers with their own transportation and infrastructure support. "The practice of sending agriculturalists, engineers, and public health nurses into the field and then having them work within a one-mile radius of their house for lack of transportation does not meet with the enthusiastic response of many governments," Bogdasavich declared. His recommendation that CUSO start budgeting for such expenditures undoubtedly reflected the kind of request he was getting from some volunteers. But it was wholly at odds with a 1966 information guide for overseas governments and agencies, which had explicitly stated that provision of "tools, materials or other equipment [including a vehicle] necessary for the volunteer's work" was the responsibility of the host agency.[11] And it ignored the reality that the typical volunteer was still a teacher. Also essential, Bogdasavich maintained, was budgeting for more full-time field staff.[12]

His 1968 address also dealt with CUSO and politics. CUSO, Bogdasavich argued, had neither the right nor the expertise to intervene in the internal affairs of developing countries. Nor, generally, should it make the politics of those countries the basis on which to decide whether or not it would provide them with volunteers. Probably with Ian Smith's 1965 Unilateral Declaration of Independence in Rhodesia in mind, he added, "The one exception we might consider making concerns the case where the colony has evolved into a state which, by its constitution, perpetuates the power of the former colonialists." Otherwise, "what is required is that all CUSO personnel should understand that the so-called developing countries must be free to shape their own development. This understanding coupled with competence, ought to be the specialty of the CUSO house." Bogdasavich was addressing the AGM in the particular context of the Nigerian civil war, over which CUSO was then sharply divided. But he clearly intended his message to be understood more generally, as was made clear by his jibe at those within CUSO who called for position-taking on all manner of other matters: "for the entrepreneur or against him ... for participatory democracy or against it ... for Vietnam or against it ... for the overthrow of the university community or against it ... for the smoking of 'pot' or against it ... for greater personal sacrifice or against it." That Bogdasavich felt strongly about not interfering in developing countries' politics was confirmed a year later when he repeated his warning in his second and final address to the AGM.[13] Whether they shared his view or not, his audience undoubtedly

recognized that in urging non-interference abroad, Bogdasavich was not indif-
ferent to the political status quo in the countries where CUSO had work but
rather expressing a view about what he saw as a strategically unsound approach
to development.

Beginning during Bogdasavich's term as executive director and continuing
into the mid-1970s under his successors, CUSO formally adopted several new
and broadly interrelated approaches to its work. Four of these innovations in
particular merit a brief introductory description, since together they established
the operational framework for many of the activities that followed. The innovations also lent themselves to the pursuit of political agendas that divided CUSO
internally and set off alarm bells among erstwhile supporters.[14]

Development Education: Plans to initiate a multi-faceted program of public or
development education within Canada were set in motion by a resolution passed
at the AGM in 1969. The resolution called on CUSO to "pursue a programme
of increasing public awareness of international development, and of Canada's
foreign relations, and also encouraging Canadians to act on that awareness."
The wording was weaker than that in a failed amendment calling for CUSO "to
become politically active *on behalf of developing countries.*" Still, the resolution
reflected the conviction of its authors – they were mainly RVs – that they had
an obligation to educate Canadians about developing-world issues, given their
experience as volunteers.[15] Although it would be several years before the Ottawa
office had a department exclusively concerned with development education,
CUSO declared in 1969 that it would be "a firm priority for the Second
Development Decade" and announced a fund to assist local committees with
development education outreach.[16]

A Projects Approach: In January 1973, CUSO officially began a new projects
division. CIDA's willingness to fund the new division reflected its satisfaction
with the conduct and outcome of a unique educational rehabilitation project
undertaken by CUSO in the former Biafra following its defeat in the Nigerian
civil war. The project approach was enthusiastically explained at CUSO's Asia
regional meeting the following year as involving "a process of co-operation
between CUSO and individuals or groups in the host countries, both private
and government, whereby a problem is clearly identified, alternative courses
of action explored and a plan of action chosen which has specific objectives set

within a given span of time ... CUSO will no longer concentrate exclusively on providing Canadian manpower; rather ... CUSO will respond to requests for human and material resources."[17] After Biafra, the new nation of Bangladesh became the site of CUSO's first major project initiatives. Other new and struggling countries also became major sites for a projects approach. And projects became vehicles for assisting liberation struggles, as is shown below. In the decade after the Projects Division was established, it accounted for some 40 percent of CUSO's overseas work, "setting CUSO significantly apart from other volunteer-sending organizations."[18]

Decentralization: The projects approach clearly lent itself to moves toward decentralization, advocacy for which had begun among staff in the ECSA region.[19] Described in CUSO's 1972 annual report as a major administrative change, decentralization involved establishing the position of regional field director (RFD) in each region where CUSO had work. Replacing the former Ottawa-based area directors, the RFDs were to arrange for regional meetings that would be the main planning groups for each area. It was envisioned that the new approach would draw on the insights of host nationals as well as staff and volunteers in each region in order to discern and act on local priorities. Also envisioned as a central feature of the decentralization approach were annual interregional meetings "where overseas and Canadian-based staff [would] get together to draw up international programme plans and budgets for the future."[20] Predictably, this shift also led to calls for decentralization of decision making *within* Canada, particularly by long-established local committees such as the one at UBC, which resented the Ottawa secretariat's tight control over such matters as volunteer selection.[21]

The Development Charter: Originating from the interregional meeting held at Dar es Salaam in April 1973 and grandly styled the Dar Declaration (probably in homage to President Nyerere's 1967 Arusha Declaration on socialist development for Tanzania), the charter was adopted as "an official CUSO stance" in 1974. Development, the charter declared, included "the liberation of peoples, not just from the constraints of poverty ... but from constraints which inhibit a person's control over his destiny, the pursuit of dignity and real equality." Among other things, CUSO individuals should, therefore, "actively identify themselves with all peoples who seek to strengthen rights and responsibilities for their

"Development Is Disturbance"

country's social development consistent with the United Nations' Universal Declaration of Human Rights." While volunteers were not required to sign the charter as a condition of appointment, they were encouraged to do so, and those involved in recruitment and orientation were urged to use it as a guide.[22]

Of the four initiatives just outlined, the Development Charter was the most overtly political in terms of seeming to call for involvement in the internal affairs of countries and regions where volunteers worked. Meanwhile, one innovation contemplated at the beginning of the 1970s, though not ultimately adopted, also warrants mention here, since it speaks to the climate of the times. This was the possibility of CUSO's becoming formally involved in domestic programming. By 1970, CUSO was frequently the target of withering criticism for seeming to ignore development problems in Canada's own backyard, particularly in regard to First Nations' communities. CUSO's acting executive director, David Catmur, acknowledged this kind of pressure early in 1971 in a memo to the chairman of the board. There could be some value, Catmur conceded, in having young people work with such groups as the Company of Young Canadians (CYC) and native associations as preparation for overseas service. The problem, however, was that CUSO's reach was rapidly exceeding its financial grasp. "If the overseas programme is to remain the core element for CUSO," Catmur wrote, "the organization must restrain its impulse to indulge in a variety of other activities, which however meritorious, will tend to detract from the central purpose of the organization."[23] Although a report on the feasibility of launching a domestic program did recommend such a step, the 1971 AGM ultimately voted against it, instead suggesting that CUSO/SUCO offer to assist with "the recruitment of volunteers and the provision of other services for Frontier College, the Grenfell Mission, the Labrador School Board, the CYC and other similar agencies." As well, would-be volunteers for overseas service with CUSO were advised to try to work with such agencies before going abroad.[24]

As shown in Chapter 1, some young men in the early cohorts had put in one or more summers with Frontier College before joining CUSO. Nor did RVs' involvement with Frontier College or analogous agencies following their two years overseas depend on the existence of a domestic volunteer program within CUSO. The idea of establishing its own domestic program was in essence an indication of how much attention was being paid within Canada at this time to creating opportunities for youth to get involved with activities that addressed social and economic disparities. But as Catmur had pointed out, CUSO was already stretched financially to meet its overseas commitments, and it was for those commitments that it received CIDA funding. While such funding had increased considerably over the years, it did not keep pace with CUSO's increasing ambitions and rising costs, with the result that in 1972 CUSO found itself in a deficit position.[25] The decision made by the AGM not to support a distinctive domestic program undoubtedly saved CUSO from spilling more red ink. It may also have saved it from the kinds of embarrassing fiascos that periodically propelled CYC projects into national headlines.

Meanwhile, CUSO was having to face the fact that there were parts of the developing world where Canadian volunteers and other Western "do-gooders" were not wanted, or where the terms or conditions of work were unacceptable. As already discussed, CUSO ended its pioneering initiatives in India in 1972. In East Africa, work was terminated in three countries, including Uganda, where Idi Amin's murderous regime made staying on untenable.[26] However, CUSO's troubles in the Caribbean had a much higher profile than those in East Africa, given the extensiveness of CUSO's early involvement in the nearer region, the initial attractiveness of placements there, and Canada's commercial and Commonwealth connections with several Caribbean countries.[27] From the late 1960s, as Black Power sentiment increased, there was a backlash against volunteers in several Caribbean sites. The growth of racial tension and resentments directed specifically at Canada and Canadians was in large part the product of discriminatory Canadian immigration practices and real or perceived exploitation by the many Canadian-owned firms operating in the region. But there was also resentment against the presence of white would-be helpers from outside the region, particularly if the volunteers were perceived as taking jobs away from qualified locals.[28] In 1969, a radical Jamaican publication, *Abeng,* accused Canadian volunteers of being, along with Peace Corps workers, spies and subversives.[29] In the same year and with much more explosive effect, the racial tensions that had developed in Montreal with the highly publicized and inequitably handled Sir George Williams University affair reached several of the islands.[30] A region that had initially been viewed as a desirable site for volunteer postings came to be a minefield of racial difficulties. Large numbers of volunteers quit their posts early, and, in the face of increasing problems, programing in the region was cut back sharply.[31] There would be further cutbacks or closures in other regions where CUSO had work in the course of the 1970s but none as high profile as those in the Caribbean.

Political Advocacy at the Home Base: Venues, Vehicles, Issues

By the last half of the 1960s, there existed a sizable number of returned volunteers and volunteers turned staff who believed that they should draw on their overseas experience and their newfound political awareness to become development activists. In October 1966, RVs held their first conference, at Ste. Agathe, Quebec. Conference organizer Josette Blais reminded her colleagues that CUSO was "at a crucial stage in its development," and while she wanted them to be "constructive," she also challenged them to "take off the white gloves."[32] (Her metaphor may have been especially meaningful to female RVs from early 1960s cohorts, whose attire at reception ceremonies for departing volunteers had sometimes still included the classic little white gloves associated with respectable mid-century femininity.) Regional RV conferences soon became annual events in the CUSO calendar, and while the 1966 gathering heard some expressions of unease about what growth and bureaucracy would do to CUSO, the conferences quickly became sites for looking forward and for challenging the status quo, for instance, by questioning existing placement practices and by presenting resolutions in favour of political activism.[33] The new tone was signalled at the Winnipeg RV conference in 1968, at which were distributed coloured sheets of paper bearing pithy ideological statements by such authors/activists as Frantz Fanon, Ivan Illich, Che Guevara, and Fidel Castro. Illich, whose radical critique of the inequitable impact of formal, Western-style education was published in 1971 as *Deschooling Society*, addressed an audience of more than 600 people when he was brought to Toronto by RV David Cayley and other organizers to speak to a teach-in on development issues.[34]

Writings by and about these and other critics and revolutionaries were now routinely part of the assigned-reading diet for newly chosen volunteers. The preliminary recommended reading list sent to new volunteers assigned to West Africa in 1971 included seven books on Canadian themes as well as seven related to Africa (they were told to expect a further "comprehensive" list!). The Canadian titles, intended to sensitize the volunteer to "the frequently overlooked soft underbelly of our own society," included Harold Cardinal's *The Unjust Society* and Pierre Vallières's *White Niggers of America*. Recipients of the reading list were assured that the books would be "readily available in bookshops."[35] This was far from being the case, especially in rural and small-town Canada. Perhaps recognizing this reality and the unreality of expecting new recruits to read the dozens of books being recommended,[36] CUSO published three volumes of

Readings in Development at the beginning of the 1970s. The readings included were mainly short articles reproduced from journals and newspapers. Not all were written from a left perspective, but the inclusion of such items as advertisements for US military aircraft and Hilton International hotels, and Mitchell Sharp's response to foreign policy critics, were intended to illustrate the exploitive and self-serving aspects of Western capitalism and foreign policy. Reflecting the anti-American mood in contemporary Canada, articles dealing with the branch-plant Canadian economy shared space in the volumes with tributes to Tanzanian President Julius Nyerere's "socialism with a human face," West Indian students' denunciations of neocolonialism in the Caribbean, and a Kenyan writer's withering scorn for the "ignorance, naiveté and arrogance" of Western volunteers. As the Introduction to Volume 1 of *Readings in Development* explained, the common theme in the collection was "very simply that the problems of development in the third world cannot be adequately or successfully overcome unless the interrelationships between development and underdevelopment are understood."[37]

Two of the three editors/compilers of *Readings in Development* were also the editors of *NEWSTATEments,* an ambitious new periodical launched by CUSO in 1971 with a view to providing a "'radical' analysis" of the relationship between development and underdevelopment. Notwithstanding its declared radical intent, the first issue of *NEWSTATEments* claimed former Prime Minister L.B. Pearson among its "associate corresponding editors," along with well-known left-leaning international and Canadian scholars and activists. (G.K. Helleiner, Gerry Caplan, and Harold Cardinal were among the Canadians listed.) The goal was to publish solicited scholarly articles along with relevant commentary, poetry, and art. Subscribers were also to receive notification about public symposiums to be organized around specific development themes.[38] True to its word, the second issue of *NEWSTATEments* reported on an Ottawa seminar featuring Paulo Freire, the Brazilian author of *Pedagogy of the Oppressed.* Freire's approach to adult literacy, referred to in English as conscientization, was being acclaimed among development advocates well beyond Latin America for its apparent ability to transform "the once inarticulate into self-conscious actors and makers of history." At the time of his appearance at the Ottawa symposium and in a follow-up interview on CBC television, Freire was head of the Educational Division of the World Council of Churches (WCC). The editors of *NEWSTATEments* clearly considered it a coup to have arranged Freire's first public appearance in Canada.[39] They were also proud to use their pages to introduce their readers to developing-world sculpture and other art forms at a time when such work was little known within Canada. Not surprisingly, given its limited audience and high cost, *NEWSTATEments* proved to be short lived. Its significance lies not in its influence but rather in what it signified about CUSO's excessive confidence at this period about its ability to be a leading voice in educating Canadians about the developing world.[40]

In the meantime, reaching its most immediate constituencies and giving them information and a voice about its work overseas and within Canada was the task of CUSO's more modest periodicals. Of these, the *Bulletin* had been around the longest, dating back to 1962. At the end of 1973, the *CUSO Forum* replaced the *Bulletin* and other more ephemeral publications.[41] The content of the first issue of the new *CUSO Forum* reflected activists' desire to make it an edgier and more political periodical. The cover page carried a challenge from David Beer, who had already become one of CUSO's best-known advocates for political activism and whose name would remain well known to friends and critics of CUSO into and beyond the 1980s. Beer's involvement with CUSO dated back to its beginnings. The son of the headmaster at Pickering College in Newmarket, Ontario, and a nephew of John Holmes, Beer had his first taste of the developing world while still a student at Pickering. For part of the summer of 1960, he travelled into the interior of British Guiana with fellow student David Milne and their mentor, Guy Arnold, who later founded Canadian Voluntary Commonwealth Service (CVCS). In 1963, the year CVCS became part of CUSO, Beer abandoned his University of Toronto studies to do youth work in a still-tranquil Jamaica. He began a three-year term in Zambia in 1964 just prior to that country's independence under President Kenneth Kaunda, and like several other CUSO activists, he literally married into the cause of nationalist activism. Writing in the *Bulletin* in 1968, Beer had explained that his Zambian brother-in-law had "lost two years of his education while supporting the nationalist struggle." Through this family link and especially through his friendships with refugees from Rhodesia living in Zambia, Beer continued, he had come to understand that national liberation required sacrifice and struggle, perhaps even, in the case of Rhodesia, "the last and most foreboding method of winning freedom ... guerilla warfare."[42] Notwithstanding its acceptance of guerilla warfare as the ultimate form of liberation struggle, Beer's 1968 *Bulletin* article had been moderate in tone and more than a little idealistic about what young Canadians could contribute in support of national struggles. By 1973, Beer was regional field director for CUSO's ECSA region, a prime mover behind the Development

Charter and decentralization, and overall, much feistier in tone and approach than his 1968 self.[43] Dismissing the former *Bulletin* as "bland," Beer urged those responsible for the new *CUSO Forum* to make it relevant and interesting and to be the vanguard in development education by introducing such topics as "the trade and aid question – exposé of Canadian trade policies which blunt or negate our aid policies." It should also stop publishing "bland generalized commentary" by agencies like CIDA and "would you believe the World Bank!"[44]

The second issue of the new *Forum* made it clear that not everyone was happy with the periodical's new look and tone. Although the editor reported a mainly positive response to the inaugural issue, she acknowledged that for some readers it had moved *too* far left. "Looks like the Communist *Daily Worker* with pictures," declared someone in the External Affairs Office. More significantly, Bill McNeill, formerly a volunteer and coordinator in Nigeria and now CUSO's director of Canadian operations, took strong issue with Beer's recommendations for the *Forum*. His acid response to Beer's remarks about the *Bulletin* reflected the personal tensions as well as the ideological differences among some CUSO staff in this period: "I would argue that Robert McNamara's concern that the World Bank should be supporting reforms in land tenure patterns, tax laws and banking regulations, is infinitely more interesting and encouraging than the minutes of most CUSO termination conferences. And, would you believe, even more helpful than the E.C.A. [East and Central Africa] Development Charter."[45] Shortly thereafter, fed up with what he regarded as the triumph of ideology over pragmatism and a concomitant lack of decisiveness in management (the board had passed over him and chosen Murray Thomson to become the new executive director), McNeill left CUSO to become the long-serving executive director of WUSC.[46]

The challenge facing the *Forum* from radicalized RVs if, in the interest of balanced coverage, it continued to print traditional, upbeat accounts from volunteers still in the field was vividly demonstrated in the spring of 1974. The April-May cover story by a young volunteer teaching English in a girls' Catholic secondary school in Malawi prompted a withering commentary from an RV who had himself taught in Malawi, a one-party capitalist state with strong ties to South Africa: "What did we spend those hours arguing about what the hell we were doing in an elitist educational system of an evidently fascist country during CUSOMAL [CUSO/Malawi] meetings in 72 and 73 if the CUSO community, never mind the general public, is to be fed rose-tinted pap such as this article? ... Why did a majority of volunteers recommend a phasing out of

"Development Is Disturbance"

education in a recent survey [?]"[47] The *Forum* continued to give space to the kind of volunteer narrative that this RV dismissed as rose-tinted pap as well as to complaints from local committees whose recruitment and fundraising tasks were made harder by the political turn, and from others in the CUSO constituency who were simply impatient with "party line jargon" and "politicization."[48] Indeed, Ted Burke, who, as director of public affairs evidently had overall responsibility for the *Forum* at this time as well as for the preparation of publicity, recruitment, and fundraising materials, seemed to some on CUSO's left to be *too* concerned with balanced coverage and too cautious himself about political activism, especially after he gave *Forum* space to the views of right-winger Peter Worthington of the *Toronto Sun*.[49] Burke's approach ultimately proved to be a poor fit with CUSO's political orientation, and by the spring of 1975, he was no longer a part of the organization.[50]

Political Advocacy and the Focus on Southern Africa

The resolution passed at the 1969 AGM calling on CUSO to get involved in development education had not, as seen, gone as far as to authorize the organization "to become politically active on behalf of developing countries." And yet some in the CUSO constituency eagerly moved in that direction several years before the organization established its controversial "Dev Ed" Department. Over time, their criticisms of particular Canadian government policies and corporate investment decisions engendered significant public concern and produced sharp internal differences over matters of tactics and strategy.

The political turn and its fallout were particularly evident in regard to position-taking on southern Africa. By 1970, the policies and politics of the region were receiving an increasing level of critical attention both internationally and within Canada. The Sharpeville massacre of 1960 had generated a rise in black militancy in South Africa and increased international criticism of apartheid, while Prime Minister Harold Macmillan's "winds of change" speech in the same year signalled a less complacent attitude within Britain toward Africa's remaining white-minority regimes. Under pressure from anti-apartheid member countries, including Canada under John Diefenbaker, South Africa withdrew from the Commonwealth. From 1961, as the Republic of South Africa, it continued to pursue racially separatist policies.[51] Under successive Trudeau administrations, Canada regularly denounced South Africa's apartheid system. And yet, as Linda Freeman observes, "official support for full economic and diplomatic relations never wavered." It was the gap between denunciation and performance, particularly after the Trudeau government published its White Paper on Foreign Policy in June 1970, which prompted CUSO to speak out.[52]

CUSO did not have volunteers in the Republic of South Africa, but programming in East and Central Africa dated back to 1964, having begun in Tanzania, Zambia, and Uganda.[53] Having work in the region inevitably fostered a strong interest in the politics of southern Africa (hence the later restyling of the short form for the region from ECA to ECSA). In November 1970, CUSO's AGM passed a resolution urging the federal government to recognize the legitimacy of southern Africa liberation movements. The resolution focused on Rhodesia/Zimbabwe and South Africa and pointed out that Sweden and the World Council of Churches had already set precedents for assisting liberation movements. A press release on behalf of CUSO's board of directors declared that while CUSO was "a technical assistance agency" and not "a political pressure group ... the sensitivity of the majority of the CUSO constituency to the southern Africa issue cannot be ignored." CUSO was preparing a brief on the southern Africa situation to present to a House of Commons committee, the press release stated, and would also use it "as a basis for discussion by university, business, government and community groups." A 1970 report to a parliamentary subcommittee on international assistance chastised the federal government for continuing to promote trade with South Africa notwithstanding its assent to a UN resolution calling on member countries to refrain from collaborating or trading with the republic. In the spring of 1971, some CUSO staff members also prepared a brief on southern Africa for presentation to the Senate Committee on External Affairs.[54]

These interventions into the political realm elicited public criticism. A *Globe and Mail* editorial, written after the AGM had passed its resolution critical of Ottawa's southern Africa policies, declared that CUSO had gone "dangerously beyond its mandate."[55] When CUSO board member and *Globe* writer Clyde Sanger, who fully supported CUSO's position-taking on southern Africa, challenged the *Globe*'s editorial stance, the newspaper followed up with a statement whose perspective appeared to be widely shared: "The Globe does not quarrel with CUSO's right to take positions on political issues. It does question the Canadian Government's right to subsidize agencies which advocate the 'liberation' of people from governments which Ottawa recognizes as legitimate." Like other media, the *Globe* viewed CUSO's advocacy on the southern Africa issue in the context of the recent FLQ crisis in Quebec and French President Charles de Gaulle's intervention in Canadian politics three years earlier. External Affairs

Minister Mitchell Sharp made a similar comparison in a conversation with the director of CUSO's East and Central Africa program, Lawrence Cumming, a few weeks after the AGM had passed the controversial resolution on southern Africa. Sharp evidently felt that he had been blindsided by the resolution and was not mollified when Cumming assured him that it did not yet reflect official CUSO policy and was in any case about "activities in Canada only and not political involvement in our host countries." Reporting on his conversation with Sharp, Cumming wrote that the minister had said that CUSO could not expect to take political positions while receiving money from the federal government and that Canada could no more interfere in the internal affairs of southern African countries than France could be permitted to interfere in Canada's.[56]

CUSO's political turn also created headaches for those within the organization responsible for public relations and private-sector fundraising. One lawyer (a Q.C.) who had been a supporter wrote, "I think the work of CUSO has been excellent but going into the political arena will destroy it." A report to CUSO's board of directors written just a month after the resolution had been passed by the 1970 AGM claimed that it had already had a serious effect on CUSO fundraising "and certainly on CUSO's fund-raising potential."[57] In the wake of this kind of fallout, steps had to be taken to mend fences with major supporters. Business leaders had been important to CUSO's positive image and its fundraising efforts from its earliest days. A national advisory committee had been established in 1966 involving such men as Thomas Bata of Bata International; W.J. Bennett, president of the Iron Ore Company of Canada; and R.W. Southam, president of the *Ottawa Citizen*.[58] Although most of CUSO's funding now came from the federal government, maintaining good relations with prominent business and community leaders remained vital. Thus, in August 1971, a seminar called "CUSO and the Business Community" was convened. Among those in attendance were Lewis Perinbam from CIDA, members of CUSO's board of directors and senior staff, the chairman of its corporate fundraising campaign, and representatives of such companies as Alcan and Imperial Oil. The aim was to arrive at an arrangement that would not muzzle RVs speaking as individuals, while ensuring that statements made in CUSO's name had the approval of "management" and did not needlessly embarrass or offend CUSO supporters.[59]

In taking a critical position on Canada's acts of omission and commission in southern Africa in 1970 and thereafter, CUSO as an organization was neither unique nor a pioneer. Mainline churches, whether speaking just for their own denominations or ecumenically, were strong voices in support of liberation movements and social justice struggles in southern Africa, Latin America, and elsewhere from the late 1960s.[60] An important target for their activism was Canadian trade policy, as was shown in 1970 in the much discussed *Black Paper: An Alternative Policy for Canada towards Southern Africa*. Though CUSO RVs Richard Williams and Hugh Winsor were contributors to *The Black Paper*, the lead authors were the United Church of Canada's Garth Legge, area secretary for Africa, Latin America, and the Caribbean on the church's Board of World Mission (BWM), and University of Toronto political science professor Cranford Pratt, a respected scholarly exponent of "humane internationalism."[61] The four authors, all of whom had worked in East Africa, were spokesmen for a group provisionally calling itself the Committee for a Just Canadian Policy Towards Africa. Their paper provided a forceful critical analysis of the federal government's proposed policies on southern Africa as set out in the Trudeau government's *Foreign Policy for Canadians*. As indicated in its subtitle, *The Black Paper* made clear proposals for a more activist, explicitly anti-racist approach, an approach that would include providing non-military aid to liberation movements, not trading with South Africa, and certainly not continuing to grant it preferential Commonwealth trade rates.[62] As veteran scholar/activist John S. Saul has observed, *The Black Paper* provided "a carefully argued and principled ... response" to the federal white paper, and its conclusions became "axioms" for the larger liberation support efforts that emerged in the 1970s.[63]

As CUSO undertook more political advocacy on developing-world issues in the 1970s in partnership with ecumenical groups and respected academics, and with regionally based advocacy groups such as the Toronto Committee for the Liberation of Portugal's African Colonies (TCLPAC) and its successor, the Toronto Committee for the Liberation of Southern Africa (TCLSAC), whose founders included RVs, it was perhaps less likely to alienate erstwhile supporters and more likely to win a hearing than when it spoke as an isolated voice (though among such groups it was sometimes singled out for media criticism).[64] Meanwhile, CUSO also demonstrated its solidarity with ecumenical groups such as GATT-Fly by publicizing their ongoing strategies for pressuring the federal government to develop more favourable aid and trade policies with the developing world.[65]

While by the early 1970s CUSO was under fire from some of its own constituency for becoming too political – even in the ECSA region some volunteers were critical of its left-leaning politics[66] – the organization was simultaneously being accused by others in the fold of remaining too cautious about political issues. In addition to those in the anglophone side of CUSO who favoured more political activism, there was also pressure from CUSO's francophone wing, SUCO. At the time of CUSO's founding in 1961, SUCO had simply stood for Service Universitaire Canadien Outre-mer, a straightforward translation of Canadian University Service Overseas. The bilingual first issue of the *CUSO Bulletin* and the composition of CUSO's first slate of officers reflected the organization's sense of itself as acting for and in Quebec as well as the rest of Canada. Likewise, when board chairman King Gordon visited an orientation for French-speaking volunteers in 1966, he was impressed by their dedication and in a letter to his friend Prime Minister Pearson predicted that they would do "a great job *for Canada* overseas."[67] The difficulties of placing volunteers in former French African colonies on the same basis as other volunteers meant that such placements began later and were more costly, but by 1967, there were ninety volunteers in French-speaking Africa, often working in institutions established by French-Canadian missionaries. Over the next few years, this number grew rapidly.[68] CUSO's efforts to be bicultural and bilingual and efforts like Gordon's to engage with the francophone volunteers were, however, no guarantee of ongoing harmony. Nor was the missionary connection a guarantee of a conservative approach to SUCO's operations either within Canada or overseas. The status quo did not hold. From the late 1960s, SUCO increasingly sought greater independence in its relationship with CUSO, and by the early 1970s its evolution increasingly mirrored, or went beyond, the politics of other left-wing and separatist elements in Quebec.

With the support of executive director Frank Bogdasavich and as formalized through constitutional change, SUCO was largely autonomous in its home-base and overseas operations from 1968 onward, although the two organizations remained a single corporate body throughout the 1970s and as such submitted a joint annual budget to CIDA.[69] Employing socialist discourse to present its vision for political change in the developing world and taking the position that Quebec, like such countries as Angola, needed to be liberated from colonialism, SUCO was, at the same time, bureaucratically ambitious and financially profligate, with a Canadian staff and budget proportionately much higher than CUSO's. Despite its lack of any effective control over SUCO, CUSO was held accountable for its francophone counterpart's financial excesses as well as its increasingly radical politics. In his account of the "SUCO Connection," Ian Smillie maintains that many CUSO staff and board members in this period were afflicted by an Anglo or liberal guilt about Quebec that made them slow to distance themselves from ill-conceived SUCO policies and actions.[70] Others, however, were strongly attracted by its radical politics.[71]

Development as Disturbance

Relations with SUCO became increasingly complex and time-consuming during Murray Thomson's term as CUSO's executive director. It was on Thomson's watch, too, that development as "disturbance" came closest to being CUSO policy. For those who subscribed to the expression "Don't trust anyone over thirty,"[72] Thomson was an unlikely apostle for a disruptive approach to development, a middle-aged "mishkid" whose maternal grandfather had served for years as secretary of the Presbyterian Church in Canada's Foreign Missions Committee and whose parents and sister had been missionaries in China, where he himself had been born. Although Thomson remained close to his family, he grew away from his Presbyterian/United Church of Canada ties during his university years and became attracted to other avenues for social service. Eventually, Thomson's most important ties became those with Quakerism and peace work in Canada and Asia. It was through the latter that he met and married his Thai wife, Suteera, an academic, fellow peace activist, and feminist. His involvement with CUSO began in 1970 when he went to Thailand, first serving as field staff officer and then as regional field director of the Southeast Asia program. He returned to Canada as CUSO's executive director in 1974.[73]

What did Thomson mean by development as disturbance? Writing in 1973, he explained that for him it involved

> disturbance to ourselves and our organization, it means trying to define, isolate and attack obstacles, barriers, roadblocks to real development: trade barriers, arms races, greedy multinational corporations, elites (including ourselves) which are screwing up the process ... the sooner we get on with tackling one or two of them, *regardless of how the funding chips fall,* the sooner we will be on the road to development.[74]

Thomson's approach was also reflected in the principles in the Development Charter, which he had helped to draft, and by emerging broad trends in the organization. Upon taking office, he summarized these trends as representing a desire for "a shift – not a lurch or drastic change, but a shift – towards a more active, more public identification with the unrepresented of the world: the poor,

"Development Is Disturbance"

the oppressed, and the powerless, and away from too close identity with the elites of the world." Acknowledging that these political-activist trends within CUSO were probably not favoured by those who were more numerous in its broad constituency and who wanted to "continue to do what we have always done – promote high quality manpower to overseas countries – only do it better," Thomson indicated that the political trend seemed "to represent a majority of CUSO's Canadian-based, decision-making bodies: the Board and the AGM." It also appeared to be "the dominant voice" of ECSA, of the Latin American program, and of SUCO.[75]

In his final year as executive director, Thomson further characterized the divisions within CUSO as those between "socialist roaders," essentially those who supported the Development Charter and the activist trends he had described in 1974, and "pragmatists," those more concerned with CUSO's traditional goals.[76] While his own inclinations were with the socialist roaders, Thomson's pacifist style of management and his view that both sides had something useful to contribute to the organization made him reluctant to assert authority as executive director,[77] either to give the socialists' views dominance or, on the other hand, to make the final break with SUCO that his predecessor had set in motion and that many in CUSO now deemed necessary. (Troubled by the national symbolism of such a break, he himself had a last-minute change of heart on the question at the thirteenth AGM and instead encouraged a majority of delegates to opt for one more effort at compromise with SUCO.)[78] Though Thomson would later be criticized for a participatory management style that resulted in delays in decision making (one staff member called his approach "participatory anarchy"[79]) and for allowing loose cannons and ideological tensions to go unchecked, even his critics remained sincere admirers of his personal commitment to the broad principles in which he believed. The photograph of Gandhi that hung above his desk and his own gentle behaviour made the label "the Mahatma," by which he was widely known, seem appropriate. As for complaints that his management style was ineffective, some of Thomson's responses to internal differences on such matters as recruitment appear in retrospect to have been deft political manoeuvres as well as evidence of an inclusive management style.[80]

By contrast, Thomson's successor as executive director, Robin Wilson, was anxious to assert his authority as a way of dealing with budget problems, with dispersed decision making within CUSO, and with the loose cannon that SUCO had become. Wilson came to CUSO as an outsider and as someone without

Murray Thomson *(left)*, who became CUSO's executive director in 1974, and Ian Smillie, who headed the organization from 1979 to 1983, brought dedication – and very different leadership styles – to the job. Photo of Thomson from *CUSO Forum,* January 1974; photo of Smillie from *CUSO Forum,* Summer 1980. Both courtesy of Cuso International.

executive experience in a development NGO. Although he had worked with the YMCA in the Caribbean, his only experience in NGO management had been with the Y in Thunder Bay.[81] Not surprisingly, given this background and his determination to take charge, the divisions within CUSO became even sharper under his management, contributing to crises that appeared for a time to threaten the organization's survival.

It was not that Wilson was opposed to the broad causes and values espoused by CUSO, or even to taking strong political positions. As executive director, for instance, he wrote in February 1977 to the president of the Royal Bank of Canada, urging that in view of Chile's flawed human rights record since 1973, the bank should reconsider being part of a consortium that was then lending money to the Chilean government.[82] After an article appeared in the *Toronto Sun* in July 1977 denouncing CUSO and CIDA and excoriating SUCO (for its anti-Zionism,

"Development Is Disturbance"

its support for the PLO, and its separatism), Wilson gamely joined his SUCO counterpart in writing a letter to the *Sun* in which the two men attempted to respond to the newspaper's charges. In the same month, Wilson tried to deal with these and other charges against CUSO/SUCO on a television program whose aggressive host made use of inflammatory SUCO documents with which Wilson was unfamiliar.[83] But even public efforts such as these to defend CUSO/SUCO could not offset the ill will that Wilson created among staff and board members. His attempts to rein in the dispersed decision making that had come about through decentralization angered the more radical elements within CUSO, while his blunt style and uncollegial approach to management made him vulnerable as an outsider to CUSO's "tribalism."[84]

Early on in his term as executive director, Wilson gave offence with his seemingly dismissive attitude to what was called the "basic strategies debate." In 1977, the *CUSO Forum* devoted two full issues to the debate, which had originated in the ECSA region. Some of the broad issues involved, particularly political activism versus pragmatism, had been under discussion for several years. By the mid-1970s, there was also considerable soul searching about the appropriateness of Western-style education and medicine in development programming. Far from being unique to CUSO, this kind of reflection was taking place in secular and faith-based NGOs across North America and Western Europe. Influenced by internationally known figures like Ivan Illich and Paulo Freire and by the kinds of initiatives associated with China's "barefoot doctors" (two of whom had attended CUSO's 1974 AGM), some NGOs, including the Christian missions that had pioneered educational and medical modernization in the developing world, were rethinking their earlier involvement in this kind of work.[85] In several countries where CUSO worked, staff and volunteers considered suspending the recruitment of secondary-school teachers and medical professionals, or actually did so. Margaret Hilson was a representative voice for this approach in the CUSO debate over health programming when, writing from a public-health posting in Honduras, she defended CUSO/Botswana's recent decision to suspend the recruitment of general practitioners. Formerly a volunteer nurse in India and later a member of the CUSO/Ottawa health team, Hilson now declared that sending another CUSO doctor to replace a volunteer predecessor in a Botswana hospital would be "counterproductive to the development of health services in that country" so long as there was "no possibility of replacing that physician with a national health worker." Hilson's opinion was "as infuriating as it is sad," countered Dr. Doug Ramsay of Molepolole, Botswana.

Like several other contributors to the published exchange, Ramsay also decried the CUSO/Botswana decision to cease recruiting teachers. Both decisions had been ideologically driven and made under pressure, he argued, and should be reconsidered in a mail-in ballot.[86] Hilson's and Ramsay's views were presented as part of a passionate and largely constructive exchange that had first taken place in the CUSO/Botswana newsletter and then been reproduced in the *Forum* as the second instalment of the basic strategies debate. Wilson, though, was perhaps reacting to more extreme positions set out in the first instalment[87] when he wrote and circulated an overview paper under the inflammatory title "Decentralization and the B.S. Debate." Predictably, it elicited anger, and sharp divisions on the issues that he introduced.[88]

Matters related to Wilson's leadership finally came to a head in January 1979 when he presented the board of directors with a controversial policy to restore to the executive director the authority to hire and fire staff. Writing several years later about the furore and Wilson's proposed policy change, Ian Smillie declared the change entirely reasonable and "long overdue." But it was misunderstood by those on the board who perceived only Wilson's lack of fit with the CUSO family and its way of doing things. After fierce internal debate, the board voted to fire Wilson.[89]

Overseas Political Activism and Its Perils

Wilson's firing exacerbated some ongoing concerns about CUSO, not only about administrative matters and the organization's failure to rein in its controversial francophone sibling, but also about CUSO's political activism within a number of developing countries. As political advocacy within Canada made clear, ECSA was the region most characteristically associated with an activist approach.[90] By the late 1960s, a number of Zambia-based volunteers and staff had personal contacts with liberation movement leaders in the refugee community from Rhodesia/Zimbabwe. Tanzania was also a site of political connections and inspiration. Independent from 1964 under its widely admired first president, Julius Nyerere, the Republic of Tanzania seemed for a time a hopeful model for the entire region. The type of socialism espoused by Nyerere, his emphasis on blending elements of modernization with village-based traditionalism *(ujamaa)*, and his openness to assistance from skilled Westerners willing to work toward the country's goal of self-reliance made it a magnet for volunteers from Europe and North America.[91] Dar es Salaam, the cosmopolitan capital, and its nearby beaches attracted vacationing CUSO volunteers from the entire region as well as those with placements in the city, and it was a base for local field staff and regional gatherings.[92] There, by 1969, representatives of several militant liberation movements were making contact with CUSO staff, who began inviting some of the militants to in-country orientations for newly arrived volunteers. In the early 1970s, using funds available for projects and taking advantage of the decentralization process in CUSO that allowed for more regional autonomy, ECSA field staff established new support programs for liberation movements in Angola, Mozambique, and Zimbabwe.[93] At the same time, advocacy for such movements was stepped up in Canada, especially through organizations like TCLPAC and TCLSAC, whose membership included Marxists like John S. Saul as well as more moderate friends of the liberation cause such as Cranford and Renate Pratt.[94]

Humanitarian assistance to liberation movements was not inconsistent with Canadian foreign policy during the mid- to late 1970s. In 1973, under pressure from African leaders and local groups, the Commonwealth Heads of Government Meeting, assembled in Ottawa, issued a communiqué recognizing the legitimacy of liberation movement struggles to win "full human rights and self-determination," though as noted later by the *Canadian Annual Review* in its account of the meeting, "The developed states, especially Canada and the United Kingdom, interpreted 'struggle' to be non-violent in nature." The following year External Affairs Minister Mitchell Sharp made it government policy to provide "peaceful humanitarian aid" (albeit not without delays in actual implementation in the face of media criticism). CIDA provided guidelines for organizations wishing to establish humanitarian and development projects in support of "the indigenous populations in southern Africa who are victims of racist and apartheid policies." Since Canada had already joined in the UN condemnation of the illegal Ian Smith regime in Rhodesia, humanitarian aid for that country's liberation struggle was relatively non-controversial, but for the next several years even the African National Congress (ANC) in South Africa was not excluded from such aid.[95] CUSO was just one of a number of secular and faith-based NGOs to apply for the new CIDA funding. It was also just one of a number of bodies, including organized labour and ecumenical groups, to facilitate visits to Canada by liberation movement leaders in the mid- and late 1970s.[96]

CUSO, however, was the NGO about which foreign-aid skeptics were often most uneasy. It was still the single largest recipient of funds from CIDA's NGO Division. Indeed, it relied overwhelmingly on annual CIDA funding for its very existence. This, together with the socialist stance of some of its most vocal RVs and staff members and the fact that liberation movements with which it was associated accepted assistance from Communist states, made it an obvious target for critics. When in 1983 an extreme right-wing group, Citizens for Foreign Aid Reform (C-FAR), belatedly published an attack on government policies that facilitated aid to such movements, it was CUSO it singled out, accusing it of using taxpayer dollars to support both "Soviet-backed terrorists in Africa" and "public relations work here in Canada on behalf of these groups" in violation of Revenue Canada guidelines.[97]

David Beer played a recurring role in or behind much of the controversy, a tireless advocate for politicized development support within Canada and a well-connected activist on the ground. Accompanied by his Zambian family, he had returned to Toronto in 1967 to resume his undergraduate studies but remained very much involved with CUSO, representing the Toronto local committee on the CUSO board of directors and acting as a key figure in the push for decentralization in the overseas regions. In 1969, he went back to Zambia as CUSO field officer, and from 1972 to 1974 he was regional field director of the ECSA region. Back in Canada, he served briefly as director of the Dev Ed Department and for a time was national fieldworker for the ecumenical development-education initiative Ten Days for World Development. In 1978, at age thirty-seven (relatively old by CUSO standards), the peripatetic Beer once again returned to Zambia.[98]

As the Lusaka-based regional representative of CUSO's ECSA programming, responsible for coordinating a budget of $1.7 million, Beer was front and centre when, in August 1979, newly elected Prime Minister Joe Clark and several other members of his short-lived government and representatives of the Canadian media came to Zambia for the Commonwealth Heads of Government Meeting being held in Lusaka. It was a time when guerilla activity in Zimbabwe had escalated in response to Ian Smith's most recent effort to undermine the independence struggle through a show of compromise with moderates. Some 60,000 Zimbabwean refugees were living in Zambia. Most were linked ethnically to ZAPU (Zimbabwe African People's Union), the militant group led by Joshua Nkomo and Edward Ndlovu and the one with which Beer and CUSO were chiefly involved. From 1976, under pressure from the Organization of African Unity, ZAPU had joined forces with Robert Mugabe's ZANU (Zimbabwe African National Union) to form the "Patriotic Front."[99] Despite Beer's efforts to prepare an itinerary for the visiting Canadians that would present the cause of Zimbabwean liberation and the work of Canadian NGOs assisting it as fully and favourably as possible, the visit brought to a head several years of frequently critical media coverage.[100] From 1976, CUSO had supported a major humanitarian program for Zimbabwean refugees in Zambia. The program included such components as a nursery and a poultry project, and other organizations (including Oxfam, the United Church of Canada, the Canadian Catholic Organization for Development and Peace, and Save the Children) also supported it. By 1979, the program was being described as CUSO's "major priority" in the ECSA region.[101]

In response to ongoing questions about CUSO's activities in southern Africa, Beer and others had repeatedly declared that CUSO funds were not spent on arms for guerilla movements in Zimbabwe or South Africa or elsewhere where liberation movements were taking place. Although most Canadian political officials and media representatives who came to Lusaka for the Commonwealth gathering were supportive of what they were learning about CUSO's humanitarian work, Beer recalls, some in the media remained skeptical. The reports they filed reflected their skepticism and were filled with inflammatory content. A *Toronto Sun* story headed "Funny 'farm'" claimed that a so-called farm was really a base for guerilla operations and that MP Doug Roche had been prevented from visiting it. A *Globe and Mail* article by Norman Webster began, "Many Canadians think all members of the Patriotic Front are terrorists. David Beer, from Newmarket, has them over for dinner. He also hands over lashings of Canadian government money to them." Webster made it clear that he did not accept Beer's claim that there was "no question of CUSO money going to buy arms or train guerillas." Predictably, the negative fallout included indignant letters to the editor.[102]

Ongoing embarrassments from SUCO, the controversial firing of Robin Wilson, and highly charged press reports from Zambia: how did CUSO survive the multiple crises? The year 1979 did prove to be something of a near-death experience for the organization, and it was reined in. Following the firing of Wilson and the internal dissent that resulted, CUSO was told by the secretary of state's office that "in light of these circumstances we have found it necessary to review the entire situation and re-assess CIDA's involvement with CUSO/SUCO." CUSO's budget was frozen at the preceding year's level, and it was asked for assurances that participation in partisan politics would end.[103] In April, Lewis Perinbam, by now a vice-president at CIDA, explained that while CIDA had no intention of taking over CUSO, it would ensure that the organization was held accountable for its use of public funds.[104] A directive from CIDA to the CUSO board followed. In the face of CUSO's internal problems, the board was asked to name an interim management group composed of two experienced non-staff persons "to administer the organization until further notice ... This group will be empowered to take all steps necessary to ensure effective management, including staff changes." The directive went on to state that CIDA's continuing contractual arrangements for CUSO's services would depend on those steps having been taken by October 1979. With CUSO's acceptance of these conditions, CIDA tentatively approved its budget, albeit with cuts.[105]

Ian Smillie became CUSO's new executive director, taking over in October from the interim director who had administered the organization's affairs since January.[106] Smillie had the background and temperament to get the organization back on track and restore government confidence. Following his two years as a volunteer in Sierra Leone, he had worked in CUSO staff positions in West Africa and then for other development organizations at home and abroad, including a period as coordinator of programs for CARE in Bangladesh. In 1975, he had co-founded a new NGO called Inter Pares. Even during his years away from CUSO, though, he had remained a concerned part of the CUSO community. More pragmatist than socialist roader in terms of Murray Thomson's categories, Smillie took several steps as the new executive director to reassure CIDA and the federal government generally that CUSO was still a worthwhile partner in development work. He participated in the selection of respected new members for the board of directors, for instance, and supported the work of independent committees to review CUSO's constitution, finances, and administration. He prepared carefully for early meetings with External Affairs Minister Flora MacDonald and her Liberal successor, Mark MacGuigan, at the same time working to shore up relationships and confidence within the CUSO family.[107] Only one important relationship was not shored up: the one with SUCO. In December 1980, the joint AGM of CUSO and SUCO unanimously passed a motion to end their connection: henceforth, they were to be two entirely separate organizations, each submitting its own budget to CIDA.[108]

Since CUSO's status was technically that of an NGO, the federal government could not simply have killed it off as it had already done with the CYC, but it could, in theory, have discontinued all funding to CUSO, as it was to do with SUCO in 1984 – in effect, starving it to death.[109] That CUSO was *not* dealt with in this way despite the crises of 1979 was not merely a matter of Smillie's reassuring presence as the new executive director. The reality was that CIDA had a history of symbiotic relationships with NGOs like CUSO; the break with SUCO was unprecedented. Writing about the period from the late 1960s to the mid-1980s, Cranford Pratt and Tim Brodhead outline the benefits such relationships brought to CIDA: "The alliance of CIDA and the NGOs," they state,

> was widely seen to assist the Canadian aid effort. CIDA accepted that the NGOs had relationships with Third World institutions and communities that were more intimate and closer to the grass roots than could ever be achieved by an official aid agency. NGOs could therefore produce projects that would reflect felt community needs and would typically reach poor communities and help meet their needs. It was also recognized that the cost of some types of development assistance, particularly of recruiting and sending volunteers overseas, was much less when undertaken by NGOs than when done directly by government or by "for profit" firms.[110]

The summer after he took over as executive director, Smillie insisted in a *CUSO Forum* interview that what the Canadian taxpayers got from CUSO through the CIDA nexus was "a heck of a bargain for their money." The CIDA grant to CUSO cost individual Canadians only about forty-five cents per year each, he maintained, and with that money, CUSO could work at a grassroots level, supporting "dozens of small projects that bring clean drinking water, better health, nutrition, education and food to people who are making [progress] towards that end themselves."[111] *CUSO Forum* at this time was being sent to MPs and diplomats as well as to CUSO's immediate constituency. The kinds of unproblematic, non-ideological grassroots benefits that Smillie stressed as outcomes in the interview were undoubtedly meant to be reassuring to this larger audience. These were visually verifiable "feel-good" outcomes.

More subtly, some within CUSO believed, the symbiotic relationship with CIDA could at times involve government use of CUSO as a kind of foreign-policy stalking horse, a means of testing Canadian public reaction to possible government involvement with particular Third World groups, places, or policies, or of making indirect and informal contacts that might later be followed up. There was speculation, for instance, in 1974, that SUCO's sponsorship of Hortensia Allende's visit to Canada following the death of her Marxist husband during the Chilean coup led by General Pinochet had the private support of Prime Minister Trudeau and was a means of trying to anticipate public reaction to accepting Chilean refugees.[112] In the same year, though External Affairs

Minister Mitchell Sharp refused to meet MPLA leader Dr. Agostinho Neto from Angola during his visit to Canada, CUSO RV Jean Pelletier, at the time SUCO's overseas operations director, arranged a private meeting for Neto with his father, Secretary of State Gérard Pelletier, and Trudeau.[113] The fundraising visit to Canada by the two Zimbabwean Patriotic Front leaders in the summer of 1979, which CUSO helped arrange and for which it was sharply criticized in the media, was known about in advance by CIDA, Smillie told *Forum* readers. Indeed, prior to the outburst of media criticism, CIDA had been "at least tacitly supportive."[114] CUSO's involvement in Cuba, advocated by some in CUSO from the early 1960s and initiated following Frank Bogdasavich's visit there in 1969 to meet Cuba's request for some specific types of high-level technical assistance, was not opposed by CIDA, even though CUSO was evidently the first NGO from a non-Communist country to send volunteers to the Communist island. CIDA in fact provided special funding to expand CUSO's university-assistance project in Cuba prior to beginning its own bilateral program there in 1974.[115] It continued to provide some funding to CUSO's agricultural and health work in Cuba for a time, even after the federal government's bilateral program was terminated in 1978. It was not until 1980 that Mark MacGuigan as external affairs minister in Trudeau's new government stopped all government aid to Cuba (notwithstanding his boss's private objections), including the small amount channeled through CUSO "so as not to indirectly subsidize Cuban adventurism abroad."[116]

Of course, in circumstances in which the relationship with CUSO ceased to be a heck of a bargain and instead became a headache for CIDA because of media and taxpayer outcry, the financial implications could go beyond ending modest funding for special projects. The annual grant could be cut severely, as had happened in 1974 when Murray Thomson was executive director, and again in the wake of the Wilson firing. Or budget approval could be delayed for a long period as an indirect way of sending a message to an errant CUSO, or simply because wary government officials at various levels were going over its budget projections with a fine-tooth comb.[117] But though the risk of government funding being denied was an ongoing source of concern, on the whole CIDA seems not to have taken that step often during these decades. As an outside commentator observed in a 1975 report, CIDA's relationship with CUSO was "a rare example of government restraint and cooperation vis a vis a non-governmental organization."[118] The cooperative relationship was undoubtedly helped by the fact that over the years so many people from CUSO, beginning with Lewis Perinbam himself, had become part of CIDA.[119]

External Affairs Minister Flora MacDonald visiting CUSO's support project for
Zimbabwean refugees while attending the Commonwealth Conference in Lusaka in
August 1979. *CUSO Forum*, Spring and Summer 1981. Courtesy of Cuso International.

Furthermore, even at the height of controversies there were politicians from
all parties who stood by CUSO and pointed to its record of positive accomplishments. They included Andrew Brewin and Pauline Jewett of the NDP; Liberals
Iona Campagnolo and even Mark MacGuigan; and Tories Gordon Fairweather,
Doug Roche, Flora MacDonald, and Walter McLean. Some, like McLean, had
long-standing and deeply personal involvement with CUSO, as did Senator
Eugene Forsey, whose daughter Helen was an RV.[120] In 1978, as an Opposition
MP visiting China, Indonesia, and Bangladesh, Roche had toured a CUSO-
supported self-help project for Bangladeshis that he subsequently praised in
Reader's Digest. CUSO Forum quoted Roche as calling Proshika "one of the best,
if not THE best, Canadian aid project[s] in the Third World."[121] Roche and Flora
MacDonald were with Prime Minister Joe Clark when he travelled to Zambia
for the Commonwealth Conference in the summer of 1979, MacDonald in her
role as external affairs minister. Both these Red Tories refuted charges made by
the *Globe* and the *Sun* claiming that CUSO supported liberation movements
militarily.[122] Roche, who was chairman of the External Affairs and Defence
Committee, declared that he had in fact visited what the *Sun* had referred to

In 1980, former Liberal cabinet minister Iona Campagnolo toured CUSO's Kampuchean refugee camp in Thailand and subsequently became actively involved in its fundraising campaign. Here *(centre),* she joins CUSO's Sharon Capeling and Ian Smillie at an Ottawa press conference. Courtesy of Cuso International.

as an out-of-bounds "Funny 'farm'" run by CUSO and that it was in fact a farm rather than a guerilla military base.[123] Flora MacDonald, who had earlier served on CUSO's Kingston local committee, opted out of an official conference event during her stay in Zambia in order to visit a CUSO-supported refugee project. Back in Canada, when a *Globe* editorial followed up on Webster's earlier article by denouncing the way that Beer and CUSO "splashed [money] about on a succession of chic or strenuously partisan causes" and by urging MacDonald to rein CUSO in, she instead praised the Beers' contributions in Zambia. More-over, through her visit to the refugee project, where she happily mingled with a group of children, she had provided CUSO with a wonderful publicity photo.[124]

There were also loyal friends in the media. In addition to prominent jour-nalists who, like Clyde Sanger, were, in a sense, part of the CUSO family,[125] there were others who, when they criticized CUSO, did so more in sorrow that its many accomplishments were being harmed or overlooked than in anger or disgust at its alleged missteps.[126] Journalists also wrote upbeat stories about the mundane, non-ideological development contributions of people such as CUSO's Betty and Ed Wilson, a middle-aged farm couple from Bracken, Saskatchewan, serving in Tanzania, where Joe Clark visited their wheat farm.[127] And small-town newspapers from various parts of Canada continued to print stories about young

"Development Is Disturbance"

– and sometimes not-so-young – volunteers from their communities who were reportedly doing good work in the early CUSO tradition and without any overt ideological involvement.[128]

The Non-Politics of Gender and Race

Questions about the roles of men and women within CUSO and about the specific problems confronting women in developing countries were not significant issues in CUSO's turbulent politics in the 1970s. These two related but distinct questions in fact received scant coverage in CUSO documents and publications before about the mid-1970s. Nor did they figure in the basic strategies debate. Indeed, even in 1985, gender issues were not sufficiently salient to receive coverage in Ian Smillie's history of CUSO (though in an otherwise glowing review he was mildly reproached by RV and feminist activist Marnie Girvan for his inattention to "the 'Women's Liberation Movement' within CUSO").[129] The impact of second-wave feminism on CUSO's organizational culture came later and differed in significant respects from feminism's impact on other institutions and organizations in the larger national landscape. Both in this regard and in terms of its awakening to the cluster of concerns associated with the term *women in development* (WID), CUSO was largely in step with other development NGOs.

As a development NGO with a disproportionately high number of female volunteers, almost all of them recent graduates of universities or professional programs, CUSO could not, of course, remain isolated from the feminist currents that became part of the *Zeitgeist* of the last half of the 1960s. Thus in 1969, some participants in an RV conference in western Canada drafted a resolution calling on CUSO to make "a concerted effort ... to increase the representation of women" as delegates to the AGM, on field staff, and in the Ottawa secretariat, given the fact that women were "disgracefully under-represented" in those groups.[130] But it was not until 1975, five years after the publication of the *Report* of the Royal Commission on the Status of Women in Canada, that the *Forum* reported on an investigation into the status of women as CUSO staff members. The report was followed up by recommendations from the interregional meeting at which it had been presented for increasing women's numbers in senior staff positions in Ottawa and abroad and ensuring that women were "centrally involved in CUSO decision-making" and equitably paid.[131] In the same year, reflecting the new mood – and perhaps editor Bob Stanley's raised consciousness – the *Forum* also printed letters to the editor that drew attention to sexism in such matters as CUSO's recruitment and advertising materials.[132]

Gender-based inequities on the work front and numerous mundane forms of sexism in Canada had by that time been receiving attention from middle-class women's organizations and from university women and feminist journalists for almost a decade.[133] In accounting for the apparently later feminist assertiveness within CUSO, it is worth recalling some aspects of gender relations touched on in Chapter 2, especially the easy camaraderie that seems to have existed between male and female volunteers in the first Development Decade and the sense of broadened horizons and expanded frontiers that came to young women through the very fact of their overseas placements. These personal development experiences appear to contrast strongly with the sense of frustration that arose among young women in New Left organizations on Canadian university campuses as they grew to resent their inferior roles and sexual exploitation in a movement nominally devoted to new and broader understandings of justice issues.[134] Furthermore, such personal-as-political activities as the production in 1968 by McGill University students of the *Birth Control Handbook,* and the Abortion Caravan that made its protesting way from BC to Ottawa in 1970,[135] did not perhaps seem as urgent to CUSO's female volunteers. A policy of making birth control pills available to single as well as married volunteers when they went abroad seems to have been approved by CUSO Health Services by the late 1960s.[136] In addition, the 1975 CUSO task force recommending the appointment of more women to staff positions contributed fairly quickly and without discernible resistance to women's increased presence in the CUSO/ Ottawa secretariat. Sharon Capeling, coordinator of orientation from 1974 to 1977, recalled that under Murray Thomson, women "got a much better shake from CUSO than they'd ever had before."[137] Likewise, as director of program funding, Marilyn Duchesne observed in 1977, "I feel that we have come a long way in CUSO over the last few years – insofar as women moving into top and middle management positions – but I don't want us to rest on our laurels." There were fewer increases in women as field staff, and no woman would hold the position of executive director until 1990, seven years after Margaret Catley-Carlson became president of CIDA.[138]

As for a focus on the specific needs of Third World women in development programming, which Duchesne also made part of her mandate,[139] it is perhaps only in retrospect that the emergence of such a focus seems to have been late in taking place in CUSO and analogous organizations. Like their Peace Corps counterparts, CUSO volunteers in the 1960s were anxious to be sensitive to the cultural norms of their host countries. As explained in Chapter 2, CUSO's early male volunteer leaders in India wanted their female counterparts to behave with circumspection so as not to transgress prevailing patriarchal norms. They were far from being unconcerned about the glaring gender inequalities that were part of everyday life in India, but at the same time they were anxious not to interfere in cultural matters and risk repeating what they believed had been everyday acts of Western cultural imperialism by their colonial and missionary predecessors.[140] How and when did things change? In conjunction with the feminism that was part of left and liberal mainstream thinking in North America and Europe in the late 1960s and early 1970s, the publication of Danish economist Ester Boserup's *Women's Role in Economic Development,* which argued that development had actually made things worse for Third World women, was a vital catalyst in raising awareness about the need for a conscious focus on women in development planning. During the next few years what would come to be called a WID approach worked its way into the discussions and conceptual frameworks of international organizations like the UN and national agencies like USAID and CIDA and numerous NGOs. In 1975, CIDA hired a special adviser on women and development.[141]

A year earlier, Margaret Hilson had sought to raise CUSO's awareness of the subject of women and development when, returning from a huge gathering of NGO delegates in Bucharest held concurrently with the UN World Population Conference, she publicized statements by both gatherings that reflected the new consciousness. (In a closing statement, the NGO gathering had declared, for instance, that governments "should take particular steps to achieve integration of women into every stage of the development process of the 2nd development decade. The economic contribution of women as mothers and providers of food both in rural and urban areas should be fully recognized.")[142] But it took the beginning of International Women's Year (IWY), 1975, to prompt the *Forum* to do a feature issue on the subject of women and development. The issue led off with an article by RV and former board member Michael Sinclair, who counselled CUSO to recognize the limitations of what it could do on the women-and-development front and instead to concentrate on "highly selective efforts – in a few places, carefully researched."[143] Yet even International Women's

David Beer *(left)* and Sithembiso Nyoni, executive officer of the Organization of Rural Associations for Progress (ORAP) in Zimbabwe. Nyoni visited CUSO's Ottawa office in 1983 after attending the World Council of Churches' gathering in Vancouver. *CUSO Forum*, November 1983. Courtesy of Cuso International.

Year was not enough to make women and development the *Forum*'s cover story in that feature issue, for the burning CUSO concern at the time was CUSO/SUCO politics at the most recent AGM.

Nor was coverage of WID issues sustained in CUSO publications during the "Women's Decade" that followed IWY despite the ongoing attention to such issues by staff members such as Marilyn Duchesne and the subsequent founding by long-time CUSO supporter Norma Walmsley of MATCH International, a pioneering Canadian NGO devoted to establishing small-scale projects for women in the developing world.[144] Significantly, the reminiscences and observations featured in the *Forum*'s twentieth-anniversary issue in the summer of 1981, all of them written by male contributors, contained only a single, passing, reference to an initiative specifically directed to women.[145] The limited coverage of women's issues and of WID projects in this period may seem all the more surprising in that during the late 1970s and early 1980s, the *Forum* editor was Sharon Capeling, who would later become a highly regarded specialist on women's issues in development with the UN.[146] Certainly, when Capeling began

"Development Is Disturbance"

publishing special *Forum* issues on each of CUSO's geographic regions, starting in 1979 with the West Africa region, accounts of projects that specifically targeted women were part of the coverage,[147] and overall, there was significantly more attention to WID-type issues by the time CUSO marked its twenty-fifth anniversary. What seems clear, however, is that topics related to macroeconomic frameworks and liberation struggles and daunting new challenges such as the Kampuchean refugee crisis in Thailand continued to outrank WID issues in terms of coverage in CUSO media even during the Women's Decade. And men's voices continued to dominate in recounting CUSO's roles in these areas.

By the late 1990s in Europe and North America, there was an abundance of writing by development specialists and feminist scholars dealing with the numerous theoretical approaches and specific projects deployed to assist developing-world women during the preceding three decades. Framed first as WID, then as WAD (women and development), and finally as GAD (gender and development), these efforts, the literature generally agreed, had made disappointingly little headway, especially in helping the poorest of the poor. CUSO alumni-turned-development-specialists were among those who contributed overviews of this vast subject.[148] There is nothing in what they or others have written to indicate that CUSO was particularly late or particularly anemic among NGOs in taking up the challenge of programming to assist women. Indeed, CUSO and CUSO alumni worked closely and cooperatively with MATCH and played leadership roles in this new and innovative NGO from the time of its founding. And Proshika, the celebrated rural self-help organization that CUSO nurtured in Bangladesh from 1975, served as a departure point when CUSO became directly involved in a women's program there at the end of the decade.[149] While CUSO's earlier involvement in family-planning in India came out of India's concern to control its population rather than as programming for women, the CUSO personnel who participated in the family-planning work were unquestionably attuned to women's special needs and concerns. A "robust masculinity"[150] may well have persisted among senior male staff in CUSO even beyond the 1970s, but that did not preclude the creation of specific WID projects or the appointment of personnel anxious to promote such projects. During the 1980s, WID became solidly established within CUSO, a "motherhood cause" rather than a source of divisiveness.

Even less than gender did race issues become part of the internal conflicts of CUSO's 1970s. Perhaps because opposition to racism as a societal phenomenon and a barrier to development was taken as a given within its organizational culture, race issues as such were not typically in the foreground in CUSO. Nor did CUSO become involved in interrogating and refashioning its practices around recruitment and staffing in a systematic and formal way even in the 1980s but rather moved forward in an ad hoc fashion. In this respect, it reflected larger national patterns wherein ripple effects from postcolonialism's consciousness-raising and changing demographics began to affect institutional practices on diversity within Canada only late in the twentieth century.[151]

As noted in Chapter 1, 1960s volunteers saw themselves as more open and sensitive than their colonial-era predecessors in regard to establishing relationships with host nationals. Race sensitivity had been encouraged both by the gentle calls for humility from early mentors such as Donald Faris and Lewis Perinbam and by the much more overt efforts at consciousness-raising at the orientations of the late 1960s. Warnings against turning to expatriate communities and especially to "Brits" for their social lives had also been part of the preparation of new volunteers.[152] High-minded pre-departure attitudes and advice from mentors were, of course, no guarantee of racial sensitivity once volunteers were on the ground, as a surviving piece of volunteer-authored racist doggerel from the mid-1960s makes clear. (Circulated among some RVs at the time of CUSO's fiftieth anniversary, it produced understandable embarrassment, although one RV acknowledged that her early letters home from that period were even more of an embarrassment.)[153] Given the fact that the young volunteers were being dispatched to help "modernize" less developed countries and that they came from a nation that had historically fashioned its immigration policy and many social policies along race lines, it would have been surprising if they had all maintained attitudes of openness in everyday encounters and eschewed racially offensive remarks in their private writings. The so-called Marjorie Michelmore affair that resulted in international headlines in 1961 when a newly arrived Peace Corps volunteer in Nigeria unknowingly dropped a postcard inscribed with negative comments on the country's sanitation practices only to have it picked up and publicized by an angry university student provided an early cautionary lesson for all volunteers, not just those in the Peace Corps.[154]

While there can be no gainsaying the fact that "the helping imperative" among young Western volunteers in development had significant legacies from the colonial past,[155] the differences in approach that resulted from the new predisposition and context and from diverse admonitions from mentors and critics should not be minimized. Indeed, an article about volunteer socializing, seemingly written with VSO personnel in East Africa particularly in mind but reprinted in the *CUSO Forum* in 1974, maintained that in their desire to distinguish themselves from their colonial predecessors young volunteers sometimes went overboard and created an unfortunate impression, especially in rural areas, by "their misjudged matey-ness" and their too-casual approach to dress and social behaviour.[156] Lewis Perinbam may well have heard stories of such excesses, and he probably had well-developed antennae for detecting falsity in racial bonhomie at all levels, but when he addressed CUSO's 1972 AGM in his capacity as director of CIDA's NGO Division, it was positive changes in attitude and practice between the West and the non-West since the bad old days of colonialism that he emphasized. And among agencies demonstrating those changes, CUSO/SUCO was a "'flagship' ... It demonstrates ... that it is possible to break through the barriers of the past, and to move from the patronising attitudes of the colonial era to those founded on equality and respect."[157] Aspirations to be more open and egalitarian in race matters in work and personal relationships than had been typical of even the most liberal of colonial-era missionaries and officials were a reality, even if they were not always met. Furthermore, in CUSO's contentious 1970s, such aspirations typified both those who favoured pragmatic development strategies and those who urged political approaches and acts of solidarity with liberation-movement struggles. Both groups regarded socioeconomic circumstances, particularly as exacerbated by centuries of colonialism, rather than race-based human deficiencies as responsible for problems of underdevelopment. That being the case, it came to seem appropriate to bring voices from the non-West into conversations about how to "do" development.

As of 1971, with the inclusion of the Thailand local committee, the AGM for the first time had voting delegates from a developing country. Staff in the ECSA region led the way in calling for representation on the board of directors from countries where CUSO had work.[158] As for efforts to inject ethnic and racial diversity into CUSO's volunteer and staff profile, these bore fruit incrementally and without being matters of formal policy. Unlike the Peace Corps, CUSO had no large "visible minority" population to which it could turn for diasporic volunteers.[159] Among black CUSO volunteers, probably one of the earliest and most remarkable was an ANC underground leader from South Africa who had fled to Canada in the early 1960s and settled in Winnipeg. Together with his wife, he went to Zambia as a CUSO teacher in 1968, subsequently becoming a field staff officer there.[160] Diasporic Africans and others from majority-world backgrounds who came into CUSO in somewhat larger numbers in the 1970s as Canadian-born or Canadian-educated volunteers or staff typically had credentials that made them stand out.[161] But they were, under-standably, a small number. Meanwhile, a planning document on recruitment from the early 1980s dealt extensively with the desirability of increasing the number of older and professionally trained volunteers in the years ahead, but it made no explicit reference to recruiting within Canada for ethnic or racial diversity.[162]

Hiring "host nationals" as volunteers and staff was potentially a more ef-fective way of bringing diversity into CUSO, and projects were one way of doing this. The annual report for 1974-75 claimed that CUSO had fielded 856 volunteers in that calendar year and supported ninety-nine new projects, which, "in turn, included support for about 200 host national 'volunteers' on a full-time basis, and an additional 100 part-time."[163] The total would have included support staff such as drivers and cleaners, however, and to that extent did not imply a significant shift to indigenous decision making in the field. Moreover, CIDA's basic annual grant to CUSO was provided on the assumption that it was essentially a placement organization geared to placing volunteers sent from Canada. Politicized field staff in the ECSA region were among the earliest CUSO staff to argue that development in their region was best served by initiatives that did not involve obligatory volunteer placements from Canada. Yet by the early 1980s, the desire to wean CIDA from a view of CUSO as simply a volunteer-sending agency and to respond more flexibly to host countries' changing needs was also evident among staff in several other regions and in the Ottawa secretariat.[164]

In the Caribbean region, where late-1960s volunteers had experienced race-based hostility both as Canadians and as "do-gooders," there was a period in the early 1980s when CUSO was again able to move forward, now with a focus on projects established or facilitated by staff born in the region. They, in turn, hired local people to work in a variety of projects and cooperated with local development agencies.[165] Dominican-born Marlene Green was one such new leader as projects officer for the Eastern Caribbean. Based in Grenada, she became responsible for the evacuation of CUSO's volunteers, a mix of Caribbean-born and white personnel, when US troops invaded the island in 1983 to depose its Marxist government and the volunteers were caught in the crossfire.[166] Later, back in Canada, where she had lived for almost two decades as a university student and a social worker involved with black and other min-ority communities, Green became a strong advocate for affirmative action in hiring by CUSO and NGOs generally as a means of increasing their racial diversity. Selena Tapper benefited directly from her advocacy and personal encouragement. A Jamaican who came into CUSO from an indigenous development agency in 1984, Tapper served for about a decade as regional field officer for the Caribbean. Like other women colleagues of Green's within CUSO during this period, she recalls that gender issues received more – and more formal – attention from CUSO than did race. Moreover, Canadian members of the board seemed less comfortable with race issues and with "overt political analysis of the overseas programme" than their overseas counterparts on the board, and remained more wedded to a "'helping' analysis." Nonetheless, "at its best," Tapper reflected, CUSO was at the forefront "or at least in the front running" in terms of addressing such new issues.[167]

That CUSO dealt with race issues in an ad hoc way rather than through formal affirmative action policies did not preclude significant progress toward making CUSO's staff more representative of the overseas constituencies it had been established to serve, especially from the late 1970s. During this period, under executive directors whose involvement with the organization went back to the 1960s and was reflected at a personal level in the marriages they had formed overseas, CUSO moved toward greater diversity in a largely uncontentious fashion.[168]

Controversy and Continuity in CUSO's Development

As this chapter has shown, by the early 1970s, the idea that young Canadian volunteers equipped with BAs and good will could, ipso facto, make a significant contribution to the developing world seemed passé. The "fine young Canadians" from the start-up years were being reconfigured in the CUSO memory bank as naive idealists. Neither those who wanted to professionalize CUSO nor those who sought to politicize it mourned their passing. By the end of the seventies, there had been more than a decade of diverse new approaches and divided opinions within the organization about how best to "do" development. Frank Bogdasavich's 1968 call for more professionalism in the training and support of volunteers was still being echoed in 1975 by *Forum* articles deploring the sending of untrained BAs as teacher volunteers.[169] By that time, though, there were plenty of CUSO activists who deplored the sending of *any* teachers to promulgate Western-style education. Like Western-style medicine with its alien values, impossible requirements, and lack of cultural fit, formal education was doing more harm than good, the politicized activists argued. CUSO should instead provide the ideological and material support, especially through a projects approach, to help marginalized people help themselves. In the ECSA region, calls for downscaling in volunteer placements were paralleled by support for liberation movements.

Though other Canadian NGOs, including ecumenical groups, also became politicized during the 1970s, they generally did so with less controversy and less call on the public purse and without the youthful swagger that sometimes marked CUSO. It was these kinds of changes that complicated the organization's original wholesome image and divided its own constituency. In the end, though, the divisions usually had more to do with style and strategy than with ultimate goals. A volunteer writing from Botswana in 1974 sought to argue this point: "For most of us, objections to politicization are pragmatic rather than philosophical, else we probably wouldn't be in CUSO."[170] Two years later, Professor C. M. "Red" Williams used his retirement as chair of CUSO's board of directors to comment on the divides within CUSO and to issue several warnings. He began not by romanticizing the good old days but rather by declaring that "CUSO/SUCO organizationally is a much superior vehicle for program delivery than ever before." Nor did he disparage the new type of idealism in the organization. But the new idealism and youthful enthusiasm were not sufficient justification for "tilting at windmills." Indeed, "to propose, or even more, to take overt part in revolutionary reforms in the Third World may well be no more than meddling or even outright arrogance when measured by the average volunteer's experience and likely ongoing commitment to take the full consequence of his action." CUSO should certainly continue to take risks in its programming, Williams believed, but it should not risk the entire organization just to take "a political stance." Furthermore, it should put an end to the debilitating debates about the CUSO/SUCO relationship, and it should do serious fundraising if it really wanted to free itself "from the constraints of Treasury and CIDA." Otherwise, it could face joining CYC "in the history books."[171]

Upon taking office as executive director in October 1979 after the several debacles earlier in the year, Ian Smillie restored a measure of stability to CUSO, but he did so without publicly distancing himself from the controversial ECSA programs.[172] When his history of CUSO was published in 1985, it revealed his impatience with what he regarded as "outspoken political posturing."[173] But Smillie's book certainly did not question the appropriateness of assisting liberation struggles or of attempting to educate Canadians and their politicians out of their parochialism and conservatism about the developing world. When, in

"Development Is Disturbance"

ending his term as executive director in 1983, Smillie both challenged the extreme charges against CUSO by C-FAR and simultaneously gave space in the *Forum* to an article by Professor Kenneth Hilborn, one of C-FAR's university-based supporters, letters to the editor both supported and criticized his actions.[174] Clearly, the question of whether CUSO should aim for "balance" or take an unambiguously political stand remained unresolved in CUSO's third decade, even as the organization remained united in its broad commitment to development.

When one turns back from particular debates and stances to on-the-ground volunteer activities, what becomes clear is the degree to which there was continuity within CUSO despite the disturbances of the 1970s. Educational placements remained the most common placements, and while the number of professionally trained teacher-volunteers increased, young, inexperienced, and untrained volunteers remained numerous. This was certainly the case in Nigeria, CUSO's largest placement country, where requests for teachers for secondary schools and teacher-training institutions increased throughout the 1970s. As for involvement in the politics of a host country, wartorn Nigeria rather than the ECSA region became the first test case, albeit in a less overtly ideological way. The next chapter follows CUSO volunteers and staff into Nigeria as they faced both the daunting challenges of that country and the pressures and reproaches that periodically reached them from other parts of the CUSO universe.

4

"Big Is Beautiful?"
The Challenges of Serving in Nigeria

"Big Is Beautiful?" was the provocative title of a 1979 article on Nigeria by Gerry Caplan. A specialist in African history and a well-known NDP activist, Caplan had been serving for two years as CUSO coordinator in Nigeria when he wrote his un-boosterish article for the *CUSO Forum*. With its wealth of natural and human advantages, he observed, Nigeria had the capacity to be the most successful nation in the Third World. Instead, the oil boom and bust of the 1970s had exacerbated the prevailing Hobbesian ethos of the country, making life for most Nigerians "short, nasty and brutish."[1] Some thirty-four years after Caplan penned his lament, a casual reference to Nigeria is even more likely to evoke negative associations among Canadians: email scam messages perhaps, or media accounts of political corruption, disputes over oil resources, and sectarian violence. Unlike India, Nigeria has not become a subject of modernizing success stories in Canadian media. When mentioned at all, it is likely to be as a troubled and troubling African nation.

In 1961, it was a very different story. Nigeria had become an independent country within the British Commonwealth a year earlier. Established constitutionally as a federal parliamentary democracy (and as a republic from 1963), Nigeria was a country rich in natural resources and market potential and, with a population of about 56 million people, Africa's most populous nation.[2] Especially by comparison with the chaotic Congo, where Canadian peace-keepers were serving, Nigeria appeared to be reassuringly stable, a promising site for useful development work by eager young Canadians.[3] In April 1962, the CUSO *Bulletin* presented the good news: the Bureau for External Aid in the Nigerian federal government had asked CUSO to provide fifty secondary-school teachers. Salary, transportation costs, and housing would be supplied by Nigeria itself. Volunteers who could teach English, science, mathematics, and French were especially needed. A teaching diploma, while desirable, was not essential.[4] In its eagerness to respond to this opportunity, CUSO initially selected fifty out of sixty-two applicants, though when it became clear that neither CUSO nor the Nigerian government was in a position to handle such a large number in that first year, the pioneering cohort was whittled down to just seven volunteers.[5]

One of the seven volunteers was Roy Fischer, newly graduated from the University of Toronto with a chemistry degree. Fischer had read about Nigeria's request in *The Varsity,* and although he had already been offered a good job at Proctor and Gamble, the corporate world did not appeal to him in the way that overseas work did. He had discussed an appointment to a mission school in the Congo with the United Church of Canada's Jim Ormiston, but they both agreed that it probably wouldn't be a good fit. Instead, that September, Fischer headed off to teach mathematics and science at a boys' secondary school in the Western Region of Nigeria with no more preparation for his new duties than some ex-perience in Sunday school teaching and a brief orientation in July at Macdonald College in Montreal.

The placement almost hadn't happened. As the summer ended, the promised contract from Nigeria and the money to cover Fischer's transportation still hadn't arrived. Indeed, he had already begun studies at the Ontario College of Education when the necessary arrangements finally fell into place. Arriving in the airport at Lagos, he was eventually met by his school principal, taken to register at the Canadian High Commission, and then driven to his new home in the bush some thirty miles from Ibadan. "Home" had kerosene lighting and running water, but there was no mosquito netting and, beyond an incongruous box of corn flakes, not much to eat. For the twenty-two-year-old Fischer, raised in downtown Toronto, it was all very baffling – but not overwhelming. On the morning after his arrival, he made a meal of the dry corn flakes and then, on his own, found his way to the school in time for assembly. He would wind up teaching some English as well as science and math and, though he was no athlete, acting as assistant games master. In those first months, he occasionally got rides into Ibadan to buy food and other supplies and in between travelled by bicycle to a village market. Later, there would be a little Austin, purchased with a loan from school officials. Though there would be few social contacts in that first year, his second year brought a more robust social life. It included tennis with young Nigerians and the Indian teacher at his school, occasional high teas with an expatriate couple in the nearby town of Oyo, and a lasting friendship with a Peace Corps volunteer.

Fischer's first CUSO appointment in Nigeria would be followed by another (1973-75), this time as a salaried field staff officer based in Ibadan. In the intervening period, there would be a job at the University of Toronto's International Student Centre, combined with committee work and public speaking for CUSO; graduate studies in anthropology at McGill; and two years on staff in Uganda, where he oversaw the closing of CUSO programming.[6] But all that was still ahead in 1962 when he was part of CUSO's pioneering cohort in Nigeria. The lack of professional preparation for his teaching duties, the haphazard beginnings, and some – though by no means all – of his experiences in that first appointment were typical of the experiences of other early CUSO volunteers in Nigeria. Like these other volunteers, Roy acquired a smattering of the local language, survived the routine hazards of Nigeria's roads and the almost-routine hazard of being robbed. Some of his fellow volunteers would die or be maimed in Nigeria – it was CUSO's most dangerous posting – and some would quit early and return home. But like Roy, most had enough luck and commitment or sheer doggedness to complete their contracts and sometimes the willingness to sign on for more. This chapter deals both with CUSO as an NGO responding to the challenges of a volatile environment and with individual volunteers' personal narratives. In 1979, when volunteer numbers there peaked, one-third of all CUSO volunteers were said to be serving in Nigeria.[7] Given that fact and the size of the country, field staff had a vital role to play in ensuring the acceptability of CUSO's work and – to the extent that they could – the safety and well-being of the volunteers. If the civil war was their most daunting test, there were numerous more mundane and morale-sapping challenges during the years between 1962, when Nigeria extended its welcome, and the mid-1980s, when the beleaguered military government effectively declared CUSO redundant. As this chapter shows, volunteers and staff alike generally rose to the challenges.

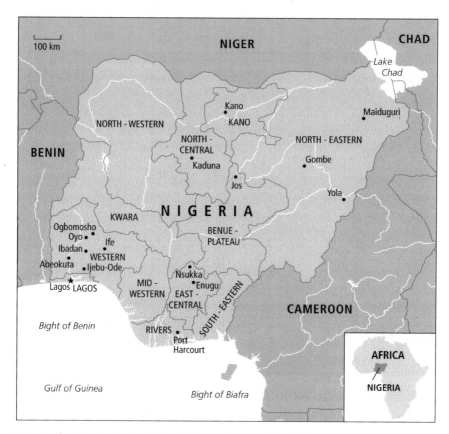

Nigeria, showing the twelve federal states on the eve of the civil war.

Starting Out in Nigeria: The McLean Era

Newly independent Nigeria was not hesitant about accepting development assistance from the West. In terms of modernizing projects, schooling was regarded as crucial. Christian missions had begun establishing schools in southern Nigeria from the mid-nineteenth century. Education had come to be seen "as a means not only of economic betterment but of social elevation." Mission teaching, however, had mainly been at an elementary level, and because of British colonial officials' concern not to antagonize the Muslim North, it was mainly confined to the South. Even there, schooling was still a scarce commodity in the decade leading up to independence (a more than 80 percent illiteracy rate even in increasingly Christian Igboland) and, at the same time, regarded as crucial to personal and national development.[8] In the decade 1952 to 1962, the total expenditure for education in the country from private and public sources more than quadrupled, and both the Eastern and Western Regions sought in the face of massive challenges to introduce free primary education. In 1961, Nigeria was reported to be seeking at least one thousand expatriate secondary-level teachers per year for the next decade.[9] It was within this broad context that Canada's federal government and CUSO became involved in Nigeria.

Encouraged by Britain and mindful of its Commonwealth obligations and the Cold War context, Canada established a High Commission in Nigeria in 1960 and promptly began providing some official development assistance, one component of which was eleven teachers, funded through the External Aid Office in 1961. In December 1961, as CUSO's acting executive director, Lewis Perinbam contacted Ottawa officials about possible roles for volunteers in assisting development in West Africa.[10] CUSO, however, would have learned about Nigeria's interest in obtaining large numbers of teachers from abroad through Canadian mission ties as well as through government and university channels. The Presbyterian Church in Canada had begun a small mission in the Eastern Region of Nigeria in the 1950s in association with the established work of Scottish Presbyterians.[11] The mission had a dynamic spokesman in the church's secretary for overseas missions, Dr. E.H. (Ted) Johnson, who in 1957 had brought a prominent Nigerian Christian leader, Dr. (later, Sir) Francis Ibiam, on a speaking tour to Canada. Among those moved by Dr. Ibiam's appeal for Canadian teachers was Walter McLean, at the time an undergraduate at the University of British Columbia. In 1961, as president of the Ottawa-based National Federation of Canadian University Students (NFCUS), McLean visited Canadian campuses and sought out potential volunteers for CUSO. He was a skilled recruiter with a strong interest in Nigeria, but there was a serious problem at the receiving end, as Roy Fischer's experience had shown: CUSO had no coordinator on the ground to meet new volunteers and facilitate their placement. Given this situation, Ted Johnson arranged a missionary appointment with the Presbyterian Church of Nigeria for the now-ordained McLean and authorized him to give as much time as necessary to the needs of CUSO.[12]

For much of the next three years, working mainly from their base in Enugu, the capital of the Eastern Region, Walter McLean and his wife, Barbara, who taught in a government girls' school, divided their time between their official jobs and their voluntary work for CUSO. On the advice of N.U. Akpan, a senior civil servant and one of many prominent Nigerians in his congregational circle

CUSO/Nigeria volunteers at reception, Enugu, September 1964, hosted by N.U. Akpan *(front row, fourth from right)*, then permanent secretary of the Ministry of Education. Coordinator Walter McLean is crouching *(front row, far left)*. Bill McNeill is three places to his right. *CUSO/SUCO Bulletin*, November 1964. Courtesy of CUSO International.

(like Ibiam, Akpan would become part of the inner circle of Biafran leaders in the forthcoming civil war), Walter met with government officials in Lagos to facilitate accreditation of volunteers for work in Nigeria. He also investigated prospective placements for volunteers, mainly in the Eastern Region, met them on their arrival, and visited them at their work sites. The garage of the house provided by Barbara's school became a kind of CUSO office and a temporary stopping place for volunteers. There were plenty of requests for the volunteers, especially from missions, which still provided much of Nigeria's schooling. Barbara recalled one memorable morning when a group of nuns who were particularly keen to get some of the new teacher-volunteers arrived at the McLeans' residence before Walter was even awake to hear their request.[13] Writing in March 1965 to his friend Duncan Edmonds, who was then special assistant to External Affairs Minister Paul Martin, Walter assured Edmonds that there was "almost no limit" to the number of teachers that CUSO could place, particularly if they had qualifications to teach the sciences or French or English. Just then, he reported, he was processing twenty-three applications for teachers.[14]

The Challenges of Expansion

The McLeans' contribution to early CUSO programming in Nigeria was, then, substantial, especially considering that it was done on an unsalaried basis. But there was a certain unease within CUSO about Walter's mission and church identity and his elite connections. And some volunteers did not take kindly to his ad hoc policies for trying to monitor their behaviour. Motorbikes, usually called Hondas and a standard acquisition for volunteers of both sexes, became an early source of friction, especially after one volunteer had an accident while travelling without permission outside the country. In any case, by the summer of 1965, volunteer numbers had grown substantially, and CUSO had access to federal funding to hire paid staff. As well, the McLeans were about to go on home leave.[15] It was clearly an opportune time to appoint a full-time coordinator. Bill McNeill, who had just completed his first year as a CUSO volunteer teaching English and history at a Catholic mission secondary school some sixty miles from Enugu, was asked by executive director Bill McWhinney to take over from McLean.[16] McLean's desire to have an ongoing connection with CUSO after his return to Nigeria from home leave was accommodated by making him Special Advisor. Both within Nigeria and back in Canada, he would continue to support CUSO strongly and in a variety of ways.

CUSO typically attempted to fill its field staff positions by turning to (male) volunteers who had a degree of maturity, regional experience, and a demonstrated sense of responsibility. McNeill was a good fit in all these respects. Raised on a Manitoba farm and at work from age fourteen, he had attended Sir George Williams University as an adult student, graduating in 1964. In that year, at age twenty-eight, he had accepted the appointment to Nigeria, notwithstanding an initial lack of much awareness about development issues and a frustrating orientation in Toronto (some of it "dreary beyond belief"). McNeill's maturity as a new volunteer had impressed McLean, who recalled that, unlike most of the new arrivals in 1964, he had offered to help out with the luggage. Though he had only one year of experience when he took over as coordinator, McNeill had already learned first-hand or through other volunteers stationed in the region about many of the difficulties of teaching in Nigeria: the paucity or absence of textbooks, for instance; the corrupt practices of some school officials; and other challenges that occasionally came with mission-school appointments. McNeill's experience in his own school had been mainly positive. He had felt supported by the Trinidadian priest who was his principal, and he was under

"Big Is Beautiful"

no compulsion to attend Mass or other church functions. But others among the volunteer teachers he had come to know in his region were not so lucky. Like the principal and several Nigerian colleagues at the school where he taught, Keith Bezanson went months without being paid by the venal chief who owned the ramshackle school and who showed up mainly to collect term fees.[17] Some conservative Protestant mission schools wanted volunteers who were committed evangelicals, and some Catholic schools wanted all their teachers to be practising Catholics. As coordinator, McNeill made it clear to evangelical school officials that most volunteers were not evangelically inclined and shouldn't be required to attend church. If Catholic school officials seemed likely to demand compliance and orthodoxy from Catholic volunteers, McNeill was inclined to send them Protestants. Later, field staff would also find ways to circumvent such requests.[18]

As CUSO/Nigeria's first full-time coordinator, McNeill relocated CUSO headquarters to Ibadan in the Western Region, where the local Ministry of Education supplied him with living and office accommodation and where a branch of the Canada-based shoe-manufacturing firm of Thomas Bata provided office furnishings. Ibadan was a better base than Enugu as McNeill sought to broaden his contacts with education officials. The requests he dealt with, however, came mainly from mission or private schools, since the fully-funded teachers provided through Canada's External Aid Office were generally placed in government schools. McNeill was committed to expanding CUSO's placements, not only into the Yoruba-dominated Western Region but also by providing teachers to the Muslim Northern Region, where schooling needs were immeasurably greater than in either of the two southern regions. Ironically, CUSO's expansion into the North would happen during Nigeria's civil war.

The War Years

Known in Canada as "the tragedy of Biafra," the civil war lasted from July 1967 to January 1970, resulting in the deaths of from 1 million to 3 million Nigerians, mostly in the Eastern Region and most of them civilian deaths from disease and starvation.[19] For CUSO, the war would prove to be the biggest and most divisive challenge it had faced since its inception. To the many within CUSO and in Canada at large who sympathized with the suffering and the national ambitions of the Igbo, the dominant group in the would-be independent state of Biafra, CUSO's decision to continue placing volunteers in federal Nigeria despite the war seemed callous, a dramatic example of pragmatic but immoral development politics. In the long run, however, the decision assured the organization of a future in Nigeria. A brief overview of the circumstances that gave rise to the war, and of the war itself, will help to provide a context for CUSO's evaluation of this challenge, its divided response, and its postwar programming.

Historian Elizabeth Isichei observes that in 1960 there was something like "a conspiracy of optimism" about Nigeria's prospects for independent nationhood. In reality, the unity of the new nation was illusory. (Looking back from 2008, novelist Chinua Achebe called the political and constitutional structure that had been put in place "virtually a trap.")[20] Regional and ethno-religious tensions predating independence were exacerbated by the corruption and the manipulation of democratic federal and regional institutions that took place from independence onward. The Northern Region feared domination by the two southern regions (increased to three in 1963 with the creation of the Mid-Western Region); the South, in turn, feared domination by the more populous and less developed North. It was against this background that the two 1966 coups took place, leading directly to the war. The first coup, carried out primarily by Igbo, targeted mainly non-Igbo leaders. The second, carried out by northerners, mainly targeted Igbo. It was in the wake of the second coup that a horrifying massacre of Igbo living in the North took place. For more than a generation, Igbos' skills and literacy had given them access to good positions in commerce and the civil service in the North. Now, many thousands of them were killed, while more than a million fled back to the East after experiencing or witnessing acts of extreme violence.[21] Meetings to bring about compromises between the leaders of the rival military/political factions were unsuccessful. On 30 May 1967, Colonel Emeka Ojukwu, the charismatic Igbo military leader of the Eastern Region, declared the region's independence as the Republic of Biafra, promising his people that "with God on our side, we shall vanquish."[22]

The Federal Military Government (FMG), headed by Army Chief of Staff Yakubu ("Jack") Gowon, a devout Christian from a minority ethnic group in the North, initially anticipated only the need for a police action to suppress what his government regarded as a local rebellion, not Biafrans' briefly successful invasion of Mid-Western state nor their determination to hold out long after the war had become a dreadful war of attrition. Even after FMG forces had captured the East's major port and airport and oil fields (most of the country's oil resources were in the East) and driven the resistance into the Igbo heartland, the would-be state of Biafra held on until January 1970, despite intense suffering and mass starvation. In its struggle, it won official recognition from very few African and Western governments, but it was aided by the International Committee of the Red Cross (ICRC), and especially by the churches, whose airlifts of humanitarian relief sometimes accompanied or provided cover for arms supplies.[23] It was also aided by a highly successful propaganda campaign, so that "many people firmly believed that Biafra was a victim of a Federal Government bent on genocide and that the war was one between Northern Muslims and Biafran Christians, despite the fact that the Federal leader was, himself, a Christian."[24]

Many CUSO volunteers appear to have been only dimly aware of or not concerned about the complex developments leading up to the outbreak of the war. In 1966, following the first coup, in January, they had merely been advised to be cautious about local travel – and to write reassuring letters to their parents! But in May 1967, four days before the Biafran declaration of independence, they received stricter instructions from CUSO/Ottawa: abide by McNeill's travel restrictions or have their contract terminated. "I realize that the present situation in Nigeria probably does not appear as tense from your vantage point as it does from Canada," Jon Church wrote in his May memo to the volunteers. "Nevertheless," he continued, "we are most anxious that everyone takes no unnecessary risks. The entire CUSO programme relies on continued financial support from the Government of Canada and from the private sector. Any injury or death to a CUSO volunteer in Nigeria could have very serious repercussions."[25] Yet even when the war was imminent, and as thousands of expatriates, including Peace Corps volunteers, prepared to leave the East, Dan Turner, the impetuous twenty-three-year-old volunteer who was to succeed McNeill as coordinator that fall and who was his Enugu-based deputy coordinator until then, at first supported the volunteers' desire to stay in the Eastern Region with "their people." These volunteers, Turner recalled, were proud to be associated with the "clever and quick" Igbo, inspired by Ojukwu's oratory, and anxious to demonstrate solidarity with the Igbo cause. As the situation in the East became increasingly volatile, Turner reluctantly oversaw the hastily improvised evacuation of the volunteers, some of whom – also reluctantly – agreed to a transfer to a CUSO posting elsewhere in West Africa. He then returned to CUSO's office in Ibadan to continue running what remained of the CUSO/Nigeria program (eight volunteers in the North and twenty-three in the West in the fall of 1967[26]). By early 1968, however, Turner had been expelled from Nigeria, for while in Ghana to attend a CUSO meeting he had expressed strong pro-Biafra sentiments, which had been reported back to the federal government.[27]

Teacher Dagmar Langer being treated by nurse Diane North at an in-service gathering for Nigeria volunteers, December 1964. North was back in Canada when the civil war began, but she returned on a private contract to work as an acting nursing tutor at Queen Elizabeth Hospital, Umuahia, Biafra. "I was the lucky one," she told *Maclean's* magazine, "because I was able to stay and help." Courtesy of Walter McLean.

Back in Canada, like many of the volunteers who had served in the Eastern Region, Turner became a passionate advocate for the Biafran cause. Canadian media had initially paid little attention to the far-off Nigerian civil war. But from mid-1968, newspapers, radio, and graphic television images aroused intense concern by exposing the suffering of beleaguered civilians in secessionist Biafra, especially the women and children. (Hence the horrified reaction when Prime Minister Trudeau responded to a reporter's question that summer with the seemingly dismissive "Where's Biafra?")[28] Like the Canadian Presbyterian missionary community with its close personal connections to the Eastern Region of Nigeria, RVs like Turner would have heard vivid first-hand reports of the violence inflicted on Igbo in the North in 1966 from the thousands of refugees returning from there in the lead-up to the war, themselves the victims or observers of horrors.[29] Architect Grant Wanzel, posted in the North, had personally witnessed acts of violence. Now, back in Canada, these Biafra sympathizers were exposed to increasing media coverage of the wartime plight of the people with

"Big Is Beautiful"

whom they had bonded. Such coverage could only increase their sense of guilt and concern for the people they felt they had abandoned. Turner vainly sought CUSO's permission to let him return to Biafra (RV Diane North *did* return as a nursing tutor on a private contract just before the war broke out), while fellow RVs, including Gayle Cooper, Turner's future wife, and future journalist David Cayley (Sarawak), engaged in pro-Biafran activism in a variety of Canadian venues, including the office of External Affairs Minister Mitchell Sharp.[30]

Notwithstanding such strong expressions of concern and support within Canada and within CUSO for the people of secessionist Biafra, staff and volunteers who had served in Nigeria, or who were still there, were by no means of one mind about how the organization should respond to the civil war. Given the uncertainty in the early months of the war, it had seemed best to redirect the 1967 contingent to the other parts of West Africa where CUSO had work (Ghana and Sierra Leone). In 1968, however, after many months of exchanges and discussion among staff on the ground and in Ottawa, it was decided to send more than seventy volunteers to federal Nigeria that year. The decision had not been taken lightly or without awareness of the need for volunteers to be selected and placed with great care. There was to be a special focus on the North, where the need for teachers was greatest, and a deputy coordinator was to be placed there. Mid-Western state, briefly a site of conflict, was declared altogether out of bounds for volunteers.[31]

For CUSO staff, the personal safety of the new volunteers was a non-issue, since they were being placed far from the conflict zone. Indeed, in some parts of Nigeria there was little to remind people that a war was even being fought. Journalist and CUSO board member Clyde Sanger, writing in 1969 following extensive travel in wartime Nigeria, observed, "It is surprising ... to find, on first arriving in Nigeria, how localized the war is ... up north in Kano the war seems more remote than it has done in London or, sometimes, Ottawa."[32] Still, given the strong feeling against continuing CUSO programming during the war – and among board members as well as emotionally engaged RVs – the case for carrying on had to be made carefully and soberly and without appearing to minimize the significance of Biafra's suffering.[33] This was the challenge that Bill McNeill took on in his "Report on the West African Programme" in October 1968.

Though he had completed his term in Nigeria and returned to Canada the previous year, McNeill had agreed to go back temporarily in January 1968 following Dan Turner's expulsion, to assist the newly appointed coordinator (who remained only briefly). When he wrote his October report, McNeill was once again back in the Ottawa office as director of CUSO's West African program. He took great pains to present the rationales behind what he recognized would be a controversial decision and one in which he had played perhaps the single most important role. He explained that he and regional coordinator Don Simpson had toured much of Nigeria early in 1968 and consulted with spokesmen for other voluntary organizations and Western government agencies about the pros and cons of continuing to work in Nigeria during wartime: "all had plans to bring in a new programme." As for the demand side, with the North now reorganized into six separate states, each with its own ministry of education, there was a new sense of responsibility about educational needs, and each of the states had asked CUSO "for large numbers of volunteers." Contributing to lessening the enormous educational deficit in the North, in however small a way, McNeill wrote, could help promote Nigeria's future stability by allowing Northerners "to feel more secure." On the larger question of whether CUSO should continue to operate in a country whose politics were unsavoury or even abhorrent, McNeill was clear: CUSO had, and was still providing, programs in many such countries, including Ghana. As for the reports of atrocities in Nigeria's conduct of the war, McNeill wrote: "I think it only fair to say that while there may be inequalities in the Nigerian situation we feel that we ought not to become involved in the internal politics of the country. Instead, we limit ourselves to an evaluation of the likely effectiveness of the work we are asked to do." He then turned to the views of the volunteers themselves: a majority of those still on the ground had voted at their termination conference in May 1968 to continue CUSO's program in Nigeria. And as for the cohort that had gone through orientation in London during the summer, none had opted to turn down the assignment to Nigeria or transfer to another country when given a chance to do so. Indeed, everyone had remained committed even though the majority of the RVs who had been on the orientation staff "had pro-Biafran leanings." Finally, McNeill concluded his justification for continuing the Nigerian program by quoting a senior international aid agency official whose views coincided with his own: "Millions of good people in Nigeria (both Christian and Moslem), on both sides, are suffering ... They have all worked hard to raise their children in the best way they can in a very confused and bloody situation involving powerful external political and economic influences. They need and deserve our assistance as much as people do in any developing country and there are no insurmountable obstacles in giving them the help they need."[34]

Another cohort of volunteers was sent to Nigeria in 1969, despite intense pressure from pro-Biafra RVs and some CUSO board members to have the program there "frozen." But the arguments made by McNeill and other staff who shared his perspective were ultimately persuasive. Tim Brodhead, who had succeeded McNeill as coordinator in Ibadan after a brief stint as deputy coordinator and, before that, three years of teaching at the University of Ife in the Western Region, was twice brought back to Canada to present to the CUSO board the case for continuing the program. Likewise, writing in March 1969 as deputy coordinator for Nigeria, Ian Smillie had urged a continuation of programming, particularly in the North. The tragedy of the 1966 killings there, he wrote, "does not obviate the very great need for CUSO in Nigeria."[35] As for executive director Frank Bogdasavich, he, too, appeared to favour remaining engaged in Nigeria, though he recognized the unpopularity of that position among some of the CUSO constituency. As seen in Chapter 3, Bogdasavich believed that as a general policy CUSO should not get involved in the internal politics of the countries in which it was serving. In the case of Nigeria, staying the course was the *least* political step to take.[36] By the end of 1969, CUSO had 119 personnel in Nigeria. There were also still about 130 volunteers from Britain and a much smaller number from France and Germany. As for the Peace Corps, whose situation in the country had become increasingly untenable, it was down to about 40 volunteers from a high of more than 800.[37]

It is possible that pressure within CUSO to freeze its programming in Nigeria would have arisen again in 1970 and perhaps increased if the war had continued. Some former CUSO staff, recalling the civil war years, believed that pro-Biafra public opinion among Canadians had grown so strong by 1970 that the Canadian government would have been forced to recognize an independent Biafran state, thereby effectively putting an end to CUSO's work in federal Nigeria. Pro-Biafra sentiment was in fact sufficiently strong that Mitchell Sharp (who called the crisis the "most distressing issue I faced in my first year as secretary of state for external affairs") had at last agreed to supply transport for relief flights in addition to food and medical aid.[38] But then, unexpectedly, in January, the civil war in Nigeria ended. After the many months of holding out against federal forces at the urging of Ojukwu and in the face of now-hopeless odds, the Biafrans' will to continue had waned. As a British war correspondent who was on the scene a week before the war ended wrote, "People are now choosing ... to risk massacre at Federal hands rather than die slowly from starvation in a shrinking enclave." Ojukwu opted to leave Biafra and turn over its government to his chief of staff, who sued for peace.[39]

As for CUSO, in piloting their organization through the divisive shoals of Nigeria's civil war, CUSO staff in Ottawa and on the ground had experienced a political coming of age. In the fashion of Prime Minister Trudeau himself, those directly responsible had opted for "reason over passion." Their hearts may have been with the Igbo people, among whom many had made friends and whose suffering had been made known to them at the time of the 1966 massacre and later through the haunting wartime media images of starving infants and emaciated nursing mothers. But they had learned to think like managers and administrators. And they knew from their years on the ground, first as volunteers and then as staff, that the issues behind the war were not as starkly black and white as they appeared to sympathetic outsiders; that not all Easterners wanted a sovereign Igbo-run state, that not all Christians were on the same side; and that not all national identities could or should find expression in independent statehood.[40] In the short term, their stand made them unpopular with those within CUSO who took a different position on how the organization should have responded. McNeill recalls being accused by one staff member in the CUSO/Ottawa office of supporting genocide, and at one CUSO speaking engagement in Canada, he was reportedly booed off the stage by RVs who had been posted in Nigeria's Eastern Region.[41] Nonetheless, their pragmatic approach had enabled McNeill and Brodhead and like-minded colleagues to carry the organization through its first political crisis, and it stood them in good stead with key figures both in Nigeria and in Canada in terms of their future work. Their non-interventionist position was praised both by Nigeria's federal education commissioner and by CIDA's Lewis Perinbam, who commended them on their "wise handling of a difficult and complex situation."[42]

Personnel and Projects in the Former Biafra: A Temporary Return to the East

Many Igbo and their sympathizers had expected a massacre, even a genocide, in the event of Biafra's collapse. Following news of the surrender, opposition politicians in Canada proposed that "a massive international relief operation" be organized and that Canadians participate in an observer team to ensure that reprisals against the secessionists were not carried out.[43] But the worst did not happen. Instead, "a general amnesty was offered to all those who had fought against the Nigerian army ... no reparations or indemnities were demanded,"[44] and steps toward rebuilding the region that had called itself Biafra were quickly undertaken or facilitated by Nigeria's federal government.[45] There was thus a supportive climate in Canada and a relatively welcoming if enormously challenging setting in which CUSO could begin contributing with personnel and material aid.

The 1966 violence against Igbo in the North had driven many skilled workers back to the East. But the war had greatly reduced their numbers and their capacity to rebuild. CUSO had begun receiving urgent pleas for help from the former Biafra almost immediately after the conflict had ended. In a report to the CUSO board in which Tim Brodhead recommended reopening work in the eastern states, Brodhead, the Ottawa-based director of CUSO's West African program, maintained that because CUSO had retained the trust of Nigerian authorities during the war, it was in "a unique position to contribute positively to post-war reconstruction." He strongly recommended that an additional thirty-five volunteers be sent to Nigeria, over and above the number originally planned for 1970, especially to assist in reopening secondary schools and teacher-training colleges in the East. Moreover, the thirty-five should be fully funded for two years. An office should be opened in Enugu in East-Central state, and capital should be provided to assist in rebuilding schools, such funds to be spent at the discretion of the Enugu-based field staff officer in consultation with local volunteers. In view of Canada's concern for Biafra during the war, Brodhead wrote, he anticipated that there would be strong popular support for CIDA to provide the necessary extra funding to CUSO for work in the war-torn region.[46] Ian Smillie, successor to Brodhead as country coordinator in Nigeria, toured the most afflicted states in the region a few months after the war ended and again with colleague Jack Pearpoint in early June. Smillie confirmed Brodhead's account of the eagerness for CUSO's help in the region, and the need, especially in the Enugu area, where damage had been extensive. Most everything had been destroyed or looted from the schools, he wrote; many schools were even without roofs. Yet despite the bleakness of the situation, "The most striking thing to an outsider is the determination with which people are getting on with their lives." This same determination prevailed at the University of Nsukka, which wanted help in re-establishing its former high standards. But given the demanding conditions, the volunteers chosen should be "rugged people with good academic qualifications."[47]

In the first years following the war, staffing assistance *was* provided to the University of Nsukka as well as, more typically, to secondary schools. Despite warnings to prospective volunteers about the rugged conditions they would face in their placements in war-ravaged locales and the extra care that was to be taken to weed out unsuitable candidates before or during orientation, record-high numbers of volunteers were placed in Nigeria overall at this time. In a progress report on CUSO's assistance to educational institutions in East-Central state some eighteen months after the war had ended, Jack Pearpoint described several forms of aid. As well as providing volunteer teachers, CUSO had helped restock several school laboratories, distributed books supplied by Canada's Overseas Book Centre, and assisted a variety of other small, local projects. Although pitifully inadequate in the face of existing needs, CUSO's assistance was significant, Pearpoint maintained, in that it was helping to fill a gap in the early postwar period when other agencies with the resources to do more and bigger things were not yet fully operational. Moreover, CUSO's aid was very much appreciated at a time when, in the face of the enormous and ongoing difficulties, students' and teachers' morale was starting to wane. "Even small reconstruction programmes are an important incentive to keep people working through this difficult period," Pearpoint wrote. "CUSO has been able to help several schools in this way and ... we hope to be able to continue injecting both aid and enthusiasm into large numbers of schools." He was particularly moved by the sight of students writing their all-important government examinations while sitting on the floor.[48]

Pearpoint was a relative newcomer to Nigeria. He had left his volunteer position in Ghana in the spring of 1970 to come to Enugu on request from CUSO to serve as the region's first postwar field staff officer. With Felix Enang, a young Nigerian who had assisted CUSO staff for several years,[49] he had travelled through the wartorn areas, sleeping in their Volkswagen van, fending off drunken ex-soldiers and requests for bribes while making contact with school principals and other local educational leaders and instigating the kinds of small initiatives described above. But in the face of the region's staggering needs and the determination of local people to re-establish schooling, Pearpoint was anxious to do something more substantial. In a meeting with the Canadian high commissioner, he made what was at the time an "outrageous" request: $1 million from CIDA over and above its regular funding so that CUSO could effectively act as CIDA's subcontractor and undertake a major educational rehabilitation project. There was a lag of several months between the time that CIDA agreed to fund this initiative and the actual signing of the contract and, later, further delays in getting money out to the field. Nonetheless, the

A group of schoolchildren in postwar "Biafra." The desks in the background were made by local carpenters with funding provided by CUSO's educational rehabilitation project.
Courtesy of Jack Pearpoint.

educational rehabilitation project proved to be one of CUSO's most successful and influential ventures.[50]

Because UNICEF had committed to primary-school reconstruction, Pearpoint and his colleagues determined that their project should focus on building desks for students and teachers. Beyond providing much-needed school furnishings, such an approach would create local jobs and put money into individual villages by having local carpenters obtain the needed materials and build the desks. Several other features of the project were designed to increase local participation and forestall problems of corruption, cronyism, and poor workmanship. After an initial meeting between a CUSO representative and the representatives of a given school, a specially established Local Educational Committee was to invite a local carpenter to examine a prototype, make a sample desk, and then, if his work met with committee approval, make a bid for producing more such desks, with all input costs included. After the desks were inspected by the local committee, the carpenter was to be paid through a voucher signed by the headmaster, a senior teacher, and another member of the school committee. CUSO staff made provision for meticulous record-keeping of sums paid out and utilized, and sought to keep its own costs under control so that more money could go directly into desk production. Thus, when travel to meet with local committees proved costly, Jean Pelletier, the acting project manager in East-Central state, found ways to reorganize visits to the different project divisions so as to have more money for the project itself. Plans were also made for the "Nigerianization" of administrative staff as a way of cutting costs and establishing a sense of ownership and engagement in the project overall. A final report to the educational authorities of one state in February 1973 by Pelletier's successor, Mike Sakamoto, provided statistics on what had been accomplished in the state: 47,204 three-seater desks for students and 6,803 teachers' desks to go to 625 schools at a cost of CDN$200,000. In terms of injecting cash into local communities, the report declared that the project had succeeded to "a remarkable degree" and was, overall, an "unqualified success." Credit for what had been accomplished was given to the state's minister of education and district education officers for their cooperation but most of all to the enthusiasm and commitment of the hundreds of local school committees.[51]

In an article about rebuilding efforts in the former Biafra for *Weekend Magazine,* journalist Ernest Hillen commented favourably on CUSO's educational rehabilitation project: about one thousand schools had been provided with desks, jobs had been created, and almost no cases of local corruption had occurred. In their determination to keep the project on track in their communities, Pearpoint affirmed, local committees had been vigilant about preventing the misappropriation of funds, and on the rare occasions when that did happen the committee itself made up the loss so that the project in their community would not be discontinued.[52] In the meantime, CUSO's skilful handling of this large and experimental CIDA-funded project won it strong support from the Canadian high commissioner in Lagos, who in turn commended it to CIDA staff. At one point the high commissioner even chastised those responsible at CIDA for delays in forwarding promised funding. There had been another potentially serious problem in CIDA's response to Pearpoint's proposal: at an early stage in the project's conception, a CIDA officer had made a suggestion that could have significantly weakened its community impact, recommending that needed goods and services be provided from Canada. In the end, however, procurement tying ("tied aid") was not forced upon the project.[53] Rather, CIDA commended Pearpoint for the project's effectiveness "in both its design and implementation." More significantly, the agency undertook to provide CUSO with funding for a permanent Projects Division. At the end of 1972, acting executive director David Catmur asked Pearpoint to return to Ottawa to become the first director of the Projects Division.[54]

The success of the educational rehabilitation project in Nigeria, Ian Smillie writes, showed CIDA "that a large-scale project could be developed efficiently and managed economically by an NGO" and that it could be done "with an alacrity unknown within government."[55] In the decade that followed, as noted in Chapter 3, some 40 percent of CUSO's overseas work would be in the form of projects. Ironically, though, a projects approach did not become significant in Nigeria. Instead, volunteers remained at the centre of CUSO programming there. And as the former Eastern Region recovered from the worst effects of the war, volunteers were increasingly placed in the North. From 56 percent of total placements in the country in 1970, the proportion in the North rose to 72 percent in 1975, and to 86 percent in 1980.[56] The vast majority of placements were in teaching. But whatever the nature of the volunteers' assignments in northern states, they were frequently in settings where local authorities were still laying the groundwork and attempting to play catch-up with the more "developed" South. The volunteers' two-year stint would reflect that reality. In the next section of this chapter, I draw heavily on volunteers' personal and retrospective accounts of their experiences both before and after the civil war and in all parts of the country in order to convey the variety and the range of their responses.

Volunteering in Nigeria: Work and Life on the Ground

When Montreal-born Bernie Lucht was assigned to a teaching position in Nigeria in 1969, he was undeterred by concerns about the civil war. Lucht was unusual among volunteers of the time in that his degree, history and political science from Sir George Williams University, had included courses on Africa. As well, at age twenty-five with several years of journalism work behind him, he had more life experience than many of his peers. He and his wife, Rita, were both eager for an assignment in Africa. Although their government-established secondary school in a tiny village in northeastern Nigeria was a small one, there was a three-person history department, where he was able to teach West African history, while Rita taught English to their Muslim and Christian students. As was common, housing was provided on the school compound. The Luchts were initially without motorbikes, but on weekends they could travel rough by lorry to visit another CUSO couple, Gordon and Nancy Campbell, with whom they had formed a friendship at orientation and who were now serving in Yola, near the Cameroon border. On longer breaks they could travel further afield. Yet Bernie Lucht wasn't yearning to get out of his village or out of Nigeria. Like many volunteers, he was troubled by the lingering colonialism of British residents and by the racism of other expatriates whom they met (mainly Lebanese and Indians in this case), but there were satisfying friendships with the Nigerian teachers and the VSO couple on staff, and there was a fascinating culture to observe. Eschewing war-related subject matter, Lucht wrote several articles about Nigeria for the *Montreal Star*. "I loved it there," he recalled. He even toyed with the idea of staying on.[57]

Beginning his Nigeria experience six years earlier and in a very different part of Nigeria, Acadia University graduate Stan Barrett was, like Lucht, fascinated and permanently affected by Nigeria. Initially interviewed for India, Barrett was reassigned and sent to an isolated village secondary school to teach English and French in Nigeria's Eastern Region. A non-believer from a Protestant family, he socialized comfortably with the easygoing Irish Catholic priests who were his colleagues and bosses. Likewise, he made friends with his Igbo teaching colleagues and picked up enough Igbo to enjoy visiting his students' home villages. His extracurricular activities included helping to build sports facilities at the school and playing soccer and other sports with the boys. On one of the long school holidays, there was a motorcycle trip through West Africa that included a visit to the fabled Timbuktu and during another holiday, a hitchhiking trip to East Africa. Back in Canada in 1965, Barrett began graduate studies in English but soon switched to anthropology (the discipline of choice for numerous Peace Corps volunteers who became academics). Through his choice of field work, he found himself back in Nigeria during the civil war, this time in a Yoruba-speaking region in the west, where, for a time, the impact of the war was palpable. In 1971, Barrett obtained his doctorate in anthropology from the University of Sussex, the circuitous outcome of a cultural curiosity that had begun with his two volunteer years in an Igbo village.[58]

The difference between a volunteer who adapted and one who merely endured – or did not – is perhaps best understood as a combination of background and personality factors and the luck of the draw in terms of placements and timing. Volunteers like Barrett and Lucht had a curiosity about and an openness to new cultural experiences, a degree of confidence, even *chutzpah*, and the sustenance of companionship. RVs who recalled their volunteer experience positively and whose future bore traces of its imprint also typically had

had satisfaction in their work, numerous frustrations notwithstanding, some sense of being valued for what they did, and engagement beyond their assigned job. What they did not necessarily have was relevant work experience or professional training or untroubled relations with CUSO staff. Barrett's pre-service work experience, for instance, was mainly in construction. And the adventurous spirit that took him on those extended motorbike journeys also led to some difficulties with the guidelines that CUSO sought to impose for the safety of its volunteers and the longevity of its country programming.[59] Here the case of Tim Brodhead, introduced earlier, is also instructive.

Brodhead was without teaching experience, just twenty-two years old, and only part-way through an MA in political science at McGill University when in 1965 he was hired to teach at the then-new university at Ife in the Western Region. He had not been slated to teach political science, but disregarding that fact, he simply showed up in the department and was taken on. He was by no means alone in not having a doctorate or teacher training among those hired in the university. Nor was his lack of knowledge of the Yoruba language a barrier in the classroom, since courses were taught in English. But he found himself in a wholly Nigerian milieu in the ancient town in terms of his social life and was thus strongly motivated to pick up enough Yoruba to follow conversations in the staff room and function at the market. Unsurprisingly, he quickly became intensely interested in the turbulent politics of Nigeria. Much to the chagrin of staff at CUSO/Ottawa, Brodhead wrote an article for the *McGill Daily*, published in February 1966, detailing the corruption that had characterized Nigerian politics since independence and that had resulted in the then-recent (and in many minds salutary) military coup. Like their counterparts in the Peace Corps, CUSO volunteers were enjoined not only to refrain from engaging in their host country's politics but also to eschew any comments on political issues that could jeopardize their organization's acceptability. Inasmuch as it identified specific politicians and regions as particularly corrupt, Brodhead's article was particularly ill-advised from the perspective of public-relations-minded staff in Ottawa (as, evidently, was a later piece intended for the *Montreal Star*), and he was firmly told that any future articles should first be submitted for clearance by CUSO's Ottawa office. Official concerns notwithstanding, Brodhead's writing demonstrated a high level of engagement with his host country and a close reading of the political situation less than a year after his arrival.[60] Far from being intimidated by the political turmoil swirling around him, he had already extended his stay for a third year at the university when he was asked to take on a coordinator role. Once in his new role, Brodhead promptly became a pragmatic and responsible staff person, ably responding to the challenges arising from the civil war and its aftermath.

What about women volunteers? Although in undertaking service with CUSO in Nigeria they may have encountered a less restrictive cultural framework overall than their counterparts in India, they faced numerous challenges. Nevertheless, after the first few years, single women outnumber single males in some volunteer cohorts and, over time, "emerged as the backbone of the Nigeria cooperant program."[61] Dagmar Langer, a German-born Canadian, was part of an early cohort, serving in Nigeria in the mid-1960s when single women made up about half the total number of CUSO volunteers in the country. Langer arrived in the Western Region in 1964, a scholarship student from the University of Toronto, newly equipped with a history degree. After a few months in a large urban school, Langer got her wish for a "bush" posting and was transferred by the state Ministry of Education to a smaller, poorer, community-financed girls' high school outside the town of Ogbomosho. Despite being a relatively large town, Ogbomosho was without industry and most amenities. "We find that we must travel the 70-odd miles into Ibadan for almost everything above and beyond those things which we can buy here in the market," Langer wrote in 1965 in the *CUSO/SUCO Bulletin*. Three years later, she provided a longer account of her experiences for *Man Deserves Man*.[62] Her skilfully crafted narrative provided rich detail about the town and her interactions with its people (the "vast majority pagan and illiterate"), but her focus was on her teaching and on the needs and responses of her pupils, which made it all feel tremendously worthwhile. While some of their parents were well-to-do, others were impoverished farmers and townspeople struggling to find the money to pay for a place for their daughter in the boarding school: "We have had up to one thousand applications for the thirty places vacant each year."[63] Langer's account of local zeal for schooling meshes well with historian Toyin Falola's memories of a Yoruba village boyhood in the same general region, where the strong emphasis on hard work for youth was "defined mainly in terms of gaining a Western education."[64]

One of just three university graduates on staff when she began at the school, Langer wound up teaching in each of the six forms and in a range of subjects, including West African history, a subject largely foreign to her but for which she developed a syllabus. She also helped develop a small library in a room in her home and, during a vacation, worked on a village health scheme whose concerns she brought back to her pupils. Although Langer's published accounts were obviously written to inspire future volunteers and placed a strong emphasis on service, there is no reason to doubt the genuineness of her commitment or the satisfaction she took from feeling useful and wanted. Despite living in a town strongly affected by the turbulent politics of 1966 (the late premier of the Western Region, murdered in the January coup, came from Ogbomosho), she chose to extend her stay for a third year.

Langer emerges from the printed page as an exemplary volunteer but perhaps not someone whose experience could be captured by the phrase *joie de vivre*. That phrase immediately came to mind, however, following an interview with Gini Dickie, who, at age twenty-one, went to Nigeria in the same cohort as Bernie and Rita Lucht, who became life-long friends.[65] Dickie taught English at a government girls' secondary school in the ancient mud-walled city of Kano, a historic centre of Islamic culture in the far north of the country. Although her professional background was limited to a general BA in political science, she had a zest for new experiences and more familiarity with a larger world than might have been expected from someone her age from small-town Ontario. A mixed-race teacher and a United Church minister had stimulated her interest in world issues, and during a Montreal summer, she had enjoyed the internationalism of working in the UN Pavilion at Expo. The following summer, she had hitchhiked through Europe, finding herself in Paris in the company of two student radicals from Columbia University and surrounded by tear gas at the time of the student uprisings. Back at McGill University for her final year, a course in Marxism had prompted her to join a radical student group, one of whose members she brought to speak to her sorority. Following graduation, she found her way to CUSO.

During her two-year stay in Kano, Dickie shared a house with Canadian and VSO volunteers and with a Hausa woman who, unusually for the time, went on to attain a university degree. Thanks to the departure of a local Peace Corps volunteer, Gini obtained a free Honda, and thanks in part to the Kano Club, she enjoyed an active social life and dated across ethnic and racial lines. Like her male counterparts, she travelled extensively during school holidays. As for the civil war, the combat zone was far from Kano and far from her daily consciousness. Looking back, Dickie reconstructed her youthful CUSO self as an exuberant if sometimes naive young woman, in tune with the spirit of the musical *Hair,* which she played for her students.

As for Dickie's students, they were a privileged few, attending a high school that mainly served elite Muslim families. Unlike many of her fellow volunteers,

Dickie remembered her students as well prepared, though few went on to the advanced courses that would have enabled them to attend university. Many Muslim fathers appeared to be educating their daughters only to increase their future value as brides. The British colonial legacy of a literary education that emphasized Shakespeare and other classics remained strong in Nigeria for the handful of students who made it to high schools like the one where Dickie taught, and in her school there were still older British staff members fully attuned to that tradition and mindful of the fact that they had to prepare their students for O- and A-level examinations that met the requirements of the West African school certificate. Dickie, however, was keen to introduce African literature. Here again she believed that her youth and naïveté had stood her in good stead: "I didn't let ... [my] lack of experience and teacher training stand in the way of battling the Brits over the teaching of African Literature. Of course, the irony was that by the time I left, every school in Kano state had started to teach the African Lit. alternatives on the syllabus." Volunteers like Dickie may have been reflecting the influence of late 1960s cultural nationalism on Canada's academic and arts communities when they sought to encourage Nigerians' awareness of and pride in their own cultural achievements.

Kitty Moses, posted to Benue-Plateau state in the same year, did something analogous, albeit in an extracurricular context (the museum in the state capital at Jos). In many other respects, however, her experience was markedly different from Dickie's, for she went to Nigeria as part of a couple. The Moses were assigned to Government College, Keffi, a boarding school for boys, where Kitty taught French while her husband taught science and physics. As a married couple, they were by no means oddities among volunteers in their cohort. Indeed, in 1970, 30 percent of volunteers were couples. When Kitty Moses looked back on two satisfying CUSO years, she reflected that in addition to well-defined jobs, holiday travel, and a social life that included local Hausa professionals as well as the many expatriates on the college staff, she and her husband had benefited from sharing their Nigeria experience as a couple: "Our CUSO experience was a great one to share at the start of a marriage and a good basis for building a lasting relationship."[66] Other RVs who had served as couples reported something similar. Yet a CUSO assignment could also strain a marriage. A significant number of relationships ended following the couple's return to Canada. As CUSO staff became aware of the tensions that could result when a newly married couple or those already in a strained relationship were thrown so wholly on each other's company in a new and difficult environment, they

"Big Is Beautiful"

alerted would-be volunteer couples to the potential risks and considered how to respond when marriages broke down in the field.[67]

Whether single or married, volunteers experienced living conditions that were markedly different from what they were used to in Canada. Even if their accommodation was a modern bungalow rather than a mud-brick house, unreliability in electricity and water supply was commonplace. Limitations in housing and amenities, a monotonous and unfamiliar diet, and the absence of Western-type stores could occasion a lot of comment by volunteers in the early period of their placement. But such things could be borne with equanimity by volunteers who felt useful and appreciated in their workplace and community and who had congenial companions. Dagmar Langer left behind a "plush existence" at a comprehensive school when she took on her bush posting. She acknowledged that the lack of stimulating companionship occasionally left her feeling intellectually isolated. But she claimed to be unfazed by the lack of modern conveniences in her small house, and experienced the absence of electricity as more of a problem in regard to the limitations it placed on her teaching. By the same token, the installation of water in the school during her stay was hailed as an encouraging sign of institutional progress.[68]

Memories shared by Dr. Ron Cyr, who served in the same general area of western Nigeria as Langer in the early 1970s, also speak to some of these aspects of the volunteer experience.[69] Cyr had his own two-bedroom house on the compound of the Anglican grammar school where he taught chemistry and math, but the water supply was haphazard, and, looking back, he couldn't recall a "proper bath or shower" during all the time that he lived on the compound. Volunteers were, of course, forewarned to expect such conditions. (Having heard tales of self-sacrificial missionary clergy from the nuns who had been his childhood teachers, Cyr had, in fact, expected to see more evidence of hardship and less of comfortable secular living than he encountered when he met Irish clergy in Ijebu-Ode, his new hometown.) What *was* intensely frustrating during his first year, though, as he struggled to do a good job of teaching chemistry (he had been doing doctoral work in the subject at the University of Toronto) was the unreliability of water, gas, and electricity at the school and "the sorry state of the lab facilities" under a likable but nonchalant instructor. In the second year, realizing that there were things he could do to make a difference, Cyr devoted weeks of evenings to cleaning up the lab and persuaded school authorities to build an underground water storage tank. Looking back, he considered the latter his most lasting contribution at the school.

Keith Bezanson *(left)* makes light of the dismal circumstances at the school compound that was his first posting in Nigeria, 1964. Courtesy of Walter McLean.

Even at their most rugged, the physical aspects of living and working conditions for CUSO volunteers in Nigeria were probably less rigorous than those experienced by their early counterparts in India (though Keith Bezanson's several months in the employ of the venal eastern Nigerian chief perhaps stands as the nadir).[70] Moreover, Nigeria volunteers typically had the assistance of a steward or house servant, a phenomenon that, as young Canadians, they encountered with profound unease. Bill McNeill recalled how shocked he and his fellow volunteers were when, arriving in 1964, they were briefed by Barbara McLean on how to deal with servants. The practice seemed so much at odds with CUSO values and philosophy that it briefly became a subject for discussion in the *CUSO Forum*. Yet in the CUSO/Nigeria guidebook for 1970, having a steward was presented as normal, a cost that could usually be managed on a volunteer's salary along with a motorbike and "at least one good holiday."[71] Like many of his fellow volunteers, Ron Cyr initially viewed the idea of hiring a

"Big Is Beautiful"

steward as a repugnant colonial holdover. But he quickly learned that he would be importuned by men seeking such employment until he agreed to take someone on and that doing without anyone to do shopping, cooking, and cleaning was impractical.

In his long and thoughtful reflections on his volunteer years, Cyr was adamant that he had never considered an early termination. Having steeled himself for the "hell-hole" he had expected postwar Nigeria to be, he instead found the reality surprisingly pleasant. However, unlike Cyr, many volunteers who ultimately experienced satisfaction and success in their Nigeria placements did consider early termination, especially in the first months of their assignment. One early volunteer who later became a coordinator mentioned, albeit perhaps partly in jest, that he would have quit early on had it not been for the embarrassment of returning home after all the send-off parties. Paul Delaney, who taught in the Gombe Emirate, a traditional state area in northern Nigeria, in 1973-75, ultimately became so involved in his teaching that he researched and wrote a booklet on the history of the Emirate for the use of his students. He considered extending his stay for a third term and, in retirement, returned by invitation for a visit that gave him great joy. Yet during his first year, Delaney suffered so much from loneliness and from his sense of having failed to connect with his students that he wanted to quit and in fact briefly went home at his own expense "to sort things out in my head."[72]

Early terminations *did* become a more common phenomenon in CUSO generally in the 1970s and 1980s, rising from an annual overall attrition rate of 7 percent as of 1971 to 20 percent for those on the two-year contract norm in 1984-85. Even if the increase was not exceptionally high in Nigeria, it appeared high because of the large total number of volunteers serving there.[73] And the reality was that in many respects conditions were worsening for CUSO in Nigeria, especially from the mid-1970s. The 1979 handbook for new volunteers was forthright about problems in the country generally and particularly in the schools, as a section on teaching, probably by Gerry Caplan, illustrated: "Volunteers should arrive expecting the worst, and will rarely be disappointed; that's why you're needed, after all; and that's the challenge. Standards are as abysmally low as apathy and indiscipline are uncontrollably great. Many students are functionally illiterate and have no foundations whatever for a secondary education." As for the students enrolled in the teachers' colleges – the second most common placement for teacher-volunteers – "only those who can't qualify for high school choose to enter." And with the federal government's introduction in 1976 of "a staggeringly ambitious program known as Universal Primary Education (U.P.E.)," the pressures on such colleges had increased.

Having alerted the new crop of volunteers to the bleakness of the conditions they would face, the section on teaching concluded on an upbeat note and threw the challenge back to them: "the rewards can be equally great. Probably never again will you have a chance to influence lives so directly and positively. And you will. And each time you do will help compensate for the difficult times. It all depends on you – your understanding of under-development, your personal motivation for becoming a volunteer, your expectations of the job. If you've got all this together, then you can handle anything Nigeria throws at you – even its schools."[74] Before turning briefly away from the schools, it is worth considering the experiences of two women who coped and survived even in the face of deteriorating conditions and even in the much maligned teachers' colleges.

Marian White went from Prince Edward Island to northern Nigeria in 1977 equipped with arts and education degrees and a set of textbooks for teaching English. Instead, the principal of the government teachers' college to which she was assigned in a tiny village south of Jos asked her to do teacher training. Many of her students in the co-educational college were already in their twenties – one woman was already a grandmother – and thus perhaps more highly motivated than the lacklustre younger students depicted in the 1979 handbook. (Looking back, she remembered her Nigerian students as more highly motivated than the youth she later briefly taught in Canada's North.) As part of her job, White drove out to villages on her Honda to find practice-teaching placements for her students. She had loved them, she remembered, and felt loved back. Retrospective sentimentality? Perhaps. But along with her professional preparation, she had been equipped with practical coping skills and a background that motivated and eased her adaptation. Raised in a large farming family, she was untroubled by the absence of modern conveniences in her bush posting, and having been taught by nuns who were globally conscious (she recalled a fastathon to raise funds for Biafra), she was, though without the nuns' religious zeal, imbued with an ethic of service.[75]

For Toronto-born Anne Simpson, posted to a teachers' college in Niger state in 1982, it was more of a struggle, but she, too, did more than merely survive. Age twenty-five and unusually well equipped professionally – she had arts and education degrees from Queen's University and a four-year diploma from the Ontario College of Art and Design – she also had experience in domestic volunteering and a strong belief in the value of volunteer work. That, and the allure of adventure, had led her to reject the offer of a secure high school teaching job at home in favour of a CUSO assignment. But along with the loneliness of the first year, there were the frustrations of the low level of teaching (rote learning with no student textbooks until she personally supplied a set) and the awfulness of being forced by the principal to join her colleagues in witnessing the public lashing of a student. "I thought of quitting and going home often," she recalled. Transferred for her second year to an advanced teachers' college in Benue state, Anne had students who were being prepared for high school teaching and, overall, a richer teaching and personal experience. In addition to feeling more at home in Nigerian society, she drew inspiration for her teaching from colleagues who were doing outstanding jobs. And as with so many others who adapted, she had sustaining friendships and exotic holiday-travel adventures, shared in her case with the CUSO volunteer who became her husband.[76]

Educational placements never fell below 80 percent in CUSO/Nigeria programming in the decades covered in this study, and by 1985 they reached 90 percent.[77] The pattern persisted despite pressure from CUSO/Ottawa to make more placements in the health, agriculture, and technology sectors and despite claims by field staff that they *did* make requests for volunteers with professional skills whom they could deploy in these sectors. Meanwhile, the minority of volunteers who served in non-teaching assignments faced challenges that could make their placements more problematic in every sense than those of the teacher-volunteers. The difficulties began before such volunteers ever left Canada. Orientations for West Africa were conducted overwhelmingly with teaching assignments in mind. The lack of comparable occupational preparation for volunteers destined for placements in medical, agricultural, and technical work was understandable, but it could leave such volunteers ill prepared for the vast differences that existed between their Canadian and Nigerian work worlds in terms of such matters as physical conditions in the workplace, indigenous workers' different levels of professional preparedness, and institutional and personal corruption. Especially in medical and technical postings, such differences had more impact than they did in teaching. How volunteers coped in such circumstances varied a good deal, reflecting such factors as motivation and maturity and the extent of the volunteers' exposure to cultural and workplace diversity prior to joining CUSO. The experiences of two male volunteers of about the same age working in technical and medical placements illustrate this point.

In his candid two-volume *Letters Home*, Andy Buhler, a CUSO laboratory technician in Nigeria in 1969-71, gives readers a window into his frustrations over the two-year period, beginning with his orientation in July 1969. It was "somewhat of a disappointment," he recalled in his introduction to the letters. Part of the orientation was a purported study week at Rochdale College in Toronto. Far from being technical preparation, it was effectively an experience in a "foreign" culture within Canadian society. An experimental free university and cooperative residence on the University of Toronto campus, Rochdale was then in the process of achieving its countercultural and drug-inflected notoriety and as such decidedly "an eye-opener for this naive country boy." Black humour continued to feature in Buhler's letters to family and friends over the next two years. The letters acknowledge bouts of depression and heavy drinking and leave the impression that, overall, his experience in Nigeria was, like the orientation, somewhat of a disappointment, not only to Buhler himself but also to CUSO field staff.[78] His first posting, at Kano City Hospital, was meant to involve him in training lab assistants for screening and treating patients in the field in order to lessen patient pressure on the hospital itself. But when the laboratory in which he was to conduct such training "had not yet been designed, much less built" months after his arrival, he pressed to be reassigned or returned home.[79] As country coordinator for Nigeria, Ian Smillie was initially impatient with Buhler's complaints. But writing in March 1970, he acknowledged the pointlessness of continuing in what was, in essence, a non-job. He also outlined the kinds of problems that could occur in trying to find appropriate placements for non-teaching personnel: "The problem with technical and agricultural requests ... is that the jobs are not often clear even in the minds of the people who make the requests, much less to the hapless Coordinator and/or volunteer. And unfortunately this only becomes evident after the volunteer arrives. For teachers there is always a class in a room that they can stand in front of."[80]

Shortly thereafter, Buhler was assigned to a new posting, a Catholic hospital in Mid-Western state that had been badly damaged by rebel occupation during the war. Smillie explained that Buhler would be expected by the nun in charge to re-establish a functioning laboratory, order equipment, train someone to assist and perhaps succeed him, and generally "help get the hospital on its feet."[81] Buhler's new posting in southern Nigeria *did* prove more satisfactory as his second volume of *Letters Home* and his helpful responses to a questionnaire attest. But while his work felt more useful, he now missed the social life he had had with fellow volunteers in Kano and, overall, seems not to have engaged with Nigeria in ways that typically took him beyond observer status. Significantly, he used his holiday to travel to Europe rather than within West Africa, and for this Smillie was reproachful, "especially as you know CUSO's feelings on the matter. I think there is a lot more to do and see here than you are likely to see on your next three trips to Europe."[82]

Looking back decades later, Buhler did not consider his two volunteer years a waste: there had been some good times, and, besides, "Nigeria gave me my lessons." One of those lessons, however, was something that CUSO hoped every would-be volunteer would understand *before* signing on: that a stint as a volunteer in development work was not something to be undertaken as a cure for dissatisfactions back home. In Buhler's case, there had been a bad job experience that had made him feel like a failure: "With that failure still freshly behind me, I suppose I envisioned, rather idealistically, that all of my training could be put to some use in a developing country." Back in Canada, Buhler eventually found his feet and went on to a satisfying life, albeit not in professional roles that bore the imprint of his Africa interlude.[83]

Like Buhler, Dr. Bill Bavington also experienced dissatisfaction with his first placement, also in northern Nigeria, but he responded to the frustration of his situation in a very different way and out of quite different personal circumstances. Bill Bavington had come to Nigeria with his wife, Grace, a nurse-volunteer, in 1968. Prior to doing so and following graduation from medical school and a year's internship, he had spent a summer in Ghana with Operation Crossroads Africa, and he had worked in general practice for six months in an isolated and medically underserviced region of Canada. Given this background, he was less ill-served than Buhler by the general lack of professional content at the orientation for West African volunteers in London. When his first posting in Nigeria, a new rural state hospital, resulted in "never-ending hospital clinical work" instead of the public health and preventive medical work in outlying communities that he had expected to make a priority, he sought a transfer. When it was not forthcoming, he orchestrated his own transfer to another rural posting, a Catholic hospital where he was able to do work that felt more productive. Bill and Grace Bavington extended their stay in Nigeria for a third year. Their subsequent professional studies and careers and their volunteer activities within Canada reflected the strong and positive impact of their three years with CUSO/Nigeria. Indeed, they would return to the country for further medical work in the late 1980s.[84]

As the preceding paragraphs make clear, relationships between volunteers and field staff could become tense. Often, the latter had only a slight edge over the former in terms of age and developing-world experience. Yet as staff they had responsibilities to the Ottawa secretariat and for the smooth functioning of CUSO's relationships with in-country state officials and employers. Such responsibilities sometimes put them in the position of having to enforce unpopular regulations or deal with potentially troublesome volunteer behaviour. CUSO's ultimate concern was to serve the needs of developing-world peoples, in however small a way, rather than cater to the expectations of its volunteers. At the same time, an ongoing supply of volunteers depended on positive responses conveyed back to Canada by each year's crop of newcomers. Generally, therefore, staff tried to support the volunteers from the time they sought out suitable placements for them, welcomed them to Nigeria, and helped them settle in until they oversaw arrangements for their return home two years later. By the early 1970s, like their counterparts elsewhere, CUSO/Nigeria staff were also responsible for an increasing amount of specialized in-country orientation activity. During this period, they could try to address volunteers' fears and concerns. At the annual Christmas-week gathering that brought volunteers together, and at termination conferences at the end of their assignments, staff could also seek feedback on everything from program development to the adequacy of volunteers' salaries and the question of whether they had felt usefully employed. In contrast to their counterparts in some other regions, particularly ECSA, CUSO/Nigeria staff generally eschewed broad ideological issues in their dealings with volunteers, focusing instead on practical concerns even if they had previously been ideologues themselves.

A concern with practicalities was evident in 1970 in the first handbook specifically prepared for Nigeria volunteers. Introduced by coordinator Ian Smillie, it contained a brief overview of Nigerian history, perhaps a tacit recognition that earlier volunteers had lacked knowledge of the broad cultural and colonial background leading up to the civil war. A reading list included works by the country's rising literary stars, making it clear to new volunteers that however "underdeveloped" Nigeria might be, it was not a cultural wasteland. This first guide also contained information about CUSO's own brief history in Nigeria, the kinds of assignments volunteers could expect, the kind of clothing they should bring, and a useful, tongue-in-cheek glossary. Two mid-1970s guidebooks dealt cautiously with the volatile politics of Nigeria's second decade of independence and sought to reassure volunteers that regime change need not make them apprehensive about living and working in Nigeria. A brief section in one of the guides was perhaps pragmatically fulsome about Nigeria's leadership on the African continent.[85] By contrast, the 1979 guide prepared on

Gerry Caplan's watch was forthright about the state of the country's politics and economy, contrasting the ill-distributed, oil-induced economic growth with the nation's worsening mass poverty, and caustic about Lagos, the federal capital and "proud perennial recipient of the World Health Organization's Filthiest City in the World award."[86] Overall, despite the variability of the guidebooks, volunteers who served during CUSO's second decade in Nigeria were forearmed with a good deal more knowledge about what they were getting into than their 1960s predecessors had possessed.

They also had more on-the-ground staff support. By 1979 there were five staff members at work in Nigeria. A deputy coordinator worked with the country coordinator out of Ibadan. Three field staff officers were placed in the North, two in Kaduna and one in Kano.[87] As well as trying to visit volunteers as frequently as time, distance, and bad roads allowed, field staff had to deal with a variety of crises. Problems related to road accidents were by far the most common. When they resulted in death, staff had the sad duty of informing the family and arranging for the return of the body to Canada for burial. Perhaps one of the worst such events occurred in 1968. A young woman had been hit while riding her Honda and left to die by the side of the highway, found only the next morning by a student.[88] There were other occurrences that also required sensitivity and prompt action, such as the volunteer in her third year of service so "completely traumatized" by a robbery and a beating that she was unwilling to stay on, and two others so seriously burned when the gas canister in their house exploded that they had to be transported from their remote location and flown to London for treatment before being returned home.[89]

Typically, however, staff concerns about volunteers were linked to more mundane issues related to their placements. Field staff trip reports from the late 1970s convey something of the range of issues that arose and provide a valuable supplement to the recollections provided decades later by the volunteers themselves. One male volunteer posted to a school of agriculture in a city in a northeast state was so frustrated with his work there and with his dealings with ministry of agriculture officials that his threats of reacting with violence were taken seriously by CUSO staff, who deemed it prudent to return him to Canada. In the same city, a reported job for a nurse-tutor in a school of nursing turned out upon investigation to have shacks for facilities, virtually no equipment, sixty unmanageable students, and a principal so frustrated that she herself was quitting just six months into her job. As shown earlier, staff expected volunteers to show a good deal of adaptability, but there were clearly situations in which they could not function usefully, and in this case the placement was deemed unviable.[90] In her December 1977 report on her trip in another part of the North, Barbara Kincaid, a Ghana RV and the first woman to serve in Nigeria in a staff position, visited some volunteers who had not yet been paid by ministry officials and were living in genuine want. Another volunteer lacked the skills to cope with a "prickly" principal, while two female volunteers had moved in with a nearby male volunteer after they were robbed and their house invaded by locusts. In what was evidently a mission placement, Kincaid found a newly arrived female volunteer experiencing hostility from a dysfunctional missionary roommate. Yet another volunteer was reportedly going through "great periods of depression," even though she was serving with her partner.[91]

Volunteers' placement problems sometimes manifested themselves in three Ds: drink, dirt, and drugs. In the report just cited, Kincaid visited one male volunteer who seemed to be drinking heavily and who lived in a "filthy house," its only decoration "neatly arranged gin bottles." She was concerned by "the distressing number of volunteers [who] live in what I consider unattractive and at times quite dirty houses," and by others who socialized with hard-living expatriates in their area who had "too much money and too little respect for Nigerians." Kincaid was by no means the only staff person to comment on what appeared to be physical manifestations of loneliness and other adjustment problems.[92] A doctoral study of personal changes in volunteers as a result of their Nigeria experience, completed in 1975 by someone who had himself served in the country a few years earlier, likewise referred to extensive marijuana and alcohol use among some groups of volunteers.[93] Comments by others, including volunteers themselves, make it clear, however, that, as with their contemporaries in Canada, their use of alcohol and drugs might sometimes be merely recreational, especially in social gatherings, rather than therapeutic or consolatory.[94]

If field staff reports and guidebooks for volunteers sometimes sounded overly concerned, priggish, or high-handed in comments related to such matters as sanitation and drug use, it was in large part a reflection of staff's responsibility for CUSO's image as well as for the well-being of their volunteers. Thus, in reference to drug use, volunteers were reminded in the 1979 guidebook that if they were caught violating Nigerian laws, neither CUSO as an organization nor the Canadian High Commission would be in a position to save them from the consequences. Indeed, they were told that "CUSO field staff officers are empowered to terminate a contract and repatriate volunteers involved with illicit drugs." The same guidebook, however, promised "a hugely decadent New Year's

Eve Party" as part of the Christmastime conference. As for other matters related to changing cultural and moral norms among Canadian youth, including the sexual revolution, CUSO was in tune with or ahead of changing mores, merely reminding women volunteers in the same guidebook that if they were using birth control pills they should bring their own supply.[95] Female volunteers' sexual activity was presumably regarded as normally a private matter rather than something that CUSO needed to monitor to protect its image or in the role of *in loco parentis*.

While the trip reports cited above contained concerns about a variety of volunteer placement problems, on the whole they were consistent with volunteers' own retrospective accounts of successful adaptations. Thus on her December 1977 tour, Barbara Kincaid visited volunteers who were coping well with officialdom and enjoying their teaching, even when schools were overcrowded and sometimes "pretty bush." Their satisfied bosses were already asking for more volunteers. Marian White and her roommate were among the volunteers on Kincaid's circuit. Both women, she reported, were coping well, "taking it all in their stride and enjoying themselves." And if some volunteers gave evidence of maladjustment in their unkempt housekeeping, there was the counterbalancing example of a young man whose coping skills and positive attitude were evident in his attractively decorated house and a garden; he had welcomed Kincaid as "a perfect host," and "whipped up a pizza in an outdoor oven." Summing up the 4,000-kilometre trip, in which she had managed to visit all the volunteers and call upon all the education ministries in her territory, Kincaid reported that she had "encountered no really major problems" and overall had had a successful and "generally pleasant trip." On a return visit to the volunteers in her area a few months later, this time accompanied by Barbara Brown from CUSO's Ottawa office, Kincaid even found that the volunteer whose drinking had been a source of concern was now doing well. Indeed, his principal had written him a letter of congratulation after he produced the school's first play. Brown, who wrote her own report on the trip, was also upbeat: while there had been some problems among the volunteers, "with very few exceptions" they were doing "excellent jobs."[96]

Dilemmas and Debates over Programming

Generally positive accounts of volunteers' contributions and experiences in Nigeria coexisted in the 1970s with debates about CUSO's role in the country and reports of morale problems. From time to time, the question of whether CUSO should even continue to operate in Nigeria was discussed. Staff members were understandably at the forefront in such discussions. They were responding to real or perceived criticisms from CUSO/Ottawa and from staff in other, more progressive, regions and sometimes out of their own frustrations and doubts about the appropriateness of their work in Nigeria.

Much of the discussion centred on the extent to which Nigeria programming remained focused on advanced formal schooling. As seen in Chapter 3, some staff in the ECSA region and elsewhere rejected formal education as a development strategy during the 1970s. In the case of Nigeria, the oil boom, which took off with the quadrupling of crude oil prices in 1973-74 and which peaked by 1977,[97] gave a new edge to the questioning, particularly when, having adopted its Universal Primary Education plan, Nigeria began recruiting thousands more expatriates, Canadians among them, to teach at regular salaries.[98] The oil wealth also contributed to ever greater levels of conspicuous consumption by elite Nigerians and to corruption on a record scale. Given these circumstances, some asked, shouldn't CUSO be directing its volunteers and its money to countries less able to help their own poor? One staff officer wrote in this vein in 1974: conceding that he was not speaking for his colleagues, he nonetheless recommended that programming in Nigeria should end, since in the new circumstances created by the oil boom, CUSO was simply providing a rich country with "cheap labour."[99]

Two years later, a critique of the Nigeria field staff's Country Plan for 1976-77 attacked the plan's narrow programming focus and charged that formal education did nothing to decrease the gap between rich and poor and provide grassroots benefits. The author of an unsigned response to the critique acknowledged the need for CUSO/Nigeria staff to re-examine the range of their programming and the rationale. But he also went on the offensive: some of their placements, indeed even some of their university placements, *did* have grassroots benefits, he argued. As for the more general criticism of formal education programming in development, it was evidently influenced by the writings of Ivan Illich and Paulo Freire, theorists whose views, however currently fashionable on the left in the West, were clearly at odds with Nigeria's own demonstrably strong commitment to formal education. (Even Cuba, the anonymous author pointed out, valued and fostered formal education!) And did anyone really think that if CUSO withdrew from Nigeria, that would change the country's approach to education? As for the charge that CUSO was duplicating what other volunteer agencies were doing, it was wide of the mark, the author felt especially since CUSO/Nigeria worked closely with VSO, the largest such outside agency.[100]

The response to the critique could have made more of the point that demand for formal education was, quite literally, a grassroots phenomenon, and of the distinct but important argument that by continuing to concentrate on volunteer placements CUSO/Nigeria was indirectly providing a benefit to CUSO overall. If a small town inhabited mainly by farmers undertook to build and support three community high schools with no help from government beyond teachers' salaries, wasn't that grassroots and thus a highly appropriate setting for a CUSO volunteer? Community-based demand of this kind was a very real phenomenon, albeit less likely in the North than the South.[101] Meanwhile, the pragmatic argument for CUSO-wide benefits from the ongoing focus on placing teacher volunteers in Nigeria was strongly made in other contexts. Such a focus had the effect of subsidizing CUSO programming in other regions, it was contended. Because the CIDA funding formula hinged on the total number of volunteers CUSO placed each year, and because Nigeria was by far the single biggest placement country, dismantling CUSO's educational programming there would result in significant financial loss to the organization. Gerry Caplan may have been overstating the case when in 1978 he wrote that "the issue may just boil down to two quite simple and stark alternatives: continue sending teachers to Nigeria or forget CUSO," but he was not alone in making the point.[102]

Given their perception of being under attack and underappreciated by the larger CUSO organization,[103] field staff valued expressions of support from Nigerian and Canadian officials. Such support also helped them cope with occasional accusations that the teacher-volunteers they supplied were no more than unqualified youth seeking to escape unemployment at home. Just such an attack was made in 1971 in an article in the *New Nigerian,* the major newspaper in the North. Written by a Nigerian student then said to be studying at the University of British Columbia, the article was endorsed by an editorial. In response, the secretary of the Bureau for External Aid in the federal Ministry of Education was at pains to assure coordinator Steve Gibbons that CUSO volunteers were in fact very much wanted and appreciated by both federal and state authorities. The fact that Nigeria almost always asked for more volunteers than CUSO could supply should, the secretary said, be taken as "undisputable proof" of that. Allan McGill of the Canadian High Commission in Lagos was also reassuring: CUSO enjoyed "a remarkable popularity in Nigeria ... commensurate with the success of their efforts." It was simply that with the departure of the Peace Corps it had become "the largest volunteer agency in Nigeria" and, as such, a natural target of "overall resentment of the colonialist past and the 'new-colonialist' present."[104]

Later in the decade, the same student wrote an even angrier piece, calling the CUSO volunteers "UNWANTED PARASITES" and drawing parallels with the infamous Marjorie Michelmore postcard affair that had rocked the early Peace Corps in his country.[105] In these circumstances, CUSO/Nigeria staff and volunteers undoubtedly welcomed a much more temperate article by another Nigerian graduate student, Eme Ekekwe, published in the *CUSO Forum* in 1979. Ekekwe, who was studying at Carleton University and doing summer work for CUSO's Orientation Department, sought to inject a dose of realism into the organization's debates about whether it should remain in the new Nigeria and what its volunteers could contribute. The frustration was understandable, but a hasty withdrawal would be unhelpful, even "self-righteous," especially since the now-fading oil boom had left millions of rural and slum-dwelling Nigerians as badly off as ever. "The loud criticism of support for formal education by CUSO in Nigeria and other places is often misplaced," Ekekwe declared. Indeed, "with all its evils ... formal education is still something I would help a Nigerian peasant acquire, especially if, in the meantime, I have nothing else to offer." Adding that elitism was "no more a mark of education in Nigeria than it is of any capitalist society, including Canada," especially at advanced levels, he recommended that CUSO should stay on at least for the next several years and "concentrate on rural postings *in the northern states.*"[106]

Such reassurances notwithstanding, some volunteers did worry that through their work they were helping to broaden opportunities for an already relatively privileged group of Nigerians. Sandra Kalmakoff, the thoughtful twenty-year-old daughter of progressive, politically minded Saskatchewan parents, was uneasy about her first placement: teaching English composition and remedial reading in a university-preparation program at a college in Kano in 1972-74. It seemed to this young honours philosophy graduate that since the college could obviously afford to hire many expatriate contract teachers and pay them "many times more than a CUSO salary," she would be better deployed in a poorer school doing more basic teaching. Extending her term for a third year, Kalmakoff transferred to a more rural posting, where she trained future primary-school teachers. While she felt better about what she was doing there, she nonetheless believed that CUSO colleagues doing rural nursing and agricultural-extension work were making more directly useful contributions.[107] Volunteers like Kalmakoff could readily observe the educational inequalities – and the fallout. Although almost half of state budgets went into education in 1973, only one in three children attended primary school, and only one in twenty-five students went on to secondary school. And yet even primary-school leavers were reluctant to return to farm settings or do manual labour, a problem already obvious in the South at independence and now a national dilemma.[108] Did the reality of such problems and the fact that it was, comparatively, the already privileged who benefited from CUSO's teaching services mean that the organization should refuse to support Nigeria's formal educational initiatives? Or would such a stance be, in Ekekwe's words, "self-righteous"? Couldn't an argument be made for eventual wider benefits? As a volunteer serving in a Methodist-run boys' high school argued in a letter to the *CUSO Forum* in 1980, the fact that he was involved in teaching boys who were, comparatively, part of a future Nigerian elite did not rule out possible developmental value from his work somewhere down the road.[109]

For those critical of the overwhelming emphasis on formal education in CUSO's work in Nigeria, or anxious to respond to the criticisms and conscious of the ethical reservations of volunteers like Kalmakoff, there seemed to be a compelling logic for moving more in the direction of a projects approach. In 1977, four years after the establishment of CUSO's Projects Division, CUSO overall had funded close to 300 major projects and more than 300 discretionary projects.[110] And yet, while the projects approach had begun in Nigeria, it did not fare well there. It had significantly greater importance in CUSO programming elsewhere, including the ECSA region, where it lent itself to CUSO staff's more politicized approach to development, and in other regions, including Bangladesh, where CUSO was able to establish effective links with and help strengthen local civil-society groups. Even in other parts of West Africa, there was more project work.[111] Was it the case, as field staff elsewhere and critics in CUSO's Ottawa secretariat had it, that CUSO/Nigeria staff lacked the initiative to move beyond the familiar routines of making educational placements? Or were they simply complying with the expressed priorities of Nigerian federal and state officials and education-minded community groups? A brief look at some project-related activities and concerns by staff and volunteers in Nigeria shows some of the challenges they faced.

There were early indications of a willingness to take advantage of the new programming opportunities available through CUSO's Projects Division. There was also a straightforward statement of purpose by staff: to "provide modest financial support to projects which help solve locally defined problems."[112] Already in the spring of 1973, as reported by coordinator Roy Fischer, CUSO/ Nigeria had approved four discretionary projects and two larger projects, and he anticipated more of the former as volunteers became aware of this new programming possibility.[113] One such proposal that year requested funds to purchase a van for use by a Nigerian physiotherapist who had seen an itinerant physiotherapy project during a stay in Canada and believed something similar would be useful in his region. A proposal put forward two years later by a volunteer couple requested discretionary funds on behalf of an ethnic-minority woman who was taking in orphaned children with no extended family to care for them. For a time, volunteers gave space in their newsletter, *Disting,* to ways of identifying feasible local projects.[114]

Field staffers Barbara Kincaid and Ron Davis began 1978 with new initiatives to promote projects and with additional sources of project funding. The Canadian High Commission had committed to $50,000, while the Nigerian Federal Government had agreed to provide a subvention to CUSO for every volunteer who completed her or his two-year contract, with the money to be used on community projects. Volunteers received a form letter and a project-description form from Kincaid and Davis encouraging them to look for useful and viable grassroots projects for their particular area. Meanwhile, as coordinator, Gerry Caplan was cautiously optimistic that the subvention fund would allow CUSO/ Nigeria "to move into projects in a serious way for the first time ever." The critical factor was achieving the number of new placements to which they had committed, and avoiding early terminations.[115] The 1979 handbook provided a simple definition of a project for the benefit of new volunteers and listed some examples of projects currently being funded: a public-health nurse, a farmers' cooperative, a slum-community project, and schools for the deaf and blind.[116]

In practice, however, it proved difficult to identify, launch, monitor, and sustain viable small-scale development projects that were more than just short-term "good works." Economist and development critic William Easterly has referred to NGOs as more likely than state or multilateral agencies to be "Searchers" rather than "Planners," that is, to be on the lookout locally for "do-able actions" leading to "specific things that help poor people."[117] Certainly, Barbara Kincaid sounded like a Searcher as she carried out her first tour in 1978, keeping an eye out for possible projects while checking in with her volunteers. Nevertheless, the main task for Kincaid and other field staff was arranging and

"Big Is Beautiful"

overseeing volunteers' placements. There would be no CUSO/Nigeria staff officer whose sole responsibility was project work until 1985.[118] And as for the volunteers, how realistic was it to think that, even in their second year, they could readily identify feasible projects, given their limited community knowledge and rudimentary language skills? (Situations like the one involving the physiotherapist, personally known to at least one volunteer through the hospital where they both worked, were probably atypical.) And who would monitor any such project once the volunteer left? Kincaid pondered the possibilities – and the risks – of approaching local officials for project ideas: what if they suggested something that CUSO deemed inappropriate and she then had to turn down their request? "There must be *some* projects out there for us," she wrote, "so we'll keep looking."[119]

The difficulty of establishing contacts with groups who could speak authentically and disinterestedly for community needs had been recognized in 1973 at a meeting of West Africa regional staff: they mainly worked with government officials, they acknowledged, and had good relations with them, but they had built up few relationships with indigenous NGOs.[120] What, then, were the options? Mindful of the fact that missions had more local knowledge than volunteers as a result of their long-term presence in many communities and less in the way of potential conflicts of interest than local community officials, Gerry Caplan wrote, following a 1978 trip to northeast Nigeria, that if CUSO wanted to see functioning projects and get project ideas it could do no better than "*cherchez l'église.*" Here, and in another report a few months later, he respectfully described good projects carried out by nuns, and referred to strong leadership in local development work provided by white Roman Catholic priests. Unfortunately, when one of the latter later saw Caplan's report on the trip, he took strong offence at the CUSO coordinator's characterization of some church-initiated projects as "basically misguided quintessential trickle-down capitalism," helping individuals rather than the community.[121]

His "trickle-down capitalism" remark notwithstanding, Caplan was decidedly out of sympathy with project policy statements from CUSO/Ottawa that seemed to come out of a vaguely left-wing view of development rather than to be cognizant of on-the-ground realities. His frustration was evident when in May 1978 he responded to a document on "Project Criteria and Use" that appeared to be a statement of official policy: if its rhetoric were to be taken seriously, the document would create "impossibly high expectations for ourselves ... for our volunteers, and for the nationals we want to serve." In response to the statement that one project goal should be to "allow the beneficiaries to understand the broader socio-economic and physical conditions under which they live," he asked, "whose job is this? Do most FSOs [field staff officers] have either the competence or the time? Do most white missionaries – who in West Africa at least are so often the intermediaries between CUSO and the project – have either the competence or the interest? Do most local spokesmen or community development workers have the grasp or the training?" The "Big Questions" being raised in such documents, Caplan charged, were "uselessly divisive redherrings." CUSO should concentrate on what it could realistically do: "We try to help a few needy people. That's all. Nothing more. They want better health or cleaner water or improved literacy or trained oxen or the competence to help others help themselves. With our laughably small number of dollars, we help a tiny number of such people achieve these very modest, very human goals. We should discuss CUSO's role within these simple, realistic and highly constraining parameters."[122] It was a far cry from the goal of conscientization that critics of modernization theory in development (including Caplan himself)[123] had taken up by the early 1970s. But it was grounded in the sobering realities of doing development work in Nigeria. For Caplan as CUSO's Nigeria coordinator and a committed democratic socialist, it was important that CUSO's projects should serve "'disadvantaged groups ... working cooperatively'" rather than just help individuals. But beyond that, the projects were simply an attempt "to make a few wretched lives more tolerable. That's not a very highfalutin ideal, I know, but it does seem accurately to reflect the limitations of CUSO's contributions to this country."[124]

Paradoxical Patterns and the End of an Era

Caplan's somewhat bleak defence of project initiatives was consistent with two interrelated points made by him and others in regard to CUSO/Nigeria programming overall: that is, the need for realism in that programming – what Nigeria mainly asked for was teachers – and for small expectations about outcomes. West African region staff had wrestled with the latter issue at one of their meetings in 1974 in the context of trying to help volunteers come to terms with placement problems and thwarted idealism. What was needed, the staff agreed, was some sort of strategy "for presenting the idea that development is a process in which a volunteer plays a very, very small role."[125] Ekekwe made a similar point in his 1979 *CUSO Forum* article specifically in reference to Nigeria when he told volunteers that their role, though worthwhile, was "bound to be peripheral." The statements in both cases, far from being dismissive of the volunteers' efforts, were intended to foster a helpful sense of proportion and a long-term perspective.

Such a perspective was especially necessary for Nigeria volunteers from the early 1970s, for beyond the deteriorating national environment in the oil era, there was the morale-sapping problem of being part of a program increasingly under attack from more "progressive" elements in the CUSO family for not being sufficiently "developmental." In addition to higher early termination rates in the 1970s, volunteer dissatisfaction was also expressed, indirectly, in annual incoming cohort sizes that sometimes fluctuated downward after the record high intake of 1971. In 1978, even an acute shortage of teaching jobs at home was not enough to bring new volunteers forward in sufficient numbers to meet the requests from Nigeria. A *Globe and Mail* article in 1977 citing the opinion of a disgruntled older volunteer that CUSO should "ditch its whole operation in Nigeria" had perhaps contributed to the recruitment problem. In any event, two *Globe* articles in 1978 reported on the problem.[126]

And yet, as shown in this chapter, personal accounts by and about volunteers attest to the fact that many continued to have positive experiences in Nigeria, even as conditions became more challenging. Likewise, some field staff from this period retain positive memories of their work, even though they were under greater pressures than the volunteers. Barbara Kincaid remembered her position as a field staff officer as one in which she thrived: it was "exhilarating and exhausting and demanding"; it also provided her with an opportunity to work with colleagues who were "generally very committed, capable and knowledgeable."[127] A fortuitous combination of personality and circumstance could allow volunteers and staff to survive, even thrive, even in chaotic and discouraging circumstances and impel them to make a case for maintaining a CUSO presence in Nigeria. Thus, in the same year that the *Globe* reported on the teacher-recruitment problem in Canada, the 120 volunteers who came together for the annual CUSO/Nigeria Christmas conference "strongly reaffirmed their conviction that the CUSO program was making a positive contribution to Nigeria" and that recruitment of teachers should continue, notwithstanding ongoing difficulties and debates. In 1979, 140 volunteers, a record-high number, left for Nigeria.[128]

Volunteer numbers remained strong for the first few years of the 1980s. There was even a new initiative with the introduction of a special focus on teaching English as a second language (TESL). By 1986, most volunteers were

TESL teachers.[129] One of them, Wayn Hamilton, arriving in 1983 with two university degrees and a TESL certificate, could certainly be said to have thrived. Hamilton, perhaps the first African Nova Scotian to serve with CUSO/Nigeria, remained involved in Nigeria and other parts of West Africa well into the 1990s.[130] The geographical concentration of volunteer placements (down to nine states from eighteen) and the continuity in management at the regional level made possible by Sharon Capeling's leadership of the entire West African program through most of the 1980s also boded well for CUSO in Nigeria, especially given Capeling's wealth of volunteer and staff experience and her familial ties to the country through her marriage to Robin Alakija. Finally, in 1980-81, Eme Ekekwe, introduced earlier, served for a year as CUSO/Nigeria coordinator.[131]

Nevertheless, CUSO's presence in Nigeria declined dramatically in the mid-1980s. Fewer than twenty – perhaps fewer than a dozen – new volunteers were sent to the country in 1985, the lowest number since the first year of the civil war.[132] CUSO's desire in the 1980s to put more emphasis on project work, especially in conjunction with local NGO partners, would likely have resulted in some decline in volunteer numbers in Nigeria as part of a more general pattern during the decade even without changes on the ground. But the immediate precipitating factor was the withdrawal of Nigeria's welcome mat for volunteers and for expatriates generally.[133] Illegal immigrants, contract workers, and other outsiders became collateral damage from deteriorating social, economic, and political conditions under the Second Republic (1979-83) and the two military regimes that succeeded it.[134] The most significant source of national dissatisfaction affecting CUSO was the high level of unemployment among educated Nigerians, the group most able to criticize government. Now, therefore, it was being asserted, there were enough Nigerian teachers to meet existing needs in the general education system. Formal authorization from the Federal Republic of Nigeria for CUSO to work in the country had lapsed in 1984, and it had still not been renewed when, as hired consultants, Ekekwe and Suzanne Veit published *CUSO/Nigeria: A 25 Year Retrospective Evaluation* in 1986. While Ekekwe and Veit tried to put the best face on the "vague and conflicting messages" emanating from the federal Ministry of National Planning about CUSO's future role in Nigeria, merely describing its treatment of CUSO as "unkind" and noting how much the organization was valued by individual Nigerians (from students to school principals and state officials), they acknowledged that most volunteer agencies had already left the country.[135] Outlining four possible options for CUSO/Nigeria, the first of which was immediate withdrawal, they instead endorsed the option adopted by staff at a January 1986 programming meeting: a decision to commit to a three-year development phase, characterized by a "shift towards fewer cooperants [volunteers], the identification of possible NGO partners, and the focussing of project work on certain key sectors in each region of the country." If after the three-year trial this approach proved unworkable, it would then be time to phase out of Nigeria "with the full knowledge of how good that association has been to Nigeria and to CUSO."[136]

Beginning in 1962 with just seven volunteers, CUSO over the years had made placements in virtually every Nigerian state. It was a testimony to the volunteers' personal resolve and to the support of field staff that the vast majority completed their contracts and in a few cases even extended them. If at times they had felt overwhelmed by the risks and frustrations, what stood out decades later in shared recollections was a quiet satisfaction that they had risen to the challenges and the opportunities of living in "an incredibly vivid place."[137] That they had had a chance to do so was, of course, a reflection of Nigeria's decades-long eagerness for volunteers to help meet its goal of modernization through education. Some two decades later, Nigerian politics and demographics had created a new and unwelcoming environment for expatriate volunteers. Whatever lay ahead, for CUSO/Nigeria, it was the end of an era.

5

"Involvement That Lasts a Lifetime"
Returned Volunteers and Canadian Society

It is my frankest opinion that the [CUSO] volunteers themselves derive the most benefit from the experience. Eventually, whether these returned volunteers become diplomats or housewives, Canada as a whole will benefit.

– returned volunteer John R. Wood, 1965[1]

As important as the professional and personal contributions which CUSO volunteers make in their country of service are the contributions which they make to Canada on their return.

– Prime Minister Pierre Elliott Trudeau, 1969[2]

CUSO is now a vital component in Canada's international development effort ... it has moved from its initial experimental and amateur status to a level of performance and professionalism which are the envy of many government and non-governmental agencies in Canada and abroad ... But CUSO has done much more. It has exposed Canadian society to the currents and cross-currents of a world in ferment. In doing so, it has helped to involve Canadians as participants instead of as spectators on the world's stage ... [and] is helping to create a more informed public.

– Lewis Perinbam, Director, Non-Governmental
Organizations Division, CIDA, 1972[3]

Claims that CUSO volunteers' personal gains and potential contributions to Canadian society equalled or exceeded their overseas contributions became something of a mantra, whether made by the returned volunteers themselves (RVs) or in laudatory remarks such as those by Trudeau and Perinbam. Writing in 1981, Tim Brodhead provocatively challenged such claims. Far from returning as an engaged citizenry, the majority of volunteers, he postulated, had simply moved on to consumerist lifestyles: "Their two years overseas was just that: two years to be remembered perhaps fondly, nostalgically, with a sigh or a shudder. But not as an expression of any longer-term commitment to the ideas which it was presumed had inspired them to the 'noble sacrifice.'" Brodhead was not, though, as disillusioned as this statement appeared to suggest: he went on to call for ongoing participation – albeit more informed and thoughtful participation – in a global struggle "to overturn structures which permit the rich to profit from the poor" and to suggest that such participation was "as relevant to our own societies as to others."[4]

Like Brodhead, other CUSO insiders conceded that many RVs had not become notably engaged on international or Canadian issues following their two years abroad.[5] Because CUSO was the earliest secular Canadian NGO to put volunteers into development work and still the largest at the end of its first quarter century, the apparently complete return to private life by so many of those youthful foot soldiers in development – they were said to number nine thousand by 1983[6] – was seen as all the more regrettable. And yet the expectations of Wood, Trudeau, and Perinbam did not go unfulfilled: many CUSO alumni *did* remain directly engaged in international matters, particularly through careers in development work. Others promoted a global consciousness within their own Canadian communities or reflected that consciousness in volunteer work and in their approach to a variety of national and community issues. Their CUSO experience may not have been solely responsible for producing their global- and civic-mindedness, but it unquestionably strengthened and confirmed pre-existing tendencies. Brodhead's own career path is instructive. He was already politically aware and interested in Africa's changing political landscape when he went to Nigeria in 1965. Following his return, he spent several years in staff positions with CUSO before going on to refugee and relief work in Sudan and the drought-ridden Sahel. Back in Canada in 1976, he joined with Ian Smillie in founding Inter Pares. From 1987 to 1992, Brodhead was executive director of the Canadian Council for International Cooperation and during that period co-authored an important research study on NGOs for the North-South Institute.

In 1995, he became president and chief executive officer of the Montreal-based J.W. McConnell Family Foundation. Looking back in 2009, Brodhead reflected that his entire career came out of his initial decision to go to Africa.[7]

Personal interviews and written contacts with other CUSO alumni confirm the ongoing salience of their initial encounter with the developing world, even if their post-CUSO careers did not have a discernible international dimension. Such sources also confirm that, for many, the volunteer experience was fundamental in giving them the confidence to take on challenging new roles as they moved on with their lives. The word "empowerment," frequently used to describe Western women's desired impact on impoverished women in the Global South, has become something of a cliché in development circles. But in terms of the impact of the overseas experience on the volunteers themselves, empowerment seems an entirely apt term, perhaps particularly so for female volunteers. Chapter 5 provides a broad and anecdotally informed survey of ways that the youthful volunteer experience played out in the professional and personal lives of male and female RVs and in the communities where they lived. The chapter confirms that the two years of overseas involvement could indeed last a lifetime and even reverberate across generations. Born for the most part during the Second World War or the baby-boom era, CUSO volunteers in the 1960s and 1970s were part of a larger demographic that has come to be associated with linear careers and prosperous, even wealthy, lifestyles. Many of the alumni who come into focus in this chapter, however, lived peripatetic lives, characterized by varied careers and multiple sites of involvement rather than by significant wealth accumulation or fixed identities. The subsections that follow should therefore be understood as organizational conveniences rather than as mutually exclusive categories for analyzing and containing their post-volunteer lives.

"The Coming Back Is Not Easy": Returning Home and Moving On

Their overseas placements had been frustrating, exhilarating, ultimately unsettling, experiences for many volunteers. The personal and career plans that some had in mind before serving overseas were now in flux or discarded. Especially if they were feeling unsettled about their future plans, it was not surprising that many seized the opportunity to extend the adventure by taking the long way home. A prolonged period of rough travel in Asia, Africa, the Middle East, or Europe became a rite of passage for many returning volunteers. Given their experience of rugged placements, they could cope readily with haphazard travel and accommodation arrangements, even in places like Afghanistan. Once back home, though, they could not always summon up the degree of enthusiasm for reunions with family, home-cooked meals, and Canadian abundance that their loved ones had eagerly anticipated, or conform, even for appearance's sake, to such former rituals as family churchgoing.

As departing volunteers they had been told to anticipate culture shock, but the early cohorts were ill prepared for its reverse. One returnee, coming back to Toronto in 1964 and seeing the city's then-new Yorkdale Shopping Centre, remembered finding it "obscene." Another likewise remembered being almost sickened by the abundance in Canadian stores.[8] If such statements sound hyperbolic now, it is worth remembering how little exposure most young Canadians had had to worlds of extreme want and difference, even via television, in the 1960s.[9] Returning from such worlds, the volunteers saw their Canadian communities through new eyes. Harry and Sandra Gaudet have no recollection of having been warned about the likelihood of reverse culture shock when they prepared as a young CUSO couple – just twenty-two and twenty, respectively – to go from Prince Edward Island to Grenada in 1968: "Because we were coming home we expected everything to be the same. What we didn't realize was that we would change."[10] Yet a tendency to be preachy and self-righteous in recounting their experiences of Third World poverty (and cultural achievements) and to comment unfavourably on Canadians' consumerism and cultural myopia, the RVs soon came to realize, often meant that once they moved beyond what one of them called "snake stories" friends and family simply tuned them out or changed the subject. "I think most volunteers felt they had experienced something momentous in their lives," Jill Morton Grant recalled, "but that people in Canada didn't quite get it, showing only polite interest, so we probably learned early on not to go on and on about our overseas experience." On his "return to the Parish," another wrote, the volunteer found Canada "one of the most parochial countries that any of us ever saw."[11] Such an assessment did not allow for the fact that there were special interest groups – churches, and organizations like Rotary clubs and 4-H, for example – that *did* want to hear about the volunteer's experience, particularly if he or she had a personal or community connection to the group or had received some financial support from it. But this was less likely to happen after the early years and in large cities or for RVs who had no established links to such groups.

In addition to having lived in a developing country that had exposed them to worlds of socio-economic difference and postcolonial aspirations, many RVs had had the experience of a cosmopolitan placement. As well as co-workers who were part of the educated indigenous elite in places like Dar es Salaam, there were other volunteers – from the US, Britain, or northern Europe, or sometimes from a comparatively more developed Asian or African country – who were also part of the expatriate mix. In newly independent Botswana, where Dr. Paul Kelly and teacher Katherine Eberl, his future wife, served in the mid-1970s, an indigenous elite was still almost non-existent in some professional fields, and hence the expatriate volunteer community was probably unusually large.[12] But even for volunteers who served in isolated placements, such as was often the case in 1960s India, there were cosmopolitan encounters at international work camps or during holiday travels. The overall effect was to expose the young Canadians to the values and aspirations of diverse peoples, as workmates, friends, and lovers. Meanwhile, the Canada to which they returned was still far from being a multicultural country, for despite the extent of postwar immigration the newcomers were mainly from European backgrounds. In these circumstances, especially for the 1960s cohorts, friendships with those who had shared their overseas experiences and the trials of re-entry remained important, frequently enduring for a lifetime. Serving on a CUSO local committee, helping out with orientation, or working on the national CUSO staff also provided something of a temporary soft landing, even for a few whose overseas experience with the organization had not been a source of satisfaction to it or themselves.[13]

CUSO was not in a position to put its RVs through psychological analysis to detect changes resulting from their overseas service and experience of "re-entry," something the Peace Corps was already doing with its volunteers by the mid-1960s. Nevertheless, it seems clear that like their US counterparts, many Canadian RVs began working or studying in areas that they hadn't previously considered and that they were "far less security minded than previous generations of young people."[14] Relevant data are most readily available for the two COV cohorts who, gathering in 1986 and 1987, respectively, for twenty-fifth anniversary celebrations, produced reunion booklets that provide revealing snapshots of their volunteer and post-volunteer lives.[15] The most striking aspect is the number who went on to graduate or professional studies within a year or so of returning: at least six of the fourteen profiled from the 1961 cohort did so (one RV had died), and fully half of the sixteen from the 1962 cohort. Few from either cohort promptly put down firm residential or occupational roots following their volunteer years. And although women made up almost half of the first

"Involvement That Lasts a Lifetime"

group, and the majority of the second group, returning to a North America where women were still marrying in their early twenties, only one of these women seems to have married in the year of her return from her placement.[16] Information on RVs from later cohorts points to similar patterns, with a period of further study in the years following their return, or, later, as preparation for career change or advancement, becoming something of a norm.

Careers in Development: Ottawa and Beyond

John Wood's 1965 speculation that male RVs might go on to become diplomats was not unreasonable: it was, after all, a path followed from the interwar era by some able sons of missionary families, who had learned from birth to be at home in other cultures.[17] Wood's expectation was in fact promptly fulfilled by his friend and fellow India volunteer Steve Woollcombe and, briefly in the 1980s, by ex-Nigeria volunteer Keith Bezanson, who served for three years as Canada's ambassador to Bolivia and Peru. Following their CUSO service, both men had gone on to graduate studies at US universities sparked by their overseas experience, and both had obtained Ford Foundation fellowships in international development to do so. After completing his MA in political science on CUSO as a case study of an NGO, the fluently bilingual Woollcombe joined Canada's Department of External Affairs as a foreign-service officer. It was the beginning of a long career in diplomacy that took him to the US and Europe as well as to positions in Cameroon, Indonesia, Venezuela, and Ottawa.[18]

Nevertheless, External Affairs proved to be an atypical career site for RVs who retained overseas interests and pursued them through official channels. Instead, as the federal government began to participate more vigorously in international aid and development work in the first Development Decade, RVs were particularly sought out by the Canadian International Development Agency (CIDA) and the International Development Research Centre (IDRC). Indeed, the longest stretch of Bezanson's career would be spent with these two organizations. Beginning as a consultant with CIDA in 1968 while still engaged in his doctoral research in Ghana, Bezanson went on to a series of senior positions with CIDA, including a vice-presidency, and, in the 1990s, to the presidency of IDRC.[19] Maurice Strong had a keen eye for such talent. He was already on CUSO's National Advisory Council and a firm believer in the organization's usefulness for Canada's overall aid program when he became head of the External Aid Office in 1966. From 1968, when the office became the much more ambitious entity CIDA, with Strong as its idealistic and entrepreneurial president, there were, as David Morrison notes, vigorous efforts to tap into the "youth, commitment, and enthusiasm" that an organization like CUSO could provide.[20] Likewise, A.F.W. Plumptre, commissioned in 1966 to do investigative groundwork for establishing the agency that became IDRC, regarded CUSO as a kind of seeding ground for future workers in international aid and other fields. Volunteers' numbers should be increased, Plumptre suggested, and following their overseas service they should be encouraged to "make full and productive use in government, in business, in education, in research, of their remarkable [and] unique experience."[21]

Undoubtedly, the most crucial and direct personal linkage in the hiring of CUSO alumni at the early CIDA was Lewis Perinbam. A CUSO founding father and interim executive secretary in CUSO's first year, Perinbam wrote the report for Strong that became the basis for CIDA's NGO program and in 1968 left his World Bank job to become the first director of the Special Programs branch, of which the NGO Division was a part. From 1974 until his retirement in 1991, Perinbam was a vice-president at CIDA.[22] The cumulative impact of Perinbam's and other officials' faith in the abilities of the volunteers was still evident at CIDA in the early 1980s, when an informal survey suggested that some 40 percent of its senior staff had come to the organization with a CUSO background. The specific figure may be exaggerated. Still, to Elizabeth McAllister, who came to CIDA about that time, it seemed that *"everyone"* had worked for CUSO.[23] Like Bezanson and Terry Glavin, a pioneer volunteer in Jamaica and an early CUSO staffer, many had joined CIDA in the late 1960s, when personnel numbers almost doubled. It was, writes Morrison, "a period of unparalleled opportunity to recruit excellent people" because of the available talent pool, the willingness of the treasury board to facilitate expansion, and a generally supportive climate.[24]

Notwithstanding the growth in opportunities at CIDA, many CUSO alumni who ultimately served with the agency did not make it their first or only post-CUSO employer. For returning male volunteers in the 1960s, there were many other opportunities in Ottawa and beyond, as the career of Bill McWhinney illustrated. McWhinney became a senior vice-president at CIDA only in 1980 after his brief stint with the Company of Young Canadians, five years as executive assistant to Liberal cabinet member Donald Macdonald, and seven years in the treasury board.[25] His fellow COVers Tom Schatzky and Dale Posgate were also latecomers to CIDA. Schatzky began a twenty-three-year career there only in 1981, after having worked for years in a variety of executive positions in organizations as varied as the Centennial International Development Program and the Shastri Indo-Canadian Institute, while political scientist Posgate came to CIDA only after a long period in academic life.[26] Furthermore, for many CUSO alumni, CIDA was just one of several sources of employment in freelance and contract work in international development. Because CIDA had so few staff members based in developing countries and building up local contacts and expertise (just fifty-five in a staff of over a thousand in 1979),[27] there were perhaps more contract opportunities for outsiders with developing-world experience in the agency than would otherwise have been the case.

To what extent did CUSO alumni turned government experts retain NGO values and loyalties? During the politically charged 1970s, some "socialist roaders" on CUSO's staff and some within SUCO worried that RVs who had attained senior positions within CIDA had forgotten their NGO roots and become too sanguine about, and comfortable with, official development policies. Given his key role in CUSO's founding, Lewis Perinbam was perhaps especially hurt by charges that CIDA prevented CUSO from achieving its potential as a development agency.[28] Yet clearly, having RVs in senior roles at CIDA – or at Treasury Board (Brian Marson played a crucial role there in the early 1970s), or as assistants to such key cabinet members as External Affairs Minister Mitchell Sharp (Jon Church's position in 1971) – could not guarantee that CUSO would invariably have smooth sailing with its evolving development interests.[29] Not only were there competing and countervailing government priorities, but also, as Chapter 3 shows, there were critics in the media and among conservative special interest groups ready to challenge what they saw as wrong-headed development policies and expenditures and to hold CIDA, and the federal government generally, accountable for the alleged misdeeds of the NGOs they funded. At the height of CUSO's political crisis in the late 1970s, Ian Smillie writes, the relationship with CIDA did become "adversarial – and unpleasant."[30] Even so, and even if some within CUSO did not see it that way at the time, it was undoubtedly helpful to have broadly sympathetic and knowledgeable insiders in CIDA, and in related government departments, insiders in a position to affect the agendas of CUSO and other NGOs. Their presence may also help to explain why among member countries in the Organization for Economic Co-operation and Development, Canada still stood second in the late 1980s in the proportion of official development assistance channelled through NGOs.[31]

As president of CIDA, Maurice Strong was a driving force in the founding of the IDRC, one of its "three midwives," along with former Prime Minister Lester B. Pearson and David Hopper. Pearson became the first chairman of the IDRC's international board of governors and Hopper the first president (1970-78), responsible for shaping its essential features, including avoidance of "research imperialism" and providing strong support for specific, problem-oriented, research projects originating in the Global South.[32] Hopper was also a key figure in bringing CUSO alumni into the new organization. During his years in India, he had been an important mentor to volunteers there and familiar with the kinds of projects in which they were engaged. RVs were regarded as having ideal attitudinal attributes – indeed "missionary zeal" – for the kind of work that IDRC wanted to undertake.[33]

Four program divisions were established at the outset, with the two natural science divisions – Agriculture, Food and Nutrition; and Population and Health – receiving the largest share of the centre's resources.[34] In truth, the number of RVs with relevant backgrounds for these two priority divisions was not large. Relatively few CUSO RVs had agricultural experience and expertise, and, of these, some had been hired by CIDA or other agencies. Still, Gordon Banta and Jeffrey Fine were among RVs who became program officers at IDRC and who were able to make culturally and politically sensitive contributions to the centre's on-the-ground agricultural research.[35] Meanwhile, within IDRC's Population and Health Division, an RV who as co-director of the CUSO/India program had had particular responsibility for health work became a planning officer in the first year of the centre's existence.[36] Wendy Marson, one of the first CUSO nurses to be involved in India's family-planning programs, began three years of work at IDRC in 1972 after having obtained master's degrees in public health and public administration from Harvard University. Like other India RVs, she remembers Hopper as a strong mentor, encouraging her to pursue a doctorate and helping her to obtain a bursary for doctoral studies at a time when some other senior development officials remained dubious about the value of facilitating advanced scholarship by women.[37] Although Hopper had been succeeded by Ivan Head by the time that Sarawak RV Christopher Smart joined IDRC in 1979, the centre's research focus and concern with practical applications remained largely unchanged. Smart had done further overseas work after serving in Sarawak and obtaining a graduate science degree from the University of Sussex, including four years of teaching at the University of Papua New Guinea and three years opening volunteer programs in Africa for

WUSC. But the IDRC had been on his "personal 'radar screen'" from his graduate school days, and following the fortuitous circumstances that led to his being hired, he remained with the centre for twenty-four years.[38]

Given the nature of IDRC's early programming priorities and the fact that the background of so many newly returned CUSO volunteers in the 1960s and 1970s was an undergraduate arts degree and a teaching placement, there were probably comparatively fewer employment opportunities for them within the centre than there were at CIDA. Nevertheless, there seems to have been a good deal of personnel cross-flow between these two federal development agencies, as well as shared and overlapping development interests. CUSO RVs were affected accordingly. The most notable example was Keith Bezanson, who succeeded Ivan Head to become the centre's third president in 1991. Bezanson was in charge at a time of drastic funding cutbacks and oversaw an almost 50 percent reduction of IDRC staff. His responses to the parlous circumstances of his presidency, IDRC historians Muirhead and Harpelle suggest, were hard-headed, creative, and necessary and probably saved the centre from "the wrecker's ball" before Bezanson's departure in 1997 for seven years to become director of the Institute of Development Studies at the University of Sussex.[39]

For former volunteers wanting ongoing involvement in international development work, CIDA and IDRC were the single biggest sites of employment within Canada. But there were plenty of opportunities in other agencies and particularly in NGOs, beginning with CUSO itself. CUSO had certainly not been envisioned as a place where volunteers or staff would build long-term careers. On the contrary, in the optimistic 1960s, there was talk, as in other NGOs, of a time when, through the success of development activities, NGOs would put themselves out of business. In the early 1970s, some looked for a similar outcome as support for autonomous Third World liberation and development strategies bore fruit.[40] Nevertheless, as Chapter 3 shows, many alumni had a continuing involvement with CUSO, as repeat volunteers or as staff. Numerous alumni also worked for other NGOs such as WUSC, Oxfam Canada, and CARE. The NGO life by its nature was not normally conducive to occupational or financial security. Given that fact and the opportunities for senior-level employment positions available to them in CIDA and IDRC, numerous male RVs gravitated to these official agencies, while many female alumni moved among NGOs and in and out of the larger agencies on contracts. At CIDA, the proportion of permanent officer positions for women was rising by the late 1970s as Public Service Commission requirements took effect. But it was evidently only in the 1980s during the presidency of Margaret Catley-Carlson and the sharper focus at that time on women in development (WID) that more, and more senior, positions for women opened up, especially following Elizabeth McAllister's pioneering and pragmatic leadership of the WID unit. Several female RVs who came into CIDA in that decade moved into WID leadership roles.[41] At IDRC, which had more of an arms-length relationship with government than CIDA and a quite different mandate, attention to WID issues and increases in the number of female project leaders came a good deal later. As for NGOs, although their awareness of WID issues certainly increased from the mid-1970s, as shown earlier and contributed to the opening up of more officer positions for women on NGO staffs, opportunities to head these organizations were slow to appear.[42] The constraints in these different workplaces notwithstanding, many of CUSO's female alumni were able to parlay their volunteer experiences and the confidence acquired overseas into rewarding development-related careers, working wherever opportunities opened up.

The confidence that came from having experienced unusual levels of testing and responsibility overseas was an especially striking phenomenon among RVs who had served as nurses. This category included the small group of women who had participated in India's family-planning program. Until Canada legalized birth control in 1969, CIDA and other federally funded agencies had considered themselves constrained from working with international family-planning and population control organizations. And within Canada, health professionals had not built up relevant skills and knowledge. Thus, when CIDA and IDRC and other agencies *did* begin supporting international family-planning and related maternal and childcare health initiatives, it made sense to consult with CUSO – as CIDA did, for instance, about funding for the Christian Medical Association of India's large family-planning project[43] – and to employ RVs with relevant experience. Sheila Ward had anticipated the ongoing benefits when she commented in her 1971 study of CUSO nurses' work on "the obvious advantage of an overseas nursing experience." Her own subsequent career was an example. Obtaining a master's degree in population planning at the University of Michigan, she worked in her field in the US for some years and then, for decades, on a freelance basis on numerous consultancies, particularly for CIDA. Her diverse assignments in project design and consulting took Ward into the age of HIV/AIDS and into Asia, Africa, and the former USSR.[44] CUSO nurses who did family planning as volunteers were by no means the only nurse alumni to go on to expansive careers in health-related fields,[45] but the specialized nature of their overseas experience opened up particular opportunities as population planning and related issues became expanding new fields in the late twentieth century.

Women who had served overseas with CUSO as teachers far outnumbered those who had been nurses. A significant number of this larger category maintained a lifelong involvement with development or analogous work. For Susanne Wise, forty years of global and national engagement began with a one-year volunteer placement as a teacher in Dominica in 1963. Thereafter, she worked variously for CUSO in Ottawa and Africa; for External Affairs (Ottawa, Dublin, Lagos) and Treasury Board; and in First Nations work for three provincial governments before beginning the longest segment of her career: fifteen years with UNICEF in Cambodia, Laos, and Malawi. Along the way she was able to complete an MBA through a Harvard-managed program in Teheran. Reflecting back on her career, Wise observed, "My tiny little one [volunteer] year with CUSO was the foundation for the rest of my life, both working and personal, both in Canada and overseas."[46]

Sharon Capeling's development career began, as Wise's had, with a teaching assignment in the Caribbean. Capeling had never been out of Saskatchewan before attending the orientation in Antigonish that preceded her departure for Barbados in 1967. She was in Barbados for three years, teaching first in a tough but rewarding comprehensive school for girls and then in an elite boys' grammar school. Despite her struggle with the "white liberal guilt" arising from her second placement, where the resentment of a Barbadian male colleague with superior credentials had been palpable, Capeling immediately took another volunteer assignment, this time in Nyerere's Tanzania, where so many CUSO hopes were invested. Back in Canada in 1972, she began almost two decades of administrative work as a member of CUSO staff, serving first as national co-ordinator of local committees and then as coordinator of orientation. In 1977, she became director of public affairs and program funding. Her new role included responsibility for editorship of the *CUSO Forum*. It also involved putting out fires at times of controversy as well as orchestrating favourable coverage and raising funds from a range of private sources. The latter was important in order to offset CUSO's image as entirely CIDA-dependent and to obtain money for projects that needed more than CIDA could provide. A pragmatist in terms of CUSO politics, Capeling was successful at getting former Liberal cabinet minister Iona Campagnolo to assist with fundraising for CUSO's project to assist Kampuchean refugees.[47] In the 1980s, as regional field officer in West Africa, Capeling had overall responsibility for CUSO programming in the region. Married and then widowed during this period, Capeling-Alakija moved on to the United Nations in 1989, where she served successively as director of UNIFEM (United Nations Development Fund for Women), director of evaluation and strategic planning at the United Nations Development Program, and finally as executive coordinator of the United Nations Volunteer Program. At a UN memorial service following her death in 2003, Secretary-General Kofi Annan spoke movingly of Capeling-Alakija's diverse contributions to international work and paid tribute to her as "a natural citizen of the world."[48]

Like Wise and Capeling-Alakija, other RVs of both sexes found their way into multilateral institutions. Some were involved only briefly with such bodies as the World Health Organization, the Food and Agriculture Organization, or other UN agencies. Others, like Nigel Fisher, who as a volunteer had taught history and economics to ex-rebel soldiers in postwar Biafra, spent decades in the multilateral sector. Beginning with the UN in 1977, Fisher lived and worked in a dozen developing countries, overseeing the UN's humanitarian and reconstruction programs in Afghanistan early in the twenty-first century and its stabilization mission in Haiti following the 2010 earthquake. Retiring in 2012, he lent his name – and his boots – to a ubiquitous UNICEF fundraising campaign.[49] Mostly, though, CUSO alumni who remained in development did so from Canadian organizational bases. As well as serving with official agencies and existing NGOs, they became involved in founding or staffing umbrella organizations for promoting development, and they were board members and sometimes founders of other NGOs. Indeed, they moved fluidly among organizations and effectively seeded themselves throughout the Canadian development community. The Canadian Council for International Cooperation (CCIC) provides an outstanding example. Established in 1968 to provide a collective voice for NGOs, its mandate evolved as the number of institutional members increased to 110 by 1988. Coordinating, educational, and advocacy functions remained central, however, even as the CCIC grew. And CIDA continued to provide it with funding, notwithstanding CCIC's frequent criticisms of such CIDA aid policies as the excessive use of food aid and tied aid generally.[50] Following his tenure as executive director of the CCIC, Tim Brodhead was succeeded by Betty Plewes, also a former Nigeria volunteer, while in 1995,

Thailand RV Rieky Stuart joined the organization as deputy director. Like Brodhead, Plewes and Stuart brought extensive experience as CUSO staff members as well as their volunteer backgrounds.

All three were also part of what Clyde Sanger called "the CUSO mafia" on the board of directors of the North-South Institute. CUSO alumni were active and in some cases long-serving or repeat board members from the time of the North-South Institute's founding in 1976. Like the CCIC, the institute became an advocate for more generous and developmentally sensitive official aid and trade policies. But whereas the CCIC functioned primarily in a coordinating, educational, and advocacy role, the main function of the North-South Institute was to provide rigorous and professional research on specific North-South policy issues from the perspective of an independent and non-partisan agency.[51] As such, it provided work opportunities for RVs who had equipped themselves with specialized technical expertise[52] as well as those who could bring broad development perspectives to positions on the board. RVs' involvements with these umbrella organizations undoubtedly facilitated further career opportunities, particularly in existing and newly established NGOs. Both Betty Plewes and Rieky Stuart, for instance, have been involved in a dizzying number of NGOs, and both have been activists and authors on WID and gender-equity issues.[53] It was this broad background that Stuart brought with her when she became executive director of Oxfam Canada in 1999. Plewes, a founding member of Partnership Africa Canada in 1986, remained involved as the organization reinvented its mandate to focus on countries where "blood diamonds" and "conflict minerals" have fuelled wars, sexual violence, and numerous forms of corruption.[54]

Finally, Stuart and Plewes and other CUSO alumni with diverse organizational and regional experience in the world of development have also become development consultants.[55] In some cases, they provide specialized areas of technical expertise and focus on particular regions, as RV Wendy Quarry has done, for instance, in the field of development communication.[56] Others, including Ian Smillie, probably Canada's best-known independent development consultant, range more broadly. The issues in which Smillie has been involved and about which he has written during the past three decades mirror unfolding new initiatives and concerns in international development work, from the emergence and growth of southern NGOs and micro-credit for impoverished South Asian women to efforts to control the trade in blood diamonds.[57]

Toward a Less Parochial Canada: Development Education

By the early 1970s, there were a few CUSO activists who, having seen the limits of what technical assistance could accomplish and influenced by such theorists as Ivan Illich and Paulo Freire, wanted to close down overseas programming altogether and instead concentrate entirely on consciousness raising in Canada through research, education, and political activism. More typically, as in other NGOs from the late 1960s onward, the new critical analysis of development strategies "gave rise to a demand for education programs to *complement* the overseas aid work." It was within this broad context that CUSO's 1969 Annual General Meeting (AGM) passed the RV-sponsored resolution that committed the organization to official involvement in development education.[58] Development education did not become a large part of the total budget of CUSO or other Canadian NGOs even after CIDA began funding it from 1971 through what later became known as its Public Participation Program.[59] Nonetheless, development education was an outreach activity that had the potential to inform and engage Canadians through a wide variety of media and forums. An ambiguous term and a difficult activity to define, *development education,* as carried out in this period, typically involved three, often overlapping, elements: information, education, and advocacy. Along with faith-based NGOs, CUSO staff and RVs became early and innovative practitioners of all these forms of development education. Indeed, they were regarded by their international colleagues as leaders in this activity.[60]

Well before the term *development education* came into vogue, other Canadians had, of course, engaged in analogous activity, beginning with the missions community almost a century earlier and, from about the mid-twentieth century, the Unitarian Service Committee's indefatigable Lotta Hitschmanova. And, as noted, when the first cohorts of COV and CUSO volunteers returned home in the early 1960s, they made presentations to Rotary clubs, church groups, and other constituencies that were interested in their experiences. These kinds of individual volunteer presentations and such advocacy as that by pro-Biafra activists in 1968 and Jean Stilwell's appeals for aid for Bengali refugees in 1971 did not come to a sudden end when CUSO took up development education as a specific organizational activity. But those behind Dev Ed, as it came to be known, were determined to go well beyond providing information and sympathetic images of the countries where its volunteers were serving. They wanted to focus on Western complicity in creating underdevelopment through self-serving trade and aid policies, and on the need to move beyond a paternalistic "good works" approach and provide support for indigenous groups in their struggles against colonialism and neocolonialism. Like RVs generally, Dev Ed activists also wanted Canadians to realize that far from being national "basket cases" in "dark" continents, the countries where volunteers were serving had rich cultures and resources of their own.

Outreach to schools was regarded by international activists as a logical component of development education and an important means of achieving long-term impact. (The ongoing commitment to development work in Scandinavian countries, where national curricula became "very strong" on such issues, suggests that this belief was not misplaced.)[61] But while such outreach began early on as an organizational activity within CUSO, it proved to be short lived. Probably several factors were responsible for its brief duration, not least the combination of naïveté and arrogance accompanying offers to "help" schools. (One RV, recalling that in 1969, she and some of her colleagues had tried to set up study groups in Toronto on Third World issues, observed, "We really thought that after two years ... we knew it all!"[62]) When CUSO's director of Canadian operations contacted educational officials in August 1969, he identified three areas in which he believed CUSO could be helpful to school boards: curriculum development, textbook appraisals, and the training of teachers. CUSO could also advise school librarians on "relevant books and periodicals and which books should be avoided."[63] Some of the measures proposed were more modest than this and more feasible in what they offered. Thus, in 1974, CUSO/Ottawa's Development Education department had a schools coordinator to do such things as put Canadian teachers in touch with CUSO personnel overseas and arrange for the sending and receiving of educational materials and cultural artifacts. In the same year, Jim Griffith of the CUSO campus committee at the University of Prince Edward Island organized a schools program whereby RVs and foreign students went into PEI schools to raise students' awareness of Third World issues.[64] This kind of outreach was feasible in a small province with a tiny population. However, the fact that in Canada schooling was a provincial rather than a federal responsibility stood as a barrier to a standardized national approach to school-level development education from CUSO/Ottawa. Ideologically, a more formidable barrier was the view of some development education workers that they should just "drop the schools," since they were hopelessly conservative institutions whose role was "to socialize kids into accepting the world as it is." CUSO evidently abandoned organized national efforts at development education through the school system in 1974. Of course, many RVs who returned as teachers to Canadian classrooms or who came into those classrooms as invited speakers were eager to communicate their interest in the problems and potential of the developing world to students and did so with or without support from CUSO/Ottawa, provincial governments, or other agencies. And sometimes their interest was contagious: John Stackhouse, the *Globe and Mail*'s first overseas development writer, recalls that his own "romance with Africa" was sparked at a school assembly in 1975 by an RV who had served in Tanzania and whose ongoing engagement with that country was palpable.[65]

As for a role for universities, some politicized advocates of development education believed that they, too, were "inherently too conservative, too formal and too bureaucratic" to be venues for effective work.[66] Nevertheless, CUSO staff and RVs contributed substantially to the establishment of university-level courses and programs related to global issues and to centres for international education and development studies. These are now such ordinary features of Canadian universities that it is difficult to conceive of how novel they were when they began in the 1960s. When the University of Western Ontario launched its Office of International Education in 1969 under the headship of Althouse College professor Don Simpson, Western's president described it as one of the first centres of its kind in Canada. In addition to his youthful leadership in establishing Crossroads Africa in Canada, Simpson had directed CUSO orientations at Althouse for West-Africa-bound volunteers in 1967 and 1968 and served as CUSO regional coordinator in West Africa during the early months of the Nigerian civil war. Western's president believed that releasing Simpson temporarily from Althouse for the West Africa assignment would help prepare him to head up the new office, which operated in collaboration with CIDA and the Association of Universities and Colleges of Canada (AUCC).[67] During the 1970s at the University of British Columbia, the President's CUSO Committee broadened its emphasis from recruiting and selecting volunteers to include development education as well, not only by ad hoc outreach to the larger community but also through on-campus development-studies programs and courses. By the fall of 1976, plans were announced for a graduate seminar titled "Strategies for Development in Third World Countries." A five-part development awareness lecture series was also begun, recommended especially for those intending to volunteer with CUSO but open to all and at no cost.[68] At the time that these steps were being taken at UBC, at least four Canadian universities already had development-studies programs: Carleton, McGill, the University of Ottawa, and the University of Toronto. The programs at the latter two were headed, respectively, by Professors King Gordon and Cranford Pratt, both valued friends of CUSO.[69] In the Maritimes, Saint Mary's University established its International Education Centre in 1972. At least two early RVs served as executive directors of the centre over the next few decades. Starting out as a resource facility for materials about developing-world countries, it also became an important resource for local ethnic-studies organizations and supported multiculturalism programs.[70]

CUSO's most innovative form of development education, the Cross-Cultural Mobile Learner Centre, was a direct offshoot of its orientation activities at Althouse College. By 1971, a substantial body of Africana had been built up at the resource centre at Althouse for use in the orientations. The collection included films, pamphlets, and cultural artefacts, as well as books and periodicals. As it expanded, the collection was used by some Canadian businesses with overseas work as well as by prospective volunteers.[71] With approval from CUSO's board of directors and with the assistance of various groups and institutions, including the School of Library Science at the University of Toronto, Don Simpson and colleague Sydney North transformed the centre from a static to a mobile resource. Launched in the fall of 1971, it was proudly described in a CUSO publicity leaflet as a "multi-media, computer-assisted information retrieval and problem-solving operation."[72] Costs of taking the centre on tour were to be shared by CIDA, Western's Office of International Education, and CUSO itself. By mid-December, the centre was receiving extensive media coverage and attracting large crowds, such that school groups eager to see its "revolutionary" technology at the National Museum of Man in Ottawa were having to be turned away.[73] By the time the mobile facility was sold to the International Education Centre at Saint Mary's University about a year later, it had toured Canada, reached some eighteen thousand people, and prompted the establishment of at least eight permanent, community-based versions of the centre across the country. Many more such centres would follow, some evolving into sites of activism and advocacy as well as information and, importantly, as with the One Sky Learner Centre in Saskatoon, addressing local social and economic issues as well as international problems and highlighting linkages between the two.[74]

As seen in Chapter 3, much of the advocacy aspect of development education as undertaken by CUSO in the 1970s was focused on southern Africa, and, along with faith-based groups, CUSO was something of a pioneer in questioning official development and foreign-policy positions and in seeking to appear before diverse government groups to make presentations and lobby. Murray Thomson's 1976 report as executive secretary suggested the variety and extent of CUSO's outreach to official Ottawa by mid-decade: "We spent more time on Parliament Hill, meeting with at least 25 Members of Parliament, submitting two Briefs to the Standing Committee on External Affairs, and one Brief to the Immigration Department. We were also involved in an Inter-Church Committee Brief on Chilean Refugees, and will soon submit the Food Brief to the Department of Agriculture. We have also increased our contacts with Government officials in the Treasury Board, External Affairs, and CIDA."[75]

Thomson was also interested in promoting innovative approaches to development education through coordinated efforts with international and umbrella organizations and, across Canada, with campus local committees and community groups. On his watch, for instance, CUSO helped finance "Five Minutes to Midnight," a two-hour film on world poverty that premiered at the UN and that CUSO urged Canada's national media to buy for prime-time use.[76] Local committees such as UBC's feisty President's CUSO Committee did not necessarily look to or accept CUSO/Ottawa's leadership on development education or other matters. While the UBC committee welcomed such innovations as the Mobile Learner Centre, it also took initiatives of its own and worked in conjunction with other local groups to exert pressure at the national, provincial, and community levels. In 1973, for instance, as part of the Southern Africa Action Coalition, a local solidarity and pressure group, the committee called for changes in federal policies "so as to remove inconsistencies between what Canada says and what Canada does." More concretely and closer to home, the committee urged BC's NDP government to stop selling South African and Portuguese wines in its liquor outlets.[77]

Whether working on its own or in conjunction with other agencies, CUSO clearly engaged in a wide, and widely varied, array of activities under the rubric of development education. Did they make any difference? In the chapter of *Land of Lost Content* dealing with development education, Ian Smillie described it as "probably the organization's most prodigious failure." Smillie was writing shortly after the completion of his term as CUSO's executive director and following the struggles required to restore CUSO's reputation after its period of public-relations disasters. It was mainly the institutionalized advocacy aspect of Dev Ed that he had in his sights and those staff for whom "the imprecise

"Involvement That Lasts a Lifetime"

principle of 'solidarity'" overrode a practical awareness of how their "increasingly controversial public positions would damage the organization's recruitment and fundraising base, as well as its delicate relationship with government." He was careful to exclude from his indictment "the individual and collective efforts of volunteers who returned to their communities with development messages."[78] Writing with more distance in *Bridges of Hope?*, and about the development education efforts of NGOs generally, Brodhead and Herbert-Copley referred to some of the same problems that Smillie had identified in CUSO's approach, including scarce financial resources spread too thin and a lack of the kind of sustained attention and expertise on complex issues of aid and trade that would allow NGOs to offer viable policy alternatives. Even when working through the CCIC, Brodhead and Herbert-Copley noted, member-NGOs' differences about what they wanted to emphasize as development priorities persisted, with predictably negative results: "Too often, the Council's policy pronouncements have been unfocused, reactive, and poorly researched."[79]

Furthermore, when it came to advocating on big development-related and foreign-policy issues, making policy critiques, and demonstrating "solidarity," CUSO and other NGOs were also up against the fact that there were many members of other Canadian constituencies – parliamentarians, bureaucrats, international business leaders, and others in the general public – whose priorities differed from those of the NGO community. They wanted Canada's development contributions to serve pragmatic national purposes as well as provide humanitarian aid. The ongoing practice of procurement tying in official development assistance (ODA), which NGOs routinely criticized, was a prime example of the pragmatism.[80] A less frequently raised issue in NGOs' development education advocacy, but also illustrating the divide between their concerns and the pragmatic concerns of the federal government, was immigration policy. In 1975, CUSO and Inter Pares jointly responded to the government's Green Paper on Immigration Policy with a booklet of their own. In it, they urged the government to look beyond narrowly national interests in framing immigration policy. They highlighted such matters as the effect of the proposed immigration policy in contributing to the brain drain from developing countries, the need for improved measures for helping refugees, and for more education in multiculturalism.[81]

In taking up advocacy positions that were at odds with longstanding or pragmatic government policies on development, or development-related issues, especially if they did so in intemperate language or from poorly researched positions, NGOs like CUSO risked embarrassing CIDA and thus biting the hand that (largely) fed them. They also risked alienating individual donors, including, occasionally, former volunteers, if they appeared – however false the perception – to be spending more time on "politics" at home than on constructive work overseas.[82] Yet despite problems in the delivery, and perception, of development education messages, there were undoubtedly positive outcomes from CUSO's involvement in this kind of activity, however difficult to quantify and, often, slow to materialize. CUSO alumni who called for a ban on South African wines from the early 1970s and for disinvestment in that country, for instance, may have seemed to be naive voices crying in the wilderness or, later, ill-informed advocates of a chic cause. But together with other civil-society groups that took up these causes internationally, they arguably contributed over time to changes in mainstream thinking and, eventually, to legislated sanctions.[83] Probably, too, they contributed at least marginally to attitudinal and policy changes in regard to dealing with refugees.[84] And in the early 1980s, along with other groups internationally, they helped raise awareness and provoke action on the so-called "bottle baby" controversy, also known as Nestlégate, by targeting and testifying about multinational corporations that promoted the use of infant formula to mothers in the Global South, despite the known deleterious effects.[85] Even if it did not have sophisticated research or economic clout to back up its advocacy positions on issues such as this, CUSO could be part of what became known as "the hassle factor."[86]

Finally, as noted, there were many CUSO alumni who brought their global awareness back to their own communities and participated there in various forms of development education. Local fundraising activities could simultaneously serve this function if they could engage Canadians without merely tugging at their heartstrings and downplaying the complex reasons for underdevelopment.[87] During the late 1960s and in the early 1970s, Miles for Millions walks were undoubtedly the most important such events. Conceived as part of the Centennial International Development Program and directed from 1968 by a coordinating committee on which CUSO was represented, the walks were held in hundreds of communities across Canada. Historian Tamara Myers writes that the majority of walkers were elementary and high school students. But many RVs were also participants. One of them was Don Lowe, a retired engineer who had volunteered in Uganda at age seventy-nine. Lowe was eighty-three by the time he took part in a walk in Vancouver's Stanley Park to raise money for

"Involvement That Lasts a Lifetime"

scholarships for technical-school students in Uganda. Following his death in 1971, a commemorative fundraising walk was organized in his memory.[88]

Fellow British Columbian Hans-Henning Mündel had many more years than Lowe in which to promote development and international awareness. Mündel paralleled his professional career in agricultural development work with recruitment for CUSO and ongoing voluntary contributions to development education in several different Canadian communities. He is undoubtedly atypical in the degree to which his professional and personal life has exemplified the "involvement that lasts a lifetime" phenomenon, but it nonetheless bears highlighting as an illustration of the range of activities that could result when a committed volunteer with a like-minded partner returned with a determination to remain engaged. In Winnipeg for three years for doctoral work at the end of the 1960s, Hans-Henning with Bev established links with other RVs and with the newly formed Manitoba Association for World Development. At the request of the provincial education department, they provided slides for use with the province's fifth-grade social studies curriculum component on India. Later, in Lethbridge, Alberta, they became charter members of the World Citizens Centre, which remained active for twenty years.[89] Located far from the radical end of the Dev Ed spectrum, the Mündels' contributions to world-mindedness were tangible, localized, and unflagging.

Domesticating Development

Although CUSO's AGM voted in 1971 not to establish its own domestic development program, it strongly encouraged RVs – and students thinking about applying to CUSO – to consider volunteering in domestic development agencies. This was the personal inclination of some RVs well before domestic development became an issue for CUSO. Dennis Edwin McDermott[90] returned early and unwell from a lonely and unproductive assignment at a YMCA in British Guiana with "no desire or intent to sign on again" and with a conviction that "there was a lot that needed to be done right in Canada." He became heavily involved in the Combined Universities Campaign for Nuclear Disarmament and the Student Union for Peace Action (SUPA). As a SUPA activist, he organized a demonstration for voting rights in Selma, Alabama, and did community organizing, first in Toronto and then in Kingston. Although the slum project he directed in Kingston became one of the community organizing models for the Company of Young Canadians, McDermott did not personally join the Company: "at the time that would have been seen by myself and my friends as selling out and becoming a 'vendue.'" In 1966, the Kingston project and McDermott personally received kindly if exceedingly condescending coverage in the special issue of the *Canadian* that profiled students from Canadian campuses who were said to be demonstrating their "youthful idealism" in projects at home and abroad.[91] The piece was probably typical of contemporary assessments of "youthful idealism" of the more "radical" sort (McDermott's) in its inability to anticipate the ways in which such idealism might eventually be transmuted into long-term social service career paths. In McDermott's case, following SUPA, the career ahead was in child and youth work, culminating eventually in a position as executive director of the Ontario Association of Child and Youth Counsellors.

McDermott's return from his CUSO assignment evidently ended the international chapter in his life. However, for many CUSO alumni who later worked in domestic development or related activities, or who supported such activities on a volunteer basis, engagement with international development remained ongoing. For these alumni, the worlds of international and domestic development were perceived not as oppositional or sharply distinct but rather as complementary and porous. Indeed, some of them passed through a revolving door of international and national involvements for years or even decades. Hans-Henning Mündel's extensive professional and volunteer work for international development, for instance, did not preclude volunteer engagement with domestic issues. In 1979, he was part of a group that organized a charity to sponsor a family of Vietnamese refugees. Later, a bylaw change allowed the group to funnel funds left from the charity to overseas work, including the establishment of a dairy herd in the Paniya colony in southern India where Mündel had had his first placement.[92] His fellow India RV Anne Jones (later Hume) of Toronto also assisted refugees on a volunteer basis, first in the settlement of Ugandan Asians and later finding jobs for refugees from Southeast Asia.[93] Other RVs were engaged in assisting refugees from Chile and other parts of Latin America through such agencies as Toronto's Cross-Cultural Communication Centre. As both Howard Adelman and Reg Whitaker have noted, Cold War politics and business interests made Ottawa exceedingly reluctant to accept refugees from Chile following General Pinochet's right-wing coup there. Especially if such refugees remained involved in the left-wing politics of their own country, assisting them could prove controversial.[94]

Working with refugees and other immigrants, whether as volunteers or paid staff, was a predictable domestic spinoff from a CUSO overseas experience. The same was true for teaching ESL (English as a second language), a skill that became increasingly important in the 1970s and 1980s in an increasingly multicultural Canada. Anne Jones Hume was one of a number of CUSO alumni whose teaching career included teaching ESL. Her volunteer year in India, she believed, "made me more receptive of students from other countries when I ... taught ESL, and made me more accessible to them." Likewise, Judy Ransom regarded her CUSO background as relevant and useful when she taught ESL to new Canadians, first at Toronto's George Brown College and later at Seneca College. Ransom was CUSO's contact at George Brown when CUSO needed ESL teachers for a pilot project in Cuba in the early 1970s and one of five from the college to take up the four-month assignments. Their task was to prepare postgraduate engineering students at the University of Havana to take courses in English taught by CIDA-sponsored Canadian engineering professors.[95]

M, one of the ESL teachers recruited by Ransom for Cuba, provides a fascinating illustration of the interweaving of related overseas and domestic assignments. M was already well travelled and interested in Latin America when the opportunity in Cuba arose. When she was refused an extended leave of absence by George Brown College after her four-month assignment ended, she resigned from the college and stayed on with the CUSO project until mid-1975. "Being in Cuba in the 70s was a marvellous experience," she wrote; "I did everything I could to learn about the politics, the political philosophies and the actual functioning of a socialist country." Chilean refugees and Cubans figured importantly in M's vibrant personal and social life, while her professional work expanded both her skills and her confidence. Following another assignment in Cuba in 1976-77, this time with CIDA, and the completion of a graduate degree in applied linguistics, M worked for several years in community organizations in Toronto. At the Cross-Cultural Communication Centre, she developed a program and resource books to assist immigrant women seeking employment. She also volunteered with the Latin American Working Group and got involved in solidarity work before signing on again with CUSO, this time for three years of community development in Bolivia. Back in Toronto once more, M did the kind of teaching and resource-preparation work with refugee women and other disadvantaged adult learners for which her previous experiences had prepared her. When financial cutbacks by Ontario's Harris government in the 1990s led to the closing of some such projects, she reluctantly returned to high school teaching. It was not the career path she wanted at that stage in her life, but she had a son as well as herself to support, and as she observed, her involvement with CUSO had taught her skills of resourcefulness and adaptability.[96]

Two decades earlier, when some CUSO insiders had been urging the establishment of a full-fledged domestic development program, providing outreach to immigrant women was not the sort of activity they envisioned. Rather, they had in mind work with institutions like Frontier College and, especially, with Aboriginal communities. In the 1970s, these became intertwined areas of involvement for RV Jack Pearpoint. As Chapter 1 shows, Frontier College had been an important influence for a significant number of early male volunteers during their university years. Although the organization had not been part of Pearpoint's undergraduate experience, he was able to play a key role as its president following his years with CUSO, serving for some sixteen years from the mid-1970s and taking the venerable but faltering institution in new directions. Despite the recognition he had achieved for his handling of the educational rehabilitation project in postwar Biafra and his subsequent managerial experience at CUSO/Ottawa as head of its new Projects Division, Pearpoint's appointment to the presidency of Frontier College was not a foregone conclusion, given his lack of personal experience as a volunteer with the organization. Still, Pearpoint greatly admired the College's history and worked hard to win the job. As Canada's oldest adult literacy organization, Frontier College had gone through some significant changes since its founding in 1899.[97] When Pearpoint took up the presidency, the college was deeply in debt and in crisis. The remote work camps where generations of volunteers had taught literacy to immigrants or illiterate Canadian-born workers had largely been made redundant by social and technological change. The college needed a new focus. Pearpoint and his colleagues, a few of whom later were also CUSO alumni, determined to take it into new settings. They met strong resistance when they tried to break into the new kinds of migrant labour camps that housed temporary agricultural workers. But they were more successful with other challenges, including literacy and driver education in a western Canadian prison where a high number of Aboriginal Canadians were incarcerated. There was also collaborative work with First Nations groups in Alberta, Saskatchewan, and the Northwest Territories. Some of the new work clearly took Frontier College beyond its traditional literacy mandate to include job training and work with street youth. On Pearpoint's watch, Frontier College also collaborated with

Aboriginal groups challenging plans for a northern gas pipeline, and it encouraged Inuit leaders to do the slow, village-by-village consultations that allowed for popular input in the eventual establishment of Nunavut.[98]

Pearpoint's Frontier College work with First Nations people was protracted and varied. A significant number of other CUSO alumni also worked with Aboriginal communities, especially in western Canada, between or following overseas involvements. Mar and Rob Thomson, for instance, were employed by Saskatchewan's NDP government in northern health services from 1974 to 1978 following placements in Malawi and Malaysia and two years at a private school in Port Hope, Ontario, that had felt "too perfect" to be a good fit with their personal values after their overseas experiences.[99] For RVs like the Thomsons, these were interludes. But for Marie Smallface Marule, one of the first "Indian" women to volunteer with CUSO, work with First Nations turned out to be a lifelong commitment. When Smallface joined CUSO in the mid-1960s as a student at the University of Alberta and a member of the Blackfoot Nation from Cardston, she experienced criticism from fellow Aboriginals for her decision to volunteer with the organization. Three years later, a twenty-four-year-old serving in Lusaka, Zambia, as a senior officer with the government's adult literacy program, she found it liberating not to be cast in the role of "an Indian spokesman. In Zambia my being Indian is irrelevant." But at the same time, working as a producer of radio programs in two Zambian languages for community development, she was becoming interested in the use of mass communication for education in Canada as well as Zambia. "When I return home," she told the *CUSO/SUCO Bulletin*, "I intend to use my African experience to help bring Canada out of its racial dark ages."[100] Back in Canada, Smallface Marule did teaching and human rights work and completed a master's degree in anthropology. As secretary-treasurer of the National Indian Brotherhood (NIB, later replaced by the Assembly of First Nations), Smallface Marule helped the NIB's executive director, George Manuel, think through the ideas that found form in his book *The Fourth World: An Indian Reality*. She was, Manuel wrote, "the first person to be able to show me, from direct and personal experience, the close relationship and common bonds between our own condition as Indian people, and the struggles of other Aboriginal people and the nations of the Third World."[101] Smallface Marule herself subsequently became executive director of the NIB. She also helped found the World Council of Indigenous Peoples and played leadership roles in a consortium for First Nations adult and higher education. In 1992, she was appointed president of Red Crow

Community College on the Blood reserve in southern Alberta, described on its website as "the first Tribally controlled community college in Canada." An honorary degree from the University of Calgary in 2010 was one of a number of honours in recognition of her work for Aboriginal people in education and community development, work that had grown organically from her youthful volunteer experience in Zambia.[102]

Where Did All the Teachers Go? Avoiding the Canadian Classroom?

> After my years with CUSO in Nigeria [1973-75] I became an elementary school teacher and found myself involved in a project where we supported a school and an orphanage and a teacher in Sierra Leone. The children got so involved that they tried to stop the war in Sierra Leone and eventually built a new secondary school and enabled the teacher to get his Master's degree. (At one point I had four of my Grade 4's with me at a children's conference at the UN and they told our story in front of Kofi Annan, Craig Kielburger and the weeping Sierra Leonean Ambassador to the UN. I was stunned.)

The project described here by RV Paul Delaney was his own initiative and a direct outcome of his volunteer experience rather than the result of any prompting from CUSO/Ottawa's development education department. Delaney was obviously deeply engaged in helping his students to learn and care about the developing world. But how many other returning volunteers went into Canadian elementary- and high-school classrooms with this kind of commitment or, for that matter, went into those classrooms at all? Most of his CUSO friends *did* go into teaching, Delaney wrote, and, he speculated, other RVs probably took classroom initiatives somewhat like his.[103] If so, their presence in Canadian schools was undoubtedly significant for raising global awareness and concern. In fact, however, RVs who made careers in teaching at the elementary- or secondary-school levels are not much in evidence in CUSO sources. The twenty-fifth anniversary booklets prepared by the two pioneering COV cohorts and mentioned earlier in this chapter are striking for this absence: it appears that only one person from the 1961 cohort taught in the school system following her return, and then only for a few years, and that only two from the 1962 cohort made careers in the system. A 1966 study containing data on 193 RVs found that only twenty-eight were teaching in Canada. RVs who settled into Canadian classrooms are exceedingly scarce in the *CUSO Forum*'s "Where are they now?"

"Involvement That Lasts a Lifetime"

series. Beginning in 1978 and continuing into the 1980s, this series tended to feature alumni in high-profile or developmentally related work. Finally, among alumni located for interviews for this project, only a minority had had careers as school teachers, despite the fact that teaching had been by far the single most common type of overseas placement.[104]

Most volunteers had, of course, gone overseas without teaching experience or professional teacher training. Following their return, CUSO tried in several ways to assist them with jobs or study plans. It sought to have school boards recognize their overseas experience and to arrange with universities and colleges for bursaries or remission of fees.[105] If despite their overseas experience and these early forms of assistance only a comparatively small number became career schoolteachers, how can that be explained? As noted earlier in this chapter, volunteers often returned home unsettled about plans for the future. Even some who had already trained as teachers moved on to different lines of work. Although Marian White was already equipped with a B.Ed. as well as a BA when she went to Nigeria in 1977, she taught only episodically after her return to Canada before turning to full-time development work in Atlantic Canada.[106] By the time she returned, there was a scarcity of full-time teaching positions. The situation had been different for RVs wanting classroom positions in the 1960s and early 1970s. But by the late 1970s, and for much of the 1980s, teaching positions were in short supply in much of southern Canada, and seniority largely determined boards' hiring policies.[107] An RV who taught in Nigeria a few years ahead of White and who trained at Althouse College following her return did not wind up in full-time teaching until 1990. In any case, by the time she graduated from Althouse, she was, she recalled, "already having second thoughts" about high school teaching in Canada and was drawn increasingly to political activism.[108]

It is worth emphasizing that, for many volunteers, taking a teaching assignment with CUSO had been an opportunity for adventure and for serving and learning abroad rather than the first step in a career that they planned to pursue for the rest of their working lives. Indeed, White recalled taking her education degree as a "stepping stone" to an overseas appointment rather than out of a sense of vocation. The experience of Chris Smart, introduced earlier, is also instructive. Chris and his wife had already been teaching for two years in a suburban Toronto high school in the late 1960s on the basis of summer school training when they were accepted for teaching assignments in a rural government secondary school in Sibu, Sarawak. It was a good and peaceful interlude, indeed, just right in terms of their own life stage and the evolution of Malaysian politics. When they left Sarawak, they were no more inclined to return to suburban Toronto classrooms than they had been when they made what they considered their "Great Escape" back in 1968. It seems likely that a good many other CUSO alumni were also unwilling to settle into the perceived routine of an ordinary teaching appointment after several years of something more exotic. Having struck out into the unknown once, they were more inclined than their stay-at-home contemporaries to do so again if conventional classroom teaching appeared likely to be, as Smart feared, "decades of the same."[109]

Academe, Journalism, Politics, and the Arts: Expressions and Degrees of Engagement

Whether or not teaching in the Canadian school system was, in reality, a road less taken by CUSO alumni, or simply a less visible road, the fact remains that alumni who became career teachers in the system do not loom large in the CUSO record. On the other hand, that record and the interviews undertaken for this book indicate that a disproportionately high number of RVs went on to obtain advanced professional and academic degrees. Of this number, some spent all or part of their subsequent careers in the Canadian universities and community colleges whose growth was such a marked feature of the 1960s and early 1970s.[110] Not surprisingly, development or developing countries became the focus of some RVs' advanced studies and careers. In such cases, they frequently, though not invariably, focused on the region where they had served.[111] Following his volunteer placement in Ghana, Jim Morrison returned to West Africa to obtain a doctorate in Nigerian history at the University of Ibadan before making his career at Saint Mary's University. As faculty members, RVs like Morrison became catalysts for an interest in race relations, development studies, and related fields in their respective Canadian universities.[112]

Some RVs who did doctoral studies related to the developing world worked in university settings only briefly before moving on to federal or international agencies, or, by contrast, like Keith Bezanson, they came to university settings after decades in such workplaces. Wendy Dobson's experience illustrates this latter pattern. After writing a doctoral thesis related to the economics of Korean development, Dobson travelled extensively, studied other developing-country economies, and worked for a period as associate deputy finance minister before joining the Rotman School of Management at the University of Toronto in the

"Involvement That Lasts a Lifetime"

early 1990s and becoming professor and director of the Institute for International Business.[113] Finally, there were CUSO alumni-turned-academics who, while not making the developing world the direct focus of their graduate studies and subsequent research, played significant roles in encouraging the establishment of development studies and international awareness at the universities where they taught. University of Waterloo historian Jim Walker, for instance, a pioneering scholar on Black Loyalists and race relations in Canada, founded the Global Community Centre at his university, served on the local CUSO committee, and participated in the educational work of Ten Days for World Development.[114] Some of these scholars and scholar bureaucrats identified strongly with the institutionalized efforts at development education begun by CUSO/Ottawa in the late 1960s. Others were undoubtedly uneasy with the tactics and ideology of Dev Ed's more politicized exponents. Arguably, though, what they all had in common was a broad-based interest in increasing Canadians' knowledge of the Global South. The same was true of RVs who became journalists, another category of alumni that CUSO tended to publicize.

Several veterans of CUSO service in Africa became nationally known and award-winning media figures. Print journalists Hugh Winsor and Dan Turner and CBC radio's Bernie Lucht had all made tentative beginnings in journalism even before becoming volunteers. Following his assignment with CUSO in Dar es Salaam "to help establish a national news agency," Winsor briefly did similar work under External Aid auspices before becoming an editorial writer and columnist at the *Globe and Mail* in 1969. Although his main focus at the *Globe* was national affairs, there was also some scope for writing about development issues. Serving on the board of the North-South Institute from its founding until 1990, Winsor used his journalistic expertise to help the institute acquire "some tricks of the trade that might be used to tease a largely insular and introspective Canadian media into paying more attention to Third World issues."[115] Dan Turner returned to Canada in 1967 following the unguarded expression of pro-Biafran sentiment that led to his expulsion from Nigeria, and thereafter worked mainly in journalism. Although he was a member of the Parliamentary Press Gallery for most of his career, he also covered international politics on location in South Africa and Zimbabwe and was briefly Africa bureau chief for *Maclean's*. Married to a fellow Nigeria RV with an ongoing career in international NGOs, Turner had a personal as well as a professional reason for maintaining a journalistic involvement in Africa issues.[116] As for Bernie Lucht, in the decade following his return from Nigeria, he made it something of a mission to increase

Canadians' awareness of Africa. CBC provided generous funding for him to prepare biographical profiles of some early nationalist leaders, and in 1973, he was able to attend a conference in Norway to interview leaders of African liberation movements for a series of broadcasts. In 1980, there was again strong support from CBC radio for an Africa Week series to mark the twentieth anniversary of the wave of the continent's independence movements.[117]

In the late 1980s, Lucht's fellow RV and CBC Radio *Ideas* colleague David Cayley still remained sufficiently interested in the broad subject of development, or, perhaps more accurately, development critiques, to re-establish the contact with Ivan Illich that had begun some two decades earlier. Cayley interviewed Illich for a series of radio broadcasts on the ailing churchman's iconoclastic views. A major theme to emerge from their conversations was Illich's conviction that institutionalizing the Christian Gospel and Good Samaritan teachings had been a great and historic evil, as were related contemporary Western development practices such as trying to institutionalize mass literacy in developing countries. As edited and fleshed out by Cayley following Illich's death in 2002, the transcripts resulted three years later in *The Rivers North of the Future,* a sympathetic introduction to Illich's ideas for a generation unfamiliar with the period when he was an internationally influential critic of conventional development theory.[118]

Like journalism, the world of politics was another venue for CUSO alumni who wanted a public platform for engaged citizenship. None achieved national leadership, as VSO's John Major did, becoming prime minister of Britain in the 1990s, or had a discernible influence on a national leader, as was evidently the case with elderly Peace Corps volunteer Bessie Lillian Carter ("Miss Lillian"), the mother of President Jimmy Carter.[119] Still, quite a few CUSO RVs did seek political office and with all parties, beginning, probably, with Jon Church, who ran unsuccessfully as a federal Liberal candidate in 1968.[120] RVs served one or more terms as mayors, city counsellors, and trustees, as members of Parliament, and, in the case of British Columbia's Gordon Campbell, as a provincial premier. Following their two teaching years in Nigeria, Gordon and Nancy Campbell maintained their CUSO connection for a time by serving on the President's CUSO Committee at UBC. Campbell cut his teeth politically at the municipal level before moving on to the provincial Liberal leadership and obtaining office as premier in 2001. Did his CUSO experience continue to have resonance for the politically ambitious Campbell? A *Maclean's* magazine profile in 1999 would suggest that it did.[121] Official online biographical profiles while he was premier also frequently made reference to his volunteer years overseas and as such signalled his desire to call attention to that aspect of his youthful identity.

To the extent that CUSO alumni aspired to or held political offices, it appears most often to have been at the municipal level. Torontonians Gordon Cressy and Joanne Campbell – another CUSO couple – remained involved with CUSO and its work decades after beginning multi-faceted careers in municipal politics and civic service. Cressy had had a volunteer placement with the YMCA in Trinidad in 1963-64, where his youthful entrepreneurial zeal had led him to order a boatload of Canadian Christmas trees to sell as a fundraiser for the purchase of equipment for the Y.[122] Joanne Campbell had spent three years in a CUSO placement at an adult education centre in Zambia a decade later. As chairman of CUSO's board of directors in 1983, Cressy visited CUSO projects in East and Central Africa with Campbell, an experience they subsequently described in enthusiastic detail in the *Toronto Star*. The same enthusiasm and engagement was still evident in 2008 when a CUSO newsletter described their latest commitment, which had brought Cressy's career "full circle": a YMCA project in Tobago.[123]

Few alumni who entered political life remained as engaged with CUSO as Gordon Cressy and Joanne Campbell. As with the CUSO alumni who became journalists, there were definite limits on the extent to which RVs in politics and other forms of public service could be advocates for development or engage otherwise in international matters when their careers were playing out on local and national stages where more immediate issues demanded attention. Still, having had a youthful experience of overseas volunteering could, at a minimum, have the effect of making alumni-turned-politicians more attuned than they might otherwise have been to global issues that affected their bailiwicks and more sensitive to the needs and concerns of community members with roots in the Global South.[124]

Whatever lines of work they took up upon returning to Canada, volunteers brought back a deeper understanding of the non-Western world. Through "serving and learning" they had come to realize, albeit sometimes haltingly, that however impoverished economically so-called underdeveloped communities might be, they were not without rich artistic, historical, and religious traditions. If surprisingly few volunteers became formal converts to Buddhism or other non-Western religious traditions at a time when it was fashionable for the young to do so in large North American cities,[125] many nonetheless became admirers and even proselytizers for the artistic expressions of their host countries' cultural and faith traditions. A remarkable early example was Ottawa-born Anne-Marie Groves, who, while teaching in Madras (Chennai) in the mid-1960s, became an avid and apt student of several styles of Indian classical dance. Subsequently, with Canada Council and Commonwealth grants, Groves (later Gaston) studied in India under some of the country's leading masters of these forms. Both before and after the completion of her Oxford University doctorate on the sociology of Indian performing arts, she continued to perform on stages in North America and Britain and in India itself, where her artistry was hailed by national media. At a time when Indian classical music and dance, and even Bollywood films, were little known in a Canada that still had relatively few immigrants from India, Anne-Marie Gaston's sensitive and skilled performances were recognized and welcomed as a form of cultural ambassadorship rather than problematized as a form of cultural appropriation.[126]

Meanwhile, CUSO's *NEWSTATEments,* launched in 1971, was meant to be a vehicle for educating a wide spectrum of Canadians about the historical and contemporary cultural resources of the non-Western world as well as about the politics of underdevelopment. "*NEW STATEments* will have art, it will have poetry," the journal's opening statement declared, and its international cast of associate corresponding editors was to be involved in making – and critiquing – selections of articles and visual materials for inclusion. As well as several poems by non-Westerners, the second issue contained dramatic black and white photographs of sculpture and paintings from Africa, India, and Mexico. *NEWSTATEments* was a short-lived venture, as Chapter 3 notes, an instance of CUSO's early-seventies political and cultural reach exceeding its financial grasp.[127] Still, the urge to promote this kind of cultural awareness did not come to an end. Africa, in particular, was a "dark continent" so far as Canadians' familiarity with its historical and modern cultural creativity was concerned. By the end of the 1970s, the *CUSO Forum* and individual volunteers and alumni were enthusiastically promoting the traditional and contemporary arts of Africa, and of West Africa in particular. Liz Kane brought Ghanaian weaver Gilbert Bobbo to Ottawa to demonstrate his family's traditional skill in weaving Ghana's famous Kente cloth. At Ottawa's Byward Market, Vicki Henry established one of the first of three Canadian stores dealing exclusively in African art. Wendy Lawrence, who had served as a junior lecturer at the University of Lagos, described for *Forum* readers the "Eclectic Circus" that was the Nigerian art scene,

"The finest non-Indian dancer of Bharata Natyam, Kuchipudi and Odissi in the world." So wrote New Delhi's *Financial Express* in reference to "Anjali," Anne-Marie Gaston (neé Groves), shown here ca. 1970. As a CUSO volunteer in India, Groves became fascinated by Indian classical dance and went on to decades of study and international performance. Courtesy of Anne-Marie Gaston.

and in 1979 at the Best of Africa Gallery in Toronto, she introduced the work of multimedia artist Bruce Onobrakpeya and provided an accompanying monograph. Lawrence also drew Canadians' attention to Nigeria's best-known pop music star, Fela Anikulapo Kuti, whose Afro-Spot nightclub she had visited with other volunteers and whose Afro-beat music and flamboyant personal life would later become internationally known. *CUSO Forum* was enthusiastic about the first-ever specialized exhibition of African art at Ottawa's National Gallery, a showing of masks and statuary. The 1979 exhibition drew heavily on the personal collection of Torontonians Barbara and Murray Frum, among the few serious Canadian collectors of African art at the time. Gerry Caplan, another early collector, made some of his work available for display at the Best of Africa Gallery while he served as CUSO's coordinator in Nigeria.[128]

Despite her low salary, Lawrence had managed to come home with works by emerging artists like Onobrakpeya, who later gained international recognition. Most CUSO volunteers were not in a position to purchase the kinds of carvings, masks, and other cultural artefacts that would be considered for inclusion in major exhibitions. But many brought home more modest works to share with family or for personal collections. Historian Sharon Cook recalls that her parents returned with wonderful masks from their placement in Papua New Guinea as well as – more disturbingly for dog-loving Sharon – a dog-tooth necklace given to her father by a student on the occasion of the birth of his first grandson.[129] Most commonly, volunteers gave personal expression to their overseas encounters with regional art and architecture through the photographs and letters they sent home to family and friends. RVs who became literature teachers in schools and university classrooms could also introduce students to emerging Asian and African writers at a time when an exclusive focus on the Western canon was only beginning to be questioned.[130] Sooner or later, a few would draw on their overseas experience for personal literary creativity. For Dave Godfrey and Audrey Thomas, both 1960s Ghana RVs, it was sooner. Teaching in Ghana at a time when the early promise of the presidency of Kwame Nkrumah had given way to his defiant determination to hold onto power, Godfrey began to sketch out what later became his dizzyingly innovative Governor General's Award–winning novel, *The New Ancestors*. Set in the fictional Lost Coast and peopled with a shape-shifting cast of Western and African characters, the novel, Godfrey later said, was deliberately intended to confound readers, for he "wanted the non-African reader in some way to experience those moments of stark incomprehension which hit even the most open-minded

"Involvement That Lasts a Lifetime"

travellers to Africa." Ghana figured importantly in Audrey Thomas's first short story and novel and, a good deal later, in *Coming Down from Wa*. In the latter, CUSO itself plays a role as the fictional aid agency COW: Thomas's central character travels to Ghana as a young graduate student in an attempt to discover what it was in his parents' 1960s volunteer experience there with COW that so profoundly and mysteriously destroyed their relationship.[131] Unlike Godfrey and Thomas and the celebrated poet Dionne Brand, who served in Grenada, there would be other RVs who, as writers, would wait decades before turning back to their placement country as a source of subject matter and inspiration.[132]

Intimate Internationalism and Ongoing Connections

Beginning with the first cohort, a significant number of volunteers entered the CUSO barque in pairs. This was especially likely to be the case if volunteers were older, like Sharon Cook's parents, already in their sixties when they left for Papua New Guinea. At the other end of the age spectrum, for a few young couples, the voyage out was also their honeymoon, and the trials of the field became the trials of a marriage. Even if they did not start out as a couple, many volunteers returned to Canada married. Occasionally, the new partner was someone from the Peace Corps or VSO serving in the same community. More often she or he was a fellow CUSO volunteer. In the early days, some of these on-the-spot marriages became social fodder for the *Bulletin,* with detailed accounts of the couple's ingenuity and community support in cobbling together wedding attire, reception requirements, and even a guest list. When Diane Davis and John Baigent married in Accra, Ghana, in 1964, the Ghanaian headmaster at John's school gave the bride away and hosted the bridal party before the wedding. The third secretary at the Canadian High Commission provided the reception, where the eight-year-old daughter of the Peace Corps director caught the bouquet.[133] Later, as intra-CUSO marriages became more common or took place back in Canada, they became less noteworthy in CUSO publications. Yet their significance was considerable for the organization as well as for the couples directly concerned, for when both marriage partners had had an overseas experience, they seem to have been more likely to join CUSO as staff, serve on their local CUSO committee, or engage in other supportive activities following their return to Canada.

Their families were probably not surprised when their CUSO son or daughter returned with a fellow volunteer as a partner. What undoubtedly took more getting used to was the number of alumni who returned with partners from the developing world. To liken this phenomenon to Canadian soldiers' earlier return with war brides is to exaggerate its demographic import. Still, while the numbers were much smaller, the significance was not negligible. "Cross-race" marriages had not been illegal in Canada as they still were in some US states even in the early 1960s. But just over a generation earlier there had been an incident in Oakville, Ontario, in which Canadian Ku Klux Klan members had burned crosses and seized a white woman from her black partner to prevent such a marriage, and in that case the Klan had acted with the clear approval of local law-enforcement officials and many others in the community.[134] And while the post–Second World War period was a time when explicit references to race as a basis for exclusion from Canada were dropped from immigration legisla-tion, as late as 1955 the director of immigration expressed the view that "coloured people" were unsuitable immigrants for Canada, a view that still appeared to be part of Canadians' "common sense" understanding on the subject of im-migration.[135] Then came the sixties and the liberalizing of attitudes on race and sexuality. The two phenomena melded in the cross-race relationships that were one aspect of the sexual revolution across the Western world and, for a great many volunteers, part of the CUSO experience in a number of placement countries.

Dating in the field seldom led to marriage. But when it did, the resulting relationship could have a significance that extended beyond the couple and their respective families. CUSO volunteers' interracial and international mar-riages may in a small way have contributed to a liberalizing of attitudes in the Canadian communities to which they returned. In 1965, the *Bulletin* featured an account of one such marriage, probably one of the earliest, that of volunteer Bob Pim and his Jamaican bride, paediatrics specialist Dr. Jean Carberry. Chris Bryant, who began as a volunteer in Grenada that same year, married several years later in Jamaica while serving as CUSO staff: "I arrived in Jamaica with one suitcase in 1969," he wrote, "and left in 1973 with a wife, a son and several suitcases!" As educated, middle-class Canadians marrying developing-world partners with elite backgrounds or professional status, volunteers like Pim and Bryant and their partners were helping to counter long-held stereotypes, about both mixed-race relationships and non-white immigrants.[136] The Carib-bean seems to have been the site of many of the earliest of these relationships. But marriages to women and (less often) men from East and West Africa were also not uncommon, while in Thailand, where CUSO began working in 1967,

"Involvement That Lasts a Lifetime"

Above: Irene Banda and David Beer, Zambia, November 1964. They married two years later. *Right:* The 1968 marriage of Judy Pullen of Oakville, Ontario, to Tsewang Choegyal Tethong. A deputy minister in the Tibetan government in exile when they met, "T.C." worked for the Dalai Lama for fifteen years. Courtesy of David Beer *(above)* and Judy Pullen Tethong *(right).*

marriages to Thais, especially by staff members, were almost a norm.[137] South Asia's dominant cultural and religious values did not easily lend themselves even to platonic relationships between Canadian volunteers and Asians of the opposite sex, much less to dating and marriages. And yet such marriages did occasionally take place. Probably the most publicized was the wedding of Judy Pullen and T.C. Tethong in 1968. The event was celebrated at the Oakville home of Pullen's prominent family, complete with the flying of Tibetan and Canadian flags. In the same way that they supported their daughter's work with Tibetan refugees in India, Judy Pullen's parents were demonstrating their support for her marital decision through the hosting of this large and high-profile event.[138]

Sooner or later, a good many CUSO marriages ended in divorce or separation.[139] Marriages involving cross-race couples were part of the pattern and indeed faced particular challenges. Even as the Canadian Charter of Rights came into operation, many Canadians remained uneasy about mixed-race marriage and about immigration generally.[140] Well-educated newcomers of "visible minority" backgrounds faced (and continue to face) frequent difficulties in finding appropriate employment in Canada. T.C. Tethong was no exception. Still, many such relationships, including the Pullen-Tethong partnership, did more than just survive: they could have positive ripple effects within and beyond their immediate communities, even in rural Canada. Ghana RV Hank Koskamp, for instance, went online in 2008 to describe and celebrate his enduring marriage to his Ghanaian partner, Rose, and the successful integration of their family into their Huron Township farming community. Two years later, an online story in the *Lucknow Sentinel* explained that Rose's ongoing fundraising initiatives for her Ghanaian village were warmly supported in the region.[141]

With or without familial bonds to draw them back, many CUSO alumni made sentimental return journeys to the site of their placement. They wanted their children to see the place that had been such an important part of their own formation as young adults, to reacquaint themselves with anyone there who might remember them, or just to see how, or if, things had changed. Perhaps reflecting the degree to which they had sought to integrate into "their" communities, India alumni were especially inclined to make these return journeys. As Chapter 2 shows, it could be a poignant experience, as it was for Gordon Banta when he went back to the leprosy community where he had invested so much labour, only to find that all those he had known there had died. Others' experiences were more positive, if varied. Besides keeping in touch by mail over the years, Jim Walker made several return visits to the remote village where as a young COVer he had had the quintessential mud-hut experience. The ashram still existed, with the daughter of the former head now in charge.[142] Fellow historian Robin Jeffrey met up with old acquaintances whose family lives, by contrast, personified modernizing, globalizing India when in 2009 he revisited Chandigarh, where he had taught in the late 1960s: "I had a great couple of days there with ex-students and teacher-colleagues ... The deputy principal of the school ... [has] a son in the US, a daughter in Canada and the youngest son an officer in the Indian Air Force. Another Sikh colleague in his 70s spends time with his kids in Vancouver occasionally."[143] Perhaps more than any of the other India volunteers, Hans-Henning Mündel remained involved over the years with his (first) placement community. As well as organizing projects in Canada to assist the Paniyas colony, Mündel made several return visits so that his family could see the settlement about which they had heard so much. Visiting with his son in 1986, he was gratified to see that "some of the real 'movers and shakers' in this Colony now were some of my former schoolchildren! Those whom I

"Involvement That Lasts a Lifetime"

enrolled in 1966!" Mündel returned once again in 2011 to see the hospital and other facilities that his international Rotary contacts and private donations had helped to bring into being.[144]

Nigeria did not inspire CUSO alumni with a similar zeal for sentimental return journeys. RVs like Bernie Lucht and Dan Turner, who went back in later years for job-related reasons, found it a disturbingly violent and depressing country.[145] Still, some veterans of Nigeria service undoubtedly entered the "Return to your CUSO posting" draw that CUSO organized as part of its twenty-fifth anniversary celebrations and that Betty Plewes publicized in describing her own enjoyable visit to the school in Kano where she had taught some fifteen years earlier. So much about Kano itself had changed, she wrote, that it "was not so much going back as going again." And yet opportunities existed to reconnect, and "old friends remain the same." Bill and Grace Bavington had a similar experience when they went back to Nigeria for a year of medical work in the 1980s. Urban growth was a striking phenomenon even in northern cities like Kano and Zaria, but revisiting their former worksites, they received a warm welcome from Nigerians with whom they had worked.[146]

The Bavingtons returned accompanied by their children. They were by no means the only CUSO couple to undertake new assignments with one or more children in tow. Generally, though, alumni with an ongoing interest in volunteering waited until they were free of family responsibilities before again taking to the global road. There were plenty of agencies through which they could work in addition to CUSO itself, including one that CUSO had presciently helped to found: Canadian Executive Service Overseas (CESO). Officially established by External Affairs minister Paul Martin Sr. in 1967, CESO was designed to facilitate late-life volunteering. The plans called for two members of its board of directors to be appointed by CUSO.[147] Alumni as different in professional backgrounds as retired farmer Hank Koskamp and former diplomat Steve Woollcombe served more than one placement with CESO in the twenty-first century and through assignments in former Soviet-bloc countries experienced first-hand sending agencies' new understanding that underdevelopment is not exclusively a phenomenon of the Global South.[148] Meanwhile, John Baigent's reengagement with overseas service a quarter century after beginning with CUSO in Ghana came about under very different circumstances. Following decades of work as a specialist in labour and constitutional law, Baigent persuaded his legal partners to inaugurate a sabbatical program; he himself went to Ethiopia with WUSC in 1988. In 2001, Baigent founded and became executive director of a new NGO, Partners in the Horn of Africa, eventually making it his full-time job and spending about half of each year in Ethiopia. As a new NGO, Partners focused both on the kinds of things that had engaged some volunteers in Baigent's youth – building schools and health clinics and digging wells – and on more recent concerns, such as establishing micro-finance programs and caring for HIV/AIDS orphans.[149]

There has also been generational continuity. The young adult children of RVs who remained active on international development issues frequently became involved in such issues themselves or demonstrated a global interest in other ways. RVs' children who were born or raised in a developing country were perhaps especially inclined to follow this kind of path, but the phenomenon has by no means been confined to them. The international outlook of the new generation could be expressed in activities as brief and as local as linking up with developing-world athletes in advance of sporting events in Canada, or in more prolonged form through the international development courses and programs that had become available at Canadian universities by the late twentieth century, thanks in part to the initiatives of their parents' generation. All three of Jill Morton Grant's children enrolled in such programs and had opportunities to study and work abroad before settling into full-time careers. The son of filmmaker and development communications specialist Neill McKee chose to do a doctorate in law on Canada's international development policy, while international themes are central to the work of his playwright daughter.[150] As for following in their parents' footsteps by actually serving with CUSO or another NGO, that was becoming almost commonplace by the beginning of the twenty-first century. Now, however, such assignments were often of shorter duration, and electronic communications had effectively shrunk the sense of distance. Catherine Duffy's father had understandably been worried when his daughter left PEI for Borneo in 1965. But forty years later, when Catherine's own son left for a six-month CUSO assignment in Laos, she could be more sanguine about his departure thanks to her own world-mindedness and her son's ability to stay in touch through such means as cell phones and email.[151]

Adult children of CUSO alumni have also followed their parents into political activism. Probably the most high-profile example has been Lhadon Tethong, youngest of the three children of Judy Pullen and T.C. Tethong. The Tethong family's involvement with the Tibetan independence movement and

"Involvement That Lasts a Lifetime"

Lhadon Tethong, daughter of Judy Pullen and T.C. Tethong, followed her parents into pro-Tibet activism. As executive director of Students for a Free Tibet (SFT), she used the Internet to publicize SFT's demonstrations in Beijing to a global audience a year prior to the Beijing Olympics (2008). Courtesy Students for a Free Tibet.

humanitarian work had remained ongoing even after they settled in Victoria following their years in India. In addition to her work with the Tibetan Refugee Aid Society, Judy had become a central figure in pro-Tibet protest activities. As the only one of the three Tethong children born in Canada, Lhadon was in the most secure position to carry her mother's activism forward. In August 2007, as director of the New York-based organization Students for a Free Tibet, Lhadon and her fellow activists made world-wide headlines in advance of the Beijing Olympics thanks to the sophisticated media techniques they used to protest and publicize China's Tibet policy. Deploying all the electronic tools at their disposal, they turned what could have been merely a locally observed moment of protest into a global story.[152]

Staying On

Paul Scott's 1977 novel about a British colonial couple who opted to stay on in India at the end of the Raj gave fictional form to real-life British colonial officials who could not face the climate, the loss of social status, and the general dreariness of a return to England as the British Empire began to wind down.[153] No such negative prospects awaited CUSO volunteers as they returned to Canada following their two years abroad. Quite the contrary, especially in the period when they were still being welcomed back as fine young Canadians and when there were still plenty of jobs for university graduates. Nevertheless, some volunteers did opt to remain in the Global South. Probably the most unusual instance was that of an Ottawa volunteer who, beginning as an electronics teacher in a Zambia trade school in 1969, held diverse volunteer and staff positions with CUSO before deciding to open a bar in The Gambia after the region became a tourist hotspot as a result of Alex Haley's book *Roots*.[154] More usually, ties of marriage intersecting with a strong interest in the politics and development of the region where the volunteers served appear to have been decisive factors. The number who made this choice was undoubtedly small, and only a few countries/regions became sites of long-term attachments. Still, such attachments provide a fascinating variation on the broad theme of this chapter.

Several volunteers who served in Zambia and who became well known within the CUSO community put down familial and career roots in East, Central, and Southern Africa (CUSO's so-called ECSA region). Ross Kidd was one such volunteer. Beginning as head of the Adult Education Department in the College of Applied Arts and Commerce in Lusaka in 1966, Kidd stayed on after his marriage to a Zambian. Later, from his new home in Botswana, he made a career as a training and community development specialist, using innovative drama techniques and working in such areas as HIV/AIDS education and rural water supply. Far from being limited by his location in Botswana, Kidd has been able to do project and consulting work in more than thirty countries and has had access to funding agencies all over the world.[155] Mary Krug began as a volunteer in the same year as Kidd. Married to Zimbabwean nationalist activist Edward Ndlovu in 1972, she lived from 1980 in Zimbabwe, where Edward was elected a member of parliament. The Ndlovus experienced both the hopefulness of the early years in newly independent Zimbabwe and, in the mid-1980s, Edward's detainment without trial as former nationalist activists in the liberation movement group that had long rivalled Robert Mugabe's fell afoul

"Involvement That Lasts a Lifetime"

of the Mugabe government for allegedly plotting its overthrow. Despite Edward's death in 1989 and the tragic political and economic decline of Zimbabwe, Mary Krug Ndlovu remained in her adopted country, working as a human rights activist and on behalf of the trust established in her husband's memory.[156] Meanwhile, as shown in Chapter 3, David Beer's connection with CUSO's ECSA region began even earlier, in 1964. As a volunteer leader with the Zambia Youth Service, Beer proudly participated in ceremonies marking the birth of the nation. His marriage to Irene Banda, one of the country's first registered nurses, took place in 1966. In the decades that followed, Beer's relationship with the region and with CUSO remained both intensely strong and decidedly peripatetic as he pursued his controversial liberation-movement activism on both sides of the Atlantic. From 1994, as an independent organizational development practitioner and consultant, Beer lived and worked mainly in South Africa. It was only in 2009, with children and grandchildren located in Canada, that he opted, at last, to retire in his own country.[157] For RVs like Beer, whose lives had been characterized by contract work, decades overseas, and activism rather than Western consumerism, retirement could be a financially challenging undertaking rather than the beginning of the "golden years." What it emphatically was not was occasion for regret at having acted on youthful idealism.

Conclusion

It may well be true that after their two years abroad many CUSO alumni simply moved on, occasionally recalling their time overseas "with a sigh and a shudder" while largely focusing on the private and material concerns of their post-CUSO lives. That does not diminish the significance of the sizable number who remained engaged by international concerns or by analogous national or community issues through their careers or voluntary activities. Nor should it be too readily concluded that those alumni who largely disappeared from view left no developmental impact on their families and communities and were not themselves permanently shaped by their experience. By way of conclusion, two final examples are suggestive.

The first involves my high-school classmate, mentioned at the beginning of this book. Following her two CUSO terms in a government boys' school in Kenya in the late 1960s, June Dingwell returned to her native Prince Edward Island and a life of teaching, marriage, and family responsibilities. In contrast to a sizable number of other CUSO RVs in PEI, June evidently had little or no long-term involvement with CUSO committee work or other development-related activities. Nevertheless, younger family members became active in Farmers Helping Farmers, a local NGO whose projects over the years, mainly in Kenya, have received strong community support and matching CIDA funds. Indeed, in 2003, Farmers Helping Farmers won CIDA's inaugural Bill McWhinney award "for excellence in volunteer programming." Shortly thereafter, as part of the specialization in international education component of his B.Ed., June's elder son travelled to Kenya for his "inter-cultural [teaching] experience." His mother's example had influenced his choice of placement, he wrote, and "I will definitely be taking her stories with me."[158] The second example is that of an RV on the other side of Canada who agreed to be interviewed only reluctantly and on condition of anonymity. In his post-CUSO years, he maintained no ongoing ties to development-related work, and he showed absolutely no desire to wax nostalgic about his two years abroad. Yet during the course of the interview, he acknowledged that the two years had been "a life-altering experience," an involvement that, even in his case, had in fact lasted a lifetime.

Conclusion
"Gnat against Elephant" and "The Time of Our Lives"

In 1986, University of British Columbia political science professor John R. Wood wrote to CUSO executive director Chris Bryant protesting the decision to close the CUSO committee office at UBC. Established early in 1961 as the President's Committee on Student Service Overseas, the committee predated the formal establishment of CUSO itself. Wood was one of several CUSO alumni distressed by the decision. Ending the UBC local committee was part of a larger CUSO pattern of moving off university campuses, another letter-writer acknowledged, and generally it made sense to do so, but UBC's pioneering committee was special: as a hub of outreach within International House, its demise would be a loss to global awareness in the large university community. The organizational name change in 1981 whereby CUSO no longer stood for Canadian University Service Overseas (it now just stood for itself) had been an earlier move in the same direction.[1] But given the UBC campus committee's long history, closing it down in CUSO's twenty-fifth anniversary year was particularly significant. It effectively symbolized the end of the era when CUSO volunteers had primarily been young, newly graduated Canadians.

Volunteers – officially called "cooperants" since 1981 – were already from a different demographic: older, on average, and with the mix of specialized skills and work experience that developing countries were now said to be seeking.

(Anecdotal evidence suggests that this pattern was already emerging by the late 1970s.) They were also destined for fewer countries than in CUSO's salad days and significantly fewer in number. Claiming more than 1,300 volunteers in forty-five developing nations in 1971, CUSO had a presence in just twenty-nine countries in 1983, and in the year following, it planned to "stabilize" new placements from Canada at just 250 per year. These demographic shifts were among a number of changes in the lead-up to what some staff were referring to in the anniversary year as "the new CUSO." Also highlighted as an aspect of this new CUSO was increasing participation in large projects initiated and wholly funded by CIDA.[2]

Like other northern NGOs, the CUSO of the mid-1980s was operating in a changed global environment. The newly decolonized nations of the early 1960s were now decades old, battered survivors of their own turbulent politics and of changing fashions in the theory and practice of development.[3] NGOs were far more numerous, with a growing number now originating in the Global South. Particularly after the appointment of the World Commission on Environment and Development, of which Canadians Maurice Strong and Jim MacNeill were important figures, environmental degradation began receiving greater attention in a new (and continually expanding) discourse on sustainable development. Meanwhile, the imposition on Southern governments of structural adjustment programs had the predictable effect of exacerbating poverty and inequality and thus increasing the need for assistance from NGOs.[4]

Insofar as CUSO itself was concerned, there was a recognition that some of the changes it was initiating, or being drawn into, might have unwelcome consequences down the road. Chris Bryant acknowledged that "our search for skilled people has left behind the very people who built CUSO – the young university graduates." Speaking more generally, Tim Brodhead warned that in accepting large sums of money to carry out government-initiated projects, NGOs risked becoming "simply ... project brokers" rather than agents of social change. Neither was recommending a return to the practices of the 1960s, when they had themselves been young volunteers. In response to changed conditions in the Global South and at home, Britain's Voluntary Service Overseas (VSO) and the US Peace Corps had also been sending fewer volunteers than in their heyday. Nevertheless, unlike CUSO, they remained firmly committed to what VSO's Dick Bird called its "central sending mission." They were also anxious to increase volunteer numbers and saw an ongoing role for the liberal arts graduate in the volunteer mix.[5] CUSO had already begun broadening its mission by the early 1970s, engaging in the politics of liberation-movement support and establishing a Projects Division. Some within the organization, beginning with left-oriented field staff, had also sought to scale down volunteer placements. But the extent to which volunteer numbers declined in the mid-1980s was not simply a triumph of a left-wing position or of an overall falling off in requests from developing countries. As Bryant frankly acknowledged in 1985, it was also a consequence of the Nigerian government's sudden new unwillingness to accept foreign workers: "The country which allowed us to define ourselves to ... CIDA as a manpower placement agency, long after mass placements had ended elsewhere, has given us a new message ... That message must mean changes for CUSO."[6] The "new CUSO" of the mid-1980s was, then, a product of the organization's own political and strategic considerations as well as of the larger development context.[7] As it observed its twenty-fifth anniversary and moved on, CUSO was both hesitant to celebrate the milestone, given the reality that in many places where it worked conditions had actually worsened rather than improved over the years, and proud of the many links it had established with partners in host countries.[8]

The "old" CUSO had been a product of a very different and more optimistic time. During its first quarter century, it had managed to send some nine thousand volunteers to the developing world. What had *that* CUSO accomplished? Insiders and specialists in the world of NGOs point out that assessing their performance is "a difficult and messy business," and therefore often not done, or not done well.[9] But what about the volunteers themselves? How did *they* view their contribution, at the time and in retrospect? As seen in Chapter 2, the earliest volunteers in India had quickly recognized that anything they could do to help needy people was a mere drop in the ocean. In "Doomsday Idealism," the concluding chapter to the otherwise generally upbeat collection of narratives in *Man Deserves Man*, Ghana RV Dave Godfrey used a more original metaphor: "Returning," he wrote, "there is only one clear, overwhelming thought: gnat against elephant." Godfrey was not belittling what his fellow volunteers had been doing so much as pointing out its minuteness, and its futility so long as those in the "castle" – the rich Western nations – continued to pursue self-serving policies in regard to the Third World.[10] In the decades that followed, there would be many new metaphors to signify development dilemmas, and a steady stream of reports, articles, and book-length indictments of harmful Western policies, targeting not only such Western capitalist practices as inequitable trade and resource-extraction policies, but also, among "postdevelopmentalists" like Escobar and Rist, "the entire [development] paradigm."[11]

As this book shows, many returned volunteers remained engaged in the cause of development despite their early recognition of their "gnat" status and their subsequent awareness of all that could and did go wrong. One of them was Keith Bezanson. In his roles at CIDA, IDRC, and the University of Sussex and as chair of the VSO International Board, Bezanson was well positioned to learn about disappointing development outcomes, and he was probably exposed to a more-than-average quantity of bleak development literature. Yet the loss of youthful innocence in former volunteers like himself, he contends, did not mean a loss of faith: "Most of us came to realize that the innocence of our zeitgeist was at quantum variance with the lessons of history, the realities of asymmetrical political and economic power and the barriers of corruption and capture. Yet ... that realization ... did not result in disillusionment or defeatism. Although it did produce more sober reflection, my impression is that most of the Peace Corps, VSO and CUSO volunteers of my generation never abandoned the ideal. To this day, many continue to work for development and to advocate for it."[12]

The willingness of so many CUSO alumni to remain engaged in work or advocacy for development and for analogous activities within Canada, and their positive reflections on their CUSO years, can also be understood, I think, in terms of an implicit acceptance of the kinds of realistic goals advocated in William Easterly's *The White Man's Burden*: "doable actions" rather than "Big Plans" and a "utopian agenda"; help to individuals rather than attempts "to transform governments or societies"; in short, "modest interventions that make people's lives better."[13] As CUSO coordinator in Nigeria, Gerry Caplan had also advocated this kind of realism, especially in frustration with others in the CUSO family who had loftier ambitions for the organization and indicted programming in Nigeria as not sufficiently developmental. What might be called retrospective realism likewise helps to explain why, despite their lack of illusions about what they had contributed to resolving the problems of the developing world, RVs, looking back decades later on their own youthful involvement, typically did not regard it as having been futile.

Especially in the early years and probably in all countries, individual volunteers had sometimes found themselves placed in non-jobs or in ill-defined or inappropriate assignments. Probably the situation was nowhere as bad as it was in the early Peace Corps, where Sargent Shriver's penchant for rapid growth and "bigness" had resulted in numerous disenchanted volunteers, with a majority in some countries such as Pakistan finding themselves in non-productive jobs.[14] Moreover, as the India experience showed, CUSO volunteers coped with ill-advised placements by contributing outside their nominal jobs and engaging creatively in the work and life of their communities rather than by quitting early. Such an approach, encouraged by their mentors, allowed them to establish lasting personal connections and broadened their cultural horizons. Immediate job satisfaction may have been strongest among volunteers who were in a position to play immediately helpful or actual life-saving roles, whether among refugees, in medical settings, or elsewhere. Such settings, however, were not the norm. The typical CUSO volunteer was, like her American and British counterpart, a classroom teacher assigned to fill a gap in a secondary school or other educational institution until a local counterpart could step in.

A sense of having contributed something worthwhile extended to this volunteer majority, though sometimes only in retrospect. It included not only RVs who became skilled and inventive at coping with ill-prepared students and scarce or not-existent curricular resources but also those who did not consider themselves to have been well-prepared or talented teachers. Reaching out to their students with enthusiasm, organizing sports or other activities, and providing services outside the classroom could amplify their contribution as teachers. Looking back on a twenty-five-year career with IDRC and the World Bank, during which time he had upgraded his qualifications through graduate studies, one such RV mused that, notwithstanding his shortcomings inside an early 1970s classroom in Trinidad, he might actually have "achieved more" during his three teaching years with CUSO on the racially tense island "than in the prestigious and more glamorous other parts of my career. Go figure." Across the Atlantic a female volunteer who taught A- and O-level English literature in a girls' school in Ghana about a decade earlier had initially sought a transfer, seeing the school as "too posh," too much like an African version of her own Havergal College background. But looking back after a long career in development and having observed numerous "well intentioned" but "misguided" development efforts that ultimately failed to strengthen local people's well-being, she had a different view. "The basic teaching job might have been the least harmful and most helpful thing that we [volunteers] could have done," she concluded. And in her own case, her personal and academic background had enabled her to fit in at her assigned school and do a good job.[15] Over the years, such RVs have had the experience of receiving letters from appreciative former

Nigeria's high commissioner to Canada, Iyorwuese Hagher, greets his former teacher, CUSO RV Diane Labelle-Davey, during CUSO's fiftieth-anniversary celebrations. Courtesy of Sean Kelly and CUSO International.

students or of revisiting their placement country and meeting students who went on to higher education and professional careers.[16] When CUSO marked its fiftieth anniversary in June 2011, one such ex-student, Nigeria's high commissioner to Canada, used the occasion to speak about the impact that a particular CUSO teacher had had on his life. Diane Labelle, teaching French in a secondary school in Jos during the civil-war years, had been an inspiration to him and several other "sassy and smart" students who went on to successful careers, the high commissioner told CBC radio listeners; "the real ambassadors were people like her."[17]

Particularly in view of criticisms of the practice of exporting Western-style education that came to the fore outside and within CUSO in the mid-1970s and the self-doubts such criticisms instilled in teacher-volunteers, these retrospective reflections are noteworthy. They resonate with Easterly's argument about the value of assisting individuals to improve their lives through modest interventions. That the students helped by CUSO teachers were often, comparatively, already privileged and that their education could serve to exacerbate socio-economic divides (or fuel resentment among those who remained unemployed) cannot be gainsaid. Yet as CUSO's experience in Nigeria showed, the desire for formal schooling in many regions was a genuinely grassroots phenomenon. This was nowhere more evident than with the educational rehabilitation project in postwar Biafra where volunteer-turned-staff-officer Jack Pearpoint and his colleagues came away with a sense of having made a difference "one village at a time."[18]

If few volunteers in any country where CUSO served were in a position to do much individually to help the very poorest of the poor, CUSO institutionally attempted to do so through project work, including small-scale initiatives undertaken through the Projects Division. Archival records reveal little about the ultimate outcomes from such initiatives. Discussing the problematic nature of measuring "success" in small NGO projects, Inter Pares's Brian Murphy observed in 1991 that "The real goal of such projects should be to organize people economically and politically so that they can understand their situation and begin to work together to change it." Other NGO activists were more skeptical about the ability of outsiders to promote that kind of understanding and transformation. Tangible project effectiveness in helping the poorest seemed most likely if CUSO could identify and work with highly motivated indigenous groups, as in the case of Proshika in Bangladesh, where, in addition to providing initial financial assistance for Proshika's work with small, rural self-help projects, CUSO served as the go-between that eventually brought Proshika millions of dollars in CIDA funding.[19]

Projects initiated by CUSO staff in conjunction with local partners were also the development vehicles of choice for those working in support of liberation movements and, later, in newly independent countries in eastern and southern Africa. For staff who had worked for years, sometimes decades, in support of the liberation movements, disappointing outcomes were acknowledged only belatedly and with difficulty.[20] As an invited guest at Zimbabwe's independence celebrations in April 1980, David Beer was proud to be able to introduce Canada's External Affairs minister, Mark MacGuigan, to men who were about to become part of Robert Mugabe's ministry and to some key figures from other new states. And in the decades that followed, he and other CUSO colleagues involved with the African National Congress were anxious to serve as "bridges" between the ANC and the Canadian government. Ultimately, Zimbabwe's decline under Mugabe was "the most disillusioning, heartbreaking part" of Beer's involvement in Africa. Still, looking back in retirement, Beer was able to put Zimbabwe's failure and problems in other post-independence ECSA countries into the perspective of someone who had remained engaged and seen, alongside the grave problems typically featured in Western media, such hopeful aspects as a vibrant press (Zambia), strong civil-society groups (South Africa), and resilient populations.[21]

As this book has shown, CUSO as an organization frequently took up development issues and regional concerns well in advance of CIDA. Moreover, as Brodhead and Pratt observe, NGOs such as CUSO in these decades "provided a public face to Canada's aid program, eliciting political support and offering an avenue for Canadians' involvement." To be sure, the NGOs were never as influential on aid-related issues as they wished to be. Nevertheless, David Morrison maintains that as part of Canada's small development community, they were often able to persuade parliamentarians and bureaucrats to support "humane internationalist values."[22] As Canada's largest volunteer-sending agency, eventually bringing home thousands of men and women with developing-world experience, CUSO had a distinctive contribution to make among Canadian NGOs, both to nation-wide development education in all its forms and to the staffing of development organizations. Over the years, hundreds of RVs brought their energy and concerns into permanent and contract positions in Canada's official development agencies and NGOs, becoming, in Clyde Sanger's phrase, a kind of "CUSO mafia." Networking with and hiring one another, they have, over time, taken the helm of agencies as different as IDRC, the Canadian Council for International Cooperation, the North-South Institute, KAIROS, Oxfam, and WUSC. They have also established new NGOs as vehicles for acting on their personal perspective on how, or where, to "do" development, and they have played significant roles in multilateral agencies.

Domestic development issues and community concerns also engaged CUSO alumni, as Chapter 5 shows. Unquestionably, there were many alumni who did not take up *any* form of public activism, international or domestic, following their volunteer years, whether because they returned disillusioned or because of other circumstances in their personal lives. Nevertheless, as a group, RVs have perhaps been unique among Canadians for the degree to which global-mindedness and domestic civic engagement have remained complementary and lifelong attributes. If this is so, it has not been because they experienced their two years overseas as a period of youthful apprenticeship in "do-goodism." Like Donald Faris, who inspired many of the earliest enthusiasts, they would have squirmed under the term "self-sacrifice" so often applied to foreign missionaries in an earlier era. Instead, as Faris had anticipated, they experienced the interval as a time when they gained more than they gave, a time of enrichment and personal growth. Statements made to this effect in the course of interviews were, I believe, not just "spin" or the result of memory's tricks. Certainly, they *did* remember homesickness and illness and assorted discomforts and, in some cases, periods of feeling useless or of resenting the resentment of indigenous co-workers. But they also came back, as one of them wrote in 1967, having done things "we never imagined we were capable of doing," with broadened horizons and new-found confidence.[23]

In 1981, as CUSO was about to mark its twentieth anniversary, John Gray's new musical, "Rock and Roll," premiered at the National Arts Centre. It began with a song whose first stanza struck a chord with organizers of anniversary events and was incorporated into their "Reminiscences":

In the time of our lives
Our footsteps were sure,
Ideals were intact,
And our motives were pure;
No failures to mourn
Or regrets to endure,
We were having the time of our lives.[24]

The anniversary organizers presumably were taken by the sixties nostalgia in Gray's lyrics rather than celebrating their own youthful virtue, for as they well knew, as volunteers starting out in that era, their footsteps had been anything but sure and their motives decidedly mixed. Still, in a time of unprecedented optimism and idealism about possibilities for contributing to a fairer world, many of them *had* experienced their volunteer years as the time of their lives. Old CUSO hands who maintain that the sense of commitment and camaraderie was strongest in that first decade are probably right.[25] Yet many volunteers and cooperants who served in later decades also experienced their two overseas years as a time of exuberance and personal growth. Part of a large company of CUSO alumni who went on to lives of engaged global and national citizenship, they became a leaven in Canadian society. As Canada's global villagers age and fall silent, the nation will be poorer for their passing.

A Note on Sources and Acknowledgments

Rather than include a bibliography of all the secondary sources used in preparation for this book, I have chosen to economize on space and instead direct
readers to the notes for each chapter. There, the works that proved most helpful
are fully cited on first use. As for written primary sources, the single most important has been the Canadian University Service Overseas (CUSO) fonds, MG
28, I 323, at Library and Archives Canada (LAC). I have experienced nothing
but kindness from the staff at LAC in making use of this fonds over a period of
several years. Indeed, several staff members went out of their way to help me.
Yet I confess that I was never able to determine the rationale by which the individual volumes in this large collection were organized. Some volumes contain
files for wholly unrelated subject matter and may simply reflect the way materials
were received from CUSO's Ottawa office, where the demands of the day took
precedence over tidy organizing. Occasionally, different pages of the same
letter or report are found in files in different volumes. If complete lists were
kept annually of such important matters as names, ages, and total number of
volunteers sent overseas, they have not become part of this collection. Gaps of
this sort have made it difficult to verify and compare data. In 1978, the *CUSO
Forum* began providing totals of all returned volunteers. The numbers seem
reasonably, but not wholly, reliable. It should also be noted that these totals
included volunteers who served with Service Universitaire Canadien Outre-
mer (SUCO) until 1981, when formal separation of the English-Canadian and
Quebec wings of what began as one organization was complete. Problems with
gaps and inconsistencies in the holdings in this fonds are noted here not by way
of complaint but rather to account for some idiosyncratic references in my
endnotes and to alert future users to the challenges as well as the richness of
the collection. Some copies of CUSO periodicals, of which the two most long-
lasting are the *CUSO/SUCO Bulletin* and the *CUSO Forum,* are found in this
fonds. Mostly they are found in the National Library. Robarts Library at the
University of Toronto also has a partial run of these periodicals and annual
reports as, probably, do some other university libraries across Canada where
CUSO had active committees.

Other, smaller, collections of CUSO materials were found in the King
Gordon fonds, MG 30, C 241, at LAC, and at several university archives, most

valuably in the John Conway fonds at the University of British Columbia Archives. This fonds is also useful for materials retained by Professor Conway on such related organizations as World University Service of Canada and the Student Christian Movement. In regard to privately held collections, the two most helpful, particularly for correspondence on the early days of CUSO, are the Donald K. Faris Family Collection and the collection of Stephen Woollcombe and the late Bill McWhinney, cited as the McWhinney/Woollcombe Collection. Both were largely uncatalogued but very much worth the trouble of sorting through for my purposes. Tim Brodhead, Roy Fischer, and Murray Thomson provided CUSO print materials from their personal files, some of which I did not find in any other holdings. Ian Smillie shared his collection of more than fifty taped interviews, conducted in preparation for writing *The Land of Lost Content: A History of CUSO* (Toronto: Deneau, 1985). The tapes, made under less than optimal auditory conditions and stored in Smillie's garage for some twenty years thereafter, are nonetheless invaluable as candid exchanges of information and opinion with founders, volunteers, and staff.

My own interviews with former volunteers were conducted in person or on the basis of a detailed questionnaire that I prepared at an early stage of my research and modified slightly thereafter. Early word-of-mouth requests for subjects to interview and a 2005 notice about my project on the CUSO Alumni website brought valuable responses, which in turn led to other contacts. Undoubtedly, these approaches resulted in my hearing from those alumni who remained most engaged with CUSO or with development generally, and who have retained the strongest bonds with one another. I have tried to keep the silence of disengaged and unreached alumni in mind in writing this book. Among those who agreed to be interviewed, and many others who provided information more briefly through correspondence and phone conversations, very few requested confidentiality. Even so, I have occasionally withheld names or used initials for respondents when it seemed prudent to do so. I have adopted the same policy with regard to potentially still-sensitive matters in correspondence and reports.

It is a pleasure to acknowledge the many forms of help I have received in working on this book. I begin with sincere thanks to the former volunteers and staff and other members of the extended CUSO family who are listed in Appendix 3. Some of them responded not once or twice but on numerous occasions over several years, and with unfailing graciousness, to requests for diverse forms of assistance. Many former volunteers and staff whom I interviewed early on read a rough draft of what became Chapter 1, as did Clyde Sanger and Keith Spicer. Welcome feedback on one or more later chapters was provided more recently by Gini Dickie, Barbara Kincaid Moore, Wendy Quarry, and Stephen Woollcombe. Stephen, David Beer, Walter McLean, Judy Pullen Tethong, Judy Ransom, and Ian Smillie provided photographs from their own collections, as did the family of the late Don Faris. For assistance with photographs from the files of what is now Cuso International, all freely given, I thank Kristie Kelly and Sean Kelly. At CUSO's Ottawa office, I was also generously assisted by Judith David and, more recently, by Executive Director Derek Evans and his assistant, Lorraine Chartrand. Former staff at the Canadian International Development Agency who responded to my questions about gender matters at the agency as they affected CUSO and the hiring of returned volunteers (RVs) include Barbara Brown, Wendy Lawrence, and Diana Rivington (themselves RVs), Elizabeth McAllister, and Carolyn McAskie. Returned volunteer Christopher Smart's long career at the International Development Research Centre made him a helpful source about CUSO connections there.

No amount of release time or research funding would have made it possible to see all the countries where CUSO volunteers worked, so I am especially grateful that I was able to visit a few of those countries, thanks to funding for my earlier research on women and missions. Grants from King's University College at Western facilitated research trips within Canada and conference presentations over a period of several years. Former King's colleagues Stephanie Bangarth and the late and much-missed Jeff Cormier kindly shared sources and leads from their own research. From within the larger academic community and beyond, I want also to thank the following for assistance that ranged from computer help, research tips, anecdotes, and conference contacts, to accommodation and hospitality: Paul Axelrod, Kevin Brushett, Marie Burge, Sharon Cook, Paul Dewar, Isabel Dingwell, Karen Dubinsky, Dawn and Don Faris and the extended Faris family, Keith Fleming, Kofi Hope, Graham Lea, Catherine Le Grand, Heather MacAndrew, Helene McFayden, Audrey McLaughlin, Brian Mclean, Dominique Marshall, Chris Miller, David Morrison, Bruce Muirhead, Inger-Marie Okkenhaug, Julius Olajos, Katherine Ridout, Renée Soulodre-La France, Val Taylor, Ryan Touhey, Marguerite Van Die, Elizabeth Waterston, and David Webster. Reaching back into the past, I would add to this list Ramsay Cook, who more than three decades ago alerted me to the rich research possibilities to be found in studying Canadian sojourners in the non-Western world. It is an honour to claim him as a mentor.

Two anonymous scholars evaluated my manuscript for UBC Press in an insightful, generous, and timely manner. Their reports have helped me to make *Canada's Global Villagers* a better book. As for UBC Press, I cannot speak too highly of the support I have received from staff there, especially through early encouragement and advice from Melissa Pitts, now the Press's director, and later from Emily Andrew and Lesley Erickson. Their editorial guidance has been clear, prompt, and reassuring.

My best thanks are to an extended network of family and friends who have been an ongoing source of support. There are, undoubtedly, many others within and beyond the CUSO community who have assisted me with the research and writing of this book but whose names do not appear here. I hope that in spite of the omission, they will find some trace of their contribution in these pages. As for errors of fact and interpretation in the book, they are no one's responsibility but my own.

Appendices

Appendix 1
Volunteer placements by region and country, September 1971[*]

Asia

India	21
Papua & New Guinea	46
Sabah	29
Sarawak	9
Thailand	40
West Malaysia	14

Caribbean

Barbados	22
Grenada & Carriacou	2
Guyana	10
Jamaica	47
St. Kitts	3
St. Lucia	10
St. Vincent	7
Trinidad & Tobago	5

Latin America

Bolivia	6
Chile	3
Colombia	53
Cuba	2
Ecuador	1
Peru	16

East and Central Africa

Botswana	24
Kenya	3
Malawi	35
Tanzania	89
Uganda	46
Zambia	91

West Africa

Ghana	83
Nigeria	164
Sierra Leone	50

Francophone Africa
(served by SUCO volunteers)

Algérie	47
Burundi	16
Cameroun	43
Congo	37
Côte d'Ivoire	34
Dahomey	1
Gabon	3
Haute-Volta	50
Madagascar	35
Mali	14
Rwanda	30
Sénégal	24
Tchad	30
Togo	21
Tunisie	18

[*] Data, including spelling of country names, taken from "CUSO Facts and Figures," issued by CUSO Fund Raising, 151 Slater Street, Ottawa.

Appendix 2
CUSO executive directors, 1961-90

1961-62	Lewis Perinbam, acting executive secretary
1962-66	Bill McWhinney
1966	Terry Glavin, acting executive secretary
1967-68	Hugh Christie
1968-70	Frank Bogdasavich
1970	John B. Wood
1970-72	[David Catmur and Bill McNeill, directors, respectively, of Overseas and Canadian Operations, served as interim executive directors]
1972-73	John Gordon
1974-76	Murray Thomson
1976-79	Robin Wilson
1979	[David Hamilton, interim executive director, January-October, 1979]
1979-83	Ian Smillie
1983-90	Chris Bryant

Appendix 3
Informants: Former CUSO volunteers and staff

Personal interviews and/or responses to questionnaires

Harry Baglole
Sally Bambridge* [Ravindra]
Gordon Banta
Stan Barrett
Bill Bavington
Grace Bavington
Linda Bean [Fischer]
David Beer
Keith Bezanson
Tim Brodhead
Chris Bryant
Andy Buhler
Nancy Callaghan
John Cameron
Christina Cassels
Allan T. Collier
Mary Corkery
Lawrence Cumming
Ron Cyr
Gini Dickie
Catherine Duffy [Mullally]
Katherine Eberl [Kelly]
Suki Falkner
Roy Fischer
Judy Fleming [Barber]
Nancy Garrett
Harry Gaudet
Sandra Gaudet
Dave Godfrey
Ellen Swartz Godfrey
Wayn Hamilton

Bonnie Hartley
Karem Hall [Wright]
Vicki Henry
Jane Hill
Margaret Hilson
David Ingram
Lois James [Chetelat]
Robin Jeffrey
Colin Bruce Johnstone
Anne Jones [Hume]
Sandra Kalmakoff
Paul Kelly
Barbara Kerfoot [Hooper]
Ross Kidd
Barbara Kincaid [Moore]
Mary Krug [Ndlovu]
Wendy Lawrence
Bernie Lucht
Dennis E. McDermott
Neill McKee
Walter McLean**
Gordon Bruce MacNeil
Bill McNeill
Brian Marson
Wendy Marson [Dobson]
Kenneth Mellish
Teresa Mellish
Jill Morton [Grant]
Jim Morrison
Kitty Moses
Hans-Henning Mündel

Adel G. Nafrawi
Jack Pearpoint
Lewis Perinbam**
Brian Perry
Patricia Phillips
Dale Posgate
Judy Pullen [Tethong]
Judy Ransom
Joyce Relyea
Wendy Salmond [Quarry]
Ozzie Schmidt
Donna Shields [Shields-Poë]
Anne Simpson
Don Simpson**
Christopher Smart
Ian Smillie
Bill Sparks
Alan Stewart
Rieky Lambregts [Stuart]
Mar Thomson
Murray Thomson**
Rob Thomson
Dan Turner
James W. St. G. Walker
Sheila Ward
Marian White
Susanne Wise
John R. Wood
Stephen Woollcombe

Emails and telephone contacts

Donna Anderson [Hudson]
Catherine Brackley
Barbara Brown
Bev Burke
Gerry Caplan**

Jon Church
Paul Delaney
Anne-Marie Groves [Gaston]
Hank Koskamp

Vandra Masemann
Betty Plewes
Diana Rivington
Tom Schatzky
Selena Tapper**

Informants Interviewed: Non-CUSO

John Conway
Barbara McLean

Cranford Pratt

Clyde Sanger

* Surnames of women are those under which they served. Current names are shown in brackets.
** Staff who had not previously served as CUSO volunteers.
Note: Interviewees who requested full confidentiality are not listed.

Notes

Preface

1   Nicolas Barry-Shaw and Dru Oja Jay, *Paved with Good Intentions: Canada's Development NGOs from Idealism to Imperialism* (Halifax: Fernwood Publishing, 2012), 6.
2   Ian Smillie, "NGOs: Crisis and Opportunity in the New World Order," in *Transforming Development: Foreign Aid for a Changing World*, ed. Jim Freedman (Toronto: University of Toronto Press, 2000), 114-33, esp. 123-24; Brian K. Murphy, "International NGOs and the Challenge of Modernity," in *Debating Development: NGOs and the Future*, ed. Deborah Eade and Ernst Ligteringen (Oxford/Oxfam International, 2001), 60-85 ("corporatisation" at 80); Samantha Nutt, *Damned Nations: Greed, Guns, Armies and Aid* (Toronto: McClelland and Stewart, 2011), Chap. 5 (see page 138 for volunteer tourism); Alison Van Rooy, "Good News! You May Be Out of a Job: Reflections on the Past 50 Years of Northern NGOs," in *Debating Development*, 19-43.

Introduction

1   "How to Be a Global Villager," *Maclean's*, February 1969, 43-48.
2   "Sixth Annual Meeting," *CUSO/SUCO Bulletin*, October 1967–January 1968, 5.
3   "Report of the Executive Secretary (Actg), 1965-66," 14, Library and Archives Canada (LAC), CUSO fonds, MG 28, I 323, vol. 75, file 4 (hereafter LAC/CUSO, MG 28, I 323, with volume and file number); "Where Are the 9,000 Now?," *CUSO Forum*, September 1985, 17. The figure includes volunteers who served with CUSO's francophone counterpart, Service Universitaire Canadien Outre-mer (SUCO), until 1981, when full separation of the two organizations took place.
4   Ruth Compton Brouwer, "When Missions Became Development: Ironies of 'NGOization' in Mainstream Canadian Churches in the 1960s," *Canadian Historical Review* 91, 4 (2010): 661-93. A similar phenomenon was occurring in Canadian Catholic mission work, as Catherine Le Grand has shown. See "Development, Liberation Theology and the Peasant Movement of Agrarian Reform: Quebec Catholic Missionaries in Honduras, 1955-1975" (paper presented to Canadian Historical Association annual meeting, Concordia University, Montreal, 31 May 2010). Michael Barnett deals masterfully with links and legacies between religion and humanitarianism in *Empire of Humanity: A History of Humanitarianism* (Ithaca, NY: Cornell University Press, 2011).
5   Gilbert Rist, *The History of Development: From Western Origins to Global Faith*, 3rd ed. (London: Zed Books, 2008); James McKay and Matthew Hilton, "Introduction," *NGOs in Contemporary Britain: Non-State Actors in Society and Politics since 1945*, ed. Nick Crowson, Matthew Hilton, and James McKay (Basingstoke, UK: Palgrave Macmillan, 2009), 3. Rist's *History of Development* is part of a vast sea of literature on the subject, much of it sharply critical of specific development ideologies and practices, or, as in the case of Rist, of the very concept of development understood as economic growth. When this literature discusses the work of NGOs, it generally portrays their contributions as more in tune with local realities and therefore less likely to do harm. See, for instance, William Easterly, *The White Man's Burden: Why the West's Efforts to Aid the Rest Have Done So Much Ill and So Little Good* (New York: Penguin Books, 2006) and Jeffrey D. Sachs, *The End of Poverty: Economic Possibilities for Our Time* (New York: Penguin Books, 2005). Remarkably, Arturo Escobar's *Encountering Development: The Making and Unmaking of the Third World* (Princeton, NJ: Princeton University Press, 1995), one of the most widely cited examples of a deconstructionist approach to development discourse, largely omits NGOs from its analysis.

6   Rist, *History of Development,* 70-71 (quotations on 71; italics are Rist's).

7   For instance, Mark H. Haefele, "Walt Rostow's Stages of Economic Growth: Ideas and Action," in *Staging Growth: Modernization, Development, and the Global Cold War,* ed. David C. Engerman, Nils Gilman, Mark H. Haefele, and Michael E. Latham (Amherst: University of Massachusetts Press, 2003), 81-103. Haefele uses the terms *economic development* and *modernization* interchangeably.

8   Vijay Prashad, *The Darker Nations: A People's History of the Third World* (New York: New Press, 2007), Introduction, 6-7, 12-13.

9   Rist, *History of Development,* Chap. 5.

10   Crowson, Hilton, and McKay, eds., *NGOs in Contemporary Britain,* 12. The original mandate of both organizations was refugee and relief work in Europe; Maggie Black, *A Cause for Our Times: Oxfam – The First 50 Years* (Oxford: Oxfam and Oxford University Press, 1992), 61.

11   Johanna M. Selles, *The World Student Christian Federation, 1895-1925* (Eugene, OR: Wipf and Stock Publishers, 2011); Arthur Gillette, *One Million Volunteers: The Story of Volunteer Youth Service* (Harmondsworth: Penguin, 1968), Preface and Chaps. 1 and 2. The goal of SCI work camps was to contribute manual labour while working alongside indigenous volunteers in a fraternal rather than a charitable or evangelizing mode.

12   Barnett, *Empire of Humanity,* 120-22 (World Vision); Clyde Sanger, *Lotta and the Unitarian Service Committee Story* (Toronto: Stoddard, 1986).

13   World University Service of Canada, *Fifty Years of Seminars* (Ottawa: World University Service of Canada, 1997). Regarding Trudeau and WUSC, see also John English, *Citizen of the World: The Life of Pierre Elliott Trudeau,* vol. 1, *1919-1968* (Toronto: Vintage Canada, 2007), 329-30.

14   Canadian Crossroads International, "Milestones," http://www.cciorg.ca/page.aspx?pid=403.

15   Gillette, *One Million Volunteers,* 179, 199.

16   Harold Jantz, "Canadian Mennonites and a Widening World," in *Religion and Public Life in Canada: Historical and Comparative Perspectives,* ed. Marguerite Van Die (Toronto: University of Toronto Press, 2001), 329-45; *Journey of Solidarity: The Story of Development and Peace* (Ottawa: Novalis 1992); Black, *Oxfam – The First 50 Years,* 100-1; Arthur Gillette, *One Million Volunteers,* and Arthur Gillette, *New Trends in Service by Youth* (New York: United Nations, 1971).

17   Cited, for instance, in Gillette, *One Million Volunteers,* title page, and "CUSO – Report of the Executive Secretary 1964-65," LAC/CUSO, MG 28, I 323, vol. 75, file 5.

18   Gillette, *New Trends,* 3.

19   Mora Dickson, ed., *A Chance to Serve* (London: Dennis Dobson, 1976), 110, and Dick Bird, *Never the Same Again: A History of VSO* (Cambridge: Lutterworth Press, 1998), Chap. 2, for Dickson and VSO's founding; Elizabeth Cobbs Hoffman, *All You Need Is Love: The Peace Corps and the Spirit of the 1960s* (Cambridge: Harvard University Press, 1998), Chap. 3, for "Peace Corps cousins."

20   David Webster, *Fire and the Full Moon: Canada and Indonesia in a Decolonizing World* (Vancouver: UBC Press, 2009), esp. Introduction and Conclusion. See Jacques Hébert and Maurice F. Strong, *The Great Canadian Building Bee: Canada a Hope for the Third World* (Don Mills: General Publishing, 1980), Part 1, for a vivid example of the myth as expressed by Hébert.

21   Significantly, in *Canada among Nations 2008: 100 Years of Canadian Foreign Policy,* ed. Robert Bothwell and Jean Daudelin (Montreal/Kingston: McGill-Queen's University Press, 2008), the chapter on aid and development is by practitioner-turned-consultant Ian Smillie. Reviewing Bothwell's *Alliance and Illusion: Canada and the World, 1945-1984* (Vancouver: UBC Press, 2007), Greg Donaghy expressed surprise that the book "spends so little time on Canada's quickening relations with the periphery, especially Asia, from the mid-1960s on"; see *Canadian Historical Review* 91, 3 (2010), 553-55, quotations at 554. Interestingly, there was more attention to aid questions seventeen years earlier in *Pirouette: Pierre Trudeau and Canadian Foreign Policy,* which Bothwell co-authored with J.L. Granatstein (Toronto: University of Toronto Press, 1990), particularly in Chap. 11.

22 Keith Spicer, *A Samaritan State? External Aid in Canada's Foreign Policy* (Toronto: University of Toronto Press, 1966); Clyde Sanger, *Half a Loaf: Canada's Semi-Role in Developing Countries* (Toronto: Ryerson Press, 1969). There is an ironic backstory to Spicer's book as I show in Chap. 1.

23 Peyton V. Lyon and Tareq Y. Ismael, eds., *Canada and the Third World* (Toronto: Macmillan, 1976); Cranford Pratt, ed., *Internationalism under Strain: The North-South Policies of Canada, the Netherlands, Norway, and Sweden* (Toronto: University of Toronto Press, 1989), and *Canadian International Development Assistance Policies: An Appraisal* (Montreal/Kingston: McGill-Queen's University Press, 1994), particularly Chap. 13.

24 David R. Morrison, *Aid and Ebb Tide: A History of CIDA* (Waterloo: Wilfrid Laurier University Press, in association with the North-South Institute, 1998); Bruce Muirhead and Ronald N. Harpelle, *IDRC: 40 Years of Ideas, Innovation, and Impact* (Waterloo: Wilfrid Laurier University Press, 2010).

25 Bill McWhinney, "The Necessary Reagent," introduction to *Man Deserves Man: CUSO in Developing Countries*, ed. Bill McWhinney and Dave Godfrey (Toronto: Ryerson Press, 1968), 1-31; Ian Smillie, *The Land of Lost Content: A History of CUSO* (Toronto: Deneau, 1985).

26 G. Stephen M. Woollcombe, "Canadian University Service Overseas: A Case Study of an Overseas Volunteer Program," (master's thesis, Pennsylvania State University, 1965); Glen C. Filson, "Major Personal Changes in a Group of Canadians Working in Nigeria," (PhD thesis, Ontario Institute for Studies in Education, 1975); Paul St. Clair McGinnes, "Major Personal Changes in Forty Returned CUSO Volunteers," (PhD thesis, Ontario Institute for Studies in Education, 1975). Barbara Heron's *Desire for Development: Whiteness, Gender, and the Helping Imperative* (Waterloo: Wilfrid Laurier University Press, 2007), written more recently and reflecting contemporary development concerns, is also based on an OISE thesis.

27 Most notably, Tim Brodhead and Brent Herbert-Copley, with Anne-Marie Lambert, *Bridges of Hope? Canadian Voluntary Agencies and the Third World* (Ottawa: North-South Institute, 1988).

28 Hans-Henning Mündel, *My Life among the Paniyas of the Nilgiri Hills* (Lethbridge: Carpe Diem Mündel Publishing, 2007); and R.A. (Andy) Buhler, *Letters Home: Glimpses of a CUSO Cooperant's Life in Northern Nigeria, 1969-70*, and *Letters Home: Glimpses of a CUSO Cooperant's Life in Southern Nigeria, 1970-71* (Victoria, BC: Trafford Publishing, 2006). See also Ross Pennie, *The Unforgiving Tides* (n.p.: Manor House Publishing, 2004), a work of "creative non-fiction" based on Pennie's two years as a young CUSO doctor in Papua New Guinea, and John S. Saul, *Revolutionary Traveller: Freeze-Frames from a Life* (Winnipeg: Arbeiter Ring Publishing, 2009). Saul spent just one year with CUSO, on a university appointment in Mozambique, but his memoir is of great value for providing insights into the larger milieu in which CUSO's more politicized strand functioned in the 1970s and 1980s.

29 Akira Iriye, *Global Community: The Role of International Organizations in the Making of the Contemporary World* (Berkeley: University of California Press, 2002).

30 Richard Peet with Elaine Hartwick, *Theories of Development* (New York: Guildford Press, 1999), esp. Chaps. 4 and 5.

31 Several of the general questions raised in this paragraph, but especially this one, are skilfully addressed in Barnett's *Empire of Humanity*.

32 Transnationalism was not part of CUSO's vocabulary in this period, and I have not used it explicitly as an analytical tool in this book. Retrospectively, however, CUSO volunteers appear to represent an almost ideal type of transnationalist. As Patricia Clavin writes in "Defining Transnationalism," it is "first and foremost about people: the social space that they inhabit, the networks they form and the ideas they exchange"; *Contemporary European History* 14, 4 (2005): 422.

Chapter 1: "Fine Young Canadians"

1 William Wordsworth, *The Prelude*, Book 11, in *The Prelude with a Selection from the Shorter Poems, the Sonnets, the Recluse, and the Excursion*, ed. Carlos Baker (New York: Holt, Rinehart and Winston, 1954), 392.

2 "What's Bugging the Committed Kids?," *The Canadian*, 21 May 1966, 3-19. The KAIROS mentioned by Alderman was a new and activist United Church of Canada young people's organization, not the ecumenical social justice organization headed by CUSO RV Mary Corkery that famously fell victim to the disapproval of Prime Minister Harper's minister for international cooperation in 2009.

3 See especially Doug Owram, *Born at the Right Time: A History of the Baby-Boom Generation* (Toronto: University of Toronto Press, 1997), Chap. 9; Bryan D. Palmer, *Canada's 1960s: The Ironies of Identity in a Rebellious Era* (Toronto: University of Toronto Press, 2009), Chap. 8; Myrna Kostash, *The Story of the Sixties Generation in Canada: Long Way from Home* (Toronto: James Lorimer and Company, 1980), Part 2.

4 Lewis Perinbam, *Opportunities for Service in Asia: Report of a Tour of Southeast Asian Countries Made during July-August 1961 by Mr. Lewis Perinbam, Acting Executive Secretary* (Ottawa: Canadian University Service Overseas, 1961), 1.

5 *Proceedings: The National Conference of Canadian Universities and Colleges, 1961*, Thirty-Seventh Meeting, 8-10 June 1961, 86-89; Perinbam, *Opportunities for Service*, inside front cover and foreword for list of officers for 1961-62.

6 Proposal, 1 June 1959, 2-5, Library and Archives Canada (LAC), CUSO fonds, MG 28, I 323, vol. 62, file 2 (note that page 1 of the proposal is in vol. 61, file 39). References hereafter to this fonds are to LAC/CUSO, MG 28, I 323, with volume and file number. Biographical material on Perinbam, including quotation, comes from his unpaginated and uncompleted memoir, "People Matter: The Life and Ideas of Lewis Perinbam," kindly provided by Nancy Garrett, who has since donated Perinbam's papers to LAC.

7 Perinbam to H.O. Moran, 3 March 1961, LAC/CUSO, MG 28, I 323, vol. 128, file 19; ibid., vol. 62, file 1, for "Canadian Programmes for Graduate Volunteers to Serve Abroad" (contains details of 20 March meeting), "Report of the Preparatory Committee for Canadian Overseas Service," and "New Agency for Overseas Service" (press release).

8 Ibid., vol. 128, file 19, Moran to Perinbam, 3 July 1961, and Perinbam to Moran, 19 April 1962. Through Moran, director general of the EAO, Perinbam received financial help and guidance on contacts for his Asia trip, but otherwise the EAO at this stage kept financial and other commitments to CUSO to a minimum. For the administrative arrangements with the UNESCO office and for assistance in Europe, see Perinbam, *Opportunities for Service*, 1, 3.

9 Ian Smillie, *The Land of Lost Content: A History of CUSO* (Toronto: Deneau, 1985), Chap. 2. See also Bill McWhinney, "The Necessary Reagent," in *Man Deserves Man: CUSO in Developing Countries*, ed. Bill McWhinney and Dave Godfrey (Toronto: Ryerson Press, 1968), for an earlier insider account of the roles of Perinbam, Spicer, and other founding figures.

10 Keith Spicer, *Life Sentences: Memoirs of an Incorrigible Canadian* (Toronto: McClelland and Stewart, 2004), 49; Donald K. Faris, *To Plow with Hope* (New York: Harper and Brothers, 1958), esp. preface and Chap. 15 (quotation 203). I deal with Faris's influence on CUSO's early volunteers in India in Chap. 2.

11 Spicer, *Life Sentences*, Chap. 5; "Submission to the Government of Canada on a Scheme for Commonwealth Graduate Volunteers," LAC/CUSO, MG 28, I 323, vol. 62, file 1. For the Memorandum of Agreement incorporating COV, 21 March 1961, see ibid., vol. 101, file 18. The submission had requested $50,000 from Colombo Plan funds for the "pilot project." Revised as "A Scheme

for Canadian Overseas Volunteers," it contained no request for government assistance. My thanks to Roy Fischer for the latter document and much else from his collection of CUSO memorabilia (hereafter Fischer Collection).

12 "Scheme for Canadian Overseas Volunteers," Schedule II; Spicer, *Life Sentences*, 50, 56-57. The departure date was August, not June, as written later by Spicer. See also G. Stephen M. Woollcombe, "Canadian University Service Overseas: A Case Study of an Overseas Volunteer Program" (master's thesis, Pennsylvania State University, 1965) and Michael Graham, "On Assignment to Help the World," *Globe Magazine*, 31 March 1962, 9-10.

13 McWhinney, "Necessary Reagent"; Smillie, *Lost Content*, Chap. 2. Unless otherwise shown, the discussion that follows of the various volunteer groups and their merger into CUSO draws on these sources.

14 "The History of CUSO – Personal Recollections, Brian Marson, May 2009," sent as an email attachment to author, and author's interview with Marson, 27 May 2009. (Unless stated otherwise, all interviews cited in this book were conducted by the author.) For the extensive correspondence between Spicer and the two students and others involved in the emerging President's Committee at UBC, see LAC/CUSO, MG 28, I 323, vol. 101, file 16, labelled "U.B.C. Correspondence with CUSO 1960-1962."

15 "CVCS," n.d., Fischer Collection. Arnold was a lecturer at Ryerson College by the time this brochure was printed.

16 McWhinney, "Necessary Reagent," 13; "The Origins of CUSO: The Personal Recollections of Dr. J.F. Leddy," 16 May 1981, 5 (Fischer Collection). Prepared for the twentieth anniversary of CUSO, Leddy's is both the most self-serving of the various accounts of CUSO's founding and the least reliable on many details.

17 Donald Wilson to John Conway, 22 March 1961, forwarding copy of Wilson's confidential memo "To Members of D.O.M. [Department of Overseas Missions of Canadian Council of Churches] Sub-Committee on 'Volunteer Service,'" John Conway fonds, University of British Columbia Archives (hereafter UBC Archives/Conway fonds), box 22, file 1 (memo contains second quotation).

18 Fred Stinson to Rev. R.M. Bennett, 27 May 1961, and Bennett to Stinson, 30 May 1961, with copies of replies received from overseas mission and indigenous church leaders. Bennett was secretary of the missions department of the CCC. This correspondence is in a largely uncatalogued collection of documents held by Stephen Woollcombe from his own files and those of the late Bill McWhinney (hereafter McWhinney/Woollcombe Collection).

19 Ruth Compton Brouwer, "When Missions Became Development: Ironies of 'NGOization' in Mainstream Canadian Churches in the 1960s," *Canadian Historical Review* 91, 4 (2010): 661-93. By contrast, the general secretary of the Church Missionary Society in Britain was uneasy with the secular character of Voluntary Service Overseas (VSO), CUSO's British counterpart, and with its short-term postings; John Stuart, "'The Real Need ... of Overseas Communities Cannot Be Met by Tourists ...': British Missionaries and the Challenge of Voluntary Service Overseas, 1957-67" (paper presented to American Historical Association, 8 January 2011, Session 215).

20 George A. McMahon Sr., ed., Preface, *Personal Papers of Dr. Francis J. Leddy*, vol. 1 (Windsor, ON, 2005).

21 See Spicer to John Conway, 26 and 28 February 1961, UBC Archives/Conway fonds, box 22, file 1, for details of what was probably just a misunderstanding with Conway about borrowed COV documents. However, Spicer seemed to have grounds for concern about Belshaw's use of COV documents. See LAC/CUSO, MG 28, I 323, vol. 101, file 16, esp. Belshaw to Spicer, 20 December 1960; Spicer to Brian Marson, 31 December 1960, enclosing Spicer to President MacKenzie, 31 December 1960; Belshaw to Spicer and to President MacKenzie, 17 January 1961; Prof. John Young

to Spicer, 23 January 1961, and Spicer to Young, 26 January 1961 (contains "perfidious" reference); and finally Belshaw to Spicer, 13 February 1961. Spicer should delay his plans for a year, Belshaw told him, until federal help and national administration could be secured through the External Aid Office and the Canadian Universities Foundation.

22 See, for example, "Report of the Preparatory Committee for Canadian Overseas Service," n.d., in ibid., and for later accounts of Stinson's objections at the CUSO founding meeting, Smillie, *Lost Content*, 17-18, and Leddy, "Origins of CUSO," 11-13.

23 For concerns about centralization, see Wilson to Professor John Conway, 22 March 1961, and Wilson to Perinbam, 25 May 1961, UBC Archives/Conway fonds, box 22, file 1.

24 Excerpt from Bissell's address to the Second National Conference of the Canadian National Commission for UNESCO, 22 February 1961, cited in "A Scheme for Canadian Overseas Volunteers," Fischer Collection.

25 For example, O.G. Schmidt to A.R. Meikle, 28 February 1962, and Stinson to Meikle, 18 August 1961, in Correspondence, India/Sarawak, 1961-62, McWhinney/Woollcombe Collection.

26 Spicer to Faris, 28 August 1961, and Stinson to Faris, 16 April and 16 May 1962, in ibid. While Faris did not rule out the possibility of returning to Canada to work with CUSO, he had been offered a renewal of his UNICEF contract in India and seemed inclined to remain there; Marion Faris to Stinson, 6 May 1962, in file on CUSO, 1962, Donald K. Faris Family Collection, privately held (hereafter Faris Collection).

27 Joint letter from COVs at Bombay to "Dear Uncle Fred," 14 February 1962, and telegram and letter from Stinson to McWhinney, 21 February and 22 February 1962, in file on volunteers, 1961, McWhinney/Woollcombe Collection.

28 McWhinney to Arthur Kroeger, 27 July 1962, McWhinney to Shri Dharampal, 27 July 31 August, 20 October 1962, and Dale Posgate to "Dear Toronto," 21 September [1962], McWhinney/Woollcombe Collection; also McWhinney, "Necessary Reagent," 16. Lewis Perinbam recalled that he and Geoffrey Andrew approached McWhinney about becoming executive secretary of CUSO and thus bringing the two groups together; author's conversation with Perinbam, 19 September 2006.

29 Copy of letter to Dale Posgate, 17 September 1962 (probably from Ozzie Schmidt), and Ozzie Schmidt to Dear – [COVs in India], 22 December 1962, in McWhinney/Woollcombe Collection. CVCS also merged with CUSO, ceasing to exist as a separate organization in 1964; McWhinney, "Necessary Reagent," 14.

30 Spicer, *Life Sentences*, 57. Spicer's thesis would eventually become a pioneering monograph on Canadian foreign aid as *A Samaritan State? External Aid in Canada's Foreign Policy* (Toronto: University of Toronto Press, 1966), but not before he toned down its idealism to make it acceptable to thesis supervisor Jim Eayrs. As Spicer later wrote in *Life Sentences*, "I became devil's advocate against my own ideals" (63).

31 Eric W. Ricker, "Report on the Development of CUSO ... September 23, 1961," LAC/CUSO, MG 28, I 323, vol. 75, file, 31; and ibid., vol. 101, file 16, for Belshaw's report on the UBC President's Committee's first year of operations, 16 April 1962. Both reports explained that before merging with CUSO, the President's Committee had raised sufficient funds to send two UBC home economics graduates to Ghana under the auspices of a US voluntary agency in the fall of 1961. Like the COV cohorts and those sponsored by CVCS, the two women, Judy Foote and Jocelyn King, were later counted as CUSO volunteers, but they remain largely invisible in published CUSO accounts.

32 Leddy, "Origins of CUSO." Smillie conducted or arranged for more than fifty taped interviews with CUSO figures in preparation for writing *The Land of Lost Content*. Of particular relevance for accounts of CUSO's founding are interviews with Geoffrey Andrew, 29 October 1980 (conducted by Barbara Hoffman); Duncan Edmonds, n.d.; Francis Leddy, n.d. (conducted by Peter Hoffman);

Barbara and Walter McLean, n.d. (conducted by Peter Hoffman); Lewis Perinbam, 10 August 1983; Fred Stinson, n.d. (conducted by Peter Hoffman). There are no taped interviews with Spicer or other early student leaders, but a lengthy interview with Jamaica RV Terry Glavin (26 May 1984), who was associate secretary in 1964, casts valuable light on the fuzzy and selective memories of some claimants to founder status. I am greatly indebted to Smillie for lending his tape collection (cited hereafter as STC [Smillie Tape Collection], with name of interviewee).

33 Fred Stinson, as interviewed by Peter Hoffman, in STC.

34 Arthur Gillette, *One Million Volunteers: The Story of Volunteer Youth Service* (Harmondsworth: Penguin, 1968), esp. Chap. 9; Scott Stossel, *Sarge: The Life and Times of Sargent Shriver* (Washington: Smithsonian Books, 2004), 252; Elizabeth Cobbs Hoffman, *All You Need Is Love: The Peace Corps and the Spirit of the 1960s* (Cambridge: Harvard University Press, 1998), Chaps. 1 and 2.

35 See, for instance, "Prefer Canadian Plan to U.S. Peace Corps," undated *Globe and Mail* article in file of newspaper and magazine clippings, McWhinney/Woollcombe Collection; and "On Assignment to Help the World/Ahead of the Peace Corps," *Globe Magazine*, 31 March 1962. On "the preference for bigness" in the Peace Corps, see Cobbs Hoffman, *All You Need Is Love*, 9. On growing cynicism among the US New Left about the real purpose behind the Peace Corps, Mark Kurlansky, *1968: The Year That Shook the World* (New York: Ballantyne Press, 2004), 166.

36 Fred Stinson to Thomas Earl[e] of CBC Press Gallery, 2 March 1961, and to Editor of *Saturday Night*, 6 March 1961, in McWhinney/Woollcombe Collection; Terry Glavin, "The Canadian Peace Corps (Canadian University Service Overseas)," *World Review*, December 1964; Cobbs Hoffman, *All You Need Is Love*, 177.

37 Perinbam, *Opportunities for Service*, 11 (for concluding remarks), 5 (for reported concerns).

38 Lewis Perinbam, "Report of the Acting Executive Secretary ... for 1961-1962," Robarts Library, University of Toronto. Regarding Wilson, see Brouwer, "When Missions Became Development," 684-85. Regarding McLean, see Canada, Library of Parliament, "Oral History Project," transcript of interview with the Honourable Walter McLean by Tom Earle, April-June 1993 (hereafter, Earle interview with McLean), 9-11.

39 McWhinney, "Necessary Reagent," 16; Woollcombe, "Case Study," 98-99.

40 In McGill University Archives, RG 75, C 34, see, for instance, file labelled "CUSO-COV and Other International Matters"; for letter of Rev. Roger Balk to CUSO Selection Committee, 18 January 1963; vol. 16 of McGill University Scrapbooks, 1, 92, and vol. 17 of Scrapbooks, 40, 345.

41 See Perinbam, "Report of the Acting Executive Secretary ... for 1961-1962," 3; D.B. Marson to Don Simpson, 10 December 1965, LAC/CUSO, MG 28, I 323, vol. 84, file 12, for on-campus cooperation between CUSO and Crossroads.

42 "Guide for Local Representatives and Co-ordinating Committees," January 1962, ibid., vol. 101, file 15.

43 Woollcombe, "Case Study," 116-17.

44 CUSO Information Form (undated, but probably early 1960s) in LAC/CUSO, MG 28, I 323, vol. 101, file 17; ibid., vol. 26, files 3, 4, 5, National Selection Committee (Minutes and Correspondence) provide examples of variability in campus committees' approach to the interview and ranking process.

45 Perinbam, "Report of the Acting Executive Secretary ... for 1961-1962," Appendix 3.

46 National Selection Committee (Minutes and Correspondence), LAC/CUSO, MG 28, I 323, vol. 26, files 3, 4, 5. While there is considerable discussion of individual applicants in these files, the actual forms completed by them are not included. In the absence of full and systematic applicant records, it is difficult to reach firm conclusions about the bases on which volunteers were selected. Nonetheless, it seems clear that academic excellence was not insisted upon at either the campus or national committee level, and that considerations of an applicant's motivation and likely suitability for a particular host country were sometimes impressionistic or based on gossipy

anecdotes. For illustrations of these patterns, see file 5, "Candidates Not Recommended by Local Committees/April 1962"; file 3, minutes of subcommittee of National Selection Committee, 24 February and 4 May 1964, and 16 March 1965.

47 Woollcombe, "Case Study," 114-16.

48 Perinbam, "Report of the Acting Executive Secretary ... for 1961-1962," 5; CUSO, "Information Guide for Overseas Governments and Agencies," n.d., Fischer Collection.

49 Perinbam, *Opportunities for Service,* 8-9; Gillette, *One Million Volunteers,* 197.

50 Canadian National Commission for UNESCO, *Secretary's Report for 1961/1962,* 11-12; Smillie interview with Lewis Perinbam, STC; Chairman's Report for 1961-62, June 9, 1962, and undated general letter from Bill McWhinney, n.d., in LAC/CUSO, MG 28, I 323, vol. 61, file 39.

51 Canadian National Commission for UNESCO, *Secretary's Report for 1961/1962,* 11-12; Perinbam, "CUSO: The Next Phase," *CUSO Bulletin,* November 1962; McWhinney, "Necessary Reagent," 14.

52 Geoffrey Andrew to Leon Lortie, 9 October 1962, LAC/CUSO, MG 28, I 323, vol. 58, file 21, for quotation; Barbara Hoffman interview with Geoffrey Andrew, STC; Leddy, "Origins of CUSO," 17.

53 Form letter by Ozzie Schmidt, 22 December 1962, Faris Collection; McWhinney, "Necessary Reagent," 19-20 (includes the sum raised). On in-kind and provincial assistance, see "Secretariat Activities," *CUSO/SUCO Bulletin,* November 1964, 4. In-kind help included books donated by publishers and medical kits and cutlery for use by volunteers.

54 "National Fund Raising Campaign," ibid.

55 Herb Moran to Guy Arnold, 28 February 1961, LAC/CUSO, MG 28, I 323, vol. 128, file 20; Lewis Perinbam to Howard Green, 3 November 1961, and Green to Perinbam, 21 Nov 1961, in ibid., vol. 61, file 38; Green to Leddy, 24 January 1963, in ibid., vol. 83, file 32.

56 Ibid., vol. 128, file 19, Perinbam to Moran, 19 April and 2 May 1962, and Moran to Perinbam, 6 June 1962. In the May letter, Perinbam pointedly observed that he had recently obtained $10,000 from the Carnegie Corporation to assist with orientation costs.

57 Ronning to Spicer, 4 May 1961, and George to Spicer, 21 February [1961], McWhinney/Woollcombe Collection.

58 David R. Morrison, *Aid and Ebb Tide: A History of CIDA and Canadian Development Assistance* (Waterloo: Wilfrid Laurier University Press in association with the North-South Institute, 1998), 28; Andrew Cohen, *While Canada Slept: How We Lost Our Place in the World* (Toronto: McClelland and Stewart, 2003), 78.

59 *CUSO Bulletin,* May 1964, 1; H.O. Moran (to McWhinney), 15 July 1965, LAC/CUSO, MG 28, I 323, vol. 128, file 17, regarding preparation of a contract for the half-million dollars.

60 Geoff Andrew to Hon. Paul Martin, 25 July 1963, in LAC/CUSO, MG 28, I 323, vol. 128, file 18; McWhinney to Bill Davis (Ontario's minister of education), 25 March 1964, and McWhinney to Moran, 7 October 1965, ibid., vol. 24, file 14, and vol. 124, file 17.

61 Form letter from McWhinney to volunteers, 25 October 1963, in ibid., vol. 102, file 16; *CUSO Bulletin,* February 1964, 1.

62 McWhinney, "Necessary Reagent," 21, and Smillie, *Lost Content,* 257-58; McWhinney to Paul Hellyer, Minister, Department of National Defence, 5 October 1965, LAC/CUSO, MG 28, I 323, vol. 24, file 11.

63 Ronning to Undersecretary of State for External Affairs, confidential memo of 5 March 1964, accompanied by "CUSO," unsigned document, probably by Arthur Kroeger, outlining the history of COV/CUSO in India, LAC/CUSO, MG 28, I 323, vol. 61, file 38. I deal with the India volunteers' relations with Canadian diplomats more fully in Chap. 2.

64 See, for instance, "Helping Our Own Peace Corps" (citing *Toronto Daily Star*) and "Editorial Comment on CUSO," reproduced in *CUSO Bulletin,* April 1962; "Universities/Getting Away from Suburbia," *Time,* 20 July 1962; "They May Learn Enough to Give Us a Conscience," editorial, *Globe and Mail,* 16 April 1965.

65 Spicer, *Life Sentences*, 57.

66 Response to questionnaire by Wendy Salmond Quarry, July 2011 (for Bata at orientation); Linda Freeman, *The Ambiguous Champion: Canada and South Africa in the Trudeau and Mulroney Years* (Toronto: University of Toronto Press, 1997), 98-100.

67 "Parliamentary Debates CUSO," *CUSO Bulletin*, November 1963; Canada, House of Commons Debates, 10 June 1963, 853-61; Fairweather, Notice of Motion, R. Gordon Fairweather fonds, Library and Archives Canada, MG 32, C72, vol. 8, file 13. My thanks to Stephanie Bangarth for sharing materials from this collection.

68 Spicer, *Life Sentences*, 50; Paul Martin, *A Very Public Life*, vol. 2, *So Many Worlds* (Toronto: Deneau, 1985), 381 (regarding his daughter).

69 Smillie, *Lost Content*, 254-58; Leddy, "Origins of CUSO," 17-18. In fact, such requests were already coming to Martin's department. When in 1964 a missionary priest asked for External Affairs funding to hire teachers for his college in Bolivia, the official who replied suggested he turn to CUSO! See Father Walter Strub to Martin, 22 December 1964, and P.M. Towe to Strub, 5 January 1965, LAC/CUSO, MG 28, I 323, vol. 83, file 31.

70 Ibid., Martin to Leddy, 16 March 1964.

71 Leddy, "Origins of CUSO," 18; Smillie interview with Duncan Edmonds.

72 See Smillie, *Lost Content*, 255-56, regarding Pearson's support for assisting CUSO and the suggestion that he put pressure on Martin to find a way of doing so.

73 "Statement by the Prime Minister on Feb. 7th," *CUSO/SUCO Bulletin*, February 1966, 4. See Smillie, *Lost Content*, 258-62, for an overview of the emergence of the CYC and the tense early relationship with CUSO. Pearson appointed Duncan Edmonds as organizing secretary for the CYC and Leddy as its chairman. In taking on these roles, both men alienated former CUSO colleagues while at the same time proving to be ill-suited to organize the very different youth culture coming into the CYC.

74 "Bill McWhinney accepte un nouveau poste," and "Close CUSO-CYC Co-operation Anticipated," *CUSO/SUCO Bulletin*, February 1966, 1 [loss of McWhinney], 5 [fundraising difficulty].

75 See LAC/CUSO, MG 28, I 323, vol. 103, file 17, CUSO Press Releases, 1961-1969, for W. Borden Spears to McWhinney, 17 December 1965, sending the *Maclean's* article. A CYC pamphlet containing excerpts from Hansard and revealing all-party support for the founding of the CYC shows that the MPs' emphasis was on CUSO and missionary work rather than the US Peace Corps as antecedents for what they supposed the CYC would be undertaking; file on CYC in Fischer Collection. Cf. Kevin Brushett, "Making Shit Disturbers: The Selection and Training of the Company of Young Canadian Volunteers, 1965-1970," in *The Sixties in Canada: A Turbulent and Creative Decade*, ed. Athena Palaeologue (Toronto: Black Rose Books, 2009).

76 McWhinney's dissatisfaction with his CYC position is discussed in his 6 July 1983 interview with Ian Smillie and in Smillie's interview with Terry Glavin (STC) . See also Ian Hamilton, *The Children's Crusade: The Story of the Company of Young Canadians* (Toronto: Peter Martin, 1970), 4, 24, 32-33.

77 Meeting of Executive Committee, 28-29 August 1966, 2, LAC/CUSO, MG 28, I 323, vol. 64, file 16. Although he had come from the EAO (initially on an interim basis), Christie was a strong supporter of an independent CUSO; see ibid., vol. 150, file 4, for copy of Christie to Maurice Strong, 6 October 1966.

78 Smillie, *Lost Content*, 111.

79 The overview that follows on volunteers' personal backgrounds makes use of data in nonrestricted records in the LAC/CUSO fonds; biographical information in published accounts or private collections; and information shared by informants in personal interviews, questionnaires, and email or telephone contacts. Information on aspects of personal identity is not consistently available in the LAC/CUSO fonds, but for the type of biographical data available in some National Selection Committee files, see LAC/CUSO, MG 28, I 323, vol. 26, files 3-5, 1962-65.

80 Reginald W. Bibby, *The Boomer Factor: What Canada's Most Famous Generation Is Leaving Behind* (Toronto: Bastian Books, 2006), 205.

81 Statistical data on "Candidates for 1967 as of May 30, 1967" (Fischer Collection) provide an interesting supplement to the information given here, since these statistical data include applications received (645 overall) as well as applicants recommended (569). Religiously, the single largest group of applicants were Catholics (236), followed by United Church of Canada adherents (111) and then Anglicans (80). There was clearly some category confusion in listing less familiar religious groups. Thus, the list of applicants included Jewish (7) *and* Hebrew (1), Islamic (1) *and* Muslim (1). Although this list of applicants also included Hindu (1) and "Evangelist" (4), I have seen no references to the appointment of Hindus or strongly evangelical Protestants during this period. Regionally, the 1967 data show Ontario universities well in the lead in terms of applicants.

82 R. Douglas Francis, Richard Jones, and Donald B. Smith, *Destinies: Canadian History since Confederation,* 5th ed. (Toronto: Thomas Nelson, 2004), Chap. 19, esp. 495-97; Paul Anisef et al., *Opportunity and Uncertainty: Life Course Experiences of the Class of '73* (Toronto: University of Toronto Press, 2000), Chaps. 2 and 6.

83 "Necessary Reagent," 25-26.

84 File on CUSO II containing list of COVs for 1962, Faris Collection; Canadian University Service Overseas, "Report of the Executive Secretary (Actg), 1965-66," Appendix, including "Applications Received," LAC/CUSO, MG 28, I 323, vol. 75, file 4.

85 McWhinney to Faris, 30 November 1964, Faris Collection; McWhinney, "Necessary Reagent," 29.

86 A few volunteers dropped out of university or delayed completing their degree in order to join CUSO, but this was not common.

87 Owram, *Born at the Right Time,* 180-81.

88 Cobbs Hoffman, *All You Need Is Love,* 67; for the term *BAGs* and early 1970s concerns about placing them, see BA Generalists, 1973, LAC/CUSO, MG 28, I 323, vol. 102, file 34.

89 CUSO, "Report of the Executive Secretary (Actg), 1965-66," Appendix, for "Applications Received," LAC/CUSO, MG 28, I 323, vol. 75, file 4. Out of the total of 571 applicants, 473 were recommended.

90 Ibid.; Kathryn McPherson, *Bedside Matters: The Transformation of Canadian Nursing, 1900-1990* (Toronto: Oxford University Press, 1996), 221, for comparative statistics in 1962 on nurses with degrees and diplomas, and 257 for moves toward more university-based training in the 1960s and 1970s.

91 This speculation and information below about RV's work experience is based mainly on author interviews with RVs who served as nurses or their responses to the questionnaire. (The questionnaire referred to here and elsewhere in the notes was prepared by the author.)

92 "Orientation 1966," *CUSO/SUCO Bulletin,* August 1966, 7, for breakdown of new volunteers by country and occupation; ibid., February-April 1967, "The CUSO Nurse," 2-3; and *Communique,* 14 April 1970, 1, in LAC/CUSO, MG 28, I 323, vol. 103, file 10.

93 For instance, Grace Bavington and Nancy Garrett had worked in cottage hospitals, where they had occasionally been called upon to deliver babies, among other non-routine tasks. Lois James had worked in the Canadian Arctic. Interview with Bavington, 30 September 2005; Garrett, 19 September 2006; Lois James Chetelat, 6 May 2007.

94 *Canadian Overseas Volunteers/1961-1986/25th Anniversary Reunion ...,* 18-20 July 1986, and *Canadian Overseas Volunteers (CUSO)/1962 Group ... 25th Anniversary Reunion,* 21-23 August 1987, both booklets in McWhinney/Woollcombe Collection (hereafter COV Reunion booklet, 1986, and COV Reunion booklet, 1987). Regarding McWhinney's concern, see McWhinney to Woollcombe, 15 May 1963, LAC/CUSO, MG 28, I 323, vol. 102, file 18. For data on volunteers by gender later in the 1960s, see "CUSO SUCO selection/RVs – Conference, 1968/ R. Guilbeault Selection-Orientation," last page, in ibid., file 3.

95 Alison Prentice et al., *Canadian Women: A History* (Toronto: Harcourt, 1988), 428, Table A.20.

96 In 1967, female applicants substantially outnumbered males (360 to 285), but among the female applicants, 50 were under twenty-one years of age, perhaps many of them secretaries, 23 of which applied. The table from which these data come, "Candidates for 1967 as of May 30, 1967" (Fischer Collection), does not show a breakdown by gender for applicants who were actually recommended. Probably few of these very young women were selected, but their applications speak to their desire for broader horizons.

97 "CUSO Selection Manual/1972," Table V, showing male candidates as 52 percent of total as of 15 September 1971, LAC/CUSO, MG 28, I 323, vol. 129, file 17; also ibid, vol. 98, files 23-25, for information about gender patterns at local committee level in mid-1970s. In Nigeria, female volunteers often outnumbered male volunteers, probably because of the ongoing concentration on placing teachers there; see Eme N. Ekekwe and Suzanne Veit, CUSO/Nigeria: A 25 Year Retrospective Evaluation, vol. 1 (Port Harcourt, Nigeria, and Victoria, Canada: Uniport Konsult and Fulcrum Consultants, 1986), 45.

98 For the impact of the Vietnam war on Peace Corps volunteering, see Paul Theroux, Fresh-Air Fiend: Travel Writings, 1985-2000 (Boston: Houghton Mifflin, 2000), 40. During the first decades, men continued to outnumber women in the Peace Corps by a ratio of more than three to one; Sargent Shriver, "The Vision," in Making a Difference: The Peace Corps at Twenty-Five, ed. Milton Viorst (New York: Weidenfeld and Nicolson, 1986), 19.

99 I discuss the experiences of some of these men in Chap. 2.

100 James H. Morrison, A Pictorial History of Frontier College: Camps and Classrooms (Toronto: Frontier College, 1989); Edmund Bradwin, The Bunkhouse Man, reissued edition with new introduction (Toronto: University of Toronto Press, 1972).

101 Information drawn from responses to author questionnaire and/or personal interviews: Godfrey, 16 September 2006; Wood, 18 December 2006; Woollcombe, 4 December 2006 and 2 July 2011; Morrison, questionnaire, November 2010, and interview, 22 January 2011; Kidd, response to questionnaire January 2012 and typescript of "My Three Summers with Frontier College – '64, '65, and '66." Selection committees attached considerable value to Frontier College experience; see National Selection Committee, Meeting of NSC sub-committee, 12 March 1964, and undated list of applicants, organized by university of origin (probably 1964), LAC/CUSO, MG 28, I 323, vol. 26, file 3.

102 McWhinney and Godfrey, eds., Man Deserves Man, Appendix 4, 452-61; "Candidates Recommended by Local Committees/April 1962/Nigeria," and Minutes of meeting of National Advisory Selection Board ... 6 April 1962, LAC/CUSO, MG 28, I 323, vol. 26, file 5; Cobbs Hoffman, All You Need Is Love, 66, 67.

103 COV's preparatory sessions for its volunteers, which I briefly discuss below, had focused mainly on cultural aspects.

104 "CUSO Orientation Programme for Africa-Bound Appointees," CUSO Bulletin, November 1962; File on Orientation, Early 1960s, Fischer Collection.

105 Memo from Executive Secretary to CUSO Personnel regarding Orientation Program to be held at University of Ottawa, Aug. 11-31, 1963, LAC/CUSO, MG 28, I 323, vol. 64, file 16; ibid., vol. 84, file 24, for Rev. R.B. Bennett to Dear Friends, 19 October 1962, regarding McWhinney's request to the CCC. For Guilbeault's long involvement, see CUSO/SUCO Bulletin, February/April 1967, 17, and CUSO Forum 1, 3 (1978): 23-24; and for his 1963 language teaching, response to questionnaire by Wendy Salmond Quarry, who recalls that the last week of their "bizarre" orientation was held at the Commonwealth Institute in London, where several volunteers promptly played truant by flying off to France.

106 "Secretariat Activities," CUSO Bulletin, August 1964, 3-4, for plans for upcoming orientations at Université de Montréal and University of Toronto; Woollcombe, "Case Study," 145, for feedback and quotations.

107 "Orientation, 1966," *CUSO/SUCO Bulletin,* August 1966, 1-6; John Baigent, "A New Approach to CUSO Orientation," ibid., August 1967, 14-15; and August-September 1967, special issue on "Orientation '67."

108 Don Simpson, "West Africa," in ibid., 4-6; Report of the 1968 CUSO West Africa Orientation by D.G. Simpson, and Report on the 1968 West Africa Orientation Course, to Don Simpson from Dan Turner, LAC/CUSO, MG 28, I 323, vol. 48, file 12.

109 Accounts by Joan Barrett and Cathy Duffy in *Man Deserves Man,* ed. McWhinney and Godfrey, 34-46, 65-72; interview with Catherine (Cathy) Duffy Mullally, 26 July 2005. See also Smillie's account of Peter Hoffman's introduction to his post in Sarawak in *Lost Content,* Chap. 1.

110 Belshaw to Stinson, 28 March 1961, LAC/CUSO, MG 28, I 323, vol. 101, file 16.

111 Perry [Anglin] of *Toronto Star* to Ozzie Schmidt, 28 February, 1962, in file on media coverage, 1961-63, McWhinney/Woollcombe Collection; Arnold Bruner, "Swahili or Culture Shock Anyone?," *Toronto Daily Star,* 27 August 1965, 7. The horror stories – how to say no in Masai country to a "blood milkshake," or to avoid being knifed for speaking Ibo in the wrong part of Nigeria – were reportedly presented to the volunteers by a "linguistics expert."

112 Morrison, *Aid and Ebb Tide,* 2.

113 Stan Barrett, for instance, was interviewed for India and then reassigned to Nigeria. Nancy Callaghan, expecting to go to Malaysia, was sent to Jamaica. In the course of a brief telephone conversation with a CUSO staff member, John Cameron had to decide between a posting in Thailand or Ghana. Barrett interview, 10 December 2005; Callaghan, 21 October 2005; Cameron, 10 August 2005.

114 On Rostow's influence see, for instance, Gibert Rist, *The History of Development: From Western Origins to Global Faith,* 3rd ed. (London: Zed Books, 2008), Chap. 6; Mark H. Haefele, "Walt Rostow's Stages of Economic Growth: Ideas and Action," in *Staging Growth: Modernization, Development, and the Global Cold War,* ed. David C. Engerman, Nils Gilman, Mark H. Haefele, and Michael E. Latham (Amherst: University of Massachusetts Press, 2003), 81-103.

115 Gillette, *One Million Volunteers,* Chap. 9; Ian Smillie, *The Alms Bazaar: Altruism under Fire; Non-Profit Organizations and International Development* (London: IT Publications, 1995), xiii.

116 Interview with Ian Smillie, 24 June 2005.

117 "Necessary Reagent," 6-7.

118 Ibid., 5, for Faris, and [v] for Radhakrishnan.

119 Response to questionnaire by Wendy Salmond Quarry.

120 Interview with Allan T. Collier, 15 September 2006.

121 Response to questionnaire by David Ingram, April 2007 [for quotation]; also Donna Anderson Hudson, email, 6 June 2012, and "Nine for Service," U of T's *Varsity Weekend Review,* March 1963.

122 Response to questionnaire by Sally Bambridge Ravindra, October 2005.

123 Interviews with John R. Wood, 4 June 2008, and with David Beer, 26 July 2011. Both spoke of Holmes as an important influence. Beer's twin brother, Charles, served with CVCS. Their younger brother, Jim, and cousin Anne Skinner also joined CUSO. On Holmes, who served for a time on CUSO's executive committee and briefed departing volunteers, see Adam Chapnick, *Canada's Voice: The Public Life of John Wendell Holmes* (Vancouver: UBC Press, 2009).

124 The motivational circumstances discussed in the preceding sentences were mentioned by one or more RVs in interviews or questionnaires.

125 Response to questionnaire by Dr. Nafrawi, and telephone conversation, December 2005.

126 Tilghman interview on CBC Radio *Ideas,* 7 February 2011; also Antonia Whyatt, "Top of the Ivy League," *Chatelaine,* February 2011, 102 (contains quoted phrase).

127 Several interviewees mentioned missionary ancestors. Dave McLean, who went to Sierra Leone with CUSO in 1968, was the great-grandson of a missionary, the son of a minister, and the brother of the Rev. Walter McLean; "CUSO Cooperant Profile/David and Dawn McLean, 1960s," n.d. (copy

supplied by Jill Morton Grant). Regarding a CUSO/India volunteer who appeared anxious to emulate the self-sacrificial behaviour of her sister, a nun, see John Wood to McWhinney, 3 November 1963, LAC/CUSO, MG 28, I 323, vol. 102, file 16.

128 For instance, Harry Baglole (interview, 28 July 2005) and Catherine Duffy Mullally, both from PEI; Dennis E. McDermott (questionnaire, December 2005), and Wendy Lawrence (questionnaire, January 2012), both from Ontario; and Sheila Ward from Manitoba.

129 Jill Morton Grant, who went to Tanzania in 1966, was uneasy about missionaries as a group, but she was one of a number of respondents who remembered a youthful admiration for Schweitzer; response to questionnaire, May 2006, and subsequent conversations. Several RVs mentioned Tom Dooley, the founder of Medico, as an influence. Though not actually a missionary, Dooley was strongly motivated by his Catholicism. His interest in medical work in the developing world had been sparked by his naval service in Southeast Asia; James T. Fisher, *Dr. America: The Lives of Thomas A. Dooley* (Amherst: University of Massachusetts Press, 1997).

130 Interview with Bonnie Hartley, January 2006; response to questionnaire by Hans-Henning Mündel, July 2006.

131 Response to questionnaire by Colin Bruce Johnstone, March 2006. Several volunteers in the late 1960s subsequently became short-term lay missionaries with the United Church in the same country where they had served with CUSO; *United Church Observer*, 15 May 1966, 33, and 1 May 1970, 36.

132 Cobbs Hoffman, *All You Need Is Love*, 125; interview with Ellen Schwartz Godfrey, 16 September 2006.

133 Brouwer, "When Missions Became Development."

134 For McWhinney's claim, see McWhinney to Rev. R.M. Bennett, 7 January 1963, in response to Bennett to McWhinney, 27 December 1962. Writing as executive secretary of the Department of Overseas Missions of the CCC and forwarding the letter of complaint from the Rev. W.J. Wood of the Christian Council in Lagos, Bennett seemed somewhat embarrassed by Wood's concern about CUSO volunteers and observed that he was "perhaps old school"; LAC/CUSO, MG 28, I 323, vol. 84, file 24. Many missions, perhaps especially Roman Catholic ones, readily accepted volunteers from different faith backgrounds and made few or no religious demands on them. This was the experience, for instance, of teachers Ellen Schwartz Godfrey in urban Ghana and Harry Baglole in Uganda. The product of a rural United Church of Canada upbringing, Baglole was well received by the Catholic brothers who ran the bush school where he taught and with whom he socialized comfortably over beer, bridge, and dinners.

135 Name withheld. When I mentioned early ties between CUSO and mission organizations to another RV, he declared that he would not have joined CUSO if he had had any inkling that it was in any way linked with Canada's mission past. See also Brouwer, "When Missions Became Development," 684-85, for Donald Wilson's 1962 report of his campus tour for CUSO: "By and large," Wilson wrote, "the university community has a complete emotional and intellectual bloc to the word 'missionary' as they understand it."

136 Stuart Macdonald, "Death of Christian Canada? Do Canadian Church Statistics Support Callum Brown's Timing of Church Decline?," *Historical Papers 2006/Canadian Society of Church History*, ed. Brian Gobbett, Bruce L. Guenther, and Robynne Rogers Healey, 135-56. Of particular significance in Macdonald's work for a focus on CUSO volunteers' backgrounds is the fact that in the Anglican, Presbyterian, and United churches, membership peaked in 1964 or 1965 before beginning a sudden and sharp decline. In all three denominations, Sunday School enrolment had reached its peak just a few years earlier, as had confirmation for United Church teenagers. For Brown's argument see Collum G. Brown, *The Death of Christian Britain: Understanding Secularization, 1800-2000* (London: Routledge, 2001). The meaning and timing of secularization in the West is, of course, much contested. Nonetheless, recent influential works as different as Brown's *Death of*

Christian Britain, Hugh McLeod's *The Religious Crisis of the 1960s* (Oxford: Oxford University Press, 2007), and Charles Taylor's *A Secular Age* (Cambridge: Harvard University Press, 2007) concur that the 1960s marked a fundamental shift in the role of religion as lived experience.

137 Owram, *Born at the Right Time,* 219. See also Catherine Gidney, *A Long Eclipse: The Liberal Protestant Establishment and the Canadian University, 1920-1970* (Montreal/Kingston: McGill-Queen's University Press, 2004). Cf. George Egerton, "Entering the Age of Human Rights: Religion, Politics, and Canadian Liberalism, 1945-50," *Canadian Historical Review* 85, 3 (2004): 451-79, esp. note 73.

138 Bezanson response to questionnaire, February 2011.

139 For instance, Barnett, *Empire of Humanity,* esp. 105-6. Barnett's is a sensitive and sophisticated analysis of some two centuries of humanitarianism but by no means the first work to ponder colonial-era legacies in the era of "neo-humanitarianism." Closer to home and much more specific in her focus, former CUSO volunteer Barbara Heron finds colonial continuities of a maternalist sort in middle-class white women who, like herself, volunteered in sub-Saharan Africa in the 1980s and early 1990s; *Desire for Development: Whiteness, Gender and the Helping Imperative* (Waterloo: Wilfrid Laurier University Press, 2007). See also *The Power of Whiteness: Racism in Third World Development and Aid* (London: Lawrence and Wishart, 2003) by British volunteer Paulette Goudge, who draws on her own experience in Nicaragua in this period, and Jawad Syed and Faiza Ali, "The White Woman's Burden: From Colonial *Civilisation* to Third World *Development,*" *Third World Quarterly* 32, 2 (2011): 349-65.

140 While Edward Said's classic, *Orientalism* (New York: Pantheon Books, 1978), provided a helpful theoretical framework for my early research on women and foreign missions (*New Women for God: Canadian Presbyterian Women and India Missions, 1876-1914* [Toronto: University of Toronto Press, 1990]), it seems to me to have little utility for explicating motivation among postcolonial volunteers like those who joined CUSO. I briefly discuss race issues in Chap. 3.

141 Form letter from J. King Gordon, 16 September 1966, sent to Donald G. Faris, inviting him to attend the forthcoming AGM; Faris Collection.

142 CIDA, *Partners in Tomorrow: Fifteen Years of CIDA's NGO Program/1968-1983,* 7-8, 10; CIDA *Annual Review '69,* 49, and CIDA *1983-84 Annual Review,* 64, Table E; Morrison, *Aid and Ebb Tide,* 68-70.

143 *CUSO 71/ Annual Review,* 12, 15, in LAC/CUSO, MG 28, I 323, vol. 74, file 33.

144 Ibid., 1 and 11 (for volunteer numbers); "Report of the Executive Secretary to the Seventh Annual Meeting [1967-68]," ibid., vol. 75, file 2.

145 "National Advertising for CUSO," *CUSO/SUCO Bulletin,* May 1966, 24.

146 For the nursing advertisement see LAC/CUSO, MG 28, I 323, vol. 101, file 20; for the other slogans and accompanying letter of advice to CUSO from Paul A. Goulet, 10 November 1967, see ibid., vol. 102, file 10, Summarized Recommendations from Stanfield, Johnson & Hull.

147 Ibid., vol. 83, file, 29, Memo from Bob and Margaret and Iain [Thomson], 18 September 1970, regarding "What we're doing"; McKee response to questionnaire, April 2011.

148 *Man Deserves Man,* 214-38, for "Adaptation" (quotation at 234), and 85-102 for "Orientation" (quotations at 91, 93, and 95). In the latter, Wood avoided the appearance of disparaging the early volunteers' accomplishments by stressing that in the absence of rigorous orientation they had met challenges through their individual adaptability (91). As for the missionaries who had participated in early orientations, they were by no means all "ancient." Former China missionary Katharine Hockin was a middle-aged SCM leader whose background and activism resulted in her name being recorded in RCMP files. My thanks to Chris Miller for this information.

149 Jeffrey response to questionnaire, October 2010; author's interview with Bill Bavington and follow-up response to questionnaire; interview with Gini Dickie, 12 March 2007. The pervasive cultural significance of highlife music in this period of Nigeria's history shows up in such recent works as

Chimamanda Ngozi Adichie's *Half of a Yellow Sun* (New York: Knopf, 2006) and Chinua Achebe's *The Education of a British-Protected Child/Essays* (New York: Knopf, 2009).

150 Names withheld.

151 Wood, "Orientation," 97-98; also Jon Church to Tim Brodhead, 1 May 1967 (copy provided by Brodhead), and Smillie's group interview, tapes 3 and 4, with Sharon Capeling, David Hamilton, Carol Seguin, and Chris Bryant (on tape 4), n.d., in STC. Some prospective volunteers actually left orientation and abandoned their plans to go overseas as a result of these sessions, according to this interview.

152 Wood, "Orientation," 99; interview with J., 16 December 2010.

153 See LAC/CUSO, MG 28, I 323, vol. 48, files 6-12, for orientation programs for various regions, and for Garrett's view, file 9, Garrett to Paul McGinnis, 22 October 1969.

154 LAC/CUSO, MG 28, I 323, vol. 48, file 9, for "Orientation Report," 5, 7, undated and unsigned, probably written following 1969 orientation programs. The "good bash" to which the writer referred almost certainly included casual sexual encounters. Smillie's group interview with Capeling and three other CUSO staff members, cited above, includes discussion of female volunteers agreeing to "prove" their lack of racism by responding to sexual pressure from young African men who were resource persons. The tape also includes discussion of sexual pressure on a female volunteer by a CUSO staff person. Several of my interviews with RVs or their responses to questionnaires confirm the orientation to have been a time of casual, perhaps first, sexual encounters. Instances of what would now be considered sexual harassment provide indications of how the sexual revolution could be manipulated in these highly charged settings.

155 *Lost Content*, 125-26. See also Rick Williams's account of the 1969 East Africa orientation in LAC/CUSO, MG 28, I 323, vol. 48, file 7. Smillie's group interview with Capeling and other RVs (in STC) provides second-hand details, including efforts to keep word of the brawl from the press. On Black Power activism in Montreal at this period and the Sir George Williams affair, see Sean Mills, *The Empire Within: Postcolonial Thought and Political Activism in Sixties Montreal* (Montreal/Kingston: McGill-Queen's University Press, 2010), Chap. 4.

156 *CUSO 71/Annual Review* 8, LAC/CUSO, MG 28, I 323, vol. 74, file 33.

157 Interview with Karem Hall Wright, 30 March 2007.

158 "CUSO information 4/International Development: An Introductory Reading List," November 1969, copy in Fischer Collection.

159 Stinson to Faris, 23 January 1961, McWhinney/Woollcombe Collection.

160 Dan Turner, for instance, recalled his 1966 orientation at McGill University as a wonderful experience despite the fact that he got thrown in jail for drinking in the wrong place and was accidentally pushed through a plate-glass window; response to questionnaire, June 2011, and follow-up conversation, 23 June 2011.

161 "National Advertising for CUSO," 24; for the 1971 data, see *CUSO Selection Manual*, 1972, Table VII, LAC/CUSO, MG 28, I 323, vol. 129, file 17.

162 *CUSO 71/Annual Review*, 1, in ibid., vol. 74, file 33.

163 Owram, *Born at the Right Time*, 181-83 (quotation at 181); Palmer, *Canada's 1960s*, Chap. 8; Anisef et al., *Opportunity and Uncertainty*, Chap. 6, and for changes at the University of Toronto, Martin L. Friedland, *The University of Toronto: A History* (Toronto: University of Toronto Press, 2002), Chap. 36.

164 Sanger, "Turbulence in CUSO over Its Goals," undated *Globe* clipping, in LAC/CUSO, MG 28, I 323, vol. 74, file 14, and *Half a Loaf: Canada's Semi-Role among Developing Countries* (Toronto: Ryerson Press, 1969), 232.

165 Response to questionnaire by Colin Johnstone, March 2006. Colin went to Sarawak with CUSO in 1962. See also "A Radical Look at Recruitment," *CUSO Forum*, Fall 1969, 1, 8, by Zambia RV Nigel Hawkesworth, whose theme was also declension in the quality and commitment of recent volunteers.

166 Notes on CUSO Regional Conference, Bangkok, 8-11 November 1969, LAC/CUSO, MG 28, I 323, vol. 122, file 17.

167 *CUSO Selection Manual*, 1972, blue Selection booklet with foreword by R. Guilbeault, ibid., vol. 129, file 17; "Dear CUSO Selector," n.d., UBC Archives/Conway fonds, box 6, file 14 (for quotation).

168 Sanger, *Half a Loaf*, 233-34. Valuable insights on Caribbean postings and volunteers sent there are also contained in Smillie's interview with Terry Glavin, STC.

169 Janice Tyrwhitt, "CUSO: Canada's Foreign Aid Extraordinary," *Reader's Digest*, January 1969, re-printed as a CUSO pamphlet; Donald Savage, review of *Man Deserves Man*, in *Canadian Forum*, October 1968, 166-67, on file with other reviews, including the one from *Canadian Reader* in LAC/CUSO, MG 28, I 323, vol. 49, files 23 and 24.

Chapter 2: A Passage to India

A portion of Chapter 2 draws on material previously published as "Ironic Interventions: CUSO Volunteers in India's Family Planning Campaign, 1960s-1970s," *Histoire sociale/Social History* 43, 86 (2010): 279-313.

1 Statement by Nehru in a meeting with newly arrived volunteers as recalled by John R. Wood. As their spokesman, Wood had expressed their sense of inadequacy about what they could do to help out in India; author interview with Wood, 4 June 2008. (Unless stated otherwise, all interviews cited in this book were conducted by the author.)

2 "Canadian Overseas Volunteers Bulletin," n.d., reproduced in CUSO-VSO 50th anniversary CD; Bill McWhinney and Dave Godfrey, eds., *Man Deserves Man: CUSO in Developing Countries* (Toronto: Ryerson Press, 1968), App. 4.

3 Bill McWhinney to Dale Posgate, 27 July 1962, evidently repeating Posgate's phrase, in Donald K. Faris Family Papers, privately held (hereafter Faris Collection).

4 "A Scheme for Canadian Overseas Volunteers," 2, in Roy Fischer Collection (hereafter Fischer Collection), and Keith Spicer, *Life Sentences: Memoirs of an Incorrigible Canadian* (Toronto: McClelland and Stewart, 2004), Chap. 5; Lewis Perinbam, *Opportunities for Service in Asia: Report of a Tour of Southeast Asian Countries Made during July-August 1961* (Ottawa: Canadian University Service Overseas, 1961). Although Perinbam's tour included Pakistan, I have not seen evidence that CUSO tried placing volunteers there.

5 Keith Spicer, *A Samaritan State? External Aid in Canada's Foreign Policy* (Toronto: University of Toronto Press, 1966), 162-65. See also David R. Morrison, *Aid and Ebb Tide: A History of CIDA and Canadian Development Assistance* (Waterloo: Wilfrid Laurier University Press in association with the North-South Institute, 1998), App. C, 456-59. India headed the list of "Top Twenty Recipients of Canadian Government–to-Government ODA at Five-Year Intervals" for every interval from 1960-61 to 1980-81. Useful overviews of the Canada-India relationship are Barrie M. Morrison, "Canada and South Asia," in *Canada and the Third World*, ed. Peyton V. Lyon and Tareq Y. Ismael (Toronto: Macmillan, 1976), 1-59, and Ryan Touhey, "Canada and India at 60," *International Journal*, Autumn 2007, 733-52. Notwithstanding extensive Canadian aid, there were significant tensions between the two countries, as both these authors show.

6 Spicer, *Samaritan State*, 54, quoting Diefenbaker for "family concern"; Benjamin Zachariah, *Nehru* (London: Routledge, 2004), esp. Chap. 6; Vijay Prashad, *The Darker Nations: A People's History of the Third World* (New York: The New Press, 2007), esp. introductory chapter and chapters (un-numbered) on Bandung and Belgrade.

7 Mark H. Haefele, "Walt Rostow's Stages of Economic Growth: Ideas and Action," in *Staging Growth: Modernization, Development, and the Global Cold War*, ed. David C. Engerman, Nils Gilman, Mark H. Haefele, and Michael E. Latham (Amherst: University of Massachusetts Press, 2003), 81-103;

Dennis Kux, *India and the United States: Estranged Democracies, 1941-1991* (New Delhi: Sage Publications, 1993), esp. Chap. 5; Brent Ashabranner, *A Moment in History: The First Ten Years of the Peace Corps* (New York: Doubleday, 1971), 37.

8   Judith M. Brown, *Nehru: A Political Life* (New Haven: Yale University Press, 2003), 300-3, and 246 for quotation.

9   Biographical sketches of the two COV cohorts that went to India, Ceylon, and Sarawak were included in booklets published for their respective twenty-fifth anniversary reunions: *Canadian Overseas Volunteers, 1961-1986,* and *Canadian Overseas Volunteers (CUSO), 1962 Group* ... (hereafter COV Reunion booklet, 1986, and COV Reunion booklet, 1987), in Bill McWhinney/Stephen Woollcombe Collection (hereafter McWhinney/Woollcombe Collection).

10 Spicer's memoir, however, suggests otherwise. He had perhaps read too much into the assurances he had received from his contacts while there. See *Life Sentences,* 53.

11 Spicer to Faris, 26 November 1960, and Don and Marion Faris Newsletter, Christmas 1963, giving a brief overview of the ANP; both in Faris Collection.

12 Spicer to Faris, 26 November 1960, and also copy of Spicer to Shri Dharampal, 6 April 1961, containing Spicer's proposed arrangements with AVARD some five months after he wrote to Faris; both in Faris Collection.

13 Faris to Spicer, 17 March 1961; also Gopal Krishna to Spicer, writing for Dharampal, 17 January 1961, and Dharampal to Spicer, 16 March 1961; Memo from Dale Posgate on COV's first year in India, October 1962, all in McWhinney/Woollcombe Collection.

14 K.N. Gangrade and R. Sooryamoorthy, "NGOs: Retrospect and Prospect," in *NGOs in Development Perspective,* ed. R.B. Jain (Delhi: Vivek Prakashan, 1995), 38.

15 Zachariah, *Nehru,* 190, 194-95.

16 Gangrade and Sooryamoorthy, "NGOs: Retrospect and Prospect," 35-39; Ajit K. Dasgupta, *Gandhi's Economic Thought* (London: Routledge, 1996), esp. Chap. 9, "The Legacy of Gandhi." See also Les Johnson's overview of the Gandhian roots of such ashrams, in one of which he served, in *Man Deserves Man,* ed. McWhinney and Godfrey, 379-90.

17 "Association of Voluntary Agencies for Rural Development ... A Note on Placement of Canadian Volunteers," in McWhinney/Woollcombe Collection. Other materials on AVARD with this document show its role in arranging the volunteers' orientation, accommodation, and travel to their placements. Regarding *zilla parishads* and the kinds of volunteers who might fit their needs, see Posgate to Dear Toronto, 21 September [1962], in McWhinney/Woollcombe Collection.

18 *To Plow with Hope* (New York: Harper and Brothers, 1958); Lewis Perinbam to Faris, 3 July 1961, Faris Collection. Also Perinbam, *Opportunities for Service,* 27-28.

19 Melvin Arnold of Harper & Brothers to Faris, 4 February 1958, in file of reviews and correspondence related to *To Plow with Hope,* Faris Collection. Other information about the reception of the book comes from this file.

20 The Netherlands connection is mentioned in Faris to Spicer, 17 March 1961, McWhinney/Woollcombe Collection.

21 *To Plow with Hope,* 202-3.

22 Elizabeth Cobbs Hoffman, *All You Need Is Love: The Peace Corps and the Spirit of the 1960s* (Cambridge: Harvard University Press, 1998), esp. Chap. 2.

23 Faris to Ozzie [Schmidt] and Bill [McWhinney], 4 February 1963; Stinson to Dharampal, 19 December 1961. See also Spicer to Dharampal, 6 April 1961, and surviving portion of letter from Dale [Posgate to Faris, first page missing], all in Faris Collection.

24 Evidence of two volunteers' initial unease in unstructured settings can be seen in letters from HL in Orissa, 20 October 1961, and from SS in West Bengal, 12 October 1961, in Faris Collection. For Mira Behn, see Kumari Jayawardena, *The White Woman's Other Burden: Western Women and South Asia during British Rule* (New York: Routledge, 1995), 203.

25 McWhinney to Arthur Kroeger, 24 March 1962, McWhinney/Woollcombe Collection. McWhinney observed that this volunteer's experience "may or may not have accentuated a process already started."

26 A.P. Choudhuri to Faris, 13 December 1961, in Faris Collection; also, Dale Posgate to Bill McWhinney, 14 May [1962], McWhinney/Woollcombe Collection, for his fellow volunteers' sympathetic but realistic views on this young colleague's struggles, which were all the more poignant for his having done his own sponsorship fundraising.

27 "Conference of Canadian Overseas Volunteers," 10-16 February 1962, to Mr. [Ozzie] Schmidt, 30 October 1962, Faris Collection.

28 Posgate's comments on volunteers' contributions are in Posgate to McWhinney, 17 July [1962], McWhinney/Woollcombe Collection. In the same collection see Dharampal to Dear Friend, 8 December 1961, and Posgate to Dear Friends, regarding the work camp. Comments on his own job and friendships are in Posgate response to questionnaire, August 2006. (The questionnaire referred to here and elsewhere in the notes was prepared by the author.)

29 McWhinney to Posgate, 27 July 1962, McWhinney/Woollcombe Collection. But see also in ibid., McWhinney to Posgate, 12 July 1962; McWhinney was initially upset by Posgate's frank remarks about the insignificance of the COVs' contributions in India.

30 McWhinney to Posgate, 17 and 27 July 1962, in ibid. Communication problems with their host institution and with AVARD and McWhinney about the reasons for their departures from their posts had initially left the women subject to criticism by Dharampal and some of their peers. Interestingly, Perinbam, having met with Dharampal during his visit to India in 1961, had anticipated the kinds of problems that could arise in placing volunteers through AVARD; see *Opportunities for Service*, 28.

31 Cook to McWhinney and Schmidt, 9 January 1963, Library and Archives Canada (LAC), CUSO fonds, MG 28, I 323, vol. 102, file 19 (hereafter LAC/CUSO, MG 28, I 323, with volume and file number).

32 Schmidt to Dear –, 22 December 1962, Faris Collection.

33 Wood to Dear Oz[zzie Schmidt] or Bill [McWhinney], 22 September 1962, McWhinney/Woollcombe Collection. Information on Wood comes from his response to my questionnaire, December 2006, personal interview, and letters to his family, which he kindly shared.

34 Dale Posgate to Dear Toronto, 21 September [1962], McWhinney/Woollcombe Collection; interview with Jim Walker, 17 January 2007.

35 Response to questionnaire from Donna Shields-Poë, January 2008, and email communication 8 March 2010. In 2009, on the day that the ashram's founder died, Donna received a personal call from his family.

36 Account by Jim and Sheila Ward in *Man Deserves Man*, ed. McWhinney and Godfrey, 368-69; interview with Sheila Ward, 29 October 2006, and follow-up correspondence. I discuss the Wards' later work below.

37 This was the experience of Suki Falkner, who taught English to high school girls in an ashram devoted to women's uplift. Falkner had been warned prior to her arrival that her main function, so far as the ashram's politically shrewd female supervisor was concerned, would be as a showpiece. Her frustration at this did not prevent her from entering into the spirit of the place and trying to fit in, wearing a *khadi* sari, oiling her hair, etc.; interview, 11 July 2007.

38 For Millar's account, see *CUSO/SUCO Bulletin*, February 1966, 14-16.

39 Dharampal to Schmidt, 30 October 1962, and Posgate to Dear Toronto, 21 September [1962], McWhinney/Woollcombe Collection. Dharampal had larger worries at this time than the volunteers: he had briefly been jailed by Nehru's government for criticizing its handling of war with China; Marilyn Cook to "Hi Everybody," 20 December 1962, LAC/CUSO, MG 28, I 323, vol. 102, file 19.

40 Woollcombe to McWhinney, ibid., vol. 102, file 17, and interview with Woollcombe, 4 December 2006; McWhinney to Dharampal, 20 October 1962, McWhinney/Woollcombe Collection.

41 Woollcombe to McWhinney, 27 July 1963, LAC/CUSO, MG 28, I 323, vol. 102, file 17.

42 Illnesses are mentioned in, for instance, Marilyn Cook to Oz, Grant, and Bill, 10 June 1963, in ibid., file 18, and in Marion Faris to Our Dearest Ones, 29 December 1962, in Faris Collection.

43 Undated newspaper clipping about Jim Walker in Clippings file, McWhinney/Woollcombe Collection, and interview with Walker. For Woollcombe's views, letter to Bill McWhinney, 27 July 1963, LAC/CUSO, MG 28, I 323, vol. 102, file 17.

44 For instance, Marion Faris to son Ken, 14 February 1963, and to Our Dear Ones, 7 June 1963, and 28 July 1963, Faris Collection; fragment of report from Steve Woollcombe to McWhinney, probably October 1963, dealing with volunteers' health problems, ways of recognizing their indebtedness to the Farises, and other matters, LAC/CUSO, MG 28, I 323, vol. 102, file 17.

45 For instance, SB to "Dear Mother and Father Faris," 3 March 1963, and M to Mamaji, 4 September 1974; also Mother [Marion] to Kenny, 13 September 1962, regarding a Toronto reception for the COVs' parents to meet Don and Marion, all in Faris Collection.

46 Copy of McWhinney to Posgate, 27 March 1962, and McWhinney to Don Faris, 28 March 1962, Faris Collection.

47 Regarding Kroeger's role, see, for instance, form letter from Ozzie Schmidt to "Dear –," 22 December 1962, in Faris Collection; handwritten letter/report, unsigned, Steve Woollcombe to Bill McWhinney, probably October 1963, in LAC/CUSO, MG 28, I 323, vol. 102, file 17; "Memo," unsigned but probably by Kroeger, regarding his views on and relationship with the volunteers, in ibid., vol. 61, file 38.

48 "Ottawa's 'dean of deputy ministers' cherished the ideals of good governance," obituary, *Globe and Mail*, 12 May 2008, S12; Minutes of National Selection Committee meeting, 8-9 February 1964, LAC/CUSO, MG 28, I 323, vol. 26, file 3; MM to Mamaji and Papaji, 24 April 1966, Faris Collection, regarding plans for an Indian meal with Kroeger and various RVs to celebrate his forthcoming wedding.

49 Confidential memo from Ronning to Undersecretary of State for External Affairs, 5 March 1964, and undated and unsigned memo on "CUSO," LAC/CUSO, MG 28, I 323, vol. 61, file 38.

50 Hopper's name occurs frequently in CUSO correspondence and in my interviews with RVs. For instance, Marilyn Cook to "Hi Everybody," 20 December, 1962, ibid., vol. 102, file 19; Stephen Woollcombe to Ozzie Schmidt and others, 11 July 1963, in ibid., file 17; interview with Suki Falkner, and with Wendy Dobson, 22 August 2007.

51 Fragment of handwritten report by Woollcombe, LAC/CUSO, MG 28, I 323, vol. 102, file 17; Dale Posgate to Bill McWhinney, 2 July [1962], regarding gathering in Kashmir, McWhinney/Woollcombe Collection.

52 Quotations from Donna Shields-Poë's response to questionnaire, January 2008. Lois James (later Chetelat), also a nurse, likewise remembered a Buddhist rest home during orientation as good preparation for what lay ahead and sounded almost nonchalant as she wrote to her family about flies, smells, board beds, and rats; details included in her unpublished manuscript, "Alice's Daughters," 397, copy kindly supplied by Chetelat.

53 Memo from McWhinney to Nobel Power, EAO, 20 July 1964, LAC/CUSO, MG 28, I 323, vol. 128, file 17, and ibid., vol. 102, file 17, for Woollcombe to McWhinney, 8 October 1963, and fragment of handwritten report by Woollcombe; letter from John R. Wood to his family, 4 September 1962 (for "Alouette!").

54 Wood to McWhinney, 15 January 1964, LAC/CUSO, MG 28, I 323, vol. 102, file 16.

55 For the makeshift filing cabinets, see ibid., and in the same file, regarding veto of a CUSO phone, McWhinney to Woollcombe and Wood, 24 October 1963. For Judy Ransom as Wood's necessarily frugal successor as coordinator, interview, 1 February 2007, and information in the next section.

56 I am grateful to several RVs for sharing observations about gender relations among volunteers in India in the early years.

57 Barbara Heron's claim that until the 1990s, few Canadian women participated in development is clearly wide of the mark; see *Desire for Development: Whiteness, Gender and the Helping Imperative* (Waterloo: Wilfrid Laurier University Press, 2007), 159n21.

58 McWhinney to Woollcombe, 15 May 1963, LAC/CUSO, MG 28, I 323, vol. 102, file 18; also, ibid., file 17, for McWhinney to Woollcombe, 18 September 1963, and to Wood, 15 November 1963.

59 "CUSO/Orientation-India/Stephen Woollcombe, May 1963," and Woollcombe to Ozzie Schmidt and McWhinney, 1 May 1963, ibid., file 18. Woollcombe's concern for CUSO's reputation was understandable: he had worked closely with Spicer in the founding of COV; moreover, his own first months of teaching in a private school had made him sensitive to the risk of misunderstanding and gossip about even the most innocuous expressions of friendship with a co-worker of the opposite sex.

60 Ibid., and, for quotation, Ozzie Schmidt to Marilyn Cook and Woollcombe, 24 May 1963.

61 There was in fact a tradition reaching back to the nineteenth century of unconventional Western women coming to India and, in part by their very "otherness," finding niches as social reformers and supporters of Indian nationalism; Jayawardena, *The White Woman's Other Burden*. Moreover, in some parts of India, most notably Kerala, where a tradition of matrilineality and, later, Communism and varied forms of activism prevailed, there were distinctive patterns of gender relations and social reforms; Robin Jeffrey, *Politics, Women and Well-Being: How Kerala Became a "Model"* (London: Macmillan Press, 1992).

62 For criticisms of SB for relocating on her own and thus giving offence, Cook to Schmidt, 24 October 1962, and Woollcombe to Schmidt and McWhinney, 1 May 1963, LAC/CUSO, MG 28, I 323, vol. 102, files 19 and 18, respectively. For appreciation of SB's contribution in her new placement, letter from Headmaster, Khalari Basic School, Angul, 23 February 1963, and for her frustration at being held up as COV's "bad example," Jim Walker to Dear Oz et al., February 1963, both in McWhinney/Woollcombe Collection. Not only had SB done useful work, the Headmaster wrote, but her presence as an outsider was also helping to broaden the horizons of the children being cared for by his institution.

63 Wood to McWhinney, 15 January 1964, LAC/CUSO, MG 28, I 323, vol. 102, file 16; account of the wedding in "The CUSO Ephemera," a handwritten CUSO newsletter [October 1964] by coordinator Judy Ransom, with added personal note to Mr. and Mrs. Faris, Faris Collection; interview with JF, 9 May 2007.

64 Response to questionnaire and interview with BH, 5 January 2006.

65 Source of information withheld on request.

66 Interview with KH, 30 March 2007, and phone conversation, February 2010.

67 One exception was Dale Posgate, who identified Cook's, as well as John Wood's and Tom Schatzky's, leadership potential soon after their arrival; Posgate to "Dear Toronto," 21 September [1962], McWhinney/Woollcombe Collection.

68 There is a large correspondence by Cook in LAC/CUSO, MG 28, I 323, vol. 102, file 19. See, for instance, Cook to Ozzie Schmidt, 24 October 1962, to Schmidt and McWhinney, 9 January 1963, to "High Gang" [the volunteers], 7 April 1963, and her postscript on Woollcombe to Schmidt, McWhinney, and Grant MacDonald, 27 June 1963. For a somewhat condescending acknowledgment of Cook's abilities, see McWhinney to Woollcombe, 3 May 1963, and Schmidt (unsigned copy) to Woollcombe, 27 June 1963. The question of Cook's leadership ability would soon become moot, for that spring she became involved with a poultry project through which she met a Peace Corps volunteer to whom she became engaged; profile in COV Reunion booklet, 1987, McWhinney/Woollcombe Collection.

69 For instance, Woollcombe to McWhinney, 27 July 1963, LAC/CUSO, MG 28, I 323, vol. 102, file 17, and Wood to McWhinney, 3 November 1963, in ibid., file 16.

70 Minutes of CUSO Executive Committee Meeting, 22 December 1964, 2, Faris Collection.

71 Ransom interview, and email, 20 March 2007. Ransom had been asked at the annual Bombay reunion to consider taking on the coordinator role, but she recalled that some volunteers who had already returned to Canada were skeptical that a woman could handle the position effectively. For their recommendation of a male volunteer from her cohort as coordinator, see Woollcombe to McWhinney, 8 October 1963, LAC/CUSO MG 28, I 323, vol. 102, file 17; John Wood to McWhinney, 3 November 1963, and McWhinney to Wood, 15 November 1963, both in file 16.

72 Ransom interview; John Stackhouse, "How Five Idealistic Young People Ventured Forth – And Didn't Save the World," *Globe and Mail*, 19 December 1998, Focus section, deals briefly with this project and the array of services it was providing when Stackhouse and a group of RVs visited it in 1998. Ransom's leadership potential was acknowledged in Schmidt to Marilyn Cook and Steve Woollcombe, 24 May 1963, LAC/CUSO, MG 28, I 323, vol. 102, file 18.

73 Interview with Ransom.

74 Introduction to section on India, *Man Deserves Man*, ed. McWhinney and Godfrey, quotation at 353-54.

75 See biographical profiles in COV Reunion booklets, 1986 and 1987, McWhinney/Woollcombe Collection.

76 For Woollcombe, Report on teaching assignment at Shreyas, 16 January 1964, LAC/CUSO, MG 28, I 323, vol. 102, file 16, and interview, 4 December 2006. For Wood, response to questionnaire, December 2006. There are numerous examples in India and elsewhere of volunteers' initiatives that took them beyond their assigned tasks. For Peace Corps expectations about going beyond one's assigned job, see Fritz Fischer, *Making Them Like Us: Peace Corps Volunteers in the 1960s* (Washington: Smithsonian Institute, 1998), 149.

77 Unless otherwise indicated, the information and quotations that follow come from Banta's responses to questionnaire, March 2007.

78 Wood to McWhinney, 15 January 1964, LAC/CUSO, MG 28, I 323, vol. 102, file 16.

79 Questionnaire completed by Mündel, July 2006; Hans-Henning Mündel, *My Life among the Paniyas of the Nilgiri Hills*, introduction by Clyde Sanger (Carpe Diem Mündel Publishing, 2007). See also Mündel's account in *Man Deserves Man*, 356-66.

80 "Tibetan Refugee School at Kangra" with attached statement by John Haysom, McWhinney/Woollcombe Collection; "Overseas Reports," CUSO/SUCO *Bulletin*, February 1964, 5-7; George Woodcock, *Faces of India* (London: Faber and Faber, 1964); and Alan Twigg, *Tibetans in Exile: The Dalai Lama and the Woodcocks* (Vancouver: Ronsdale Press, 2009), 19-22.

81 Interview with Pullen, 7 August 2008; Pullen's journal-based account in *Man Deserves Man* (quotation at 409); and, for background details, Lois James Chetelat, chapter on "CUSO, India and Tibetan Refugees," in "Alice's Daughters," unpublished manuscript.

82 What follows draws on Chetelat's "CUSO, India and Tibetan Refugees" and on interview with Chetelat, 6 May 2007.

83 "CUSO, India and Tibetan Refugees," 430.

84 Ibid., 449, 451 (for quotation); see also Lois James Chetelat's account in Stackhouse, "How Five Idealistic Young People Ventured Forth – And Didn't Save the World."

85 "CUSO Report of the Executive Secretary (Actg), 1965-66," LAC/CUSO, MG 28, I 323, vol. 75, file 4.

86 "Personal Recollections" provided by Marson to author, May 2009.

87 "Annual Report on the India Programme," by Marson, accompanying "1966-67 Report of the Executive Secretary," Robarts Library, University of Toronto; also Christina Cassels, "CUSO-India/ Education Programme/1966-69," 1, copy kindly supplied by Cassels.

88 There is a large literature on the green revolution and on the unanticipated and harmful effects on poor farmers unable to benefit from its contributions to agricultural productivity. For a recent work focused on US self-interest and depicting the green revolution as "a legendary success in name only," see Nick Cullather, *Hungry World: America's Cold War Battle against Poverty* (Cambridge: Harvard University Press, 2010), quotation at 269.

89 Hans-Henning Mündel's account in *Man Deserves Man*, 356-66; *My Life*; response to questionnaire, July 2006.

90 Account by Jim and Sheila Ward in *Man Deserves Man*, 367-78; interview with Sheila Ward, 29 October 2006.

91 David Van Praagh, "CUSO Project/Saskatchewan Farmer Grows Seeds in India," *Globe and Mail*, 19 July 1966; table with summaries of volunteers and staff in Asia, 13 January 1971, LAC/CUSO, MG 28, I 323, vol. 108, file 24 on Overseas Operations.

92 "India," in "CUSO-Asia Report/Sept. 1968," by Brian Marson, in LAC/CUSO, MG 28, I 323, vol. 102, file 3; *CUSO/SUCO Bulletin*, May-July 1968, special issue on "The CUSO Agriculturalist," who, as featured here, had specialized training and comprised two women. For the Peace Corps, see Ashabranner, *Moment in History*, 151, 271-72. In the mid-1960s, Ashabranner writes, the Peace Corps's commitment to growth resulted in the acceptance of numerous BA generalists, some of whom, placed in agricultural assignments in India, embarrassed themselves and disappointed their hosts with their lack of fit. He gives the example of a history major who praised what he thought was a field of wheat, only to be politely corrected by the block development officer, who said that, yes, it was "excellent barley."

93 I elaborate more fully on the larger context in "Ironic Interventions: CUSO Volunteers in India's Family Planning Campaigns, 1960s-1970s," *Histoire sociale/Social History* 43, 86 (2010): 279-313.

94 Judith R. Seltzer, *The Origins and Evolution of Family Planning Programs in Developing Countries* (Santa Monica, CA: RAND, 2002), 15; Gayl D. Ness and Hirofumi Ando, *The Land Is Shrinking: Population Planning in Asia* (Baltimore: Johns Hopkins University Press, 1984), 74-100; Brown, *Nehru*, 300-1, 314-15.

95 Matthew Connelly, *Fatal Misconception: The Struggle to Control World Population* (Cambridge: Harvard University Press, 2008), Chap. 6, esp. 221.

96 Brouwer, "Ironic Interventions," 290-92. For an excellent study of the problems that have constrained Indian nurses' professional development, see Madeleine Healey, "Indian Sisters: A History of Nursing Leadership and the State, 1907-2007" (PhD thesis, Politics Program, School of Social Sciences, La Trobe University, 2007).

97 Marilyn Cook to "High Gang," 7 April 1963; LAC/CUSO, MG 28, I 323, vol. 102, file 18; "Prefer Canadian Plan to U.S. Peace Corps," undated *Globe and Mail* article, in file of clippings, McWhinney/Woollcombe Collection, for volunteer Tom Schatzky's statements about birth control opportunities. See also profiles of Reggie Modlich and Sue Hamilton Van Iterson in COV Reunion booklet, 1987, McWhinney/Woollcombe Collection.

98 Interview with Ward.

99 Brouwer, "Ironic Interventions," 302-3.

100 Interview with Brian Marson, 27 May 2009, and with Wendy Dobson (who served with CUSO as Wendy Marson), 22 August 2007.

101 Interview with Dobson. Her article was published in November 1967 and reprinted in a multi-themed collection of readings on family planning prepared by Brian Marson and S.L. Perkin; for "Family Planning," in "India Reader," see LAC/CUSO, MG 28, I 323, vol. 26, file 20.

102 This comment and the paragraphs that follow draw on my interviews with six of the CUSO nurses who had family-planning assignments as well as on other interviews and archival sources.

103 What follows draws on Phillips's responses to questionnaire, interview, 19 September 2006, and follow-up correspondence.

104 Phillips, "Follow-up Visit," *Journal of the Christian Medical Association of India* (hereafter CMAI *Journal*), 45, 11 (1970): 681-85.

105 Joyce Relyea, "A New Concept in Family Planning Education," CMAI *Journal*, 43, 10 (1968), 513-17. Other information about Relyea's role comes from interview, 11 July 2008, and from follow-up correspondence and documentation. Stilwell's report is in CMAI *Journal* 46, 10 (1971): 577-78.

106 Ruth Compton Brouwer, "Learning and Teaching about Birth Control: The Cautious Activism of Medical Missionaries in 1930s India," in *Rhetoric and Reality: Gender and the Colonial Experience in Asia*, ed. Avril A. Powell and Siobhan Lambert-Hurley (New Delhi: Oxford University Press, 2006), 154-84; Dr. Prakash Narain, "Role of Voluntary Organizations in Public Health Programs," CMAI *Journal* 48, 7 (1973), 300-2; Eric R. Ram, "Church Hospitals and Primary Health Care," ibid., 54, 2 (1979), 58-67; Leela Damodara Menon, "The Role of Voluntary Agencies in Family Planning," in *Family Planning in India: Policy and Administration/Proceedings of Three Seminars* (New Delhi: Indian Institute of Public Administration, 1973), 214.

107 *Man Deserves Man*, ed. McWhinney and Godfrey, 452.

108 "India," in "CUSO-Asia Report/Sept. 1968," by Brian Marson. For the reassigned teacher, see Marson's "Annual Report on the India Prorgramme," 1966-67.

109 For Garrett, response to questionnaire, interview, 19 September 2006, and follow- up communications. For Henry, email communication, 22 July 2009. For Ward, interview and follow-up communications.

110 For details see "Orientation In-Country Asia 1968," LAC/CUSO, MG 28, I 323, vol. 108, file 12, which also contains information on the 1967 orientation.

111 "CUSO-India/Field Officer's Report," 2, 5, 13, in ibid., vol. 26, file 24, "India Reader."

112 Asia Regional Meeting/Bangkok, 7-10 May 1972, 3, ibid., vol. 122, file 16.

113 Morrison, "Canada and South Asia," 46-47. See also Clyde Sanger, *Lotta and the Unitarian Service Committee Story* (Toronto: Stoddart, 1986), 189-91. USC phased out its support to its partner agencies in India over the period 1971-75.

114 Written comments from Phillips to author, 17 July 2009.

115 Dick Bird, *Never the Same Again: A History of VSO* (Cambridge: Lutterworth Press, 1998), 97-98; Ashabranner, *Moment in History*, 271-72; Kux, *India and the United States*, Chap. 7, esp. 307-8. Kux writes that the Peace Corps later phased out of India entirely.

116 Many of the contributors to *Man Deserves Man* had served in India. See also "What's Bugging the Committed Kids?," by Tom Alderman in *The Canadian*, 21 May 1966, for several accounts and photographs of CUSO/India volunteers.

117 Marson's "Annual Report on the India Programme," 1967, 5-6; account by Les Johnson in *Man Deserves Man*, 379-90; interview with Collier, 15 September 2006. Collier's second teaching placement was a much happier experience, but in this case the school was serving an already relatively privileged student population.

118 Report by Susan Caplan, 1968, in LAC/CUSO, MG 28, I 323, vol. 26, file 26, "India Reader"; Barbara Kerfoot response to questionnaire, February 2010. For problems experienced by CUSO teachers in India in the late 1960s and particularly in the institution in Chandigarh, where Caplan briefly and unhappily served, see Cassels, "CUSO-India/Education Programme." Regional and state governments briskly directed CUSO, VSO, and Peace Corps teachers to this institution, but they were frequently resented by staff and by the government teachers they were meant to retrain.

119 Katherine Frank, *Indira: The Life of Indira Nehru Gandhi* (Boston: Houghton Mifflin, 2002), 404-7; Connelly, *Fatal Misconception*, 318-26.

120 See, for instance, an article from *The Economist*, included in CUSO's "Readings in Development," LAC/CUSO, MG 28, I 323, vol. 44, file 21; also ibid., vol. 148, file 18, for "A Black Perspective on Family Planning," in "Capsule, 1970." The latter was a newsletter for CUSO health personnel.

121 Memo from Ragan, April 1970, and Garrett's reply, 18 May 1970, ibid., vol. 148, file 18. See also Brouwer, "Ironic Interventions," 308-9. Like Oxfam Canada, Oxfam UK, and agencies in Norway and Sweden, CIDA *did* support the CMAI's family-planning work in the 1970s.

122 Interview with Phillips and Phillips's CV; interview with Garrett, 4 June 2008, and email to author, 14 November 2008. So far as nursing was concerned, the perception that indigenous professionals could now meet existing needs in family-planning leadership was perhaps unduly sanguine, at least outside the CMAI. See Healey, "Indian Sisters," regarding the ongoing fragility of India's nursing profession.

123 Interview with Marson.

124 Jean Stilwell, "The full-time business of existing," *CUSO Bulletin* 3, 1971, cover story; Phillips's interview with author and CV. Much of what follows on Bangladesh in this paragraph draws on Smillie, *Lost Content,* Chap. 13.

125 Smillie, *Lost Content,* Chap. 13.

126 Information drawn from Phillips's CV.

127 Cobbs Hoffman, *All You Need Is Love,* 156.

128 G. Stephen M. Woollcombe, "Canadian University Service Overseas: A Case Study of an Overseas Volunteer Program" (master's thesis, Pennsylvania State University, 1965), 66; MA to Don and Marion Faris, 21 July 1965, Faris Collection.

129 Rosemary Speirs, "Realism Replaces Idealism among CUSO Volunteers," *Globe and Mail,* 28 August 1979, as saved in "CUSO in the News," vol. 2, 1979, LAC/CUSO, MG 28, I 323, vol. 50, file 5.

130 "A Challenge to the Returned Volunteer," [2], LAC/CUSO, MG 28, I 323, vol. 102, file 3.

131 Woollcombe, "Case Study," 70.

132 Response to questionnaire by Sally Bambridge Ravindra, October 2005.

133 "How Five Idealistic Young People Ventured Forth."

134 Anne Jones Hume response to questionnaire, 21 February 2006; written communication from Phillips, 17 July 2009.

Chapter 3: "Development Is Disturbance"

1 "Talk Delivered at the Conference on Inter-American Student Projects (CIASP), Cuernavaca, Mexico, April 20, 1968, by Monsignor Ivan Illich," included in "Ancillary Papers" with reports from CUSO's Seventh Annual General Meeting (AGM) in Roy Fischer Personal Collection (hereafter Fischer Collection). Despite the title, Illich had not been able to deliver his talk in person. For the second quotation, see Elizabeth Cobbs Hoffman, *All You Need Is Love: The Peace Corps and the Spirit of the 1960s* (Cambridge: Harvard University Press, 1998), 218.

2 Looking back in 1983 as he ended his term as CUSO's executive director, Ian Smillie recalled the organization's transition from early "unquestioning enthusiasm" to a stage at which it became "almost paralyzed by our sense of inadequacy"; "The Way Ahead ... ," *Forum,* June 1983, 1. Frantz Fanon's *The Wretched of the Earth* (New York: Grove Press, 1963), perhaps the most widely cited book on CUSO reading lists from the late 1960s, may not actually have been read by everyone in the CUSO community, but it was certainly widely discussed, and its very title (translated from the French *Les damnés de la terre*) could foster white liberal guilt. Fanon was writing about decolonization rather than development, but by dismissing the European socio-economic and cultural model with such vehemence, rejecting the notion of "catch[ing] up," and declaring that the colonized "must turn over a new leaf ... work out new concepts, and try to set afoot a new man," he provided would-be helpers with few road maps beyond rejecting the modernization theory of the first Development Decade (254, 255 for quoted passages).

3   Six of the seven Ottawa staff positions were held by RVs at the beginning of 1966; *CUSO/SUCO Bulletin,* February 1966, 6.

4   "CUSO to Begin Research," *CUSO/SUCO Bulletin,* August 1967, 9-11, and "Introducing ... CUSO National," December 1968, 3-4. See also *CUSO '69,* 10: a new Canadian Operations Division employed three full-time staff for recruitment and for communication with CUSO's now seventy local committees, located on university and college campuses across Canada. As acting executive director in 1971, David Catmur would express concern to the AGM about "the trend towards beginning to pay for things we traditionally got through free voluntary service"; *CUSO Bulletin* 4, 1971, 4.

5   *CUSO/SUCO Bulletin,* February 1966, 6; "Introducing ... CUSO National."

6   "They're Taking a Constitutional," *CUSO/SUCO Bulletin,* Summer 1969, 1, and "Development Is Our Business," *CUSO/SUCO Bulletin,* December 1968, 1.

7   "Development Is Our Business"; *CUSO '69,* statement by Bogdasavich, 1; Louis Sabourin, "An Insider Evaluation of CUSO by an Outsider," *CUSO/SUCO Bulletin,* February-April 1968, 9, 10 (for "realism" and "a functional approach"). See also "Proposal for Board Training Programme," draft 2 (1968 or 1969), in Library and Archives Canada (LAC), King Gordon fonds, MG 30-C241, vol. 40, file 7 (hereafter LAC/Gordon fonds with volume and file number).

8   Terry Glavin, "'A Dangerous Drift Towards a Placement Agency,'" *CUSO/SUCO Bulletin,* August 1967, 18-19; Normand Tellier, "CUSO/In Search of an Identity," and letter from Joyce Andrews, Achimota, Ghana, in *CUSO/SUCO Bulletin,* October 1967–January 1968, 12-14, 24. See also Robert N. Thompson, "The Importance of Being Private," in *CUSO/SUCO,* February-April 1967. Thompson, a Social Credit MP from Alberta and an early supporter of CUSO, favoured retaining the early CUSO spirit. Glavin, Tellier, and Andrews advocated what they saw as a more realistic and less sentimental approach to the volunteer's role. India RV John R. Wood, who went on to a long career as a political science professor at UBC, stopped serving on the university's local committee when CUSO "became 'too professional' for my taste"; response to questionnaire, December 2006. (The questionnaire referred to here and elsewhere in the notes was prepared by the author.) For a 1969 call to replace "volunteer" with "cooperant," see "CUSO Montreal Returned Volunteer Conference/Resolutions," LAC/Gordon fonds, vol. 40, file 9.

9   RV Marjorie Dawson, for example, explained that when she joined CUSO in 1972, the concepts of volunteerism and altruism were no longer "in"; "What Now CUSO," *CUSO Forum,* Summer 1974, 23.

10   That the "hair shirts versus professionals" tensions predated the "pragmatic" versus "political" alignments and that both these ideological divides were sometimes exacerbated by personal conflicts is made clear in Ian Smillie's taped interviews with Dr. Ed Ragan, n.d., and Tim Brodhead, 26 July 1983, in Smillie Tape Collection (hereafter STC).

11   "Development Is Our Business," 2, 4; *Information Guide for Overseas Governments and Agencies,* undated pamphlet [1966], in Fischer Collection.

12   "Development Is Our Business," 1, 2, 4.

13   Ibid., 2; excerpts from Bogdasavich's address to AGM, *CUSO Forum,* Winter 1969-70, 2. Interference in the internal struggles of developing nations, he worried, could even "be conceived by them as a racialist slander."

14   Malawi RV Terrance Cox acknowledged these possibilities in "New Roles for Canada's Overseas Volunteers: CUSO, by Now a National Institution, Faces Some Fresh Challenges," *Saturday Night,* June 1974, 24-28. Cox's article was reproduced in *CUSO Forum,* Spring 1975, 13-15.

15   "AGM Approves Public Education," *CUSO Forum,* 1969-70, cover story. Italics added.

16   *CUSO '69,* 11. See also Jean Christie, "A Critical History of Development Education in Canada," *Canadian and International Education* 12, 3 (1983), 8-20.

17   Proceedings of the Asia Regional Meeting, November 3-9, 1974, quotation from p. 4 of booklet titled *Project Programming: CUSO Asia's Response,* in LAC, CUSO fonds, MG 28, I 323, vol. 122, file 14 (references hereafter to this fonds are to LAC/CUSO, MG 28, I 323, with volume and file number). See also "CUSO Projects: A New Dimension," *CUSO Forum,* Christmas 1973, 18.

18   Ian Smillie, *The Land of Lost Content: A History of CUSO* (Toronto: Deneau, 1985), 86.

19   David Catmur, "Overseas Operations," *CUSO 71/Annual Review,* 2, in LAC/CUSO, MG 28, I 323, vol. 74, file 33.

20   *Annual CUSO/SUCO Reports 1972,* section on Overseas Programmes (for quotations); "There've Been Some Changes Made," *Communique* [1973?], in University of British Columbia Archives, John Conway fonds, box 6, file 13 (hereafter UBC Archives/Conway fonds, with box and file number). Within months, the new RFD structure was coming under fire from some of those most directly affected; see Bruce Miller, "A Critical Review of the R.F.D. Structure," November 1972, LAC/CUSO, MG 28, I 323, vol. 22, file 10.

21   Letter from Tom Morton, *CUSO Forum,* January 1974, 6; Smillie interview with Father Romeo Guilbeault, n.d., STC.

22   "Passed Development Charter," *CUSO Forum,* January 1974, 3, and "CUSO Charter Is General Guide," February-March 1974, 6 (for quotations).

23   Draft memo from Catmur to Gérard Aubry regarding domestic program, 2 February 1971, LAC/CUSO, MG 28, I 323, vol. 22, file 8.

24   Ibid., for Barbara Hoffman, "Domestic Programming Report" and "Some Thoughts on Proposed Domestic Programme"; and ibid., vol. 29, file 13, for "Minutes of the Tenth Annual General Meeting of the Canadian University Service Overseas," Carleton University, 26-28 November 1971, 10. See also "Be It Resolved That ..." *CUSO Bulletin* 4 (1971): 7.

25   Chairman's Report in *CUSO Annual Review/72,* LAC/CUSO, MG 28, I 323, vol. 74, file 32.

26   See *CUSO 71/Annual Review,* 8, regarding Kenya and Ethiopia, and *CUSO Forum,* Spring and Summer 1981, 24, for Clyde Sanger's personal retrospective on ECSA and the termination of the Kenya and Uganda programs as "[t]he first shuffle of countries." David Beer, ECSA regional field director when the Uganda program was terminated, discussed the circumstances behind the decision in an interview with the author, 26 July 2011. (Unless stated otherwise, all interviews cited in this book were conducted by the author.)

27   J.L. Granatstein and Robert Bothwell, *Pirouette: Pierre Trudeau and Canadian Foreign Policy* (Toronto: University of Toronto Press, 1990), 261-62, 275-76; Smillie, *Lost Content,* Chap. 3, for an overview of the CUSO experience in the Caribbean.

28   Smillie interview with Sharon Capeling, 29 October 1983, STC; Rommel Lawrence, "Caribbean Volunteer Corps?," *CUSO Forum,* January 1975, 16.

29   *Abeng,* 3 May 1969, reproduced in CUSO's *Readings in Development,* vol. 1, ed. Robert D.H. Sallery, Mary L. McDonald, and Paul Duchesne, sec. XVI, n.p., n.d.

30   Sean Mills, *The Empire Within: Postcolonial Thought and Political Activism in Sixties Montreal* (Montreal/Kingston: McGill-Queen's University Press, 2010), 104-8; Smillie interview with Capeling, STC; Smillie, *Lost Content,* 37-38.

31   "Overseas Programmes," in *CUSO Annual Review/72*; "Annual CUSO/SUCO Reports," 1972, LAC/CUSO, MG 28, I 323, vol. 74, file 32; Smillie interview with Terry Glavin, STC; "Paradise Lost? No Fun in the Caribbean Sun," *CUSO Bulletin,* Spring 1970, 12. CUSO's Frank Bogdasavich and regional coordinator Father Howard Gardiner were asked to speak to the Senate Committee on Foreign Affairs in February 1970 about the likely causes of strained Caribbean-Canadian relations. Regarding volunteer cutbacks in the region in the 1970s, and for CUSO's new approach and new problems in the early 1980s, see Smillie, *Lost Content,* 42-52. In regard to CUSO's troubles in the Caribbean, it is worth recalling Clyde Sanger's concern, discussed in Chap. 1, about ill-considered early volunteer placements and consequent high attrition rates.

32 "Returned Volunteers' Conference," *CUSO/SUCO Bulletin,* November 1966/January 1967, cover story.

33 CUSO Returned Volunteer Conference, University of Manitoba, 11-14 October 1968, LAC/CUSO, MG 28, I 323, vol. 35, file 4, and Resolutions from Returned Volunteer Conferences, Southwestern Ontario, 16-18 October 1970, in ibid., vol. 36, file 3; *CUSO Forum,* Summer 1970; *CUSO Forum,* Christmas 1973, 8.

34 Returned Volunteers Conference, Winnipeg, 12-14 October 1968, LAC/CUSO, MG 28, I 323, vol. 76, file 29; *Rivers North of the Future: The Testament of Ivan Illich as Told to David Cayley* (Toronto: Anansi, 2005), 11. Illich's *Deschooling Society,* which had come out of his experiences in Puerto Rico in the 1950s, had a powerful impact on educators concerned with First World as well as Third World social inequalities.

35 Memo to "Volunteers Assigned to West African Programme" accompanying letter by Tim Brodhead to Ron Cyr, 22 April 1971. My thanks to Dr. Ron Cyr for sharing this material.

36 "International Development: An Introductory Reading List," CUSO information leaflet 4, published in 1969, listed dozens of works, ranging from Lester Pearson's *Partners in Development* to Eldridge Cleaver's *Soul on Ice;* copy of leaflet in Fischer Collection.

37 *Readings in Development,* vol. 1, Introduction, sec. II (aircraft ad.), III (branch-plants), XV (Mitchell Sharp), XIV (Kenya), XVI (West Indian students); vol. 2, 2 (for Hilton ad) and 115 (for Nyerere). Copies from Fischer Collection.

38 *NEWSTATEments* 1, 1 (1971), 1, introductory statement. Copies are available in Thomas Fisher Collection, Robarts Library, University of Toronto.

39 Ibid, 1, 2 (1971), 2 (for quotation), 4-7, for transcript of television interview with Freire. See also Eber F. Ferrer, "The Conscientization Process in Brazil," 8-10.

40 No issues of *NEWSTATEments* were published in 1972, and when it reappeared briefly in 1973 and 1974, it had been purchased from CUSO by former editor-in-chief Robert Sallery, who, while retaining many of the earlier corresponding editors, hoped also to involve them in "a variety of action programs," including development training and project design; "A Note to Readers," *NEWSTATEments* 2, 1 (1973) 3.

41 The *CUSO Forum,* December 1973, 24, stated that it was replacing the *Bulletin, Forum, Communique,* and *Memo. Communique,* published from 1969 to 1971, was intended as a vehicle for communication between CUSO/Ottawa and local committees. Not only did CUSO periodicals come and go; they also made frequent changes in regard to such matters as stylizing titles, providing dates of issues, and even pagination.

42 David Beer, "Zimbabwe: The Thoughts of a CUSO Volunteer from Zambia," *CUSO/SUCO Bulletin,* October 1967–January 1968, 20-21. Unlike Zimbabwe, Zambia, formerly Northern Rhodesia, won its independence through a long campaign of civil disobedience rather than protracted guerrilla warfare.

43 In 1968, Beer had contributed a section to *Man Deserves Man* (338-51), the content and tone of which, he told Ian Smillie in an early 1980s interview, now made him cringe; STC.

44 *CUSO Forum,* Christmas, 1973, cover story.

45 Ibid., January 1974, 4, 7.

46 Ibid., February-March 1974, 11; interview with McNeill, 22 September 2008; Smillie, *Lost Content,* 101-2.

47 "New Problems, Challenges Face Margo in Malawi," *CUSO Forum,* April-May 1974, and letter to editor from Terrance Cox, June 1974 issue, 5. See also Fall 1974 issue, 20, for discussion of the appropriateness – or not – of publishing a letter that Margo had written in good faith for her sponsor (a Saskatoon United Church Women's group) and then allowing it to be ridiculed in print.

48 "Soo Committee Expressed Strong Opinion," letter to editor, *CUSO Forum*, February-March 1974, 4; "Do It Yourself Kit Proposed," letter to editor, *CUSO Forum*, Summer 1974, 10; and "A Non-Declaration on Politicization," Fall 1974, 22.

49 See *CUSO Forum*, January 1974, 4, for "Point Made Point Taken"; February-March 1974, 4, for "Thought CUSO Was a Progressive Organization" and "Ted Burke Answers"; April-May 1974, 19-21, for "Public Affairs Updated," letter from David Gallagher, and unsigned follow-up comment, seemingly by Burke.

50 See footnote to "New Roles for CUSO Volunteers," *CUSO Forum*, Spring 1975, 15.

51 T.R.H. Davenport, *South Africa: A Modern History*, 3rd ed. (Toronto: University of Toronto Press, 1987), Chaps. 15, 16; Linda Freeman, *The Ambiguous Champion: Canada and South Africa in the Trudeau and Mulroney Years* (Toronto: University of Toronto Press, 1997), 19-29, for Diefenbaker's involvement.

52 Freeman, *Ambiguous Champion*, 55. On the generally contradictory tone of the white paper, see Robert Bothwell, *Alliance and Illusion: Canada and the World, 1945-1984* (Vancouver: UBC Press, 2007), 292-94.

53 *CUSO 71/Annual Review*, 8, LAC/CUSO, MG 28, I 323, vol. 74, file 33. See also "CUSO's Who's Who in the Field," *CUSO Forum*, Summer 1974, 16. CUSO's East and Central Africa volunteers were by then in Botswana, Malawi, Tanzania, and Zambia.

54 AGM Minutes, 1970, 7-8, in LAC/CUSO, MG 28, I 323, vol. 70, file 14; ibid., vol. 103, file 17, for press release; vol. 75, file 17, for Report to Parliamentary Sub-Committee on Development Assistance; vol. 50, files 27-29, for CUSO Brief on Southern Africa, 1970-1971, and related correspondence; and vol. 102, file 2, "Presentation to the Senate Commission on Foreign Affairs Representing Asia," by R.D.H. Sillery and David Catmur. The first document in the latter file dealt with southern Africa as well as Asia.

55 *Globe*, 14 November 1970.

56 LAC/CUSO, MG 28, I 323, vol. 75, file 16, for Sanger and the *Globe*'s response to him, and for Cumming to David Catmur and John Wood, 2 December 1970.

57 Ibid., for 11 December 1970 letter from lawyer, and file 14, for "Report to Board of Directors," 4-5 December 1970; vol. 50, file 27, memo from Iain [Thomson] to Bill, 27 May 1971; also vol. 102, file 5, for "Working Paper/CUSO Regional Meeting/Fund Raising."

58 *CUSO/SUCO Bulletin*, February 1966, 7.

59 UBC Archives, Conway fonds, box 6, file 11, CUSO, 1971, for report on the seminar.

60 For instance, Bonnie Greene, ed., *Canadian Churches and Foreign Policy* (Toronto: James Lorimer, 1990); John S. Saul, "Liberation Support and Anti-Apartheid Work as Seeds of Global Consciousness," in *New World Coming: The Sixties and the Shaping of Global Consciousness*, ed. Karen Dubinsky et al. (Toronto: Between the Lines, 2009), 135-36; David Sheinin, "Cuba's Long Shadow: The Progressive Church Movement and Canadian-Latin American Relations, 1970-87," in *Our Place in the Sun: Canada and Cuba in the Castro Era*, ed. Robert Wright and Lana Wylie (Toronto: University of Toronto Press, 2009), 121-42. For the leading roles of Western churches generally, see Organization for Economic Co-operation and Development, *Voluntary Aid for Development: The Role of Non-Governmental Organizations* (Paris: OECD, 1988), 19-21.

61 For more on Legge see Ruth Compton Brouwer, "When Missions Became Development: Ironies of 'NGOization' in Mainstream Canadian Churches in the 1960s," *Canadian Historical Review* 91, 4 (2010): 661-93, and for Pratt and "humane internationalism," *Internationalism under Strain: The North-South Policies of Canada, the Netherlands, Norway and Sweden*, ed. Cranford Pratt (Toronto: University of Toronto Press, 1989).

62 Garth Legge et al., *The Black Paper: An Alternative Policy for Canada towards Southern Africa*, published in September 1970 issue of *Behind the Headlines* and then made available in pamphlet

form through the Canadian Institute of International Affairs. Readers of the *CUSO Bulletin* were provided with a summary of the *Black Paper* in the Fall 1970 issue.

63 Saul, "Liberation Support," 135.

64 See ibid., 136-37, for TCLPAC and TCLSAC, and Saul, *Revolutionary Traveller: Freeze-Frames from a Life* (Winnipeg: Arbeiter Ring Publishing, 2009). Already in 1973 there were what CUSO called "action groups" on apartheid in six major Canadian cities. By the late 1970s, the number of such groups and the range of alliances had broadened; see, for instance, "What's On," *CUSO Forum*, December 1973, 24, and "CUSO, Labor, and Churches Join Forces in Anti-Apartheid Campaign," *CUSO Forum* 6, 2 (1978): 4. On CUSO as a particular target for criticism, see Smillie, *Lost Content*, 218-19.

65 "GATT-Fly Probes Our Trade Issues," *CUSO Forum*, February-March 1974, 10-11.

66 For instance, copy of Lorne Lewis to Mitchell Sharp, 29 April 1974, forwarded to Murray Thomson, LAC/CUSO, MG 28, I 323, vol. 115, file 23; John Ewing, "A Non-Declaration on Politicization," *CUSO Forum*, Fall 1974, 22. CUSO was being "used" by Communist-controlled international terrorism, Lewis wrote.

67 King Gordon to "Mike," 12 July 1966, in LAC/Gordon fonds, vol. 41, file 2 (italics added).

68 Smillie, *Lost Content*, 284. Interestingly, in 1967, four of SUCO's volunteers were anglophones; emails from Barbara Brown, 11 December 2011 and 18 January 2012. Brown was a TESL teacher in Madagascar.

69 "Report of the Executive Secretary," to Seventh AGM, 8-14 November 1968, 6-7; "The Seventh Annual Meeting," *CUSO/SUCO Forum*, January 1969, 5; Smillie, *Lost Content*, Chap. 23.

70 Smillie interview with Wendy Quarry, 26 May 1984, STC, and Smillie, *Lost Content*, Chap. 23. SUCO domestic staff had increased to ninety by 1972, Smillie writes, and "CUSO/SUCO had run up a deficit of almost a million dollars, most of it on the SUCO side" (289). Yet there were some within SUCO, including, in 1974, its unpopular executive director, Ron Leger, and overseas director Jean Pelletier, who were themselves unhappy with its extravagance, radical rhetoric and ideology, and lack of accountability (289, 294-301, 308). See also Bob Stanley, "AGM Rejects CUSO-SUCO Split," *CUSO Forum*, January 1975, 1: "The differences are not so much cultural and linguistic as ideological."

71 For instance, Rob Dumont, "CUSO ... As Respectable as Motherhood?," *CUSO Forum*, Summer 1974, 20; also Smillie interview with Robin Wilson, 10 August 1983, STC.

72 Mark Kurlansky, challenging the cliché, points out that some of the leading radicals in the US in 1968 were in fact over thirty. See Kurlansky, *1968: The Year That Rocked the World* (NY: Ballantine Books, 2004), 178.

73 "Murray Thomson Is New Director," *CUSO Forum*, January 1974, 2, and "Suteera Thomson," *CUSO Forum*, Summer 1980, 34; Smillie, *Lost Content*, Chap. 7; interview with Thomson, 21 June 2005, and follow-up conversations.

74 Smillie, *Lost Content*, 100, quoted passage cited in endnote 11, 376, as communication from Thomson to Smillie, 4 October 1973. My italics.

75 "CUSO Trends in 1974," *CUSO Forum*, January 1974, 2-3.

76 "Executive Secretary's Report to Mini-IRM," 31 May 1976, LAC/CUSO, MG 28, I 323, vol. 61, file 17.

77 Significantly, Thomson favoured the original term *executive secretary* over *executive director*. Looking back some thirty years later, Thomson believed that terms like *socialist* or *New Left* and *capitalist* or *pragmatist* had not accurately reflected the shades of opinion about development within CUSO at this period and affirmed that both factions had contributed something useful; personal conversations 21 June 2005, 31 October 2006, and 9 May 2007.

78 Stanley, "AGM Rejects CUSO-SUCO Split," 1; Thomson to Dear – [Staff], 13 December 1974, copy provided by Thomson; and interview with Thomson. Oxfam Canada avoided a similar protracted

struggle by formally agreeing in 1973 to the creation of a wholly independent Oxfam Québec; John MacFarlane, "The Consequences of Bilingual and Bicultural Tensions on the Canadian Aid Programme from 1968 to 1976" (master's thesis, Laval University, 1990), 71-74.

79 Quoted in Smillie, *Lost Content*, 107.

80 Consider, for instance, Thomson's gentle yet shrewd response to "Group Dislikes Bus Ads," in *CUSO Forum*, Summer 1974, 10.

81 *CUSO Forum* 5, 1 (1977): 6.

82 Wilson to W.E. McLoughlin, 3 February 1977, in LAC/CUSO, MG 28, I 323, vol. 61, file 5, CUSO/ SUCO Board Meetings – Miscellaneous Documents/1976-1977.

83 LAC/SUCO, MG 28, I 323, vol. 61, file 4, CUSO/SUCO – Board Meetings: Documentation – Media/1977, for "CUSO in the News," containing *Sun* article, 8 July 1977, and response of Wilson and Yvon Madore, 19 July 1977. Smillie's interview with Wilson (10 August 1983 in STC) contains detailed discussion of Wilson's disastrous appearance on Morton Shulman's CITY-TV program, which was followed the day after by the resignation of the businessman who was to have headed CUSO's national fundraising campaign. See also Smillie, *Lost Content*, 133-34.

84 Smillie, *Lost Content*, 115-18; Smillie's interviews with Stan Percival, 21 June 1983, and Lewis Perinbam, 10 August 1983, STC. For evidence that Wilson alienated even moderates within CUSO, see Memo to Wilson from Ginger MacColl, 26 July 1978, LAC/CUSO, MG 28, I 323, vol. 61, file 3.

85 In the early 1970s, the Christian Medical Commission (CMC) of the World Council of Churches sharply attacked medical missions' historic emphasis on trained professionals and infrastructure; see, for instance, address by Dr. William H. Foege, "Community Medicine," reprinted by CMC, ca. 1970, and included in sec. IX of "CUSO Readings in Health," LAC/CUSO, MG 28, I 323, vol. 45, file 1. While there was general agreement among faith-based and secular development specialists on the need for an increasing emphasis on preventive and public health measures, there was strong resistance to the extreme position that medical professionals should no longer be sent from the West, as the CUSO debate on health issues showed. On "barefoot doctors" at the AGM, see John Lute, "Barefoot Doctors Aid Professionals," *The Citizen (Ottawa)*, 9 December 1974, 2.

86 "The Basic Strategies Debate Continues," *CUSO Forum* 5, 2 (1977): 2 (Hilson), 3, 7 (Ramsay), and 3-6 (other contributors). See also Michael Oliver to Robin Wilson, 24 April 1978, and Wilson to Oliver, 7 June 1978, LAC/CUSO, MG 28, I 323, vol. 27, file 19. While visiting Tanzania from Carleton University, a long-time centre of support for CUSO, President Oliver was dismayed to learn from Tanzanian officials that CUSO/Tanzania proposed to stop placing secondary-school teachers in their country, a decision the officials regarded as a form of arrogant left-wing colonialism. Similar concerns about the decision-making processes behind the closing of programs in Malawi and Zambia are expressed in Ian Smillie's taped interview with Sharon Capeling (STC), in Smillie, *Lost Content*, 112-14, and in a letter from Malawi RV Rick Sutton, *CUSO Forum*, Winter 1979, 24-25.

87 Wilson may have been particularly frustrated by the suggestion that CUSO's overseas regions should function as genuinely "worker-controlled" structures (with CUSO in Canada playing only an advisory role), and that these "workers" should serve only in states striving to build socialism; "CUSO Forum Supplement," published with *CUSO Forum* 5, 1 (1977): 11-18. Ozzie Schmidt recalls that, as one of the two field staff officers in Botswana at this time, he was sometimes frustrated by the rigidity and moral certainty of some on the left in these debates, notwithstanding his own general sympathy with the left-leaning orientation of CUSO's ECSA region (response to questionnaire, April 2007).

88 Memos from Wilson, 9 May 1977, on CUSO/"Decentralization and the B.S. Debate," and 12 August 1977, acknowledging strong criticisms of his approach ("hierarchical, dictatorial, anti-democratic, and counter to everything CUSO stands for"), in LAC/CUSO, MG 28, I 323, vol. 98, file 8.

89 Smillie, *Lost Content*, 116-18 (quotation at 117), and Smillie, interview with Stan Percival, 21 June 1983, STC.

90 For distinctive insider overviews of CUSO's involvement in the region, see Smillie, *Lost Content,* Chaps. 15-17, and Christopher Neal, David Beer, John van Mossel, John Saxby, and Joan Anne Nolan, "CUSO and Liberation Movements in Southern Africa: An Appeal for Solidarity," in *Aid as Peacemaker: Canadian Development Assistance and Third World Conflict,* ed. Robert Miller (Ottawa: Carleton University Press, 1992), 123-41.

91 Ali A. Mazrui and Michael Tidy, *Nationalism and New States in Africa from about 1935 to the Present* (London: Heinemann, 1984), 294-96; quoted statement by Nyerere in *CUSO/SUCO Bulletin,* February-April 1968, n.p.; Smillie interview with Sharon Capeling, 29 October 1983, STC. Capeling had sought out Tanzania as a desirable cross-posting after serving in Barbados, but following her arrival in 1970, she became disillusioned by the gap between Nyerere's socialist aspirations and his achievements, and by what she regarded as the political naïveté of CUSO local field staff.

92 Smillie, *Lost Content,* Chap. 15; "Focus on Tanzania," *CUSO/SUCO Bulletin,* May 1966, cover story, and 16-17 for narrative account by Rudy Carter, one of several Canadians among many other expatriates teaching at the University College of Dar.

93 Saul, *Revolutionary Traveller;* "Beer Back in Zambia," *CUSO Forum,* Winter 1979, 41; Smillie interview with David Beer, n.d., STC. In the interview, Beer explained that most connections with and support for the Angolan movement were through SUCO.

94 Saul, *Revolutionary Traveller;* interview with Cranford Pratt, 20 February 2007.

95 John T. Saywell, ed., *Canadian Annual Review of Politics and Public Affairs, 1973* (Toronto: University of Toronto Press, 1974), 262-63; Freeman, *Ambiguous Champion,* 123, 124.

96 Freeman, *Ambiguous Champion,* 123, regarding CIDA aid to NGOs. Zimbabwean leader Edward Ndlovu, for instance, visited Canada in the early 1970s and again later in the decade with colleague Joshua Nkomo; interview with Mary Krug Ndlovu, 23 September 2010, and "Report from the Front/Nkomo Visits Canada," *CUSO Forum* 6, 1 (1978): 11-12.

97 Branka Lapajne, *CUSO and Radicalism* (Toronto: Citizens for Foreign Aid Reform, 1983), quotations from introduction by Research Director Paul Fromm. Five years earlier, Oxfam Canada's political activism had resulted in a warning from Ottawa that it could lose its charitable status if it continued to speak out; MacFarlane, "Consequences," 75.

98 "Beer Back in Zambia," 41-42; CV dated June 2009 as provided by Beer.

99 Mazrui and Tidy, *Nationalism,* 144-51, for the war of independence in Zimbabwe and the ethnic, ideological, and personality disputes between ZAPU and ZANU.

100 Smillie interview with Beer, STC, and author interview with Beer.

101 LAC/CUSO, MG 28, I 323, vol. 50, file 5, "CUSO in the News," issue 2, for copy of article by Ron MacGillivray, "CUSO Steps up Relief to Rhodesian Refugees," from *Connections: News about Canada and the Third World.* See also "Report From Lusaka," *CUSO Forum* 6, 1 (1978): 11-13, for other CUSO projects in southern Africa aiding liberation movements in the late 1970s.

102 Author interview with Beer; Smillie, *Lost Content,* 219-24. Examples of the media coverage can be found in LAC/CUSO, MG 28, I 323, vol. 50, file 5, "CUSO in the News," issues 1 and 2, 1979. The two articles cited are in issue 2.

103 Luc Bertrand to Bishop Russell F. Brown, 18 April, 1979, in LAC/CUSO, MG 28, I 323, vol. 115, file 23 (for quotation); Memo from Colin Freebury to Field Staff, 3 August 1979, in ibid., vol. 21, file 1, Administration: General Correspondence; Smillie interview with Stan Percival, STC, and Smillie, *Lost Content,* 118-19. See also Diane Francis, "Go Abroad, Young Man, the Home Front's Hell," *Maclean's,* 26 March 1979, 45-46, on the internal dissent, particularly over SUCO extremism, and possible consequences for funding.

104 "CUSO Is Worth Shoring Up," *London Evening Free Press,* 28 March 1979; letter from Perinbam to *Regina Leader-Post,* 7 April 1979.

105 LAC/CUSO, MG 28, I 323, vol. 61, file 34, CUSO Executive Director's Office – Miscellaneous Correspondence, 1977-1981, for CIDA – statement/Appendix A/"CUSO/SUCO – The Next Steps";

Globe and Mail, 8 June 1979, for "CIDA Lifts Financial Ban on CUSO after Management Moves Accepted."

106 "Smillie Named CUSO Director in Shakeup over Quebec Wing," *Globe and Mail,* 25 August 1979; "Message from the Executive Director," *CUSO Forum* 1, 2 (1979): 47.

107 "Message from the Executive Director," and "Inter Pares and CUSO on the Same Wavelength," *CUSO Forum* 6, 3 (1978): 22-23. Smillie does not discuss his own CUSO roles in *Land of Lost Content,* but there are references to this period in Chaps. 8 and 26, esp. 119, 358. Regarding new appointments to the board and the independent committees, see LAC/CUSO, MG 28, I 323, vol. 58, file 1, CUSO Board of Directors Correspondence, for Smillie to JM, 8 Nov 1979. For the meetings with the two ministers, see ibid., vol. 171, file 13, report on "Meeting with the Honourable Flora MacDonald," n.d., and "Meeting with Mark MacGuigan, May 1, 1980."

108 Smillie, *Lost Content,* 305-6. After all the ink and energy that had been expended over CUSO/ SUCO controversies, the reference in the *CUSO Forum* to the new relationship was brief and anodyne; "Important Dates in CUSO's History," Spring and Summer issue, 1981, 16.

109 Smillie, *Lost Content,* 307-8; MacFarlane, "Consequences," 90. A different and much smaller SUCO was later reborn; SUCO, "Historique," http://suco.org/suco/solidarite-union-cooperation/ historique/.

110 "Paying the Piper: CIDA and Canadian NGOs," in *Canadian International Development Assistance Policies: An Appraisal,* ed. Cranford Pratt (Montreal/Kingston: McGill-Queen's University Press, 1994), 91-92. See also David R. Morrison, *Aid and Ebb Tide: A History of CIDA and Canadian Development Assistance* (Waterloo: Wilfrid Laurier University Press in association with the North-South Institute, 1998), 68-70, and Tim Brodhead and Brent Herbert-Copley with Anne-Marie Lambert, *Bridges of Hope? Canadian Voluntary Agencies and the Third World* (Ottawa: North-South Institute, 1988), 4. Writing in 1991 about the evolving relationship between the federal government and development NGOs, Brian K. Murphy argued that many of the latter had effectively been co-opted by their increased dependency on government funding; "Canadian NGOs and the Politics of Participation," in *Conflicts of Interest Canada and the Third World,* ed. Jamie Swift and Brian Tomlinson (Toronto: Between the Lines, 1991), 161-211. For such relationships in international perspective, see Terje Tvedt, *Angels of Mercy or Development Diplomats? NGOs and Foreign Aid* (Trenton, NJ: Africa World Press, 1998).

111 "Canadians Get a Heck of a Bargain for the Money," interview with Smillie, *CUSO Forum,* Summer 1980, 39-41 (quotations on 41).

112 Untitled commentary, probably by Ted Burke, *CUSO Forum,* April-May 1974, 20-21.

113 Smillie, *Lost Content,* 206.

114 Smillie, "Heck of a Bargain," 41. See Tvedt, *Angels of Mercy,* 46, for something similar: Norway's use of NGOs as "alternative channels [for providing aid to or establishing contacts with] politically sensitive areas and groups."

115 Smillie interview with Bogdasavich, STC, and Smillie, *Lost Content,* Chap. 11; LAC/CUSO, MG 28, I 323, vol. 36, file, 32, for contract involving CUSO, CIDA, and several Canadian universities in the provision of teaching services in Cuba, and ibid., vol. 129, file 16, for "Summary of CUSO/ SUCO Activities in 1976-77," 29, 31. See also Robert Wright, *Three Nights in Havana: Pierre Trudeau, Fidel Castro and the Cold War* (Toronto: Harper, 2007), 122-23.

116 Whitney Lackenbauer, *An Insider's Look at External Affairs: The Memoirs of Mark MacGuigan* (Calgary: University of Calgary Press, 2002), 128-29 (quotation); "CUSO Cuba: After 12 Years Future Uncertain," *CUSO Forum,* Spring-Summer 1981, 38-41.

117 Copy of form letter from Murray Thomson to all staff, 13 December 1974; Ian Smillie's "Points for Discussion with Hon. Flora MacDonald," n.d., in LAC/CUSO, MG 28, I 323, vol. 171, file 13.

118 Report on CUSO by Dr. Irene [? illeg.] Pinkau of International Secretariat for Volunteer Service, 1975, in LAC/CUSO, MG 28, I 323, vol. 76, file 9.

119 I discuss RVs' presence in CIDA in Chap. 5. During the late twentieth century, the governments of other donor countries in the North also developed collaborative relationships with NGOs, but personnel movement from NGOs into state agencies seems to have been especially common in Canada. For the relationships in other countries, see Tvedt, *Angels of Mercy,* Chap. 2, and *Stakeholders: Government-NGO Partnerships for International Development,* ed. Henny Helmich and Ian Smillie in collaboration with Tony German and Judith Randel (London: Earthscan Publications, 1999), esp. Chap. 2.

120 See "Development Education under Fire," *CUSO Forum* 5, 1 (1983): 39, for reference to some of these MPs and others as CUSO's defenders in the face of right-wing attacks. See also *CUSO Forum* November 1983, 13, "CUSO Friend Dies," regarding Brewin; and, for Forsey and others, LAC/CUSO, MG 28, I 323, vol. 171, file 7, Senator/MP Campaigns 1976-1979. In 1976, Forsey organized a luncheon for some fifteen MPs with an interest in CUSO. I thank Stephanie Bangarth for sharing relevant documents from the R. Gordon Fairweather fonds at LAC, MG 32 C72, vol. 8, file 13.

121 "Proshika ... Canada's Best Aid Project," *CUSO Forum* 6, 3 (1978): 20-21. See also "Proshika Phase II," and "Roche in Asia: An Unusual Travelogue," *CUSO Forum* 2, 3 (1980): 13, 15-16.

122 See Robert MacDonald, "A Hardnosed Senator," *Toronto Sunday Sun,* 19 August 1979, for this journalist's view that both Roche and Flora MacDonald had been "sucked in by the local propaganda machine in the four African countries visited."

123 Smillie, *Lost Content,* 223-24; author interview with David Beer.

124 "Taxpayer Dollars in Guerilla Warchests?," *Globe and Mail,* 9 August 1979; LAC/CUSO, MG 28, I 323, vol. 50, file 6, Public Affairs: CUSO, n.d., for CUSO reports September-October '79, and ibid, vol. 171, file 13, for Ian Smillie's account of his meeting with Flora MacDonald and her supportive comments about CUSO's work in refugee camps and about David and Irene Beer. Later, especially in response to hostile public opinion, Conservative policy on aid to southern Africa and particularly to the ANC *did* become more restrictive, a pattern continued by the Liberals when they returned to government; Freeman, *Ambiguous Champion,* 123-26.

125 See *CUSO Forum,* Summer 1981, 24, for Sanger's retrospective on CUSO and his own involvement. David Beer remembered Michael Valpy as another supportive journalist.

126 For instance, Richard Gwyn, "Is This the Way to Spend Our Money?," *Toronto Star,* 20 January 1979; Rosemary Speirs, "Realism Replaces Idealism among CUSO Volunteers," *Globe and Mail,* 28 August 1979; "CUSO Is Worth Shoring Up," *London Evening Free Press,* 28 March 1979.

127 Marilyn Dulop, "African Frontier Tests Mettle of Canadians," *Toronto Star,* 28 August 1979.

128 LAC/CUSO, MG 28, I 323, vol. 50, file 5, "CUSO in the News," 1 and 2, 1979, contains copies of stories from papers like the *Eastern Graphic* of Montague, PEI.

129 Review in *CUSO Forum,* November 1985, 6.

130 Handwritten drafts of proposed resolutions, seemingly prepared at BC RV conference for AGM, LAC/CUSO, MG 28, I 323, vol. 85, file 18.

131 "Women and CUSO," *CUSO Forum,* Spring 1975, 2-3.

132 Ibid., 4, and January 1975, 11.

133 For a broad overview of second-wave feminism in Canada, see Alison Prentice et al., *Canadian Women: A History* (Toronto: Harcourt Brace Jovanovich, 1988), Chaps. 13, 14, and for more specialized attention, Nancy Adamson, Linda Briskin, and Margaret McPhail, *Feminist Organizing for Change: The Contemporary Women's Movement in Canada* (Toronto: Oxford University Press, 1998), and Mills, *Empire Within,* Chap. 5.

134 Myrna Kostash, *Long Way from Home: The Story of the Sixties Generation in Canada* (Toronto: James Lorimer and Company, 1980), chapter titled "The Rising of the Women"; Bryan D. Palmer, *Canada's 1960s: The Ironies of Identity in a Rebellious Era* (Toronto: University of Toronto Press, 2009), 297-304.

135 Kostash, *Long Way from Home*, 171-79, and Palmer, *Canada's 1960s*, 302-3; Adamson, Briskin, McPhail, *Feminist Organizing for Change*, 45-46, 201.

136 See LAC/CUSO, MG 28, I 323, vol. 101, file 14, for Minutes of Meeting of Area Review Board, 23 September [1969] containing "CUSO Policy on Payment of Birth Control Pills"; it was agreed that CUSO would pay for all pills, "no distinction being made between married and single women, and that we would try to get as many free supplies as feasible." But for some unease about unreservedly providing the pill to single "girls," see paper showing discussion of dental and contraceptive policy in ibid., vol. 35, file 3, Health Services: Advisory Review Board, 1968-1970.

137 Smillie interview with Capeling.

138 "New Faces in CUSO Ottawa," *CUSO Forum* 4, 3 (1976): 5, showing that of eight recently appointed staffpersons, four were women; Duchesne to Betty Plewes, 23 August 1977, LAC/CUSO, MG 28, I 323, vol. 169, file 11, Women – General, 1976-1979, for quotation. See "First Impressions," *CUSO Forum*, November 1990, 1, regarding Ghana RV Lyse Blanchard as CUSO's first female and first francophone executive director. For Catley-Carlson, see Morrison, *Aid and Ebb Tide*, esp. Chap. 7.

139 LAC/CUSO, MG 28, I 323, vol. 169, file 11, for Memo to all FSOs from Duchesne, 10 September 1976, regarding plans to prepare a brochure that would deal with women in all aspects of CUSO, from their presence in the Ottawa office to targeting their needs in specific projects.

140 See Chapter 2, 72-73. Jonathan Zimmerman writes that while straining to be sensitive to local cultures, young Peace Corps men were often woefully sexist in responding to the particular issues and needs facing their female counterparts; *Innocents Abroad: American Teachers in the American Century* (Cambridge: Harvard University Press, 2006), 103-5. I did not hear of or read about a similar degree of insensitivity in CUSO.

141 Ester Boserup, *Women's Role in Economic Development* (New York: St. Martin's Press, 1970); Paul Kennedy, *The Parliament of Man: The Past, Present, and Future of the United Nations* (Toronto: Harper Collins, 2006), esp. Chap. 5; Devaki Jain, *Women, Development and the UN: A Sixty-Year Quest for Equality and Justice* (Bloomington: Indiana University Press, 2005); Betty Plewes and Rieky Stuart, "Women and Development Revisited: The Case for a Gender and Development Approach," 107-32, in *Conflicts of Interest*.

142 Margaret Hilson, "World Population Conference and Tribune – Bucharest," *CUSO Forum*, Fall 1974, 6-8 (quotation on 7).

143 Michael Sinclair, "'I Just Saw God.' 'What Did He Look Like?' 'She's Black,'" *CUSO Forum*, January 1975, 8-10.

144 Morrison, *Aid and Ebb Tide*, 239; Plewes and Stuart, "Women and Development Revisited," 125; profile of Walmsley in *CUSO Forum*, February 1988, 4. As a young political science professor, Walmsley had attended CUSO's founding meeting in June 1961 and served for six years as campus chairperson at Brandon University.

145 *CUSO Forum*, twentieth anniversary edition, Spring and Summer, 1981. Clyde Sanger referred to CUSO's plans for assisting in agricultural projects and proposals put forward by a women's group in newly independent Zimbabwe (24).

146 I discuss Capeling's career more fully in Chap. 5.

147 Norman Simon, "Spreading the Word among Women," and Betty Plewes, "The Market Mammies of West Africa," *CUSO Forum*, Winter 1979, 17-19, 21. See also *CUSO Forum*, Summer 1980, for special Asia edition, and *CUSO Forum*, Winter 1980, for special issue on Latin America, esp. 15-16, for Virginia Smith, "The Triple Day," on women's lives in the shanty towns of Peru.

148 Plewes and Stuart, "Women and Development Revisited," and *Two Halves Make a Whole: Balancing Gender Relations in Development* (Ottawa: Canadian Council for International Cooperation and MATCH International, 1991); Ian Smillie, "The Pink Elephant: Empowerment and the Status of Women," in Smillie, *The Alms Bazaar: Altruism under Fire; Non-Profit Organizations and International Development* (London: IT Publications, 1995).

149 Morrison, *Aid and Ebb Tide*, 239; Plewes and Stuart, "Women and Development Revisited," 125-26; "Area I," *CUSO Forum*, Summer 1980, 5.

150 This is Sean Mills's apt phrase from his introduction to *The Empire Within* (15).

151 See, for instance, Martin L. Friedland, *The University of Toronto: A History* (Toronto: University of Toronto Press, 2002), 629-30. Although about half the student body at U of T self-identified as non-white by 1994, ad hoc practices rather than an official policy of affirmative action to assist members of visible minorities to obtain faculty positions continued notwithstanding some student protests.

152 For instance, Tim Scorer, "Volunteerism – Outdated in the 70s," *CUSO Forum*, Winter 1969-70, 14.

153 My thanks to the RV who shared this information and the verse, written in the style of an award-winning novelty tune from 1964, "Hello Muddah, Hello Fadduh (A Letter from Camp)."

154 Scott Stossel, *Sarge: The Life and Times of Sargent Shriver* (Washington: Smithsonian Books, 2004), 251-55; PeaceCorpsWriters.org, "The Infamous Peace Corps postcard," at http://www.peacecorps writers.org/pages/2000/0001/001pchist.html.

155 Barbara Heron, *Desire for Development: Whiteness, Gender, and the Helping Imperative* (Waterloo: Wilfrid Laurier University Press, 2007).

156 Nesta Wyn Ellis, "Complaints about Volunteers," *CUSO Forum*, June 1974, 7. See also ibid., January 1975, 16, for Barbadian journalist Rommel Lawrence's "Caribbean Volunteer Corps?" While Lawrence praised volunteers who came from outside the region, he speculated that behind the façade of friendliness there was a "general shunning of things West Indian." The "answer to social and economic uplift," he believed, was neither Black Power nor outside volunteer assistance but rather an indigenous Caribbean Volunteer Corps.

157 Perinbam address, 2 December 1972, 3, in Gordon fonds, MG 30-C 241, vol. 40, file 13.

158 *CUSO Bulletin*, 4/71, 2, regarding the Thailand committee; email from Chris Bryant, 25 June 2012, for ECSA's initiative regarding board representation.

159 Jonathan Zimmerman, "Beyond Double Consciousness: Black Peace Corps Volunteers in Africa, 1961-1971," *Journal of American History* 82, 3 (1995): 999-1028. While the Peace Corps was eager to attract African-American volunteers, it eschewed questions about race on application forms. CUSO and other Canadian volunteer-sending agencies would not have had a significant number of potential volunteers from majority-world backgrounds until near the end of the twentieth century; see, for instance, "Leading Source Countries of Immigrants, Selected Years," in R. Douglas Francis, Richard Jones, Donald B. Smith, *Destinies: Canadian History since Confederation*, 5th ed. (Toronto: Thomson Nelson, 2004), 497. In *Generation NGO* (Toronto: Between the Lines, 2011), ix, editors Alisha Nicole Apale and Valerie Stam suggest that even in the twenty-first century there has not been a dramatic change in the ethnic and socio-economic background of volunteers. Cuso International's recently implemented diaspora volunteering program reflects a creative effort at broadening its outreach.

160 Information on Dennis September supplied by David Beer in email to author, 2 July 2012.

161 For instance, Dr. Rawle Frederick and Gloria Frederick, Montrealers from the Caribbean who volunteered with CUSO in Tanzania in the mid-1970s and, while there, were invited to attend meetings of the sixth Pan African Congress as guests of a congress organizer; *CUSO Forum*, May 1975, 1, for photos and biographical profiles, and 2-3, 5, for their article on the congress.

162 Undated document, 21 pages, title page missing, beginning "Introduction," LAC/CUSO, MG 28, I 323, vol. 52, file 4, titled "ECSA Coordinators' Meetings," 1981-82.

163 See *1974-1975 Annual Report*, LAC/CUSO, MG 28, I 323, vol. 40, file 17.

164 See, for instance, ibid., vol. 52, file 2, for memo from Ian Smillie, 18 September 1981, to Board Executive Committee regarding "Program Approach Phase II," and vol. 51, file 31, for undated memo from CF to field staff officers regarding "Program Planning in CUSO – 1982-1985." The

latter memo indicated that a "smokescreen of numbers" was sometimes used in communicating with CIDA in order to overstate volunteer involvement in some overseas programs.

165 Smillie, *Lost Content,* Chap. 3.
166 Ibid., 24, 43-45, 50-51; *CUSO Forum,* January 1984, 19, for article on the US invasion and the evacuation of volunteers. One of the evacuees was Trinidad-born writer Dionne Brand, who later wrote about the invasion in *Chronicle of the Hostile Sun* and at least one other work; Athabasca University, "Canadian Writers," http://www2.athabascau.ca/cll/writers/english/writers/dbrand/dbrand.php.
167 My thanks to Selena Tapper for speedy and helpful reflections on her involvement with CUSO (email, 30 June 2012), and to Bev Burke and Betty Plewes for facilitating this contact and sharing their recollections about the late Marlene Green and the comparative salience of gender and race issues in CUSO at this period (Burke, email and phone conversation, 27 and 28 June 2012; Plewes, phone conversation, 28 June 2012).
168 Emails from Ian Smillie, executive director 1979-83 (23 June 2012) and Chris Bryant, executive director 1983-90 (25 June 2012), both of whom Kindy shared personal information and added to my stock of information about CUSO staff members from majority-world backgrounds.
169 Frank A. Hegel, "Stop Recruiting B.A. Generalists," and Margaret Paterson, "Recruiter Replies," *CUSO Forum,* January 1975, 13-14.
170 John Ewing, "A Non-Declaration on Politicization," *CUSO Forum,* Fall 1974, 22.
171 "Open Letter from the Chairman of the Board," *CUSO Forum,* July 1976, 7.
172 Smillie, "Canadians Get a Heck of a Bargain for the Money."
173 *Lost Content,* Chap. 9, quotation at 134. Smillie's impatience with what he then regarded as needlessly inflammatory rhetoric is even more evident in the interviews he conducted with various CUSO staff in preparation for writing the book.
174 "Message from CUSO's Executive Director" and "Development Education under Fire," and Hilborn's "CUSO Politics and Soviet Strategy," *Forum,* Winter 1983, 1, 7-8, 39; ibid., June 1983, 16, for letters from John F. Godfrey and Paul Puritt. Godfrey, a member of the CUSO Board of Directors and the President of University of King's College, Halifax, criticized Smillie for comparing apartheid to the Holocaust, while Puritt, Oxfam Canada's program development officer for Southern Africa, was scathing about the "obscenity" of giving space to a letter by Hilborn.

Chapter 4: "Big Is Beautiful"

1 *CUSO Forum,* Winter 1979, 30-31.
2 Toyin Falola and Matthew M. Heaton, *A History of Nigeria* (Cambridge: Cambridge University Press, 2008), Chap. 7; Michael Crowder, *The Story of Nigeria* (London: Faber and Faber, 4th ed., 1978), 12, for population figure.
3 Kevin A. Spooner, *Canada, the Congo Crisis, and UN Peacekeeping, 1960-64* (Vancouver: UBC Press, 2009). Writing in 1962, a US development specialist on Africa described Nigeria as an "oasis of democratic development in an arid desert of authoritarian-inclined African states"; Larry Grubbs, *Secular Missionaries: Americans and African Development in the 1960s* (Amherst: University of Massachusetts Press, 2009), 69.
4 "CUSO Seeks 50 Teachers for Nigeria," *CUSO Bulletin,* April 1962, cover.
5 "Chairman's Report – 1961-62," 9 June 1962, and undated form letter from Bill McWhinney, Library and Archives Canada (LAC), CUSO fonds, MG 28, I 323, vol. 61, file 39 (hereafter LAC/CUSO, MG 28, I 323, with volume and file number). See also ibid., vol. 26, file 5, for "Canadian Candidates Recommended by C.U.S.O. for Teaching Positions in Nigeria," and "Minutes of the Meeting of National Advisory Selection Board," 16 April 1962, for Lewis Perinbam's comments on Nigeria's request, and Ian Smillie, *The Land of Lost Content: A History of CUSO* (Toronto: Deneau, 1985), 57.

6   Interview with Roy Fischer, 30 August 2007, and Fischer response to questionnaire. (Unless stated otherwise, all interviews cited in this book were conducted by the author. The questionnaire referred to here and elsewhere in the notes was prepared by the author.)

7   Eme N. Ekekwe and Suzanne Veit, *CUSO/Nigeria: A 25 Year Retrospective Evaluation*, vol. 1 (Port Harcourt, Nigeria, and Victoria, Canada: Uniport Konsult and Fulcrum Consultants, 1986), 9.

8   Crowder, *Story of Nigeria*, 195 (for quotation); Elizabeth Isichei, *A History of the Igbo People* (London: Macmillan, 1976), Chaps. 11, 12 (199 for illiteracy rate).

9   A. Babs Fafunwa, *History of Education in Nigeria* (London: George Allen and Unwin, 1974), Chap. 6, and 204-5 for expenditures; see also Lamin Sanneh, *West African Christianity: The Religious Impact* (Maryknoll: Orbis Books, 1995), 151-58. Regarding the search for one thousand teachers, see H.O. Moran, "Canada's Educational Aid Programmes Including Service Abroad for Canadian Teachers," 5, in LAC/CUSO, MG 28, I 323, vol. 128, file 20.

10   Robin O. Matthews, "Canada and Anglophone Africa," in *Canada and the Third World*, eds. Peyton V. Lyon and Tareq Y. Ismael (Toronto: Macmillan, 1976), 60-132, esp. 90-91, 104-7; Moran, "Canada's Educational Aid Programmes," 4 (for eleven teachers); Perinbam to C.R. Patterson, 4 December 1961, in LAC/CUSO, MG 28, I 323, vol. 24, file 15.

11   Geoffrey Johnston, *Of God and Maxim Guns: Presbyterianism in Nigeria, 1846-1966* (Waterloo: Wilfrid Laurier University Press, 1988).

12   Canada, Library of Parliament, "Oral History Project," transcript of interview with McLean conducted by Tom Earle, April-June 1993 (hereafter, Earle interview with McLean), 9-11; author interview with Barbara and Walter McLean, 23 March 2007. See also Smillie, *Lost Content*, 58-60.

13   Interview with Barbara and Walter McLean, and Earle interview with Walter McLean. See also Presbyterian Church in Canada, Archives, Toronto (hereafter PCA), box 1989-101/103-G-13, Presbyterian Church of Nigeria/McLean Walter, for correspondence between Ted Johnson, McLean, and others dealing with McLean's appointment and activities. Included there is "McLean Newsletter No. 2," June 1963, containing references to elite Nigerian government officials in McLean's church.

14   Walter McLean to Edmonds, 29 March 1965, LAC/CUSO, MG 28, I 323, vol. 83, file 31, External Affairs Correspondence. McLean also reported having placed a doctor, nurses, and laboratory workers in the previous year.

15   Smillie, *Lost Content*, 59, and Smillie interview with Bill McNeill, 25 July 1983, in Smillie Tape Collection (hereafter STC); author interview with Walter McLean. Motor bikes gave volunteers a means to escape the confines of their posting and link up with fellow volunteers on weekends and holidays. While they were instructed by CUSO not to have automobiles unless they were work requirements, motorbikes were recognized as a reasonable acquisition. CUSO even arranged for loans to help volunteers purchase bikes, at the same time instructing them to obtain crash helmets and driving permits. These arrangements appear to have been regularized by McLean's successor; D.B. Marson to Timothy Brodhead, 12 November 1965, and accompanying loan form and undated memorandum from Bill McNeill (probably Autumn 1965) to "All volunteers," copies provided by Brodhead.

16   Interview with Bill McNeill, 22 September 2008. Unless otherwise shown, information about McNeill is drawn from this interview.

17   Bezanson, response to questionnaire, February 2011. When Bezanson finally quit in frustration, CUSO arranged a transfer for him to a much better school in the Western Region, the memory of which remained "a permanent joy."

18   Interview with Ian Smillie, 24 June 2005. As noted in Chap. 1, many mission placements made few or no religious demands on volunteers. No doubt this was partly an outcome of careful placement practices by field staff.

19   John T. Saywell, ed., *Canadian Annual Review for 1968* (Toronto: University of Toronto Press, 1969), 259-68, for "The Tragedy of Biafra"; Falola and Heaton, *A History of Nigeria*, 180, for estimate

of deaths. Writing soon after the war, journalist John de St. Jorre, who made three visits to Biafra during the conflict, gave a much lower estimate, as did fellow journalist Guy Arnold in 2005; see de St. Jorre, *The Nigerian Civil War* (London: Hodder and Stoughton, 1972), 412, and Arnold, *Africa: A Modern History* (London: Atlantic Books, 2005), 213.

20 Isichei, *History of the Igbo People*, 241, quoting John Ovinbo, and Chap. 15 for background to war and the war years; Chinua Achebe, *The Education of a British-Protected Child* (New York: Knopf, 2009), 30.

21 Estimates of the number killed in the massacre vary widely. Falola and Heaton, *A History of Nigeria*, 120, cites a range of between 7,000 and 50,000. Isichei, *A History of the Igbo People*, 473, writes that "perhaps six to eight thousand" were killed in what some began calling a pogrom. Meanwhile, Igbo living in the Western Region also became part of the refugee flight back to the homeland.

22 Falola and Heaton, *A History of Nigeria*, 122. The division of the country into twelve states by the federal government was viewed by Ojukwu as a further and final act of provocation.

23 De St. Jorre, *Nigerian Civil War*, Chaps. 7-9. De St. Jorre writes that "the relief operation began to grow [in 1968] until by the summer of 1969 it had surpassed all similar crises since the Second World War ... Both bodies worked on each side of the line but the I.C.R.C. played the larger part in Nigeria and the Churches the most effective role in Biafra" [238-39].

24 Crowder, *Story of Nigeria*, Chap. 18, quotations at 272, 276. Moreover, during the war years many Igbo evidently continued to live safely in federally held territory; Falola and Heaton, *History of Nigeria*, 177.

25 Memo from John Baigent to all volunteers, 16 January 1966, and from Jon Church, 26 May 1967. Baigent was responsible for the West Africa desk at CUSO/Ottawa until he was succeeded by Church. Both memos provided by Brodhead.

26 Turner newsletter to volunteers, written from Ibadan, n.d., copy provided by Brodhead.

27 Smillie interview with Turner, n.d., STC; author interview with Turner, June 2011. Quoted phrases are from the Smillie interview. Subsequent references to Turner's involvement come from these interviews unless otherwise shown.

28 Robert Bothwell, *Alliance and Illusion: Canada and the World, 1945-1984* (Vancouver: UBC Press, 2007), 307.

29 One much-told story about a mother who arrived naked on a packed refugee train from the North carrying her child's severed head was included in Chimamanda Ngozi Adichie's novel about the civil war, *Half of a Yellow Sun* (New York: Knopf, 2006). Walter McLean's friend N.U. Akpan writes of having personally witnessed the arrival of the infamous train; *The Struggle for Secession, 1966-1970: A Personal Account of the Nigerian Civil War* (London: Frank Cass, 1972), xii.

30 Smillie, *Lost Content*, Chap. 5; Donald Barry, "Interest Groups and the Foreign Policy Process: The Case of Biafra," in *Pressure Group Behaviour in Canadian Politics*, ed. A Paul Pross (Toronto: McGraw-Hill-Ryerson, 1975), 115-47; "The Tragedy of Biafra." For the references to Wanzel and North, see "How to Be a Global Villager," and "The Girl Who Wouldn't Leave Biafra," *Maclean's*, February 1969, 45, 48.

31 For the 1968 volunteer appointments see D.G. Simpson, "Report of the 1968 CUSO West Africa Orientation," 2, in LAC/CUSO, MG 28, I 323, vol. 48, file 12. For the need for caution in selecting volunteers, see ibid., vol. 85, file 5, for Simpson's memo to Jon Church, stamped 20 December 1967; ibid., file 8, for Simpson to Church, 28 April 1968, regarding the Midwest, and file 7 for Simpson memo to West Africa volunteers, 14 May 1968, regarding Brodhead's appointment. As CUSO's temporary regional coordinator, based in Ghana, Simpson had visited parts of Nigeria in November 1967 and would do so again with Bill McNeill early in 1968.

32 A memo from Canada's External Affairs Department in the fall of 1967 had assured CUSO's Jon Church that northern Nigeria was considered a safe area for foreign nationals; see ibid., vol. 85, file 6, for West Africa Regional Co-ordinator, memo of 17 October 1967 from Church to Don

Simpson. For Sanger's view, see his *Half a Loaf: Canada's Semi-Role in Developing Countries* (Toronto: Ryerson Press, 1969), 1.

33 Tim Brodhead's recollection is that perhaps as many as 90 percent of the board was pro-Biafran; interview with author, 22 June 2009.

34 McNeill, "Report on the West African Programme," 5-10, copy in Fischer Collection.

35 For Brodhead, Smillie, *Lost Content,* 75-76, and author interview with Brodhead. For Smillie quotation, see conclusions to Lynn Taylor's "West Africa Programme/Paper for CUSO Executive Committee Meeting, April 10, 1969," in LAC/CUSO, MG 28, I 323, vol. 11, file 21.

36 Smillie interview with Bogdasavich, 27 July 1983, STC.

37 Numerical data about volunteers are from "Information Guide: Nigeria," n.d. [1970], 22, in LAC/CUSO, MG 28, I 323, vol. 47, file 27. In some parts of the federation, volunteers generally, and Peace Corps volunteers in particular, were suspected of being spies; memo to Jon Church from Don Simpson, received 20 December 1967, in ibid., vol. 85, file 5. The Peace Corps would later phase out in Nigeria.

38 Mitchell Sharp, *Which Reminds Me ... A Memoir* (Toronto: University of Toronto Press, 1994), 207; "Biafra," in *Canadian Annual Review,* 1970, 357-58. The Canadian government had previously been aiding both sides through the ICRC.

39 De St. Jorre, *Nigerian Civil War,* Chap. 15, quoting unidentified correspondent at 395.

40 For Trudeau's response to the Nigerian civil war see John English, *Just Watch Me: The Life of Pierre Elliott Trudeau, 1968-2000* (Toronto: Alfred A. Knopf, 2009), 64-67, and for the association of his name with the slogan "Reason over Passion," Chap. 4. My comments here about CUSO field staff who set aside personal and emotional responses in favour of a pragmatic approach to the war are based on my interviews with several of them as well as on various document sources.

41 Smillie interviews with McNeill, 25 July 1983, and with Dr. Ed Ragan and Dan Turner (n.d.), STC. Looking back, Turner acknowledged that he had probably been too ready to view the conflict exclusively from a pro-Biafran perspective.

42 "Report to the Board on Proposals for Reopening CUSO Programme in Eastern States of Nigeria," by Tim Brodhead (1970), including letter from Perinbam, in LAC/CUSO, MG 28, I 323, vol 12, file 9.

43 "Biafra," in *Canadian Annual Review,* 1970, 358.

44 Crowder, *Story of Nigeria,* 277.

45 Chinua Achebe's *There Was a Country: A Personal History of Biafra* (New York: Penguin Press, 2012) disputes the claim that an olive branch was extended to the former Biafra by the Nigerian federal government and is, overall, more critical of positions taken by the federalists than in some of his earlier work.

46 Brodhead, "Report to the Board," 1970, in LAC/CUSO, MG 28, I 323, vol. 12, file 9. See also *CUSO Bulletin,* Spring 1970, 6, for Brodhead's report on West Africa.

47 Copy of report of trip to East-Central, Rivers, and South-Eastern states by Ian Smillie and Jack Pearpoint, 7-13 June 1970, in LAC/CUSO, MG 28, I 323, vol. 12, file 9.

48 Ibid., "Progress Report/Assistance to Educational Institutions in the East Central State of Nigeria," by Pearpoint [June 1971].

49 On Enang's long involvement with CUSO, culminating in a position as assistant to the field staff officer in Calabar, see Ekekwe and Veit, *Retrospective Evaluation,* 31-32.

50 This paragraph and what follows draws on my interview with Jack Pearpoint, 16 December 2010, and on Smillie, *Lost Content,* 81-87, unless otherwise noted.

51 M.A. Sakamoto, "CUSO-CIDA Education Rehabilitation Programme/Final Report/Presented to the State School Board on Feb. 9th, 1973," LAC/CUSO, MG 28, I 323, vol. 100, file 5. See file 6 for Pelletier's Report II, suggesting cost-saving measures; file 1 for Pearpoint to L.R. Waldock, 8 May 1972, on "nigerianization in staffing"; and files 1-5 and 7-8 for additional information on this project, including a detailed form for the project and an account book.

52 Ernest Hillen, "Nigeria: A Time to Heal," *Weekend Magazine*, 30 September 1972, 2-4, 6-7; interview with Pearpoint.

53 Memo, 12 January 1972, seemingly from Brodhead to Bruce Miller in Ibadan, LAC/CUSO MG 28, I 323, vol. 100, file 1, regarding the high commissioner's criticism of CIDA for delays in funding; Smillie, *Lost Content*, 84, for musings at CIDA about supplying labour and material inputs for the project from Canada. On Canada's long history of making its overseas aid conditional on the purchase of needed goods and services from within Canada itself, see Stephen Brown, "Aid Effectiveness and the Framing of New Canadian Aid Initiatives," in *Struggling for Effectiveness: CIDA and Canadian Foreign Aid,* ed. Stephen Brown (Montreal/Kingston: McGill-Queen's University Press, 2012), 83-84.

54 L.R. Waldock to Pearpoint, 25 May 1972, LAC/CUSO, MG 28, I 323, vol. 100, file 1, for quotation; author interview with Pearpoint regarding the invitation to head up the new Projects Division.

55 Smillie, *Lost Content*, 86.

56 Ekekwe and Veit, *Retrospective Evaluation*, 44, Figure 2.

57 Interview with Bernie Lucht, 15 February 2011.

58 Interview with Stan Barrett, 10 December 2005. For Peace Corps alumni as anthropologists, see Brian E. Schwimmer and D. Michael Warren, eds., *Anthropology and the Peace Corps: Case Studies in Career Preparation* (Ames: Iowa State University Press, 1993).

59 Walter McLean to Doug Small, Canadian High Commission, Lagos, 30 January 1964, in LAC/CUSO, MG 28, I 323, vol. 84, file 7. See also note 15 in this chapter and p. 142.

60 Brodhead, "Nigeria Reborn," *McGill Daily*, 25 February 1966, 6; Diane Baigent letter to Brodhead, 22 February 1966. See also Louise Lorcas writing for Jon Church to Brodhead, 22 November 1966, explaining why articles he had submitted to CUSO/Ottawa with a view to having them published in the *Montreal Star* would not in fact be forwarded, given their political content. Copies of *McGill Daily* article and correspondence kindly supplied by Brodhead. For Peace Corps warnings against political statements in the context of the Nigerian civil war see Fritz Fischer, *Making Them Like Us: Peace Corps Volunteers in the 1960s* (Washington: Smithsonian Institute Press, 1998), 84.

61 Ekekwe and Veit, *Retrospective Evaluation*, 45, Figure 3, for comparative data for five-year intervals from 1965 on volunteers' gender and marital status, and 48 for quotation. As Ekekwe and Veit acknowledge, problems with CUSO sources make it difficult to compare statistical data over time. Still, Figure 3 is probably broadly accurate in presenting gender and marital patterns.

62 "Dagmar Langer, Teacher, Western Nigeria," *CUSO/SUCO Bulletin*, May 1965, 21-22; Bill McWhinney and Dave Godfrey, eds., *Man Deserves Man: CUSO in Developing Countries* (Toronto: Ryerson Press, 1968), 173-87. What follows on Langer draws mainly on her account in *Man Deserves Man* unless otherwise shown.

63 McWhinney and Godfrey, eds., *Man Deserves Man*, 174, 177.

64 Toyin Falola, *A Mouth Sweeter Than Salt: An African Memoir* (Ann Arbor: University of Michigan Press, 2004), 144. Getting an education, Falola wrote, was even made the subject of songs. See also Sanneh, *West African Christianity*, 151-58, regarding the early zeal for grammar schools in places like Ogbomosho.

65 What follows is based on my interview with Dickie, 12 March 2007, and on follow-up emails.

66 Response to questionnaire by Kitty Moses, April 2007; Ekekwe and Veit, *Retrospective Evaluation*, 45, Figure 3.

67 "Information Guide: Nigeria," n.d. [1970], 47, in LAC/CUSO, MG 28, I 323, vol. 47, file 27; ibid., vol. 11, file 20, for "West Africa Programme/Regional Field Staff Meeting, Ibadan, Aug. 24-25, 1971," 3, and "Response ..." rough draft, 10 September 1971, from David Catmur, 2-3. Catmur recommended dealing with marriage breakdowns in the field on a case-by-case basis. In the early 1970s, CUSO also became cautious about appointing volunteers who had recently separated or divorced, fearing that they might be seeking an escape from unhappiness and ultimately leaving themselves

vulnerable far from home. My thanks to Paul Axelrod for sharing his experience of this kind of response from CUSO when he applied to teach English in Botswana in 1973; email, 12 February 2007.

68 Langer account in *CUSO/SUCO Bulletin,* May 1965, 22, and in *Man Deserves Man,* 175, 183-85.

69 Response to questionnaire provided by Dr. Cyr, January 2006. I am indebted to Cyr for the fullness and thoughtfulness of his responses and for sharing copies of correspondence, photos, etc.

70 See page 143 for reference to Bezanson, and Smillie, *Lost Content,* Chap. 12, for details of Bezanson's terrible first placement: a school lacking even the most basic of provisions for its teachers and boarding students and no accommodation for Bezanson, who wound up sharing a room and a bed with the principal, himself newly hired, in a thatch and mud house.

71 Smillie interview with McNeill, STC; Gundi Robertson, "Who Needs a Steward?," *CUSO Forum,* April-May 1974, 16, and "Reader Agrees with Viewpoint on Servants," ibid., June 1974, 5; "Information Guide: Nigeria," n.d. [1970], 33-34, LAC/CUSO, MG 28, I 323, vol. 47, file 27, for information for volunteers on cost of living.

72 Information provided by Paul Delaney, including email of 18 September 2011, for the quoted phrase, and copy of his reprinted booklet *History of the Emirate.*

73 Ekekwe and Veit, *Retrospective Evaluation,* 49-52, specific data on 50. Early returns also increased in VSO in the 1970s; Dick Bird, *Never the Same Again: A History of VSO* (Cambridge: Lutterworth Press, 1998), 170.

74 "Teaching in Nigeria," in *Nigeria,* 14, LAC/CUSO, MG 28, I 323, vol. 47, file 31. See also ibid., vol. 12, file 16, for "Report on Caplan-Gillis Trip to North-East Nigeria, 25-30 January 1978," by Gerry Caplan, which referred to the increasing use of soldiers in secondary schools in the region to deal with discipline problems.

75 Interview with Marian White, 2 August 2007.

76 Response to questionnaire by Anne Simpson, December 2010. The patterns of adaptation to housing and working conditions discussed in the preceding pages are generally consistent with patterns reported by Ekekwe and Veit on the basis of their small case studies of three "waves" of volunteers: generally, problems with physical facilities mattered more in their work than in their home lives, and volunteers' adjustment problems were exacerbated when there were few or no other volunteers in their area for support and companionship; *Retrospective Evaluation,* 63-73.

77 Ekekwe and Veit, *Retrospective Evaluation,* 47, Fig. 5.

78 R.A. (Andy) Buhler, *Letters Home: Glimpses of a CUSO Cooperant's Life in Northern Nigeria, 1969-70* (Victoria, BC: Trafford Publishing, 2006), 9 (for quotations), also 105, regarding "six weeks of non-programme [at Orientation] for technicians," 144, on "medics" being "thrown in almost as an afterthought," and 102-5, for tensions with FSOs. Regarding depression and drinking, see, for instance, 83, 112, 137-38. In his July 2009 response to my questionnaire, Buhler acknowledged that during his time in northern Nigeria he drank more than he had done before or since. For his second assignment, see *Letters Home: Glimpses of a CUSO Cooperant's Life in Southern Nigeria, 1970-71* (Victoria, BC: Trafford Publishing, 2006).

79 Buhler, *Letters Home ... Northern Nigeria,* 137-38; response to author's questionnaire.

80 As reproduced in *Letters Home ... Northern Nigeria,* 141-42.

81 Smillie to Andy, 25 April 1970, reproduced in ibid., 178.

82 Ibid.

83 Buhler responses to questionnaire.

84 Interviews with Bill and Grace Bavington, 30 September 2005; questionnaire completed by Bill Bavington, September 2006.

85 LAC/CUSO, MG 28, I 323, vol. 47, file 27, *Information Guide: Nigeria,* n.d. [1970], and file 29, *CUSO Nigeria,* 1974-75. Of the two information booklets in file 29, one, *CUSO Nigeria,* was evidently written in 1976 or later, though the year 1974 is pencilled on the cover; it included an admiring

account of "Nigeria's Position in the Black World." *CUSO-Nigeria,* dated 1975, breaks off a section on General Gowon (overthrown that year in a bloodless coup) in mid-sentence with new information crudely pasted in. Both guidebooks appear to have been written with a cautious awareness that they might be read by Nigerian political officials.

86 *Nigeria,* in ibid, file 31, quotation at 8.

87 Ibid., 10.

88 Memo from Don Simpson to CUSO volunteers, 13 February 1968, in ibid., vol. 85, file 4.

89 Ibid., vol. 12, file 17, for Southern Nigeria Tour report by Bamishe and Caplan, 19-24 September 1977; file 15, "Report of Trip to London, April 5-8th" [1978]. This report on the evacuation and transport of the two burn victims suggests the complexity of such arrangements.

90 Frank Gillis, "Trip Report 28 Oct-6 Nov 1977," in ibid., file 17.

91 Barbara [Kincaid], "Trip Report," 20 December 1977, in ibid., file 16.

92 See also, for instance, ibid., Ron Davis, "Tour Report," 18-21 April 1978, and "West Africa Trip Report, March 1, 1978 to April 8, 1978" (unsigned, evidently by Barbara Brown from the Ottawa secretariat).

93 Glen C. Filson, "Major Personal Changes in a Group of Canadians Working in Nigeria," (PhD thesis for Department of Educational Theory, Ontario Institute for Studies in Education," 1975). See, for instance, 15, 21, 108. Filson believed that his "hippie" appearance when he visited volunteers in their placements for research purposes may have contributed to the readiness of some to offer marijuana and perhaps exaggerate its use [21].

94 One interviewee who served with her husband remembered a good deal of recreational marijuana at CUSO social gatherings. Although they did not themselves use alcohol or drugs because of their religious beliefs, they did not hesitate to attend such events and in fact drove long distances over bad roads to be part of them.

95 *Nigeria* (guidebook), 11, 13, 15, in LAC/CUSO, MG 28, I 323, vol. 47, file 31.

96 [Kincaid], trip report of 20 December 1977, and of 20 March 1978, in ibid., vol. 12, file 16, and file 15, for Brown's unsigned "West Africa Trip Report, March 1, 1978 to April 8, 1978."

97 Falola and Heaton, *A History of Nigeria,* Chap. 9, esp. 138. In the 1970s, revenue from oil made Nigeria the thirtieth wealthiest nation in the world.

98 In 1977, Nigeria was said to be seeking 27, 000 teachers from around the world; see Gerry Caplan, "Report of Live-and-Learn Trip to Nigeria, July 11-July 29, 1977," LAC/CUSO, MG 28, I 323, vol. 12, file 17.

99 Greg Spendjian, "A Re-assessment of the CUSO-Nigeria Programme" [Aug. 1974], with accompanying memo to Roy Fischer and others, 8 August 1974, LAC/CUSO, MG 28, I 323, vol. 12, file 8. Spendjian recommended that a debate on CUSO's future in Nigeria be made the main item at the next AGM and the matter resolved quickly in order to end the demoralization resulting from uncertainty about CUSO/Nigeria's future. The minutes of the 1975 AGM *did* record a resolution calling for an end to sending secondary-school teachers to Nigeria; ibid., vol. 98, file 10, for Minutes of 1975 AGM.

100 Ibid., files 11 and 12. "CUSO in Nigeria/A Reply to Critique of Nigeria Country Plan, 1976/77" is in the latter. The critique itself is missing from these files.

101 For the struggles and satisfactions of a young volunteer-teacher in one such town, only the second white person ever to live there, see Smillie, *Lost Content,* 363-69. See also the case of Dagmar Langer, above.

102 "More Golden Oldies," Caplan to Sharon Capeling, 19 June 1978, LAC/CUSO, MG 28, I 323, vol. 12, file 14. See also Ekekwe and Veit, *Retrospective Evaluation,* 91, 96-97.

103 "We worked so damn hard," one former staff member recalled, "yet we were always on the defensive"; quoted in Ekekwe and Veit, *Retrospective Evaluation,* 96, together with several similar

expressions of grievance by former staff. See also Gerry Caplan, "CUSO Expansion in Nigeria," 21 September 1978, in LAC/CUSO, MG 28, I 323, vol. 12, file 13.

104 T.F. Aiyepeku to S. Gibbons, 28 July 1971, and memo of 22 June 1971, from Allan McGill, Canadian High Commission, to Under-Secretary of State for External Affairs, Ottawa, regarding "CUSO and Nigeria," in LAC/CUSO, MG 28, I 323, vol. 58, file 19. See also undated memo from Steve Gibbons to "All Volunteers" regarding the article and editorial. The article itself, "CUSO Volunteers Should Go Home – Thanks CUSO but Get Out," by Tundey Yusuf, is missing from the file, but the editorial is included.

105 Tundey Yusuf, "CUSO – Go Home!" n.d, in ibid., vol. 12, file 16 [1977-78]. Yusuf claimed that he had been the keynote speaker at the previous AGM but that CUSO officials had withheld information about his address in a subsequent communiqué. The Michelmore dropped-postcard incident is discussed on page 130.

106 Eme N. Ekekwe, "Home Thoughts from Abroad," *CUSO Forum*, Winter 1979, 39-40. Ekekwe would later serve as CUSO coordinator in Nigeria and in 1986 co-author the *Retrospective Evaluation* cited frequently in this chapter.

107 Response to questionnaire by Sandra Kalmakoff, August 2006. In the late 1970s, Kalmakoff had a CUSO placement in Papua New Guinea, where her assignment felt more useful and effective.

108 Nigeria Country Plan prepared by field staff, November 1973, LAC/CUSO, MG 28, I 323, vol. 11, file 17 (5 for statistics); Crowder, *Story of Nigeria*, 252, for educational problems at independence; Caplan, "Big Is Beautiful?," 31, for present and projected problems for primary-school leavers.

109 Letter to the editor, *CUSO Forum*, Summer 1980, 43. See also Steve Haber, "Sponsor's Report," LAC/CUSO, MG 28, I 323, vol. 157, file 39. VSO struggled with similar ethical dilemmas in this period; Bird, *Never the Same Again*, 125.

110 CUSO/SUCO Brief to the Sub-Committee on International Development, April 1977, 9-10, LAC/CUSO, MG 28, I 323, vol. 129, file 16. As initially conceived, discretionary projects, that is, those that could be approved at the discretion of national staff, would involve sums of $500 or less, a figure that was later raised to $1,000 and then $2,000; see *Annual CUSO/SUCO Report, 1973*, and "CUSO Projects: A New Dimension," *CUSO Forum*, Christmas issue, 1973, 18, for brief introductions to the new division, and Ekekwe and Veit, *Retrospective Evaluation*, Chap. 6, for the later period. Although CIDA remained the chief source of funding for projects, CUSO also got assistance from other sources and sometimes did fundraising for specific projects.

111 Ekekwe and Veit, *Retrospective Evaluation*, Chap. 6, esp. 133, 135-36. Regarding effective links in Bangladesh, especially through coordinator Ray Cournoyer, a veteran worker in the area, see Smillie, *Lost Content*, 172-86.

112 Nigeria Country Plan, November 1973, n.p., LAC/CUSO, MG 28, I 323, vol. 11, file 17.

113 Ibid., file 19, "West Africa Regional Meeting, March 23-26, 1973," 3, for Fischer.

114 Ibid., vol. 91, file 4, for physiotherapist proposal submitted by Marlene Redekop, 17 September 1973, and related staff correspondence; and vol. 86, file 30, for application from Murray and Gerri Dickson, January 1975, for funds for "Makurdi Voluntary Foster Home Project." For project discussion in *Disting*, see October 1976 issue in ibid., vol. 12, file 18.

115 Ibid., vol. 12, file 16, for form letter to "Dear People" and Project Description form; and for Caplan, "Total Placements in Nigeria, 1977-78," 17 January 1979, and "Situation Report: Nigeria and CUSO, March 1978."

116 *Nigeria* (handbook), 10, LAC/CUSO, MG 28, I 323, vol. 47, file 31.

117 William Easterly, *The White Man's Burden: Why the West's Efforts to Aid the Rest Have Done So Much Ill and So Little Good* (New York: Penguin Books, 2006), 18.

118 Ekekwe and Veit, *Retrospective Evaluation*, 142.

119 Kincaid, "Trip Report – Kano – Jos – January 22-25 [1978]," LAC/CUSO, MG 28, I323, vol. 12, file 16.

120 Ibid., vol. 11, file 19, for "Regional Overview," Appendix 2 to "Minutes of the West Africa Regional Meeting held at Busua Beach, Ghana, November 22-27, 1973." See also Ekekwe and Veit, *Retrospective Evaluation,* 151, for the criticism, made in 1986, that CUSO/Nigeria was still "not localized enough."

121 "Report of Caplan-Gillis Trip to North-East Nigeria, January 25-30, 1978," and "Report of Trek to South-East Nigeria," n.d. [February-March 1978], LAC/CUSO, MG 28, I 323, vol. 12, file 16; and file 15 for Caplan to Frank Gillis, 1 April 1978, regarding the response of the angry priest, the co-ordinator of social welfare for his diocese. See also in this file Caplan's "Cardoso Community Project, Ajegunle, Lagos (Proj. 105-5/8)," 9 May 1978; Caplan believed the Cardoso project, initiated by a nun to help post-primary-school teenagers, had wider potential benefits.

122 Gerry Caplan, "Project Criteria," memo to Robin Wilson and others, 10 May 1978, in Roy Fischer Collection.

123 See Dean Walker, ed., *Canada and the Third World: What Are the Choices?,* papers from forty-fourth Couchiching Conference of the Canadian Institute of International Affairs (Toronto: Yorkminster Publishing, 1975), 79-81, for the views of a younger Caplan.

124 Caplan, "Project Criteria." CUSO/Nigeria did in fact participate in several major projects, but some of them may have been initiated by CIDA or carried out in conjunction with other agencies; see Ekekwe and Veit, *Retrospective Evaluation,* 143-52.

125 "Minutes of the West Africa Regional Meeting, Ibadan, Nigeria, November 24-28, 1974," LAC/CUSO, MG 28, I 323, vol. 11, file 18.

126 For reference to the *Globe* article citing the disgruntled volunteer and related correspondence, see Cam Bowes to various CUSO staff, 15 July 1977, and to Secretary/Bureau for External Aid for Education [Nigeria], 19 July 1977, and Gerry Caplan to Bob Dyck, 16 August 1977, in ibid., vol. 12, file 17. See ibid., vol. 50, file 5, for "CUSO in the News," issues 1 and 2, 1979, for *Globe* clippings from 1 August and 14 August 1978 reporting the recruitment shortfall. The latter article mentioned the shortfall in the context of reporting that Nigeria was using a consulting firm to hire 300 secondary-school teachers in Canada.

127 Kincaid response to questionnaire, August 2011.

128 *Nigeria,* Handbook, 1979, 10, LAC/CUSO, MG 28, I 323, vol. 47, file 31; Ekekwe and Veit, *Retrospective Evaluation,* 9 and 16.

129 Ekekwe and Veit, *Retrospective Evaluation,* 106, 115.

130 Hamilton response to questionnaire, September 2011; Hamilton profile in CUSO/VSO Calendar, 2011-12, featured for month of February.

131 Ekekwe and Veit, *Retrospective Evaluation,* 106, for the concentration of placements, and "Preface" for Ekekwe as CUSO coordinator, 1980-81. Capeling was based in Togo. Her development career is discussed further in Chap. 5.

132 Ekekwe and Veit, *Retrospective Evaluation,* 16, puts the number at seventeen. Executive Director Chris Bryant gave the lower figure in "Reflections on Development," *CUSO Forum,* September 1985, 1.

133 Bryant, "Reflections on Development," 1, and Ekekwe and Veit, *Retrospective Evaluation,* xi, and Chap. 7, "The Future of CUSO in Nigeria."

134 Falola and Heaton, *A History of Nigeria,* Chaps. 11-12, provides an overview of ever-worsening conditions in this period.

135 *Retrospective Evaluation,* Chap. 7, including 156, for quotations; also, 103-4 for details of lapsed contract arrangements.

136 Ibid., 156-58. Although they were not uncritical of CUSO/Nigeria, conceding that its programming had often lacked a coherent organizational framework to tie all its placements and projects together logically, Ekekwe and Veit (a former volunteer in the Ivory Coast) believed that it had made a

valuable contribution to Nigeria and to CUSO overall, notwithstanding the years of criticism from inside the organization.
137 The phrase is that of RV Anne Simpson.

Chapter 5: "Involvement That Lasts a Lifetime"

1 Address by Wood to Fourth National Conference of Canadian National Commission for UNESCO, 9-12 March 1965, 4, Library and Archives Canada (LAC), CUSO fonds, MG 28, I 323, vol. 85, file 13 (references hereafter to this fonds are to LAC/CUSO, MG 28, I 323, with volume and file number).
2 *CUSO/SUCO Bulletin*, Summer 1969, front page.
3 Perinbam, Notes on an address on "The Quest for Justice," 1, 5, 10, Carleton University, in LAC/CUSO, MG 28, I 323, vol. 32, file 21, 11th Annual General Meeting of CUSO, 2 December 1972.
4 Tim Brodhead, "Smiling Faces Going Places with CUSO," *CUSO Forum*, Spring-Summer, 1981, 18-20, later reissued as a CUSO leaflet.
5 For instance, Nigel Hawkesworth, "A Radical Look at Recruitment," *CUSO Forum*, Fall 1969, cover story; "Report on Meetings in Ottawa – January 20-22, 1977," by Donna Peaker, and "Dear CUSO Member," 14 November 1978, in University of British Columbia Archives, John Conway fonds, box 8, file 13, CUSO – Miscellaneous, 1975-80 (hereafter UBC Archives/Conway fonds with box and file number).
6 "Where Are the 9,000 Now?," *Forum*, November 1983.
7 Interview with Brodhead, 22 June 2009, and email communications. (Unless stated otherwise, all interviews cited in this book were conducted by the author.) The study referred to is *Bridges of Hope? Canadian Voluntary Agencies and the Third World*, by Brodhead and Brent Herbert-Copley with Anne-Marie Lambert (Ottawa: North-South Institute, 1988). For the McConnell Foundation, see the J.W. McConnell Family Foundation website, "History," http://www.mcconnellfoundation. ca/en/about/history.
8 Response to questionnaire by Dennis E. McDermott, December 2005, and by Bill Bavington, September 2006. (The questionnaire referred to here and elsewhere in the notes was prepared by the author.)
9 Peace Corps volunteers had similar experiences even decades later. Susan Lowerre, serving in Senegal in the 1980s, writes of returning home on sick leave and discovering that "My Mom and Dad were rich, unbelievably, luxuriously rich, and I had never realized it before"; Lowerre, *Under the Neem Tree* (Seattle: University of Washington Press, 1991), 101.
10 Response to questionnaire by Harry and Sandra Gaudet, February 2010.
11 Walter Herring, "I'm Back – I Think," *CUSO/SUCO Bulletin*, November 1966/January 1967, 18-19; Donna Bailey, "Home Sweet Home," *CUSO/SUCO Bulletin*, August 1967; interview with Catherine Duffy Mullally, 26 July 2005 ("snake stories"); response to questionnaire by Jill Morton Grant, 31 May 2006; Frans Koch, "Return to the Parish," *CUSO/SUCO Bulletin*, August-September 1967, 23-24. The articles cited appeared in a *Bulletin* series, "Au retour," on the nature and challenges of readjusting to Canada.
12 Interviews with Dr. Kelly and Katherine Eberl Kelly, 8 August 2009. (The quotation in the heading of this section comes from my interview with Dr. Kelly.)
13 Herring, "Au retour," 19. Les Johnson joined the CUSO national staff as interim director of the Asia program in 1967 (and later served on the CUSO board), notwithstanding the problematic nature of his own volunteer experience as presented in *Man Deserves Man*; see Bill McWhinney and Dave Godfrey, eds., *Man Deserves Man: CUSO in Developing Countries* (Toronto: Ryerson Press, 1968), 379-90, and "CUSO Staff '68," *CUSO/SUCO Bulletin*, October 1967–January 1968, 18. I deal later in this chapter with the many volunteers who had significant long-term staff involvements with CUSO.

14 "Returning Volunteers Are Valuable Citizens," *CUSO/SUCO Bulletin*, May 1965, 11. See also Charles A. James, foreword, *Anthropology and the Peace Corps: Case Studies in Career Preparation*, ed. Brian E. Schwimmer and D. Michael Warren (Ames: Iowa State University Press, 1993), x.

15 *Canadian Overseas Volunteers /1961-1986 /25th Anniversary Reunion*, 18-20 July 1986; *Canadian Overseas Volunteers (CUSO) /1962 Group ... 25th Anniversary Reunion*, 21-23 August 1987 (hereafter COV Reunion booklet, 1986, and COV Reunion booklet, 1987). The booklets are in a collection held by Steve Woollcombe containing papers from his own files and those of the late Bill McWhinney (hereafter McWhinney/Woollcombe Collection).

16 For average age of women's first marriage in Canada at this period see Alison Prentice et al., *Canadian Women: A History*, 2nd ed. (Toronto: Harcourt Brace and Company, 1996), 468. For the lone COV example, see COV Reunion booklet, 1987, 6, McWhinney/Woollcombe Collection.

17 See, for instance, J.L. Granatstein, "Canada and Peacekeeping: Image and Reality," in *Canadian Foreign Policy: Historical Readings*, ed. J.L. Granatstein (Toronto: Copp Clark Pitman, 1986), 237-38, and Ivan L. Head and Pierre Elliott Trudeau, *The Canadian Way: Shaping Canada's Foreign Policy, 1968-1984* (Toronto: McClelland and Stewart, 1995), 225. Such prominent diplomats as Chester Ronning and Arthur Menzies were "mishkids," their careers continuing well into the 1960s.

18 Interview with Woollcombe, 4 December 2006; COV Reunion booklet, 1986, McWhinney/Woollcombe Collection.

19 Response to questionnaire by Bezanson, 3 February 2011, and attached CV.

20 Regarding Strong's early regard for CUSO, see Strong to Prime Minister Pearson, 9 February 1967, Strong to Frank Bogdasavich, 10 April 1969, Bogdasavich to "Dear Maurice," 30 June 1970, and other relevant documents in LAC/CUSO MG 28, I 323, vol. 150, file 4. For Morrison, see *Aid and Ebb Tide: A History of CIDA and Canadian Development Assistance* (Waterloo: Wilfrid Laurier University Press in association with the North-South Institute, 1998), 57. See also *Partners in Tomorrow: Fifteen Years of CIDA's Non-Governmental Organizations Program, 1968-1983* (Ottawa: Minister of Supply and Services, 1984), 10.

21 Bruce Muirhead and Ronald N. Harpelle, *IDRC: 40 Years of Ideas, Innovation, and Impact* (Waterloo: Wilfrid Laurier University Press, 2010), 31.

22 Morrison, *Aid and Ebb Tide*, 69.

23 Ian Smillie interview with Murray Thomson, n.d., Smillie Tape Collection (hereafter STC); email from Elizabeth McAllister, 19 January 2012. See also Brodhead and Herbert-Copley with Lambert, *Bridges of Hope?*, 75.

24 For Glavin, see Smillie, *Lost Content*, 168, and *Globe and Mail* obituary for Terrence "Terry" Michael Glavin, 1 November 2011, S7. For Morrison quotation, see *Aid and Ebb Tide*, 64.

25 "Where Are the 8,000 Now?," *CUSO Forum*, Spring and Summer, 1981, 37, for feature on McWhinney.

26 COV Reunion booklet, 1987, McWhinney/Woollcombe Collection; email from Tom Schatzky, 25 June 2007; Dale Posgate response to questionnaire, 18 August 2006.

27 Douglas Roche, *What Development Is All About: China, Indonesia, Bangladesh* (Toronto: NC Press, 1979), 160.

28 Perinbam to Hugh Nangle, Editor, *CUSO Forum*, 9 August 1976, LAC/CUSO, MG 28, I 323, vol. 5, file 7, responding to a letter from two ECSA staff members, and ibid., vol. 84, file 10, for Perinbam to Jacques Jobin, 13 January 1972: "In all humility I suggest that you are greatly mistaken if you think that those of us who serve in CIDA are less sincere, less committed or less honest than those who work for SUCO and other non-governmental organizations." See also Smillie, *Lost Content*, 266.

29 Brian Marson, whose Treasury Board responsibilities included the CIDA file, sometimes found himself at odds with CUSO's executive over its budget submissions, and Treasury Board sometimes

reduced spending allocations that CIDA had already approved; Marson, "The History of CUSO – Personal Recollections," sent with email, and interview, 27 May 2009. For concerns about cuts at Treasury Board level, see, for example, C.M. Williams (CUSO/SUCO board chairman) to Allan J. MacEachen, 24 October 1975, in LAC/CUSO, MG 28, I 323, vol. 115, file 23. For CUSO concerns relating to RV Jon Church in his role as executive assistant to Mitchell Sharp in 1971, see Smillie, *Lost Content,* 202-3.

30   *Lost Content,* 357.
31   Brodhead and Herbert-Copley with Lambert, *Bridges of Hope?,* 56. See also Robert Bothwell, *Alliance and Illusion: Canada and the World, 1945-1984* (Vancouver: UBC Press, 2007), 300. Reflecting on CIDA's relationship with NGOs over its forty-year history, Bothwell described them as "fervent, opinionated, and often impractical ... [CIDA's] greatest support and its greatest handicap."
32   Muirhead and Harpelle, *IDRC,* Preface, Introduction, Chap. 1 (quotations at 14).
33   Ibid., 75.
34   Canada, *The International Development Research Centre: A Brief History* (Ottawa [2005]), 6.
35   Muirhead and Harpelle, *IDRC,* 67, 151, 178. On Banta's work as a volunteer in India see Chap. 2, and, for Fine as a volunteer in Nigeria, his "A Reappraisal of Common Assumptions Concerning Agricultural Development in Nigeria," *CUSO/SUCO Bulletin,* May-July 1968, 10-11.
36   *CUSO Bulletin,* vol. 3, 1971, 6-7, for Carol McPherson at IDRC.
37   Interview with Wendy Dobson, who served in India as Wendy Marson, 22 August 2007.
38   Response to questionnaire by Christopher Smart, 5 January 2011.
39   Muirhead and Harpelle, *IDRC,* Chap. 5 (267 for "wrecker's ball"), and 279, 281, 357; Bezanson response to questionnaire, 3 February 2011.
40   Mary Krug Ndlovu recalls that in 1971, even though she and some of her fellow RVs were involved in development education and orientation programs, they also believed that "CUSO should come to an end within 5 years. We were into the writings of Walter Rodney, Andre Gunder Frank and Ivan Illich"; response to questionnaire, September 2010.
41   Morrison, *Aid and Ebb Tide,* 238-43; emails from Diana Rivington (5 December 2011), Barbara Brown (30 November 2011 and 18 January 2012), Wendy Lawrence (18, 19, 20 January 2012), and Elizabeth McAllister (19 January 2012). RVs Brown and Lawrence and Marnie Girvan all joined CIDA's WID unit in the eighties with Girvan eventually becoming director of the renamed Women in Development and Gender Equity unit. While WID work at CIDA certainly led to increased opportunities for female staff, McAllister observes that advances in the goals of the unit did not hinge on specially designated female staff: "It really was in the beginning broadly owned ... with most male and female staff supporting WID."
42   Muirhead and Harpelle, *IDRC,* 44, 185-87. The early opportunities for female alumni in IDRC's Population and Health Division, mentioned above, are best understood as a reflection of the priority given at the time to population control as an urgent international issue rather than as a women's issue. Regarding NGOs see, for example, Betty Plewes and Rieky Stuart, *Gender Work Is Never Done: A Study of NGO Capacity in Gender and Development* (Ottawa: Canadian Council for International Development and Canadian International Development Agency, 1992), i. As noted in Chap. 3, it was only in 1990 that CUSO had its first female executive director.
43   Dr. E.J. Ragan (CUSO Medical Director) to Gen. D.C. Spry, Consultant, CIDA, Special Programs Division, 6 May 1970, LAC/CUSO, MG 28, I 323, vol. 150, file 3. Although Spry had sought advice about funding Oxfam Canada's work with the Christian Medical Association of India (CMAI), Ragan advised that CIDA should instead provide financial support directly to the CMAI, something it did in the 1970s; email from Dr. Eric Ram to author, 15 February 2006.
44   "Sheila Ward – Report on Nursing, 1969-1971," LAC/CUSO, MG 28, I 323, vol. 148, files 12, 13, 14 (quotation from file 13, 22); Sheila Ward, interview, 29 October 2006, and CV. See Brouwer, "Ironic

Interventions: CUSO Volunteers in India's Family Planning Campaign, 1960s-1970s," *Histoire sociale/Social History* 43, 86 (2010): esp. 311-13, regarding future training and career paths among other RVs in addition to Ward.

45 Donna Shields-Pöe, for instance, obtained two masters degrees and eventually became a deputy director with the Canadian Institutes of Health Research; response toquestionnaire, June 2007, and CV. Lois James Chetelat served in Honduras and Indonesia with Care-Medico (later absorbed into CARE) in the late 1960s and early 1970s before marrying and returning to Canada and eventually obtaining a doctorate in anthropology; interview, 6 May 2007.

46 Response to questionnaire, August 2009, and emails. Perhaps not surprisingly, Wise experienced her two years with Treasury Board as a poor fit with her international interests.

47 Smillie, *Lost Content*, 34-35, 36-39, 338; Smillie interview with Capeling, 29 October 1983 (STC); Carol Cooper, "Canada's champion volunteer," *Globe and Mail*, 8 December 2003, R7.

48 Ibid. For UNIFEM, established in 1976, see Devaki Jain, *Women, Development, and the UN: A Sixty-Year Quest for Equality and Justice* (Bloomington: Indiana University Press, 2005), 94-95, 127-31. For Kofi Annan's remarks, see "Sharon Capeling-Alakija's Life Driven By 'Sense of Solidarity and Social Justice,' Secretary-General Says at Memorial Ceremony"; http://www.unis.unvienna. org.unis/pressrels/2003/sgsm9056.html (accessed 29 October 2010).

49 See United Nations website, http://www.un.org/News/Press/docs/2010/sga1233.doc.htm, and other websites that deal with Fisher's career. For the UNICEF campaign, see, for instance, "These Boots Saved 987,250 Children's Lives," *Globe and Mail*, 30 October 2012, A16.

50 Morrison, *Aid and Ebb Tide*, 70, 129, 182, 362; Brodhead and Herbert-Copley, with Lambert, *Bridges of Hope?*, 19, 53-56. However, CIDA *did* make funding cuts to CCIC when its position-taking seemed particularly likely to embarrass the agency (Morrison, 129).

51 *Review/The North-South Biannual Newsletter*, Fall-Winter 2001, twenty-fifth anniversary issue, esp. 2, for "CUSO Mafia," and 21, for alphabetical list of former board members. See also Morrison, *Aid and Ebb Tide*, 111. Under its current president, SUCO alumnus Joseph Ingram, the institute has twice been ranked as the world's top international development think tank with an operating budget under $5 million. See the institute's website.

52 For instance, Réal Lavergne, who, following his two years with CUSO in Peru in the mid-1970s and the completion of a doctorate in economics, joined the institute and in the 1980s participated in a pioneering and influential evaluation of CIDA's bilateral aid program, co-authoring the country study of Senegal; see "Réal and Val Lavergne – RVs Who Stayed Involved," CUSO *Forum*, August 1983, 17; Morrison, *Aid and Ebb Tide*, 215, 428-29; *Review/The North-South Biannual Newsletter*, 8.

53 See references to their publications above and in Chap. 3. Illustrating the strong links that could exist between NGO activists and CIDA, Elizabeth McAllister recalls that Plewes, Stuart, Tim Brodhead and other "'CUSO graduates'" were "huge supports from the outside" when CIDA was developing its WID policy; email to author from McAllister, 19 January 2012.

54 Response to questionnaire by Rieky Stuart, April 2011. Information on Plewes and Stuart and their organizational involvements can be found on several websites, including that for the McLeod Group. See also Partnership Africa Canada's website and Ian Smillie, *Blood on the Stone: Greed, Corruption and War in the Global Diamond Trade* (London: Anthem Press and International Development Research Centre, 2010).

55 E.T. Jackson and Associates is an example of a development consultancy firm whose roster of "key people" includes such RVs as Richard Marquardt, John Saxby, and Paul Turcot, as well as Rieky Stuart; E.T. Jackson and Associates website, "Our Key People."

56 In 1981, Quarry received an IDRC fellowship to learn how to adapt her decade of experience in radio and television to communication needs in development work; response to questionnaire, July 2011. See also Wendy Quarry and Ricardo Ramírez, *Communication for Another Development: Listening before Telling* (London: Zed Books, 2009).

57   See, for instance, Ian Smillie and John Hailey, *Managing for Change: Leadership, Strategy and Management in Asian NGOs* (London: Earthscan Publications, 2001), Smillie, *Freedom from Want: The Remarkable Success Story of BRAC, the Global Grassroots Organization That's Winning the Fight against Global Poverty* (Sterling, VA: Kumarian Press, 2009), and Smillie, *Blood on the Stone*.

58   Jean Christie, "A Critical History of Development Education in Canada," *Canadian and International Education* 12, 3 (1983), 8-20 (quotation at 9; italics added). Christie worked in CUSO's Development Education Department in the mid-1970s. The 1969 resolution is discussed above in Chap. 3.

59   Christie, "Critical History," 10, 14; CIDA, *1983-84 Annual Review*, 31-32.

60   Christie, "Critical History," 15; Brodhead and Herbert-Copley, with Lambert, *Bridges of Hope?*, 17-18, 91.

61   John Clark, *Democratizing Development: The Role of Voluntary Organizations* (West Hartford, CT: Kumarian Press, 1991), 125; Alison Van Rooy, *The Global Legitimacy Game: Civil Society, Globalization, and Protest* (London: Palgrave Macmillan, 2004), 48-49 (for Scandinavia).

62   Response to questionnaire from Mary Krug Ndlovu, and interview, 23 September 2010.

63   Letter of Bruce Bailey, 5 August 1969. For this and much other correspondence attempting to interest boards of education and other bodies in CUSO's assumed expertise, see LAC/CUSO, MG 28, I 323, vol. 103, file 18, Publications-Correspondence, 1969-1971. See also *CUSO/SUCO Bulletin*, October 1967–January 1968, 2, for resolutions passed at a recent RV conference, one of which proposed to "negotiate immediately with Provincial Governments" about making the experience and resources of RVs available for teacher training programs.

64   "Schools Program," *CUSO Forum*, February-March 1974, 23-24. For Griffith's initiative, see "In Brief" item in ibid., 12.

65   The "drop the schools" view is quoted in Brodhead and Herbert-Copley, with Lambert, *Bridges of Hope?*, 97. See Christie, "Critical History," 11, on the termination of CUSO's development education work in schools, and, for Stackhouse, *Out of Poverty and into Something More Comfortable* (Toronto: Random House, 2000), 60-61. I am grateful to Professor Vandra Masemann of OISE, a 1960s Ghana RV, for her views on barriers to implementing development education in the schools; personal conversation, 25 June 2011, and email, 29 June 2011.

66   Wilma Van Berkel, "Universities and Development Education in Canada," *Canadian and International Education* 12, 3 (1983), 97-110 (quotation at 109), and, in the same issue, Matthew Zachariah, "Editorial: The State of the Art of Development Education," 6. Neither writer was personally espousing this negative view.

67   "Don Simpson to International Education Post," *CUSO Forum*, Summer 1969, 5; Simpson, "A Canadian Odyssey (1957-1993)/A Personal and National Journey Towards Cross-Cultural Harmony," draft outline for planned memoir, 10 August 2009, 3. St. Francis Xavier University's Coady International Centre, established in 1959, was perhaps the first such centre.

68   UBC Archives/Conway fonds, box 8, file 13, Miscellaneous, 1975-80, for UBC CUSO President's Committee Minutes, 26 February 1976; notice of meeting, 21 September 1976, regarding forthcoming graduate seminar; September 1976 notice of forthcoming Development Awareness program; and April 1977 document by Bev MacDougall regarding a second Development Awareness series and the suggestion of implementing a registration fee in view of the series' popularity. As CUSO's executive director at this period, Murray Thomson was anxious to encourage universities and colleges to integrate overseas volunteer work into their curricula; "Executive Secretary's Report to the CUSO Committee," 23 April 1976, 4; these and other documents, cited below, from Thomson's personal files kindly provided to the author.

69   *Development Studies – CUSO List*, 1971 booklet in LAC/CUSO, MG 28, I 323, vol. 83, file 24.

70   *The First Decade: International Education Centre, 1972-1982*, booklet kindly provided by RV Jim Morrison, who headed the centre from 1979 to 1983; interview with Morrison, 22 January 2011.

71 Orientation Report, 1971, by Ian Smillie, LAC/CUSO, MG 28, I 323, vol. 49, file 13; Simpson, outline for "Canadian Odyssey," 4.

72 "We're Putting Wheels on the Learner Centre"/"CUSO Communique," 12, 1971, UBC Archives/ Conway fonds, box 6, file 11.

73 "Cross-Cultural Learner Centre/Ottawa: 22 November–11 December 1971," LAC/CUSO, MG 28, I 323, vol. 29, file 13; Smillie, *Lost Content,* 130, for "revolutionary" technology.

74 Minutes of meeting of board of directors, Saturday, 18 November 1972, 1, LAC/CUSO, MG 28, I 323, vol. 29, file 29; Smillie, *Lost Content,* 130-31. See also Brodhead and Herbert-Copley, with Lambert, *Bridges of Hope?,* 5, and Morrison, *Aid and Ebb Tide,* 128.

75 Thomson, "Executive Secretary's Report to the CUSO Committee," 23 April 1976, 3.

76 Form letter from Thomson to "All RFDs and FSOs," 14 October 1975, 3 (for film); Thomson, "Trip to Western Canada, 21-27 March 1974"/Confidential, and "Executive Secretary's Report to the CUSO Committee," 23 April 1976, 3.

77 "CUSO-VAN," March 1972, 2, 11 July 1973, 6, and September 1973, in UBC Archives/Conway fonds, box 6, file 12 and file 15. On the wine issue, see also CUSO report by Tom Morton for Vancouver committee, *CUSO Forum,* January 1974, 6.

78 Smillie, *Lost Content,* Chap. 9, quotations at 124, 132-33.

79 Brodhead and Herbert-Copley, with Lambert, *Bridges of Hope?,* 54.

80 For critiques see, for instance, Roche, *What Development Is All About,* 161-64, and Robert Carty, Virginia Smith, and LAWG [Latin American Working Group], *Perpetuating Poverty: The Political Economy of Canadian Foreign Aid* (Toronto: Between the Lines, 1981), 86-94.

81 "The Third Imperative for Canadian Immigration Policy: Interdependence with the Third World," 1975, in LAC/CUSO, MG 28, I 323, vol. 50, file 4. Remarkably, in 2011 the role of the brain drain in undermining the effectiveness of Canadian official development assistance was being discussed as a "new" issue; "Brain Drain of African Doctors Saved Canada $400-million," *Globe and Mail,* 26 November 2011, A24.

82 Christie, "Critical History," 14; Brodhead and Herbert-Copley, with Lambert, *Bridges of Hope?,* 50-51, 66-68. The case of a former physician-volunteer who joined in this criticism by writing to his MP was a cause of concern to CUSO staff in 1978; memo from Ginger McCall to Dave Pollack, Robin Wilson, and others, 30 June 1978, and reply from Marnie Girvan, 4 July 1978, in LAC/CUSO, MG 28, I 323, vol. 171, file 7.

83 Linda Freeman, *The Ambiguous Champion: Canada and South Africa in the Trudeau and Mulroney Years* (Toronto: University of Toronto Press, 1997), esp. Chaps. 6 and 7. Kofi Hope's doctoral thesis, which I read after my manuscript had been accepted for publication, focuses on anti-apartheid activism by CUSO and the United Church of Canada and argues for significant impact notwith-standing Canadian groups' comparatively late involvement; Hope, "In Search of Solidarity: International Solidarity Work between Canada and South Africa, 1975-2010" (PhD thesis, St. Antony's College, Oxford University, 2011).

84 Howard Adelman, "Canadian Refugee Policy in the Postwar Period: An Analysis," in *Refugee Policy: Canada and the United States,* ed. Howard Adelman (Toronto: York Lanes Press, 1991), esp. 195-98.

85 "CUSO in the Eighties," UBC Archives/Conway fonds, box 8, file 14; "Dev. Ed. Newsletter/Nestle Boycott Suspended," CUSO *Forum,* May 1984, 13. See also Clark, *Democratizing Development.* Clark argues that well-orchestrated lobbying campaigns by NGOs on issues such as this one "can lead to quite significant policy shifts" (131, for quotation, and 135-37).

86 On the "hassle factor," see Freeman, *Ambiguous Champion,* 136.

87 Brodhead and Herbert-Copley, with Lambert, *Bridges of Hope?,* 83-85. See also Clark, *Democratizing Development,* 38: "It is always the famine appeals which bring in the money. Raising funds for development is never as lucrative."

88 Tamara Myers, "Blistered and Bleeding, Tired and Determined: Visual Representations of Children and Youth in the Miles for Millions Walkathon," *Journal of the Canadian Historical Association*, new series, 22, 1, (2011): 245-75. On CUSO's and Lowe's involvement, see "Get Out and Walk!" and "82 Years Young," *CUSO/SUCO Bulletin*, Winter 1969-70, 3, 14, and 10-11. See also "We Shall Remember Him," UBC Archives/Conway fonds, box 6, file 11.

89 Mündel, response to questionnaire, July 2006.

90 Not to be confused with the prominent late-twentieth-century Canadian labour leader of the same name. Information and quotations in what follows come from McDermott's responses to questionnaire and accompanying email message, 14 December 2005.

91 Tom Alderman, "What's Bugging the Committed Kids?," *The Canadian*, 21 May 1966. For the segment on the Kingston project, "Help for the Poor at Home – Whether They Want It or Not," see 9-11.

92 Mündel, response to questionnaire.

93 Anne Jones Hume response to questionnaire, 21 February 2006.

94 Adelman, "Canadian Refugee Policy," 195-98, and Reg Whitaker, *Double Standard: The Secret History of Canadian Immigration* (Toronto: Lester and Orpen Denys, 1987), 254-61, which indicates that fewer than 1,200 Chilean refugees had been accepted by early 1975. Several CUSO alumni had personal relationships with the Chileans and/or were drawn into controversial solidarity work in Latin America or Toronto. Their names have been withheld by request.

95 Jones Hume response to questionnaire; interview with Judy Ransom, 1 February 2007, and follow-up email communications. After the Cuba interlude, Ransom had longer ESL teaching assignments with CIDA in Indonesia and China interspersed with her community college work.

96 Written responses to questionnaire and personal interview with M, 15 February 2007.

97 Unless otherwise shown, what follows on Pearpoint and Frontier College draws on my interview with Pearpoint, 16 December 2010, and on James H. Morrison, *A Pictorial History of Frontier College: Camps and Classrooms* (Toronto: Frontier College Press, 1989). Morrison is researching a full history of Frontier College.

98 Following his retirement from Frontier College, Pearpoint undertook very different work, albeit still in the not-for-profit sector; Inclusion website, "Inclusion Associates," http://www.inclusion.com/aspearpoint.html.

99 Interview with Mar and Rob Thomson, 29 July 2005. Following their retirement from teaching careers in 2005, this couple again joined CUSO, serving for two years in the Solomon Islands; email, 1 July 2007.

100 "CUSO Volunteer Wants More Indians to Go Overseas," *CUSO/SUCO Bulletin*, December 1968, 9.

101 George Manuel and Michael Posluns, *The Fourth World: An Indian Reality* (Toronto: Collier-Macmillan, 1974), xv.

102 Red Crow Community College website, "History," http://www.redcrowcollege.com/history.htm, (accessed 22 September 2010), for quotation. Regarding Smallface Marule's honorary degree, see "University Celebrates Its Aboriginal Graduates," http://www.ucalgary.ca/news/utoday/june15-2010/graduates.

103 Paul Delaney emails to author, 28 June 2011 (contains quotation) and 30 November 2011.

104 COV Reunion booklets, 1986 and 1987, McWhinney/Woollcombe Collection; "Post-Service Activities of CUSO Volunteers (prepared 1966)," LAC/CUSO, MG 28, I 323, vol. 50, file 13. For my methods of contacting interviewees, see the "Note on Sources."

105 See *CUSO/SUCO Bulletin*, October 1967–January 1968, 5-6 for "Sixth Annual Meeting," Resolution A, regarding request for bursaries and remission of fees, and, 16, "CUSO Staff '68"; also "Especially for Teachers," *CUSO Forum* 2, 1972.

106 Interview with Marian White, 2 August 2007; emails, 23 and 24 November 2011.

107 Ibid., and My Podcast World website, http://marianwhite-cuso-vso.mypodcastworld.com/, for White's September 2011 podcast interview with Charlottetown RV Ray MacCormack, who recalled being hired immediately in the earlier period on the strength of his overseas experience; "Bleak Prospects for Canadian Teachers," *Forum*, Winter 1979, 14; R.D. Gidney, *From Hope to Harris: The Reshaping of Ontario's Schools* (Toronto: University of Toronto Press, 1999), 111, and email on job shortages from R.D. Gidney and Wyn Millar, 24 November 2011.

108 Name withheld on request.

109 Smart response to questionnaire, 5 January 2011, and email, 13 January 2011. Writing from western Canada about her own experience and that of others in her circle, CC reported attitudes and patterns similar to those described in this paragraph; email, 3 December 2011.

110 Doug Owram, *Born at the Right Time: A History of the Baby-Boom Generation* (Toronto: University of Toronto Press, 1997), 181; Berta Vigil Laden, "Ontario's Colleges: Looking Ahead to 2015 and Turning 50," presentation to Association of Colleges of Applied Arts and Technology of Ontario, 20-21 February 2005, accessed online 29 November 2011. The first Ontario community college opened in 1966; within two years, eighteen were in operation.

111 For instance, Dick Hamilton, John Wood, and Robin Jeffrey, who served in 1960s India, all made that country the object of their doctoral research (in economics, political science, and history, respectively), with Wood and Jeffrey becoming career academics. For Hamilton, see COV Reunion booklet, 1986, McWhinney/Woollcombe Collection; Wood response to questionnaire, December 2006, and later interview; Jeffrey response to questionnaire, October 2010.

112 Jim Morrison, response to questionnaire, November 2010, and interview, 22 January 2011.

113 Bezanson response to questionnaire and attached CV; Dobson, *Gravity Shift: How Asia's New Economic Powerhouses Will Shape the 21st Century* (Toronto: University of Toronto Press, 2009), 222, and interview, 22 August 2007.

114 Interview with Jim Walker, 17 January 2007. Like India RVs who taught at several other Canadian universities, Walker was also involved for many years with the Shastri Indo-Canadian Institute. Meanwhile, nearby at McMaster University, Trinidad-born Gary Warner, who directed CUSO's Sierra Leone program in the 1970s, promoted international development and international connections for McMaster and pioneered courses on French-African and Caribbean literature; see Who's Who in Black Canada website, "Dr. Gary Warner," http://www.whoswhoinblackcanada.com/2010/10/16/dr-gary-warner/.

115 Winsor contribution to *Man Deserves Man*, ed. McWhinney and Godfrey, 316-25 (321 for first quotation), and to *Review/The North-South Biannual Newsletter*, 7 (second quotation). For Winsor's involvement on specific development issues see references in Morrison, *Aid and Ebb Tide*.

116 Turner response to questionnaire, and follow-up conversation with Turner and Gayle Cooper, June 2011; also website for "Dan Turner Creative."

117 Interview with Bernie Lucht, 15 February 2011.

118 David Cayley, *The Rivers North of the Future: The Testament of Ivan Illich as Told to David Cayley*, foreword by Charles Taylor (Toronto: Anansi Press, 2005).

119 Bird, *Never the Same Again*, 184-85. As prime minister of Britain, Major encouraged the Overseas Development Administration to launch what became its Overseas Training Programme in association with fourteen academic institutions. Regarding "Miss Lillian," see Jimmy Carter, *A Remarkable Mother* (New York: Simon and Schuster, 2008).

120 Smillie, *Lost Content*, 202.

121 For the Campbells' continuing involvement on the UBC campus, see list of returned volunteers on President's Committee, UBC Archives/Conway fonds, box 6, file 12. Campbell worked several references to his CUSO experience into Chris Wood's interview with him; see Wood's "A Premier in Waiting?," *Maclean's*, 3 May 1999, 28-30.

122 Smillie, *Lost Content*, 30-32.

123 Gordon Cressy and Joanne Campbell, "CUSO Revisited," *CUSO Forum*, November 1983, 1, 10-11. The article, an edited version of the *Star* piece, also listed Cressy's past civic and NGO involvements, including presidency of the National Council of YMCAs and membership in the Urban Alliance on Race Relations. For the couple's three-year commitment in Tobago, see "Gordon Cressy's Latest Adventure Brings Career Full Circle," *CUSO News*, issue 08-1, 3-4 (copy received as CUSO promotional material).

124 I am grateful to Paul Dewar, foreign affairs critic for the NDP, for a helpful conversation related to this subject (13 July 2012). Following the completion of his BA, Dewar had a short-term volunteer assignment with Tools for Peace in Nicaragua, influenced in part by the development interests of his mother, former Ottawa mayor Marion Dewar. Brief as it was, the placement had a "profound impact" on his subsequent ongoing interest in the Global South and on his belief that politicians can and should do more to recognize and advance Canadians' interest in development-related issues. As a candidate for the federal NDP leadership in 2012, Dewar was unique in his attention to such issues.

125 One of the RVs interviewed for this project spoke of her conversion to Buddhism as a significant factor in her personal life, but conversion in this case seems to have taken place years after her overseas placement. Several other volunteers who served in Asian countries spoke of reading extensively about Hinduism, and especially Buddhism, and of studying and adopting meditation practices. However, the increasing secularization of Canada and other Western countries from the 1960s onward may have lessened the likelihood that RVs would become strong adherents of *any* faith practice.

126 Profile of Anne-Marie Groves Gaston in "Where Are the 6,000 Now?," *CUSO Forum*, Summer 1980, 17. I am grateful to Gaston for a conversation (24 June 2011) and print information about her ongoing career as an artistic director and a scholar of Indian classical dance forms. For an instance of the scholarly aspect, see her *Bharata Natyam: From Temple to Theatre* (New Delhi: Manohar, 1997).

127 *NEWSTATEments* is available in the Thomas Fisher Collection, Robarts Library, University of Toronto.

128 "African Art Gets Canadian Recognition At Last," and Wendy Lawrence, "The Eclectic Circus," *CUSO Forum*, Winter 1979, 24-25 and 32-33, and Lawrence response to questionnaire and emails, January 2012. Vicki Smith Henry, probably one of the few volunteers with some formal background study in non-Western art, worked decades later with acquisitions from "culturally diverse communities in Canada" for the Art Bank collection in Ottawa; response to questionnaire, September 2009.

129 Email from Sharon Cook, 7 August 2005. I am grateful to Sharon for lending copies of her parents' letters, diaries, and tapes recording their experiences in a region of Papua New Guinea still at an early stage of its encounter with modernity. A profile of Nigeria RV William Zambusi in "Lives Lived," *Globe and Mail*, 30 March 2011, L8, makes it clear that a volunteer's personal collection could retain a lifelong importance.

130 Gini Dickie, for instance, having introduced her Nigerian students to the work of poet and novelist Wole Soyinka in the early 1970s, did something similar decades later in Canada, using a poem by Soyinka as part of her presentation on "The Arts as Meaning Makers" when she was applying for a position in the Faculty of Education at Toronto's York University; email from Dickie, 15 March 2007.

131 Dave Godfrey, *The New Ancestors* (Toronto: McClelland and Stewart, 1984, orig. ed. 1970); A.C. Morrell, "The I and the Eye in the Desert: The Political and Philosophical Key to Dave Godfrey's *The New Ancestors*," in *Studies in Canadian Literature* 12, 2 (1987), for Godfrey's statement about

wanting to confound readers. For an overview of Thomas's work, including *Coming Down from Wa* (Toronto: Viking, 1995), see the George Woodcock Lifetime Achievement Award website, "Audrey Thomas 2003," http://www.georgewoodcock.com/audreythomas.html.

132 Regarding Brand, see above, see 278n66. For Anne Simpson, who volunteered in Nigeria's Muslim north in the early 1980s and who later became a well-known poet, it would be the twenty-first century before she felt ready to revisit her time in Nigeria to begin a novel set partly in that country. Response to questionnaire by Simpson, December 2010, and "Upcoming Writer-in-Residencies for Anne Simpson," http://www.stfx.ca/news/view/2792/.

133 Account by Diane Davis Baigent, teacher, Ghana, *CUSO/SUCO Bulletin*, November 1964, 9-11. See also Smillie, *Lost Content*, 95, for an anecdote about the Bangkok wedding reception for Rieky and Colin Stuart, hosted by the Canadian ambassador, where passionate political discussion about the omnipresent Vietnam War threatened to upstage the celebration.

134 James W. St. G. Walker, *"Race," Rights and the Law in the Supreme Court of Canada: Historical Case Studies* (Waterloo: Osgoode Society for Canadian Legal History and Wilfrid Laurier University Press, 1997), 135-37. For more detail on this case, see Constance Backhouse, *Colour-Coded: A Legal History of Racism in Canada, 1900-1950* (Toronto: The Osgoode Society for Canadian Legal History and University of Toronto Press, 1999), Chap. 6.

135 Walker, *"Race," Rights and the Law*, Chap. 5, quotations at 285, 300.

136 "Secretariat Activities," *CUSO/SUCO Bulletin*, May 1965, 5-6 (Pim marriage); response to questionnaire by Chris Bryant, July 2011.

137 Regarding Thailand marriages, see Smillie, *Lost Content*, 331. Thailand was also a country where, for a time, an unmarried volunteer could adopt a child, as JH did while teaching there in the early 1970s (phone conversation, and response to questionnaire, November 2011). However, adoption appears not to have been a common volunteer practice in any placement country.

138 Interview with Judy Pullen Tethong, 7 August 2008; Smillie, *Lost Content*, 56.

139 More than half of the first COV cohort were separated or divorced by the time of their 1986 reunion (COV Reunion booklet, 1986, in McWhinney/Woollcombe Collection). While this was an unusually high rate, anecdotal evidence suggests that marriage breakdown among RVs generally was higher than in the overall Canadian population. For data on the latter, see *Canadian Women: A History*, Prentice et al., Figure A.3, 469.

140 Walker, *"Race," Rights and the Law*, Afterword.

141 Koskamp to Megan, 30 November 2008, as part of the Meg in Ghana blog, "Overseas Success Story," http://meginghana.blogspot.com/2008/07/overseas-success-story.html (accessed 7 December 2010); Koskamp, Facebook entry "Ripley is the BEST village in Canada" (accessed 26 January 2011); Sara Bender, "Finlayson's Village Dining Hosting Charity Event," *Luck Now Sentinel*, 14 June 2010, http://www.lucknowsentinel.com/.

142 Interview with Jim Walker.

143 Response to questionnaire, 24 October 2010.

144 Response to questionnaire; *My Life among the Paniyas*, 151 (for quotation); email from Mündel to Christopher Smart, 6 January 2011.

145 Interview with Lucht; email from Dan Turner, 20 June 2011.

146 "Betty Plewes, "Fulfilling a Dream," *CUSO Forum*, May 1986, 5; email from Grace Bavington, 22 November 2005; response to questionnaire by Bill Bavington, September 2006. On 10 January 2012, CBC Radio's *Metro Morning* featured an interview with Dr. Adrian Sohn, an RV whose experience illustrates and complicates the theme of this paragraph. Dr. Sohn has made several return visits to "Buzu Village" to carry out personal aid projects since teaching high school near the village in 1980 and was about to make another such visit when a new wave of violence fuelled by ethnic tensions and economic problems forced him to delay his plans.

147 "Why CUSO Encouraged the formation of CESO," King Gordon fonds, LAC, MC 30-C241, vol. 40, file 1; "Canadian Executive Service Overseas," *CUSO/SUCO Bulletin,* October 1967-January 1968, 23-24. Focusing initially on "a limited area in East Africa," CESO over time expanded the range of its work and the countries in which it served, eventually offering its services to Canadian Aboriginal organizations as well as to overseas countries; Jim Lotz, *Sharing a Lifetime of Experience: The CESO Story* (Lawrencetown Beach, NS: Pottersfield Press, 1997). CESO is now known as Canadian Executive Service Organization.

148 Email from Koskamp, 28 August 2005; Olivia Ward, "Spirit of Altruism Lives On," *Toronto Star,* 5 June 2011, IN1, IN 49 (references to Woollcombe and other early volunteers). After retiring from farming in 2002, Koskamp had served in Armenia and as an election observer in El Salvador. Despite having suffered from a brain tumour in 2004, followed by extensive rehabilitation, he went to Senegal with CESO three years later as a cooperatives and agricultural consultant.

149 "John Baigent, LLB '69/Partners in the Horn of Africa' Founder Wins Dalhousie Award for Public Service" http://law.da.ca/Alumni_and_Friends/Awards/John_Baigent.php (accessed 24 January 2011).

150 Grant response to questionnaire, 31 May 2006; McKee response to questionnaire, April 2011.

151 Interview with Catherine Duffy Mullally, 26 July 2005. All three children of Sarawak RV Colin Johnstone, the youngest born in Brazil, did one or more short-term service projects overseas; response to questionnaire, March 2006.

152 Interview with Judy Pullen Tethong, 7 August 2008. For coverage of the 2007 protests in China, see, for instance, "Cut off from Canada for 36 hours," and "Protest Received Worldwide Publicity," *Globe and Mail,* 9 August 2007, 1, 8.

153 Paul Scott, *Staying On* (London: Heinemann, 1977).

154 Note on Nigel Florida, aka Muhammad Lamin Florida, in "Where Are the 9,000 Now?," *CUSO Forum,* January 1987, 13. One former colleague remembered Florida as a brilliant educator and an early proponent of the concept of appropriate technology.

155 Email from Kidd, 9 December 2011, response to questionnaire, January 2012, and updated CV.

156 Responses to questionnaire by Mary Krug Ndlovu and personal interview, September 2010; information sheet on Mary Ndlovu; and, for the trust, http://www.artforaidsinternational.org/portfolio-items/edward-ndlovu-memorial-trust-past/. Female volunteers seem to have married and stayed on less often than their male counterparts, but see also the "Where Are They Now?" feature, *CUSO Forum,* May 1987, 13, for Uganda volunteer Barbara Matiru, who married a Kenyan civil servant and established a family and a publishing career in Nairobi.

157 CV for David Beer; response to questionnaire, and interview, July 2011. Details of Beer's career are also available in his early 1980s interview with Ian Smillie (STC).

158 June Dingwell Lea died in 1999. Information about her CUSO years is based on letters and diaries kindly shared by family members. For the involvement of younger family members in Farmers Helping Farmers and regarding the Bill McWhinney award, see *Farmers Helping Farmers* newsletter, 30 July 2003, 12 (for CIDA award), and May 2006, 1. My thanks to Graham Lea for conversations and email correspondence in 2004 about his mother's influence and his own teacher-training plans.

Conclusion

1 Wood to Bryant, 17 February 1986, Peter Herd to Bryant, 26 February 1986, and other letters and a poem on the planned closure, located in University of British Columbia Archives, John Conway fonds, box 8, file 14, CUSO – Miscellaneous, 1981-86. See also Library and Archives Canada, CUSO fonds, MG 28, I 323, vol. 157, file 39, U.B.C. Faculty/Local Committee (5 of 5), 1966-1980,

correspondence and reports, for evidence of longstanding and effective efforts to involve faculty in fundraising for CUSO. For the organizational name change, see "No-Name CUSO," *CUSO Forum*, February 1989, 3.

2   Maureen Johnson, "Is the 'New' CUSO Already Here?," *CUSO Forum*, June 1986, 16 (new types of cooperants) ; Chris Bryant, "The New CUSO – A Working Paper," ibid., March 1986, 4-5; and "Large Projects – A New Trend for CUSO or More Emphasis on an Old Theme?," ibid., September 1985, 4-5. For 1971 country and volunteer numbers, see "CUSO Facts and Figures," box 6, file 11, UBC Archives/Conway fonds. See *CUSO Annual Review 1982-1983*, 1, for country numbers in 1983, and Rieky Stuart, "VSO – from a CUSO Perspective," *CUSO Forum*, September 1984, 8, for planned cooperant numbers. Stuart reminded readers that volunteers from Canada would be joining host nationals and "transnational[s]," the latter posted between Third World countries. For an overview of patterns and problems in the 1980s changes, and the context, see Joy Woolfrey, Research Coordinator, *CUSO/Technical Assistance Review: CUSO Cooperants in the 1990s: Part of the Solution or Part of the Problem?*, June 1990.

3   Richard Peet with Elaine Hartwick, *Theories of Development* (New York: Guildford Press, 1999), esp. Chaps. 4 and 5.

4   For these and other changes from the mid-1980s on, see, for instance, Tim Brodhead and Cranford Pratt, "Paying the Piper: CIDA and Canadian NGOs," in *Canadian International Development Assistance Policies: An Appraisal*, ed. Cranford Pratt (Montreal/Kingston: McGill-Queen's University Press, 1994), esp. 96-119; Michael Edwards and David Hulme, eds., *Making a Difference: NGOs and Development in a Changing World* (London: Earthscan Publications, 1992), Introduction; Gilbert Rist, *The History of Development: From Western Origins to Global Faith*, 3rd ed. (London: Zed Books, 2008), esp. Chap. 10. Rist contends that much of the theorizing about causes of under-development, including dependency theory, in fact resulted in few "concrete policies" and that despite much talk in the 1970s about a "basic needs" approach, its "concrete effects [were] quite limited"; see 110, 162. On NGOs picking up the slack as structural adjustment programs resulted in cuts in state social services, see, for instance, Ian Smillie, "NGOs: Crisis and Opportunity in the New World Order," in *Transforming Development: Foreign Aid for a Changing World*, ed. Jim Freedman (Toronto: University of Toronto Press, 2000), 118-119.

5   Bryant, "The New CUSO," 5; Tim Brodhead, "NGOs: The Next 25 Years," *CUSO Journal*, 1986, 21-23, quotation at 23; Dick Bird, *Never the Same Again: A History of VSO* (Cambridge: Lutterworth Press, 1998), 154, and also "Hands across the Water," *CUSO Forum*, September 1984, 8; John W. Sewell, "In a Changing World," 185-90, and C. Payne Lucas and Kevin Lowther, "The Experience: Africa," 113, in *Making a Difference: The Peace Corps at Twenty-Five*, ed. Milton Viorst (New York: Weidenfeld and Nicolson, 1986).

6   Chris Bryant, "Reflections on Development," *CUSO Forum*, September 1985, 1.

7   Although those involved in "the new CUSO" could not know it, even greater changes lay ahead: unprecedented cuts in government funding for official development assistance in the 1990s – part of an international pattern – and, in the first decade of the twenty-first century, CUSO's merger with VSO, an outcome that, ironically, took it back to a focus on placing volunteers. See Morrison, *Aid and Ebb Tide*, Chap. 10, on 1990s cuts to CIDA funding and to NGO programs.

8   "A Message from the Executive Director as CUSO Turns 25," *CUSO Forum*, May 1986, 2, and "Message from the Executive Director," *CUSO Annual Report 1986/87*, 5-6.

9   Michael Edwards and David Hulme, eds., *Beyond the Magic Bullet: NGO Performance and Accountability in the Post-Cold War World* (West Hartford, CT: Kumarian Press, 1976), Introduction, 1, for quotation.

10   In Bill McWhinney and Dave Godfrey, eds., *Man Deserves Man: CUSO in Developing Countries* (Toronto: Ryerson Press, 1968), 415-41, quotation at 415.

11 Peet with Hartwick, *Theories of Development*, Chap. 5 (159 for Escobar on "rejection of the entire paradigm").

12 Bezanson response to questionnaire, February 2011. (The questionnaire referred to here and elsewhere in the notes was prepared by the author.)

13 *The White Man's Burden: Why the West's Efforts to Aid the Rest Have Done So Much Ill and So Little Good* (New York: Penguin Books, 2006), 18, 368, 375.

14 Scott Stossel, *Sarge: The Life and Times of Sargent Shriver* (Washington: Smithsonian Books, 2004), Chap. 22.

15 Dan Turner, who quickly recognized that he was singularly unprepared for university-teaching assignments in Nigeria, nevertheless came to believe later that he had been at least "marginally useful"; response to questionnaire, June 2011. For the Trinidad volunteer, response to questionnaire by Gordon MacNeil, August 2006; for Ghana, response to questionnaire by Wendy Salmond Quarry, July 2011.

16 For instance, Quarry response to questionnaire, and "A Thank You and a Hello," *CUSO Forum*, September 1984, 20, regarding RV Jim McFetridge's return visit to Thailand.

17 "Blood, Sweat and Volunteers. On the Fiftieth Anniversary of CUSO, a Nigerian Diplomat Tells Us How the Organization Changed His Life," program segment on *As It Happens*, 10 June 2011, featuring the diplomat and Diane Labelle-Davey. During the anniversary year, Donna Anderson Hudson likewise had a personal thank you from a former Nigerian student who went on to a diplomatic career. In the years following her return to Canada in 1978, she had had frequent letters from Mohammed, "one of my most diligent correspondents." In Ottawa to sign a trade agreement, he contacted her and arranged a visit; email from Hudson to author, 11 June 2012.

18 Interview with Jack Pearpoint, 16 December 2010. (Unless stated otherwise, all interviews cited in this book were conducted by the author.)

19 Brian K. Murphy, "Canadian NGOs and the Politics of Participation," 189, in *Conflicts of Interest: Canada and the Third World*, ed. Jamie Swift and Brian Tomlinson (Toronto: Between the Lines, 1991). As Ian Smillie explained in *The Land of Lost Content: A History of CUSO* (Toronto: Deneau, 1985), 182-86, CUSO's ability to assist Proshika owed most to the gruff pragmatism and local knowledge of the ex-missionary priest who was CUSO staffperson in Bangladesh at the time this connection was established.

20 For example, "CUSO's Head Office Receives Distinguished Visitor," *CUSO Forum*, August 1988, 1. That a lack of frankness about problematic liberation movement outcomes could create difficulties for CUSO's Ottawa-based staff is suggested in Ian Smillie's interview with Sharon Capeling, 29 October 1983, Smillie Tape Collection (hereafter STC).

21 Tape made by Beer describing independence celebrations, and Smillie interview with Beer, n.d., both in STC; Beer response to questionnaire, and personal interview, 26 July 2011; and Christopher Neal, David Beer, et al., "CUSO and Liberation Movements in Southern Africa: An Appeal for Solidarity," 123-41, in *Aid as Peacemaker: Canadian Development Assistance and Third World Conflict*, ed. Robert Miller (Ottawa: Carleton University Press, 1992), "bridges" at 141.

22 Brodhead and Pratt, "Paying the Piper," 96; Morrison, *Aid and Ebb Tide*, Chap. 11, 441 (quoted phrase), also 427, 441-43, 447-48, 451.

23 Don Faris to son Ken, 19 July 1960 ("how I squirmed under missionary 'self-sacrifice'"), Faris Collection; Frans Koch, "Return to the Parish," *CUSO/SUCO Bulletin*, August-September 1967, 24.

24 As reproduced in "Reminiscences," *CUSO Forum*, Spring and Summer, 1981, 21.

25 Statistics on early terminations among volunteers (which, as noted earlier, increased in the 1970s) and patterns of attendance at the fiftieth-anniversary events in Ottawa in 2011 appear to support their contention.

Index

26, 68-69, 71; in Nigeria, 137, 140, 152, 154, 170, 173, 176; in Thailand, 296*n*133

Canadian Institute of International Affairs (CIIA), 14

Canadian Institute of Public Affairs, 13

Canadian International Development Agency. *See* CIDA (Canadian International Development Agency)

Canadian National Commission for UNESCO, 12, 15, 23

Canadian Nurse, 43, 84

Canadian Overseas Book Centre, 152

Canadian Overseas Volunteers (COV). *See* COV (Canadian Overseas Volunteers)

Canadian Reader, 51

Canadian Universities Foundation (CUF), 22, 23, 25

Canadian University Service Overseas. *See* CUSO (Canadian University Service Overseas)

Canadian Voluntary Commonwealth Service (CVCS), 15, 78, 105, 248*n*31

Capeling, Sharon, 124(i); as CUSO staff, 126, 128-29, 193-94, 286*n*131; in UN agencies, 194; as volunteer, 193, 273*n*91

Capeling-Alakija, Sharon. *See* Capeling, Sharon

Caplan, Gerry, 104; background, 136, 286*n*123; as coordinator in Nigeria, 136, 163-64, 169, 173, 176, 177-78, 230

Carberry, Jean, 218

Cardinal, Howard, 103, 104; *The Unjust Society,* 103

CARE, 120, 191

Caribbean region, 277*n*156; Canadian connections with, 102, 268*n*31; placements in, 15, 78, 102, 132-33, 193; as site of race-based tensions, 102, 132; volunteers from, 277*n*161. *See also names of individual countries*

Carleton University, 22, 174, 272*n*86

Carter, Bessie Lillian ("Miss Lillian"), 212

Carter, Jimmy, 212

Carter, Rudy, 273*n*92

Cassels, Christina, 76

Castro, Fidel, 103

Cateley-Carlson, Margaret, 126, 192

Catholic Church: and missions, 111; officials of in early CUSO committees, 12, 22; as

religious background of volunteers, 28, 252*n*81. *See also* Canadian Catholic Organization for Development and Peace; churches; Leddy, Francis; missionaries; missions

Catmur, David, 101, 102, 241, 267*n*4, 282*n*67

Cayley, David, 103, 147, 212; *The Rivers North of the Future,* 212

CCIC (Canadian Council for International Cooperation). *See* Canadian Council for International Cooperation (CCIC)

Centennial International Development Program, 189, 202

Ceresole, Pierre, 3

Ceylon (Sri Lanka), 24, 53, 55, 62, 77

C-Far. *See* Citizens for Foreign Aid Reform (C-Far)

Chandigarh, 89

Chetelet, Lois. *See* James, Lois

Chile, 114, 121, 204

Christian Aid, 3, 244*n*10

Christian Council of Nigeria, 40, 255*n*134

Christian Medical Association of India (CMAI), 84-86, 87, 89, 90, 192, 266*nn*121-22, 289*n*43

Christie, Hugh, 28, 96, 251*n*77

Christie, Jean, 291*n*58

Church, Jon, 43, 145, 189, 212

Church, Mary Lou, 43

churches, 2, 6, 16, 69, 110, 145, 185, 243*n*4, 270*n*60, 280*n*23. *See also* Canadian Council of Churches; ecumenical groups; missionaries; missions; *names of individual denominations*

CIDA (Canadian International Development Agency), 5, 126, 200, 202, 234; aid to Bangladesh, 233; aid to CMAI, 266*n*121, 289*n*43; aid to Cuba, 122, 205; aid to postwar Biafra, 151, 152, 154-55, 282*n*53; begins funding NGOs, 41; criticisms of, 114, 118, 189, 290*n*50; and development-education support, 196, 198, 199; establishment of, 187-88; and family planning, 90, 192, 289*n*43; funding of CUSO, 6, 41, 51, 102, 117, 132, 152, 154-55, 193, 285*n*110, 286*n*124; increasing opportunities in for senior female staff, 191-92; relations with CUSO, 6, 96, 119-20, 121, 122, 134, 150, 189, 192, 194, 228, 229; RVs and, 187-89,

175, 177-78, 180-81, 230; consultative meeting (March 1961), 13, 15, 16; and COV, 15-19, 21; criticisms of, 6, 49, 101, 107, 108-9, 118-20, 134; criticizes Canadian aid and foreign policies, 107-8, 109-10, 200, 201; and Cuba, 122; and cultural imperialism as concern, 127; and CYC, 26-27, 101, 251*n*73, 251*n*75; Dar Declaration, 100; decentralization, 100, 106, 115, 116, 117, 118; Development Charter, 100-1, 105-6, 112, 113; development education, 6, 99, 107, 196-202; domestic development programming considered, 101, 203; educational rehabilitation project, 152-55; expansion in placement countries, 28, 90-91, 95; and expectations of volunteers regarding informal services, 77; family planning in India supported, 81, 129; female volunteer numbers, 72; field staff, 75, 76, 81, 91, 117, 126, 132-33, 272*n*87, 273*n*91; field staff/Nigeria, 138, 142, 145, 147, 149, 150, 152, 166, 167-71, 172-73, 175, 176-78, 179, 181; founding meeting, 12, 15; founding period, 11-19; and fundraising in private sector, 23-24, 41-42, 109, 202, 272*n*83; government funding of begins, 24-27; and "host nationals," 132; increases in volunteer numbers, 28, 42, 95; ideological divisions, 7, 99, 107, 110, 113, 115, 119, 134, 267*n*10, 273*n*103; in India, 53-55, 58, 81, 88-90; labels and slogans, 1, 8, 49-50, 97, 228, 229; local committees, 21, 43, 46, 48, 50, 51, 100, 124, 131, 186, 200, 217, 227; media coverage of, 26, 27-28, 34, 38, 47, 49, 51, 108, 114-15, 119, 123-25; medical assignments debated, 115, 133; and mission placements, 40, 255*n*134; name changes, 7, 227; National Advisory Council, 109, 187; National Selection Committee, 22-23, 48, 68; national staff, 28, 95, 126, 150, 160-61, 175; new idealism in, 134; and Nigerian civil war, 97, 143-44, 145, 147-50; orientations, 32-34, 44-48, 142, 165-66, 193, 198, 199, 253*n*105, 257*n*151, 257*nn*154-55; orientations, in-country, 117, 168; and Peace Corps, 19-20, 46; personality conflicts in, 97, 106, 267*n*10; politicians' support for, 26, 51, 123-24, 275*n*124; politicization in, 51, 95-96, 99,

103-4, 106-8, 110-11, 112-19; and postwar Biafra, 151-55; pragmatists in, 95, 113, 120, 193; professionalization of, 42-43, 95, 96, 97, 133; programming changes in, 81, 90-91, 102, 180-81; programming continuity in, 135; project funding, 285*n*110; Projects Division, 99-100, 155, 175, 206, 229, 233; public support for, 26, 51; race issues in, 46-48, 102, 129-33, 257*nn*154-55, 278*n*167; recruitment, 42-43, 48, 132, 140; regional and inter-regional conferences, 50, 88, 99, 100; relations with church and mission personnel, 13, 15, 16; relations with federal government, 24-26, 108-9; self-criticism in, 94-95; "socialist roaders" in, 113, 120, 189; and SUCO, 96, 97, 111-12, 113, 114-15, 119, 120, 134, 271*n*70, 273*n*103; teaching assignments debated, 115, 133; terminates program in India, 88; and Treasury Board, 134, 189, 200, 288*n*29; and volunteers' marriages, 160-61, 282*n*67; and WID, 125, 126-29, 276*n*139; and women as staff, 125-26, 276*n*139; writings about by RVs, 5-6. *See also* COV (Canadian Overseas Volunteers); RVs; volunteers, CUSO; volunteers, CUSO/India; volunteers, CUSO/Nigeria

CUSO alumni. *See* RVs (returned volunteers)

CUSO Bulletin and *CUSO/SUCO Bulletin*. See *Bulletin*

CUSO Forum. See *Forum*

Cuso International, 7, 277*n*159

"CUSO mafia," 195, 234

CUSO/Nigeria: A 25 Year Retrospective Evaluation, 180-81, 286*n*136

CUSO-VSO, 7

CVCS (Canadian Voluntary Commonwealth Service). *See* Canadian Voluntary Commonwealth Service (CVCS)

CYC (Company of Young Canadians), 11, 27-28, 101, 102, 120, 134, 188, 204, 251*n*73, 251*n*75

Cyr, Ron, 161, 162-63

Dalai Lama, 79, 80, 219
Dalits, 32
Dar es Salaam, 96, 100, 116-17, 186
Davis, Diane, 217

Nestlégate (bottle-baby controversy), 202, 292n85
Netherlands, 60
Neto, Augustino (MPLA leader), 122
"new CUSO," the, 228, 229
New Delhi, 66, 67, 71, 73, 87
New Left, 12, 28, 126, 249n35
New Nigerian, 173
NEWSTATEments, 104-5, 214, 269n40
New Trends in Service by Youth (Gillette), 4
NGOs (nongovernmental organizations):
    changed global environment for by mid-1980s, 228, 298n4; children of RVs in, 222-23; emergence of in development work, 3-4, 5; faith-based, 117, 196, 200, 272n85; in international campaigns, 202, 292n85; leadership roles for women in, 192; liberation movement support by, 117, 118, 119; nature of careers in, 191; optimism of in 1960s, 191; performance assessment, 229, 233, 234; politicization of, 51, 94-95; RVs in, 191, 194, 221-22; southern, 177, 180, 195, 228; symbiotic relationships with CIDA, 121-22, 189, 274n110; umbrella organizations for, 194-95; views on development issues opposed, 201; and WID issues, 125, 127, 129, 192. *See also names of individual NGOs*
Nigeria, 7, 38, 49, 139(m), 181, 232, 280n32;
    arts of promoted in Canada by CUSO and RVs, 214, 216; Benue-Plateau state, 160; Bureau for External Aid, 137, 173; Canada and, 140, 143, 146, 147, 149, 150, 280n32; civil war, 8, 143, 144-45, 149-50, 151; colonial era, 139-40, 282n64; corruption, 144, 157, 172; coups in, 144, 157; demand for teachers and formal education in, 137, 140, 141, 151, 173, 175, 233, 284n98, 286n126; as depicted in CUSO guidebooks, 168-69, 283n85; East-Central state, 151, 152, 154; Eastern Region, 140, 141, 143, 146, 150, 155, 156; expulsion of expatriates, 180; Gombe Emirate, 163; images of at independence, 136, 137, 278n3; as largest field for CUSO, 138; Mid-Western region, 144; Mid-Western state, 147; missions' roles in, 139, 177, 178, 286n121; Muslim region, 139, 143; negative

images of, 36, 136, 221; new states created, 148, 280n22; NGOs in, 177, 180; Niger state, 164; Northern Region, 144; oil wealth, 172, 284n97; oil-fuelled economic and social problems, 172, 179; optimism of early years, 136-37; political organization and resources at independence, 136-37; population of, 137; regional differences and divisions, 139, 144, 148, 155, 173 ; requests CUSO volunteers, 137, 148; return trips by RVs, 221, 296n146; universal primary education plan adopted, 164; Western Region, 140, 143, 149, 157, 159. *See also* Biafra; volunteers, CUSO/Nigeria
Nilgiri Adivasi Welfare Association (NAWA), 78, 82
Nkomo, Joshua, 118, 273n96
Nkrumah, Kwame, 216
nongovernmental organizations (NGOs).
    See NGOs
North, Diane, 146(i), 147
North, Sydney, 199
North-South Institute, 183, 195, 211, 234, 290n51
Northern Rhodesia. *See* Zambia
Norway, 266n121, 274n114
nurses, 252n90; Indian, 83-84, 85-86, 90, 264n96; 266n122
nurses, CUSO: background and preparation of, 30-31, 39, 44, 47, 48, 85; in India, 63, 65, 73, 79, 80, 85, 87; recruitment of, 43, 48; as RVs, 192-93. *See also* volunteers, CUSO/India, family planning *and* medical work
Nyerere, Julius, 100, 104, 116, 193, 273n91
Nyoni, Sithembiso, 128 (i)

ODA. *See* official development assistance
OECD (Organization for Economic Co-operation and Development). *See* Organization for Economic Co-operation and Development (OECD)
official development assistance (ODA), 189, 201
Ogbomosho, 158, 159, 282n64
Ojukwu, Emeka, 144, 145, 149, 150
Oliver, Michael, 272n86
One Sky Learner Centre, 199

Onobrakpeya, Bruce, 216
Operation Crossroads Africa. *See* Crossroads
Africa; Crossroads International
Organization for Economic Co-operation
and Development (OECD), 189, 270*n*60
organized labour, 117
orientations. *See* COV, orientations for; CUSO,
orientations
Orissa, 65, 77, 89
Ormiston, Jim, 137
Ottawa Citizen, 109
Owram, Doug, 40-41, 49
Oxfam, 3, 244*n*10, 266*n*121. *See also* Oxfam
Canada
Oxfam Canada, 4, 6, 7, 91; careers for RVs
in, 191, 195, 234; and creation of Oxfam
Quebec, 271*n*78; funding threatened by
political activism, 273*n*97; supports pro-
jects for Zimbabwean refugees, 119; and
work in India, 88, 266*n*121, 289*n*43
Oxford University, 214

Pakistan, 57, 88, 91, 231, 258*n*4
Pan African Congress, 277*n*161
Paniyas, 78, 82, 93, 204, 220-21
Papua New Guinea (PNG), 58, 90-91, 216,
217
Partners in the Horn of Africa, 222
Partnership Africa Canada, 195
paternalism, 41
Patriotic Front (Zimbabwe), 118, 119, 122
Peace Corps: 23, 46, 49, 61, 63, 77, 212, 230,
287*n*9; and accusations of spying, 102,
281*n*37; backgrounds of volunteers in,
30, 31, 32; and black volunteers, 131,
277*n*159; changes in by mid-1980s, 228-
29; Committee of Returned Volunteers,
94; cultural sensitivity as concern of,
127; founding of, 4, 19; gender distribution in, 253*n*98; in India, 57, 58, 69-70,
80, 88, 264*n*92, 265*nn*115, 118; influence
on other volunteer youth groups, 19, 41;
in Nigeria, 130, 145, 149, 159, 174, 281*n*37;
psychological testing of on return, 186;
relations with COV and CUSO, 20, 69-
70, 217; RVs as anthropologists, 156; and
sexism, 276*n*140
"Peace Corps cousins," 4, 20, 63

Pearpoint, Jack, 151, 152, 154-55, 206-7, 233,
293*n*98
Pearson, Geoffrey, 71
Pearson, Lester B., 24, 25(i), 26-27, 104, 111,
190; *Partners in Development,* 269*n*36
Pelletier, Gérard, 91, 122
Pelletier, Jean, 91, 122, 154, 271*n*70
Perinbam, Lewis, 22(i), 246*n*6, 246*n*8, 248*n*28;
at CIDA, 18, 41, 119-20, 122, 131, 150, 182,
188, 189, 288*n*28; as CUSO interim exec-
utive secretary, 12-13, 18, 20-23, 55, 57,
60, 130, 140, 258*n*4, 269*n*30
Peru, 276*n*147, 290*n*52
Phillips, Patricia: in India, 82, 85-86, 90, 91,
93; as RV, 91
Pim, Bob, 76, 218
Pinochet, Augusto, 121, 204
Planning Commission (India), 59, 70
Plewes, Betty, 194-95, 221, 290*n*53
Plumtre, A.F.W., 188
PNG (Papua New Guinea). *See* Papua New
Guinea (PNG)
Posgate, Dale: as volunteer, 62, 63, 64, 66, 67,
92, 262*n*67; as RV, 188-89
postcolonialism, 130
Prashad, Vijay, 3
Pratt, Cranford, 5, 110, 117, 121, 199, 234
Pratt, Renate, 117
Presbyterian Church in Canada, 112; mission
in Nigeria, 140; Nigerian civil war, 146;
support for CUSO, 16, 140
President's Committee on Student Service
Overseas (UBC), 15, 16, 19, 81, 227,
248*n*31. *See also* UBC President's CUSO
Committee
Princeton University, 38
Proshika, 129, 233, 299*n*19
Pullen, Judy, 77, 78-80, 93, 219(i), 220, 222-23
Punjab, 92
Puritt, Paul, 278*n*174

Quakerism, 112
Quarry, Wendy. *See* Salmond, Wendy
Queen's University, 164

race issues and CUSO. *See under* CUSO *and*
volunteers, CUSO
Radhakrishnan, Sarvepalli, 37, 70(i), 71, 88

Ragan, Ed, 90, 289n43
Ramsay, Doug, 115-16
Ransom, Judy, 70(i), 75-76, 205, 263nn71-72, 293n95
Ratlam, 84
Ravindra, Sally. *See* Bambridge, Sally
Read Margaret, 32-33
Reader's Digest, 51, 123
Readings in Development, 104
Red Crow Community College, 207-8
Redekop, Marlene, 285n114
refugees, aid and advocacy for, 202, 205; Bengali, 91, 196; Chilean, 121, 200, 204, 293n94; Kampuchean, 124, 129, 194; Tibetan, 77, 79-81, 93, 219; Vietnamese, 204; Zimbabwean, 124
Relyea, Joyce, 86
returned volunteers (RVs). *See* RVs (returned volunteers)
Rhodesia, 98, 105, 108, 116. *See also* Zimbabwe
Rist, Gilbert, 3, 230, 243n5, 298n4
Rivington, Diana, 289n41
Rochdale (Toronto), 166
Roche, Doug, 119, 123-24, 275n122
Rockefeller, Foundation, 81
Rodney, Walter, 289n40
Ronning, Chester, 24, 26, 68-69, 288n17
Rostow, Walt, 35
rotary clubs, 185, 196, 221
Royal Bank of Canada, 114
Royal Canadian Air Force (RCAF), 24, 26
Royal Commission on the Status of Women in Canada, 125
Royal Commonwealth Society, 14
RVs (returned volunteers), 8, 49-50, 55; as academics, 189, 210-11, 294n111; and the arts, 214-17; in CIDA, 187-89, 191, 205; conferences of, 103, 125; and cross-race personal relationships, 218-20; as CUSO staff, 95, 105, 115, 118, 148, 170, 186, 191, 193-94; as development consultants, 195, 290nn55-56; in development education, 196-99, 202-3, 211, 291n63, 291n68; in domestic development, 101, 203-8; empowered and cosmopolitanized by overseas placements, 184, 185-86, 235; in External Affairs, 187; in family-planning work, 190, 192-93; and fiftieth anniversary of CUSO, 299n25; and First Nations work, 206-8; and gendered career paths in development, 191-92; graduate and professional studies, 186, 187, 210, 290n45, 294n111; high expectations for, 182-83; in IDRC, 187, 188, 190-91; in international development work, 187-95, 234; in journalism, 211-12; lifelong friendships among, 186; on local committees, 186, 217; marriage and divorce, 217-20, 296n139; in multilateral agencies, 194; in NGOs, 191; numbers of, 7, 183; nurses as, 192-93; ongoing friendships of, 68; and politicization, 49, 51, 103, 106-7, 109, 118, 209, 222; in politics, 212-13; as repeat volunteers, 191, 205; retrospective perspectives on contributions, 230, 231-34; return visits to host countries, 167, 220-21; reverse culture shock, 185-86; staying on in developing countries, 224-25; stereotypes of developing countries challenged by, 8, 197, 213; as teachers in Canada, 208-10; as transnational citizens, 10; in umbrella organizations, 194-95. *See also* CUSO; volunteers, CUSO; volunteers, CUSO/India; volunteers, CUSO/Nigeria

Sachs, Jeffrey, 243n5
Said, Edward, 256n140
Saint Mary's University, 199, 210
Sakamoto, Mike, 154
Sallery, Robert, 269n40
Salmond, Wendy, 195, 253n105, 290n56, 299nn15-16
Sanger, Clyde, 5, 49, 51, 108, 124, 147, 195, 234, 268n26
Sarawak, 34, 39, 190, 209, 210
Saul, John S., 110, 117, 245n28
Sauvé, Jeanne, 22(i)
Sauvy, Albert, 3
Savage, Donald, 45(i), 51-52
Save the Children, 119
Schatzky, Tom, 32, 188-89, 262n67, 264n97
"Scheme for Canadian Overseas Volunteers," 55
"Scheme for Commonwealth Graduate Volunteers," 14
Schmidt, Ozzie, 17, 64, 72, 272n87
Schweitzer, Albert, 37, 39, 255n129

SCM (Student Christian Movement), 12, 15, 21, 32, 40-41
Scott, Paul: *Staying On,* 224
second-wave feminism, 125, 126, 127
Second World War, 184
secularization, 10, 40, 255n136, 295n125. *See also* CUSO, relations with church and mission personnel
Senate Committee on External Affairs, 108, 268n31
Seneca College, 205
September, Dennis, 131, 277n160
Service Civil International (SCI), 3, 244n11
Service Universitaire Canadien Outre-mer (SUCO). *See* SUCO (Service Universitaire Canadien Outre-mer)
Sevagram, 61, 62, 63
Sharp, Mitchell, 104, 109, 117, 122, 147, 149, 189
Sharpeville massacre, 107
Shastri Indo-Canadian Institute, 189, 294n114
Shastri, Lal Bahadur, 66, 83
Shields, Donna, 260n35, 261n52, 290n45
Shields-Pöe, Donna. *See* Shields, Donna
Shreyas, 76-77
Shriver, Sargent, 61, 230-31
Shulman, Morton, 272n83
Sierra Leone, 35, 36, 38-39, 120, 147, 208
Simpson, Anne, 164-65, 287n137, 296n132
Simpson, Don, 33-34, 148, 198, 280n31
Sinclair, Michael, 127
Sir George Williams University, 47, 102, 142, 155
sixties, the: idealism and optimism in, 5, 235; and social change, 95, 218; youth movements in, 11-12
ska (Jamaican), 44
Smallface, Marie, 29(i), 207-8
Smart, Chris, 190-91, 209-10
Smillie, Ian, 47, 114(i), 124(i), 244n21, 278n168; as author of CUSO history, 5, 13, 19, 116, 125, 134, 155, 189, 274n107; career overview, 35-36, 120; on C-FAR, 135; as CUSO executive director, 120, 121, 122, 134, 266n2; as development consultant, 195; on development education, 200-1; as Nigeria field staff, 149, 151, 166, 167, 168; on the "SUCO connection," 111-12; as volunteer, 35-36
Smith, Ian, 98, 117, 118

Sohn, Adrian, 296n146
Somers, H.J., 12
South Africa, 26, 107, 110, 117, 119, 131, 225, 234
South Asia, 13, 14, 55
Southeast Asia, 13, 14, 55
Southern Africa Action Coalition, 200
Southam, R.W., 109
southern Africa, 107, 108
Soyinka, Wole, 295n130
Spendjian, Greg, 284n99
Spicer, Keith: as author, 5, 248n30; and COV, 14, 15, 16, 17, 61; and CUSO, 16, 17, 18, 19, 22(i); and Faris, 13, 58-59, 60; in India, 55, 57, 259n10
Speirs, Rosemary, 275n126
Stackhouse, John, 93, 198
Stam, Valerie, 277n159
Stanley, Bob, 126
St. Francis Xavier University, 12, 291n67
Stilwell, Jean, 86, 89, 91, 196
Stinson, Fred, 14, 16, 17-18, 22(i), 26, 48, 61, 63
Strong, Maurice, 41, 187-88, 190, 228
Stuart, Rieky Lambregts, 195, 290n53, 296n133, 298n2
Students for a Free Tibet (SFT), 223
structural adjustment programs (SAPs), 228, 298n4
Student Christian Movement (SCM). *See* SCM (Student Christian Movement)
Student Union for Peace Action (SUPA). *See* SUPA (Student Union for Peace Action)
Student Volunteer Movement for Foreign Missions (SVM), 15
SUCO (Service Universitaire Canadien Outre-mer), 28, 122, 189, 243n3, 271n68, 271n70; Angolan liberation movement supported, 273n93; background and radicalization of, 111; relations with CUSO, 96, 97, 111-12, 113, 114-15, 116, 119, 120, 121, 122, 273n103; separatism in, 111, 115; termination of government funding for, 120, 121, 274n109
SUPA (Student Union for Peace Action), 11, 203-4
sustainable development, 228
Sweden, 108, 266n121

Tanzania, 49, 96, 104, 108, 124, 198, 270n53, 277n161; socialist development model of admired, 100, 116, 193, 273n91; teaching placements in debated, 272n86

Tapper, Selena, 133

TCLPAC (Toronto Committee for the Liberation of Portugal's African Colonies), 110, 117

TCLSAC (Toronto Committee for the Liberation of Southern Africa), 110, 117

teachers, CUSO, 191, 193; appreciation for expressed, 232; backgrounds of, 32, 135, 138, 209; continuing placements of debated, 115, 133, 172-74, 175, 179; demand for in Nigeria, 137, 140, 141, 151, 155, 165, 172-73, 178, 179; as gap fillers, 35, 231; high numbers of in Nigeria said to subsidize other CUSO programs, 173; orientations for, 32-33, 148, 165, 174; recruitment problems, 179; redundancy concerns of in India, 89. *See also* RVs; volunteers, CUSO; volunteers, CUSO/India; volunteers, CUSO/Nigeria

Tellier, Norman, 267n8

Ten Days for World Development, 118, 211

TESL (teaching English as a second language), 179-80. *See also* ESL (English as a second language)

Tethong, Lhadon, 222-23, 223(i)

Tethong, Tsewang Choegyal ("T.C."), 79-80, 219(i), 220, 222

Thailand, 112, 129, 131, 218, 296n137

Thant, U, 4

Third World (as term), 3

Third World countries, 35. *See also names of individual countries*

Thomas, Audrey, 216; *Coming Down from Wa*, 217

Thompson, Robert N., 267n8

Thomson, Mar and Rob, 207, 293n99

Thomson, Murray, 114(i); background of, 112; as executive director of CUSO, 106, 112-13, 120, 122, 126, 200, 271n77, 291n68; pacifism of, 112

Thomson, Suteera, 112

Tibet, 79, 223; government-in-exile, 79, 80, 219; refugees, 77, 79, 80-81, 93

Tibetan Refugee Aid Society (TRAS), 79, 223

tied aid, 154, 194, 201, 282n53

Tilghman, Shirley. *See* Caldwell, Shirley

Timbuktu, 156

"To Serve and Learn," 8, 49

Toronto Star, 26, 34, 213

Toronto Sun, 107, 114-15, 119, 123-24

Toronto Telegram, 25

transnationalism, 245n32

treasury board, 134, 188, 189, 200; RVs in, 189, 193, 288n29, 290n46

Trinidad, 213, 231

Trudeau, Pierre Elliott, 3, 108, 121, 122, 146, 150, 182, 183

Truman, Harry, 2

Turner, Dan: on orientation, 257n160; as RV, 211, 221; as volunteer and staff in Nigeria, 145-46, 147, 280n27, 281n41, 299n15

UBC President's CUSO Committee, 21, 198, 212. *See also* President's Committee on Student Service Overseas

Uganda, 102, 108, 138, 202, 203

Ugly American, The, 48

ujamaa, 116

UN (United Nations), 2, 60, 108, 127, 128, 194, 200, 208

UN World Population Conference, 127

UNESCO, 60

UNESCO, Canadian National Commission for. *See* Canadian National Commission for UNESCO

UNICEF, 58, 67, 153, 193, 194

UNIFEM (United Nations Development Fund for Women), 194

Unitarian Service Committee (USC), 3, 75, 88, 196, 265n113

United Church of Canada, 13, 112, 255n131; anti-apartheid activism of, 110, 292n83; as denominational background of volunteers, 28, 39; and liberation movement support, 110, 119; missionary work of, 84, 137; support for COV and CUSO, 16; supports Crossroads Africa, 4

United Nations (UN). *See* UN (United Nations)

United Nations Development Decade, 3, 19. *See also* Development Decades

United Nations Development Program, 194

United Nations Volunteer Program, 194

United States: aid to India, 57, 83; invasion of Grenada, 132; resentment of in India over Pakistan war, 88. *See also* Agency for International Development (AID)

universities, 15, 48-49, 198-99, 210-11, 255n135.
See also names of individual universities
University of Alberta, 207
University of British Columbia (UBC), 15, 21,
43, 100, 173. *See also* UBC President's
CUSO Committee; President's Commit-
tee on Student Service Overseas
University of Havana, 205
University of Ibadan, 210
University of Ife, 149, 157
University of Michigan, 192
University of Nsukka, 151
University of Ottawa, 33, 199
University of Papua New Guinea, 190
University of Prince Edward Island, 197
University of Saskatchewan, 12
University of Sussex, 156, 190, 191
University of Toronto (U of T), 72, 199, 210-11,
277n151; as alma mater of volunteers, 78,
105, 161; International Student Centre of,
138; orientations at, 33; roles of faculty
and students in establishing COV and
CUSO, 12, 17, 18, 21, 43, 47
University of Waterloo, 211
University of Western Ontario, 33, 44, 198, 199.
See also Althouse College
University of Windsor, 27
Uttar Pradesh, 66

Vallières, Pierre, 103; *White Niggers of America,*
103
Valpy, Michael, 275n125
Van Iterson, Sue Hamilton, 264n97
Varanasi, 92
Varsity (University of Toronto), 38, 137
Veit, Suzanne, 180, 282n61, 286n136
Vietnam War, 98, 296n133
Volontaires Canadiens Outre-mer (Laval
University), 15
Voluntary Service Overseas (VSO). *See* VSO
(Voluntary Services Overseas)
Volunteer Graduate Scheme (Australia), 4, 14
volunteers, 4, 58, 149, 228-29, 281n37
volunteers, CUSO: age of, 29-30, 31, 48, 217,
227; assigned readings for, 47, 103; be-
coming field staff, 75, 76, 91, 105, 138,
142, 145, 149, 170; class and ethnic/race
backgrounds, 28-29, 184, 251n79, 252n81;
declining numbers of by 1980s, 228,

229; early terminations by, 163, 179;
educational/professional backgrounds
of, 30-32; gender ratios in, 31, 72, 253nn96-
97; "host nationals as," 132; and idealism,
9-10, 12, 36-37, 39-40, 225, 230, 235; marriages of, 133, 160-61, 217; and mission
placements, 40, 89, 141, 142, 255n134;
and missionary connections and support,
37, 39, 79, 140, 177, 254n127; motivation,
35-41, 49-50; openness about placements,
34-35; and optimism, 35; and orientations,
32-34, 35, 44-48; perceived declension in,
49-51, 247n165; politicization of, 49, 51,
95; and race issues, 41, 46-48, 130-31,
256n139; recruitment and selection of,
21-23, 48, 249n44, 249n46; religions
of, 28; religious influences on, 37, 39-40;
secularization and, 40-41, 255n135; sensitivity training for, 34, 44-45, 257n151;
service beyond assigned jobs encouraged,
77, 231, 263n76; and sexuality issues, 38,
257n154; tempering expectations in, 50,
178. *See also* CUSO; RVs; volunteers,
CUSO/India; volunteers, CUSO/Nigeria
volunteers, CUSO/India: adaptation of, 58,
61-62, 65, 66, 67; agricultural work of,
65, 77-78, 81-83, 93 ; aims and roles of
discussed, 62-66; arrival, 53-54; assistance for on the ground, 66-71; and
community-development work, 59,
61-62, 75; conferences and reunions of,
62, 76, 263n71; cross-cultural dating,
73-74; cultural imperialism as concern,
127; diplomats' support for, 68-69, 71;
early philosophy of, 7, 53, 61, 92; and
family planning, 81, 83, 84-87, 89-90;
and gender matters, 62, 71-76, 126,
127, 262nn59; health and medical work
of, 65, 73, 74, 76, 79, 80; and illnesses
among, 67, 88; images of as naive, 55, 92;
living conditions of, 55, 65, 66, 67; and
mission placements, 73, 89; and national
development priorities, 59, 81; and
orientations, 69, 70, 71; and Peace Corps,
69-70; positive images of, 7, 53, 69; realism of about contributions, 55, 92-93,
229; redundancy as concern of, 64, 90,
93; in refugee work, 77, 78-81, 91; relations with Indian government, 86, 87,

88, 90; roles of in finding placements, 64, 76; as "status symbols" in indigenous organizations, 65-66; and teaching, 66, 76-77, 79, 87, 89, 93, 265nn117, 118; and ties to India as ongoing, 54, 93; variety in assignments of, 54; in villages, 65. *See also* CUSO; RVs; volunteers, CUSO
volunteers, CUSO/Nigeria, 7-8, 141(i); adaptation patterns, 156-57, 158, 159, 160, 161-63, 164-65, 165-68, 169-71, 283n76; alcohol and drug issues, 170-71, 284nn93-94; assignments of criticized for teaching emphasis, 172-75, 179; and civil war, 145, 146-47, 148, 149, 150; conferences and reunions, 170-71, 179, 284n94; criticisms of by Nigerians, 173-74, 285n105; difficulties for in teaching, 142-43, 163-64, 165, 283n70, 283n74; early terminations by, 163; and field staff, 166, 167-68, 169-71, 176-77; and gender patterns, 158, 170, 171, 253n97, 282n61; guidebooks for, 162, 163-64, 168-69, 170-71, 176; living conditions of, 161-63, 170-71; as married couples, 160-61; and mission placements, 141, 142-43, 156, 161, 166, 167, 170, 175; nonteaching assignments of, 165-67, 174-75; numbers of, 142, 179, 180, 181; oil wealth as source of new challenges, 172, 179; and postwar Biafra, 151, 152, 155; and projects approach, 175-77; requests for by Nigerian government, 137, 140, 173; resilience of, 181; and servants, 162-63; sexual activity of treated as personal matter, 171; teachers as priority, 137, 140, 141, 148, 151, 155, 165; teaching placements, 141, 151-52, 155, 156, 157, 158-60, 161, 163, 164-65, 171, 174-75; and withdrawal of welcome mat for, 180-81. *See also* CUSO; RVs; volunteers, CUSO
VSO (Voluntary Service Overseas), 13, 130, 217, 230; begins, 4; early terminations in, 283n73; in India, 46, 58, 88, 265n118; merges with CUSO, 7; in Nigeria, 173, 285n109; ongoing commitment to sending volunteers, 228-29
VSO International Board, 230

Walker, Jim, 211, 220, 261n43, 294n114, 296n135

Walmsley, Norma, 128, 276n144
Wanzell, Grant
Webster, Norman, 119, 124
Weekend Magazine, 154
Western University. *See* University of Western Ontario
WAD (women and development). *See* women and development (WAD)
Wanzel, Grant, 146
Ward, Barbara, 48
Ward, Jim, 82
Ward, Sheila: background, 255n128; in India, 82, 84, 87; as RV, 192
Warner, Gary, 294n114
West Africa, 160, 166
West Africa (CUSO placement region), 54, 103, 129, 140, 145, 147; orientations for, 198; project work in, 175; regional field staff and meetings, 177, 178, 180, 194
Whitaker, Reg, 204
White, Marian, 164, 171, 209
WID (women in development). *See* women in development (WID)
Williams, C.M. ("Red"), 134
Williams, Richard, 110
Wilson, Betty and Ed, 124
Wilson, Donald, 12, 15-16, 16-17, 21, 32
Wilson, Robin: background of, 113-14; as executive director of CUSO, 113-16, 119, 122, 272nn83-84, 272nn87-88
Winsor, Hugh, 110, 211, 294n115
Wise, Susanne, 193, 290n46
women and development (WAD), 129
women in development (WID), 76, 125, 126-29, 195, 289n41, 290n53
Women's Decade, 128, 129
Women's Role in Economic Development (Boserup), 127
Wood, John B. (executive director), 241
Wood, John R. (volunteer): background of, 32, 254n123; as contributor to *Man Deserves Man,* 43-44, 45-46, 256n148; in India, 64, 71, 75, 258n1, 262n67; as RV, 182, 183, 187, 227, 267n8, 294n111
Woodcock, George
Woollcombe, Stephen (Steve): background of, 32; in India, 66-67, 70, 71, 72, 74, 76-77, 262n59; as RV, 187, 221
work camps, 3, 63, 77, 244n11

World Bank, 106, 188, 231
World Citizens Centre, 203
World Commission on Environment and
    Development, 228
World Council of Churches, 104, 108, 128,
    272n85
World Health Organization, 194
World Student Christian Federation, 3
World University Service (WUS), 3, 13. *See
    also* WUSC (World University Service
    of Canada)
World University Service of Canada (WUSC).
    See WUSC (World University Service of
    Canada)
World Vision, 3
Worthington, Peter, 107
WUSC (World University Service of Canada),
    3-4, 15, 21, 38, 106, 191, 222, 234

YMCA, 114, 203, 213
Yola,
York University, 34, 44

Yorkdale Shopping Centre, 185
Yusuf, Tundey, 285nn104-5

Zachariah, Benjamin, 59
Zambia, 108, 124, 207, 234, 270n53;
    Commonwealth Heads of Government
    meeting in, 1979, 118-19, 123; independ-
    ence of, 105, 269n42; site of CUSO con-
    tacts with liberation movement leaders,
    116-17; teaching placements in debated,
    272n86
Zambusi, William, 295n129
ZANU (Zimbabwe African National Union),
    118
ZAPU (Zimbabwe African People's Union),
    118
Zaria, 221
zilla parishads, 59, 259n17
Zimbabwe, 108, 116, 117, 118-19, 122, 123, 128,
    224-25, 233-34
Zimmerman, Jonathan, 276n140

Printed and bound in Canada by Friesens

Set in Meta, Trajan, and Minion by Artegraphica Design Co. Ltd.

Copy editor: Catherine Plear

Proofreader: Jillian Shoichet

Cartographer: Eric Leinberger

CALCULATIONS IN CERAMICS

CALCULATIONS IN CERAMICS

by

R. Griffiths
B.Sc., F.I.Ceram.

and

C. Radford
B.Sc., F.R.I.C., F.I.Ceram.

MACLAREN AND SONS LTD.
LONDON, ENGLAND

©

R. GRIFFITHS and C. RADFORD, 1965

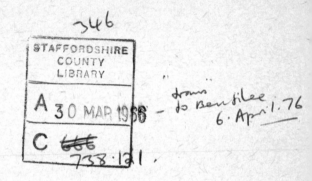
Made and printed in England by
LIVESEY LTD., ST. JOHN'S HILL, SHREWSBURY

PREFACE

This book is intended to meet the needs of ceramic technologists and managers insofar as fundamental calculations are concerned.

Each type of problem is preceded by an explanation of its relevance to ceramic processing and many completely worked examples are included.

A fundamental treatment is given to the calculations on "Suspensions" and "Dilution", and, in addition, the long-established calculating techniques (*e.g.* Brongniarts' Formula) are fully explained.

The glaze calculations include examples containing frits used in current industrial practice.

An attempt has been made (in Chapter I) to assist the reader whose knowledge of basic arithmetic is inadequate; at the end of the book there is a brief introduction to some of the calculations necessary for the statistical assessment of test data.

Our acknowledgements are due to the Principal and Governors of the North Staffordshire College of Technology for permission to use questions set in examinations at the College of Ceramics.

We are also indebted to Mr. G. Slinn and to members of the staff at the College of Ceramics for their assistance.

College of Ceramics   R. GRIFFITHS
November 1964   C. RADFORD

FOREWORD

It is some years since a book appeared devoted to the various calculations that the ceramic technologist has to make from time to time. While no revolutionary changes have occurred in the interval there have been some changes in materials used and in specifications for carrying out tests.

Since the authors have now been teaching the subject for many years, it seems appropriate that they should undertake the production of this volume.

Realizing that many juniors who have to calculate results in laboratories are not always well grounded in mathematics, they have devoted the opening chapter to basic arithmetic. Thereafter the text is illustrated with examples drawn as far as possible from everyday experience.

The book should be a very great help to students and to workers in industry, and since a great deal of work has gone into its preparation I hope that it will be well received.

W. L. GERMAN,
D.Sc., Ph.D., F.R.I.C., F.I.Ceram.

Head of College of Ceramics,
North Staffordshire College of Technology,
Stoke-on-Trent

CONTENTS

CHAPTER I

Basic Arithmetic

Numbers; Significance; Approximations; Logarithms;
Ratio, Proportion, Percentage

B Y its very nature, a number has only one characteristic— MAGNITUDE. Practically all the numbers used in this book lie within the range 0·001 to 100,000.

Much of the art of calculating depends upon an appreciation of:

(1) The relative values of the figures which make up the number (SIGNIFICANCE);

(2) The size of numbers relative to each other;

(3) What happens when numbers are subjected to the basic operations of addition, subtraction, multiplication, and division.

(1) Significance

For all normal calculations a decimal system of numbers is employed (based upon the use of ten digits).

Consider the number   44·444

The same digit is used five times, and yet each time it has a different value by virtue of its position. The importance (or significance) of a digit value decreases from left to right. Each 4, in the above example, is ten times the value of the 4 on its immediate right, and is worth only one-tenth of the value of the 4 next to it on the left.

The three most significant figures are 44·4, and the removal of the two right-hand 4's makes little difference to the value of the number as a whole.

For most calculations, numbers may be reduced to three significant figures without seriously affecting the result. By this means the arithmetic is simplified and the errors introduced are only of the order of 1 in 1,000.

The general rule for reducing a number to its 3 most significant figures is:

If the fourth significant figure is 5 or greater, increase the third significant figure by 1; if it is less than 5 it may be neglected, together with all other figures to the right of it.

Examples

Number	Number (reduced to 3 significant figures)
38·29	38·3
74·619	74·6
5,618	5,620
3·14159	3·14
0·2965	0·297
214,628	215,000
0·02067	0·0207
69·96	70·0

Note that the decimal point remains in the same place relative to the more significant figures, and that this is achieved by the insertion of noughts in the appropriate places.

(2) Relative Magnitude of Numbers

Numbers should be instantly recognized for their size in relation to other numbers.

126·4	is much greater than	2·0618
3·9	is slightly greater than	3·88
0·026	is much less than	0·10
1·04	is only a little greater than	0·969
2·50	is 100 times greater than	0·025

The two important classes of numbers are:

(A) Those greater than 1·00 (*e.g.* 14·6, 2·941);

(B) Those less than 1·00, but greater than zero (*e.g.* 0·824, 0·006).

An error of, say, 0·008 on a Class (A) number is insignificant, but the same error on a Class (B) number could have considerable effect.

(3) Operating with Numbers

The processes of addition and subtraction are simple and usually well understood.

The effects of multiplication and division, however, are not so widely appreciated. Some of these are:

(a) *Any number, when multiplied by a Class (B) number, becomes less.*

(i) $14 \times 0 \cdot 8 = 11 \cdot 2$. *(The operation is the same as evaluating $\frac{8}{10}$ths of 14.)*

(ii) $0 \cdot 06 \times 0 \cdot 007 = 0 \cdot 00042$. *(Hence the product of two Class (B) numbers is often of negligible magnitude).*

2

(b) *Any number, when divided by a Class (B) number, becomes greater.*

$$(i) \quad \frac{14}{0 \cdot 2} = 70$$

$$(ii) \quad \frac{0 \cdot 06}{0 \cdot 8} = 0 \cdot 075$$

Approximations

Whatever technique is used for a calculation—straightforward arithmetic, slide-rule or logarithms—it is good practice to estimate an "approximate answer", as a check upon the result. This practice helps to avoid the very serious errors due to "incorrect positioning" of the decimal point.

Some examples of approximation are given below:

[The symbol $\simeq$ means "is approximately equal to".]

$$(i) \quad \frac{25 \cdot 82}{0 \cdot 83} \simeq \frac{24 \cdot 0}{0 \cdot 8} \simeq \frac{240}{8} \simeq 30$$

$$(ii) \quad 0 \cdot 463 \times 212 \cdot 6 \simeq \frac{1}{2} \text{ of } 200 \simeq 100$$

$$(iii) \quad \frac{62 \cdot 37}{17 \cdot 2} \simeq \frac{62}{17} \simeq 4$$

$$(iv) \quad \frac{0 \cdot 635}{28} \simeq \frac{0 \cdot 6}{25} \simeq \frac{2 \cdot 4}{100} \simeq 0 \cdot 024$$

$$(v) \quad 3 \cdot 9 \times 0 \cdot 18 \times 62 \cdot 6 \simeq 4 \times \frac{1}{5} \times 60 \simeq 48$$

$$(vi) \quad \frac{0 \cdot 625 \times 3 \cdot 18}{420 \cdot 3} \simeq \frac{0 \cdot 6 \times 3}{400} \simeq \frac{2}{400} \simeq \frac{0 \cdot 5}{100} \simeq 0 \cdot 005$$

$$(vii) \quad \frac{3 \cdot 4 \times 2{,}160 \times 9 \cdot 5}{0 \cdot 391 \times 47 \cdot 8} \simeq \frac{3 \times 2{,}000 \times 10}{0 \cdot 4 \times 50} \simeq 3{,}000$$

$$(viii) \quad \frac{609 \times 0 \cdot 52 \times 76 \cdot 8}{0 \cdot 18 \times 47 \cdot 2 \times 88 \cdot 5} \simeq \frac{600 \times 0 \cdot 5}{0 \cdot 2 \times 50} \simeq \frac{300}{10} \simeq 30$$

Logarithms

The full processes of multiplication and division, using straightforward arithmetic, are time-consuming and tedious.

Consider the evaluation of:

$$\frac{62 \cdot 38 \times 0 \cdot 562 \times 714 \cdot 6}{3 \cdot 142 \times 836 \times 25 \cdot 37}$$

This involves four separate multiplications, followed by a division. Even the reduction to three significant figures, at the various stages, leaves a great amount of arithmetic to be done—and the possibility of errors is quite considerable.

Such a calculation may be completed quickly, and with less chance of error, using LOGARITHMIC TABLES.

A full treatment of the theory and use of logarithms is beyond the scope of this book—however, all the multiplication and division, encountered in the problems to follow, may be dealt with using a simplified short-form logarithmic technique:

The four stages are:

(1) Changing the numbers to logarithmic form;
(2) Adding (or subtracting) the logarithms;
(3) Converting the final logarithm into a number;
(4) Inserting the decimal point—on the evidence provided by an approximate estimate of the answer.

STAGE (1). Changing numbers into logarithms

Consider the number   284·6

Using four-figure logarithmic tables (see page 154) the first two figures of the number, i.e. 28, define the horizontal line in the tables along which the logarithm is to be found. The third figure, 4, fixes the vertical column and yields a logarithm, 4533.

The fourth figure, 6, provides a further increase in the logarithm, which is to be found in the sixth column on the right-hand side of the table. In this case the required increment is shown as 9. Hence the logarithm of 284·6 is 4533+9 or 4542.

Similarly the logarithm of 61·53 is 7889+2 or 7891.

In this short form technique, the logarithm of any number is merely a four-figure code group.

Further examples are:

Number	Logarithm
6·438	8087
39	5911
0·063	7993
114·8	0600
84·6	9274
0·403	6053
0·020	3010

STAGE (2). Adding (or subtracting) the logarithms

If the numbers are to be multiplied together, then their logarithms must be added.

4

(i) $$24 \cdot 36 \times 0 \cdot 687$$

Number	Logarithm
24·36	3867
0·687	8370
	2237

The logarithms are added—any figure to the left of the final four-figure group is neglected.

If the numbers are to be divided, their logarithms are subtracted.

(ii) $$\frac{36 \cdot 32}{5 \cdot 48}$$

Number	Logarithm
36·32	5601
5·48	7388
	8213

The logarithms are subtracted giving the final four-figure group 8213. Note that the logarithm 7388 must be taken away from the logarithm 5601. To do this the 5 is augmented (as in the normal subtraction process) so that the final logarithm is always positive.

STAGE (3). Converting the final logarithm into a number

This conversion is achieved by using tables of anti-logarithms (see page 156).

The final four-figure logarithm is used to enter the antilog tables in the same way as was described in Stage (1). Hence:

	Final Logarithm		Number
(i)	2237	→	1,674
and *(ii)*	8213	→	6,627

STAGE (4). Inserting the decimal point

(i) An approximate evaluation of $24 \cdot 36 \times 0 \cdot 687$ is 15, hence, in the number 1674, the decimal point is placed between the 6 and the 7, giving an answer 16·74 (or 16·7 to three significant figures).

(ii) $$\frac{36 \cdot 32}{5 \cdot 48} \simeq \frac{35}{5} \simeq 7$$

Therefore the number 6627 is finally written as 6·627 (or 6·63 to three significant figures).

5

Other examples:

(iii)
$$2 \cdot 481 \times 76 \cdot 42 \times 0 \cdot 0028$$

Number		Logarithm
2·481	→	3947
76·42	→	8832
0·0028	→	4472
5,310	←	7251

An approximate value is $2 \times 75 \times \dfrac{3}{1000} \simeq 0 \cdot 5$.

Hence the required answer is $0 \cdot 5310$ (or $0 \cdot 531$ to three significant figures).

(iv)
$$\frac{16 \cdot 38}{65 \cdot 5} \times 79 \cdot 31$$

Number		Logarithm
16·38	→	2144
79·31	→	8994
		1138 Adding
65·5	→	8162
1,985	←	2976 Subtracting

An approximate value is $\dfrac{16}{64} \times 80 \simeq 20$.

Hence the required value is $19 \cdot 9$ (to three significant figures).

(v)
$$\frac{48 \cdot 62 \times 100 \times 36 \cdot 35}{12,000 \times 0 \cdot 094 \times 2,240}$$

Number		Logarithm
48·62	→	6868
100	→	0000
36·35	→	5605
		2473 Adding
12,000	→	0792
0·094	→	9731
2,240	→	3502
		4025 Adding
		2473
		4025
6,995	←	8448 Subtracting

Approximate value is
$$\frac{50 \times 100 \times 40}{12,000 \times 0 \cdot 1 \times 2,000} \simeq \frac{5 \times 1 \times 40}{12 \times 200} \simeq \frac{1}{12} \text{ or } 0 \cdot 08$$

The required evaluation is, therefore, $0 \cdot 06995$ ($0 \cdot 070$ to three significant figures).

Ratio, Proportion, Percentage

The magnitude of two quantities (expressed in the same units), may be compared in two ways:

    (1) by their difference;
    (2) by the ratio between them, *i.e.* the number of times that one is greater (or smaller) than the other.

If object A *weighs 12 lb and object* B *weighs 3 lb then:*

Comparing A *with* B

    *By method (1) Their difference is 9 lb (*A *is 9 lb heavier than* B*).*

    By method (2) The ratio between them is $\frac{12\ lb}{3\ lb} = \frac{4}{1}$ *(sometimes written 4:1) (*A *is four times heavier than* B*).*

    or

Comparing B *with* A

    *By method (1) Their difference is 9 lb (*B *is 9 lb lighter than* A*).*

    By method (2) The ratio between them is $\frac{3\ lb}{12\ lb} = \frac{1}{4}$ *(or 1:4)*

    *(*B *is a quarter of the weight of* A*).*

Comparisons using the ratio between two quantities [method (2)], have a very wide application in ceramic calculations: many laboratory measurements need converting to the larger units.

What is the ratio between the two quantities: A = 8 *lb and* B = 4 *tons?*

Express the quantities in the same units, and then divide A *by* B*:*

$$\frac{A}{B} = \frac{8\ lb}{4 \times 2,240\ lb} = \frac{1}{1,120}$$

the ratio A:B *is 1:1,120.*

N.B. The rate between two quantities, expressed in the same units, becomes a pure number. It is the number of times one is greater (or less than) the other.

The density of a material is 314·6 lb per cu ft. Compare it with water which has a density of 62·32 lb per cu ft.
The ratio between their densities is

$$\frac{314·6}{62·32}$$

or   5·048:1

Hence the material has a density 5·048 times greater than water.

    [The result of comparing densities in this way is called the SPECIFIC GRAVITY *of the material (see Chapter III).]*

Proportion

Some properties are so related to each other that corresponding values of them always have the same ratio. This kind of relationship is called DIRECT PROPORTION.

Consider an object moving at a steady speed of 30 m.p.h. Then

$$\frac{Any\ Distance\ Travelled\ (in\ miles)}{Corresponding\ Time\ (in\ hours)} = 30\ m.p.h.$$

e.g.
$$300\ miles\ in\ 10\ hours$$
$$45\ miles\ in\ 1\tfrac{1}{2}\ hours$$
$$30\ miles\ in\ 1\ hour$$
$$9\cdot6\ miles\ in\ 0\cdot32\ hours$$

hence

$$\frac{300\ miles}{10\ hours} = \frac{45\ miles}{1\tfrac{1}{2}\ hours} = \frac{30\ miles}{1\ hour} = \frac{9\cdot6\ miles}{0\cdot32\ hours} = 30\ m.p.h.$$

This simple relationship enables us to find the distance corresponding to any particular time or the time corresponding to any particular distance.

Many calculations in ceramics involve this principle of direct (or simple) proportion:

(i) *A pint of slip weighs 34 oz. What is* (a) *the weight of 15½ pt of slip?* (b) *the volume of 214 lb of slip?*

Now $\frac{Weight\ of\ slip\ (in\ ounces)}{Volume\ of\ slip\ (in\ pints)} = 34\ oz\ per\ pt$

Therefore:

(a) $\frac{Weight\ of\ slip\ (in\ ounces)}{15\tfrac{1}{2}} = 34\ oz\ per\ pt$

Hence, *Weight of slip* $= 34 \times 15\tfrac{1}{2} = 527\ oz$

(b) $\frac{214 \times 16}{Volume\ of\ slip\ (in\ pints)} = 34\ oz\ per\ pt$

Hence,

$$Volume\ of\ slip = \frac{214 \times 16}{34} = 100\cdot7\ pt$$

(ii) *One molecule of stone contains $0\cdot16$ molecules of K_2O.* (a) *How many molecules of K_2O are there in $0\cdot426$ molecules of stone?* (b) *How many molecules of stone contain $0\cdot015$ molecules of K_2O?*

Now $\frac{Number\ of\ molecules\ of\ stone}{Number\ of\ molecules\ of\ K_2O} = \frac{1}{0\cdot16}$

8

Therefore:

(a)
$$\frac{0 \cdot 426}{\text{Molecules of } K_2O} = \frac{1}{0 \cdot 16}$$

Hence,

$$\text{Molecules of } K_2O = 0 \cdot 426 \times 0 \cdot 16 = 0 \cdot 068$$

(b)
$$\frac{\text{Molecules of stone}}{0 \cdot 015} = \frac{1}{0 \cdot 16}$$

Hence,

$$\text{Molecules of stone} = \frac{0 \cdot 015}{0 \cdot 16} = 0 \cdot 094$$

(iii) *A depth of $2\frac{1}{2}$ in. of slip in a mixing ark corresponds to 450 lb of dry body. (a) What depth of slip would you associate with 1 ton of dry body? (b) What weight of dry body corresponds to a depth of 1 in.?*

$$\frac{\text{Depth of slip (in.)}}{\text{Weight of dry body (lb)}} = \frac{2\frac{1}{2}}{450}$$

Therefore:

(a)
$$\frac{\text{Depth of slip (in.)}}{2{,}240} = \frac{2 \cdot 5}{450}$$

$$\text{Depth of slip} = \frac{2 \cdot 5}{450} \times 2{,}240 = 12 \cdot 45 \text{ in.}$$

(b)
$$\frac{1}{\text{Weight of dry body (lb)}} = \frac{2 \cdot 5}{450}$$

$$\text{Weight of dry body} = \frac{450}{2 \cdot 5} = 180 \text{ lb}$$

(iv) *A frit kiln is charged with the following raw materials: 57·6 lb borax; 20·6 lb flint; 56·0 lb felspar; 35·3 lb whiting; and 7·8 lb china clay. After the fritting process, 133·4 lb of frit are obtained. (a) What quantities of raw materials would be required to make $1\frac{1}{2}$ tons of frit? (b) What weight of finished frit would be associated with 100 lb of whiting?*

Now
$$\frac{\text{Weight of borax (lb)}}{\text{Weight of frit (lb)}} = \frac{57 \cdot 6}{133 \cdot 4}$$

and
$$\frac{\text{Weight of flint (lb)}}{\text{Weight of frit (lb)}} = \frac{20 \cdot 6}{133 \cdot 4}$$

9

Therefore:

(a)
$$\frac{\text{Weight of borax (lb)}}{1\frac{1}{2}\times 2,240} = \frac{57\cdot6}{133\cdot4}$$

Hence,

$$\text{Required weight of borax} = \frac{57\cdot6}{133\cdot4}\times 3,360$$
$$= 1,451 \text{ lb}$$

Also
$$\frac{\text{Weight of flint (lb)}}{1\frac{1}{2}\times 2,240} = \frac{20\cdot6}{133\cdot4}$$

Hence,

$$\text{Required weight of flint} = \frac{20\cdot6\times 3,360}{133\cdot4} = 519 \text{ lb}$$

Similarly each of the other charge weights must be multiplied by the factor

$$\frac{3,360}{133\cdot4}$$

i.e.

$$\text{Required weight of felspar} = 56\cdot0\times\frac{3,360}{133\cdot4} = 1,410 \text{ lb}$$

$$\text{Required weight of whiting} = 35\cdot3\times\frac{3,360}{133\cdot4} = 889 \text{ lb}$$

and

$$\text{Required weight of china clay} = 7\cdot8\times\frac{3,360}{133\cdot4} = 196 \text{ lb}$$

(b)
$$\frac{\text{Weight of whiting (lb)}}{\text{Weight of frit (lb)}} = \frac{35\cdot3}{133\cdot4}$$

$$\therefore \quad \frac{100}{\text{Weight of frit (lb)}} = \frac{35\cdot3}{133\cdot4}$$

$$\text{Weight of frit} = \frac{133\cdot4}{35\cdot3}\times 100 = 378 \text{ lb}$$

Percentage

Since we employ a decimal system of numbers (based on 10 digits), it is a simple operation to divide (or multiply) numerical values by 10, or 100, or 1,000, etc.—this merely involves moving the decimal point.

e.g.
$$\frac{134}{10} = 13\cdot4$$

$$\frac{614\cdot2}{100} = 6\cdot142$$

$$\frac{3\cdot25}{1,000} = 0\cdot00325$$

Percentages are based upon the "break-up" of some fundamental quantity into 100 parts, so that further calculations are simplified, and the magnitudes of the components are readily appreciated.

Many scales of measurement employ this principle, *e.g.* the Centigrade degree is one-hundredth of the fundamental temperature interval between the melting point of ice and the boiling point of water.

By supposing that a given quantity is divided into 100 parts we may refer to "50% (fifty per cent) of the quantity", meaning $\frac{50}{100}$ or $\frac{1}{2}$ of it. Similarly, $3 \cdot 5\%$ of some particular quantity means $\frac{3 \cdot 5}{100}$ of it.

Simple examples are as follows:

(i) $\qquad 3\% \text{ of } 1 \text{ ton} = \frac{3}{100} \times 2{,}240 \text{ lb} = 67 \cdot 2 \text{ lb}$

(ii) $\qquad 5\% \text{ of } £1 = \frac{5}{100} \times 20 = 1 \text{ shilling}$

(iii) $\qquad 63 \cdot 8\% \text{ of } 19 \cdot 3 \text{ gm} = \frac{63 \cdot 8}{100} \times 19 \cdot 3 = 12 \cdot 3 \text{ gm}$

(iv) A body contains $28 \cdot 7\%$ of china clay. How much china clay is there in $3 \cdot 6$ tons of body?

$$\frac{28 \cdot 7}{100} \times 3 \cdot 6 = 1 \cdot 033 \text{ tons} = 2{,}314 \text{ lb}$$

To Express Component Quantities as a Percentage

If 40 lb of a mixture contains 20 lb of material A, it is self-evident that the mixture contains 50% of material A. This result is obtained arithmetically by multiplying the ratio $\dfrac{\text{Weight of component}}{\text{Weight of mixture}}$ by 100.

i.e. $\qquad \dfrac{20 \text{ lb}}{40 \text{ lb}} \times 100 = 50\% \text{ of material } A$

In general, then, percentages are found by using the expression:

$$\frac{\text{Part Quantity}}{\text{Total Quantity}} \times 100$$

N.B. Both quantities in the above ratio must be expressed in the same units.

Examples

(i) 38 gm of a material contain 7 gm of iron. Express this as a percentage.

$$\frac{7}{38} \times 100 = 18 \cdot 4\%$$

Hence the material contains $18 \cdot 4\%$ of iron.

(ii) Three tons of dry body contain 1,800 lb of flint. What is the percentage of flint in the body?

$$\frac{1,800}{3 \times 2,240} \times 100 = 26 \cdot 8\%$$

The body contains 26·8% of flint.

(iii) 500 pt of water and 1,200 lb of dry powder are made into a slip. What is the moisture content of the slip, expressed as a percentage by weight? (1 pt of water weighs 20 oz).

$$Weight\ of\ water = \frac{500 \times 20}{16} = 625\ lb$$

$$Total\ weight\ of\ slip = 625 + 1,200 = 1,825\ lb$$

$$Hence,\ Moisture\ content = \frac{625}{1,825} \times 100 = 34 \cdot 25\%$$

(iv) A particle size analysis on a 2 gm sample of clay shows that 1·284 gm consist of particles less than 1 micron diameter. Express this as a percentage.

$$\frac{1 \cdot 284}{2} \times 100 = 64 \cdot 2\%$$

Hence 64·2% (by weight) of the particles are less than 1 micron diameter.

(v) A body mix consists of 215 lb ball clay, 210 lb china clay, 275 lb flint and 150 lb stone. Express the recipe as a percentage.

The total mix weighs 850 lb. Hence there is:

$$\frac{215}{850} \times 100 = 25 \cdot 29\%\ Ball\ clay$$

$$\frac{210}{850} \times 100 = 24 \cdot 71\%\ China\ clay$$

$$\frac{275}{850} \times 100 = 32 \cdot 35\%\ Flint$$

$$\frac{150}{850} \times 100 = 17 \cdot 65\%\ Stone$$

$$Total = 100 \cdot 00\%$$

Note that if the percentages are evaluated to three significant figures only, then the total becomes 100·1%. This small error is due to approximation.

DIMENSIONAL CHANGES IN PERCENTAGE FORM

During the many stages of processing, ceramic materials change in size, weight, composition, etc. These changes are often expressed in the form of percentages. There are three simple ideas involved in this procedure:

(1) The change in a property is assessed by the difference between its final value and its initial value.

Thus, a body of initial length 70 units and final length 74 units has suffered a change (gain) of 74−70 = 4 units.

Also, a body of weight 38·6 gm, which, on heating becomes 36·2 gm, has undergone a change (loss) of 38·6−36·2 gm = 2·4 gm.

(2) The fractional change in the property is given by the ratio:

$$\frac{\text{Change in value}}{\text{Initial value}}$$

Hence, using the above figures:

$$\text{Fractional change in length (gain)} = \frac{74-70}{70} = \frac{4}{70}$$

$$\text{Fractional change in weight (loss)} = \frac{38\cdot6-36\cdot2}{38\cdot6} = \frac{2\cdot4}{38\cdot6}$$

(3) The percentage change in the property is defined as:

$$\frac{\text{Change in Value}}{\text{Initial Value}} \times 100$$

i.e. Percentage change = Fractional change × 100

For the figures under consideration:

$$\text{Percentage change in length} = \left(\frac{74-70}{70}\right) \times 100$$
$$= 5\cdot72\% \text{ (gain)}$$

$$\text{Percentage change in weight} = \left(\frac{38\cdot6-36\cdot2}{38\cdot6}\right) \times 100$$
$$= 6\cdot22\% \text{ (loss)}$$

Examples

(i) *A rod, of initial length 4·00 in., attains a length of 4·12 in. when heated to 1,200°C. What is its percentage expansion?*

$$\text{Percentage change} = \left(\frac{4\cdot12-4\cdot00}{4\cdot00}\right) \times 100 = 3\cdot0\%$$

The percentage expansion of the rod is 3·0%

(ii) *A brick of length 12·4 cm contracts on heating to a final length of 12·1 cm. Express this as a percentage.*

$$\text{Percentage change} = \left(\frac{12 \cdot 4 - 12 \cdot 1}{12 \cdot 4}\right) \times 100 = 2 \cdot 42\%$$

Hence, the percentage contraction is 2·42%

(iii) *A sample of crushed stoneware weighs 5·832 gm. After acid treatment, its weight becomes 5·794 gm. What is the percentage loss in weight?*

$$\text{Percentage change in weight}$$
$$= \left(\frac{5 \cdot 832 - 5 \cdot 794}{5 \cdot 832}\right) \times 100 = 0 \cdot 652\%$$

The percentage loss in weight is 0·652%

(iv) *A test piece of initial length 8·40 cm expands 1·35% on heating. What will be its final length?*

$$\left(\frac{\text{Change in length}}{\text{Initial length}}\right) \times 100 = \text{Percentage change}$$

$$\therefore \quad \left(\frac{\text{Final length} - 8 \cdot 40}{8 \cdot 40}\right) \times 100 = 1 \cdot 35$$

$$\text{Final length} - 8 \cdot 40 = \frac{1 \cdot 35}{100} \times 8 \cdot 40$$

$$= 0 \cdot 113 \text{ cm}$$

$$\therefore \quad \text{Final length} = 8 \cdot 513 \text{ cm}$$

Note: *First the actual amount of change is found by evaluating 1·35% of the initial length. This quantity (0·113 cm) is then added to the initial length to obtain the final length.*

A shortened form of this type of calculation is shown in the following examples.

(v) *24·68 gm of whiting undergo a 44% loss in weight on heating. What is the final weight of the sample?*

$$\text{Actual change in weight} = \frac{44}{100} \times 24 \cdot 68$$

$$= 10 \cdot 86 \text{ gm}$$

$$\therefore \quad \text{Final weight} = 24 \cdot 68 - 10 \cdot 86 = 13 \cdot 82 \text{ gm}$$

(vi) *An earthenware body has a thermal expansion of 0·38% over a temperature range 20–500°C. If a test piece measures 3·827 in. at 20°C what will be its length at 500°C?*

$$Change\ in\ length = \frac{0·38}{100} \times 3·827 = 0·0145\ in.$$

$$\therefore\ Length\ at\ 500°C = 3·827 + 0·0145 = 3·8415\ in.$$

Suppose that information is given concerning the percentage change and the final value. How is the initial value calculated? Consider the following examples:

(vii) *A clay body undergoes a total shrinkage of 8% during processing. If the final length of the product is 15 cm, what was the initial length?*

As before:

$$Actual\ change\ in\ length = \frac{8}{100} \times Initial\ length$$

In this case, the initial length is unknown, let it be represented by I. *[As in previous examples the change* $\left(\frac{8}{100} I\right)$ *is applied to the initial value in order to get the final value.]* Then:

$$I - \frac{8}{100} I = 15$$

$$\frac{100\,I - 8\,I}{100} = 15$$

$$\frac{92}{100} I = 15$$

$$I = \frac{100}{92} \times 15 = 16·3\ cm$$

(viii) *On heating in oxygen a material shows a 14% increase in weight. At the end of the process the charge weight is 608 lb. What was the initial weight of charge?*

If I *is the initial weight*

$$Change\ in\ weight = \frac{14}{100} I\ (lb)$$

15

$$Then \quad I + \frac{14}{100}I = 608$$

$$\frac{114}{100}I = 608$$

$$I = 608 \times \frac{100}{114} = 533 \cdot 3 \; lb$$

Further specialized examples involving percentages are discussed in the next chapter.

Problems

(1) Use logarithms to evaluate the following expressions (to three significant figures).

(a) $\qquad\qquad 0 \cdot 482 \times 318 \cdot 7$

(b) $\qquad\qquad \dfrac{0 \cdot 624}{12 \cdot 02}$

(c) $\qquad\qquad \dfrac{41 \cdot 96 \times 2 \cdot 35}{0 \cdot 621}$

(d) $\qquad\qquad \dfrac{28 \cdot 35}{16 \cdot 9 \times 2{,}240}$

(e) $\qquad\qquad \dfrac{0 \cdot 3 \times 18 \cdot 62 \times 520}{16 \cdot 8 \times 0 \cdot 061 \times 88}$

(f) $\qquad\qquad \dfrac{20 \times 0 \cdot 007 \times 30 \cdot 8}{0 \cdot 214 \times 0 \cdot 84 \times 0 \cdot 093}$

(2) A glaze has a formula PbO, $0 \cdot 15$ Al_2O_3, $1 \cdot 95$ SiO_2. What is the $SiO_2 : Al_2O_3$ ratio?

(3) A laboratory body mix has a total charge weight of 86 lb. The corresponding industrial charge weighs $4\frac{1}{2}$ tons. What is the weight ratio between the two?

(4) A cobalt stain is to be added to an earthenware body in the ratio 1 : 20,000. How many lb of stain must be added to 8 tons of the body?

(5) One molecule of red lead contains three molecules of PbO.

(a) How many molecules of red lead are associated with $0 \cdot 186$ molecules of PbO?

(b) How many molecules of PbO are contained in $0 \cdot 089$ molecules of red lead?

16

(6) A kiln has a total capacity of 1,500 cu ft. The volume of ware in the setting is 1,140 cu ft.

    (a) What percentage of the kiln space is occupied by the ware?

    (b) What is the numerical value of the ratio:

        Volume of ware : Dead space

(7) The weight recipe of a flux is: 8 parts red lead; 2 parts borax; 3 parts flint; 1 part stone. Express this in percentage form.

(8) In a test to determine the "Linear Change on Reheat" of a refractory brick, the following observations are made:

        Initial length   14·187 cm
        Final length   14·125 cm

What is the percentage change in length of the specimen?

(9) A clay after heating weighs 32·41 gm. If the weight loss is known to be 12·6%, what was the initial weight?

(10) The recipes for two glazes are:

	Glaze A	Glaze B
Lead Bisilicate	77·5	58·1
Borax Frit	189·9	203·2
Flint	54·0	19·3
China Clay	12·9	31·5

Express the recipes in percentage form and hence find which contains the greater proportion of lead bisilicate.

CHAPTER II

Dimensional Change

Shrinkage; Moisture Content; Loss-on-Ignition

Drying Shrinkage (Wet–Dry Contraction)

DURING the drying of clayware physically held moisture is removed and this is accompanied by a contraction of the product. In general, products having a high moisture content at the beginning of the drying process undergo high drying shrinkages. The process is normally carried out at temperatures up to 110°C.

Consider a product made from plastic clay such that:

Length (wet state) = 8·0 in.
Length (dry state) = 7·4 in.

Then the change in length is 0·6 in. and this may be expressed in percentage form as follows:

$$\text{Percentage drying shrinkage} = \frac{0\cdot6}{8\cdot0}\times100 = 7\cdot5\%$$

Strictly speaking, this should be referred to as the linear drying shrinkage, since the measurements are taken along a single line.

In the laboratory, it is often convenient to mark a line (of length, say 5·0 cm) upon the trial piece whilst it is in the wet state. A further measurement, after drying, determines the wet–dry contraction.

e.g.
Length (wet state) = 5·0 cm = 50 mm
Length (dry state) = 4·7 cm = 47 mm
Change in length = 0·3 cm = 3 mm

∴ *Percentage drying shrinkage* $= \dfrac{3}{50}\times100 = 6\cdot0\%$

If the original length is given and the percentage drying shrinkage is known, a calculation yields a value for the length after drying.

E.g. *The diameter of a plate in the mould during plastic shaping is 9·8 in. If the drying shrinkage is 6·4%, what will be the plate diameter after drying?*

$$\begin{array}{c}\textit{Change in length}\\ \textit{(along the diameter)}\end{array} = \frac{6\cdot4}{100}\times9\cdot8 = 0\cdot627\ in.$$

Hence, *Diameter (after drying)* $= 9\cdot8 - 0\cdot627 = 9\cdot173\ in.$

18

Suppose that the dried size and the percentage drying shrinkage are known. How may the initial size be calculated? [Details of this kind of problem have been discussed in Chapter I—however, a further example is given below.]

A brick has a "dried length" of 16·1 cm. The wet–dry contraction of the product is 5·8%. What was the length of the brick in the plastic state?

Let I *represent the initial length of the brick*, i.e. *its length in the plastic state*

Then, $\qquad$ *the change in length* $= \dfrac{5 \cdot 8}{100} \times I \ (cm)$

Now $\qquad$ $I - \dfrac{5 \cdot 8}{100} I = 16 \cdot 1$

$\qquad\qquad\qquad \dfrac{94 \cdot 2}{100} I = 16 \cdot 1$

$\qquad\qquad\qquad\qquad I = 16 \cdot 1 \times \dfrac{100}{94 \cdot 2} = 17 \cdot 1 \ cm$

Firing Shrinkage (Dry-fired Contraction)

After drying, ceramic products are fired—usually to temperatures above 900°C. During this heat treatment, the melting of the more fusible components causes a further shrinkage of the product. This firing shrinkage is entirely dependent upon the composition of the mix and the firing schedule employed.

Calculations concerning this dry-fired contraction are similar to those already encountered during the drying process.

E.g. *The "dried length" of a porcelain insulator is 6·53 cm. After firing, its length becomes 6·18 cm. Calculate the percentage firing shrinkage.*

$$\text{Change in length} = 0 \cdot 35 \ cm$$

$$\text{Percentage firing shrinkage} = \frac{0 \cdot 35}{6 \cdot 53} \times 100 = 5 \cdot 36\%$$

Total Shrinkage (Wet-fired Contraction)

The total shrinkage of a ceramic product takes into account the effects of both drying and firing.

Consider the marked length of a trial specimen at the various stages of processing:

e.g. $\qquad\qquad$ *Length (wet state)* $= 50 \ mm$
$\qquad\qquad\qquad$ *Length (dry state)* $= 46 \ mm$
$\qquad\qquad\qquad$ *Length (fired state)* $= 41 \ mm$
$\qquad\qquad$ *Total change in length* $= \ \ 9 \ mm$

$$\text{Percentage total shrinkage} = \frac{9}{50} \times 100 = 18 \cdot 0\%$$

Also:

$$\text{Percentage drying shrinkage} = \frac{4}{50} \times 100 = 8 \cdot 0\%$$

and $\qquad \text{Percentage firing shrinkage} = \dfrac{5}{46} \times 100 = 10 \cdot 9\%$

N.B. *The sum of the percentage drying shrinkage and percentage firing shrinkage is not equal to the percentage total shrinkage (since the percentage firing shrinkage is based upon 46 whereas the others are evaluated on a basis of 50).*

The required diameter of a finished product is 9 in. If the firing contraction is $4 \cdot 62\%$ and the drying contraction is $3 \cdot 15\%$, calculate

(a) *the diameter after drying;*
(b) *the original mould diameter;*
(c) *the percentage total contraction.*

(a) *The dry-fired contraction is $4 \cdot 62\%$. Let D be the length of the diameter after drying. Then:*

$$D - \frac{4 \cdot 62}{100} D = 9$$

$$\frac{95 \cdot 38}{100} D = 9$$

$$D = \frac{100}{95 \cdot 3} \times 9 = 9 \cdot 43 \text{ in.}$$

The diameter after drying is $9 \cdot 43$ in.

(b) *The wet–dry contraction is $3 \cdot 15\%$. Let M be the original mould diameter. Then:*

$$M - \frac{3 \cdot 15}{100} M = 9 \cdot 43$$

$$\frac{96 \cdot 85}{100} M = 9 \cdot 43$$

$$M = 9 \cdot 74 \text{ in.}$$

The original mould diameter is $9 \cdot 74$ in.

(c) *The total change in diameter* $= 9 \cdot 74 - 9 \cdot 00 = 0 \cdot 74$ in.

$\therefore$ *Percentage total shrinkage* $= \dfrac{0 \cdot 74}{9 \cdot 00} \times 100 = 8 \cdot 22\%$

Volume Shrinkage

A more reliable assessment of shrinkage can sometimes be obtained, by considering changes in the volume of the clay product, at the various stages in its processing. [Linear shrinkages may be different according to the dimension considered, *e.g.* the percentage linear shrinkage measured along the length of a brick may differ from that which obtains across the width.]

Volume shrinkage calculations involve the principles used in previous examples. It may be noted, however, that the magnitude of a volume shrinkage is approximately three times the linear shrinkage of the same material. This fact may be demonstrated by considering a cube of the material, each side of which is "x" units of length, in the original state. Suppose that, after processing, each side undergoes a change equal to "a" units of length. Then:

$$\text{Percentage linear shrinkage} = \frac{a}{x} \times 100$$

To find the percentage volume shrinkage:

$$\text{Original volume} = x^3 \text{ cubic units}$$
$$\text{Final volume} = (x-a)^3 \text{ cubic units}$$

$$\text{Percentage volume shrinkage} = \frac{x^3-(x-a)^3}{x^3} \times 100$$
$$= \frac{x^3-(x^3-3ax^2+3a^2x-a^3)}{x^3} \times 100$$
$$= \frac{3ax^2-3a^2x+a^3}{x^3} \times 100$$
$$= \left[\frac{3a}{x}-3\left(\frac{a}{x}\right)^2+\left(\frac{a}{x}\right)^3\right] \times 100$$

Now, since "a" is much smaller than "x", the quantity $\frac{a}{x}$ is small (it is a Class (B) number—see Chapter I). Moreover, the quantities $\left(\frac{a}{x}\right)^2$ and $\left(\frac{a}{x}\right)^3$ must be very small indeed, and in an approximation these terms may be neglected. Hence:

$$\text{Percentage volume shrinkage} \simeq \frac{3a}{x} \times 100$$

which is 3 times the value of the percentage linear shrinkage.

Moisture Content

The weight of physically-held water in a sample of raw material is an important factor in assessing its economic value; suitability for processing; actual composition, etc.

Also it is necessary to measure and to control the moisture content of ceramic products at the various manufacturing stages.

Moisture content is determined by the loss in weight of a sample of the material after drying at 110°C.

21

"WET" OR "DRY" BASIS FOR THE EXPRESSION OF PERCENTAGE MOISTURE CONTENT

Example

A sample of china clay weighing 12·61 gm is dried at 110°C to a constant weight of 10·84 gm. What is its moisture content?

$$Loss\ in\ weight = 1·77\ gm$$

$$Percentage\ moisture\ content = \frac{1·77}{12·61} \times 100 = 14·0\%$$

N.B. The basis of this calculation is the initial weight of china clay, i.e. the "wet" weight. This is in accordance with the definition of percentage change discussed in the previous chapter. It is the commonly accepted basis for calculating percentage moisture content.

In some cases, however, it is convenient to calculate the percentage moisture content on a "dry" basis. [The position is analogous to that of a tradesman who may reckon his profit, based upon either the selling or the buying price.]

Consider a 250 gm sample of plastic ball clay consisting of 200 gm of dry clay and 50 gm of water. Then:

(a) Percentage moisture content ("Wet" basis) $= \frac{50}{250} \times 100 = 20\%$

(b) Percentage moisture content ("Dry" basis) $= \frac{50}{200} \times 100 = 25\%$

The numerical difference between the percentages is appreciable. It is important, therefore, that whenever the dry basis is used for the expression of percentage moisture contents, the fact must be stated.

Example

One hundredweight of plastic clay has a moisture content of 38% (calculated on the "dry" basis). Find the weights of water and dry clay involved in the mix, and calculate the percentage moisture content on the "wet" basis.

A 38% moisture content ("dry" basis) means that there is 38 parts by weight of water to every 100 parts by weight of dry clay. Hence:
In 112 lb of plastic clay there is

$$\frac{38}{138} \times 112 = 30·8\ lb\ of\ water$$

and $\frac{100}{138} \times 112 = 81·2\ lb\ of\ dry\ clay$

$$Percentage\ moisture\ content\ ("Wet"\ basis) = \frac{38}{138} \times 100 = 27·5\%$$

RELATIONSHIP BETWEEN PERCENTAGE MOISTURE CONTENT (DRY BASIS) AND VOLUME SHRINKAGE

The changes both in size and weight of a material during the drying process may be neatly illustrated on the same diagram. This method of presentation is often used in brochures to depict the drying characteristics of different types of clays.

Consider a sample of plastic clay consisting of 100 gm of dry clay and 40 gm of water. The percentage moisture content (dry basis) is 40%.

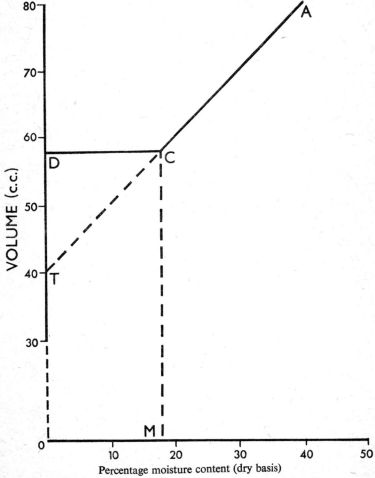

Fig. 1. Drying characteristics (based on 100 gm of dry clay)

Suppose that the volume of the plastic clay is 80 cc (point A on the diagram, Fig. 1). Then in the early stages of drying, if the plastic clay loses 3 gm of water, the percentage moisture content (dry basis) will be reduced to 37% and the volume of the plastic clay becomes 77 cc. There will be a simple relationship between the two properties, *viz.* the size of the plastic mass and the weight of water associated with it reduce by the same amounts, numerically. The point C, on the diagram, is of considerable importance. It is associated with:

(a) a moisture content (dry basis) of 18% at M. This is known as the CRITICAL MOISTURE CONTENT—below this value drying may proceed more rapidly since no further contraction takes place;

(b) a volume of 58 cc which remains constant and is the final volume reached in the shrinkage process.

During the drying from C to D, no shrinkage occurs, since the solid particles are touching one another. The moisture in between the particles is gradually removed and the moisture content is reduced to zero at the point D.

The point T (reached by the extension of AC) indicates the volume of the dry clay particles alone. It is the theoretical volume to which the clay would contract if the particles fitted together perfectly. [This volume may be used to calculate the TRUE DENSITY of the clay, *i.e.* $\frac{100 \text{ gm}}{40 \text{ cc}} = 2 \cdot 50$ gm per cc.]

The volume difference between D and T (*i.e.* 18 cc) represents the air space in the completely dried sample of clay—and hence indicates the "packing characteristics" of the material.

The diagram, therefore, provides a considerable amount of information concerning the physical properties of the clay. In particular, the shrinkage may be found for a drying operation between any required limits of moisture content.

E.g. *What contraction occurs if the clay is completely dried from a moisture content (dry basis) of 32%?*

$$\text{Original volume} = 72 \text{ cc}$$
$$\text{Final volume} = 58 \text{ cc}$$
$$\therefore \quad \text{Percentage volume shrinkage} = \frac{14}{72} \times 100 = 19 \cdot 5 \%$$

The percentage linear shrinkage will be approximately
$$\frac{19 \cdot 5}{3} = 6 \cdot 5 \%$$

Loss-on-Ignition

The chemical analysis of a ceramic material is usually determined on a sample which has been dried at 110°C, *i.e.* from which all physically-held water has been removed. To determine the loss-on-ignition, a known weight of the dried sample is heated to about 1,000°C and then reweighed.

The loss-on-ignition, then, is the percentage loss in weight occurring over the temperature range 110–1,000°C. It is due to the loss of chemically combined water, to the combustion of carbonaceous materials, and to the breakdown of such compounds as calcium carbonate. It, therefore, corresponds to the weight loss of the material from the dry state to the fired state.

A sample of dried ball clay weighs 1·2869 gm. After ignition its weight is 1·1682 gm. What is the percentage loss-on-ignition?

$$Percentage\ loss\text{-}on\text{-}ignition = \frac{0·1187}{1·2869} \times 100 = 9·22\%$$

The percentage loss-on-ignition, together with the percentage weights of SiO_2, Al_2O_3, CaO, and other "permanent" oxides, constitutes the chemical analysis of the material. In practice, the total of these percentage weights is seldom exactly 100·0 because of small inherent errors in the determination, and the difficulties involved in removing traces of reagents and in detecting minute amounts of impurities. (Totals between 99·5 and 100·5 are commonly accepted.)

Suppose that the analysis of a material is reported as:

$$SiO_2 = 52·6\%$$
$$Al_2O_3 = 21·4\%$$
$$Loss\text{-}on\text{-}ignition = 9·3\%$$
$$Other\ \text{"permanent"}\ oxides = 16·7\%$$

If this material were fired it would then consist of:

$$SiO_2 = 52·6\ parts\ by\ weight$$
$$Al_2O_3 = 21·4\ parts\ by\ weight$$
$$Other\ oxides = 16·7\ parts\ by\ weight$$
$$Total = 90·7\ parts\ by\ weight$$

Converting this to percentage form:

$$SiO_2 = \frac{52·6}{90·7} \times 100 = 58·0\%$$

$$Al_2O_3 = \frac{21·4}{90·7} \times 100 = 23·6\%$$

$$Other\ oxides = \frac{16·7}{90·7} \times 100 = 18·4\%$$

$$Total = \overline{100·0\%}$$

N.B. Although the actual weight of silica (SiO_2) remains unaltered during the firing, the fired material contains a greater proportion of silica than the dried material because of the loss-on-ignition.

To reduce the percentage of defective ware, it is advisable to test and control materials in the earlier stages of production. Hence, analytical data are often obtained on the unfired product and, by calculations, the properties of the final article may be predicted.

E.g. For adequate craze resistance a fired earthenware body is required to have a total silica content within the range 72–75%. If a sample of unfired body has 67·8% SiO_2 and a loss-on-ignition of 7·3%, will it satisfy the necessary requirement?

$$\begin{array}{ccc} \textit{100 gm unfired body} & & \textit{92·7 gm fired body} \\ \textit{(containing 67·8 gm } SiO_2) & \rightarrow & \textit{(containing 67·8 gm } SiO_2) \end{array}$$

$$\therefore \quad \begin{array}{l}\textit{Percentage total silica}\\ \textit{(calculated on the fired body)}\end{array} = \frac{67·8}{92·7} \times 100 = 73·1\%$$

Hence the requirement is met.

It is now possible to predict the final analysis of the fired product if sufficient information is given concerning the body components. To illustrate this, consider the following example:

A body recipe is: Ball clay, 25; china clay, 25; flint, 35; stone, 15.

Analytical data:

	Ball clay	China clay	Flint	Stone
SiO_2	48·4%	47·3%	98·5%	71·6%
Loss-on-ignition	11·5%	12·1%	0·2%	1·2%

Calculate the percentage total silica in the fired body.

	Dry weight	Fired weight	Weight of silica in fired material*
Ball clay	25	$\frac{88·5}{100} \times 25 = 22·1$	$\frac{48·4}{100} \times 25 = 12·1$
China clay	25	$\frac{87·9}{100} \times 25 = 22·0$	$\frac{47·3}{100} \times 25 = 11·8$
Flint	35	$\frac{99·8}{100} \times 35 = 34·9$	$\frac{98·5}{100} \times 35 = 34·5$
Stone	15	$\frac{98·8}{100} \times 15 = 14·8$	$\frac{71·6}{100} \times 15 = 10·7$
		Total $\overline{93·8}$	Total $\overline{69·1}$

* *The actual weight of silica in the fired material is the same as that in the unfired material.*

Hence 93·8 units of weight of fired body contain 69·1 units of weight of silica.

$$\therefore \quad \begin{array}{l}\textit{Percentage total silica}\\ \textit{(calculated on the fired body)}\end{array} = \frac{69·1}{93·8} \times 100 = 73·7\%$$

Problems

(1) A test piece of bone china body has a "marked" length of $5 \cdot 0$ cm in the plastic state. After drying, the distance between the marks is $4 \cdot 80$ cm and after firing $4 \cdot 35$ cm. Calculate the percentage drying shrinkage, the percentage firing shrinkage, and the percentage total shrinkage.

(2) A product has a fired length of $9 \cdot 2$ in., a drying shrinkage of $5 \cdot 6 \%$ and a firing shrinkage of $8 \cdot 5 \%$. Calculate *(a)* the "wet" length, *(b)* the "dry" length, and *(c)* the percentage total contraction. [Check the results by using the calculated values for the "wet" and "dry" lengths to produce the given value for percentage drying shrinkage.]

(3) The "die" size of a brick is $9 \cdot 4$ in. $\times 3 \cdot 8$ in. $\times 2 \cdot 4$ in. If the total volume shrinkage is $21 \cdot 5 \%$, what is *(a)* the volume, and *(b)* the approximate length of the fired brick?

(4) A partially dried product has a moisture content of $6 \cdot 0 \%$. If $4\frac{1}{2}$ tons of such product are now dried completely, what weight (in lb) of physically-held water is liberated?

(5) The "dry" recipe of a bone china body is: Bone 50; China clay 25; Stone 25. If the raw materials have moisture contents of $4 \cdot 2 \%$, $8 \cdot 1 \%$, and $2 \cdot 5 \%$ respectively, what actual weights should be used to make 100 lb of dry body?

(6) Use Fig. 1 (page 23) to calculate the approximate percentage linear shrinkage if the clay is completely dried from a moisture content (dry basis) of 25%.

(7) Four tons of plastic clay has a moisture content of $45 \cdot 0 \%$ (dry basis). Calculate *(a)* the weight of dry clay, *(b)* the weight of water, and *(c)* the percentage moisture content (wet basis).

(8) What weights of dry clay and water must be mixed to yield 2 kg of plastic clay having a moisture content of $48 \cdot 0 \%$ (dry basis)?

(9) $5 \cdot 0$ gm of plastic clay after drying at $110°C$ weigh $4 \cdot 216$ gm. When fired at $1,100°C$, the weight becomes $3 \cdot 927$ gm. Calculate *(a)* the percentage moisture content, and *(b)* the percentage loss-on-ignition.

(10) A partial analysis on a sample of unfired earthenware body shows $68 \cdot 42 \%$ SiO_2 and a loss-on-ignition of $7 \cdot 18 \%$. Calculate the percentage silica in the fired body.

CHAPTER III

Density and Specific Gravity

Definition of Density and Specific Gravity;
Simple Calculations Applicable to "Ideal" Solids and Liquids

IN the study of the physical properties of a ceramic material, a knowledge of its density is of fundamental importance.

The DENSITY OF A BODY is defined by the relationship between its mass and its volume.

i.e.
$$\text{Density} = \frac{\text{Mass}}{\text{Volume}}$$

The mass of a body is the amount of matter in it, and it is measured by comparing its gravity pull (weight) with that of standard masses (boxes of weights). For routine work in factories and laboratories, the mass of a body is numerically the same as its weight:

e.g.   An object weighing 16·4 lb has a mass of 16·4 lb

The basic units of mass are:

The "pound" (1 lb) in the British system
The "gramme" (1 gm) in the metric system
The volume of a body is a measure of its "over-all" size, *i.e.* the amount of space it occupies.

The basic units of volume are:

The "cubic foot" (1 cu ft) in the British system
The "cubic centimetre" (1 cc) in the metric system
Any related measurements of mass and volume carried out on the same quantity of matter will serve to establish the density of the material.

Examples

(i) *If 100 gm of mercury occupy a volume of 7·35 cc.*

$$\textit{Then the density of mercury} = \frac{\textit{Mass}}{\textit{Volume}} = \frac{100 \textit{ gm}}{7·35 \textit{ cc}}$$
$$= 13·6 \textit{ gm per cc}$$

(ii) *A piece of steel wire, length 20 in. and cross section 0·2 sq in., weighs 1·12 lb. What is its density?*

28

$$Volume = 20 \times 0 \cdot 2 = 4 \ cu \ in.$$

$$\therefore \qquad Density \ of \ steel \ wire = \frac{Mass}{Volume} = \frac{1 \cdot 12 \ lb}{4 \ cu \ in.}$$

$$= 0 \cdot 28 \ lb \ per \ cu \ in.$$

or

Since 1 cu ft ≡ 1,728 cu in.

$$Volume = \frac{4}{1,728} \ cu \ ft$$

and $\qquad Density = \dfrac{1 \cdot 12 \ lb}{\dfrac{4}{1,728} \ cu \ ft} = 483 \cdot 8 \ lb \ per \ cu \ ft$

Both of the above answers are correct statements expressing the density of the steel wire; it, therefore, becomes obvious that when stating the density of a material, the units employed must always be quoted.

In most cases, the density of a material is written in terms of lb per cu ft or gm per cc, but any other convenient units of mass and volume may be used. In particular, it is common practice in the British ceramic industry to quote the density of a slip in terms of ounces and pints (a slip is a suspension of solid particles in a liquid medium). Hence, the statement that "a slip has a pint weight of $35\frac{1}{2}$ oz" is merely an expression of its density.

Pure water is accepted internationally as a standard material with which other materials may be compared. Some of the commonly used expressions for the density of water are as follows:

The density of water is 62·32 lb per cu ft
or The density of water is 1·00 gm per cc
or The density of water is 20 oz per pt

[N.B. The above values are approximately true at room temperatures. For scientifically accurate statements concerning the density of a solid, liquid or gas, the relevant temperature should be quoted, since the volume of a given mass of a substance is dependent upon its temperature.]

Comparison of Densities

In comparing the densities of two materials it is essential that the same units be employed. It may be necessary to change data from one system of units to another so that there is a common basis for the comparison.

E.g. *Which has the greater density, litharge (9·2 gm per cc) or red lead (536 lb per cu ft)?*

Since a density of 62·32 lb per cu ft is equivalent to a density of 1 gm per cc, then:

$$Density\ of\ red\ lead = \frac{536}{62·32} = 8·6\ gm\ per\ cc$$

It now becomes clear that litharge is the denser material.

Specific Gravity or Relative Density

The above principles may be combined to establish a neat and simple system for the comparison of densities, using water as the basic reference material.

Thus:

The specific gravity (or relative density) of a material

$$= \frac{Density\ of\ the\ material}{Density\ of\ water}$$

e.g.

(i) If a sample of quartz has a density of 2·62 gm per cc, then:

$$Specific\ gravity\ of\ quartz = \frac{2·62\ gm\ per\ cc}{1·0\ gm\ per\ cc} = 2·62$$

(ii) If the density of a liquid is 83·4 lb per cu ft, then:

$$Specific\ gravity\ of\ the\ liquid = \frac{83·4\ lb\ per\ cu\ ft}{62·32\ lb\ per\ cu\ ft} = 1·34$$

N.B. The units used for the expression of the density of water are the same as those quoted for the material under consideration; hence the units cancel out, and the specific gravity of the material becomes simply a number. It is the answer to the question "How many times is the density of the material greater than the density of water?".

The usefulness of the specific gravity principle lies in the fact that, since it is a ratio, the weight of <u>any</u> volume of the material may be considered, provided that it is compared with the weight of the <u>same</u> volume of water, *i.e.*

$$Specific\ gravity\ of\ a\ material = \frac{Weight\ of\ any\ volume\ of\ the\ material}{Weight\ of\ same\ volume\ of\ water}$$

Examples

(iii) If 3 pt of a liquid weigh 105·6 oz, what is its specific gravity?

Since 3 pt of water weigh 60 oz, then:

$$Specific\ gravity\ of\ liquid = \frac{105·6\ oz}{60\ oz} = 1·76$$

(iv) *A piece of glass weighs 14·26 gm and has a volume of 5·8 cc. What is its specific gravity?*

$$5·8 \text{ cc of glass weigh } 14·26 \text{ gm}$$
$$5·8 \text{ cc of water weigh } 5·8 \text{ gm}$$

$$\therefore \quad \text{Specific gravity of glass} = \frac{14·26 \text{ gm}}{5·8 \text{ gm}} = 2·46$$

(v) *A 50 ml specific gravity bottle filled with a salt solution weighs 95·286 gm. The weight of the bottle is 42·341 gm. What is the specific gravity of the salt solution?*

$$50 \text{ ml of salt solution weigh } 52·945 \text{ gm}$$
$$50 \text{ ml of water weigh } 50 \text{ gm}$$

$$\therefore \quad \text{Specific gravity of salt solution} = \frac{52·945 \text{ gm}}{50 \text{ gm}} = 1·059$$

(vi) *A 1 lb metal weight has a volume of 71·5 cc. What is its specific gravity? (1 lb ≡ 453·6 gm.)*

$$71·5 \text{ cc of the metal weigh } 1 \text{ lb}$$
$$71·5 \text{ cc of water weigh } \frac{71·5}{453·6} \text{ lb}$$

$$\therefore \quad \text{Specific gravity of metal} = \frac{1}{\frac{71·5}{453·6}} = 6·35$$

(vii) *A vitreous brick has a specific gravity of 2·82 and weight 2·4 kg. What is its volume in cu in.? (1 cu in. ≡ 16·39 cc.)*

Since its specific gravity is 2·82, then its density = 2·82 gm per cc.

Now
$$\text{Density} = \frac{\text{Weight}}{\text{Volume}}$$

$$\therefore \quad 2·82 = \frac{2{,}400 \text{ gm}}{\text{Volume}}$$

$$\text{Volume} = \frac{2{,}400}{2·82} \text{ cc} = \frac{2{,}400}{2·82 \times 16·39} = 51·9 \text{ cu in.}$$

Archimedes Principle

In measuring the specific gravity of solid bodies it is convenient to use ARCHIMEDES' PRINCIPLE which states that:

When a body is immersed in a fluid, its apparent loss in weight (upthrust) is equal to the weight of fluid displaced.

[With conventional laboratory equipment the volume of a solid material cannot be measured accurately, whereas weighings can be made with greater precision. The application of Archimedes' Principle avoids the direct measurement of the volume of the solid body.]

If D = the "dry" weight of the body; and
I = the weight of the body when immersed in water (often called the "suspended" weight); then
$D-I$ = the weight of water having the same volume as the body.

Hence, Specific gravity of the body $= \dfrac{D}{D-I}$.

E.g. *A solid piece of metal weighs 24·63 gm in air, and 19·86 gm when immersed in water. What is its specific gravity?*

$$\text{Specific gravity of metal} = \frac{\text{Weight of metal}}{\text{Weight of same volume of water}}$$

$$= \frac{D}{D-I}$$

$$= \frac{24\cdot63}{24\cdot63-19\cdot86} = 5\cdot16$$

If a liquid other than water is used in determining the volume of the test material, then the density of the liquid itself must be taken into account.

E.g. *A test piece weighs 20·42 gm. When immersed in paraffin (of density 0·813 gm per cc) its weight is 15·37 gm. What is the density of the test material?*

By Archimedes' Principle, the apparent loss in weight (5·05 gm) is equal to the weight of paraffin displaced.

Now, since
$$\text{Volume} = \frac{\text{Weight}}{\text{Density}}$$

the volume of paraffin displaced $= \dfrac{5\cdot05}{0\cdot813}$

$$= 6\cdot21 \text{ cc}$$

and this is also the volume of the test piece.

Hence, Density of test material $= \dfrac{20\cdot42}{6\cdot21}$

$$= 3\cdot29 \text{ gm per cc}$$

Summary

$$\text{Density} = \frac{\text{Mass}}{\text{Volume}} \quad \text{[units must be stated]}$$

$$\text{Specific gravity (or relative density)} = \frac{\text{Density of material}}{\text{Density of water}}$$

$$= \frac{\text{Weight of any volume of material}}{\text{Weight of same volume of water}}$$

$$= \frac{D}{D-I}$$

where the solid body of weight (D) has an immersed weight in water (I).

The materials so far considered have been simple, uniform substances, existing in only one physical state, *i.e.* entirely as a solid or entirely as a liquid.

Many ceramic materials are more complex, since they are often mixtures of components which have different physical states. The two main categories are:

(1) PoROUS SOLIDS [Chapter IV]—composed of solid material interspersed with pore spaces, *e.g.* a fired earthenware body; a plaster mould.

(2) SUSPENSIONS [Chapter V]—consisting of solid particles in a liquid medium (usually water), *e.g.* a casting slip; a glaze suspension.

Problems

(1) Complete the following table by calculating the appropriate values of mass, volume or density:

	Material	Weight (mass)	Volume	Density
a	Glass	41·66 gm	16·8 cc	
b	Paraffin	39·2 gm	50 cc	
c	Alumina	84·3 gm		3·75 gm per cc
d	Water		10 gall	20 oz per pt
e	Kaolin		62·4 cc	2·50 gm per cc
f	Steel	1 ton		484 lb per cu ft

(2) Find the specific gravity of:

(a) A material having a density of 316 lb per cu ft.

(b) A piece of vitreous ware weighing 52·67 gm and having a volume of 18·6 cc.

(c) A liquid of pint weight 29·4 oz.

(d) A piece of glass weighing 3·262 gm in air and 1·958 gm when suspended in water.

(3) A vessel weighing 48·6 gm is completely filled with a liquid of density 31·5 oz per pt. If the gross weight is then 216·3 gm, what is the capacity of the vessel (in cc)?

(4) In the Rees–Hugill flask (see BS.1902 : 1952) 100 gm of a powdered material are added to a fixed quantity of xylene. What volume of liquid is displaced if the device indicates that the specific gravity of the powder is 2·35?

CHAPTER IV

Porous Solids

*Effect of Porosity on the Function of Ceramic Materials: Pore
Structure, Density—Apparent, True, Apparent, Solid;
Apparent Porosity: Water Absorption, True Porosity*

Effect of Porosity on the Function of Ceramic Materials

THE amount of pore space in a ceramic material has far-reaching
effects on its properties.

A dense, non-porous material tends to dunt far more readily than
a porous one, since the latter is capable of relieving stresses within
the pore structure.

Highly porous materials should not be used where there is a risk
of corrosion, since the cavities provide centres of attack and a large
overall surface area. Similarly, such materials have a low resistance
to erosion and abrasion.

In general terms, ware with high porosity has less mechanical
strength than a similar vitreous product.

Porosity plays an important role in the drying rates of clay goods.
As might be expected, an open porous body can be dried rapidly. In
the heavy clay industries highly plastic clays, which form close-
packed, dense bodies, are difficult to dry at an economical rate. For
this reason, many clays have to be heavily grogged, so that, without
cracking or distorting, they can be dried more quickly.

The amount of air phase present influences thermal conductivity.
Materials with high porosity are generally good heat insulators and
also have low electrical conductivity.

The viscosity and pint weight of a glaze suspension may need
adjustment according to the porosity of the ware, in order to
regulate the "pick-up" of glaze.

A 10 in. earthenware plate is highly porous and may have an
available internal surface area approaching 3,000 sq ft. Outbreaks
of "spit-out" may occur in decorated ware of this type. Completely
vitreous ware does not suffer from this fault.

The vitrification characteristics of a ceramic material are often
illustrated by a diagram showing the porosity of the material at
many different firing temperatures.

Pore Structure

Most ceramic products can be classed as porous solids, in which the continuity of the solid matter is interrupted by voids of different kinds.

In general there are two main types of pores: open and sealed pores.

Open pores are voids which are accessible (at the surface of the article) to penetration by a fluid. They exist because of the imperfect packing of the individual particles of the material and also to the escape of gases during drying and firing processes.

Sealed pores are formed on firing when bubbles of gas are frozen into the glassy matrix, or when open pores are sealed by molten material.

Some clays and bodies "bloat" when overfired. This is due to the melting action of the fluxes, together with the evolution of gases from such impurities as calcium sulphate. Large numbers of bubbles and blisters are formed, and the article expands, becoming a mass of sealed pores as the bloating continues.

Density of Porous Solids

The density of a material has been defined as a relationship between its mass (weight) and its volume.

For a vitreous object there is only one weight and one volume involved.

For a porous solid, however, there are different ways of expressing its volume, and these must be defined before any precise meaning can be given to its density.

There are three volume expressions in common use:

(1) APPARENT VOLUME

This is the "envelope" volume of the porous solid (sometimes referred to as the BULK VOLUME), and includes the volume of the solid component, open pores and sealed pores.

It may be determined by:

(a) Physical measurements of the test piece in suitable cases, *e.g.* a porous brick of sides 9 in. × 4 in. × 3½ in. has an apparent volume of 126 cu in.

(b) Using a mercury displacement method, *e.g.* a volumeter (the mercury does not enter the small open pores).

(c) The difference between the soaked weight (S) and the immersed weight (I) of the piece. If water is used as the fluid medium, then the numerical value of ($S-I$) gm gives the apparent volume in cc.

(2) TRUE VOLUME

This refers to the volume of the solid component only. It may be determined by crushing the piece into powder form—so that all the pores are destroyed—and then using a "density bottle" method.

(3) APPARENT-SOLID VOLUME

This volume lies in between (1) and (2). It is the volume of the solid component and sealed pores only, and is obtained from the difference between the dry weight (D) and the immersed weight (I) of the piece.

$$\left[\begin{array}{l} S-I \text{ gives the volume of open pores} + \text{sealed pores} + \text{solid} \\ S-D \text{ gives the volume of open pores} \\ \qquad \therefore \quad \text{by subtraction} \\ D-I \text{ gives the volume of sealed pores} + \text{solid} \end{array}\right]$$

A piece of porous material has only one weight (since the weight of air in the pore system may be neglected). Consequently there are three expressions of density, corresponding to the three volume expressions defined above.

$$\text{Apparent (or bulk) density} = \frac{\text{Weight}}{\text{Apparent volume}}$$

$$\text{True density} = \frac{\text{Weight}}{\text{True volume}}$$

$$\text{Apparent-solid density} = \frac{\text{Weight}}{\text{Apparent-solid volume}}$$

For all density expressions, the units employed must be clearly stated as lb per cu ft; gm per cc; etc.

If the units chosen are gm and cc, then the numerical value of the density will be the same as the appropriate specific gravity value.

E.g. A material having an apparent density of $3 \cdot 2$ gm per cc, has an apparent specific gravity of $3 \cdot 2$.

Hence, using gm and cc:

$$\text{Apparent (bulk) specific gravity} \equiv \text{Apparent (bulk) density} = \frac{D}{S-I}$$

$$\text{True specific gravity} \equiv \text{True density} = \frac{D}{\text{True volume of solid}}$$

$$\text{Apparent-solid specific gravity} \equiv \text{Apparent-solid density} = \frac{D}{D-I}$$

where D = weight of the dry piece (gm);
$\quad\quad S$ = weight of the soaked piece (gm);
$\quad\quad I$ = weight of the immersed piece (gm).

E.g. *A porous ceramic test piece has weight (dry) = 14·62 gm; weight (soaked) = 16·25 gm; and weight (immersed) = 8·37 gm.*

Calculate

(a) *its apparent density;* (b) *its apparent-solid specific gravity.*

(a) *Apparent density* $= \dfrac{D}{S-I} = \dfrac{14·62}{7·88} = 1·85$ *gm per cc*

(b) *Apparent-solid specific gravity* $= \dfrac{D}{D-I} = \dfrac{14·62}{6·25} = 2·34$

Porosity

This property is measured by comparing the volume of the pores with the dimensions of the piece itself.

Once again, it is important to define clearly what is meant by "pores" and whether the test piece is to be measured in terms of weight or volume.

The two most widely used expressions are APPARENT POROSITY and WATER ABSORPTION.

Apparent porosity is the ratio of open pore volume to total volume. Hence:

$$\text{Percentage apparent porosity} = \frac{\text{Open pore volume}}{\text{Total volume}} \times 100$$

$$= \frac{S-D}{S-I} \times 100$$

Water absorption is the ratio of open pore volume to the weight of the test piece. Therefore:

$$\text{Percentage water absorption} = \frac{\text{Open pore volume}}{\text{Weight}} \times 100$$

$$= \frac{S-D}{D} \times 100$$

The determination of water absorption is often used for "works control" purposes because it is simpler and less time-consuming than the measurement of apparent porosity (the immersed weight of the piece is not required in the water-absorption test).

The difference between absorption per unit volume (apparent porosity) and absorption per unit weight (water absorption) is illustrated in the following example:

A trial piece weighs 210 gm; after soaking in water it weighs 250 gm; and when suspended in water its weight is 150 gm. Calculate the percentage apparent porosity and the percentage water absorption.

$$\textit{Percentage apparent porosity} = \frac{S-D}{S-I} \times 100 = \frac{250-210}{250-150} \times 100$$

$$= 40 \cdot 0\%$$

$$\textit{Percentage water absorption} = \frac{S-D}{D} \times 100 = \frac{250-210}{210} \times 100$$

$$= 19 \cdot 0\%$$

For most ceramic materials, the apparent porosity is approximately twice the value of the water absorption. [The relationship depends upon the apparent (or bulk) density of the material since apparent porosity is based upon apparent volume whereas water absorption is based on the weight of the material.]

Apparent porosity measurements provide a better basis for the comparison of ceramic materials in general—the value of the "open pores per unit volume" is directly related to such properties as glaze "pick-up", and, upon this basis, the ceramist may make a fair comparison between porous materials of different bulk densities, *e.g.* an earthenware body and a high-alumina body.

Determination of Apparent Porosity

Most laboratories use paraffin, rather than water, since it has better penetrating properties and a lower rate of evaporation. [The method is described in BS.1902 : 1952, page 22.]

The same formula for apparent porosity is used, *i.e.*

$$\text{Percentage apparent porosity} = \frac{S-D}{S-I} \times 100$$

where D = weight of dry test piece;
  S = weight of test piece after soaking in paraffin;
  I = weight of immersed test piece (suspended in paraffin).

In fact, the apparent porosity formula applies whatever liquid is used, since the ratio

$$\frac{\text{Weight of liquid filling the open pores}}{\text{Weight of liquid having the same apparent volume as the test piece}}$$

remains the same.

[For the determination of the density (or specific gravity) of a ceramic material, the density of any liquid used in the measuring process must be taken into account (see Chapter III).]

True Porosity

For the complete assessment of the porosity of a material all the pores (open and sealed) must be considered. In this case the true porosity of the material is determined:

$$\text{Percentage true porosity} = \frac{\text{Volume of all pores}}{\text{Total volume of the test piece}} \times 100$$

$$= \frac{\text{Apparent volume} - \text{True volume}}{\text{Apparent volume}} \times 100$$

$$= \left(1 - \frac{\text{True volume}}{\text{Apparent volume}}\right) \times 100$$

$$\left[\frac{\text{True volume}}{\text{Apparent volume}} = \frac{\dfrac{\text{Weight}}{D_t}}{\dfrac{\text{Weight}}{D_a}} = \frac{D_a}{D_t} \right]$$

$$= \left(1 - \frac{D_a}{D_t}\right) \times 100$$

where $D_a = $ Apparent density $= \dfrac{\text{Weight}}{\text{Apparent volume}}$

$D_t = $ True density $= \dfrac{\text{Weight}}{\text{True volume}}$

or

If relative densities are used:

$$\text{Percentage true porosity} = \left(1 - \frac{S_a}{S_t}\right) \times 100$$

where $S_a = $ Apparent specific gravity;

$S_t = $ True specific gravity.

It is evident that the determination of true porosity involves a knowledge of the true density (or true specific gravity) of the material. This latter property of the material can only be assessed by using a sample which has been crushed into fine powder form, *i.e.* in which all the pore system has been destroyed.

Sealed Pores

The volume of sealed pores in the material is obtained by difference:

Percentage sealed pores $=$ Percentage true porosity$-$ Percentage apparent porosity

Examples

(i) A brick 9 in. $\times$ 4$\frac{1}{2}$ in. $\times$ 3 in. weighs 10 lb. If the true density is 2·78 gm per cc, calculate the percentage true porosity. (1 cu in. = 16·4 cc; 1 lb = 454 gm).

$$\text{Percentage true porosity} = \left(1 - \frac{D_a}{D_t}\right) \times 100$$

40

$$Apparent\ density = \frac{10}{9 \times 4\frac{1}{2} \times 3}\ lb\ per\ cu\ in.$$

$$= \frac{10 \times 454}{9 \times 4\frac{1}{2} \times 3 \times 16 \cdot 4} = 2 \cdot 28\ gm\ per\ cc$$

$$\therefore \quad Percentage\ true\ porosity = \left(1 - \frac{2 \cdot 28}{2 \cdot 78}\right) \times 100$$

$$= 18 \cdot 0\%$$

(ii) The external dimensions of a porous test piece are 4 in. × 4 in. × 2 in. The weight in air is 1,300 gm; after soaking in water, it weighs 1,410 gm. Calculate the bulk density and percentage apparent porosity of the material.

$$Bulk\ density = \frac{Weight}{Apparent\ volume}$$

$$= \frac{1,300}{4 \times 4 \times 2 \times 2 \cdot 54^3} = 2 \cdot 48\ gm\ per\ cc$$

$$Percentage\ apparent\ porosity = \frac{Volume\ of\ open\ pores}{Apparent\ volume} \times 100$$

$$= \frac{110}{4 \times 4 \times 2 \times 2 \cdot 54^3} = 21 \cdot 0\%$$

Problems

(1) A brick, after pressing, measures 9 in. × 4½ in. × 2½ in. The total linear contraction of the brick is 5%, and after firing it weighs 5·83 lb and has a true specific gravity of 2·70. Calculate the percentage true porosity. (453·6 gm = 1 lb; 16·39 cc = 1 cu in.)

(2) Calculate *(a)* the bulk density, and *(b)* the percentage apparent porosity, of the test pieces from the following data:

	(A)	(B)
Weight dry (gm)	120	92
Weight soaked in water (gm)	146	105
Weight suspended in water (gm)	72	43

(3) Calculate *(a)* the percentage apparent porosity, *(b)* the percentage water absorption, and *(c)* the apparent-solid density, of a trial brick, given that:

Weight dry = 280 gm
Weight soaked in water = 342 gm
Weight suspended in water = 149 gm

(4) A test-piece weighs 84·1 gm in air and 47·3 gm when immersed in water. If the percentage apparent porosity is 23·6 % calculate the bulk density.

(5) The dimensions of a trial silica brick are 4 cm×4 cm×2 cm, and the true specific gravity is 2·39. If its weight (dry) is 72 gm, calculate the percentage true porosity.

(6) A sample of flint (specific gravity = 2·63) is heated to 1,450°C. After calcination, the specific gravity is 2·34. What is the percentage increase in volume of the original flint sample?

(7) The apparent specific gravity of a brick is 1·70 and the true specific gravity 2·40. If a test piece has dimensions 3 cm×4 cm×2 cm, calculate the weight of water it may absorb (assuming no sealed pores).

(8) A porous test piece weighs 47·3 gm and displaces 312 gm of mercury from a volumeter. What is the bulk density of the material? (Density of mercury is 13·6 gm per cc.)

CHAPTER V

Suspensions

Density of a Slip; Calculations relating to Mixtures of Solid Particles and Water; Dilution Problems; Brongniarts' Formula; Standard Slop Pecks

IN the British ceramic industry, a suspension of solid particles in a fluid is often referred to as a SLIP. The solid component may be clay, flint, quartz, stone, felspar, colour, etc., and the liquid component is usually water. As mentioned previously, it is common practice to quote the density of a slip in oz per pt.

E.g. *A flint slip at 31 oz per pt*

   or

   An earthenware body slip at 27½ oz per pt

The specific gravity of the slip may be obtained by comparing it with water (which has a density of 20 oz per pt). Hence:

A flint slip at 31 oz per pt has a specific gravity of $\frac{31}{20}$ oz = 1·55 and its density is therefore 1·55 gm per cc.

To find the pint weight of a small quantity of slip:

In most laboratories, the metric system is used for the measurement of weights and volumes. It is convenient, therefore, to weigh 200 cc of the slip (using a 250 ml measuring cylinder).

E.g. *If 200 cc of the slip weighs 326 gm*

$$\text{then the density of the slip} = \frac{326 \text{ gm}}{200 \text{ cc}}$$

$$= 1 \cdot 63 \text{ gm per cc}$$

and the specific gravity of the slip = 1·63

Hence, 1 pt of the slip is 1·63 times heavier than 1 pt of water.

∴   *Pt weight of slip = 1·63 × 20 oz = 32·6 oz*

It is convenient to use 200 cc of the suspension, since its weight (in grams) divided by 10 gives the pt weight (in oz) directly.

Consider a slip made from solid particles of stone (specific gravity 2·60) and water (specific gravity 1·00). What are the maximum and minimum density limits of all the possible slips that could be made from these two components?

43

Clearly the maximum density slip is obtained in the theoretical case when it consists of a solid block of stone (no water at all), and the density would be $2 \cdot 60 \times 20$ oz = 52 oz per pt.

The minimum density slip would be entirely water (no stone particles) and hence its density would be 20 oz per pt.

If specified amounts of water and powdered material are mixed, what will be the density of the resultant slip?

This type of problem may be solved using the relationship

$$\text{Density} = \frac{\text{Weight}}{\text{Volume}}$$

Then   Density of slip $= \dfrac{\text{Total weight of components}}{\text{Total volume of components}}$

A slip is made from 37 lb stone (specific gravity 2·60) and 2 gall of water. What is its density (oz per pt)?

Working in oz and pt the calculation is conveniently set out in tabular form:

$$\textit{Weight} = \textit{Volume} \times \textit{Density}$$

	Material	Weight (oz)	Volume (pt)	Density (oz per pt)
(i)	Stone	592	[11·4]	52
(ii)	Water	[320]	16	20
(iii)	Slip	[912]	[27·4]	[33·3]

The known facts are shown in the table (in roman type). Proceed as follows:

(i)   *The volume of stone* $= \dfrac{(16 \times 37) \ oz}{(2 \cdot 6 \times 20) \ oz \ per \ pt} = 11 \cdot 4 \ pt$

(ii) *Calculate the weight of water*
        Weight of water $= 16 \ pt \times 20 \ oz \ per \ pt = 320 \ oz$

(iii) *Then*
        Density of slip $= \dfrac{592 + 320}{11 \cdot 4 + 16} = \dfrac{912}{27 \cdot 4} = 33 \cdot 3 \ oz \ per \ pt$

Hence, the weight, volume and density of each material is known and the table may be completed.

N.B. *The mental picture of 1 pt of stone particles is, at first, somewhat difficult to appreciate. A simple approach is to visualize the particles fitting together perfectly into a solid block having a volume of 1 pt. In this case 1 pt of stone would weigh 52 oz.*

Further example

In the laboratory a suspension is made using 20 gm of dry clay *(specific gravity = 2·62) and 30 cc of water. What is its density (gm per cc), specific gravity, and pint weight?*

Working in the metric system:

	Material	Weight (gm)	Volume (cc)	Density (gm per cc)
(i)	Dry clay	20	[7·63]	2·62
(ii)	Water	[30]	30·0	1·00
(iii)	Slip	[50]	[37·63]	[1·33]

(i) 20 gm of dry clay would occupy a volume of $\dfrac{20}{2\cdot62} = 7\cdot63$ cc

(ii) $\qquad$ Weight of water $= 30 \times 1\cdot00 = 30$ gm

(iii) $\qquad$ Density of slip $= \dfrac{20+30}{7\cdot63+30} = 1\cdot33$ gm per cc

Hence, $\qquad$ Specific gravity of slip $= 1\cdot33$

and $\qquad$ Pint weight of slip $= 1\cdot33 \times 20 = 26\cdot6$ oz

Other types of problems using the above principles are as follows:

(a) *What volume of water must be added to 3 cwt of dry glaze (specific gravity = 2·80) to obtain a glaze slip at 32 oz per pt?*

Working in oz and pt: Let x *pt of water be the required volume.*

	Material	Weight (oz)	Volume (pt)	Density (oz per pt)
(i)	Dry glaze	5,376	[96]	56
(ii)	Water	[20x]	[x]	20
(iii)	Slip	[5,376+20x]	[96+x]	32

(i) $\qquad$ Volume of dry glaze $= \dfrac{5,376}{56} = 96$ pt

(ii) $\qquad$ Weight of water $= 20x$ oz

(iii) *Since*

$$\text{Density of slip} = \frac{\text{Total weight of components}}{\text{Total volume of components}}$$

45

Then
$$32 = \frac{5{,}376+20x}{96+x}$$
$$\therefore \qquad 3{,}072+32x = 5{,}376+20x$$
$$12x = 2{,}304$$
$$x = 192$$

Hence 192 pt of water are required.

(b) *A flint suspension of density 1·54 gm per cc is made from 80 gm of dry flint and 55 cc of water. What is the specific gravity of the flint?*

Material	Weight (gm)	Volume (cc)	Density (gm/cc)
Dry flint	80	$\left[\dfrac{80}{d}\right]$	[d]
Water	[55]	55	1·0
Suspension	[135]	$\left[\dfrac{80}{d}+55\right]$	1·54

Let "d" be the density of dry flint (gm per cc).

(i) $\qquad$ *Volume of flint* $= \dfrac{80}{d}$ *cc*

(ii) $\qquad$ *Weight of water* $= 55$ *gm*

Since density of suspension $= \dfrac{\text{Total weight of components}}{\text{Total volume of components}}$

$$1·54 = \frac{135}{\dfrac{80}{d}+55}$$

$$\therefore \qquad \frac{123·2}{d}+84·7 = 135$$
$$123·2+84·7d = 135d$$
$$123·2 = 50·3d$$
$$d = \frac{123·2}{50·3} = 2·45 \text{ gm per cc}$$

∴ The specific gravity of the flint is 2·45.

(c) *Equal weights of water and a powder material of specific gravity 2·50 are made into a slip. What will be its pint weight?*

Let d $=$ *density of slip (gm per cc); and*
x $=$ *weight of water (gm)*
∴ $\quad$ x $=$ *Weight of dry material*

Material	Weight (gm)	Volume (cc)	Density (gm/cc)
Dry powder	[x]	$\left[\dfrac{x}{2 \cdot 50}\right]$	2·50
Water	[x]	[x]	1·00
Slip	[2x]	$\left[\dfrac{x}{2 \cdot 50}+x\right]$	[d]

$$d = \frac{2x}{\dfrac{x}{2 \cdot 50}+x} = \frac{2x}{x\left(\dfrac{1}{2 \cdot 50}+1\right)}$$

$$\therefore \quad d = \frac{2}{\dfrac{1}{2 \cdot 50}+1} = \frac{5}{3 \cdot 5} = 1 \cdot 43 \ gm/cc$$

Hence, the pint weight of slip = 28·6 oz

(d) *An ark contains 40 gall of slip at 33 oz pint weight. What weight of plastic clay (moisture content = 20%) must be added to increase the pint weight to 36 oz? (Specific gravity of dry clay = 2·50.)*

A simple calculation, based on 100 gm of plastic clay, will establish its density:

Material	Weight (gm)	Volume (cc)	Density (gm/cc)
Dry clay	80	[32]	2·50
Water	20	20	1·00
Plastic clay	100	[52]	[1·923]

$$\therefore \quad \text{Density of plastic clay} = 1 \cdot 923 \ gm \ per \ cc$$
$$= 38 \cdot 46 \ oz \ per \ pt$$

Then:

Material	Weight (oz)	Volume (pt)	Density (oz/pt)
Slip	[10,560]	320	33
Plastic clay	[x]	$\left[\dfrac{x}{38 \cdot 46}\right]$	38·46
Final slip	[10,560+x]	$\left[320+\dfrac{x}{38 \cdot 46}\right]$	36

47

$$\frac{10{,}560+x}{320+\dfrac{x}{38\cdot46}} = 36$$

$$10{,}560+x = 11{,}520+\frac{36}{38\cdot46}x$$

$$0\cdot064x = 960$$

$$x = \frac{960}{0\cdot064} = 15{,}000 \ oz$$

Hence 938 lb of plastic clay are required.

(e) *Casting slip is blunged in an ark, 14 ft in diameter, with a maximum working depth of 7 ft, to a constant pint weight of 35 oz.*

It is the normal factory practice to blunge and repress casting scraps to form press cakes with a moisture content of 25%. If the slip in the above ark is 6 ft 6 in. deep at 35 oz/pt, what weight of press cakes (lb) and volume of water (pt) must be added to the ark to bring the depth up to 7 ft and maintain the pint weight at 35 oz? (1 cu ft = 6·23 gall; specific gravity of dry body = 2·50.)

Final slip $\begin{cases} Volume = \pi\times7^2\times\frac{1}{2}\times6\cdot23\times8 = 3{,}837\ pt \\ Weight = 3{,}837\times35 = 134{,}300\ oz \\ Density = 35\ oz\ per\ pt \end{cases}$

Find the density of the plastic clay as follows:

Material	Weight (oz)	Volume (pt)	Density (oz/pt)
Dry clay	75	[1·50]	50
Water	25	[1·25]	20
Plastic clay	100	[2·75]	[d]

Density of plastic clay (d) $= \dfrac{100}{2\cdot75} = 36\cdot37\ oz\ per\ pt$

Let x = *weight of plastic clay (lb); and*

y = *volume of water (pt).*

Material	Weight (oz)	Volume (pt)	Density (oz/pt)
Water	[20y]	[y]	20
Plastic clay	[16x]	[0·44x]	36·37
Slip	134,300	3,837	35

Now

$$20y + 16x = 134,300 \quad \ldots\ldots\ldots\ldots\ldots\ldots(1)$$

$$y + 0·44x = 3,837 \quad \ldots\ldots\ldots\ldots\ldots(2)$$

Solving these simultaneous equations:

$$x = 7,997$$

$$y = 318$$

Hence 7,997 lb of plastic clay and 318 pt of water are required.

All the problems in this chapter may be solved using the technique already described. There are, however, other methods, long established in ceramics practice, which are useful in dealing with specific types of problem. Some of these are illustrated below:

Dilution Problems

The density of a slip is reduced by the addition of water. Calculations involving the quantities of slip and water, and the corresponding change in density, may be treated as follows:

To reduce 1 pt of slip at A oz per pt to the lower density B oz per pt, add $\frac{A-B}{B-20}$ pt of water.

E.g. *How much water must be added to 10 gall of slip at 36 oz per pt to obtain a slip at 32 oz per pt?*

For 1 pt of slip at 36 oz per pt, the amount of water required is

$$\frac{36-32}{32-20} = \frac{1}{3} pt$$

Hence, for 80 pt of slip, $80 \times \frac{1}{3} = 26\frac{2}{3}$ pt of water are required.

The above formula is easily proved, using the principles previously established:

CALCULATIONS IN CERAMICS

Consider 1 pt of slip at A oz per pt. Let x pt be the volume of water which must be added to produce a slip of density B oz per pt.

Then:

Material	Weight (oz)	Volume (pt)	Density (oz/pt)
Slip A	A	1	A
Water	$20x$	x	20
Slip B	$A+20x$	$1+x$	B

Since, Density of mixture $= \dfrac{\text{Weight of components}}{\text{Volume of components}}$

$$B = \frac{A+20x}{1+x}$$
$$B+Bx = A+20x$$
$$Bx-20x = A-B$$
$$x = \frac{A-B}{B-20}$$

Further example

A mixing ark contains 220 gall of slip at $27\frac{3}{4}$ oz per pt. How much water must be added to reduce the pint weight to 27 oz per pt?

For 1 pt of slip add $\dfrac{27\cdot75-27\cdot0}{27-20} = \dfrac{0\cdot75}{7}$ pt of water

$\therefore$ Total water required $= 220\times8\times\dfrac{0\cdot75}{7}$

$= 189$ pt

It is important to note that the formula $\frac{A-B}{B-20}$ yields a quantity of water (in pt) to be added to every pint of the high density slip.

Suppose slip is to be diluted from 35 oz per pt to 30 oz per pt.

Then:

$\frac{1}{2}$ pt of water must be added to each pt of the original slip or $\frac{1}{2}$ gall of water must be added to each gall of the original slip

Clearly, the quantity of water is directly proportional to the quantity of original slip. Hence, the use of the formula may be extended.

(a) *A blunger contains 80 buckets of slip at 36 oz per pt. How many buckets of water would be required to dilute the slip to 35 oz per pt?*

$$\frac{36-35}{35-20} = \frac{1}{15}$$

∴ $\frac{1}{15}$th *buckets of water are needed for every bucket of slip.*

Total water required $= \frac{1}{15} \times 80 = 5\frac{1}{3}$ *buckets*

(b) *If 10 buckets of water reduced the pint weight of a slip from 32 oz to 31 oz, how many more buckets of water would be needed to reduce it to 30 oz per pt?*

$$\frac{32-31}{31-20} = \frac{1}{11}$$

∴ $\frac{1}{11}$th *bucket of water was needed for each bucket of slip.*

I.e. *1 bucket of water was needed for each 11 buckets of slip. Since 10 buckets of water were used, the volume of slip (at 32 oz per pt) must have been*

$$10 \times 11 = 110 \text{ buckets}$$

∴ *After this first dilution there is* $110+10 = 120$ *buckets of slip at 31 oz per pt.*

For the second dilution:

$$\frac{31-30}{30-20} = \frac{1}{10}$$

Hence $120 \times \frac{1}{10} = 12$ *buckets of water are required.*

The formula may also be modified to deal with quantities and densities expressed in the metric system. In this case, the appropriate density expression for water is 1·0 gm per cc and the necessary dilution is $\frac{E-F}{F-1}$ cc of water added to every cc of slip at E gm per cc to give a resultant slip at F gm per cc.

E.g. *How much water must be added to 480 cc of slip (density 1·80 gm per cc) to reduce its density to 1·65 gm per cc?*

$$\frac{1 \cdot 80 - 1 \cdot 65}{1 \cdot 65 - 1 \cdot 0} = \frac{0 \cdot 15}{0 \cdot 65} \text{ cc of water for each cc of "original" slip}$$

Hence, total water required $= \frac{0 \cdot 15}{0 \cdot 65} \times 480 = 111$ *cc.*

Brongniart's Formula

Calculations involving the liquid and solid components of a slip are often simplified by using BRONGNIART'S FORMULA, which is:

$$W = (P-20)\frac{s}{s-1}$$

where W = Weight (oz) of the solid components in 1 pt of slip;
P = Density of the slip (oz per pt); and
s = Specific gravity of the solid component.

E.g. What is the dry content of 8 gall of flint slip having a pint weight of 31 oz? (The specific gravity of the dry flint is 2·50.)

Using Brongniart's Formula, the dry content in 1 pt of slip is:

$$W = (31-20)\frac{2\cdot50}{2\cdot50-1} = 18\cdot33 \ oz$$

Hence the dry content of 64 pt of slip is

$$= 64 \times 18\cdot33 \ oz$$
$$= 73\cdot3 \ lb$$

A proof of Brongniarts' Formula is as follows:

Consider 1 pt of slip (density P oz per pt).

Let W oz be the dry content; and

s be the specific gravity of the solid component.

Material	Weight (oz)	Volume (pt)	Density (oz/pt)
Solid component	W	$\left[\dfrac{W}{20s}\right]$	$20s$
Water	$[P-W]$	$\left[1-\dfrac{W}{20s}\right]$	20
Slip	$[P]$	1	P

Weight of water in the slip $= P-20$ oz

Volume of water in the slip $= 1-\dfrac{W}{20s}$ pt

Hence $$20 = \frac{P-W}{1-\dfrac{W}{20s}}$$

$$20-\frac{W}{s} = P-W$$

$$W - \frac{W}{s} = P - 20$$

$$W\left(1 - \frac{1}{s}\right) = P - 20$$

$$W = (P - 20)\frac{s}{s-1}$$

The formula establishes a relationship between the three variables *W*, *P* and *s*. It follows that, if any two of these are known, the remaining one may be found by calculation. (In all cases the liquid component is water.)

Examples

(i) *What is the weight of dry material in 1 pt of slip at 32 oz per pt? (Specific gravity of dry material = 2·50.)*

$$W = (32 - 20)\frac{2 \cdot 50}{2 \cdot 50 - 1}$$

$$= 12 \times \frac{5}{3} = 20 \ oz$$

$$\left[\text{Note} \quad \frac{2 \cdot 50}{2 \cdot 50 - 1} = \frac{2 \cdot 50}{1 \cdot 50} = \frac{5}{3} \right]$$

(ii) *A pint of slip contains 18 oz of dry clay (specific gravity = 2·60). What is the pint weight of the slip?*

Substituting the given values in Brongniart's Formula:

$$18 = (P - 20)\frac{2 \cdot 60}{2 \cdot 60 - 1}$$

$$P - 20 = 18 \times \frac{1 \cdot 60}{2 \cdot 60}$$

$$P = 18 \times \frac{1 \cdot 60}{2 \cdot 60} + 20 = 31 \cdot 1 \ oz$$

The pint weight of the slip is 31·1 oz.

(iii) *Four pints of slip (density 1·60 gm per cc) contain 78·8 oz of dry material. What is the specific gravity of the solid component?*

$$P = 1 \cdot 60 \times 20 = 32 \ oz \ per \ pt$$

$$W = \frac{78 \cdot 8}{4} = 19 \cdot 7 \ oz$$

Substituting in Brongniart's Formula:

$$19 \cdot 7 = (32-20)\frac{s}{s-1}$$
$$19 \cdot 7\,(s-1) = 12s$$
$$19 \cdot 7s - 19 \cdot 7 = 12s$$
$$7 \cdot 7s = 19 \cdot 7$$
$$s = \frac{19 \cdot 7}{7 \cdot 7} = 2 \cdot 56$$

The principle employed in Brongniart's Formula has a much wider use, since it may be applied to any volume of slip and any system of units. In general it becomes:

Weight of dry material = ("Weight of slip" − "Weight of water") $\frac{s}{s-1}$

N.B. In the above formula, the "Weight of slip" and "Weight of water" must have the same volume.

E.g. *300 cc of slip weigh 462 gm. The solid component is flint (specific gravity = 2·50). Calculate the dry content of the slip.*

300 cc of slip weigh 462 gm
300 cc of water weigh 300 gm

Hence, Dry content $= (462-300)\frac{2 \cdot 5}{2 \cdot 5-1} = 270\,gm$

The above principle is often used in particle size measurement (*e.g.* the hydrometer method) for calculating the dry content of a sample in slip form. It is convenient to use a specific gravity bottle as the containing vessel. The bottle is half-filled with the slip to be tested, then water is added to fill the bottle completely—it is then weighed. The weight of the bottle completely filled with water is obtained, and, since the weight of the bottle is the same in both cases, it follows that:

Weight of particles in sample $= \left[(\text{Wt. bottle}+\text{slip}) - (\text{Wt. bottle}+\text{water})\right]\frac{s}{s-1}$

where s = specific gravity of the dry material. *E.g.*

(a) *In a hydrometer test on a sample of wet-ground alumina,*
Weight of bottle+ slip = 124·6 gm
and   Weight of bottle+water = 95·8 gm

What weight of dry alumina (specific gravity = 3·64) was used in the test?

Weight of dry alumina $= (124 \cdot 6-95 \cdot 8)\frac{3 \cdot 64}{2 \cdot 64}$
$= 39 \cdot 71\,gm$

54

(b) *A bucketful of flint slip weighs 31 lb 10 oz. When filled with water its weight is 22 lb 4 oz. What is the weight of dry flint (specific gravity = 2·48) in the slip?*

$$Weight\ of\ dry\ flint = (506-356)\frac{2·48}{1·48}\ oz = 251·4\ oz$$

The "Standard" Slop Peck

Transactions concerning milled materials in slip form are based primarily upon the weights of dry material involved.

When a consignment of slip is delivered to a factory, it is weighed and its pint weight is checked—the dry content may then be calculated and this forms the basis upon which its value is assessed.

A STANDARD SLOP PECK is equivalent to 16 pt of slip at 32 oz per pt, having a solid component of specific gravity 2·50. Such a quantity of slip would have a dry content of 20 lb (since 1 pt would contain 20 oz of dry material). Hence a Standard Slop Peck is associated with a dry content of 20 lb.

In practice, a slip consignment may have a pint weight other than 32 oz, and the specific gravity of its solid component may differ from 2·50, but every 20 lb of dry material it contains will be invoiced as one S.S.P. and its value assessed accordingly. Hence, any quantity of slip containing 20 lb of dry material is equivalent to a Standard Slop Peck.

E.g. *A consignment of flint slip weighs 2¼ tons. The pint weight is 31½ oz (specific gravity of dry flint = 2·50). How many S.S.P.'s should be invoiced? What is its value at 3s 6d per S.S.P.?*

$$Total\ weight\ of\ slip = 5{,}600 \times 16\ oz$$

Now, since each pint weighs 31½ oz:

$$Total\ volume\ of\ slip = \frac{5{,}600 \times 16}{31\frac{1}{2}}pt$$

$$Dry\ content\ of\ 1\ pt = (31\tfrac{1}{2}-20)\frac{2·5}{1·5} = \frac{115}{6}\ oz$$

Hence, $$Total\ dry\ content = \frac{5{,}600 \times 16}{31\frac{1}{2}} \times \frac{115}{6}\ oz$$

$$= \frac{5{,}600 \times 115}{31\frac{1}{2} \times 6}\ lb$$

Since 1 S.S.P. ≡ 20 lb of dry material, dividing the total weight (in lb) by 20 lb will yield the required number of S.S.P.'s.

∴ $$No.\ of\ S.S.P.'s = \frac{5{,}600 \times 115}{31\frac{1}{2} \times 6 \times 20} = 170$$

The consignment is worth 170 × 3s 6d = £29 15s 0d.

Example

On testing, a pint measure was found to hold only $19\frac{3}{4}$ oz of water. A ton of flint slip was delivered which gave, with the false measure, $31\frac{1}{4}$ oz per pt. If the price of flint was 4s per Standard Slop Peck, what would be the true value of the consignment?

The false measure holds $19\frac{3}{4}$ oz of water or $31\frac{1}{4}$ oz of slip.

Hence, $$\text{Specific gravity of slip} = \frac{31\frac{1}{4}}{19\frac{3}{4}}$$

$\therefore$ $$\text{Density of slip} = \frac{31\frac{1}{4}}{19\frac{3}{4}} \times 20 = 31 \cdot 64 \text{ oz per pt}$$

Assuming that the specific gravity of the dry flint is $2 \cdot 50$, then the dry content of 1 pt of the slip is:

$$(31 \cdot 64 - 20)\frac{5}{3} = 19 \cdot 4 \text{ oz}$$

$$\text{Total dry content} = \frac{2{,}240 \times 16}{31 \cdot 64} \times 19 \cdot 4 \text{ oz}$$

$$= \frac{2{,}240}{31 \cdot 64} \times 19 \cdot 4 \text{ lb}$$

$$\text{No. of S.S.P.'s} = \frac{2{,}240 \times 19 \cdot 4}{31 \cdot 64 \times 20}$$

$$\text{Correct value} = \frac{2{,}240 \times 19 \cdot 4}{31 \cdot 64 \times 20} \times 4 \text{ shillings}$$

$$= \text{£13 15s 0d}$$

Problems

(1) 200 cc of slip weigh 298 gm. What is its pint weight?

(2) What is the pint weight of a mixture of 45 lb of dry clay (specific gravity $2 \cdot 50$) and 15 lb of water?

(3) Equal volumes of water and a powder material of specific gravity $2 \cdot 50$ are made into a slip. What will be its pint weight?

(4) A slip is made from 28 lb of dry flint (specific gravity $2 \cdot 50$) and 12 pt of water. What is its density (oz per pt)?

(5) What volume of water (cc) must be added to 40 gm of dry glaze (specific gravity $2 \cdot 90$) to yield a slip at 30 oz per pt?

(6) How many lb of dry clay (specific gravity $2 \cdot 50$) would you mix with 16 pt of water to produce a slip at 34 oz per pt?

(7) A blunger contains 60 gall of slip at 34 oz per pt. What weight of dry clay (lb), of specific gravity $2 \cdot 50$, must be added to increase the pint weight to 36 oz?

(8) How much water must be added to 5 gall of slip at 32 oz per pt to reduce its density to 30 oz per pt?

(9) An ark containing slip at 31 oz per pt required 24 gall of water to reduce the slip to 29 oz per pt. A cobalt stain is added to the slip, which is at 29 oz per pt, so that there is 0.5% of CoO, calculated on the dry body. The stain contains 40% CoO and is at a pint weight of 28 oz. (Specific gravity of dry stain is 2.80; specific gravity of dry body $= 2.50$.)

Calculate the original volume of slip at 31 oz per pt, and the number of gall of cobalt stain required.

(10) Use Brongniart's formula to calculate the missing values in the following table:

	W (oz)	P (oz per pt)	s
a		30	2·6
b		26·5	2·65
c	15		2·5
d	18		2·6
e	20	32	
f	19	30	

(11) A litre of slip weighs 1,578 gm. The solid component has a specific gravity of 2.60. Calculate the dry content of the slip.

(12) A vessel weighs 92.6 gm when filled with slip, and 67.4 gm when filled with water. What is the weight of solid particles in the slip? (Specific gravity of the dry material is 3.26.)

(13) A consignment of flint slip weighs 24 cwt. The pint weight of the slip is 32 oz and the specific gravity of the dry flint is 2.40. How many Standard Slop Pecks should be invoiced?

(14) The recipe of a body is:

12½ Dorset ball clay
12½ South Devon ball clay
25 China clay
35 Flint
15 Cornish stone

The production is 5 tons of plastic body per week, containing 22% moisture (wet basis). What weights of dry ball clays and china clay would be required per year (50 weeks)?

If the pint weight of flint and stone is 32 oz and the specific gravity of these dry materials is 2.50, how many Standard Slop Pecks of these materials would be required per year?

CHAPTER VI

Body Calculations

"Dry" and "Wet" Measurement of Materials for Body Mixing;
"Wet-Inches"; Effect of Specific Gravity; Density of the Body Slip;
Dimensions of the Mixing Ark; Adjustments to the Wet Recipe;
Additions of Body Stain

Body Mixing

IN the manufacture of all ceramic products the requisite quantities of components (flint, stone, ball clay, china clay, bone, etc.), are measured in terms of weight or volume then subjected to a mixing process.

For most ceramic bodies, the actual mixing takes place in slip form, which ensures an intimate blending of the constituents and hence a uniform product. The original quantity of each component may, however, be measured out in the dry state or in slip form.

"Dry" Measurement

The component powder materials are simply weighed out then transferred to the mixing ark—due allowance being made for any moisture content (see Chapter II).

An older technique, sometimes used in the manufacture of bone china, is to fill and level-off a "standard box" with the dry powder component. A specified number of boxes of each material is then used in the body mix. This of course, is an attempt to measure the dry materials on a volume basis. It suffers from errors due to inconsistent packing, and variable moisture contents of the raw materials.

"Wet" Measurement

The most widely used method, in British practice, is to obtain a stock of each constituent material in slip form. If the consistency (pint weight) of each slip is known, then a given volume may be pumped into the mixing ark—and it is a simple matter to calculate the dry material involved.

E.g. *A mixing consists of 960 pt of fireclay slip (at 25 oz per pt) and 120 pt of flint slip (at 30 oz per pt). What is the percentage dry recipe of the mix [assume that both components have a specific gravity (dry) of 2·50]?*

Using Brongniart's Formula:

1 pt of fireclay slip has a dry content of $\dfrac{5 \times 5}{3} = 8\frac{1}{3}$ *oz*

and   *1 pt of flint slip has a dry content of* $10 \times \dfrac{5}{3} = 16\frac{2}{3}$ *oz*

$\therefore$ *Total amount of dry fireclay* $= 960 \times \dfrac{25}{3} = 8{,}000$ *oz*

and   *Total amount of dry flint* $= 120 \times \dfrac{50}{3} = 2{,}000$ *oz*

i.e. *the dry recipe is 80% fireclay; 20% flint*

The volume of each component slip may be measured in any convenient units: pints, gallons, litres, cubic feet, etc. In particular, the simplest method is to use a "dip-stick" in the mixing ark to measure the depth of each component slip as it is added to the mix. Provided that the ark has a uniform cross-sectional area, the depths, in inches (often referred to as "wet inches"), correspond to volumes. Hence a "wet" recipe takes the form:

14 in. ball clay at 24 oz per pt
$8\frac{1}{2}$ in. china clay at 26 oz per pt
5 in.   flint   at 30 oz per pt
$2\frac{1}{4}$ in.   stone   at 32 oz per pt

If other units of volume are substituted for "wet inches" the composition of the final mix is unaltered. There will, of course, be a change in the total quantity of body slip in the mix. Nevertheless, the recipe may be written as:

14 pt   ball clay at 24 oz per pt
$8\frac{1}{2}$ pt china clay at 26 oz per pt
5 pt   flint   at 30 oz per pt
$2\frac{1}{4}$ pt   stone   at 32 oz per pt

and it now becomes a simple matter to convert this into the corresponding "dry" recipe. Assuming that the specific gravity of each of the component materials is 2·50, the dry recipe becomes:

Ball clay $14 \times (24-20)\frac{5}{3} = 93\cdot3$
China clay $8\frac{1}{2} \times (26-20)\frac{5}{3} = 85\cdot0$
Flint $5 \times (30-20)\frac{5}{3} = 83\cdot3$
Stone $2\frac{1}{4} \times (32-20)\frac{5}{3} = 45\cdot0$

and the percentage dry recipe is:

Ball clay	30·4%
China clay	27·7%
Flint	27·2%
Stone	14·7%
	100·0%

A further simplification is possible if the specific gravity of all the dry components is the same. In the above example, the specific gravity of each component was 2·50, and the factor $\frac{5}{3}$ appeared in the expression of each dry content. This constant factor ($\frac{5}{3}$) may be omitted, since it does not affect the ratios between the weights of the component materials.

Dry recipe

E.g.

Ball clay	$14 \times (24-20) =$	56
China clay	$8\frac{1}{2} \times (26-20) =$	51
Flint	$5 \times (30-20) =$	50
Stone	$2\frac{1}{4} \times (32-20) =$	27

This is virtually the same dry recipe, which is clearly seen when it is converted to percentage form, giving:

Ball clay	30·4%
China clay	27·7%
Flint	27·2%
Stone	14·7%
	100·0%

In general, then, if the specific gravity of each component is the same, to convert from a "wet" recipe to a "dry" recipe, apply the formula "Wet inches" $\times (P-20)$ to each component.

E.g. *Calculate the percentage dry recipe of the following mix:*

$10\frac{1}{2}$ in. ball clay at 24 oz per pt
$6\frac{1}{4}$ in. china clay at 26 oz per pt
4 in.   flint   at 32 oz per pt
$2\frac{1}{2}$ in.   stone   at 32 oz per pt

Dry recipe

$$Ball\ clay = 10\frac{1}{2} \times\ 4 = 42$$
$$China\ clay = 6\frac{1}{2} \times\ 6 = 39$$
$$Flint = 4\ \times 12 = 48$$
$$Stone = 2\frac{1}{2} \times 12 = 30$$

Percentage dry recipe is:

Ball clay	26·4%
China clay	24·5%
Flint	30·2%
Stone	18·9%

Effect of Specific Gravity

The assumption that all the components have a specific gravity of 2·50 is never strictly true. Materials, such as ball clay, china clay and stone, have a reasonably constant specific gravity and consequently cause very little variation in the final body from batch to batch.

Flint, however, has a variable specific gravity, dependent upon the calcination process. Calcining is necessary to make the flints brittle and, therefore, easier to grind; but, during calcination, the specific gravity of the material could be reduced, theoretically, from approximately 2·65 to 2·30.

In a well-controlled calcination process, the fall in specific gravity is arrested at the value 2·50; on the other hand under-calcined flint has a higher specific gravity and over-calcined flint a lower specific gravity than 2·50.

Such variations may cause errors in the body mix if a "wet" recipe is used. To illustrate this, compare the dry contents of the following flint slips:

Slip A 1 pt at 32 oz per pt (specific gravity of dry flint = 2·50); and
Slip B 1 pt at 32 oz per pt (specific gravity of dry flint = 2·40)

$$\text{Dry content of Slip A} = (32-20) = \tfrac{2 \cdot 5}{1 \cdot 5} \, 20 \text{ oz}$$

$$\text{Dry content of Slip B} = (32-30) \tfrac{2 \cdot 4}{1 \cdot 4} = 20 \cdot 57 \text{ oz}$$

Both the volumes and the pint weights of the two slips are the same, and it becomes clear that a reduction in the specific gravity of the dry powder material causes an increase in the dry content of the slip.

A "wet" recipe determines the volume and pint weight of the slip to be added to the mixing ark, but, even if these instructions are followed implicitly, errors in the body composition will occur if the specific gravity of the dry component changes.

Consider the recipe:

$$\begin{array}{lll} 14 \text{ in.} & \text{ball clay} & \text{at 24 oz per pt} \\ 8\tfrac{1}{2} \text{ in.} & \text{china clay} & \text{at 26 oz per pt} \\ 5 \text{ in.} & \text{flint} & \text{at 30 oz per pt} \\ 2\tfrac{1}{4} \text{ in.} & \text{stone} & \text{at 32 oz per pt} \end{array}$$

Assuming a specific gravity of 2·50 for each of the dry components, it has been shown that the dry recipe for the mix is:

$$\begin{array}{lr} \text{Ball clay} & 30 \cdot 4\% \\ \text{China clay} & 27 \cdot 7\% \\ \text{Flint} & 27 \cdot 2\% \\ \text{Stone} & 14 \cdot 7\% \end{array}$$

Suppose, now, that a batch mix was made using under-calcined flint (specific gravity = 2·60). What effect would this have upon the dry recipe?

The calculation becomes:

$$\text{Ball clay} = 14 \times (24-20) \; \tfrac{5}{3} = 93\cdot3$$
$$\text{China clay} = 8\tfrac{1}{2} \times (26-20) \; \tfrac{5}{3} = 85\cdot0$$
$$\text{Flint} = 5 \times (30-20) \tfrac{2\cdot6}{1\cdot6} = 81\cdot25$$
$$\text{Stone} = 2\tfrac{1}{4} \times (32-20) \; \tfrac{5}{3} = 45\cdot0$$

and the percentage dry recipe is now:

Ball clay 30·6%
China clay 27·9%
Flint 26·7%
Stone 14·8%

i.e. the use of under-calcined flint has led to a reduction of 0·5% in the free silica content of the body.

The general ceramic implications of this effect may be summarized as follows:

Under-calcination of flint → Less SiO_2 in body → Tendency to craze the applied glaze

Over-calcination of flint → More SiO_2 in body → Tendency to peel the applied glaze

Density of the Body Slip

The component slips each have a density which ensures that its fluid properties are suitable for mixing. The final body slip usually has a density of about 27 oz per pt—appropriate for further processing (lawning, magnetting, etc.).

The pint weight of the final body slip may be calculated from the "wet" recipe.

E.g. *An earthenware body is made from:*

18 in. ball clay at 24 oz per pt
11 in. china clay at 26 oz per pt
7½ in. flint at 30 oz per pt
4½ in. stone at 32 oz per pt

What is the density of the body slip?

   Write the recipe as:

> 18 pt of ball clay slip at 24 oz per pt
> 11 pt of china clay slip at 26 oz per pt
> $7\frac{1}{2}$ pt of   flint   slip at 30 oz per pt
> $4\frac{1}{2}$ pt of   stone   slip at 32 oz per pt

Then:

  Volume of body slip $= 18 + 11 + 7\frac{1}{2} + 4\frac{1}{2} = 41\,pt$

and

  Weight of body slip $= (18 \times 24) + (11 \times 26) + (7\frac{1}{2} \times 30) + (4\frac{1}{2} \times 32)$
$$= 1,087\,oz$$

Hence,   *Density of body slip* $= \dfrac{1,087}{41} = 26 \cdot 5\,oz\ per\ pt$

Dimensions of the Mixing Ark

If the cross-sectional area of the ark is known, then, the actual quantities of slip in the mix may be calculated from the "wet" recipe:

E.g. A mixing ark has vertical sides and a uniform cross-sectional area of 36 sq ft. The body mix is:

> 15 in. ball clay at 24 oz per pt
> 9 in. china clay at 26 oz per pt
> 5 in.   flint   at 32 oz per pt
> 3 in.   stone   at 32 oz per pt

Calculate the total volume of body slip in the mix, and the actual weights of dry materials involved (1 pt = 34·6 cu in.). Assume specific gravity of each dry component is 2·50.

> *Cross-sectional area* $= 36 \times 144$ *sq in.*
> *Total depth of slip* $= 32$ *in.*
> *Total volume of slip* $= 36 \times 144 \times 32$ *cu in.*
> $$= \frac{36 \times 144 \times 32}{34 \cdot 6}\,pt \simeq 4,800\,pt$$

N.B. $\dfrac{\textit{Cross-sectional area (sq in.)} \times \textit{Depth (in.)}}{34 \cdot 6} = \textit{Number of pt}$

Hence, for this mixing ark, the factor

$$\frac{36 \times 144}{34 \cdot 6} = 150$$

converts any depth in "wet" inches, into pints.

Then:

Material	Dry recipe	Number of pt	Dry content per pt (oz)	Total "dry" weight of each component (lb)
Ball clay	15×4 $= 60$	150×15 $= 2{,}250$	$4 \times \dfrac{5}{3} = 6\frac{2}{3}$	$\dfrac{2{,}250 \times 20}{16 \times 3}$ $= 937 \cdot 6$
China clay	9×6 $= 54$	150×9 $= 1{,}350$	$6 \times \dfrac{5}{3} = 10$	$\dfrac{1{,}350 \times 10}{16}$ $= 843 \cdot 7$
Flint	5×12 $= 60$	150×5 $= 750$	$12 \times \dfrac{5}{3} = 20$	$\dfrac{750 \times 20}{16}$ $= 937 \cdot 6$
Stone	3×12 $= 36$	150×3 $= 450$	$12 \times \dfrac{5}{3} = 20$	$\dfrac{450 \times 20}{16}$ $= 562 \cdot 5$
		Totals 4,800 pt		3,281·4 lb

The above computation may be checked by evaluating the pint weight of the body slip and proceeding as follows:

$$\text{Pint weight of body slip} = \frac{850}{32} = 26 \cdot 6 \ oz$$

$$\text{Dry content of 1 pt of body slip} = 6 \cdot 6 \times \frac{5}{3} = 11 \cdot 0 \ oz$$

$$\text{Total dry weight of body} = \frac{4{,}800 \times 11 \cdot 0}{16}$$

$$= 3{,}300 \ lb$$

[as compared with 3,281·4 lb obtained above].

Note. *The above calculation emphasizes the need for "an appreciation of significant errors". E.g. Any error made on the value of the pint weight of the body slip is multiplied by $\dfrac{5}{3}$ and then by $\dfrac{4{,}800}{16}$, i.e. the error is magnified 500 times.*

To get a more precise value, the pint weight of the body slip should be expressed as:

$$\frac{850}{32} = 26 \cdot 5632 \ oz$$

Then,   *the dry content of 1 pt of slip* $= 6 \cdot 5632 \times \dfrac{5}{3}$

$$= 10 \cdot 938 \ oz$$

and   *Total dry weight* $= \dfrac{4{,}800 \times 10 \cdot 9838}{16}$

$$= 3{,}281 \ lb$$

[which agrees closely with the value calculated in the table].

Adjustments to the "Wet" Recipe

Suppose that a body recipe demands 9 in. of china clay at 26 oz per pt, and that the actual stock of china clay slip is at 27 oz per pt. Of course, the china clay stock could be diluted to give a density of 26 oz per pt and then the recipe could be followed. It is often more convenient, however, to leave the slip density at 27 oz per pt and merely to change the number of "wet inches" to be added to the mixing ark. The basis of this adjustment is that the amount of dry china clay added should remain the same.

To convert to the dry form use the formula:

$$\text{Wet inches} \times (P{-}20) = \text{Parts by weight (dry)}$$

The recipe is:

$$9 \text{ in. at 26 oz per pt} \rightarrow 9 \times (26{-}20)$$
$$= 54 \text{ parts by weight of dry china clay}$$

Let x in. be the required depth of china clay at the new density (27 oz per pt).

Then, $x \times (27{-}20) = 54$

$$x = \frac{54}{7} = 7 \cdot 71 \text{ in.}$$

I.e. If the china clay slip is at 27 oz per pt, an addition of $7 \cdot 71$ wet in. is required.

For china clay slip at 25 oz per pt, the adjusted depth would be

$$\frac{54}{5} = 10 \cdot 8 \text{ in.}$$

and a table may be drawn up to show the required depths over a range of densities covering the situations met with in practice. Such a "ready reckoner" is called a SLIPMAKERS' CARD.

The Slipmakers' Card

				Body Recipe				
23	23¼	23½	23¾	Ball Clay 24 oz per pt 18 "wet in."	24¼	24½	24¾	25
24	22·2	20·6	19·2		16·9	16·0	15·2	14·4
25	25¼	25½	25¾	China Clay 26 oz per pt 12 "wet in."	26¼	26½	26¾	27
14·4	13·7	13·1	12·5		11·5	11·1	10·7	10·3
31	31¼	31½	31¾	Flint 32 oz per pt 7½ "wet in."	32¼	32½	32¾	33
8·2	8·0	7·8	7·7		7·3	7·2	7·1	6·9
31	31¼	31½	31¾	Stone 32 oz per pt 4 "wet in."	32¼	32½	32¾	33
4·4	4·3	4·2	4·1		3·9	3·8	3·8	3·7

Additions of Body Stain

Small amounts of cobalt stain are often added to bodies to improve their whiteness. The insoluble form of cobalt stain is prepared from cobalt oxide, china clay, stone, flint, etc.—the mixture being calcined, wet-ground, and passed through very fine sieves. This prepared stain, in the form of a slip is then added to the mixing ark (1 part of dry stain to about 20,000 parts of dry body).

Other stains, for the production of coloured bodies (yellow, blue, green, etc.), are added in a similar manner, but are required in much higher concentrations, e.g. 2% by weight or 1 part of stain to 50 parts of dry body.

(a) *One pt of stain at 31 oz per pt is added to every 200 cu ft of a wet body mixing. The dry recipe of the stain is*

$$CoO \quad 60$$
$$Flint \quad 24$$
$$Stone \quad 16$$

The specific gravity of the dry stain is 3·0. Calculate the weight of CoO per 20,000 parts by weight of dry body. The dry content of the body slip is 13·2 oz per pt. (1 cu ft = 6·23 galls.)

Stain:

$$Dry\ content\ per\ pt = (31-20)\tfrac{3}{2} = 16\cdot5\ oz$$

66

Since 60% of the stain is CoO

$$1 \text{ pt of stain contains } \frac{60}{100} \times 16 \cdot 5$$

$$= 9 \cdot 9 \text{ oz } CoO$$

Body:

There are $\qquad 13 \cdot 2$ *oz of dry material in* $\quad 1$ *pt of slip*

$\therefore \qquad 13 \cdot 2 \times 8$ *oz of dry material in* $\quad 1$ *gall of slip*

and $\qquad 13 \cdot 2 \times 8 \times 6 \cdot 23$ *oz of dry material in* $\quad 1$ *cu ft of slip*

and $\therefore \quad 13 \cdot 2 \times 8 \times 6 \cdot 23 \times 200$ *oz of dry material in 200 cu ft of slip*

Then:

To $(13 \cdot 2 \times 8 \times 6 \cdot 23 \times 200)$ *oz of dry body* $9 \cdot 9$ *oz CoO are added;*

$\therefore$ *To 20,000 parts by weight of dry body* $\dfrac{9 \cdot 9 \times 20,000}{13 \cdot 2 \times 8 \times 6 \cdot 23 \times 200}$

parts by weight of CoO area dded $= 1 \cdot 51$ *parts by weight of CoO*

(b) *It is necessary to stain a body of the following recipe:*

$\qquad$ *15 in.* $\quad$ *ball clay* $\quad$ *at 24 oz per pt*
$\qquad$ *10 in.* $\quad$ *china clay at 26 oz per pt*
$\qquad\;\;$ *8 in.* $\qquad$ *flint* $\qquad$ *at 32 oz per pt*
$\qquad\;\;$ *3 in.* $\qquad$ *stone* $\quad\;\;$ *at 32 oz per pt*

with an insoluble stain, and 1% of stain (calculated on the dry body) is to be added. The stain is made up to a pint weight of 28 oz, the specific gravity of the dry stain being $3 \cdot 0$. *The mixing ark has a uniform cross-sectional area of 36 sq ft and is filled to a depth of 5 ft 6 in. How many gallons of stain must be used for such a mixing? (Specific gravity of dry body* $= 2 \cdot 5$.)

Body slip:

$$\text{Total volume} = 5\tfrac{1}{2} \times 36 = 198 \text{ cu ft}$$

$$= 198 \times 6 \cdot 23 \times 8 \text{ pt}$$

$$\text{Density of body slip} = \frac{972 \text{ oz}}{36 \text{ pt}} = 27 \text{ oz per pt}$$

$\therefore \qquad$ *Dry material per pt* $= (27 - 20)\tfrac{5}{3} = 11\tfrac{2}{3}$ *oz*

$$\text{Total weight of dry body} = 198 \times 6 \cdot 23 \times 8 \times 11\tfrac{2}{3} \text{ oz}$$

$$\text{Dry stain required} = \frac{1}{100} \times 198 \times 6 \cdot 23 \times 8 \times 11\tfrac{2}{3} \text{ oz}$$

Now 1 pt of stain contains $(28 - 20)\tfrac{3}{2} = 12$ *oz dry material*

$$\therefore \quad \textit{Volume of stain required} = \frac{198 \times 6 \cdot 23 \times 8 \times 11\frac{2}{3}}{100 \times 12} \, pt$$

$$= \frac{198 \times 6 \cdot 23 \times 8 \times 11\frac{2}{3}}{100 \times 12 \times 8} \, gall$$

$$= 12 \cdot 0 \, gall$$

Further examples of calculations on the wet mixing process are as follows:

(c) *An earthenware body has a dry recipe:*

Ball clay	25%
China clay	30%
Flint	30%
Stone	15%

The pint weights used in the mixing are 24 oz, 26 oz, 32 oz, and 30 oz respectively. One mixing requires 300 gall of flint which normally has a specific gravity of 2·50 and pint weight of 32 oz. The slipmaker runs a mixing to the ark before the laboratory report is received that the flint in stock is really at 32½ oz per pt, and has a specific gravity of 2·45. How could (i) this error be corrected and (ii) 1,350 gall of flint slip left in stock be used for subsequent mixes?

(i) *The normal flint has a dry content of* $(32-20)\frac{5}{3}$

$$= 20 \textit{ oz per pt}$$

A normal mix requires $\dfrac{300 \times 8 \times 20}{16}$

$$= 3,000 \textit{ lb of dry flint}$$

The incorrect flint has a dry content of $(32\frac{1}{2}-20)\frac{2\cdot45}{1\cdot45}$

$$= 21 \cdot 12 \textit{ oz per pt}$$

The incorrect mix contains $\dfrac{300 \times 8 \times 21 \cdot 12}{16}$

$$= 3,168 \textit{ lb of dry flint}$$

The mix, therefore, contains 168 lb of flint in excess of the normal requirement.

To correct the charge in the mixing ark, proportionate amounts of ball clay, china clay, and stone must be added.

BODY CALCULATIONS

	Dry recipe	Required addition
Ball clay	25	$25 \times \dfrac{168}{30} = 140\ lb$
China clay	30	$30 \times \dfrac{168}{30} = 168\ lb$
Flint	30	
Stone	15	$15 \times \dfrac{168}{30} = 84\ lb$

These additions, of course, are made in slip form and to find the volume requirement for each slip proceed as follows:

Material	Dry content per pt	Volume required
Ball clay	$(24-20)\dfrac{5}{3} = \dfrac{20}{3}\ oz$	$\dfrac{140 \times 16}{\dfrac{20}{3}} = 336\ pt$
China clay	$(26-20)\dfrac{5}{3} = 10\ oz$	$\dfrac{168 \times 16}{10} = 269\ pt$
Flint		
Stone	$(30-20)\dfrac{5}{3} = \dfrac{50}{3}\ oz$	$\dfrac{84 \times 16}{\dfrac{50}{3}} = 80 \cdot 6\ pt$

i.e. the charge in the mixing ark may be corrected by a further addition of 336 pt of ball clay slip, 269 pt of china clay slip, and 80·6 pt of stone slip (each at the pint weights normally used).

(ii) *For future mixings*

There is a considerable stock of incorrect flint remaining. This may be used in two ways:

(1) By temporarily adjusting the wet recipe so that the correct amount of dry flint goes in to each charge.

(2) By diluting the incorrect stock so that it contains the same dry content per pt as the flint slip normally used. If this is done the normal "wet" recipe may be followed.

Method (1)

A normal charge introduces 3,000 lb of dry flint by the addition of 2,400 pt of flint slip, having a dry content of 20 oz per pt.

Using the incorrect flint slip, the addition per charge should now be:

$$\frac{3,000 \times 16}{21 \cdot 12} \simeq 2,270 \text{ pt}$$

$$\simeq 284 \text{ gall}$$

(instead of the normal 300 gall).

Method (2)

$21 \cdot 12$ oz of dry flint are contained in 1 pt of incorrect slip;

$\therefore$ 20 oz of dry flint are contained in $\dfrac{20}{21 \cdot 12} = 0 \cdot 947$ pt of incorrect slip.

If $0 \cdot 053$ pt of water are now added to each pint of the incorrect slip, then every pint of the new slip will contain 20 oz of dry flint.

Hence, the total water requirement is

$$1,350 \times 8 \times 0 \cdot 053 = 572 \text{ pt}$$

N.B. The dilution formula $\frac{A-B}{B-20}$ is not applicable in this case, since the specific gravity of the dry flint in the incorrect slip is different from that normally used.

(d) *The recipe of a body is:*

$$
\begin{array}{lll}
25 \text{ in.} & \text{ball clay} & \text{at 24 oz per pt} \\
16\frac{2}{3} \text{ in.} & \text{china clay} & \text{at 26 oz per pt} \\
11\frac{2}{3} \text{ in.} & \text{flint} & \text{at 32 oz per pt} \\
5 \text{ in.} & \text{stone} & \text{at 32 oz per pt}
\end{array}
$$

Analytical data of the components is:

	% SiO_2	% Loss-on-ignition
Ball clay	$50 \cdot 5$	$10 \cdot 2$
China clay	$49 \cdot 5$	$11 \cdot 8$
Flint	$97 \cdot 0$	$0 \cdot 5$
Stone	$72 \cdot 6$	$1 \cdot 5$

What increase in flint ("wet in.") is required to give a 1% increase in the percentage silica (calculated on the fired body)?

BODY CALCULATIONS

Material	Dry recipe	Fired weight	Weight of SiO_2 in fired material
Ball clay	25×4 $= 100$	$\dfrac{89 \cdot 8}{100} \times 100$ $= 89 \cdot 8$	$\dfrac{50 \cdot 5}{100} \times 100$ $= 50 \cdot 5$
China clay	$16\frac{2}{3} \times 6$ $= 100$	$\dfrac{88 \cdot 2}{100} \times 100$ $= 88 \cdot 2$	$\dfrac{49 \cdot 5}{100} \times 100$ $= 49 \cdot 5$
Flint	$11\frac{2}{3} \times 12$ $= 140$	$\dfrac{99 \cdot 5}{100} \times 140$ $= 139 \cdot 3$	$\dfrac{97}{100} \times 140$ $= 135 \cdot 8$
Stone	5×12 $= 60$	$\dfrac{98 \cdot 5}{100} \times 60$ $= 59 \cdot 1$	$\dfrac{72 \cdot 6}{100} \times 60$ $= 43 \cdot 6$
		Totals $376 \cdot 4$	$279 \cdot 4$

$$\text{Percentage silica (calculated on fired body)} = \frac{279 \cdot 4}{376 \cdot 4} \times 100$$
$$= 74 \cdot 22\%$$

Let x in. be the depth of flint slip required to give $75 \cdot 22\%$ silica (calculated on the fired body). Then:

Material	Dry recipe	Fired weight	Weight of SiO_2 in fired material
Ball clay	25×4 $= 100$	$\dfrac{89 \cdot 8}{100} \times 100$ $= 89 \cdot 8$	$\dfrac{50 \cdot 5}{100} \times 100$ $= 50 \cdot 5$
China clay	$16\frac{2}{3} \times 6$ $= 100$	$\dfrac{88 \cdot 2}{100} \times 100$ $= 88 \cdot 2$	$\dfrac{49 \cdot 5}{100} \times 100$ $= 49 \cdot 5$
Flint	$x \times 12$ $= 12x$	$\dfrac{99 \cdot 5}{100} \times 12x$ $= 11 \cdot 94x$	$\dfrac{97}{100} \times 12x$ $= 11 \cdot 64x$
Stone	5×12 $= 60$	$\dfrac{98 \cdot 5}{100} \times 60$ $= 59 \cdot 1$	$\dfrac{72 \cdot 6}{100} \times 60$ $= 43 \cdot 6$
	Totals	$237 \cdot 1 + 11 \cdot 94x$	$143 \cdot 6 + 11 \cdot 64x$

and
$$\frac{143\cdot6+11\cdot64x}{237\cdot1+11\cdot94x}\times100 = 75\cdot22$$

Solving this equation gives x = *13·04 in.*

i.e. *there must be an increase of 13·04—11·67 = 1·37 in.
of flint slip.*

Problems

[Unless otherwise stated, assume that the specific gravity of all dry components is 2·50.]

(1) Calculate the percentage dry recipe of the following mix: 500 gall of fireclay slip at 24 oz per pt and 60 gall of flint slip at 32 oz per pt.

(2) A mixing has the recipe:

> 6 in. ball clay at 24 oz per pt
> 5 in. china clay at 26 oz per pt
> 2½ in. flint at 31 oz per pt
> 1¼ in. stone at 32 oz per pt

What is the percentage dry recipe?

(3) A recipe calls for 12 in. of flint slip at 32 oz per pt (specific gravity of dry material 2·50). If a stock of flint slip is to be used at 31 oz per pt (the dried material having a specific gravity of 2·45), how many wet in. should be added?

(4) The recipe of an earthenware body is:

> 17½ in. ball clay at 24 oz per pt
> 14 in. china clay at 26 oz per pt
> 6½ in. flint at 32 oz per pt
> 4 in. stone at 30½ oz per pt

Calculate the percentage dry recipe and the pint weight of the body slip.

(5) A mixing ark has vertical sides of height 6 ft and a uniform cross-sectional area of 40 sq ft. The dry recipe of the body mix is ball clay 20, china clay 24, flint 30, stone 10. If the total charge is 1,000 gall, what is the "wet" recipe of the mix, using component slips at 24 oz per pt, 26 oz per pt, 32 oz per pt and 30 oz per pt respectively. (1 pt = 34·6 cu in.)

(6) *(a)* An ark contains a body slip at 30 oz per pt. This must be reduced to 27 oz per pt. When 10½ buckets of water are added to the slip (at 30 oz per pt) it gives a slip at 28 oz per pt. How many more buckets are required to produce slip at 27 oz per pt?

(b) If, in the above situation, one bucket holds 2 gall, how many pints of cobalt stain must be added to the slip (at 27 oz per pt) in the ark, so that there is 0·25% CoO calculated on the dry body? The stain contains 50% of CoO and is at a pint weight of 29 oz (specific gravity of the dry stain is 2·80).

(7) The recipe of a body is:

> 14 in. ball clay at 24 oz per pt
> 9 in. china clay at 26 oz per pt
> 5½ in. flint at 32 oz per pt
> 2½ in. stone at 32 oz per pt

Analytical data is:

	Ball clay	China clay	Flint	Stone
Percentage SiO_2	52·30	47·31	97·25	71·52
Percentage loss-on-ignition	11·48	12·85	0·81	1·64

What is the percentage silica (calculated on the fired body)?

(8) If the flint slip in the following body is increased from 8 in. to 9 in., what increase in the percentage of silica would you expect the fired body to show when analysed? The recipe of the body is:

> 14 in. ball clay at 24 oz per pt
> 10 in. china clay at 26 oz per pt
> 8 in. flint at 32 oz per pt
> 4 in. stone at 32 oz per pt

The silica content and loss-on-ignition of the raw materials are as follows:

	% SiO_2	% Loss
Ball clay	51·0	11·0
China clay	49·0	12·0
Flint	97·0	0·5
Stone	73·0	1·5

(9) The usual pint measure could not be found and a new one had to be substituted. Through an oversight, the counterbalance for the old measure was used and the error was not realized until the component slips had been run into the mixing ark. It was then found that the new measure was ½ oz heavier than the old one. All the materials were tested in the new measure according to the recipe. How would you rectify the mixing?

The body recipe on the factory is:

> 24 in. ball clay at 24 oz per pt
> 18 in. china clay at 26 oz per pt
> 10 in. flint at 32 oz per pt
> 8 in. stone at 31 oz per pt

(10) An earthenware body has the following dry recipe: Ball clay, 25; china clay, 25; flint, 35; stone, 15. How many tons of plastic clay with a moisture content of 20% could be produced from 224 Standard Slop Pecks of flint, assuming that the ball clay, china clay and stone are readily available?

The above body is stained with cobalt stain, one part of which is used for 20,000 parts of dry body. The body stain contains 40% CoO.

What weight of soluble cobalt chloride $CoCl_2 \cdot 6H_2O$ (in lb) would be needed to replace the cobalt stain in 10 tons of the above plastic body, assuming no cobalt chloride is lost in the press water?

CHAPTER VII

Introduction to Glaze Calculations

Molecular Weights, Formulae and Use of Chemical Equations, Oxides;
Percentage Composition and Formula; Calculation of a Recipe from
a Simple Glaze Formula; Given the Recipe of a Glaze Calculate the
Formula

CHEMICAL equations are often used in ceramic calculations. The great importance of chemical equations lies not so much in their being a convenient symbol to express the nature of the reagents and products of a chemical change, but in the fact that all chemical calculations are based on the use of formulae and equations in conjunction with atomic weights.

It is important to understand the use of these fundamental calculations as applied to ceramic materials. Once the formula of a compound is known, then it is a simple matter to calculate the molecular weight.

To calculate the molecular weight of soda ash, Na_2CO_3. Using the atomic weights of each atom,

$$
\begin{aligned}
two\ atoms\ of\ sodium &= 2\times 23 = 46 \\
one\ atom\ of\ carbon &= 1\times 12 = 12 \\
three\ atoms\ of\ oxygen &= 3\times 16 = \underline{48} \\
& \overline{106}
\end{aligned}
$$

The molecular weight = 106

To calculate the molecular weight of white lead, $Pb(OH)_2.2PbCO_3$,

$$
\begin{aligned}
3\ atoms\ of\ Pb &= 3\times 207 = 621 \\
8\ atoms\ of\ O &= 8\times 16 = 128 \\
2\ atoms\ of\ H &= 2\times 1 = 2 \\
2\ atoms\ of\ C &= 2\times 12 = \underline{24} \\
&\phantom{= 2\times 12 = } \overline{775}
\end{aligned}
$$

The molecular weight of white lead = 775

Use of Chemical Equations

Chemical equations describe not only the nature of the atoms and molecules of substances taking part in a chemical change, but also the <u>quantitative</u> relationship between them.

75

For example, consider the equation

$$CaCO_3 = CaO + CO_2$$

The weight of one molecule of calcium carbonate expressed in grams $= 40 + 12 + (3 \times 16) = 100$. The gram-molecular weight of CaO $= 56$ and the gram-molecular weight of $CO_2 = 44$.

This means that 100 gm of calcium carbonate on heating will yield 56 gm of lime and 44 gm of carbon dioxide.

The equation also indicates the volume of gas liberated. This is based on the fact that the molecular weight of any gas, expressed in grams occupies $22 \cdot 4$ litres at N.T.P. (Normal Temperature and Pressure), *i.e.* 0°C and 760 mm pressure (reference Avogadro's Hypothesis). In the above equation 100 gm of calcium carbonate on heating would liberate $22 \cdot 4$ litres of carbon dioxide at N.T.P.

These principles are used in the following examples:

If one ton of china clay is calcined to 1,100°C, what is the loss in weight in lb?

The equation for this reaction may be written

$$Al_2O_3.2SiO_2.2H_2O = Al_2O_3 + 2SiO_2 + 2H_2O$$

The loss in weight is due to the vaporization of the chemically combined water.

∴ *258 parts by weight of china clay suffers a loss in weight of 36 parts by weight of chemically combined water;*

258 tons of china clay loses 36 tons of water;

1 ton of china clay loses $\frac{36}{258}$ tons of water;

or $\frac{36}{258} \times 2,240\ lb = 312 \cdot 6\ lb$

Note. A list of important ceramic materials, together with their formulae and molecular weights is given in the Appendix.

A frit mixture contains 100 lb of calcium carbonate. Calculate the volume of carbon dioxide (cu ft) which will be liberated on fritting at a temperature of 1,000°C. (28·32 litres = 1 cu ft; 453·6 gm = 1 lb.)

$$44\ gm\ CO_2 \equiv 22 \cdot 4\ litres\ at\ N.T.P.$$

$$44\ lb\ CO_2 \equiv \frac{22 \cdot 4 \times 453 \cdot 6\ cu\ ft}{28 \cdot 32}$$

Applying Charles' Law:

$$\frac{22\cdot4\times453\cdot6}{28\cdot32}\times\frac{1{,}000+273}{273} = 1{,}673 \; cu\,ft \; CO_2 \; at \; 1{,}000°C$$

Oxides

An oxide can be defined as a compound of two elements, one of which is oxygen.

The molecular formulae of glazes and frits are given in terms of molecular parts of the constituent oxides. The oxides are classified into three main groups:

(1) Acidic Oxides

They are the oxides of non-metals. If soluble in water, they combine with it, forming an acid,

e.g. $$SO_3+H_2O = H_2SO_4$$

They combine with bases to form salts.

An example, using the acidic oxide CO_2, is given below:

$$Ca(OH)_2+CO_2 = CaCO_3+H_2O$$

Silica (SiO_2) and boric oxide (B_2O_3) are the two main acidic oxides used in frits and glazes. They combine with other elements to form silicate and borate glasses.

(2) Basic Oxides

They may be considered as the oxides of metals. They react with acids to form a salt and water only:

$$CaO+2HCl = CaCl_2+H_2O$$

If soluble in water they yield hydroxides:

$$Na_2O+H_2O = 2NaOH$$
$$CaO+H_2O = Ca(OH)_2$$

The main basic oxides used in the ceramic industry are listed below:

K_2O CaO BaO PbO Na_2O MgO ZnO

(3) Amphoteric Oxides

An amphoteric oxide may exhibit either basic or acidic properties. Alumina, Al_2O_3, reacts with dilute hydrochloric acid to yield aluminium chloride and water, and thus behaves as a basic oxide:

$$Al_2O_3+6HCl = 2AlCl_3+3H_2O$$

but with sodium hydroxide, alumina reacts as an acidic oxide and forms sodium aluminate:

$$Al_2O_3+2NaOH = 2NaAlO_2+H_2O$$

Alumina is the main amphoteric oxide in frits and glazes.

Relationship between Percentage Composition and Formula

The chemical analysis of a pure compound determines the nature and quantity of each constituent chemical substance. The result of a quantitative analysis is given in terms of percentage composition, or proportion by weight of each element present, *e.g.* a compound containing carbon, hydrogen, nitrogen and sulphur on analysis is found to have the following percentage composition:

$$C = 41 \cdot 4\%$$
$$H = 5 \cdot 8\%$$
$$N = 16 \cdot 1\%$$
$$S = 36 \cdot 7\%$$

If the figures for the percentage composition are divided by the atomic weights of the elements concerned, then the result of this calculation gives the simplest possible formula to the compound. The "empirical" or "simplest possible" formula only indicates the proportions of the atoms in the molecules, but does not give their actual number.

A compound containing carbon and hydrogen only was found to have the following percentage composition:

$$C = 92 \cdot 31\% \quad H = 7 \cdot 69\%$$

Calculate the empirical formula. (Atomic weights: C = 12; H = 1.)

The ratio of the number of carbon atoms to the number of hydrogen atoms

$$= \frac{92 \cdot 31}{12} : \frac{7 \cdot 69}{1}$$
$$= 7 \cdot 69 : 7 \cdot 69$$

The ratio is therefore 1 : 1 and the empirical formula = CH

Although the "simplest possible" formula has been established as CH, compounds C_2H_2, C_3H_3, C_4H_4, etc., would give identical results. Further evidence for this particular compound, derived from vapour density measurements, shows that the true formula is in fact C_6H_6 (benzene). However, the use of such data is outside the scope of this book, and it is only necessary to appreciate that the percentage composition when divided by the appropriate atomic weight gives the "simplest possible" formula and that this is adequate for most ceramic materials, since the correct ratio between the constituent elements is maintained.

A volatile liquid has the following percentage composition:

$$Carbon = 10 \cdot 05$$
$$Hydrogen = 0 \cdot 84$$
$$Chlorine = 89 \cdot 11$$

Calculate the empirical formula.

The relative number of atoms in the compound is:

$$Carbon = \frac{10 \cdot 05}{12} = 0 \cdot 84$$

$$Hydrogen = \frac{0 \cdot 84}{1} = 0 \cdot 84$$

$$Chlorine = \frac{89 \cdot 11}{35 \cdot 5} = 2 \cdot 51$$

Dividing throughout by the smallest number (0·84) the "simplest formula" becomes $CHCl_3$,

$$empirical\ formula = CHCl_3$$

Other chemical evidence shows that it is also its true formula, and the compound is in fact chloroform ($CHCl_3$).

So far the examples have dealt with pure chemical compounds, but the same considerations apply to ceramic materials, although the formulae of some of them are expressed in terms of oxides, *e.g.* potash felspar, $K_2O . Al_2O_3 . 6SiO_2$.

The percentage composition of china clay is given as:

$$SiO_2 = 46 \cdot 51$$
$$Al_2O_3 = 39 \cdot 53$$
$$H_2O = 13 \cdot 96$$

Calculate its molecular formula.

$$SiO_2\ \ 46 \cdot 51 \div 60 = 0 \cdot 775$$
$$Al_2O_3\ \ 39 \cdot 53 \div 102 = 0 \cdot 387$$
$$H_2O\ \ 13 \cdot 96 \div 18 = 0 \cdot 775$$

Dividing throughout by the smallest number (0·387) the empirical formula $= Al_2O_3 . 2SiO_2 . 2H_2O$.

The molecular formula for china clay $= Al_2O_3 . 2SiO_2 . 2H_2O$

In the above example the percentage composition is given in terms of oxides, molecular weights of which must be used in place of atomic weights. Similar principles apply in calculating the molecular formula of a glaze from its percentage composition.

A simple glaze has the following percentage composition:

$$PbO = 63 \cdot 90$$
$$Al_2O_3 = 5 \cdot 87$$
$$SiO_2 = 30 \cdot 23$$

Dividing the percentage composition of each oxide by its molecular weight the ratios become:

$$\frac{63 \cdot 90}{223} PbO : \frac{5 \cdot 87}{102} Al_2O_3 : \frac{30 \cdot 23}{60} SiO_2$$
$$= 0 \cdot 287\ PbO : 0 \cdot 058\ Al_2O_3 : 0 \cdot 504\ SiO_2$$

In calculating the empirical formula, each molecular part would have been divided by the smallest number (in this case 0·058). However, in ceramics a convention is adopted with glazes, that the sum of the basic oxides be equal to unity. This puts all glaze formulae on a basis which enables the many different types of glazes to be compared, one with another. A knowledge of glaze formulae used in this form is of paramount importance to the glaze technologist. He can forecast such physical properties as fusibility, solubility, etc., from such information.

In the above calculation, the basic oxide is PbO and dividing throughout by 0·287 the glaze formula becomes:

$$1 \text{ PbO}; \ 0·202 \text{ Al}_2\text{O}_3; \ 1·756 \text{ SiO}_2$$

The oxides are usually written in the order as shown, *i.e.* basic, amphoteric, and acidic.

Later, the "molecular weight" of glazes is referred to. It should be noted that this weight is not the "true molecular weight", but is really a "formula weight". It is an arbitrary figure calculated from the formula obtained by using the above convention. The "molecular weight" figure as used in glaze calculations has no true significance, since it has been computed from this artificially devised formula.

Given the Formula, Calculate the Percentage Composition

The reverse procedure to that used in the previous problem is shown below:

Given the formula of sodium carbonate, Na_2CO_3, calculate the percentage composition in terms of

(a) *the elements Na, C, and O; and* (b) *the oxides Na_2O and CO_2.*

The molecular weight of $Na_2CO_3 = 106$.

(a) Sodium $\dfrac{46}{106} \times 100 = 43·4\%$

Carbon $\dfrac{12}{106} \times 100 = 11·3\%$

Oxygen $\dfrac{48}{106} \times 100 = 45·3\%$

(b) Na_2O $(2 \times 23) + 16 = 62$

$\dfrac{62}{106} \times 100 = 58·5\%$

CO_2 $12 + (2 \times 16) = 44$

$\dfrac{44}{106} \times 100 = 41·5\%$

Further example

Given the formula of a glaze as:

$$\left.\begin{matrix} 0\cdot 6\, PbO \\ 0\cdot 4\, Na_2O \end{matrix}\right\} 0\cdot 25\, Al_2O_3 \left\{\begin{matrix} 1\cdot 9\, SiO_2 \\ 0\cdot 4\, B_2O_3 \end{matrix}\right.$$

Calculate the percentage composition.

$$
\begin{array}{llll}
PbO & 0\cdot 6 & \times 223 = & 133\cdot 8 \\
Na_2O & 0\cdot 4 & \times\ 62 = & 24\cdot 8 \\
Al_2O_3 & 0\cdot 25 & \times 102 = & 25\cdot 5 \\
SiO_2 & 1\cdot 9 & \times\ 60 = & 114\cdot 0 \\
B_2O_3 & 0\cdot 4 & \times\ 70 = & \underline{28\cdot 0} \\
& & & 326\cdot 1
\end{array}
$$

326·1 represents the "molecular weight" of the glaze.

Note. *As stated previously it is not a "true molecular weight", but, in fact, a "formula weight".*

By multiplying throughout by $\dfrac{100}{326\cdot 1}$ *the percentage composition is:*

$$
\begin{array}{ll}
PbO & 41\cdot 04 \\
Na_2O & 7\cdot 59 \\
Al_2O_3 & 7\cdot 82 \\
SiO_2 & 34\cdot 96 \\
B_2O_3 & 8\cdot 59
\end{array}
$$

It can be seen in the above calculation that

MOLECULAR WEIGHT × MOLECULAR PARTS = PARTS BY WEIGHT

Using sodium oxide as an example:

$$
\begin{array}{ll}
Na_2O & \text{molecular weight} = 62 \\
& \text{molecular parts} = 0\cdot 4 \\
& \text{and their product} = 24\cdot 8
\end{array}
$$

This relationship is used throughout glaze calculations.

Recipe of a Glaze

It has been shown that the chemical analysis of a glaze (*i.e.* the weights of the constituent oxides present) can be written in terms of a molecular formula. Also, that given the molecular formula of a glaze the percentage composition (or analysis) may be computed. Could these weights of the various oxides actually be used to manufacture the glaze?

On a small scale in the laboratory, it may be possible to obtain and weigh out the PbO, Al_2O_3, etc., and to make the glaze. The percentage composition would then become the actual working recipe of the glaze.

For industrial-scale production however, it is both uneconomical and impractical to manufacture glazes from raw oxides. Other materials are, therefore, used to introduce these oxides.

The choice of raw materials depends upon many factors, such as:

(1) Availability of the material in a pure state. The compound need not be 100% pure, but it should be available in a form which does not have variable amounts of impurities from batch to batch.

(2) Cost of raw material.

(3) Suitability of the material for continuous use under factory conditions. For example, certain lead compounds may prove to be poisonous and to have a cumulative effect when used by operatives over long periods of time.

Given a Glaze Formula, Calculate a Recipe

A simple glaze has the following formula:

$$PbO; 0 \cdot 2\, Al_2O_3; 2 \cdot 9\, SiO_2$$

Lead oxide (PbO). The following compounds contain PbO which could, theoretically, be used to introduce this oxide into the glaze:

Litharge	PbO
Red lead	Pb_3O_4
White lead	$Pb(OH)_2 . 2PbCO_3$
Lead bisilicate	$PbO . 2SiO_2$

Litharge and red lead do not suspend well, are costly and present the risk of lead poisoning.

White lead was, in the past, used as a source of PbO because of its suspending properties and availability. However, its use has been prohibited in British potteries since October 1949. White lead is a potential source of lead poisoning, because it is soluble in the hydrochloric acid contained in the gastric juices.

Lead frits are generally used today to introduce the PbO content. Lead bisilicate is a common form of lead frit extensively used because it is virtually insoluble in dilute hydrochloric acid.

Alumina (Al_2O_3). Two commercially available compounds containing Al_2O_3 are:

Bauxite	$Al_2O_3 . 2H_2O$
China clay	$Al_2O_3 . 2SiO_2 . 2H_2O$

China clay is preferred because it is a comparatively cheap product. Its flaky structure also helps in the suspension of the glaze.

Silica (SiO_2). In this country, flint is the main form of SiO_2, but quartz sand of high purity is sometimes used.

The three raw materials which may be used to compound this glaze would then be:

Lead bisilicate
China clay
Flint

The calculation of the recipe for this glaze is shown in the table below:

Material	Molecular weight	Molecular parts	Parts by weight	PbO	Al_2O_3	SiO_2
Lead bisilicate	343	1·0	343	1·0		2·0
China clay	258	0·2	51·6		0·2	0·4
Flint	60	0·5	30·0			0·5
				1·0	0·2	2·9

The "parts by weight" column gives the final recipe:

Lead bisilicate 343·0
China clay 51·6
Flint 30·0

Glaze calculations are best written out in the table form as shown above and this method is used throughout the book.

All data to the left of the double vertical line refer to the material as a whole. Data to the right refer to the oxide components involved.

Note. 0·2 molecular part of china clay brings in 0·2 molecular part of Al_2O_3 and 0·4 molecular part of SiO_2.

The general rule:

MOLECULAR WEIGHT × MOLECULAR PART = PARTS BY WEIGHT

is used and these values are set out as shown in the second, third and fourth columns of the table.

In the past white lead may have been used in the calculation instead of lead bisilicate, then the result would have been:

Material	Molecular weight	Molecular parts	Parts by weight	PbO	Al_2O_3	SiO_2
White lead	775	0·333	258	1·0		
China clay	258	0·200	52		0·2	0·4
Flint	60	2·500	150			2·5
				1·0	0·2	2·9

In the molecular parts column, 0·333 molecule of white lead is required to produce one molecule of PbO in the finished glaze for the following reason:

One molecule of white lead produces three molecules of lead oxide on calcination.

$$Pb(OH)_2 . 2PbCO_3 = 3PbO + 2CO_2 + H_2O$$

CO_2 and H_2O are non-permanent oxides and do not form compounds with other glaze constituents.

Many compounds used in frits and glazes behave in a similar manner. A list of compounds is given in the Appendix. The table gives the formula, molecular weight and permanent oxides obtained on heating these compounds.

A further example of calculating the recipe of a glaze is given below. The principle is exactly the same as in the previous example but, in many glaze calculations, more arithmetic is involved. This is due in some cases to such felspathic rocks as stone which are not pure chemical compounds. There are many different varieties of stone, each having its own composition and formula.

The formula of a glaze is:

$$\left. \begin{array}{l} 0·081 \ K_2O \\ 0·028 \ Na_2O \\ 0·293 \ CaO \\ 0·598 \ PbO \end{array} \right\} 0·232 \ Al_2O_3; \ 4·065 \ SiO_2$$

Calculate a recipe using the following raw materials:

Whiting, lead bisilicate, china clay, flint, and stone; the stone has a molecular formula:

$$\left. \begin{array}{l} 0·412 \ K_2O \\ 0·143 \ Na_2O \\ 0·180 \ CaO \end{array} \right\} 1·0 \ Al_2O_3; \ 7·1 \ SiO_2$$

Writing out the calculation in the usual table form:

Material	Molecular weight	Molecular parts	Parts by weight	PbO	K₂O	Na₂O	CaO	Al₂O₃	SiO₂
Lead bisilicate	343	0·598	205·1	0·598					1·196
*Stone	585·7	0·197	115·4		0·081	0·028	0·035	0·197	1·399
Whiting	100	0·258	25·8				0·258		
China clay	258	0·035	9·0					0·035	0·070
Flint	60	1·400	84·0						1·400
				0·598	0·081	0·028	0·293	0·232	4·065

The recipe is

$$
\begin{array}{rr}
\textit{Lead bisilicate} & 205 \cdot 1 \\
\textit{Stone} & 115 \cdot 4 \\
\textit{Whiting} & 25 \cdot 8 \\
\textit{China clay} & 9 \cdot 0 \\
\textit{Flint} & 84 \cdot 0 \\
\end{array}
$$

* In the above calculation the molecular weight of the stone was calculated in the same way as the molecular weight of any other compound, *i.e.*

$$
\begin{array}{lll}
K_2O & 94 \times 0 \cdot 412 = & 38 \cdot 7 \\
Na_2O & 62 \times 0 \cdot 143 = & 8 \cdot 9 \\
CaO & 56 \times 0 \cdot 180 = & 10 \cdot 1 \\
Al_2O_3 & 102 \times 1 \cdot 000 = & 102 \cdot 0 \\
SiO_2 & 60 \times 7 \cdot 100 = & 426 \cdot 0 \\
\hline
& & 585 \cdot 7 \\
\end{array}
$$

The stone is used as a raw material essentially to introduce the alkali content.

Considering K_2O,

$0 \cdot 412$ molecular part $K_2O \equiv 1$ molecule of stone

$1 \quad$ molecular part $K_2O \equiv \dfrac{1}{0 \cdot 412}$ molecule of stone

$0 \cdot 081$ molecular part $K_2O \equiv \dfrac{1}{0 \cdot 412} \times 0 \cdot 081$ molecule of stone

$\qquad\qquad\qquad\qquad = 0 \cdot 197$ molecular parts of stone

The calculation shows that $0 \cdot 197$ molecular part of stone is required to introduce the requisite molecular part of K_2O, namely $0 \cdot 081$. If $0 \cdot 197$ molecular part of stone is used, then at the same time, the following amounts of other oxides are introduced.

$$
\begin{array}{lll}
Na_2O & 0 \cdot 143 \times 0 \cdot 197 = 0 \cdot 028 \\
CaO & 0 \cdot 180 \times 0 \cdot 197 = 0 \cdot 035 \\
Al_2O_3 & 1 \cdot 000 \times 0 \cdot 197 = 0 \cdot 197 \\
SiO_2 & 7 \cdot 100 \times 0 \cdot 197 = 1 \cdot 399 \\
\end{array}
$$

The K_2O and Na_2O are now equivalent to the molecular parts as required by the glaze formula. Since stone is a flux and the alkalis are the active part of the flux, then the stone is introduced to satisfy the K_2O and Na_2O requirements. $0 \cdot 197$ molecular part of stone, in this case meets the requirements of K_2O and Na_2O. This is so because the question has been formulated in such a way that the alkali oxides are in the correct ratio to each other. If this was not the case, some other material would have to be introduced to make up for the deficiency of one of the oxides.

Given the Recipe of a Glaze, Calculate the Formula

A simple example is given which is the reverse procedure of the previous one.

Calculate the formula of a glaze which has the following recipe:

Lead bisilicate	50
China clay	28
Flint	10

Using the glaze calculation table:

Material	Molecular weight	Molecular parts	Parts by weight	PbO	Al₂O₃	SiO₂
Lead bisilicate	343	0·146	50	0·146		0·292
China clay	258	0·108	28		0·108	0·216
Flint	60	0·167	10			0·167
				0·146	0·108	0·675

Bringing the basic oxides to unity, divide throughout by 0·146.

Glaze formula PbO; 0·740 Al₂O₃; 4·623 SiO₂.

Note. 0·146 molecular part for lead bisilicate is calculated by dividing the parts by weight (obtained from the recipe) by the molecular weight: $\frac{50}{343} = 0·146$. The molecular parts for china clay and flint are calculated in a similar manner.

Further example

Calculate the formula of a glaze which has the following recipe:

Lead bisilicate	171·5
Whiting	23·0
Stone	120·4
China clay	32·2
Flint	30·0

The formula of the stone is:

$$\left. \begin{array}{l} 0·28\ CaO \\ 0·62\ K_2O \\ 0·10\ Na_2O \end{array} \right\} Al_2O_3 . 7SiO_2$$

Material	Molecular weight	Molecular parts	Parts by weight	PbO	CaO	K₂O	Na₂O	Al₂O₃	SiO₂
Lead bisilicate	343	0·500	171·5	0·500					1·000
Whiting	100	0·230	23·0		0·230				
Stone	602·2	0·200	120·4		0·056	0·124	0·020	0·200	1·400
China clay	258	0·125	32·2					0·125	0·250
Flint	60	0·500	30·0						0·500
				0·500	0·286	0·124	0·020	0·325	3·150

To calculate the molecular weight of the stone:

$$CaO \quad 56 \times 0 \cdot 28 = \quad 15 \cdot 68$$
$$K_2O \quad 94 \times 0 \cdot 62 = \quad 58 \cdot 28$$
$$Na_2O \quad 62 \times 0 \cdot 10 = \quad 6 \cdot 20$$
$$Al_2O_3 \quad 102 \times 1 \cdot 0 = 102 \cdot 00$$
$$SiO_2 \quad 60 \times 7 \cdot 0 = 420 \cdot 00$$
$$\overline{602 \cdot 16}$$

Dividing throughout by 0·930 to bring basic oxides to unity, the glaze formula is:

$$\left. \begin{array}{l} 0 \cdot 538 \, PbO \\ 0 \cdot 307 \, CaO \\ 0 \cdot 133 \, K_2O \\ 0 \cdot 022 \, Na_2O \end{array} \right\} 0 \cdot 349 \, Al_2O_3 \left\{ 3 \cdot 387 \, SiO_2 \right.$$

Problems

(1) Calculate the empirical formula from the percentage composition of the following compounds:

    (a) Fe = 72·4   *(b)* Fe = 77·78   *(c)* K = 38·61
           O = 27·6   O = 22·22   N = 13·86
                                                  O = 47·53

(2) Calculate the percentage composition of the following compounds, in terms of oxides (including water):

    (a) Borax crystals $Na_2B_4O_7.10H_2O$
    (b) Lead bisilicate $PbO.2SiO_2$
    (c)   Felspar $K_2O.Al_2O_3.6SiO_2$
    (d)   Silicic acid H_2SiO_3

(3) If one ton of whiting is calcined to 1,000°C, what is the loss in weight in lb?

(4) A kiln of 150 cu ft capacity contains 10 tons of bricks with a moisture content of 10%. Calculate the volume of water vapour (cu ft) at 100°C, which will be liberated in the initial stages of firing. (28·32 1 = 1 cu ft; 453·6 gm = 1 lb.)

(5) A glaze is analysed and found to have the following percentage composition:

$$SiO_2 \; = 66 \cdot 96 \qquad CaO = 10 \cdot 94$$
$$Al_2O_3 = 14 \cdot 23 \qquad K_2O = \; 7 \cdot 87$$

Calculate the molecular formula.

(6) The analysis of a glaze is given as follows:

$$\begin{array}{ll} \text{PbO} & 53 \cdot 24\,\% \\ \text{CaO} & 5 \cdot 72\,\% \\ \text{Al}_2\text{O}_3 & 5 \cdot 21\,\% \\ \text{SiO}_2 & 35 \cdot 81\,\% \end{array}$$

Calculate the molecular formula.

(7) The percentage composition of a glaze is found by analysis to be:

$$\begin{array}{ll} \text{PbO} & 22 \cdot 80 \\ \text{Na}_2\text{O} & 6 \cdot 96 \\ \text{K}_2\text{O} & 11 \cdot 54 \\ \text{Al}_2\text{O}_3 & 9 \cdot 70 \\ \text{SiO}_2 & 41 \cdot 00 \\ \text{B}_2\text{O}_3 & 8 \cdot 00 \end{array}$$

Report these results as a glaze formula.

(8) A glaze on analysis is found to have the following percentage composition:

$$\begin{array}{ll} \text{SiO}_2 & 51 \cdot 6 \\ \text{Al}_2\text{O}_3 & 8 \cdot 7 \\ \text{PbO} & 33 \cdot 6 \\ \text{K}_2\text{O} & 6 \cdot 1 \end{array}$$

Calculate:

(a) the glaze formula; and
(b) a recipe for the glaze

using china clay, lead bisilicate, potash felspar and flint.

(9) Calculate the working recipe for a glaze of molecular formula:

$$\left. \begin{array}{l} 0 \cdot 6\,\text{PbO} \\ 0 \cdot 3\,\text{CaO} \\ 0 \cdot 1\,\text{K}_2\text{O} \end{array} \right\} 0 \cdot 18\,\text{Al}_2\text{O}_3; \; 2 \cdot 0\,\text{SiO}_2$$

using lead bisilicate and potash felspar for two of the materials.

(10) Calculate the recipe of a frit:

$$\left. \begin{array}{l} 0 \cdot 72\,\text{PbO} \\ 0 \cdot 28\,\text{Na}_2\text{O} \end{array} \right\} \begin{array}{l} 0 \cdot 90\,\text{SiO}_2 \\ 0 \cdot 56\,\text{B}_2\text{O}_3 \end{array}$$

using red lead, borax, and flint.

(11) What is the recipe of a lead frit PbO; $0 \cdot 2\,\text{Al}_2\text{O}_3$; $2 \cdot 0\,\text{SiO}_2$ using red lead, china clay, and flint?

(12) Given the following lead frit formula, calculate a recipe using red lead, felspar, china clay, and flint:

$$\left.\begin{array}{l} 0 \cdot 9 \, PbO \\ 0 \cdot 1 \, K_2O \end{array}\right\} 0 \cdot 3 \, Al_2O_3; \ 2 \cdot 2 \, SiO_2$$

(13) Calculate the recipe for the frit of formula:

$$\left.\begin{array}{l} 0 \cdot 30 \, Na_2O \\ 0 \cdot 10 \, K_2O \\ 0 \cdot 60 \, CaO \end{array}\right\} 0 \cdot 18 \, Al_2O_3 \left\{\begin{array}{l} 2 \cdot 00 \, SiO_2 \\ 0 \cdot 60 \, B_2O_3 \end{array}\right.$$

using borax, whiting, felspar, china clay, and flint.

(14) A glaze has the following formula:

$$\left.\begin{array}{l} 0 \cdot 538 \, PbO \\ 0 \cdot 307 \, CaO \\ 0 \cdot 133 \, K_2O \\ 0 \cdot 022 \, Na_2O \end{array}\right\} 0 \cdot 349 \, Al_2O_3; \ 3 \cdot 387 \, SiO_2$$

Calculate a recipe for this glaze using lead bisilicate, whiting, stone, china clay, and flint.

The formula of the stone is:

$$\left.\begin{array}{l} 0 \cdot 3 \, CaO \\ 0 \cdot 6 \, K_2O \\ 0 \cdot 1 \, Na_2O \end{array}\right\} Al_2O_3 . 6SiO_2$$

(15) Compare the formulae of the two glazes given below:

Recipe modern type glaze:

   80·11 lb lead frit [PbO; $0 \cdot 078 \, Al_2O_3$; $1 \cdot 30 \, SiO_2$];
   4·95 lb china clay;
   2·89 lb flint.

Original raw type glaze:

   65 lb white lead;
   10 lb china clay;
   20 lb flint.

CHAPTER VIII

Fritted Glazes

Given the Formula, Calculate a Recipe; Fritting Factors; Given the Recipe, Calculate a Formula; Given the Recipe, Calculate Percentage Composition of the Mill Batch

MOST commercial glazes contain one or more frits. By fritting various components together it confers many desirable properties to the glaze.

The main reasons for fritting are:

(1) Soluble compounds, when fritted with other selected materials in the correct proportion, become insoluble. Glaze components should be insoluble, otherwise they tend to migrate into the pores of the biscuit ware and the glaze when fired may have a "starved" appearance. Even if vitreous ware is used with a glaze that is slightly soluble, the components will segregate as the drying process proceeds.

(2) Although lead compounds available to the ceramic industry are generally insoluble in water, they may have considerable solubility in dilute acids. If the compounds are soluble in dilute hydrochloric acid then they are toxic, since the gastric juices are highly acidic [0·17% hydrochloric acid].

Lead compounds are fritted to produce glaze components which are virtually insoluble in dilute acids.

(3) A glaze with a high proportion of clay substance may crack on drying. Chemically combined water has still to be released during the glost fire and these conditions may lead to a poor glost finish. Part of the plastic material should, therefore, be fritted, and part (approximately 10%) used raw for glaze suspension.

(4) Some compounds, such as calcium carbonate, liberate a gas on heating. Any compound that behaves in this way is fritted, so that the glaze is not likely to suffer from pin-holing and bubbling.

It is common practice to use two frits, *i.e.* a lead frit and a borax frit. If lead and B_2O_3 compounds are fritted together, then the lead does not generally reach satisfactory limits of insolubility. However, recent research has shown that lead borosilicate can be produced satisfactorily when the ratio of $PbO : B_2O_3$ is carefully selected.

Another point to consider is that the frit must mature at a reasonably low temperature. It follows then that the raw materials for a frit have to be selected to meet many requirements.

Experience has shown that the following limits, when applied to a frit, produce a product which has the necessary properties required for glaze manufacture. The basic to acidic oxide ratio should be within the range 1 : 1 to 1 : 3. Amphoteric to acidic oxide ratio 1 : 10 to 1 : 20.

Such compounds as CaO and MgO are often fritted with other materials to make them less soluble.

Synthesis of a Fritted Glaze

Oxides may be introduced into a fritted glaze in many forms. Some typical oxides are discussed below and the reasons stated for the choice of particular compounds.

K_2O. Compounds commercially available are: Pearl ash K_2CO_3, potassium nitrate KNO_3, potash felspar $K_2O.Al_2O_3.6SiO_2$ and stone. K_2O could be introduced by any of the above compounds. However, potash felspar is a likely choice: although it is insoluble and inert, it would introduce the required amounts of Al_2O_3 and SiO_2 to the frit.

Na_2O. Soda ash Na_2CO_3, borax $Na_2B_4O_7.10H_2O$, soda felspar $Na_2O.Al_2O_3.6SiO_2$, and stone. Since borax is cheap and a readily available compound and B_2O_3 is also required, then the Na_2O could be introduced into the frit as borax.

CaO. Invariably introduced as whiting ($CaCO_3$) since this compound is extremely abundant and cheap.

PbO. Generally introduced as a lead bisilicate frit. Ideal formula $PbO.2SiO_2$.

Al_2O_3. Introduced as china clay $Al_2O_3.2SiO_2.2H_2O$. Part is put into the frit to give insolubility and some is left over for mill batch additions.

SiO_2. Introduced in this country as flint (SiO_2).

B_2O_3. Borax ($Na_2B_4O_7.10H_2O$) is used wherever possible because of price and availability.

Other compounds may be used, such as boric acid (H_3BO_3) and borocalcite $CaB_4O_7.6H_2O$.

The synthesis of a fritted glaze is illustrated by the following example:

A glaze has the formula:

$$\left.\begin{array}{l} 0\cdot10\ K_2O \\ 0\cdot20\ Na_2O \\ 0\cdot44\ CaO \\ 0\cdot26\ PbO \end{array}\right\} 0\cdot27\ Al_2O_3 \left\{\begin{array}{l} 2\cdot65\ SiO_2 \\ 0\cdot40\ B_2O_3 \end{array}\right.$$

Calculate a recipe.

Considering the rules for manufacturing a suitable frit, then the following formula for the borax frit might be:

$$\left.\begin{array}{l} 0\cdot10\ K_2O \\ 0\cdot20\ Na_2O \\ 0\cdot44\ CaO \end{array}\right\} 0\cdot15\ Al_2O_3 \left\{\begin{array}{l} 1\cdot60\ SiO_2 \\ 0\cdot40\ B_2O_3 \end{array}\right.$$

Ratios:

Basic to acidic oxides $= 0\cdot74 : 2\cdot0 = 1 : 2\cdot7$
Amphoteric to acidic oxides $= 0\cdot15 : 2\cdot0 = 1 : 13\cdot3$

This purely arbitrary formula gives the ratios within the prescribed limits for a suitable frit.

To calculate the frit recipe:

Material	Molecular weight	Molecular parts	Parts by weight	K_2O	Na_2O	CaO	Al_2O_3	SiO_2	B_2O_3
Felspar	556	0·10	55·6	0·10			0·10	0·60	
*Borax	382	0·20	76·4		0·20				0·40
Whiting	100	0·44	44·0			0·44			
China clay	258	0·05	12·9				0·05	0·10	
Flint	60	0·90	54·0					0·90	
				0·10	0·20	0·44	0·15	1·60	0·40

*Note. Use of borax $Na_2B_4O_7.10H_2O = Na_2O + 2B_2O_3 + 10H_2O$
1 molecule $\equiv$ 1 mol. + 2 mols.
$\therefore$ $0\cdot2$ molecule $\equiv 0\cdot2$ mol. + $0\cdot4$ mol.

Considering the original glaze formula then the oxides required in addition to the frit are:

Material	K_2O	Na_2O	CaO	PbO	Al_2O_3	SiO_2	B_2O_3
Glaze	0·10	0·20	0·44	0·26	0·27	2·65	0·40
Borax frit	0·10	0·20	0·44		0·15	1·60	0·40
Oxides required				0·26	0·12	1·05	

The remaining oxide requirements may be met using lead bisilicate, china clay and flint.

To calculate the glaze recipe:

Material	Molecular weight	Molecular parts	Parts by weight	K_2O	Na_2O	CaO	PbO	Al_2O_3	SiO_2	B_2O_3
*Borax frit	185·7	1·00	185·7	0·10	0·20	0·44		0·15	1·60	0·40
Lead bisilicate	343·0	0·26	89·2				0·26		0·52	
China clay	258·0	0·12	31·0					0·12	0·24	
Flint	60·0	0·29	17·4						0·29	
				0·10	0·20	0·44	0·26	0·27	2·65	0·40

The molecular weight of borax frit:

$$
\begin{array}{llll}
K_2O & 94 \times 0 \cdot 1 & = & 9 \cdot 40 \\
Na_2O & 62 \times 0 \cdot 2 & = & 12 \cdot 40 \\
CaO & 56 \times 0 \cdot 44 & = & 24 \cdot 64 \\
Al_2O_3 & 102 \times 0 \cdot 15 & = & 15 \cdot 30 \\
SiO_2 & 60 \times 1 \cdot 60 & = & 96 \cdot 00 \\
B_2O_3 & 70 \times 0 \cdot 40 & = & 28 \cdot 00 \\
\hline
& & & 185 \cdot 74
\end{array}
$$

The recipe of the glaze is:

Borax frit	185·7
Lead bisilicate	89·2
China clay	31·0
Flint	17·4

and the recipe of the borax frit:

Felspar	55·6
Borax	76·4
Whiting	44·0
China clay	12·9
Flint	54·0

The recipe of the borax frit gives the weights of materials used in the fritting process, producing the borax frit needed in the glaze recipe. This is a completely separate manufacturing operation.

The recipe of the glaze is, in fact, the mill batch, since it determines the quantities of materials which are ground together to produce the finished glaze.

It can be seen that the china clay used in the mill batch is approximately 10% of the total recipe weight.

In the above glaze recipe calculation, the borax and lead frits are treated in exactly the same way as any other complex material. Once the formula of a material is known its molecular weight may be found and the computation proceeds as for stone in previous examples.

Fritting Factors

Consider the following frit:

Felspar	55·6 lb
Borax	95·5 lb
Whiting	35·0 lb
China clay	25·8 lb
Flint	42·0 lb
Total weight	253·9 lb

In practice, it is found that 253·9 lb of this frit recipe produce 189·9 lb of frit after heating.

The theoretical weight of frit produced can also be derived by calculation.

$$
\begin{array}{lrcl}
\text{Felspar} & 55 \cdot 6 \times 1 & = & 55 \cdot 6 \\
\text{Borax} & 95 \cdot 5 \times 0 \cdot 529 & = & 50 \cdot 5 \\
\text{Whiting} & 35 \cdot 0 \times 0 \cdot 560 & = & 19 \cdot 6 \\
\text{China clay} & 25 \cdot 8 \times 0 \cdot 860 & = & 22 \cdot 2 \\
\text{Flint} & 42 \cdot 0 \times 1 & = & 42 \cdot 0 \\
\hline
& & & 189 \cdot 9
\end{array}
$$

The factors used above, *e.g.* borax $0 \cdot 529$, are referred to as "fritting factors".

<u>Felspar</u> has a fritting factor of 1 (one) because it does not lose weight on heating.

<u>Borax</u> has a fritting factor of $0 \cdot 529$. It is calculated as follows:

$$Na_2B_4O_7 \cdot 10H_2O = Na_2O + 2B_2O_3 + 10H_2O$$
$$382 \equiv 202$$
$$1 \equiv \frac{202}{382} = 0 \cdot 529$$

202 is the combined molecular weight of one molecule of Na_2O and two molecules of B_2O_3.

<u>Whiting:</u>

$$CaCO_3 = CaO + CO_2$$
$$100 \equiv 56$$
$$1 \equiv \frac{56}{100} = 0 \cdot 56$$
$$\therefore \quad \text{Fritting factor} = 0 \cdot 56$$

<u>China clay:</u>

$$Al_2O_3 \cdot 2SiO_2 \cdot 2H_2O = Al_2O_3 + 2SiO_2 + 2H_2O$$
$$258 \equiv 222$$
$$1 \equiv \frac{222}{258} = 0 \cdot 86$$
$$\therefore \text{Fritting factor} = 0 \cdot 86$$

A list of fritting factors for various compounds is given in the Appendix.

Examples using fritting factors:

(1) Calculate the weight of frit produced from the following frit recipe:

69 lb flint   172 lb red lead
22 lb whiting   60 lb boric acid

Using the appropriate fritting factors:

$$
\begin{array}{lll}
SiO_2 & 69 \times 1 & = 69 \cdot 0 \\
CaCO_3 & 22 \times 0 \cdot 56 & = 12 \cdot 3 \\
Pb_3O_4 & 172 \times 0 \cdot 977 & = 168 \cdot 1 \\
H_3BO_3 & 60 \times 0 \cdot 565 & = 33 \cdot 9 \\
& & \overline{283 \cdot 3}
\end{array}
$$

283·3 lb of frit.

(2) *A frit has the following recipe:*

$$
\begin{array}{ll}
38 \cdot 4 & borax \\
13 \cdot 7 & flint \\
37 \cdot 3 & felspar \\
23 \cdot 5 & whiting \\
5 \cdot 2 & china\ clay
\end{array}
$$

Ten tons of this frit are produced each week. How many tons of each raw material must be stocked for one year's production (50 weeks)?

Using fritting factors:

$$
\begin{array}{llll}
Borax & 38 \cdot 4 \times 0 \cdot 529 & = 20 \cdot 3 \\
Flint & 13 \cdot 7 \times 1 & = 13 \cdot 7 \\
Felspar & 37 \cdot 3 \times 1 & = 37 \cdot 3 \\
Whiting & 23 \cdot 5 \times 0 \cdot 56 & = 13 \cdot 2 \\
China\ clay & 5 \cdot 2 \times 0 \cdot 86 & = 4 \cdot 5 \\
Total\ weights = & \overline{118 \cdot 1} & \overline{89 \cdot 0}
\end{array}
$$

Considering one component—borax—the calculation shows that 38·4 tons of borax are required in the production of 89·0 tons of frit. Similarly, 13·7 tons of flint are used in the production of 89·0 tons of frit.

Therefore, by multiplying each amount of raw material by $\frac{10}{89}$ gives the number of tons required per week. Multiplying by 50 converts the weekly to yearly amounts.

$$
\left.
\begin{array}{lll}
Borax & 38 \cdot 4 \times \dfrac{10}{89} = 4 \cdot 31 \\[2mm]
Flint & 13 \cdot 7 \times \dfrac{10}{89} = 1 \cdot 54 \\[2mm]
Felspar & 37 \cdot 3 \times \dfrac{10}{89} = 4 \cdot 19 \\[2mm]
Whiting & 23 \cdot 5 \times \dfrac{10}{89} = 2 \cdot 64 \\[2mm]
China\ clay & 5 \cdot 2 \times \dfrac{10}{89} = 0 \cdot 58
\end{array}
\right\} (\times 50)
\quad
\begin{array}{l}
215 \cdot 5\ tons \\[2mm]
77 \cdot 0\ tons \\[2mm]
209 \cdot 5\ tons \\[2mm]
132 \cdot 0\ tons \\[2mm]
29 \cdot 0\ tons
\end{array}
$$

Given the Recipe Calculate the Formula for a Fritted Glaze

Many recipes for glazes are known, but to the technologist it is difficult, from the recipe alone, to forecast or to correlate their properties. If a recipe can be stated in terms of a molecular formula, then this can be used as a basis for the comparison and classification of various types of glazes.

Example

The recipe of a glaze is:

Borax frit   60
Lead frit   30
China clay   10

The lead frit is $PbO.2SiO_2$ and the borax frit formula:

$$\left.\begin{array}{l} 0\cdot6\,CaO \\ 0\cdot3\,Na_2O \\ 0\cdot1\,K_2O \end{array}\right\} 0\cdot18\,Al_2O_3 \left\{\begin{array}{l} 2\cdot06\,SiO_2 \\ 0\cdot60\,B_2O_3 \end{array}\right.$$

Calculate the formula of the glaze.

Material	Molecular weight	Molecular parts	Parts by weight	PbO	CaO	Na$_2$O	K$_2$O	Al$_2$O$_3$	SiO$_2$	B$_2$O$_3$
Borax frit	245·6	0·244	60		0·146	0·073	0·024	0·044	0·503	0·146
Lead frit	343·0	0·087	30	0·087					0·174	
China clay	258·0	0·039	10					0·039	0·078	
				0·087	0·146	0·073	0·024	0·083	0·755	0·146

The molecular weight of the borax frit is calculated in the usual way:

CaO	$0\cdot60\times\ 56 =$	$33\cdot6$
Na_2O	$0\cdot30\times\ 62 =$	$18\cdot6$
K_2O	$0\cdot10\times\ 94 =$	$9\cdot4$
Al_2O_3	$0\cdot18\times102 =$	$18\cdot4$
SiO_2	$2\cdot06\times\ 60 =$	$123\cdot6$
B_2O_3	$0\cdot60\times\ 70 =$	$42\cdot0$
		$\overline{245\cdot6}$

$\frac{60}{245\cdot6} = 0\cdot244$ *and since 1 molecule of borax frit $\equiv 0\cdot6\,CaO$, then $0\cdot244$ molecules of borax frit $\equiv 0\cdot6\times0\cdot244 = 0\cdot146$ molecular part CaO. The molecular parts for the other oxides are calculated on a similar basis.*

Bring basic oxides to unity by dividing throughout by $0\cdot330$:

$$\left.\begin{array}{l} 0\cdot442\,CaO \\ 0\cdot221\,Na_2O \\ 0\cdot073\,K_2O \\ 0\cdot264\,PbO \end{array}\right\} 0\cdot25\,Al_2O_3 \left\{\begin{array}{l} 2\cdot288\,SiO_2 \\ 0\cdot442\,B_2O_3 \end{array}\right.$$

96

Further example

The recipe for a glaze is as follows:

Mill batch		Lead frit	Borax frit	
Lead frit	137·2	$PbO.2SiO_2$	Borax	76·4
Borax frit	131·2		Whiting	20·0
Whiting	10·0		Felspar	55·6
China clay	51·6		Flint	24·0
Flint	36·0			

Calculate the glaze formula.

To find the formula of the borax frit:

Material	Molecular weight	Molecular parts	Parts by weight	CaO	K_2O	Na_2O	Al_2O_3	SiO_2	B_2O_3
Borax	382	0·2	76·4			0·2			0·4
Whiting	100	0·2	20·0	0·2					
Felspar	556	0·1	55·6		0·1		0·1	0·6	
Flint	60	0·4	24·0					0·4	
				0·2	0·1	0·2	0·1	1·0	0·4

Calculated from this formula, the molecular weight of the borax frit = 131·2. To calculate the glaze formula:

Material	Molecular weight	Molecular parts	Parts by weight	PbO	CaO	K_2O	Na_2O	Al_2O_3	SiO_2	B_2O_3
Lead frit	343	0·4	137·2	0·4					0·8	
Borax frit	131·2	1·0	131·2		0·2	0·1	0·2	0·1	1·0	0·4
Whiting	100	0·1	10·0		0·1					
China clay	258	0·2	51·6					0·2	0·4	
Flint	60	0·6	36·0						0·6	
				0·4	0·3	0·1	0·2	0·3	2·8	0·4

The sum of the basic oxides as shown in the table above is, in fact, unity. Therefore the final formula of the glaze is:

$$\left.\begin{array}{l} 0·4\,PbO \\ 0·3\,CaO \\ 0·1\,K_2O \\ 0·2\,Na_2O \end{array}\right\} 0·3\,Al_2O_3 \left\{\begin{array}{l} 2·8\,SiO_2 \\ 0·4\,B_2O_3 \end{array}\right.$$

Given the Recipe, Calculate the Percentage Composition of the Mill Batch

It has been demonstrated that the glaze formula can be calculated from the recipe. The percentage composition of the mill batch for a given glaze can also be calculated and this is best shown by considering the previous example.

97

The recipe for the mill batch was:

$$
\begin{array}{ll}
\text{Lead frit} & 137 \cdot 2 \\
\text{Borax frit} & 131 \cdot 2 \\
\text{Whiting} & 10 \cdot 0 \\
\text{China clay} & 51 \cdot 6 \\
\text{Flint} & 36 \cdot 0 \\
\hline
& 366 \cdot 0 = \text{Total recipe weight}
\end{array}
$$

The glaze formula was found to be:

$$
\left.\begin{array}{l}
0 \cdot 4\,PbO \\
0 \cdot 3\,CaO \\
0 \cdot 1\,K_2O \\
0 \cdot 2\,Na_2O
\end{array}\right\}\, 0 \cdot 3\,Al_2O_3 \left\{\begin{array}{l}
2 \cdot 8\,SiO_2 \\
0 \cdot 4\,B_2O_3
\end{array}\right.
$$

If the unfired glaze was analysed, then the report would include a certain figure for loss-on-ignition, and this would be due to loss of CO_2 and H_2O from the whiting and china clay respectively.

The fritting factor for whiting is $0 \cdot 56$, which means that there is a 44% loss in weight on heating this material. Similarly the fritting factor for china clay is $0 \cdot 86$ and the loss in weight = 14%.

Since the loss-on-ignition of the other materials is negligible, the percentage loss on the mill batch is:

$$
\begin{array}{lll}
\text{Whiting} & 10 \quad \times 0 \cdot 44 = & 4 \cdot 4 \\
\text{China clay} & 51 \cdot 6 \times 0 \cdot 14 = & 7 \cdot 2 \\
& \text{Total} = & \overline{11 \cdot 6}
\end{array}
$$

∴ 366 (total weight of mill batch recipe) suffers a total loss of $11 \cdot 6$ parts by weight,

$$
\text{as a percentage} = 11 \cdot 6 \times \frac{100}{366} = 3 \cdot 170
$$

and the sum of the permanent oxides $= 100 - 3 \cdot 17$
$$
= 96 \cdot 83
$$

The glaze formula can be used to give the composition of the permanent oxides:

$$
\begin{array}{llll}
PbO & 0 \cdot 4 \times 223 = & 89 \cdot 2 \\
CaO & 0 \cdot 3 \times 56 = & 16 \cdot 8 \\
K_2O & 0 \cdot 1 \times 94 = & 9 \cdot 4 \\
Na_2O & 0 \cdot 2 \times 62 = & 12 \cdot 4 \\
Al_2O_3 & 0 \cdot 3 \times 102 = & 30 \cdot 6 \\
SiO_2 & 2 \cdot 8 \times 60 = & 168 \cdot 0 \\
B_2O_3 & 0 \cdot 4 \times 70 = & 28 \cdot 0 \\
\hline
& & \overline{354 \cdot 4}
\end{array}
$$

Each permanent oxide must now be multiplied by the factor $\frac{96 \cdot 83}{354 \cdot 40}$ and this gives a final answer for the percentage composition of the mill batch:

PbO	24·37
CaO	4·59
K_2O	2·57
Na_2O	3·39
Al_2O_3	8·36
SiO_2	45·90
B_2O_3	7·65
Loss-on-ignition	3·17

Problems

(1) A glaze has the formula:

$$\left.\begin{array}{l} 0 \cdot 475\ CaO \\ 0 \cdot 237\ Na_2O \\ 0 \cdot 079\ K_2O \\ 0 \cdot 209\ PbO \end{array}\right\} 0 \cdot 285\ Al_2O_3 \left\{\begin{array}{l} 2 \cdot 255\ SiO_2 \\ 0 \cdot 475\ B_2O_3 \end{array}\right.$$

Borax frit		Lead frit	
Whiting	180·0	Red lead	685
Borax	343·8	Flint	360
Felspar	166·8		
China clay	77·4		
Flint	216·0		

Calculate the recipe for the glaze.

(2) The formula of a glaze is:

$$\left.\begin{array}{l} 0 \cdot 33\ PbO \\ 0 \cdot 40\ CaO \\ 0 \cdot 27\ Na_2O \end{array}\right\} 0 \cdot 20\ Al_2O_3 \left\{\begin{array}{l} 2 \cdot 4\ SiO_2 \\ 0 \cdot 4\ B_2O_3 \end{array}\right.$$

This is prepared from borax frit, lead frit, china clay and flint. The formulae of the frits are:

Borax frit   Lead frit

$$\left.\begin{array}{l} 0 \cdot 6\ CaO \\ 0 \cdot 4\ Na_2O \end{array}\right\} 0 \cdot 2\ Al_2O_3 \left\{\begin{array}{l} 2 \cdot 1\ SiO_2 \\ 0 \cdot 6\ B_2O_3 \end{array}\right. \quad PbO;\ 0 \cdot 1\ Al_2O_3;\ 2 \cdot 0\ SiO_2$$

Calculate the recipe of the glaze.

(3) The formula of a borax frit is:

$$\left.\begin{array}{l}0\cdot25\ Na_2O\\0\cdot22\ K_2O\\0\cdot53\ CaO\end{array}\right\}0\cdot34\ Al_2O_3\left\{\begin{array}{l}2\cdot61\ SiO_2\\0\cdot50\ B_2O_3\end{array}\right.$$

Calculate a working recipe using borax, felspar, whiting, china clay, and flint. What weights of raw materials would be required to produce 40 tons of finished frit?

(4) How many tons of red lead are required in the production of 10 tons of lead bisilicate frit ($PbO.2SiO_2$)?

(5) A frit has the following recipe:

Borax	40
Flint	14
Felspar	40
Whiting	20
China clay	6

Calculate the number of lb of each material required to charge the kiln to produce 1 ton of finished frit.

(6) The recipe for a glaze is:

Mill batch		Borax frit	
Borax frit	60	Borax	152
Lead bisilicate	40	Whiting	76
China clay	10	Stone	80
		Flint	80
		China clay	20

The cost of the raw materials per ton is:

Borax	£39	0s	0d
Ground stone	£13	0s	0d
Ground flint	£11	0s	0d
Whiting	£9	0s	0d
China clay	£7	10s	0d
Lead bisilicate frit	£98	0s	0d

The cost of grinding is £8 0s 0d per ton of finished glaze. What is the cost per ton of finished glaze?

(7) A borax frit has the following recipe:

$$\begin{array}{ll} \text{Borax} & 40\cdot0 \\ \text{Flint} & 12\cdot6 \\ \text{Felspar} & 35\cdot8 \\ \text{Whiting} & 24\cdot0 \\ \text{China clay} & 7\cdot2 \end{array}$$

Eight tons of this frit are produced each week. How many tons of each raw material must be stocked for one year's production (50 weeks)?

(8) The analysis of a glaze is:

PbO	28·54	Al_2O_3	7·14
K_2O	4·23	SiO_2	43·08
Na_2O	3·65	B_2O_3	6·30
CaO	5·99	loss	1·12

Calculate the recipe of the mill batch using:

Lead frit $\left.\begin{array}{l} 0\cdot9\,\text{PbO} \\ 0\cdot1\,\text{Na}_2\text{O} \end{array}\right\} 0\cdot05\,\text{Al}_2\text{O}_3 \Big\{ 2\cdot1\,\text{SiO}_2$

Borax frit $\left.\begin{array}{l} 0\cdot6\ \ \text{CaO} \\ 0\cdot25\,\text{Na}_2\text{O} \\ 0\cdot25\,\text{K}_2\text{O} \end{array}\right\} 0\cdot18\,\text{Al}_2\text{O}_3 \left\{\begin{array}{l} 2\cdot0\,\text{SiO}_2 \\ 0\cdot5\,\text{B}_2\text{O}_3 \end{array}\right.$

(9) The recipes of a borax frit and lead frit used in a low sol. glaze are:

Borax frit		Lead frit	
Borax	36	Red lead	65
Potash felspar	25	Flint	35
Flint	12		
China clay	10		
Whiting	5		

The mill batch is:

$$\begin{array}{ll} \text{Borax frit} & 150 \\ \text{Lead frit} & 100 \\ \text{China clay} & 35 \\ \text{Flint} & 30 \end{array}$$

Calculate

(a) the glaze formula; and

(b) percentage composition of the raw glaze.

CHAPTER IX

Miscellaneous Glaze Calculations

Substitution; Addition of Colouring Oxides to Glazes and Frits; To Calculate a Glaze Formula when the Percentage Composition of the Components is Given; Miscellaneous Example

Substitution

IT is often found necessary in works practice to substitute one component of a glaze for another. These circumstances may arise because of the unavailability of one product or because a cheaper and more suitable compound has come on to the market.

In glaze development work, one compound is often substituted for another in order to confer more desirable properties on the glaze, *e.g.* a lower thermal expansion.

A factory may produce a frit for a glaze for many years, then find that the glaze has been superseded. Large stocks of this frit may be on hand and the technologist has then to calculate the amount of this frit, which may be used in another glaze without altering its basic formula, and hence physical properties.

The following is a typical substitution problem.

The recipe of a frit is:

Pearl ash	13·8
Boric acid	25·7
Soda ash	26·5
China clay	92·9
Flint	174·0

Calculate a new recipe using felspar ($K_2O.1\cdot1Al_2O_3.6\cdot2SiO_2$) and borax to replace the pearl ash and boric acid.

It is necessary to find the molecular formula of the frit in terms of oxides which are affected by the substitution. In this particular case all the components have to be considered.

Material	Molecular weight	Molecular parts	Parts by weight	K_2O	Na_2O	Al_2O_3	SiO_2	B_2O_3
Pearl ash	138	0·100	13·8	0·100				
Boric acid	62	0·414	25·7					0·207
Soda ash	106	0·250	26·5		0·250			
China clay	258	0·360	92·9			0·360	0·720	
Flint	60	2·900	174·0				2·900	
				0·100	0·250	0·360	3·620	0·207

Substituting felspar and borax:

Material	Molecular weight	Molecular parts	Parts by weight	K_2O	Na_2O	Al_2O_3	SiO_2	B_2O_3
Borax	382	0·104	39·7		0·104			0·207
Soda ash	106	0·146	15·5		0·146			
Felspar	578·2	0·100	57·8	0·100		0·110	0·620	
China clay	258	0·250	64·5			0·250	0·500	
Flint	60	2·500	150·0				2·500	
				0·100	0·250	0·360	3·620	0·207

The new recipe is:

Borax	39·7
Soda ash	15·5
Felspar	57·8
China clay	64·5
Flint	150·0

Further example of substitution involving a glaze containing a frit.

The recipe of a glaze is:

Borax frit		Mill batch	
Borax	573·0	Borax frit	132·7
Felspar	556·0	Lead bisilicate	103·0
Whiting	350·0	China clay	38·6
China clay	77·5	Flint	72·0
Flint	205·0		

It is proposed to substitute the following lead frit

$$\left.\begin{array}{l}0\cdot85\,PbO\\0\cdot15\,K_2O\end{array}\right\}0\cdot12\,Al_2O_3\left\{2\cdot3\,SiO_2\right.$$

for the lead bisilicate. Calculate the new recipe.

(1) The first step is to find the formula of the glaze in terms of the oxides which are going to be affected by the substitution, i.e. PbO, K_2O, Al_2O_3, and SiO_2.

Material	Molecular weight	Molecular parts	Parts by weight	PbO	K_2O	Al_2O_3	SiO_2
Lead bisilicate	343	0·300	103·0	0·300			0·600
*Felspar	556	0·100	55·6		0·100	0·100	0·600
China clay	258	0·150	38·6			0·150	0·300
Flint	60	1·200	72·0				1·200
				0·300	0·100	0·250	2·700

*Note. Felspar is the only compound which introduces K_2O. The felspar is a component of the borax frit of which 132·7 parts by weight are used in the mill batch.

The following calculation shows that the inclusion of 132·7 borax frit to the mill batch is equivalent to adding 55·6 felspar. Using fritting factors on the borax frit recipe:

$$
\begin{array}{lll}
\textit{Borax} & 573 \cdot 0 \times 0 \cdot 529 = & 303 \cdot 1 \\
\textit{Felspar} & 556 \cdot 0 \times 1 \quad\;\; = & 556 \cdot 0 \\
\textit{Whiting} & 350 \cdot 0 \times 0 \cdot 56 = & 196 \cdot 0 \\
\textit{China clay} & 77 \cdot 5 \times 0 \cdot 86 = & 66 \cdot 6 \\
\textit{Flint} & 205 \cdot 0 \times 1 \quad\;\; = & 205 \cdot 0 \\
\hline
& & 1,326 \cdot 7
\end{array}
$$

1,326·7 parts by weight borax frit ≡ 556 parts by weight of felspar

∴ *132·7 borax frit ≡ 55·6 felspar*

(2) The molecular weight of the new lead frit is calculated and the table is rewritten using this component.

Materials	Molecular weight	Molecular parts	Parts by weight	PbO	K_2O	Al_2O_3	SiO_2
Lead frit	353·9	*0·353	124·9	0·300	0·053	0·042	0·812
Felspar	556	0·047	26·1		0·047	0·047	0·282
China clay	258	0·161	41·5			0·161	0·322
Flint	60	1·284	77·0				1·284
				0·300	0·100	0·250	2·700

From the formula of the lead frit

1 molecule lead frit ≡ 0·85 molecule PbO

∴ *1 molecule PbO ≡ $\dfrac{1}{0 \cdot 85}$ molecules lead frit*

but 0·300 molecule PbO is required

∴ $\left(\dfrac{1}{0 \cdot 85} \times 0 \cdot 300 \right) = 0 \cdot 353$ *molecular part of lead frit*

Similarly, the molecular parts of K_2O, Al_2O_3 and SiO_2 as shown in the lead frit formula, are multiplied by the factor 0·353, e.g. for K_2O

$$0 \cdot 15 \times 0 \cdot 353 = 0 \cdot 053$$

(3) The glaze now requires 26·1 parts by weight felspar, as against the original 55·6. Therefore the borax frit recipe must be modified.

Originally 556 felspar ≡ 1,327 borax frit. But now, 261 of felspar is required (556−261 = 295) and subtracting this figure (295) from *the original weight of borax frit, i.e. (1,327—295) = 1,032. Since $\frac{1}{10}$ of the borax frit recipe is used in the mill batch the new recipe is:*

Borax frit		Mill batch	
Borax	573	Borax frit	103·2
Felspar	261	Lead frit	124·9
Whiting	350	China clay	41·5
Flint	205	Flint	77·0
China clay	77·5		

Glaze Calculations involving the Addition of a Colouring Oxide

A coloured glaze may be produced by the addition of a small percentage of stain.

Example

The recipe of a glaze is:

Mill batch		Borax frit recipe	
Borax frit	300	Borax	200
Lead frit	500	Stone	128
Stone	30	Whiting	88
China clay	70	China clay	73
Flint	30	Flint	126

2 parts by weight of yellow stain are required per 100 parts of mill batch.

Calculate the weight of stain which must be added to the borax frit recipe. (Recipe quoted in lb weight.)

The mill batch contains 930 lb of material, i.e. the sum of the constituents.

$$\frac{2}{100} \times 930 = 18·6 \text{ lb of stain required.}$$

Applying the appropriate fritting factors to the borax frit recipe:

Borax	$200 \times 0·529$	= 105·8
Stone	128×1	= 128·0
Whiting	$88 \times 0·56$	= 49·3
China clay	$73 \times 0·86$	= 62·8
Flint	126×1	= 126·0
		471·9

Therefore, when the frit is made, each batch produces 471·9 lb of frit, but 300 lb of frit should contain in addition 18·6 lb of yellow stain.

$\therefore$ *471·9 lb of frit require $\frac{18·6}{300} \times 471·9$ lb of stain = 29·26 lb which is the amount of stain to be added to the borax frit recipe.*

To Calculate the Glaze Formula when the Components of the Glaze are Quoted in Terms of Percentage Composition

Example

The recipe of a glaze is:

Lead bisilicate	90
Stone	50
China clay	6
Flint	12

The percentage composition of the materials is as follows:

Lead bisilicate		Stone		China clay		Flint	
PbO	$64 \cdot 0$	SiO_2	$75 \cdot 0$	Al_2O_3	$39 \cdot 0$	SiO_2	96
SiO_2	$36 \cdot 0$	Al_2O_3	$18 \cdot 4$	SiO_2	$46 \cdot 4$	CaO	4
		CaO	$0 \cdot 5$	H_2O	$14 \cdot 6$		
		K_2O	$3 \cdot 1$				
		Na_2O	$3 \cdot 0$				

Calculate the formula of the glaze.

Material	Molecular weight	Molecular parts	Parts by weight	PbO	CaO	K_2O	Na_2O	Al_2O_3	SiO_2
Lead bisilicate	*100	$0 \cdot 90$	90	$0 \cdot 258$					$0 \cdot 540$
Stone	100	$0 \cdot 50$	50		$0 \cdot 004$	$0 \cdot 016$	$0 \cdot 024$	$0 \cdot 090$	$0 \cdot 625$
China clay	100	$0 \cdot 06$	6					$0 \cdot 023$	$0 \cdot 046$
Flint	100	$0 \cdot 12$	12	$0 \cdot 008$					$0 \cdot 192$
				$0 \cdot 258$	$0 \cdot 012$	$0 \cdot 016$	$0 \cdot 024$	$0 \cdot 113$	$1 \cdot 403$

The final formula is obtained by bringing basic oxides to unity (divide throughout by $0 \cdot 310$).

$$\left. \begin{array}{l} 0 \cdot 832 \, PbO \\ 0 \cdot 038 \, CaO \\ 0 \cdot 051 \, K_2O \\ 0 \cdot 079 \, Na_2O \end{array} \right\} 0 \cdot 364 \, Al_2O_3 \left\{ 4 \cdot 525 \, SiO_2 \right.$$

*The molecular weight of each compound is quoted in the table as 100. A detailed explanation of why this is possible is given below, using lead bisilicate as an example.

$$PbO = 64\%$$
$$SiO_2 = 36\%$$

By dividing the percentage composition of each oxide by its molecular weight, the ratio of each oxide becomes:

$$\frac{64}{223} \, PbO : \frac{36}{60} \, SiO_2$$

$$= 0 \cdot 287 \, PbO : 0 \cdot 600 \, SiO_2$$

In calculating the empirical formula, each molecular part would have to be divided by the smallest number, in this case $0 \cdot 287$:

$$\frac{0 \cdot 287}{0 \cdot 287} \text{PbO} : \frac{0 \cdot 600}{0 \cdot 287} \text{SiO}_2$$

The formula would then be:

$$\text{PbO} : 2 \cdot 09 \text{ SiO}_2$$

The "molecular weight" or more accurately the "formula weight", for this compound using this particular formula $= 349$.

If the previous formula is used, *i.e.* $0 \cdot 287$ PbO; $0 \cdot 6$ SiO$_2$, then the molecular weight $= 100$. Since

$$
\begin{array}{llr}
\text{PbO} & 0 \cdot 287 \times 223 = & 64 \\
\text{SiO}_2 & 0 \cdot 600 \times 60 = & \underline{36} \\
& & 100
\end{array}
$$

Therefore, as a general rule any formula that is calculated directly from percentage composition must automatically give a molecular weight of 100. This fact is used as a method of eliminating tedious and unnecessary work in this type of calculation.

Having established that the particular formula for lead bisilicate $= 0 \cdot 287$ PbO; $0 \cdot 6$ SiO$_2$, then

$$
\begin{array}{l}
1 \text{ molecule} \equiv 0 \cdot 287 \text{ molecule PbO} \\
0 \cdot 9 \text{ molecule} \equiv 0 \cdot 287 \times 0 \cdot 9 \text{ molecule PbO} \\
\phantom{0 \cdot 9 \text{ molecule}} = 0 \cdot 258 \text{ PbO}
\end{array}
$$

Similarly $0 \cdot 9 \times 0 \cdot 6 \,(\text{SiO}_2) = 0 \cdot 540 \text{ SiO}_2$

It must be emphasized that, using a molecular weight of 100, calculated from percentage composition, is only a "short cut" method. It is equally valid to use the formula PbO; $2 \cdot 09$ SiO$_2$ with a molecular weight of 349, since:

$$\frac{90}{349} = \text{molecular part lead bisilicate required}$$

$$= 0 \cdot 258$$

and since the formula $=$ PbO; $2 \cdot 1$ SiO$_2$

$$
\begin{array}{l}
1 \times 0 \cdot 258 = \text{PbO} = 0 \cdot 258 \\
2 \cdot 1 \times 0 \cdot 258 = \text{SiO}_2 = 0 \cdot 540
\end{array}
$$

Repeating the procedure for china clay:

$$
\begin{array}{lll}
\text{Al}_2\text{O}_3 & 39 \cdot 0 \div 102 = 0 \cdot 382 \\
\text{SiO}_2 & 46 \cdot 4 \div 60 = 0 \cdot 773
\end{array}
$$

It is not necessary to consider the H$_2$O, since it is a non-permanent oxide.

$$
\begin{array}{l}
1 \text{ molecule china clay} \equiv 0 \cdot 382 \text{ molecule Al}_2\text{O}_3 \\
0 \cdot 06 \text{ molecule china clay} \equiv 0 \cdot 382 \times 0 \cdot 06 \text{ molecule Al}_2\text{O}_3 \\
\phantom{0 \cdot 06 \text{ molecule china clay}} = 0 \cdot 023 \text{ Al}_2\text{O}_3
\end{array}
$$

Similarly $\qquad 0 \cdot 06 \times 0 \cdot 773 = 0 \cdot 046 \text{ SiO}_2$

Flint:

$$SiO_2 \quad 96 \div 60 = 1 \cdot 600$$
$$CaO \quad 4 \div 56 = 0 \cdot 072$$
$$1 \text{ molecule flint} \equiv 0 \cdot 072 \, CaO$$
$$0 \cdot 12 \text{ molecule flint} \equiv 0 \cdot 072 \times 0 \cdot 12 \, CaO$$
$$= 0 \cdot 008 \, CaO$$

and
$$0 \cdot 12 \times 1 \cdot 6 = 0 \cdot 192 \, SiO_2$$

Stone:

$$SiO_2 \quad 75 \cdot 0 \div 60 = 1 \cdot 250$$
$$Al_2O_3 \quad 18 \cdot 4 \div 102 = 0 \cdot 180$$
$$CaO \quad 0 \cdot 5 \div 56 = 0 \cdot 009$$
$$K_2O \quad 3 \cdot 1 \div 94 = 0 \cdot 033$$
$$Na_2O \quad 3 \cdot 0 \div 62 = 0 \cdot 048$$

0·5 molecular part of stone is required. Multiplying throughout by 0·5.

$$SiO_2 = 0 \cdot 625$$
$$Al_2O_3 = 0 \cdot 090$$
$$CaO = 0 \cdot 004$$
$$K_2O = 0 \cdot 016$$
$$Na_2O = 0 \cdot 024$$

Miscellaneous Example

This example is an actual works problem involving the use of stocks of frit A that had become obsolete.

Frit B has the following percentage composition:

$$
\begin{array}{ll}
Na_2O & 2 \cdot 3 \\
K_2O & 1 \cdot 7 \\
CaO & 4 \cdot 6 \\
PbO & 16 \cdot 3 \\
ZnO & 4 \cdot 2 \\
Al_2O_3 & 5 \cdot 9 \\
SiO_2 & 44 \cdot 4 \\
B_2O_3 & 9 \cdot 3 \\
ZrO_2 & 11 \cdot 3 \\
\end{array}
$$

It is to be compounded from frit A, felspar C which has the formula:

$$\left. \begin{array}{l} 0 \cdot 72 \, K_2O \\ 0 \cdot 28 \, Na_2O \end{array} \right\} 1 \cdot 13 \, Al_2O_3 \left\{ 7 \cdot 8 \, SiO_2 \right.$$

and other raw materials which are used in the production of frit A.

The recipe of frit A is:

$$
\begin{array}{rl}
\text{Pyrobor } (Na_2B_4O_7) & 5 \cdot 3 \\
\text{Felspar C} & 10 \cdot 9 \\
\text{Whiting} & 7 \cdot 3 \\
\text{Red lead} & 27 \cdot 7 \\
\text{Boric acid} & 14 \cdot 5 \\
\text{China clay} & 2 \cdot 5 \\
\text{Flint} & 29 \cdot 3 \\
\text{Zircon} & 2 \cdot 5 \\
\end{array}
$$

0·1 molecular part of frit A is to be used in the production of frit B. Calculate the quantity of frit A that will be required to produce 100 tons of frit B.

To find the formula of frit B from the percentage composition:

$$
\begin{array}{rll}
Na_2O & 2 \cdot 3 \div\ 62 & = 0 \cdot 0371 \\
K_2O & 1 \cdot 7 \div\ 94 & = 0 \cdot 0181 \\
CaO & 4 \cdot 6 \div\ 56 & = 0 \cdot 0822 \\
PbO & 16 \cdot 3 \div 223 & = 0 \cdot 0731 \\
ZnO & 4 \cdot 2 \div\ 81 & = 0 \cdot 0518 \\
Al_2O_3 & 5 \cdot 9 \div 102 & = 0 \cdot 0578 \\
SiO_2 & 44 \cdot 4 \div\ 60 & = 0 \cdot 7400 \\
B_2O_3 & 9 \cdot 3 \div\ 70 & = 0 \cdot 1328 \\
ZrO_2 & 11 \cdot 3 \div 123 & = 0 \cdot 0919 \\
\end{array}
$$

Dividing by 0·2623 to bring basic oxides to unity:

$$
\left.
\begin{array}{l}
0 \cdot 141\ Na_2O \\
0 \cdot 069\ K_2O \\
0 \cdot 314\ CaO \\
0 \cdot 279\ PbO \\
0 \cdot 197\ ZnO \\
\end{array}
\right\}
0 \cdot 220\ Al_2O_3
\left\{
\begin{array}{l}
2 \cdot 821\ SiO_2 \\
0 \cdot 506\ B_2O_3 \\
0 \cdot 350\ ZrO_2 \\
\end{array}
\right.
$$

To calculate the molecular weight of frit A, the recipe has to be converted to a formula. The molecular weight of the frit is then calculated in the usual way by multiplying the molecular parts by the appropriate molecular weights of each oxide.

Material	Mol. weight	Mol. parts	Parts by wt.	Na_2O	K_2O	CaO	PbO	Al_2O_3	SiO_2	B_2O_3	ZrO_2
Pyrobor	202	0·0262	5·3	0·0262						0·0524	
Felspar C	668·4	0·0163	10·9	0·0046	0·0117			0·0184	0·1271		
Whiting	100	0·0730	7·3			0·0730					
Red lead	685	0·0404	27·7				0·1214				
Boric acid	62	0·2340	14·5							0·1170	
China clay	258	0·0097	2·5					0·0097	0·0194		
Flint	60	0·4883	29·3						0·4883		
Zircon	183	0·0137	2·5						0·0137		0·0137
				0·0308	0·0117	0·0730	0·1214	0·0281	0·6485	0·1694	0·0137

109

Bring basic oxides to unity by dividing by $0\cdot2369$:

$$\left.\begin{array}{l} 0\cdot130\ Na_2O \\ 0\cdot049\ K_2O \\ 0\cdot308\ CaO \\ 0\cdot512\ PbO \end{array}\right\} 0\cdot119\ Al_2O_3 \left\{\begin{array}{l} 2\cdot737\ SiO_2 \\ 0\cdot715\ B_2O_3 \\ 0\cdot058\ ZrO_2 \end{array}\right.$$

The molecular weight of frit $A = 377\cdot7$.

To calculate a recipe for frit B (this is shown in the "parts by weight" column):

Material	Mol. weight	Mol. parts	Parts by wt.	Na_2O	K_2O	CaO	PbO	ZnO	Al_2O_3	SiO_2	B_2O_3	ZrO_2
Frit A	377·7	0·1	37·8	0·013	0·005	0·031	0·051		0·012	0·274	0·072	0·006
Felspar C	668·4	0·089	59·4	0·025	0·064				0·101	0·694		
Pyrobor	202	0·103	20·8	0·103							0·206	
Boric acid	62	0·456	28·3								0·228	
Red lead	685	0·076	52·1				0·228					
Whiting	100	0·283	28·3			0·283						
Zinc oxide	81·4	0·197	16·0					0·197				
China clay	258	0·107	27·6						0·107	0·214		
Zircon	183	0·344	63·0							0·344		0·344
Flint	60	1·295	77·7							1·295		
Total		411·0		0·141	0·069	0·314	0·279	0·197	0·220	2·821	0·506	0·350

Applying fritting factors to determine the residual weight after fritting 411 parts by weight of frit mixture B.

$$\begin{array}{lrcl} \text{Frit A} & 37\cdot8\times1 & = & 37\cdot8 \\ \text{Felspar C} & 59\cdot4\times1 & = & 59\cdot4 \\ \text{Pyrobor} & 20\cdot8\times1 & = & 20\cdot8 \\ \text{Boric acid} & 28\cdot3\times0\cdot565 & = & 16\cdot0 \\ \text{Red lead} & 52\cdot1\times0\cdot977 & = & 50\cdot9 \\ \text{Whiting} & 28\cdot3\times0\cdot560 & = & 15\cdot8 \\ \text{China clay} & 27\cdot6\times0\cdot860 & = & 23\cdot7 \\ \text{Zinc oxide} & 16\cdot0\times1 & = & 16\cdot0 \\ \text{Zircon} & 63\cdot0\times1 & = & 63\cdot0 \\ \text{Flint} & 77\cdot7\times1 & = & 77\cdot7 \\ \hline & & & 381\cdot1 \end{array}$$

$\therefore$ 411 frit B mixture $\equiv 381\cdot1$ of frit B (after fritting) and this requires $37\cdot8$ of frit A.

$\therefore$ $381\cdot1$ frit B $\equiv 37\cdot8$ frit A

$$100\ \text{frit B} \equiv \frac{37\cdot8}{381\cdot1}\times100\ \text{frit A}$$

$$= 9\cdot919\ \text{tons frit A}$$

Note. In this problem it is essential to bring basic oxides to unity in both frit A and frit B since a fixed amount of frit A ($0\cdot1$ molecular parts) is to be introduced to frit B.

Problems

(1) A glaze has the following recipe:

Borax frit 421
Lead frit 295
Stone 271
China clay 32
Flint 12

The formula of the lead frit is $PbO.2SiO_2$. It is found necessary to substitute this lead frit for one which has the formula $PbO; 0\cdot1\ Al_2O_3; 2\cdot1\ SiO_2$. Calculate a new recipe for the glaze.

(2) The recipe for a glaze using a borax frit which has been prepared on the works is as follows:

Works recipe of borax frit

Borax 76·4
Whiting 20·0
Felspar 55·6
Flint 24·0

Glaze recipe

Lead frit ($PbO.2SiO_2$) 137·2
Works borax frit 131·2
Whiting 10·0
China clay 51·6
Flint 36·0

It is found necessary to purchase a borax frit to substitute for the one which has been prepared on the works. Calculate a new recipe for the glaze using the purchased borax frit of the formula:

$$\left.\begin{array}{l} 0\cdot50\ CaO \\ 0\cdot33\ Na_2O \\ 0\cdot17\ K_2O \end{array}\right\} 0\cdot16\ Al_2O_3 \left\{\begin{array}{l} 1\cdot66\ SiO_2 \\ 0\cdot66\ B_2O_3 \end{array}\right.$$

and other pure raw materials.

(3) Substitute Cornish stone of formula:

$$\left.\begin{array}{l} 0\cdot4\ K_2O \\ 0\cdot1\ Na_2O \\ 0\cdot1\ CaO \end{array}\right\} Al_2O_3 . 7\cdot2\ SiO_2$$

for potash felspar in the following frit, and make the necessary adjustments to the recipe.

Borax frit recipe

Borax crystals 200
Potash felspar 100
Whiting 80
China clay 90
Flint 150
Soda ash 40

Mill batch

Frit 850
China clay 60

(4) A glaze is made using the borax frit of formula:

$$\left.\begin{array}{l} 0\cdot6\,CaO \\ 0\cdot2\,Na_2O \\ 0\cdot2\,K_2O \end{array}\right\} 0\cdot18\,Al_2O_3 \left\{\begin{array}{l} 2\cdot00\,SiO_2 \\ 0\cdot40\,B_2O_3 \end{array}\right.$$

The recipe for the glaze is:

$$
\begin{array}{rr}
\text{Borax frit} & 137\cdot37 \\
\text{Whiting} & 15\cdot00 \\
\text{China clay} & 42\cdot57 \\
\text{Flint} & 70\cdot20 \\
\text{Zinc oxide} & 8\cdot10
\end{array}
$$

Make this into a raw glaze using calcium borate, $(2CaO.3B_2O_3.4H_2O)$ and other pure raw materials.

(5) A glaze has the formula:

$$\left.\begin{array}{l} 0\cdot400\,PbO \\ 0\cdot426\,CaO \\ 0\cdot174\,Na_2O \end{array}\right\} 0\cdot200\,Al_2O_3 \left\{\begin{array}{l} 2\cdot500\,SiO_2 \\ 0\cdot348\,B_2O_3 \end{array}\right.$$

This is compounded from borax frit of formula:

$$\left.\begin{array}{l} 0\cdot29\,Na_2O \\ 0\cdot71\,CaO \end{array}\right\} 0\cdot14\,Al_2O_3 \left\{\begin{array}{l} 2\cdot00\,SiO_2 \\ 0\cdot58\,B_2O_3 \end{array}\right.$$

lead bisilicate $(PbO.2SiO_2)$ and other pure raw materials.

It is desired to increase the Al_2O_3 in the original glaze by $0\cdot27$ molecular parts by means of china clay. What should the new recipe be, and what percentage increase in china clay is necessary?

(6) The recipe for a glaze is:

Mill batch		Borax frit	
Borax frit	173·1	Borax	76·4
Lead frit	171·5	Whiting	30·0
China clay	25·8	China clay	25·8
		Flint	36·0

What weight of cobalt oxide (CoO) must be added to the borax frit recipe, so that the glaze contains $0\cdot02$ molecular parts CoO in addition to the molecular parts of the oxides already present.

112

(7) The recipe for a glaze is:

Mill batch		Borax frit	
Borax frit	164·8	Whiting	60·0
Lead frit	105·3	Felspar	55·6
China clay	36·1	Flint	72·0
Flint	29·4	Borax	114·6
		China clay	25·8

The glaze is stained with 3% cobalt stain made up from:

CoO, 50; china clay, 30; flint, 20; which is calcined and ground before use. This is to be replaced by adding the necessary CoO to the borax frit. Calculate the amount of CoO to be incorporated in the borax frit recipe.

(8) Calculate a recipe for the glaze:

$$\left.\begin{array}{l} 0\cdot4\,CaO \\ 0\cdot4\,PbO \\ 0\cdot2\,K_2O \end{array}\right\} 0\cdot26\,Al_2O_3 \left\{\begin{array}{l} 2\cdot4\,SiO_2 \end{array}\right.$$

using felspar, whiting, china clay, flint and lead bisilicate of the following composition:

$$PbO \quad 61\cdot2\%$$
$$Al_2O_3 \quad 1\cdot8\%$$
$$SiO_2 \quad 37\cdot0\%$$

(9) The recipe of a glaze is:

Lead bisilicate	30
Borax frit	45
China clay	8
Flint	10
Stone	7

The laboratory reports that the analyses of the materials are:

Lead bisilicate	Borax frit	China clay	Flint	Stone
PbO 65	CaO 13·70	Al$_2$O$_3$ 39·0	SiO$_2$ 98·2	SiO$_2$ 75·0
SiO$_2$ 35	Al$_2$O$_3$ 7·49	SiO$_2$ 46·6	CaCO$_3$ 1·8	Al$_2$O$_3$ 18·5
	SiO$_2$ 48·96	K$_2$O 0·6		CaO 0·4
	B$_2$O$_3$ 17·12	H$_2$O 13·8		K$_2$O 6·1
	Na$_2$O 5·06			
	K$_2$O 7·67			

What is the formula of the glaze?

(10) What is the formula of a glaze obtained by mixing 100 lb of No. 1 frit, 156 lb of No. 2 frit and 20 lb of china clay? The percentage composition of No. 1 frit is: PbO, 62·2; SiO_2, 33·5; Al_2O_3, 4·3. The formula of No. 2 frit:

$$\left.\begin{array}{l} 0\cdot1\ K_2O \\ 0\cdot6\ CaO \\ 0\cdot3\ Na_2O \end{array}\right\} 0\cdot3\ Al_2O_3 \left\{\begin{array}{l} 2\cdot8\ SiO_2 \\ 0\cdot6\ B_2O_3 \end{array}\right.$$

(11) Calculate a recipe for the glaze:

$$\left.\begin{array}{l} 0\cdot3\ \ CaO \\ 0\cdot4\ \ PbO \\ 0\cdot15\ K_2O \\ 0\cdot15\ ZnO \end{array}\right\} 0\cdot20\ Al_2O_3 \left\{\ 1\cdot85\ SiO_2\right.$$

using felspar, whiting, zinc oxide, china clay, flint and lead bisilicate of composition:

$$\begin{array}{ll} PbO & 63\% \\ Al_2O_3 & 1\% \\ SiO_2 & 36\% \end{array}$$

(12) The recipe of a glaze is:

$$\begin{array}{ll} \text{Lead frit} & 32 \\ \text{Borax frit} & 58 \\ \text{China clay} & 10 \end{array}$$

The percentage composition of lead frit:

$$\begin{array}{ll} PbO & 61\cdot7 \\ Al_2O_3 & 3\cdot4 \\ SiO_2 & 34\cdot9 \end{array}$$

and the formula of borax frit:

$$\left.\begin{array}{l} 0\cdot55\ CaO \\ 0\cdot45\ Na_2O \end{array}\right\} 0\cdot20\ Al_2O_3 \left\{\begin{array}{l} 1\cdot80\ SiO_2 \\ 0\cdot50\ B_2O_3 \end{array}\right.$$

Calculate the formula of the glaze.

(13) A glaze is made from a borax frit, zinc oxide, china clay, and flint. The analysis of glaze and borax frit is:

	Glaze	Borax frit
K_2O	5·0	8·9
MgO	0·5	0·9
CaO	6·0	10·7
BaO	2·0	3·6
ZnO	6·5	—
B_2O_3	1·9	3·4
Al_2O_3	13·6	18·3
SiO_2	64·5	54·2

Suggest a recipe for this glaze.

114

CHAPTER X

Ultimate and Rational Analysis

The Meaning of Proximate and Rational Analysis; Calculated Rational Analyses of Clays; The Felspar and Mica Conventions; The Calculated Rational Analysis of Stone and Felspar; The Substitution of Clays in Body Recipes

THE chemical analysis of a clay is usually expressed in terms of percentage composition of the constituent oxides.

Example

SiO_2	61·30
Al_2O_3	20·20
Fe_2O_3	3·40
TiO_2	0·20
MgO	0·24
CaO	0·34
Na_2O	1·05
K_2O	2·35
loss	10·90

This type of chemical analysis is generally obtained by "rapid" methods, which have now been modified by use of the spectrophotometer. The analysis of a clay may be completed within a period of 8 hr. The result, given in terms of percentage composition, is referred to as the ULTIMATE ANALYSIS.

Since the clay does not occur naturally in the form of oxides it is of some importance to know its mineralogical composition. The main mineral constituents are clay substance, felspar (mica) and quartz.

The ultimate analysis can be converted to its mineral constituents by means of a simple calculation. The result is known as a PROXIMATE ANALYSIS.

In the past, special chemical methods were used for estimating directly the minerals in clays, based on the rates at which the various minerals were attacked and dissolved by different reagents. This method was known as a RATIONAL ANALYSIS. The difficulties involved in conducting a satisfactory rational analysis were very great, and the method is now seldom used.

Nowadays, the term rational analysis is often used to describe the mineral composition obtained by calculation from the ultimate analysis. Therefore, in accordance with accepted terminology, rational analysis and proximate analysis will be assumed to have the same meaning, *i.e.* an analysis given in terms of mineral constituents calculated from the ultimate analysis.

To Calculate the Rational Analysis of a Clay

FELSPAR CONVENTION

(1) Using this convention it is assumed that the alkalis (K_2O and Na_2O) are derived entirely from felspars.

$$1 \text{ molecule } K_2O \equiv 1 \text{ molecule potash felspar}$$
$$\equiv K_2O \cdot Al_2O_3 \cdot 6SiO_2$$
$$94 \text{ parts } K_2O \equiv 556 \text{ parts potash felspar}$$
$$1 \text{ part } K_2O \equiv \frac{556}{94} \text{ parts potash felspar}$$
$$= 5 \cdot 92 \text{ potash felspar or orthoclase}$$

A similar calculation for soda spar (albite)
$$Na_2O \cdot Al_2O_3 \cdot 6SiO_2$$
yields a factor of 8·45. However, it is common practice to take the sum of the percentage of K_2O and Na_2O and to use the factor of 5·92 to convert these oxides to mineral felspar. This treatment should only be applied to clays when the total alkalis are small (2–4%) and the amount of K_2O is approximately twice the Na_2O content.

Considering the ultimate analysis quoted at the beginning of the chapter,

$$(K_2O \ 2\cdot35 + Na_2O \ 1\cdot05) = 3\cdot40 \text{ total alkali content}$$
$$3\cdot40 \times 5\cdot92 = 20\cdot13\% \text{ felspar}$$

(2) *(a)* $\quad 1 \text{ molecule } K_2O \cdot Al_2O_3 \cdot 6SiO_2 \equiv 1 \text{ molecule } Al_2O_3$
$$556 \equiv 102$$
$$1 \text{ part felspar} \equiv \frac{102}{556} \text{ parts } Al_2O_3$$
$$= 0\cdot183 \ Al_2O_3$$
$$20\cdot13 \times 0\cdot183 = 3\cdot68 \text{ parts } Al_2O_3$$
$$\text{in felspar}$$

(b) Similarly, $\quad 556 \text{ felspar} \equiv 6 \times 60 \ SiO_2$
$$1 \text{ felspar} \equiv \frac{360}{556} \ SiO_2$$
$$= 0\cdot647 \ SiO_2$$
$$20\cdot13 \times 0\cdot647 = 13\cdot02 \text{ parts } SiO_2$$
$$\text{in felspar}$$

(3) $\qquad$ Total $Al_2O_3 = 20\cdot20$ (ref. ultimate analysis)

$-Al_2O_3$ in felspar $= -3\cdot68$

$\overline{16\cdot52} = Al_2O_3$ in clay substance

1 molecule $Al_2O_3 \equiv$ 1 molecule $Al_2O_3.2SiO_2.2H_2O$

$102 \equiv 258$

1 part $Al_2O_3 \equiv \dfrac{258}{102}$ parts clay substance

$= 2\cdot53$ clay substance

$\therefore \qquad 16\cdot52 \times 2\cdot53 = \underline{41\cdot79\%$ clay substance}

(4) $\quad$ 1 molecule $Al_2O_3.2SiO_2.2H_2O \equiv$ 2 molecules SiO_2

$258 \equiv 2 \times 60$

1 clay substance $\equiv \dfrac{120}{258} SiO_2$

$= 0\cdot465 SiO_2$

$\therefore \qquad SiO_2$ in clay substance $= 41\cdot79 \times 0\cdot465$

$= 19\cdot43\% SiO_2$ in clay substance

Free quartz $=$ Total SiO_2

$-(SiO_2$ in clay substance $+ SiO_2$ in felspar)

$= 61\cdot30 - (19\cdot43 + 13\cdot02)$

$= \underline{28\cdot85\%$ free quartz}

Summary

Total alkalis $\times 5\cdot92 = \%$ felspar

Felspar $\times 0\cdot183 = Al_2O_3$ in felspar

Felspar $\times 0\cdot647 = SiO_2$ in felspar

(Total $Al_2O_3 - Al_2O_3$ in felspar) $\times 2\cdot53 = \underline{\%$ clay substance}

Clay substance $\times 0\cdot465 = SiO_2$ in clay

Total $SiO_2 - (SiO_2$ in clay $+ SiO_2$ in felspar) $= \underline{\%$ quartz}

Further information can be obtained from the percentage loss-on-ignition. The first step is to calculate the loss due to the chemically combined water in the clay molecule.

1 molecule $Al_2O_3.2SiO_2.2H_2O \equiv$ 2 molecules H_2O

$258 \equiv 2 \times 18$

1 part clay $\equiv \dfrac{36}{258}$ parts water

$= 0\cdot140$ part water

$\therefore \qquad 41\cdot78 \times 0\cdot140 = 5\cdot83$ loss due to H_2O in clay molecule

(Total loss $-$ loss due to H_2O in clay) $=$ loss due to organic matter, CO_2, etc.

$(10\cdot90 - 5\cdot83) = \underline{5\cdot07\%$ loss due to organic matter, CO_2, etc.}

Therefore, the final rational analysis may be written as:

Clay substance 41·8
Felspar 20·1
Quartz 28·8
Fe_2O_3 3·4
TiO_2 0·2
MgO 0·2
CaO 0·3
Organic matter, CO_2, etc. 5·1

Note. A simpler treatment is to obtain the "organic matter, CO_2, etc." by difference, *e.g.* in the above case it would be 5·2 making the total exactly 100·0. This is permissible because a calculated rational analysis is only an approximation. Its assumptions are not necessarily correct in every case since oxides may exist in modified forms of the pure minerals.

MICA CONVENTION

Recent work using X-ray diffraction techniques suggests that the alkali mineral associated with kaolinite is mica and not felspar. This has led to a change in the method used for calculating the rational analysis.

Since the felspar convention has been used successfully for so many years in recipe calculations, it is often found that the results of a calculated rational analysis are expressed in terms of both mica and felspar content.

The mica convention is concerned with the minerals

potash mica $(K_2O.3Al_2O_3.6SiO_2.2H_2O)$
and soda mica $(Na_2O.3Al_2O_3.6SiO_2.2H_2O)$

Using the ultimate analysis from the previous example:

(1)   1 molecule $K_2O \equiv$ 1 molecule $K_2O.3Al_2O_3.6SiO_2.2H_2O$
$$94 \equiv 796$$

$$1 \text{ part } K_2O \equiv \frac{796}{94} \text{ parts mica}$$

$$1 \text{ part } K_2O = 8 \cdot 47 \text{ parts potash mica}$$

Similarly the factor for converting Na_2O content to soda mica $= 12 \cdot 32$.

$$K_2O = 2 \cdot 35 \% \text{ (ref. ultimate analysis)}$$
$\therefore$ $2 \cdot 35 \times 8 \cdot 47 = \underline{\text{potash mica}} = 19 \cdot 91 \%$
and $1 \cdot 05 \times 12 \cdot 32 = \underline{\text{soda mica}} = 12 \cdot 93 \%$

(2)   1 molecule potash mica $\equiv$ 3 molecules Al_2O_3

$$796 \equiv 306$$
$$1 \equiv \frac{306}{796}$$

$\therefore$ 1 part potash mica $\equiv 0\cdot384$ parts Al_2O_3

$19\cdot91\times0\cdot384 = 7\cdot64 = Al_2O_3$ in potash mica

1 molecule potash mica $\equiv$ 6 molecules SiO_2

$$796 \equiv 6\times60$$
$$1 \equiv \frac{360}{796}$$

1 part potash mica $\equiv 0\cdot452$ parts SiO_2

$\therefore$ $19\cdot91\times0\cdot452 = 9\cdot00 = SiO_2$ in potash mica

Similarly for soda mica:

$$12\cdot93\times0\cdot400 = 5\cdot17 = Al_2O_3 \text{ in soda mica}$$
$$12\cdot93\times0\cdot471 = 6\cdot09 = SiO_2 \text{ in soda mica}$$

(3) Total Al_2O_3 (ref. ultimate analysis) = $\quad 20\cdot20$

$- Al_2O_3$ in micas $(7\cdot64+5\cdot17) = -12\cdot81$

Al_2O_3 in clay substance = $\quad \overline{7\cdot39}$

$7\cdot39\times2\cdot53 = \underline{18\cdot69\%}$ clay substance

(4) SiO_2 in clay $= 18\cdot69\times0\cdot465 = 8\cdot69$

SiO_2 in clay $+ SiO_2$ in micas $= (8\cdot69+9\cdot00+6\cdot09)$

$$= 23\cdot78$$

$\therefore$ Free quartz $= 61\cdot30 - 23\cdot78 = \underline{37\cdot52\%}$

The final rational analysis is:

Potash mica	19·9
Soda mica	12·9
Clay substance	18·7
Quartz	37·5
Organic matter, CO_2, etc., by difference	6·9
Fe_2O_3	3·4
TiO_2	0·2
MgO	0·2
CaO	0·3

Summary

$$K_2O\times8\cdot47 = \underline{\text{potash mica}}$$
$$Na_2O\times12\cdot32 = \underline{\text{soda mica}}$$
$$\text{Potash mica}\times0\cdot384 = \overline{Al_2O_3 \text{ in potash mica}}$$
$$\text{Potash mica}\times0\cdot452 = SiO_2 \text{ in potash mica}$$
$$\text{Soda mica}\times0\cdot400 = Al_2O_3 \text{ in soda mica}$$
$$\text{Soda mica}\times0\cdot471 = SiO_2 \text{ in soda mica}$$
$$(\text{Total } Al_2O_3 - Al_2O_3 \text{ in micas})\times2\cdot53 = \underline{\text{clay substance}}$$
$$\text{Clay substance}\times0\cdot465 = \overline{SiO_2 \text{ in clay}}$$
$$\text{Total } SiO_2 - (SiO_2 \text{ in clay} + SiO_2 \text{ in micas}) = \underline{\text{Free quartz}}$$

Calculated Rational Analysis of Stone and Felspar

A stone has the following ultimate analysis:

	%
SiO_2	71·44
TiO_2	0·13
Al_2O_3	16·54
Fe_2O_3	0·31
MgO	0·09
CaO	2·02
K_2O	4·13
Na_2O	3·10
loss	1·87

The total alkali content of a stone is of the order 7–10% (felspar 10–14%). Since the percentage K_2O is approximately the same as the percentage Na_2O, it is common practice to calculate the rational analysis in terms of potash felspar and soda felspar as separate minerals.

(1) 1 molecule $K_2O \equiv$ 1 molecule $K_2O.Al_2O_3.6SiO_2$

$$94 \equiv 556$$
$$1 \equiv \frac{556}{94}$$

1 part $K_2O \equiv 5·92$ parts potash felspar

$\therefore$ $4·13 \times 5·92 = \underline{24·45\%}$ potash felspar (orthoclase)

Similarly,
$$3·10 \times 8·45 = \underline{26·20\%} \text{ soda felspar (albite)}$$

(2) *(a)* For potash felspar:

$$\text{Orthoclase} \times 0·183 = Al_2O_3 \text{ in orthoclase}$$
$$24·45 \times 0·183 = 4·475$$
$$\text{Orthoclase} \times 0·647 = SiO_2 \text{ in orthoclase}$$
$$24·45 \times 0·647 = 15·82$$

(b) For soda felspar:

$$\text{Albite} \times 0·195 = Al_2O_3 \text{ in albite}$$
$$26·2 \times 0·195 = 5·11$$
$$\text{Albite} \times 0·687 = SiO_2 \text{ in albite}$$
$$26·2 \times 0·687 = 18·00$$

(3) Total $Al_2O_3 = $ 16·54 (ref. ultimate analysis)
$-Al_2O_3$ in felspars $= -9·59$

$$\overline{6·95} = Al_2O_3 \text{ in clay substance}$$
$$6·95 \times 2·53 = \underline{17·58\%} \text{ clay substance}$$

(4)
$$17 \cdot 58 \times 0 \cdot 465 = SiO_2 \text{ in clay}$$
$$= 8 \cdot 18$$

Total $SiO_2 - (SiO_2$ in clay$+SiO_2$ in felspars$) =$ free quartz

$$71 \cdot 44 - (8 \cdot 18 + 15 \cdot 82 + 18 \cdot 00) = 29 \cdot 44$$
$$\underline{\% \text{ free quartz} = 29 \cdot 44 \%}$$

The final result of the rational analysis is:

	%
Orthoclase	24·4
Albite	26·2
Clay substance	17·6
Quartz	29·4
Fe_2O_3	0·3
MgO	0·1
CaO	2·0
TiO_2	0·1

Summary

$$K_2O \times 5 \cdot 92 = \underline{\text{orthoclase}}$$
$$Na_2O \times 8 \cdot 45 = \underline{\text{albite}}$$
$$\text{Orthoclase} \times 0 \cdot 183 = Al_2O_3 \text{ in orthoclase}$$
$$\text{Orthoclase} \times 0 \cdot 647 = SiO_2 \text{ in orthoclase}$$
$$\text{Albite} \times 0 \cdot 195 = Al_2O_3 \text{ in albite}$$
$$\text{Albite} \times 0 \cdot 687 = SiO_2 \text{ in albite}$$
$$(\text{Total } Al_2O_3 - Al_2O_3 \text{ in felspars}) \times 2 \cdot 53 = \underline{\text{clay substance}}$$
$$\text{Clay substance} \times 0 \cdot 465 = \underline{SiO_2 \text{ in clay}}$$
$$\text{Total } SiO_2 - (SiO_2 \text{ in clay} + SiO_2 \text{ in felspars}) = \underline{\text{free quartz}}$$

Substitution of Clays in Body Recipes

A considerable number of ball clays are commercially available. They differ from each other in terms of mineral composition, physical properties, economic value, etc.

If one ball clay in a body is to be replaced by another, having a different rational analysis, the body recipe should be adjusted using the following principles:

(1) The substitution is based on maintaining the percentage of clay substance introduced by the ball clay; and

(2) The total weights of clay substance felspar and quartz in the body should be maintained at their original values.

Example

An earthenware body has the following recipe:

Ball clay I	25
China clay	25
Flint	35
Stone	15

If ball clay I is to be substituted by ball clay II calculate a new recipe given that the rational analysis of the raw materials are:

	% clay substance	% felspar	% quartz
Ball clay I	81·33	12·77	2·98
Ball clay II	74·63	11·40	12·00
Stone	17·58	50·65	29·44

China clay and flint are assumed to be pure clay substance and quartz respectively.

		Clay substance	Felspar	Quartz
(1) Old recipe:				
Ball clay I	25·00	20·33	3·19	0·74
China clay	25·00	25·00		
Flint	35·00			35·00
Stone	15·00	2·64	7·60	4·42
Total		47·97	10·79	40·16
(2) New recipe:				
Ball clay II	27·24	20·33	3·11	3·27
China clay	24·97	24·97		
Flint	32·42			32·42
Stone	15·17	2·67	7·68	4·47

New recipe:

Ball clay II	27·2
China clay	25·0
Flint	32·4
Stone	15·2

Considering section (1) above:

The old recipe was used to calculate the mineral constituents of the body in terms of clay substance, felspar and quartz.

From the rational analyses:

100 ball clay I ≡ 81·33 parts clay substance
25 ball clay I ≡ 20·33 clay substance

Similarly, $12 \cdot 77 \times \dfrac{25}{100} = 3 \cdot 19$ felspar

and $2 \cdot 98 \times \dfrac{25}{100} = 0 \cdot 74$ quartz

The clay substance, felspar, and quartz are calculated for stone in a similar way.

In section (2):

$$100 \text{ ball clay II} \equiv 74 \cdot 63 \text{ parts clay substance}$$

$$\therefore \quad 1 \text{ clay substance} \equiv \frac{100}{74 \cdot 63} \text{ ball clay II}$$

$$20 \cdot 33 \text{ clay substance} \equiv 20 \cdot 33 \times \frac{100}{74 \cdot 63} \text{ ball clay II}$$

$$= 27 \cdot 24 \text{ ball clay II}$$

Therefore, $27 \cdot 24$ parts of ball clay II are required and this must automatically introduce

$$27 \cdot 24 \times \frac{11 \cdot 4}{100} = 3 \cdot 11 \text{ parts felspar}$$

and

$$27 \cdot 24 \times \frac{12 \cdot 00}{100} = 3 \cdot 27 \text{ parts quartz}$$

The stone content must now be adjusted so that

$$\text{Total felspar} = 10 \cdot 79$$

$$\therefore \quad 10 \cdot 79 - 3 \cdot 11 = 7 \cdot 68 \text{ parts felspar required}$$

Since

$$100 \text{ stone} \equiv 50 \cdot 65 \text{ felspar}$$

$$1 \text{ felspar} \equiv \frac{100}{56 \cdot 65} \text{ stone}$$

and

$$7 \cdot 68 \text{ felspar} \equiv 7 \cdot 68 \times \frac{100}{56 \cdot 65} \text{ stone}$$

$$= 15 \cdot 17 \text{ stone}$$

$15 \cdot 17$ parts stone introduces $15 \cdot 17 \times \dfrac{17 \cdot 58}{100}$ parts of clay substance $= 2 \cdot 67$.

$$15 \cdot 17 \times \frac{29 \cdot 44}{100} = 4 \cdot 47 \text{ parts of quartz}$$

The requisite amounts of china clay and flint are calculated so that the clay substance and quartz remain at their original values.

Problems

(1) Given the ultimate analyses of clays A and B calculate their rational analyses using the felspar convention.

	A	B
SiO_2	62·95	67·83
Al_2O_3	21·10	22·30
TiO_2	2·37	1·07
Fe_2O_3	2·20	0·83
CaO	0·22	0·17
MgO	0·17	0·16
K_2O	0·13	0·58
Na_2O	0·13	0·12
loss	9·98	7·42

(2) Given the ultimate analysis of the following clays calculate their rational analyses using the mica convention.

	Ball clay	China clay
SiO_2	53·71	47·80
Al_2O_3	30·74	35·14
TiO_2	0·60	0·24
Fe_2O_3	1·18	1·25
CaO	0·11	0·13
MgO	0·34	0·34
K_2O	1·56	2·21
Na_2O	0·24	0·45
loss	10·64	11·48

(3) Given the ultimate analysis of the following materials calculate their rational analyses in terms of clay substance, orthoclase, albite, and quartz.

	Stone I	Stone II	Felspar
SiO_2	72·07	73·14	68·28
TiO_2	0·10	0·10	0·04
Al_2O_3	16·30	14·89	18·16
Fe_2O_3	0·15	0·22	0·10
MgO	0·17	0·20	0·06
CaO	1·86	1·63	0·47
K_2O	3·96	4·24	9·98
Na_2O	3·29	3·26	3·25
loss	1·86	1·84	0·49

(4) An earthenware body has the following recipe:

Ball clay I	30
China clay	27
Flint	28
Stone	15

Ball clay I is to be substituted by ball clay II. Calculate a new recipe, given that the rational analyses of the ball clays and stone are:

	% clay substance	% felspar	% quartz
Ball clay I	76·3	10·8	12·9
Ball clay II	72·0	12·1	15·9
Stone	14·0	67·2	18·8

China clay and flint are assumed to be pure clay substance and quartz respectively.

CHAPTER XI

Miscellaneous Calculations

Mensuration Problems; Sodium Silicate; Simple Statistical Assessment of Observed Data; Mean Value; Standard Deviation; Coefficient of Variation

Mensuration

A CYLINDRICAL vessel has an internal diameter of $1\cdot8$ in. and internal height $= 3\cdot7$ in.

Calculate the dimensions of a similarly shaped vessel, having the same diameter : height ratio, but a capacity of 1 pt.

Let d = internal diameter of vessel; and h = internal height.

$$\text{Volume of cylinder} = \frac{\pi d^2 h}{4}$$

$$1\text{ pt} = 34\cdot6 \text{ cu in.}$$

It is required that:

$$\frac{\pi d^2 h}{4} = 34\cdot6 \quad\dots\dots\dots\dots\dots\dots(1)$$

and

$$\frac{d}{h} = \frac{1\cdot8}{3\cdot7} \quad\dots\dots\dots\dots\dots\dots(2)$$

from equation (2)

$$d = \frac{1\cdot8h}{3\cdot7}$$

Substituting in equation (1)

$$\frac{\pi\left(\dfrac{1\cdot8\,h}{3\cdot7}\right)^2 h}{4} = 34\cdot6$$

$$\frac{3\cdot142\times1\cdot8^2\times h^3}{3\cdot7^2\times4} = 34\cdot6$$

$$h^3 = \frac{34\cdot6\times3\cdot7^2\times4}{3\cdot142\times1\cdot8^2}$$

$$h = 5\cdot71 \text{ in.}$$

Then

$$d = \frac{1\cdot8\times5\cdot71}{3\cdot7} = 2\cdot78$$

$$d = 2\cdot78 \text{ in.}$$

125

SETTING DENSITY

The setting density of a kiln is the weight of ware per unit volume of kiln space. It is usually expressed in lb per cu ft and provides information for estimating the amount of fuel required.

Example (1)

The setting volume of a barrel-shaped kiln of 16 chambers is approximately 32,000 cu ft. If there are 17,200 bricks (9 in. × 4½ in. × 2 in.) in each chamber, what is the setting density of (a) the green bricks and (b) the fired bricks, if the loss-on-ignition of the dry brick is 16·5% and the average weight 8·1 lb?

(a) $$Volume\ of\ one\ chamber = \frac{32,000}{16}$$
$$= 2,000\ cu\ ft$$
$$\therefore\quad Setting\ density\ (green\ bricks) = \frac{17,200 \times 8·1}{2,000}$$
$$= 69·7\ lb\ per\ cu\ ft$$

(b) $$Setting\ density\ of\ fired\ bricks = \frac{17,200 \times \left(8·1 \times \frac{83·5}{100}\right)}{2,000}$$
$$= 58·1\ lb\ per\ cu\ ft$$

Example (2)

100 acres of clay land is available for development and the average thickness of the clay is 15 ft. How many years reserve of clay exist for a production unit making 25 million bricks per year? (Volume of one pressed brick = 100 cu in.; 4 tons of clay occupy 2¾ cu yd).

$$1\ acre = 4,840\ sq\ yd$$
$$Total\ volume\ of\ clay = 100 \times 4,850 \times 5\ cu\ yd$$
$$= (100 \times 4,850 \times 5) \times 3^3 \times 12^3\ cu\ in.$$
$$Volume\ of\ bricks\ made\ per\ year = 100 \times 25,000,000\ cu\ in.$$
$$\therefore\quad Number\ of\ years\ reserve = \frac{100 \times 4,850 \times 5 \times 36^3}{100 \times 25,000,000}$$
$$= 45\ years$$

Sodium Silicate

Alkaline casting is well established as a shaping process, especially for products of intricate shape. For consistent results, the additions of alkalis (soda ash, sodium silicate, etc.) to the body materials must be carefully controlled. Regulating the soda ash addition is straightforward since it is readily obtained in the anhydrous form (sodium carbonate Na_2CO_3)—a white powder, which is soluble in water and has few impurities. A given sample should be tested periodically to determine the percentage of combined water which may be present. This is because the anhydrous form may revert to the stable mono-hydrate on exposure to the atmosphere.

On the other hand, sodium silicate has no fixed composition. It is supplied in the form of water glass, a viscous liquid, having a general formula $Na_2O.xSiO_2.yH_2O$ which allows for many possible variations.

For the manufacture of earthenware-type products (*i.e.* those which contain considerable amounts of ball clay), sodium silicate of the form $Na_2O.2 \cdot 06SiO_2.yH_2O$ is often used. For bone china casting slips, the sodium silicate has a much higher $SiO_2 : Na_2O$ ratio typified by the formula $Na_2O.3 \cdot 3SiO_2.yH_2O$.

Variations in the supply of viscous sodium silicate may be detected by chemical analysis. The calculation for converting percentage composition into molecular formula employs the principles described in Chapter VII.

Example

The analysis of a sample of sodium silicate is Na_2O 8·63%; SiO_2 27·6%; H_2O 63·8%. What is its molecular formula?

$$Na_2O \quad \frac{8 \cdot 63}{62} = 0 \cdot 139$$

$$SiO_2 \quad \frac{27 \cdot 6}{60} = 0 \cdot 460$$

$$H_2O \quad \frac{63 \cdot 8}{18} = 3 \cdot 54$$

Hence the formula may be written as:

$$0 \cdot 139 \, Na_2O; \, 0 \cdot 460 \, SiO_2; \, 3 \cdot 54 \, H_2O$$

or dividing throughout by $0 \cdot 139$

$$Na_2O.3 \cdot 31SiO_2.*25 \cdot 5H_2O$$

Another check on the viscous sodium silicate is afforded by measuring its specific gravity, using a hydrometer. A convenient scale devised by Twaddell is in common use, and the Twaddell degrees (°Tw) are converted to specific gravity using the following formula:

$$°Tw = (s-1) \, 200$$

* The water is not chemically combined, but it is convenient to express it in this form.

Example

If a sample of water glass shows a reading of 140°Tw then its specific gravity is given by:

$$140 = (s-1)\,200$$
$$s = \frac{140}{200}+1 = 1\cdot70$$
$$s = 1\cdot7$$

For a given type of sodium silicate a simple relationship (practically linear) exists between its specific gravity and the percentage by weight of sodium silicate it contains. Hence hydrometer readings indicate the percentage composition of the material.

Example

Given the data for $Na_2O.2\cdot06SiO_2.yH_2O$ as follows:

Specific gravity	% ($Na_2O.2\cdot06SiO_2$)
1·70	54·0
1·65	51·2
1·60	48·3
1·56	45·9
1·50	42·0

Calculate the percentage composition of a sample of the same type of water glass which gives a hydrometer reading of 108°Tw.

$$108°Tw = (s-1)\,200$$
$$Specific\ gravity = 1\cdot54$$

By plotting the graph of specific gravity against percentage $Na_2O.2\cdot06SiO_2$ from the above data it is seen that $s = 1\cdot54$ corresponds to a value of 44·5% $Na_2O.2\cdot06SiO_2$.

From the formula of the sodium silicate under consideration:
$$Na_2O.2\cdot06SiO_2$$
$$62+2\cdot06\times60 = 185\cdot6$$

it follows that
$$185\cdot6\ parts\ sodium\ silicate \equiv 62\ parts\ Na_2O$$

Hence, $44\cdot5\ parts\ of\ sodium\ silicate \equiv \dfrac{62}{185\cdot6}\times44\cdot5$
$$= 14\cdot9\ parts\ Na_2O$$

Similarly,
$$185\cdot6\ parts\ sodium\ silicate \equiv 123\cdot6\ parts\ SiO_2$$

and $44\cdot5\ parts\ sodium\ silicate \equiv \dfrac{123\cdot6}{185\cdot6}\times44\cdot5\ parts\ SiO_2$
$$= 29\cdot6\ parts\ SiO_2$$

Therefore the composition of the sodium silicate is:

14·9% Na_2O
29·6% SiO_2
55·5% H_2O *(by difference)*

Statistical Assessment of Observed Data

Single measurements of the properties of ceramic materials are seldom sufficiently precise to enable decisions to be taken confidently. Tests on a large number of specimens are required in many cases, *e.g.* craze resistance, modulus of rupture, etc.

The interpretation of the observed data often demands statistical assessment, and some of the simpler aspects of this are explained as follows:

MEAN VALUE

In most cases the "mean value" of a set of observations is simply their "average value" or "arithmetic mean".* This is defined as follows:

If $x_1, x_2, x_3, ..., x_n$ are the values of "n" separate observations, then

$$\bar{x} = \frac{x_1+x_2+x_3+ ... +x_n}{n} = \frac{\Sigma x}{n}$$

$\bar{x}$ = mean value;
Σ is "the sum of";
Σx is "the sum of all the separate values of x".

Example

If, in a test for craze resistance, the individual pieces craze after 6, 8, 4, 5, 6 and 8 cycles respectively, then the mean value for the craze resistance of the ware is:

$$\bar{x} = \frac{\Sigma x}{n} = \frac{6+8+4+5+6+8}{6} = \frac{37}{6} = 6·17 \text{ cycles}$$

DISPERSION (OR SCATTER)

Consider the following two sets of observations:

A	46·5 cm	59·2 cm	74·3 cm
B	59·8 cm	60·3 cm	59·9 cm

Both sets have the same mean value (60 cm). In which set would you place most confidence? Clearly Set B is the most reliable since the individual values are each very near to the mean value of the group. By the same token, Set A is a somewhat doubtful collection

---

* Other mean values such as the "geometric mean" and "harmonic mean" are used in special cases.

of data, since the individual values are widely scattered about the mean value. Some means of estimating the dispersion (or scatter) of a set of observations is therefore required.

A simple approach is to measure the "range" of each group, *i.e.* the difference between the highest and the lowest. This is often used for small groups in statistical quality control systems. For larger groups the range is not a reliable measure of dispersion since it depends entirely upon "freak" values, and fails to give due regard to the many individual measurements which may well be very near to the mean value.

STANDARD DEVIATION (σ)

A much better measure of the dispersion of a set of observations is afforded by calculating the standard deviation. This is often laborious, in terms of the arithmetic involved, but the technique may be illustrated by using simplified data. [Rapid methods for calculating σ and $\bar{x}$ are to be found in textbooks on statistics. In practice a computer is of considerable value for these calculations.]

Standard deviation is defined as the root mean square (R.M.S.) value of the individual deviations from the mean.

Taking the data from Set A:

Individual value = x cm	Deviation = D $D = (x - \bar{x})$ cm	D^2 sq cm
46·5	−13·5	182·3
59·2	−0·8	0·6
74·3	+14·3	204·5
		387·4

$\Sigma D^2 = 387·4$

$\dfrac{\Sigma D^2}{n} =$ The mean of the squares of the deviations

$= \dfrac{387·4}{3} = 129·1$ sq cm

$\sigma = \sqrt{\dfrac{\Sigma D^2}{n}} =$ R.M.S. value of the deviations

$= \sqrt{129·1} = 11·36$

The standard deviation of Set A is 11·4 cm.

For Set B:

x cm	$D = (x - \bar{x})$ cm	D^2 sq cm
59·8	−0·2	0·04
60·3	+0·3	0·09
59·9	−0·1	0·01
		0·14

$$\Sigma D^2 = 0 \cdot 14$$

$$\frac{\Sigma D^2}{n} = \frac{0 \cdot 14}{3} = 0 \cdot 0467 \text{ sq cm}$$

$$\sigma = \sqrt{\frac{\Sigma D^2}{n}} = \sqrt{0 \cdot 0467} = 0 \cdot 216 \text{ cm}$$

The standard deviation of Set B is $0 \cdot 216$ cm.

The statistical calculations for the two sets of observations are:

	Mean ($\bar{x}$) cm	Scatter (σ) cm
Set A	60	11·4
Set B	60	0·216

and it is obvious that a greater measure of confidence may be placed upon the Set B measurements.

COEFFICIENT OF VARIATION

Suppose that two sets of data are to be compared statistically and their respective mean values and standard deviations are as follows:

	Mean ($\bar{x}$) gm	Scatter (σ) gm
Set E	864	47
Set F	93	11

Which of the above sets is the more consistent? Certainly Set E has the greater "scatter value", in the absolute sense, but it also has a much higher mean value. Surely the "errors" must be considered in proportion to the size of the measured characteristic.

To achieve this, the coefficient of variation is calculated:

$$\text{Coefficient of variation} = \frac{\sigma}{\bar{x}} \times 100$$

$$\text{For Set E Coefficient of variation} = \frac{47}{864} \times 100 = 5 \cdot 44\%$$

$$\text{For Set F Coefficient of variation} = \frac{11}{93} \times 100 = 11 \cdot 8\%$$

The statistician would conclude that there is less "relative variation" amongst the individual members of Set E than there is amongst Set F.

The coefficient of variation enables all sets of data to be compared in a simple manner.

Further example

The individual values for the modulus of rupture of a ball clay are: 692, 586, 571, 608, 659, 614, 664, 632, 640, 611, 642, and 671 lb per sq in. Calculate (a) the mean value, (b) the standard deviation, and (c) the coefficient of variation of the data.

(a) $\qquad Mean\ value\ \bar{x} = \dfrac{7,590}{12} = 632 \cdot 5\ lb\ per\ sq\ in.$

(b)

Individual values lb per sq in.	Deviation	(Deviation)^2
692	+59·5	3,540·0
586	−46·5	2,163·0
571	−61·5	3,783·0
608	−24·5	600·3
659	+26·5	702·1
614	−18·5	342·3
664	+31·5	992·2
632	−0·5	0·3
640	+7·5	56·3
611	−21·5	462·2
642	+9·5	90·2
671	+38·5	1,483·0
		14,214·9

$$\frac{\Sigma D^2}{n} = 1{,}184 \cdot 6$$

$$\sigma = \sqrt{1{,}184 \cdot 6} = 34 \cdot 4\ lb\ per\ sq\ in.$$

(c) $\qquad Coefficient\ of\ variation = \dfrac{\sigma}{\bar{x}} \times 100$

$$= \frac{34 \cdot 4}{632 \cdot 5} \times 100 = 5 \cdot 44\%$$

[This represents a very high degree of precision for a test of this kind.]

Problems

(1) *(a)* A cylindrical vessel is required to hold 8 oz of water and to have an internal diameter of 2 in. What must be the internal height?

   (b) Using the same height : diameter ratio as in *(a)*, calculate the internal dimensions of a cylindrical vessel to hold 14 oz of water.

(2) A tunnel kiln is 90 ft long and is used to fire flooring tiles (measuring 6 in. $\times$ 6 in. $\times \frac{1}{2}$ in. in the fired state). Each truck is 6 ft long and carries 60 bungs of tiles; each bung containing 72 tiles.

   Calculate *(a)* the total area in sq yd of fired tiles produced per week, and *(b)* the width of the die used for producing these tiles. Assume that the trucks move at 2 ft per hr and that the linear total contraction is 6%.

(3) A barrel-arch kiln has 26 chambers each having an average volume of 2,100 cu ft and a setting capacity for 20,000 bricks. The pressed to fired volume contraction of the clay is 12%; the fired brick measures 9 in. $\times 4\frac{1}{2}$ in. $\times 3$ in. and weighs 7·4 lb.

   Calculate *(a)* the setting density (fired state) lb per cu ft, and *(b)* the free space per chamber (green state) cu ft.

(4) A factory produces 50 million pressed bricks per annum. The clay from the pit is taken from a seam with an average thickness of 25 ft.

   Calculate the acreage of clay that will be required for one year's production, given that a fired brick has a volume of 100 cu in. and that the pressed to fired volume contraction is 15%. (Assume that the clay as mined has the same density as the unfired pressed brick.)

(5) Calculate the percentage composition of sodium silicate of the form $Na_2O.2\cdot06SiO_2.yH_2O$ which gives a hydrometer reading of 126°Tw (use the data given in the chapter).

(6) The individual pieces in a test for craze resistance fail after 9, 12, 9, 14, 8, 6, 11, 11, 10, and 9 cycles respectively. Calculate the coefficient of variation for the observed data.

(7) Modulus of rupture tests on a ball clay and a china clay give the following data:

       Ball clay   864, 882, 927, 745, 832, 850 lb/sq in.
       China clay   115, 128, 124, 111, 121, 124 lb/sq in.

   Calculate the standard deviation and coefficient of variation for each set of measurements.

Answers to Problems

CHAPTER I (page 16)

(1) *(a)* 154   *(b)* 0·0519   *(c)* 159
    (d) 0·000749   *(e)* 32·2   *(f)* 258

(2) 13 : 1

(3) 1 : 117·1

(4) 0·896 lb

(5) *(a)* 0·062   *(b)* 0·267

(6) *(a)* 76%   *(b)* 3·17 : 1

(7) Red lead 57·14%   Borax 14·29%
    Flint   21·43%   Stone 7·14%

(8) 0·437%

(9) 37·08 gm

(10) Glaze A 23·18%   Glaze B 18·62%

CHAPTER II (page 27)

(1) 4·0%   9·4%   13·0%

(2) *(a)* 10·7 in.   *(b)* 10·1 in.   *(c)* 14·0%

(3) *(a)* 67·3 cu in. *(b)* 8·7 in.

(4) 605 lb

(5) 52·2 lb bone   27·2 lb china clay 25·6 lb stone

(6) 3·6%

(7) *(a)* 6,180 lb   *(b)* 2,780 lb   *(c)* 31·0%

(8) 1,351 gm dry clay   649 gm water

(9) *(a)* 15·7%   *(b)* 6·86%

(10) 73·7%

CHAPTER III (page 33)

(1) *(a)* 2·48 gm per cc   *(b)* 0·784 gm per cc
    (c) 22·5 cc   *(d)* 100 lb
    (e) 156 gm   *(f)* 4·63 cu ft

(2) *(a)* 5·07   *(b)* 2·83
    (c) 1·47   *(d)* 2·50

(3) 106·4 cc

(4) 42·55 cc

CHAPTER IV (page 41)

(1) 31·2%
(2) *(a)* A 1·62 gm per cc   B 1·49 gm per cc
    (b) A 35·1%   B 21·0%
(3) *(a)* 32·1%   *(b)* 22·1%   *(c)* 2·14 gm per cc
(4) 1·75 gm per cc
(5) 5·9%
(6) 12·4%
(7) 7 gm
(8) 2·06 gm per cc

CHAPTER V (page 56)

(1) 29·8 oz
(2) 36·4 oz per pt
(3) 35·0 oz per pt
(4) 32·8 oz per pt
(5) 38·6 cc
(6) 43¾ lb
(7) 214 lb
(8) 8 pt
(9) 864 pt   2·0 gall
(10) *(a)* 16·25 oz   *(b)* 10·4 oz   *(c)* 29 oz per pt
     (d) 31·1 oz per pt   *(e)* 2·50   *(f)* 2·11
(11) 939 gm
(12) 36·4 gm
(13) 86·4 S.S.P.'s
(14) 24·4 tons of each ball clay
     48·8 tons of each china clay
     76·4 S.S.P. flint
     3,275 S.S.P. stone

CHAPTER VI (page 72)

(1) Fireclay 73·5%   Flint 26·5%
(2) Ball clay 24·9%   China clay 31·1%
    Flint   28·5%   Stone   15·5%
(3) 12·9 in.
(4) Ball clay 25·5%   China clay 30·7%
    Flint   28·5%   Stone   15·3%
    Pint weight 26·5 oz

135

(5) 19·2 in. ball clay at 24 oz per pt
    15·4 in. china clay at 26 oz per pt
     9·6 in. flint at 32 oz per pt
     3·8 in. stone at 30 oz per pt

(6) *(a)* 7½ buckets   *(b)* 4 pt

(7) 73·3%

(8) From 75·8% to 76·8%

(9) Add 3·43 in. ball clay at 23½ oz per pt
        1·64 in. china clay at 25¼ oz per pt
        0·43 in. flint at 31¼ oz per pt
        0·38 in. stone at 30½ oz per pt

(10) 7·14 tons   1·13 lb

CHAPTER VII (page 87)

(1) *(a)* Fe_3O_4 *(b)* FeO   *(c)* KNO_3

(2) *(a)* $Na_2O = 16·2$ $B_2O_3 = 36·6$ $H_2O = 47·1$
    (b) PbO $= 65·0$ $SiO_2 = 35·0$
    (c) $K_2O = 16·9$ $Al_2O_3 = 18·3$ $SiO_2 = 64·7$
    (d) $SiO_2 = 76·9$ $H_2O = 23·1$

(3) 985·6 lb

(4) 60,980 cu ft

(5) $\left.\begin{array}{l} 0·7\,CaO \\ 0·3\,K_2O \end{array}\right\} 0·5\,Al_2O_3 \left\{ 4·0\,SiO_2 \right.$

(6) $\left.\begin{array}{l} 0·70\,PbO \\ 0·30\,CaO \end{array}\right\} 0·15\,Al_2O_3 \left\{ 1·75\,SiO_2 \right.$

(7) $\left.\begin{array}{l} 0·303\,PbO \\ 0·333\,Na_2O \\ 0·364\,K_2O \end{array}\right\} 0·282\,Al_2O_3 \left\{ \begin{array}{l} 2·026\,SiO_2 \\ 0·339\,B_2O_3 \end{array} \right.$

(8) *(a)* $\left.\begin{array}{l} 0·699\,PbO \\ 0·301\,K_2O \end{array}\right\} 0·395\,Al_2O_3 \left\{ 3·98\,SiO_2 \right.$

    (b) Lead bisilicate   239·7
           Felspar   167·4
       China clay   24·2
             Flint   35·3

(9) Lead bisilicate 205·8
         Whiting   30·0
         Felspar   55·6
     China clay   20·6
           Flint   2·4

(10) Red lead 164·4
     Borax 107·0
     Flint 54·0

(11) Red lead 228·3
  China clay 51·6
     Flint 96·0

(12) Red lead 205·5
   Felspar 55·6
  China clay 51·6
     Flint 72·0

(13)   Borax 114·6
   Whiting 60·0
   Felspar 55·6
  China clay 20·6
     Flint 74·4

(14) Lead bisilicate 184·5
   Whiting 24·1
    Stone 120·0
  China clay 32·8
    Flint 43·6

(15) Modern type PbO; $0·151 Al_2O_3$; $1·633 SiO_2$
  Original type PbO; $0·155 Al_2O_3$; $1·631 SiO_2$

Chapter VIII (page 99)

(1) Borax frit 192·8
  Lead frit 71·7
  China clay 32·8
    Flint 0·2

(2) Borax frit 164·5
  Lead frit 116·6
  China clay 8·8
    Flint 16·3

(3)   Borax 95·5 (13·1)
   Felspar 122·3 (16·7)
   Whiting 53·0 (7·3)
  China clay 31·0 (4·2)
    Flint 63·0 (8·6)

The figures in brackets are the tons of raw materials required to produce 40 tons of finished frit.

(4) 6·658 tons

(5)   Borax $979 \cdot 0$ lb
           Flint $342 \cdot 6$ lb
       Felspar $979 \cdot 0$ lb
      Whiting $489 \cdot 5$ lb
  China clay $146 \cdot 9$ lb

(6) £60 2s 0d

(7)   Borax $179 \cdot 5$ tons
          Flint $56 \cdot 5$ tons
      Felspar $160 \cdot 6$ tons
     Whiting $107 \cdot 6$ tons
  China clay $32 \cdot 3$ tons

(8)   Lead frit $48 \cdot 0$
    Borax frit $44 \cdot 3$
    China clay $8 \cdot 0$

(9) (a) $\left. \begin{array}{l} 0 \cdot 408 \, PbO \\ 0 \cdot 141 \, K_2O \\ 0 \cdot 156 \, CaO \\ 0 \cdot 295 \, Na_2O \end{array} \right\} 0 \cdot 456 \, Al_2O_3 \left\{ \begin{array}{l} 3 \cdot 642 \, SiO_2 \\ 0 \cdot 590 \, B_2O_3 \end{array} \right.$

    (b) PbO $20 \cdot 46$
           CaO $1 \cdot 96$
           K_2O $2 \cdot 98$
          Na_2O $4 \cdot 12$
          Al_2O_3 $10 \cdot 47$
          SiO_2 $49 \cdot 16$
          B_2O_3 $9 \cdot 29$
           loss $1 \cdot 56$

CHAPTER IX (page 111)

(1)   Borax $421 \cdot 0$
      Lead frit $308 \cdot 9$
        Stone $271 \cdot 0$
    China clay $9 \cdot 8$
         Flint $17 \cdot 2$

(2)   Lead frit $137 \cdot 2$
  New borax frit $137 \cdot 3$
     China clay $52 \cdot 4$
        Flint $35 \cdot 2$

(3)   Stone $262 \cdot 5$
    Soda ash $35 \cdot 3$
    Whiting $75 \cdot 5$
  China clay $20 \cdot 4$
      Flint $52 \cdot 8$

(4) Calcium borate 39·4
    Soda spar 78·6
    Potash spar 83·4
    Flint 72·0
    Whiting 40·0

(5) Borax frit 139·6
    Lead bisilicate 137·2
    China clay 48·0
    Flint 7·7

Percentage increase in china clay = 60·32%.

(6) Weight of CoO = 1·0

(7) 7·78

(8) Lead bisilicate 145·7
    Felspar 111·2
    Whiting 40·0
    China clay 8·8
    Flint 14·0

(9) $\left.\begin{array}{l} 0\cdot315\ PbO \\ 0\cdot402\ CaO \\ 0\cdot133\ Na_2O \\ 0\cdot150\ K_2O \end{array}\right\} 0\cdot276\ Al_2O_3 \left\{\begin{array}{l} 3\cdot065\ SiO_2 \\ 0\cdot394\ B_2O_3 \end{array}\right.$

(10) $\left.\begin{array}{l} 0\cdot350\ PbO \\ 0\cdot065\ K_2O \\ 0\cdot390\ CaO \\ 0\cdot195\ Na_2O \end{array}\right\} 0\cdot344\ Al_2O_3 \left\{\begin{array}{l} 2\cdot71\ SiO_2 \\ 0\cdot390\ B_2O_3 \end{array}\right.$

(11) Lead bisilicate 141·6
    Felspar 83·4
    Whiting 30·0
    Zinc oxide 12·2
    China clay 9·3
    Flint 1·7

(12) $\left.\begin{array}{l} 0\cdot254\ PbO \\ 0\cdot334\ Na_2O \\ 0\cdot412\ CaO \end{array}\right\} 0\cdot290\ Al_2O_3 \left\{\begin{array}{l} 2\cdot1\ SiO_2 \\ 0\cdot37\ B_2O_3 \end{array}\right.$

(13) Borax frit 55·1
    Zinc oxide 6·51
    China clay 8·8
    Flint 30·6

Chapter X (page 123)

(1)

	A	B
Clay substance	52·7	54·5
Felspar	1·5	4·1
Quartz	37·4	39·8
Organic matter, CO_2, etc., by difference	3·4	Nil
TiO_2	2·4	1·1
Fe_2O_3	2·2	0·8
CaO	0·2	0·2
MgO	0·2	0·2

(2)

	Ball clay	China clay
Clay substance	61·9	65·1
Potash mica	13·2	18·7
Soda mica	3·0	5·5
Quartz	17·6	6·5
Organic matter, CO_2, etc., by difference	2·1	2·4
TiO_2	0·6	0·2
Fe_2O_3	1·2	1·2
CaO	0·1	0·1
MgO	0·3	0·3

(3)

	Stone I	Stone II	Felspar
Clay substance	16·7	12·5	5·1
Orthoclase	23·4	25·1	59·1
Albite	27·8	27·6	27·5
Quartz	30·0	32·2	8·8

(4)
Ball clay II 31·8
China clay 27·1
Flint 27·0
Stone 14·1

Chapter XI (page 133)

(1) *(a)* 4·40 in. *(b)* Diameter = 2·41 in.
Height = 5·30 in.

(2) *(a)* 6,720 sq yd *(b)* 6·38 in.

(3) *(a)* 70·5 lb per cu ft *(b)* 502 cu ft

(4) 3·13 acres

(5) 16·7% Na_2O 33·3% SiO_2 50·0% H_2O

(6) 21·4%

(7) Ball clay 55·5 lb per sq in.; 6·53%
China clay 5·79 lb per sq in.; 4·81%

Appendix

ERRATUM

A number of Elements have been inadvertently omitted (between Hafnium and Radium), from the list of International Atomic Weights published on page 143. They are as follows :

Substance	Sym.	At. Wt.	Substance	Sym.	At. Wt.
Helium . .	He	4·003	Mercury . .	Hg	200·61
Holmium .	Ho	164·94	Molybdenum	Mo	95·95
Hydrogen .	H	1·008	Neodymium .	Nd	144·27
Indium . .	In	114·76	Neon . .	Ne	20·183
Iodine . .	I	126·92	Nickel . .	Ni	58·69
Iridium . .	Ir	193·1	Nitrogen .	N	14·008
Iron . .	Fe	55·85	Osmium . .	Os	190·2
Krypton . .	Kr	83·7	Oxygen . .	O	16·000
Lanthanum ·	La	138·92	Palladium .	Pd	106·7
Lead . .	Pb	207·21	Phosphorus .	P	30·98
Lithium . .	Li	6·940	Platinum . .	Pt	195·23
Lutecium .	Lu	174·99	Potassium .	K	39·096
Magnesium .	Mg	24·32	Praseodymium	Pr	140·92
Manganese .	Mn	54·93	Protactinium	Pa	231

INTERNATIONAL ATOMIC WEIGHTS

Substance	Sym.	At. Wt.	Substance	Sym.	At. Wt.
Aluminium .	Al	26·97	Radium . .	Ra	226·05
Antimony .	Sb	121·76	Radon . .	Rn	222
Argon . .	A	39·944	Rhenium. .	Re	186·31
Arsenic . .	As	74·91	Rhodium .	Rh	102·91
Barium . .	Ba	137·36	Rubidium .	Rb	85·48
Beryllium .	Be	9·02	Ruthenium .	Ru	101·7
Bismuth . .	Bi	209·00	Samarium .	Sm	150·43
Boron . .	B	10·82	Scandium .	Sc	45·10
Bromine . .	Br	79·916	Selenium .	Se	78·96
Cadmium .	Cd	112·41	Silicon . .	Si	28·06
Calcium . .	Ca	40·08	Silver . .	Ag	107·880
Carbon . .	C	12·010	Sodium . .	Na	22·997
Cerium . .	Ce	140·13	Strontium .	Sr	87·63
Cesium . .	Cs	132·91	Sulphur . .	S	32·06
Chlorine . .	Cl	35·457	Tantalum .	Ta	180·88
Chromium .	Cr	52·01	Tellurium .	Te	127·61
Cobalt . .	Co	58·94	Terbium . .	Tb	159·2
Columbium .	Cb	92·91	Thallium .	Tl	204·39
Copper . .	Cu	63·57	Thorium .	Th	169·4
Dysprosium .	Dy	162·46	Tin . . .	Sn	118·70
Erbium . .	Er	167·2	Titanium. .	Ti	47·90
Europium .	Eu	152·0	Tungsten. .	W	183·92
Fluorine . .	F	19·00	Uranium .	U	238·07
Gadolinum .	Gd	156·9	Vanadium .	V	50·95
Gallium . .	Ga	69·72	Xenon . .	Xe	131·3
Germanium .	Ge	72·60	Ytterbium .	Yb	173·04
Gold . . .	Au	197·2	Yttrium . .	Y	88·92
Hafnium .	Hf	178·6	Zinc . . .	Zn	65·38
			Zirconium .	Zr	91·22

COMPOUNDS USED IN GLAZE CALCULATIONS WITH THEIR
PERMANENT OXIDES AND FRITTING FACTORS

The approximate molecular weights that are commonly used are shown in brackets.

Compound and Fritting Factor		Formulae and Molecular Weights
Borax	0·529	$Na_2B_4O_7 . 10H_2O . (382) \rightarrow Na_2O(62) + 2B_2O_3(2 \times 70)$
Boric acid	0·564	$2H_3BO_3(2 \times 62) \rightarrow B_2O_3(70)$
China clay	0·861	$Al_2O_3 . 2SiO_2 . 2H_2O . (258) \rightarrow Al_2O_3(102) + 2SiO_2(2 \times 60)$
Felspar	1·00	$K_2O . Al_2O_3 . 6SiO_2(556) \rightarrow K_2O(94) + Al_2O_3(102) + 6SiO_2(6 \times 60)$
Flint	1·00	$SiO_2(60)$
Lead bisilicate	1·00	$PbO . 2SiO_2 . (343) \rightarrow PbO(223) + 2SiO_2(2 \times 60)$
Pearl ash	0·681	$K_2CO_3(138) \rightarrow K_2O(94)$
Red lead	0·977	$Pb_3O_4(685) \rightarrow 3PbO(3 \times 223)$
Soda ash	0·585	$Na_2CO_3(106) \rightarrow Na_2O(62)$
Whiting	0·560	$CaCO_3(100) \rightarrow CaO(56)$
White lead	0·863	$Pb(OH)_2 . 2PbCO_3(775) \rightarrow 3PbO(3 \times 223)$

APPENDIX

TABLE OF MINERALS

Name	Description	Formula
Agate	A form of crystalline silica	SiO_2
Albite	Soda felspar	$Na_2O.Al_2O_3.6SiO_2$ [$Na.Al.Si_3O_8$]
Amphiboles	Silicates with chains of silicon–oxygen linkages	$n(Si_4O_{11})^{6-}$
Anatase	A natural form of titanium dioxide	TiO_2
Anhydrite	Anhydrous calcium sulphate	$CaSO_4$
Anorthite	Lime-felspar	$CaO.Al_2O_3.2SiO_2$ [$Ca.Al_2.Si_2O_8$]
Apatite	Halogen derivative of calcium phosphate	$Ca_3(Cl.F.OH)(PO_4)_3$
Aragonite	A natural form of calcium carbonate	$CaCO_3$
Baddeleyite	A naturally occurring zirconia mineral	
Barytes	Heavy spar. Barium sulphate	$BaSO_4$
Bauxite	A natural form of hydrated alumina	$Al_2O_3.2H_2O$
Bentonite	An extremely fine grained montmorillonite type of clay	
Beryl	An example of the ring structure silicates	$3BeO.Al_2O_3.6SiO_2$ [$Be_3Al_2Si_6O_{18}$]
Boracite	A naturally occurring borate mineral	$6MgO.MgCl_2.8B_2O_3$
Borocalcite	Natural form of calcium diborate	$CaO.2B_2O_3.6H_2O$
Brookite	A natural form of titania	TiO_2
Calcite	A natural form of calcium carbonate	$CaCO_3$
Carborundum	A synthetic compound of silicon carbide	SiC
Chert	Chalcedonic silica	SiO_2
China clay	A primary clay essentially kaolinite	$Al_2O_3.2SiO_2.2H_2O$ [$Al_2(OH)_4(Si_2O_5)$]
Chromite	A chrome mineral of the spinel group	$FeO.Cr_2O_3$
Cobaltite	A sulphide containing cobalt and arsenic	$Co.As.S$
Corundum	A crystalline form of alumina	Al_2O_3
Cristobalite	Highest temperature form of crystalline silica	SiO_2
Cryolite	Mineral sodium aluminium fluoride	Na_3AlF_6
Dolomite	A double salt of calcium magnesium carbonate	$CaCO_3.MgCO_3$
Felspar	See orthoclase, albite and anorthite	

145

Name	Description	Formula
Flint	Crypto - crystalline chalcedonic silica	SiO_2
Fluorspar	Calcium fluoride	CaF_2
Fullers Earth	Clay similar to bentonite with high absorbing powers	
Galena	Natural lead sulphide	PbS
Ganister	A fine grained quartz rock	SiO_2
Gypsum	Calcium sulphate dihydrate	$CaSO_4.2H_2O$
Haematite	A naturally occurring form of iron oxide	Fe_2O_3
Iceland Spar	See calcite	
Iron Pyrites	Iron sulphide	FeS_2
Kaolinite	Clay substance	$Al_2O_3.2SiO_2.2H_2O$ $[Al_2(OH)_4(Si_2O_5)]$
Kieselguhr	Diatomaceous earth; remains of the diatom animal	SiO_2
Kyanite	An alumino-silicate	$Al_2O_3.SiO_2$
Lepidolite	A micaceous form of lithium mineral	$(Li.K.Na)_2(F.OH)_2$ $Al_2O_3.3SiO_2$
Lignite	A low-grade brown coal	60–70% carbon
Limonite	Hydrated iron oxide	$Fe_2O_3.xH_2O$
Magnesite	A naturally occurring form of magnesium carbonate	$MgCO_3$
Magnetite	Magnetic iron oxide	Fe_3O_4
Marcasite	Ferrous sulphide	FeS_2
Mica	See muscovite	
Montmorillonite	A type of clay substance	$Na.Al_5.Mg.Si_{24}.O_{60}.(OH)_{12}$
Mullite	A crystalline constituent of some fired bodies	$3Al_2O_3.2SiO_2$
Muscovite	Potash mica	$K_2O.3Al_2O_3.6SiO_2.2H_2O$
Nepheline	A low silica flux	$3(Na_2O).K_2O$ $[4Al_2O_3.8SiO_2]$
Nepheline Syenite	A rock consisting of nepheline and felspar	
Thivier's Earth	A clay high in iron oxide	
Tourmaline	A complex boro-silicate of Al and Na, plus traces of Li, Fe and Mg	
Tremolite	A calcium magnesium silicate. Amphibole type	$CaO.3MgO.4SiO_2$
Tridymite	An intermediate crystalline form of silica	SiO_2
Vermiculite	Hydrous mica	$3MgO.(Fe.Al)_2O_3.3SiO_2$
Willemite	Zinc silicate of the olivine type	$2ZnO.SiO_2$
Witherite	A natural form of barium carbonate	$BaCO_3$
Wollastonite	Calcium metasilicate	$CaO.SiO_2$
Whiting	Calcium carbonate	$CaCO_3$
Zircon	Zirconium silicate	$ZrO_2.SiO_2$
Zirconia	Zirconium oxide	ZrO_2

TYPICAL ANALYSES OF CERAMIC MATERIALS

	Alumina brick	Black ball clay	Blue ball clay	Bone ash	China clay	Chrome ore	Dolomite
SiO_2	13·73	46·86	50·56	0·31	47·00	2·10	0·24
TiO_2	2·88	0·68	0·87		0·10	0·21	
Al_2O_3	81·54	34·80	33·40	0·06	37·05	16·45	0·10
Fe_2O_3	1·41	0·80	1·25	0·13	0·59	16·50	0·05
MgO	0·10	0·32	0·40	1·26	0·28	16·26	21·20
CaO	0·11	0·32	0·59	54·26	0·15	0·12	31·20
K_2O	0·36	1·47	3·10		1·78	0·01	0·07
Na_2O	0·11	0·30	0·64	0·34	0·30	0·18	0·13
Loss	0·14	14·30	9·66	1·38	12·55	1·02	47·47
P_2O_5				42·12			
Cr_2O_3						46·70	

	E'thware body	Felspar	Flint	Fireclay brick	Molochite	Pegmatite	Plaster
SiO_2	69·93	68·00	97·97	55·27	54·81	72·23	0·54
TiO_2	0·01	0·02	0·01	1·04	0·10	0·03	0·02
Al_2O_3	19·53	16·85	0·39	35·30	42·31	17·83	0·14
Fe_2O_3	0·63	0·18	0·06	4·94	0·75	0·28	0·06
MgO	0·07	0·13	0·05	1·16	0·12	0·12	0·30
CaO	0·73	0·37	0·62	0·37	0·20	0·90	38·59
K_2O	1·60	10·64	0·02	1·63	1·73	1·90	0·03
Na_2O	0·62	2·58	0·04	0·39	0·11	5·96	0·08
Loss	5·75	0·41	0·65	0·34		0·53	7·88
SO_3							52·51

	Sand	Silica brick	Slate	Red clay	Stone	Whiting
SiO_2	95·02	95·90	51·54	37·68	72·76	0·04
TiO_2	0·13	0·17	0·94	0·52	0·05	
Al_2O_3	2·07	0·85	19·63	12·51	15·36	0·11
Fe_2O_3	0·21	0·79	8·26	5·00	0·16	0·01
MgO	0·12	0·06	1·99	1·94	0·16	0·04
CaO	0·15	1·75	1·44	19·34	1·57	56·06
K_2O	0·91	0·12	3·20	2·75	4·33	
Na_2O	0·16	0·08	1·31	0·25	3·17	0·03
Loss	0·37		5·08	20·12	1·93	43·83
SO_3						0·30
Cl						0·02

CONE VALUES

Approximate Squatting Temperatures of Harrison Cones

Cone No.	Deg. C	Deg. F	Cone No.	Deg. C	Deg. F	Cone No.	Deg. C	Deg. F
022	600	1,110	02	1,060	1,940	12	1,350	2,460
022A	625	1,155				13	1,380	2,515
021	650	1,200	02A	1,070	1,960	14	1,410	2,570
020	670	1,240	01	1,080	1,975			
			01A	1,090	1,995	15	1,435	2,615
019	690	1,275	1	1,100	2,010	16	1,460	2,660
018	710	1,310				17	1,480	2,695
017	730	1,345	1A	1,110	2,030	18	1,500	2,730
016	750	1,380	2	1,120	2,050			
			2A	1,130	2,065	19	1,520	2,770
015	790	1,455	3	1,140	2,085	20	1,530	2,785
014	815	1,500				26	1,580	2,875
013	835	1,535	3A	1,150	2,100	27	1,610	2,930
012	855	1,570	4	1,160	2,120			
			4A	1,170	2,140	28	1,630	2,965
011	880	1,615	5	1,180	2,155	29	1,650	3,000
010	900	1,650				30	1,670	3,040
09	920	1,690	5A	1,190	2,175	31	1,690	3,075
08	940	1,725	6	1,200	2,190			
			6A	1,215	2,220	32	1,710	3,110
08A	950	1,740	7	1,230	2,245	33	1,730	3,145
07	960	1,760				34	1,750	3,180
07A	970	1,780	7A	1,240	2,265	35	1,770	3,220
06	980	1,795	8	1,250	2,280			
			8A	1,260	2,300	36	1,790	3,255
06A	990	1,815	8B	1,270	2,320	37	1,825	3,315
05	1,000	1,830				38	1,850	3,360
05A	1,010	1,850	9	1,280	2,335	39	1,880	3,415
04	1,020	1,870	9A	1,290	2,355			
			10	1,300	2,370	40	1,920	3,490
04A	1,030	1,885	10A	1,310	2,390	41	1,960	3,560
03	1,040	1,905				42	2,000	3,630
03A	1,050	1,920	11	1,320	2,410			

Fahrenheit temperatures are calculated from the Centigrade figures and are shown to the nearest 5°.

Temperature Chart of Bullers Firing Trial Rings

Approximate Guide over a Normal Firing Cycle

Temperature Degrees C	Low Temp. Ring No. 55 (Brown)	Standard Ring No. 27 (Green)	High Temp. Ring No. 72 (Natural)	High Temp. Ring No. 26 (Pink)
960	3	0	0	
970	7	1	1	
980	11	2½	2	
990	15	4	3	
1,000	18	5½	4	
1,010	21	7	5	
1,020	24	8½	6	
1,030	27	10	7	
1,040	30	11½	8½	
1,050	32	13	10	
1,060	34	14	11	
1,070	36	15½	12½	
1,080	37	17	14	
1,090	38	18½	15½	
1,100	39	20	17	
1,110		21½	18½	
1,120		23	20	
1,130		24½	21	
1,140		26	22	
1,150		27	23	
1,160		28½	24½	
1,170		30	26	
1,180		31½	27	
1,190		33	28	
1,200		34½	29	
1,210		36	30	
1,220		37½	31	
1,230		38½	32	
1,240		40	33	38
1,250		41½	34½	39½
1,260			36½	41
1,270			38½	42½
1,280			40	44
1,290			42	46
1,300			44	48
1,320			46	50
1,340				52
1,360				53
1,380				54
1,400				55

These figures should be used with a measure of reserve dependent on the firing cycle for which the rings are being used.

BENDING TEMPERATURES OF HOLDCROFT'S THERMOSCOPE BARS

Bar No.	Degrees Centigrade	Bar No.	Degrees Centigrade	Bar No.	Degrees Centigrade	Bar No.	Degrees Centigrade
1	600	11	890	22	1,080	30	1,325
2	650	12	905	23	1,100	31	1,350
3	670	13	920	24	1,120	32	1,380
4	700	14	935	25	1,140	33	1,430
5	730	15	950	25a	1,170	34	1,460
6	760	16	960	26	1,200	35	1,475
7	790	17	970	26a	1,230	36	1,490
7a	810	18	985	27	1,250	37	1,505
8	840	19	1,000	27a	1,270	38	1,520
9	860	20	1,040	28	1,280	39	1,535
10	875	21	1,060	29	1,300	40	1,550

APPENDIX

INDUSTRIAL SIEVES

Apertures per Linear in.	Aperture (in.)	
	BS. 481 : 1933	I.M.M. (BS. 410 : 1943)
5	*0·144 0·160	0·100
8	0·085 0·097	0·062
10	0·068 0·078	0·050
12	0·055 0·063	0·0416
16	0·0461	0·0312
20	0·0352	0·025
30	0·0217	0·0166
40	0·0158	0·0125
50	0·0120	0·010
60	0·0097	0·0083
70	0·0083	0·0071
80	0·0073	0·0062
90	0·0063	0·0055
100	0·0056	0·005
120	0·0047	0·0042
150		0·0033
200	0·0030	0·0025
300	0·0021	

* *Note.* Provision has been made for two or more sizes of wire in the coarser meshes.

The British Standard Specification for test sieves is BS. 410 : 1962.

Useful Data

British   *Metric*

1 in. $= 2 \cdot 54$ cm
$39 \cdot 37$ in. $= 1$ metre

1 sq in. $= 6 \cdot 451$ sq cm
$0 \cdot 155$ sq in. $= 1$ sq cm

1 cu in. $= 16 \cdot 39$ cc
1 pt $= 568 \cdot 2$ cc
$1 \cdot 76$ pt $= 1$ litre
1 gall $= 4 \cdot 546$ litres

1 oz $= 28 \cdot 35$ gm
1 lb $= 453 \cdot 6$ gm
$2 \cdot 2$ lb $= 1$ kgm
1 ton $= 1,016$ kgm

$62 \cdot 32$ lb per cu ft $= 1$ gm per cc
20 oz per pt $= 1$ gm per cc

CONVERSION FACTORS
(British System of Units)

1 pt $= 34 \cdot 6$ cu in.
1 cu ft $= 6 \cdot 23$ gall
1 gall water $= 10$ lb
1 pt water $= 20$ oz
1 lb water $= 0 \cdot 016$ cu ft

MENSURATION FORMULAE

Areas

Triangle $A = \frac{1}{2}ad$

where $a =$ length of any side; and
 $d =$ perpendicular distance from that side (or its extension) to the opposite vertex.

Trapezium $A = \frac{1}{2}(a+b)\,d$

where "a" and "b" are the lengths of the two parallel sides; and
 $d =$ perpendicular distance between them.

Circle

$$A = \pi r^2 = \frac{\pi d^2}{4}$$

where r = radius; and
d = diameter.

Ellipse

$$A = \frac{\pi ab}{4}$$

where a = length of major axis; and
b = length of minor axis.

Volumes

Right Prism

$$V = hA$$

where h = perpendicular height; and
A = area of base.

Cylinder

$$V = \pi r^2 h$$

where h = perpendicular height; and
r = radius of base.

Pyramid

$$V = \tfrac{1}{3}hA$$

where h = perpendicular height; and
A = area of base.

Cone

$$V = \tfrac{1}{3}\pi r^2 h$$

where h = perpendicular height; and
r = radius of base.

Sphere

$$V = \frac{4}{3}\pi r^3 = \frac{\pi d^3}{6}$$

where r = radius; and
d = diameter.

Surface Areas

Cylinder (Right Circular)

$$S = 2\pi r(h+2)$$

where r = radius of base; and
h = perpendicular height.

Cone (Right Circular)

$$S = \pi r\sqrt{r^2+h^2+2}$$

where r = radius of base; and
h = perpendicular height.

Sphere

$$S = 4\pi r^2 = \pi d^2$$

where r = radius; and
d = diameter.

LOGARITHMS

N	0	1	2	3	4	5	6	7	8	9
10	0000	0043	0086	0128	0170	0212	0253	0294	0334	0374
11	0414	0453	0492	0531	0569	0607	0645	0682	0719	0755
12	0792	0828	0864	0899	0934	0969	1004	1038	1072	1106
13	1139	1173	1206	1239	1271	1303	1335	1367	1399	1430
14	1461	1492	1523	1553	1584	1614	1644	1673	1703	1732
15	1761	1790	1818	1847	1875	1903	1931	1959	1987	2014
16	2041	2068	2095	2122	2148	2175	2201	2227	2253	2279
17	2304	2330	2355	2380	2405	2430	2455	2480	2504	2529
18	2553	2577	2601	2625	2648	2672	2695	2718	2742	2765
19	2788	2810	2833	2856	2878	2900	2923	2945	2967	2989
20	3010	3032	3054	3075	3096	3118	3139	3160	3181	3201
21	3222	3243	3263	3284	3304	3324	3345	3365	3385	3404
22	3424	3444	3464	3483	3502	3522	3541	3560	3579	3598
23	3617	3636	3655	3674	3692	3711	3729	3747	3766	3784
24	3802	3820	3838	3856	3874	3892	3909	3927	3945	3962
25	3979	3997	4014	4031	4048	4065	4082	4099	4116	4133
26	4150	4166	4183	4200	4216	4232	4249	4265	4281	4298
27	4314	4330	4346	4362	4378	4393	4409	4425	4440	4456
28	4472	4487	4502	4518	4533	4548	4564	4579	4594	4609
29	4624	4639	4654	4669	4683	4698	4713	4728	4742	4757
30	4771	4786	4800	4814	4829	4843	4857	4871	4886	4900
31	4914	4928	4942	4955	4969	4983	4997	5011	5024	5038
32	5051	5065	5079	5092	5105	5119	5132	5145	5159	5172
33	5185	5198	5211	5224	5237	5250	5263	5276	5289	5302
34	5315	5328	5340	5353	5366	5378	5391	5403	5416	5428
35	5441	5453	5465	5478	5490	5502	5514	5527	5539	5551
36	5563	5575	5587	5599	5611	5623	5635	5647	5658	5670
37	5682	5694	5705	5717	5729	5740	5752	5763	5775	5786
38	5798	5809	5821	5832	5843	5855	5866	5877	5888	5899
39	5911	5922	5933	5944	5955	5966	5977	5988	5999	6010
40	6021	6031	6042	6053	6064	6075	6085	6096	6107	6117
41	6128	6138	6149	6160	6170	6180	6191	6201	6212	6222
42	6232	6243	6253	6263	6274	6284	6294	6304	6314	6325
43	6335	6345	6355	6365	6375	6385	6395	6405	6415	6425
44	6435	6444	6454	6464	6474	6484	6493	6503	6513	6522
45	6532	6542	6551	6561	6571	6580	6590	6599	6609	6618
46	6628	6637	6646	6656	6665	6675	6684	6693	6702	6712
47	6721	6730	6739	6749	6758	6767	6776	6785	6794	6803
48	6812	6821	6830	6839	6848	6857	6866	6875	6884	6893
49	6902	6911	6920	6928	6937	6946	6955	6964	6972	6981
50	6990	6998	7007	7016	7024	7033	7042	7050	7059	7067

Mean differences (proportional parts), columns 1 – 9:

1	2	3	4	5	6	7	8	9
4	9	13	17	21	26	30	34	38
4	8	12	16	20	24	28	32	37
4	8	12	15	19	23	27	31	35
4	7	11	15	19	22	26	30	33
3	7	11	14	18	21	25	28	32
3	7	10	14	17	20	24	27	31
3	7	10	13	16	20	23	26	30
3	7	10	12	16	19	22	25	29
3	6	9	12	15	18	21	24	28
3	6	9	12	15	17	20	23	26
3	6	9	11	14	17	20	23	26
3	5	8	11	14	16	19	22	25
3	5	8	11	14	16	19	22	24
3	5	8	10	13	15	18	21	23
3	5	8	10	13	15	18	20	23
2	5	7	10	12	15	17	19	22
2	5	7	9	12	14	16	19	21
2	5	7	9	11	14	16	18	21
2	4	7	9	11	13	16	18	20
2	4	6	8	11	13	15	17	19
2	4	6	8	11	13	15	17	19
2	4	6	8	10	12	14	16	18
2	4	6	8	10	12	14	15	17
2	4	6	7	9	11	13	15	17
2	4	5	7	9	11	12	14	16
2	3	5	7	9	10	12	14	15
2	3	5	7	8	10	11	13	15
2	3	5	6	8	9	11	13	14
2	3	5	6	8	9	11	12	14
1	3	4	6	7	9	10	12	13
1	3	4	6	7	9	10	11	13
1	3	4	6	7	8	10	11	12
1	3	4	5	7	8	9	11	12
1	3	4	5	6	8	9	10	12
1	3	4	5	6	8	9	10	11
1	2	4	5	6	7	9	10	11
1	2	4	5	6	7	8	10	11
1	2	3	5	6	7	8	9	10
1	2	3	5	6	7	8	9	10
1	2	3	4	5	7	8	9	10
1	2	3	4	5	6	8	9	10
1	2	3	4	5	6	7	8	9
1	2	3	4	5	6	7	8	9
1	2	3	4	5	6	7	8	9
1	2	3	4	5	6	7	8	9
1	2	3	4	5	6	7	8	9
1	2	3	4	5	6	7	7	8
1	2	3	4	5	5	6	7	8
1	2	3	4	4	5	6	7	8
1	2	3	3	4	5	6	7	8

LOGARITHMS

	0	1	2	3	4	5	6	7	8	9	1	2	3	4	5	6	7	8	9
51	7076	7084	7093	7101	7110	7118	7126	7135	7143	7152	1	2	3	3	4	5	6	7	8
52	7160	7168	7177	7185	7193	7202	7210	7218	7226	7235	1	2	2	3	4	5	6	7	7
53	7243	7251	7259	7267	7275	7284	7292	7300	7308	7316	1	2	2	3	4	5	6	6	7
54	7324	7332	7340	7348	7356	7364	7372	7380	7388	7396	1	2	2	3	4	5	6	6	7
55	7404	7412	7419	7427	7435	7443	7451	7459	7466	7474	1	2	2	3	4	5	5	6	7
56	7482	7490	7497	7505	7513	7520	7528	7536	7543	7551	1	2	2	3	4	5	5	6	7
57	7559	7566	7574	7582	7589	7597	7604	7612	7619	7627	1	2	2	3	4	5	5	6	7
58	7634	7642	7649	7657	7664	7672	7679	7686	7694	7701	1	1	2	3	4	4	5	6	7
59	7709	7716	7723	7731	7738	7745	7752	7760	7767	7774	1	1	2	3	4	4	5	6	7
60	7782	7789	7796	7803	7810	7818	7825	7832	7839	7846	1	1	2	3	4	4	5	6	6
61	7853	7860	7868	7875	7882	7889	7896	7903	7910	7917	1	1	2	3	4	4	5	6	6
62	7924	7931	7938	7945	7952	7959	7966	7973	7980	7987	1	1	2	3	3	4	5	6	6
63	7993	8000	8007	8014	8021	8028	8035	8041	8048	8055	1	1	2	3	3	4	5	5	6
64	8062	8069	8075	8082	8089	8096	8102	8109	8116	8122	1	1	2	3	3	4	5	5	6
65	8129	8136	8142	8149	8156	8162	8169	8176	8182	8189	1	1	2	3	3	4	5	5	6
66	8195	8202	8209	8215	8222	8228	8235	8241	8248	8254	1	1	2	3	3	4	5	5	6
67	8261	8267	8274	8280	8287	8293	8299	8306	8312	8319	1	1	2	3	3	4	5	5	6
68	8325	8331	8338	8344	8351	8357	8363	8370	8376	8382	1	1	2	3	3	4	4	5	6
69	8388	8395	8401	8407	8414	8420	8426	8432	8439	8445	1	1	2	2	3	4	4	5	6
70	8451	8457	8463	8470	8476	8482	8488	8494	8500	8506	1	1	2	2	3	4	4	5	6
71	8513	8519	8525	8531	8537	8543	8549	8555	8561	8567	1	1	2	2	3	4	4	5	5
72	8573	8579	8585	8591	8597	8603	8609	8615	8621	8627	1	1	2	2	3	4	4	5	5
73	8633	8639	8645	8651	8657	8663	8669	8675	8681	8686	1	1	2	2	3	4	4	5	5
74	8692	8698	8704	8710	8716	8722	8727	8733	8739	8745	1	1	2	2	3	4	4	5	5
75	8751	8756	8762	8768	8774	8779	8785	8791	8797	8802	1	1	2	2	3	4	4	5	5
76	8808	8814	8820	8825	8831	8837	8842	8848	8854	8859	1	1	2	2	3	3	4	5	5
77	8865	8871	8876	8882	8887	8893	8899	8904	8910	8915	1	1	2	2	3	3	4	4	5
78	8921	8927	8932	8938	8943	8949	8954	8960	8965	8971	1	1	2	2	3	3	4	4	5
79	8976	8982	8987	8993	8998	9004	9009	9015	9020	9025	1	1	2	2	3	3	4	4	5
80	9031	9036	9042	9047	9053	9058	9063	9069	9074	9079	1	1	2	2	3	3	4	4	5
81	9085	9090	9096	9101	9106	9112	9117	9122	9128	9133	1	1	2	2	3	3	4	4	5
82	9138	9143	9149	9154	9159	9165	9170	9175	9180	9186	1	1	2	2	3	3	4	4	5
83	9191	9196	9201	9206	9212	9217	9222	9227	9232	9238	1	1	2	2	3	3	4	4	5
84	9243	9248	9253	9258	9263	9269	9274	9279	9284	9289	1	1	2	2	3	3	4	4	5
85	9294	9299	9304	9309	9315	9320	9325	9330	9335	9340	1	1	2	2	3	3	4	4	5
86	9345	9350	9355	9360	9365	9370	9375	9380	9385	9390	1	1	2	2	3	3	4	4	5
87	9395	9400	9405	9410	9415	9420	9425	9430	9435	9440	0	1	1	2	2	3	3	4	4
88	9445	9450	9455	9460	9465	9469	9474	9479	9484	9489	0	1	1	2	2	3	3	4	4
89	9494	9499	9504	9509	9513	9518	9523	9528	9533	9538	0	1	1	2	2	3	3	4	4
90	9542	9547	9552	9557	9562	9566	9571	9576	9581	9586	0	1	1	2	2	3	3	4	4
91	9590	9595	9600	9605	9609	9614	9619	9624	9628	9633	0	1	1	2	2	3	3	4	4
92	9638	9643	9647	9652	9657	9661	9666	9671	9675	9680	0	1	1	2	2	3	3	4	4
93	9685	9689	9694	9699	9703	9708	9713	9717	9722	9727	0	1	1	2	2	3	3	4	4
94	9731	9736	9741	9745	9750	9754	9759	9763	9768	9773	0	1	1	2	2	3	3	4	4
95	9777	9782	9786	9791	9795	9800	9805	9809	9814	9818	0	1	1	2	2	3	3	4	4
96	9823	9827	9832	9836	9841	9845	9850	9854	9859	9863	0	1	1	2	2	3	3	4	4
97	9868	9872	9877	9881	9886	9890	9894	9899	9903	9908	0	1	1	2	2	3	3	4	4
98	9912	9917	9921	9926	9930	9934	9939	9943	9948	9952	0	1	1	2	2	3	3	4	4
99	9956	9961	9965	9969	9974	9978	9983	9987	9991	9996	0	1	1	2	2	3	3	3	4

CALCULATIONS IN CERAMICS

ANTILOGARITHMS

	0	1	2	3	4	5	6	7	8	9	1	2	3	4	5	6	7	8	9
·00	1000	1002	1005	1007	1009	1012	1014	1016	1019	1021	0	0	1	1	1	1	2	2	2
·01	1023	1026	1028	1030	1033	1035	1038	1040	1042	1045	0	0	1	1	1	1	2	2	2
·02	1047	1050	1052	1054	1057	1059	1062	1064	1067	1069	0	0	1	1	1	1	2	2	2
·03	1072	1074	1076	1079	1081	1084	1086	1089	1091	1094	0	0	1	1	1	1	2	2	2
·04	1096	1099	1102	1104	1107	1109	1112	1114	1117	1119	0	1	1	1	1	2	2	2	2
·05	1122	1125	1127	1130	1132	1135	1138	1140	1143	1146	0	1	1	1	1	2	2	2	2
·06	1148	1151	1153	1156	1159	1161	1164	1167	1169	1172	0	1	1	1	1	2	2	2	2
·07	1175	1178	1180	1183	1186	1189	1191	1194	1197	1199	0	1	1	1	1	2	2	2	2
·08	1202	1205	1208	1211	1213	1216	1219	1222	1225	1227	0	1	1	1	1	2	2	2	3
·09	1230	1233	1236	1239	1242	1245	1247	1250	1253	1256	0	1	1	1	1	2	2	2	3
·10	1259	1262	1265	1268	1271	1274	1276	1279	1282	1285	0	1	1	1	1	2	2	2	3
·11	1288	1291	1294	1297	1300	1303	1306	1309	1312	1315	0	1	1	1	2	2	2	2	3
·12	1318	1321	1324	1327	1330	1334	1337	1340	1343	1346	0	1	1	1	2	2	2	2	3
·13	1349	1352	1355	1358	1361	1365	1368	1371	1374	1377	0	1	1	1	2	2	2	3	3
·14	1380	1384	1387	1390	1393	1396	1400	1403	1406	1409	0	1	1	1	2	2	2	3	3
·15	1413	1416	1419	1422	1426	1429	1432	1435	1439	1442	0	1	1	1	2	2	2	3	3
·16	1445	1449	1452	1455	1459	1462	1466	1469	1472	1476	0	1	1	1	2	2	2	3	3
·17	1479	1483	1486	1489	1493	1496	1500	1503	1507	1510	0	1	1	1	2	2	2	3	3
·18	1514	1517	1521	1524	1528	1531	1535	1538	1542	1545	0	1	1	1	2	2	2	3	3
·19	1549	1552	1556	1560	1563	1567	1570	1574	1578	1581	0	1	1	1	2	2	3	3	3
·20	1585	1589	1592	1596	1600	1603	1607	1611	1614	1618	0	1	1	1	2	2	3	3	3
·21	1622	1626	1629	1633	1637	1641	1644	1648	1652	1656	0	1	1	2	2	2	3	3	3
·22	1660	1663	1667	1671	1675	1679	1683	1687	1690	1694	0	1	1	2	2	2	3	3	3
·23	1698	1702	1706	1710	1714	1718	1722	1726	1730	1734	0	1	1	2	2	2	3	3	4
·24	1738	1742	1746	1750	1754	1758	1762	1766	1770	1774	0	1	1	2	2	2	3	3	4
·25	1778	1782	1786	1791	1795	1799	1803	1807	1811	1816	0	1	1	2	2	2	3	3	4
·26	1820	1824	1828	1832	1837	1841	1845	1849	1854	1858	0	1	1	2	2	3	3	3	4
·27	1862	1866	1871	1875	1879	1884	1888	1892	1897	1901	0	1	1	2	2	3	3	3	4
·28	1905	1910	1914	1919	1923	1928	1932	1936	1941	1945	0	1	1	2	2	3	3	4	4
·29	1950	1954	1959	1963	1968	1972	1977	1982	1986	1991	0	1	1	2	2	3	3	4	4
·30	1995	2000	2004	2009	2014	2018	2023	2028	2032	2037	0	1	1	2	2	3	3	4	4
·31	2042	2046	2051	2056	2061	2065	2070	2075	2080	2084	0	1	1	2	2	3	3	4	4
·32	2089	2094	2099	2104	2109	2113	2118	2123	2128	2133	0	1	1	2	2	3	3	4	4
·33	2138	2143	2148	2153	2158	2163	2168	2173	2178	2183	0	1	1	2	2	3	3	4	4
·34	2188	2193	2198	2203	2208	2213	2218	2223	2228	2234	1	1	2	2	3	3	4	4	5
·35	2239	2244	2249	2254	2259	2265	2270	2275	2280	2286	1	1	2	2	3	3	4	4	5
·36	2291	2296	2301	2307	2312	2317	2323	2328	2333	2339	1	1	2	2	3	3	4	4	5
·37	2344	2350	2355	2360	2366	2371	2377	2382	2388	2393	1	1	2	2	3	3	4	4	5
·38	2399	2404	2410	2415	2421	2427	2432	2438	2443	2449	1	1	2	2	3	3	4	4	5
·39	2455	2460	2466	2472	2477	2483	2489	2495	2500	2506	1	1	2	2	3	3	4	5	5
·40	2512	2518	2523	2529	2535	2541	2547	2553	2559	2564	1	1	2	2	3	4	4	5	5
·41	2570	2576	2582	2588	2594	2600	2606	2612	2618	2624	1	1	2	2	3	4	4	5	5
·42	2630	2636	2642	2649	2655	2661	2667	2673	2679	2685	1	1	2	2	3	4	4	5	6
·43	2692	2698	2704	2710	2716	2723	2729	2735	2742	2748	1	1	2	3	3	4	4	5	6
·44	2754	2761	2767	2773	2780	2786	2793	2799	2805	2812	1	1	2	3	3	4	4	5	6
·45	2818	2825	2831	2838	2844	2851	2858	2864	2871	2877	1	1	2	3	3	4	5	5	6
·46	2884	2891	2897	2904	2911	2917	2924	2931	2938	2944	1	1	2	3	3	4	5	5	6
·47	2951	2958	2965	2972	2979	2985	2992	2999	3006	3013	1	1	2	3	3	4	5	5	6
·48	3020	3027	3034	3041	3048	3055	3062	3069	3076	3083	1	1	2	3	4	4	5	6	6
·49	3090	3097	3105	3112	3119	3126	3133	3141	3148	3155	1	1	2	3	4	5	6	6	6

156

APPENDIX

ANTILOGARITHMS

	0	1	2	3	4	5	6	7	8	9	1	2	3	4	5	6	7	8	9
·50	3162	3170	3177	3184	3192	3199	3206	3214	3221	3228	1	1	2	3	4	4	5	6	7
·51	3236	3243	3251	3258	3266	3273	3281	3289	3296	3304	1	2	2	3	4	5	5	6	7
·52	3311	3319	3327	3334	3342	3350	3357	3365	3373	3381	1	2	2	3	4	5	5	6	7
·53	3388	3396	3404	3412	3420	3428	3436	3443	3451	3459	1	2	2	3	4	5	6	6	7
·54	3467	3475	3483	3491	3499	3508	3516	3524	3532	3540	1	2	2	3	4	5	6	6	7
·55	3548	3556	3565	3573	3581	3589	3597	3606	3614	3622	1	2	2	3	4	5	6	7	7
·56	3631	3639	3648	3656	3664	3673	3681	3690	3698	3707	1	2	3	3	4	5	6	7	8
·57	3715	3724	3733	3741	3750	3758	3767	3776	3784	3793	1	2	3	3	4	5	6	7	8
·58	3802	3811	3819	3828	3837	3846	3855	3864	3873	3882	1	2	3	4	4	5	6	7	8
·59	3890	3899	3908	3917	3926	3936	3945	3954	3963	3972	1	2	3	4	5	5	6	7	8
·60	3981	3990	3999	4009	4018	4027	4036	4046	4055	4064	1	2	3	4	5	6	6	7	8
·61	4074	4083	4093	4102	4111	4121	4130	4140	4150	4159	1	2	3	4	5	6	7	8	9
·62	4169	4178	4188	4198	4207	4217	4227	4236	4246	4256	1	2	3	4	5	6	7	8	9
·63	4266	4276	4285	4295	4305	4315	4325	4335	4345	4355	1	2	3	4	5	6	7	8	9
·64	4365	4375	4385	4395	4406	4416	4426	4436	4446	4457	1	2	3	4	5	6	7	8	9
·65	4467	4477	4487	4498	4508	4519	4529	4539	4550	4560	1	2	3	4	5	6	7	8	9
·66	4571	4581	4592	4603	4613	4624	4634	4645	4656	4667	1	2	3	4	5	6	7	9	10
·67	4677	4688	4699	4710	4721	4732	4742	4753	4764	4775	1	2	3	4	5	7	8	9	10
·68	4786	4797	4808	4819	4831	4842	4853	4864	4875	4887	1	2	3	4	6	7	8	9	10
·69	4898	4909	4920	4932	4943	4955	4966	4977	4989	5000	1	2	3	5	6	7	8	9	10
·70	5012	5023	5035	5047	5058	5070	5082	5093	5105	5117	1	2	4	5	6	7	8	9	11
·71	5129	5140	5152	5164	5176	5188	5200	5212	5224	5236	1	2	4	5	6	7	8	10	11
·72	5248	5260	5272	5284	5297	5309	5321	5333	5346	5358	1	2	4	5	6	7	9	10	11
·73	5370	5383	5395	5408	5420	5433	5445	5458	5470	5483	1	3	4	5	6	8	9	10	11
·74	5495	5508	5521	5534	5546	5559	5572	5585	5598	5610	1	3	4	5	6	8	9	10	12
·75	5623	5636	5649	5662	5675	5689	5702	5715	5728	5741	1	3	4	5	7	8	9	11	12
·76	5754	5768	5781	5794	5808	5821	5834	5848	5861	5875	1	3	4	5	7	8	9	11	12
·77	5888	5902	5916	5929	5943	5957	5970	5984	5998	6012	1	3	4	5	7	8	10	11	12
·78	6026	6039	6053	6067	6081	6095	6109	6124	6138	6152	1	3	4	6	7	8	10	11	13
·79	6166	6180	6194	6209	6223	6237	6252	6266	6281	6295	1	3	4	6	7	9	10	11	13
·80	6310	6324	6339	6353	6368	6383	6397	6412	6427	6442	1	3	4	6	7	9	10	12	13
·81	6457	6471	6486	6501	6516	6531	6546	6561	6577	6592	2	3	5	6	8	9	11	12	14
·82	6607	6622	6637	6653	6668	6683	6699	6714	6730	6745	2	3	5	6	8	9	11	12	14
·83	6761	6776	6792	6808	6823	6839	6855	6871	6887	6902	2	3	5	6	8	9	11	13	14
·84	6918	6934	6950	6966	6982	6998	7015	7031	7047	7063	2	3	5	6	8	10	11	13	15
·85	7079	7096	7112	7129	7145	7161	7178	7194	7211	7228	2	3	5	7	8	10	12	13	15
·86	7244	7261	7278	7295	7311	7328	7345	7362	7379	7396	2	3	5	7	8	10	12	13	15
·87	7413	7430	7447	7464	7482	7499	7516	7534	7551	7568	2	3	5	7	9	10	12	14	16
·88	7586	7603	7621	7638	7656	7674	7691	7709	7727	7745	2	4	5	7	9	11	12	14	16
·89	7762	7780	7798	7816	7834	7852	7870	7889	7907	7925	2	4	5	7	9	11	13	14	16
·90	7943	7962	7980	7998	8017	8035	8054	8072	8091	8110	2	4	6	7	9	11	13	15	17
·91	8128	8147	8166	8185	8204	8222	8241	8260	8279	8299	2	4	6	8	9	11	13	15	17
·92	8318	8337	8356	8375	8395	8414	8433	8453	8472	8492	2	4	6	8	10	12	14	15	17
·93	8511	8531	8551	8570	8590	8610	8630	8650	8670	8690	2	4	6	8	10	12	14	16	18
·94	8710	8730	8750	8770	8790	8810	8831	8851	8872	8892	2	4	6	8	10	12	14	16	18
·95	8913	8933	8954	8974	8995	9016	9036	9057	9078	9099	2	4	6	8	10	12	15	17	19
·96	9120	9141	9162	9183	9204	9226	9247	9268	9290	9311	2	4	6	8	11	13	15	17	19
·97	9333	9354	9376	9397	9419	9441	9462	9484	9506	9528	2	4	7	9	11	13	15	17	20
·98	9550	9572	9594	9616	9638	9661	9683	9705	9727	9750	2	4	7	9	11	13	16	18	20
·99	9772	9795	9817	9840	9863	9886	9908	9931	9954	9977	2	5	7	9	11	14	16	18	20

The copyright of that portion of the above table which gives the logarithms of numbers from 1,000 to 2,000 is the property of Macmillan and Co. Ltd., who have authorised the use of the form in this publication.